ACCA

ADVANCED TAXATION (ATX – UK)

FA 2018

WITHDRAWN

BPP Learning Media is an **ACCA Approved Content Provider**. This means we work closely with ACCA to ensure this Study Text contains the information you need to pass your exam.

In this Study Text, which has been reviewed by the **ACCA examining team**, we:

- **Discuss** the best strategies for studying for ACCA exams
- **Highlight** the most important elements in the syllabus and the **key skills** you will need
- **Signpost** how each chapter links to the syllabus and the study guide
- **Provide** lots of **exam focus points** demonstrating what is expected of you in the exam
- **Emphasise key points** in regular **fast forward summaries**
- **Test your knowledge** in **quick quizzes**
- **Examine your understanding** in our **practice question bank**
- **Reference** all the **important topics** in our **full index**

BPP's **Practice & Revision Kit** also supports the Advanced Taxation (ATX – UK) syllabus.

FOR EXAMS IN JUNE 2019, SEPTEMBER 2019, DECEMBER 2019 AND MARCH 2020

BPP LEARNING MEDIA

First edition 2007
Twelfth edition October 2018

ISBN 9781 5097 2297 6
(Previous ISBN 9781 5097 1533 6)
eISBN 9781 5097 2298 3

British Library Cataloguing-in-Publication Data
A catalogue record for this book is available
from the British Library

Published by

BPP Learning Media Ltd
BPP House, Aldine Place
142-144 Uxbridge Road
London W12 8AA

www.bpp.com/learningmedia

Printed in the United Kingdom

Your learning materials, published by BPP Learning Media
Ltd, are printed on paper obtained from traceable
sustainable sources.

Contents

BPP
LEARNING MEDIA

Helping you to pass

BPP Learning Media – ACCA Approved Content Provider

As an ACCA **Approved Content Provider**, BPP Learning Media gives you the **opportunity** to use study materials reviewed by the ACCA examining team. By incorporating the examining team's comments and suggestions regarding the depth and breadth of syllabus coverage, the BPP Learning Media Study Text provides excellent, **ACCA-approved** support for your studies.

These materials are reviewed by the ACCA examining team. The objective of the review is to ensure that the material properly covers the syllabus and study guide outcomes, used by the examining team in setting the exams, in the appropriate breadth and depth. The review does not ensure that every eventuality, combination or application of examinable topics is addressed by the ACCA Approved Content. Nor does the review comprise a detailed technical check of the content as the Approved Content Provider has its own quality assurance processes in place in this respect.

The PER alert

Before you can qualify as an ACCA member, you not only have to pass all your exams but also fulfil a three-year **practical experience requirement** (PER). To help you to recognise areas of the syllabus that you might be able to apply in the workplace to achieve different performance objectives, we have introduced the '**PER alert**' feature. You will find this feature throughout the Study Text to remind you that what you are **learning to pass** your ACCA exams is **equally useful to the fulfilment of the PER requirement**.

Your achievement of the PER should be recorded in your on-line *My Experience* record.

Tackling studying

Studying can be a daunting prospect, particularly when you have lots of other commitments. The **different features** of the Study Text, the **purposes** of which are explained fully on the **Chapter features** page, will help you whilst studying and improve your chances of **exam success**.

Developing exam awareness

Our Study Texts are completely **focused** on helping you pass your exam.

Our advice on **Studying Advanced Taxation (ATX – UK)** outlines the **content** of the syllabus and the **necessary skills** you are expected to be able to demonstrate and any **brought forward knowledge** you are expected to have.

Exam focus points are included within the chapters to highlight when and how specific topics were examined, or how they might be examined in the future.

Exam references are provided. Up to June 2015, full exams were released by ACCA and questions from these exams are referenced by the exam in which they appeared eg 6/15 for June 2015. Subsequently, only sample questions have been released by ACCA and these have been referred in relation to the month in which they were released eg 12/17 for the September/December 2017 sample questions, which is not necessarily the same as the exam in which they actually appeared. The references should be taken as a guide. BPP Learning Media and ACCA do not advocate question spotting.

Testing what you can do

Testing yourself helps you develop the skills you need to pass the exam and also confirms that you can recall what you have learnt.

We include **Questions** – lots of them – both within chapters and in the **Practice Question Bank**, as well as **Quick Quizzes** at the end of each chapter to test your knowledge of the chapter content.

Chapter features

Each chapter contains a number of helpful features to guide you through each topic.

Topic list

Topic list	Syllabus reference

Tells you what you will be studying in this chapter and the relevant section numbers, together with ACCA syllabus references.

Introduction

Puts the chapter content in the context of the syllabus as a whole.

Study Guide

Links the chapter content with ACCA guidance.

Exam Guide

Highlights how examinable the chapter content is likely to be and the ways in which it could be examined.

> Knowledge brought forward from earlier studies

What you are assumed to know from previous studies/exams.

> FAST FORWARD

Summarises the content of main chapter headings, allowing you to preview and review each section easily.

Examples

Demonstrate how to apply key knowledge and techniques.

Key terms

Definitions of important concepts that can often earn you easy marks in exams.

Exam focus points

Tell you when and how specific topics were examined, or how they may be examined in the future.

Formula to learn

Formulae that are not given in the exam but which have to be learnt.

This gives you a useful indication of syllabus areas that closely relate to performance objectives in your Practical Experience Requirement (PER).

 Question

Give you essential practice of techniques covered in the chapter.

Chapter Roundup

A full list of the Fast Forwards included in the chapter, providing an easy source of review.

Quick Quiz

A quick test of your knowledge of the main topics in the chapter.

Practice Question Bank

Found at the back of the Study Text with more comprehensive chapter questions. Cross referenced for easy navigation.

Studying Advanced Taxation (ATX – UK)

As the name suggests, this module examines Advanced Taxation. It builds on the foundations of Taxation (TX – UK) in two ways. First, it introduces more advanced taxation topics in relation to inheritance tax and specialised personal and corporate tax. Second, it requires the ability to communicate clearly with clients, HM Revenue & Customs and other professionals in a clear and professional manner. It is an optional module, which is often chosen by both those working in a tax environment and also those with an interest in tax.

1 What Advanced Taxation (ATX – UK) is about

The Advanced Taxation (ATX – UK) syllabus builds on the basic knowledge of core taxes gained from Taxation (TX – UK) and introduces candidates to additional capital taxes in the form of stamp duty, stamp duty reserve tax and stamp duty land tax. It also extends knowledge of income tax, inheritance tax, corporation tax and capital gains taxes, including overseas aspects, taxation of trusts and additional exemptions and reliefs.

The emphasis of the module is on the candidate's skills of analysis and interpretation of information provided and communication of recommendations in a manner appropriate to the intended audience eg clients. Computations will normally only be required in support of explanations or advice and not in isolation.

2 What skills are required?

- Be able to **calculate** tax charges in support of explanations or advice.

- Be able to **explain** the tax charges in a particular scenario: what taxes are applicable and why.

- Be able to **analyse** a set of facts to ascertain when tax charges arise and any options that may be available to the taxpayer to mitigate such charges.

- Be able to **evaluate** your results and **recommend** a course of action, justifying your recommendations and setting out any other factors which the taxpayer should take into account when reaching his decision.

3 How to improve your chances of passing

Study the **entire** syllabus. 60 of the marks available to you are contained in the case-study Section A questions. Section B questions allow you to show more **specialised knowledge** and allow the examining team to test a wide range of topics.

Practice as many questions as you can under **timed conditions** – this is the best way of developing good exam technique. Make use of the **Practice Question Bank** at the back of this text. **BPP's Practice and Revision Kit** contains numerous exam-standard questions (many of them taken from past exams) as well as three mock exams for you to try.

Answer selectively – the examining team will expect you to consider carefully what is relevant and significant enough to include in your answer. Don't include unnecessary information.

Present your answers in a **professional** manner – use subheadings and leave spaces between paragraphs, make sure that your numerical workings are clearly set out.

Answer all parts of the question – leaving out a five-mark part may be the difference between a pass and a fail.

4 Brought forward knowledge

The Advanced Taxation (ATX – UK) syllabus covers almost every topic that was included in Taxation (TX – UK), with a few minor exceptions. Since tax law changes every year, this text includes all the topics covered at Taxation (TX – UK) again, updated to the latest Finance Act. At the start of each chapter, we highlight topics which have changed between the latest Finance Act and the previous Finance Acts. We also highlight new topics which you have not studied at Taxation (TX – UK).

5 Gaining professional marks

As Advanced Taxation (ATX – UK) is a Strategic Professional module, **four professional marks** will be awarded in Question 1. Professional marks will usually be awarded for **overall presentation** of the required **letter or memorandum**, the **provision of relevant advice** and the **effectiveness with which the information is communicated**.

Whatever the form of communication requested, you need to **present your advice as clearly as possible**. **Spelling and grammar** are important elements in getting your message across to the reader. Also think carefully, am I saying things that are **appropriate in a business communication**?

The exam

Computer-based exams

With effect from the March 2020 sitting, ACCA have commenced the launch of computer-based exams (CBEs) for this module with the aim of rolling out into all markets internationally over a short period. Paper-based examinations (PBE) will be run in parallel while the CBEs are phased in. BPP materials have been designed to support you, whichever exam option you choose. For more information on these changes and when they will be implemented, please visit the ACCA website.

Exam duration

The **time allowed** for both the CBE and PBE exams is 3 hours and 15 minutes.

The exam consists of two sections:

Section A consists of two compulsory case-study questions. Question 1 has 35 marks, including four professional marks, and question 2 has 25 marks. Section A questions require you to analyse the information provided and to use any guidance given to help address the requirements. Because Section A questions are relatively large, careful time management is important, and you should use the number of marks allocated to each requirement to determine how much time to spend on each part. Both questions are likely to deal with a number of different taxes and one question will require a report, letter, memo or meeting notes as part of the answer. There will be five ethics marks available in Section A. In order to score well on the professional marks, you first have to satisfy the requirement in relation to the style and format of the document requested. Further marks are then available for providing clear explanations and coherent calculations. There are no set topics for Section A questions, but you should expect to see coverage of technical taxation topics new in Advanced Taxation (ATX – UK), such as international aspects, and tax planning and interaction of taxes as well as application of technical aspects from Taxation (TX – UK).

Section B consists of two compulsory questions. Each question will have 20 marks covering both business and personal tax issues. Section B questions contain an introductory paragraph, which outlines the technical areas within the question, together with concise structured information and sub-headings to make them easier to assimilate and navigate. Again, there are no set topics, but you might expect to find more specialist questions concentrating on such areas as advanced corporation tax (eg, dealing with close companies or advising on the tax effects of purchase of own shares by a company), advanced personal tax (eg, advising on tax advantaged share schemes) or advanced capital taxes (eg, dealing with trusts).

Throughout the exam, you will be expected to identify issues, as well as demonstrate detailed knowledge of the tax system. In line with this emphasis on practicality, questions may require you to address 'the UK tax consequences' of a given situation without indicating which particular taxes to consider. It is up to you to identify the relevant taxes, and the issues in respect of those taxes, before beginning your answer.

Calculations are normally only required in support of explanations and advice, and not in isolation. Again, it is often up to you to decide what calculations to produce in order to do this in the most efficient manner. Advice on how to approach a given problem may be provided in the question.

There is no specific allocation of numerical calculation versus narrative balance within TX – UK and ATX – UK. However, in practice, TX – UK is weighted towards numerical calculation approximately 60% to 85% whereas ATX – UK is weighted 60% to 70% towards narrative explanations. In both exams, your ability to explain your treatment of tax issues and to present your opinions is vital. It is important to note that this does not mean that you need to have perfect grammar or spelling; it means that you need to make yourself understood.

Tax rates, allowances and information on certain reliefs will be given in the exam. These will be the same as shown in the Tax Tables at the end of this Study Text. You should familiarise yourself with the information provided so that you know how to find it quickly in the exam.

Analysis of past exams

The table below provides details of when each element of the syllabus has been examined in the ten most recent sittings and the question number and section in which each element was examined. Note that in exams before June 2018 there were three questions in Section B (of which two had to be answered) so that five questions in total are referenced.

Covered in text chapter		Mar/ Jun 2018	Sep/ Dec 2017	Mar/ Jun 2017	Sep/ Dec 2016	Mar/ Jun 2016	Sep/ Dec 2015	June 2015	Dec 2014	June 2014	Dec 2013
	INCOME TAX										
1	Principles of income tax	1(ii)	2(a), 5(b)	1(i)		2(b), 5(a), 5(b)	1(a), 2(b), 5(a)	3(b), 5(a)	1(b)	1(a), 4(a), 5(c)	5(a)
2	Pensions and other tax efficient investment products	4(c)	2(a), 5(b)	1(iii)			5(a), 5(b)				3(b)
3	Property and other investment income						4(b)	4(b)		4(a)	5(a)
4	Employment income	1(ii)	2(a)	1(i)	4(b)	2(b), 3(c)	1(a), 4(a)	5(a)		3(a), 5(c)	4(c)
5	Employment income: additional aspects	4(a)	3(c)	4(a)	4(a)	5(b)			5(b)	3(b), 3(c)	5(b)
6	Trade profits	1(ii)	4(a)	1(i)	2(a), 3(b)	1(a), 5(a)	1(a)	5(b)	4(a)	1(a)	
7	Capital allowances			1(i)	3(b)	1(a)		3(a)	2(a)	1(a), 5(b)	1(b)
8	Trading losses	4(b)	4(b)	1(i)			1(a)	1(b)	1(b)		
9	Partnerships and limited liability partnerships	4(b)	4(b)			5(a)					
10	Overseas aspects of income tax	3(a)		3(b)	2(b), 4(c)			1(a)	4(b)		
	CAPITAL GAINS TAX										
11	Chargeable gains: an outline	1(i)	2(a)	4(b)	2(a)	1(b), 3(a)		4(a)	1(a), 3(d)	1(a)	1(b), 3(b), 5(a)
12	Shares and securities					1(b)					3(b)
13	Chargeable gains: reliefs	3(a), 3(c)	2(a), 5(a)	1(iii), 3(b), 4(b)	2(a)	3(a), 4(a)	2(b)	1(c), 4(b)	3(c)	1(a), 5(b)	1(b), 3(b), 5(a)
14	Chargeable gains: additional aspects	3(b)		3(b), 5(c)	2(a), 2(c)	1(b), 3(a)		1(c), 3(a), 4(b), 5(c)	3(d)	4(b)	
	TAX ADMINISTRATION FOR INDIVIDUALS										
15	Self assessment for individuals and partnerships					1(a)			1(b)		

BPP
LEARNING MEDIA

Covered in text chapter		Mar/Jun 2018	Sep/Dec 2017	Mar/Jun 2017	Sep/Dec 2016	Mar/June 2016	Sept/Dec 2015	June 2015	Dec 2014	June 2014	Dec 2013
	INHERITANCE TAX										
16	An introduction to inheritance tax	1(i)	5(a)	1(ii), 3(a)		1(b), 3(b)	5(b)	4(b)	1(a), 3(a)	1(b)	1(b), 3(a)
17	Inheritance tax: valuation, reliefs and the death estate	3(a)	2(b), 5(a)	3(a)	3(a)	3(b)	1(b)	4(c)	3(b)	1(b)	3(a)
18	Inheritance tax: additional aspects	3(a)		1(ii), 3(a)	2(c)			1(d), 4(c)	3(c)	4(c)	1(b), 3(c)
	STAMP TAXES										
19	Stamp taxes		1(i)	2(b)				2(a)			
	CORPORATION TAX										
20	Corporation tax computation	2(c)	3(a)	5(a)		2(a), 4(b)	2(a), 3(a), 4(a)	2(b)	2(a), 2(b)		2(a), 2(b)
21	Chargeable gains for companies		1(i), 1(iii)	5(c)	1(a), 5(a)	2(a)	2(b), 3(b)	2(a)	2(a), 2(c)	2(b)	2(a)
22	Corporation tax administration	2(a)	3(b)	2(a)	1(a)	2(a)	2(a)		5(a)		2(a)
23	Administration, winding up, purchase of own shares			4(b)	5(a)	4(a)					
24	Losses and deficits on non-trading loan relationships	2(c)		5(b)		4(b)			2(a)		
25	Close companies and investment companies				4(b)			3(a)		5(c)	2(b)
26	Groups and consortia	2(a)	1(i), 1(ii)	2(a), 2(b), 5(c)	1(a)	2(a)	2(b), 3(a), 3(c)	2(a), 2(c)	2(a)	2(a)	2(a)
27	Overseas aspects of corporate tax	2(c)							5(c)		4(b)
	VALUE ADDED TAX										
28	Value added tax 1	2(b)	1(iv), 4(c)	2(c), 5(d)	1(b), 5(b)	1(a), 4(c)	2(b), 2(c)	1(d)	1(d)		
29	Value added tax 2	1(ii)		5(d)		4(c)	4(c)	3(c)	2(c)	1(a), 5(a)	2(c), 4(a)
	IMPACT OF TAXES AND TAX PLANNING										
30	Impact of taxes and tax planning	1(iii)	2(a), 2(b), 2(c), 3(c)	1(i), 2(d), 4(c)	1(c)	2(b), 2(c)	1(a)	2(d)	1(c)	1(a), 2(c)	1(a), 5(a)

Syllabus and Study Guide

The complete Advanced Taxation (ATX – UK) syllabus and study guide can be found by visiting the exam resource finder on the ACCA website:

www.accaglobal.com/uk/en/student/exam-support-resources.html

Income tax and national insurance contributions

1

Principles of income tax

Topic list	Syllabus reference
1 Income tax computation	A1(a)B4, B5, B7, A1(e)(ii)
2 Computing income tax payable	A1(a)B5, A1(f)(i), A1(g)(i),(ii)
3 Families	A1(e)(i),(f)(ii)

Introduction

We start our study of taxation with a look at income tax, which is a tax on what individuals make from their jobs, their businesses and their savings. We see how to collect together all of an individual's income in a personal tax computation, and then work out the tax on that income.

We also look at the family aspects of income tax, how joint income of spouses/civil partners is taxed and the anti-avoidance provisions for minor children.

In later chapters, we look at particular types of income in more detail.

Study Guide

		Intellectual level
A1	**Income and income tax liabilities in situations involving further overseas aspects and in relation to trusts, and the application of exemptions and reliefs**	
(a)	The contents of the Taxation - United Kingdom (TX – UK) study guide for income tax and national insurance, under headings:	2
•	B4 Property and investment income	
•	B5 The comprehensive computation of taxable income and the income tax liability	
•	B7 The use of exemptions and reliefs in deferring and minimising income tax liabilities	
(e)	Property and investment income:	3
(i)	Advise on the tax implications of jointly held assets	
(ii)	Recognise the tax treatment of savings income paid net of tax	
(f)	The comprehensive computation of taxable income and the income tax liability:	3
(i)	Understand the allocation of the personal allowance to different categories of income	
(ii)	Advise on the income tax position of the income of minor children	
(g)	The use of exemptions and reliefs in deferring and minimising income tax liabilities:	3
(i)	Understand and apply the rules relating to investments in the seed enterprise investment scheme and the enterprise investment scheme	
(ii)	Understand and apply the rules relating to investments in venture capital trusts	

Exam guide

Although you are unlikely to have to perform a complete income tax computation in the exam, you need to understand how the computation is put together as, for example, you may be asked to calculate the after tax income that would be derived from a particular new source. Do not overlook the effect of an increase in income on the amount of the personal allowance.

The chapter also introduces tax planning concepts. Note the treatment of joint income of spouses/civil partners and the anti-avoidance rules that apply if a parent gives funds to a minor child.

Knowledge brought forward from earlier studies

This chapter revises the basic income tax computation that you will already have met in Taxation (TX – UK). The examining team has identified essential underpinning knowledge from the Taxation (TX – UK) syllabus which is particularly important that you revise as part of your Advanced Taxation (ATX – UK) studies. In this chapter, the relevant topics are:

		Intellectual level
B5	**The comprehensive computation of taxable income and income tax liability**	
(b)	Calculate the amount of personal allowance available	2
(d)	Compute the amount of income tax payable	2

The changes in 2018/19 from 2017/18 in the material you have previously studied in Taxation (TX – UK) are that the personal allowance has been increased to £11,850, the transferable personal allowance has increased to £1,190, the basic rate limit has been increased to £34,500 and the dividend nil rate band has been reduced to £2,000. The child benefit tax charge is not examinable in Advanced Taxation (ATX – UK).

If you studied Taxation (TX – UK) before Finance Act 2016, it is important that you are aware of major changes to the personal tax computation that apply from 2016/17. Bank and building society interest is now received gross and there is no tax credit for dividends. There is a new savings income nil rate band and a new dividend nil rate band. The rates of tax for dividend income are now 7.5%, 32.5% and 38.1%. The order of set off of the personal allowance will continue usually to be against non-savings income, savings income and dividend income in that order, but in some cases it should be set against dividend income in priority to savings income. It is important that you work through all the tax computation questions in this chapter to familiarise yourself with the new rules.

Topics that will be new to you in this chapter are the additional ISA allowance for surviving spouses, tax reducers (other than the transferable personal allowance) and the taxation of families.

1 Income tax computation

1.1 Aggregation of income

One of the competencies you require to fulfil Performance Objective 15 Tax computations and assessments of the PER is to extract and analyse data from financial records and filing information relevant to the preparation of tax computations and related supporting documents. You can apply the knowledge you obtain from this section of the text to help to demonstrate this competence.

As a general rule, income tax is charged on receipts which might be expected to recur (such as weekly wages or profits from running a business). **An individual's income from all sources is brought together (aggregated) in a personal tax computation for the tax year.**

Key terms

The **tax year**, or **fiscal year**, or **year of assessment** runs from 6 April to 5 April. For example, the tax year 2018/19 runs from 6 April 2018 to 5 April 2019.

Here is an example. All items are explained later in this text.

RICHARD: INCOME TAX COMPUTATION 2018/19

	Non-savings income £	Savings income £	Dividend income £	Total £
Income from employment	54,485			
Building society interest		1,000		
Company loan stock interest		860		
UK dividends			3,000	
Total income	54,485	1,860	3,000	59,345
Less qualifying interest paid	(2,000)			
Net income	52,485	1,860	3,000	57,345
Less personal allowance	(11,850)			
Taxable income	40,635	1,860	3,000	45,495

	£	£
Income tax on non savings income		
£34,500 × 20%		6,900
£6,135 (40,635 − 34,500) × 40%		2,454
Tax on savings income		
£500 × 0% (savings income nil rate band)		0
£1,360 (1,860 − 500) × 40%		544
Tax on dividend income		
£2,000 × 0% (dividend nil rate band)		0
£1,000 (3,000 − 2,000) × 32.5%		325
		10,223
Less: tax reducer		
investment under the EIS £10,000 × 30%		(3,000)
Tax liability		7,223
Less: tax suffered		
PAYE tax on salary (say)	6,528	
Tax deducted at source on company loan stock	172	
		(6,700)
Tax payable		523

Total income is all income subject to income tax. Each of the amounts which make up total income is called a component. **Net income** is total income less qualifying interest and trade losses. **Taxable income** is net income less the personal allowance. The **tax liability** is the amount charged on the individual's income. **Tax payable** is the balance of the liability still to be settled in cash.

1.2 Types of income

Most savings income is received without deduction of tax. Dividends are also received gross. There are a number of sources of exempt income.

1.2.1 Classification of income

All income received must be **classified** according to the nature of the income. This is because different computational rules apply to different types of income. The main types of income are:

- Income from employment, pensions and some social security benefits
- Income from trades, professions and vocations (trading income)
- Income from property businesses
- Savings and investment income, including interest and dividends
- Miscellaneous income (eg casual earnings)

1.2.2 Non-savings income

The rules for computing **employment income**, **trading income** and **property business income** will be covered in later chapters. These types of income are **non-savings income**. Pension income is also non-savings income.

There is a **trading income allowance** which wholly or partially exempts small amounts of trading income and a **property business income allowance** which wholly or partially exempts small amounts of property business income. These allowances are **not examinable** in Advanced Taxation (ATX − UK).

1.2.3 Savings income

Savings income is interest. Interest is paid on bank and building society accounts, on Government securities, such as Treasury Stock, and on company loan stock.

The following savings income is **received gross**.

(a)   Bank, building society and National Savings & Investments interest paid to individuals

(b)   Interest from company loan stock which is listed on a recognised stock exchange

(c)   Interest on Government securities (these are also called 'gilts')

The following savings income is received net of 20% tax. **This is called income taxed at source.**

(a)   Interest paid to individuals by companies on company loan stock which is not listed on a recognised stock exchange and on other loans made by individuals to companies

(b)   Savings income from non discretionary trusts (dealt with later in this text)

The amount received is grossed up by multiplying by 100/80 and is included gross in the income tax computation. The tax deducted at source is deducted in computing tax payable and may be repaid.

Exam focus point

> In examinations you may be given either the net or the gross amount of such income: read the question carefully. If you are given the net amount (the amount received or credited), you should gross up the figure at the rate of 20%. For example, net company loan stock interest of £160 is equivalent to gross income of £160 × 100/80 = £200 on which tax of £40 (20% of £200) has been suffered.

1.2.4 Dividend income

Dividends on UK shares is dividend income and is received gross.

1.2.5 Exempt income   12/17

> One of the competencies you require to fulfil Performance Objective 17 Tax planning and advice of the PER is to mitigate and/or defer tax liabilities through the use of standard reliefs, exemptions and incentives. You can apply the knowledge you obtain from this section of the text to help to demonstrate this competence.

Some income is exempt from income tax. Several of these exemptions are mentioned at places in this Text where the types of income are described in detail, but you should note the following types of exempt income now.

(a)   **Scholarships** (exempt as income of the scholar. If paid by a parent's employer, a scholarship may be taxable Income of the parent)

(b)   Betting and gaming winnings, including **premium bond prizes**

(c)   Interest or terminal bonus on **National Savings & Investments Certificates**

(d)   Certain social security benefits

(e)   Income on investments made through **Individual Savings Accounts (ISAs)**

Key term

> **Individual savings accounts ISAs** are tax efficient savings accounts. There are two types of ISA.
>
> 1   Cash ISA (which only has a cash component)
>
> 2   Stocks and shares ISA (which only has a stocks and shares component, although uninvested cash may be held in a stocks and shares of ISA if the provider allows this)

The investor must be resident in the UK in the year the investment is made. The investor must normally be 18 years or over. However, a cash ISA can be held by individuals aged 16 or 17.

The annual subscription limit for ISAs is £20,000 for 2018/19. This can be invested in cash, stocks and shares, or any combination of the two.

If an individual has a **flexible cash ISA** they can **withdraw money** and **replace it in the same tax year without the replaced cash counting towards the ISA subscription limit.**

Where the holder of one or more ISAs dies, their spouse/civil partner is entitled to an additional ISA allowance equal to the value of the ISAs held by the deceased person at their death.

Investments within ISAs are exempt from both income tax and capital gains tax. The introduction of the savings income nil rate band and the dividend nil rate band means that ISAs are not as advantageous as they were previously. However, **additional rate taxpayers and individuals who have already used their savings income nil rate band will still benefit from using a cash ISA**. The **main benefit of using a stocks and shares ISA** is the **capital gains tax exemption** where an individual already uses the annual exempt amount.

Exam focus point

> The help-to-buy ISA, the innovative finance ISA and the lifetime ISA are **not examinable** in Advanced Taxation (ATX – UK).

1.3 Qualifying interest

6/15, 3/16

FAST FORWARD

> Qualifying interest is deducted from total income to compute net income.

An individual who pays interest on a loan in a tax year is entitled to relief in that tax year if the loan is for one of the following purposes:

(a) **Loan to buy plant or machinery for partnership use.** Interest is allowed for three years from the end of the tax year in which the loan was taken out. If the plant is used partly for private use, the allowable interest is apportioned.

(b) **Loan to buy plant or machinery for employment use.** Interest is allowed for three years from the end of the tax year in which the loan was taken out. If the plant is used partly for private use, the allowable interest is apportioned.

(c) **Loan to acquire any part of the ordinary share capital of a close company (other than a close investment-holding company) or to lend money to such a company which is used wholly and exclusively for the purpose of its business or that of an associated close company.** A close company is a company controlled by its shareholder-directors or by five or fewer shareholders (see later in this Text). For a company to be a close company, it must be resident in the UK. However, for the purposes of relief for interest payments, this definition is extended to include companies which are resident in an European Economic Area (EEA) state other than the UK which would be a close company if it was UK resident.

When the interest is paid, the borrower must **either** hold some shares in the close company and work the greater part of their time in the actual management or conduct of the company (or of an associated company) **or** have a material interest in the close company (ie hold more than 5% of the shares). Also, the individual usually must not have recovered any capital from the company.

Relief is not available if Enterprise Investment Scheme (EIS) relief (see later in this Text) is claimed on the shares.

(d) **Loan to buy interest in employee-controlled company.** The company must be an unquoted trading company resident in the UK or another EEA state and not resident outside the EEA, with at least 50% of the voting shares held by employees.

(e) **Loan to invest in partnership.** The investment may be a share in the partnership or a contribution to the partnership of capital or a loan to the partnership. The individual must be a partner (other than a limited partner) and relief ceases when they cease to be a partner.

(f) **Loan to invest in a co-operative.** The investment may be shares or a loan. The individual must spend the greater part of their time working for the co-operative.

Tax relief is given by deducting the interest from total income to calculate net income for the tax year in which the interest is paid. It is usually deducted from **non-savings income first, then from savings income and lastly from dividend income.** We deal with the situation where it may be deducted from dividend income in priority to savings income later in this chapter.

There is a **limit on the amount of deductions from total income, including qualifying interest,** which an individual taxpayer can make in a tax year. This limit is discussed in the chapter on trading losses later in this Text.

1.4 Personal allowance

FAST FORWARD

> All persons are entitled to a personal allowance. It is usually deducted from net income, first against non savings income, then against savings income and lastly against dividend income. The personal allowance is reduced by £1 for every £2 that adjusted net income exceeds £100,000 and can be reduced to nil.

Once income from all sources has been aggregated and any qualifying interest deducted, the remainder is the taxpayer's net income. An allowance, the **personal allowance,** is **deducted from net income.** Like qualifying interest, it usually reduces **non savings income first, then savings income and lastly dividend income.** We deal with the situation where it may be deducted from dividend income in priority to savings income later in this chapter.

All individuals (including children) **are entitled to the personal allowance of £11,850.**

However, if the **individual's adjusted net income exceeds £100,000,** the **personal allowance is reduced by £1 for each £2 by which adjusted net income exceeds £100,000 until the personal allowance is nil (which is when adjusted net income is £123,700 or more).**

Key term

> **Adjusted net income** is net income less the gross amounts of personal pension contributions (and gift aid donations – not in your syllabus).

Exam focus point

> The limit of £123,700 will be given to you in the Tax Rates and Allowances available in the exam.

We will look at personal pension contributions later In this Text and revisit this topic again then. At the moment, we will look at the situation where net income and adjusted net income are the same amounts.

Question

Personal allowance

In 2018/19, Clare has employment Income of £97,000, and receives bank interest of £8,000 and dividends of £7,500.

Calculate Clare's taxable income for 2018/19.

Answer

	Non-savings income £	Savings income £	Dividend income £	Total £
Employment income	97,000			
Bank interest		8,000		
Dividends			7,500	
Net income	97,000	8,000	7,500	112,500
Less personal allowance (W)	(5,600)			
Taxable income	91,400	8,000	7,500	106,900

Working

Net income	112,500
Less income limit	(100,000)
Excess	12,500
Personal allowance	11,850
Less half excess £12,500 × ½	(6,250)
	5,600

BPP LEARNING MEDIA

Where an individual has an adjusted net income between £100,000 and £123,700, the effective rate of tax on the income between these two amounts will usually be 60%. This is calculated as 40% (the higher rate on income) plus 40% of half (ie 20%) of the excess adjusted net income over £100,000 used to restrict the personal allowance. The individual should consider **making personal pension contributions to reduce adjusted net income to below £100,000**.

2 Computing income tax payable

12/13, 6/14, 9/15, 3/16, 6/16, 6/17, 12/17, 6/18

2.1 Income tax liability

Income tax is worked out on taxable income. First tax non-savings income, then savings income and then dividend income. There are nil rate bands for savings income and dividend income.

One of the competencies you require to fulfil Performance Objective 15 Tax computations and assessments of the PER is to prepare or contribute to the computation or assessment of tax computations for individuals. You can apply the knowledge you obtain from this section of the text to help to demonstrate this competence.

2.1.1 Tax rates

Income tax payable is computed on an individual's taxable income, which comprises net income less the personal allowance. The tax rates are applied to taxable income on non-savings income first, then to savings income and finally to dividend income.

Exam focus point

There are different rates of income tax on non-savings income for Scottish taxpayers. These are **not examinable** in Advanced Taxation (ATX – UK) but questions may state that a taxpayer is, for example, living in England, to establish that the Scottish income tax rates do not apply.

2.1.2 Savings income starting rate band

There is a **tax rate of 0% for savings income within the savings income starting rate band (£5,000 for 2018/19)**. This rate is called the **savings income starting rate**.

The savings income starting rate only applies where the savings income falls wholly or partly below the starting rate limit. Remember that income tax is charged first on non-savings income. So, in most cases, an individual's non-savings income will exceed the starting rate limit and the savings income starting rate will not be available on savings income.

The **savings income starting rate band** counts towards the **basic rate limit of £34,500**.

2.1.3 Savings income nil rate band

There is a **tax rate of 0%** for **savings income** within the **savings income nil rate band.** The savings income nil rate band for 2018/19 is **£1,000** if the individual is a **basic rate taxpayer** and **£500** if the individual is a **higher rate taxpayer**. There is **no savings income nil rate band** for **additional rate taxpayers**.

The **savings income nil rate band** counts towards the **basic rate limit of £34,500**.

Exam focus point

The detailed rules for establishing whether an individual is a higher rate or additional rate taxpayer for the purpose of computing the availability of the savings income nil rate band are quite complicated and are **not examinable** in Advanced Taxation (ATX – UK). Therefore, in any question involving the savings income nil rate band, it will be quite clear which tax rate is applicable.

In 2018/19 Alicia, who lives in England, has trading income of £14,450 and receives bank interest of £8,000. Calculate Alicia's tax liability for 2018/19.

Answer

	Non-savings income £	Savings income £	Total £
Trading income	14,450		
Bank interest		8,000	
Net income	14,450	8,000	22,450
Less personal allowance	(11,850)		
Taxable income	2,600	8,000	10,600

Income tax	£
Non-savings income	
£2,600 × 20%	520
Savings income	
£2,400 (5,000 – 2,600) × 0% (savings starting rate band)	0
£1,000 × 0% (savings income nil rate band – basic rate taxpayer)	0
£4,600 (8,000 – 2,400 – 1,000) × 20%	920
Tax liability	1,440

In order **to prevent the waste of the savings starting rate band and the savings income nil rate band**, it may be advisable to **consider increasing non-savings income to ensure that full use is made of the personal allowance against such income rather than against savings income.**

2.1.4 Dividend nil rate band

There is a **tax rate of 0%** for **dividend income** within the **dividend nil rate band.** The dividend nil rate band for 2018/19 is **£2,000** for **all taxpayers.**

The **dividend nil rate band** counts towards the **basic rate limit of £34,500 and the higher rate limit of £150,000.**

2.1.5 Basic rate

The **basic rate** of tax is **20%** for 2018/19 for both **non-savings income and savings income.**

The **basic rate** of tax is **7.5%** for 2018/19 for **dividend income.**

The **basic rate limit** for 2018/19 is **£34,500.**

2.1.6 Higher rate

The **higher rate** of tax is **40%** for 2018/19 for **non-savings and saving income.**

The **higher rate** of tax is **32.5%** for 2018/19 for **dividend income.**

The **higher rate limit** for 2018/19 is **£150,000.**

In 2018/19 Joe, who lives in Northern Ireland, has employment income of £43,150 and receives bank interest of £5,200. Calculate Joe's tax liability for 2018/19.

	Non-savings income £	Savings income £	Total £
Employment income	43,150		
Bank interest		5,200	
Net income	43,150	5,200	48,350
Less personal allowance	(11,850)		
Taxable income	31,300	5,200	36,500

Income tax	£
Non-savings income	
£31,300 × 20%	6,260
Savings income	
£500 × 0% (savings income nil rate band – higher rate taxpayer)	0
£2,700 (34,500 – 31,300 – 500) × 20%	540
£2,000 (5,200 – 500 – 2,700) × 40%	800
Tax liability	7,600

Question — Savings and dividend nil rates, basic rate and higher rate

In 2018/19 Margery, who lives in Wales, has employment income of £56,800, and receives building society interest of £1,600 and dividends of £12,000. Calculate Margery's tax liability for 2018/19.

Answer

	Non-savings income £	Savings income £	Dividend income £	Total £
Employment income	56,800			
BSI		1,600		
Dividends			12,000	
Net income	56,800	1,600	12,000	70,400
Less personal allowance	(11,850)			
Taxable income	44,950	1,600	12,000	58,550

Income tax	£
Non-savings income	
£34,500 × 20%	6,900
£10,450 (44,950 – 34,500) × 40%	4,180
Savings income	
£500 × 0% (savings income nil rate band – higher rate taxpayer)	0
£1,100 (1,600 – 500) × 40%	440
Dividend income	
£2,000 × 0% (dividend nil rate band)	0
£10,000 (12,000 – 2,000) × 32.5%	3,250
Tax liability	14,770

2.1.7 Additional rate

The **additional rate** of tax is **45%** for 2018/19 for **non-savings and saving income**.

The **additional rate** of tax is **38.1%** for 2018/19 for **dividend income**.

The **additional rate** of tax applies to **taxable income in excess of £150,000**.

Question — *Additional rate tax*

In 2018/19 Julian, who lives in England, has employment income of £148,000, and receives bank interest of £6,250 and dividends of £17,000. Calculate Julian's tax liability for 2018/19.

Answer

	Non-savings income £	Savings income £	Dividend income £	Total £
Employment income	148,000			
Bank interest		6,250		
Dividends			17,000	
Net income/taxable income (no PA available)	148,000	6,250	17,000	171,250

Julian is not entitled to the personal allowance as his net income exceeds £123,700.

	£
Income tax	
Non-savings income	
£34,500 × 20%	6,900
£113,500 (148,000 – 34,500) × 40%	45,400
Savings income	
£2,000 (150,000 – 148,000) × 40%	800
£4,250 (6,250 – 2,000) × 45%	1,912
Dividend income	
£2,000 × 0%	0
£15,000 (17,000 – 2,000) × 38.1%	5,715
Tax liability	60,727

Julian is not entitled to the savings income nil rate band because he is an additional rate taxpayer.

2.1.8 Set off of qualifying interest and personal allowance

FAST FORWARD

> Qualifying interest and the personal allowance are usually set off first against non-savings income, then against savings income and then against dividend income. However, in some cases it is more beneficial to set these against dividend income in priority to savings income.

The **usual order** of set off of **qualifying interest** (to compute net income) and the **personal allowance** (to compute taxable income) is against **non-savings income first, then savings income and lastly dividend income**.

However, taxpayers should **set them against dividend income in priority to savings income** where this **preserves the use of the savings starting rate band and the savings income nil rate band**. This is not a matter of tax planning or a claim but just the correct way to set off qualifying interest and the personal allowance to minimise the individual's tax liability.

Question — *Set off of personal allowance*

In 2018/19 Wayne, who lives in England, has trading income from a partnership of £6,650, and receives bank interest of £8,400 and dividends of £17,000. Calculate Wayne's tax liability for 2018/19.

	Non-savings income £	Savings income £	Dividend income £	Total £
Trading income	6,650			
Bank interest		8,400		
Dividends			17,000	
Net income	6,650	8,400	17,000	32,050
Less personal allowance (N)	(6,650)	(2,400)	(2,800)	
Taxable income	0	6,000	14,200	20,200

Note. Follow these steps to set off the personal allowance correctly.

Step 1 Set off the maximum amount of personal allowance against non-savings income ie £6,650.

Step 2 Work out how much savings income should be taxable in order to use the savings starting rate band and the savings income nil rate band ie £5,000 + £1,000 (basic rate taxpayer) = £6,000.

Step 3 Work out difference between net savings income and taxable savings income ie £8,400 – 6,000 = £2,400. This is the amount of the personal allowance to be set off against savings income.

Step 4 Work out the amount of the remaining personal allowance to be set off against dividend income ie £11,850 – 6,650 – 2,400 = £2,800.

	£
Income tax	
Savings income	
£5,000 × 0% (starting rate band)	0
£1,000 × 0% (savings income nil rate band – basic rate taxpayer)	0
Dividend income	
£2,000 × 0% (dividend nil rate band)	0
£12,200 (14,200 – 2,000) × 7.5%	915
Tax liability	915

2.1.9 Tax reducers

FAST FORWARD

Tax reducers reduce tax on income at a set rate of relief.

Tax reducers do not affect income; they reduce tax on income. The tax reducers are:

(a) Investments in **venture capital trusts (VCTs)**
(b) Investments under the **enterprise investment scheme (EIS)**
(c) Investments under the **seed enterprise investment scheme (SEIS)**
(d) **Transferable personal allowance** (marriage allowance). This topic is dealt with later in this section
(e) **Property business income finance costs**. This topic is dealt with later in this text

Tax reducers are deducted in computing an individual's income tax liability. The tax liability can only be reduced to zero: a tax reducer cannot create a repayment.

Investments in VCTs and under the EIS and SEIS qualify for tax reducers as a percentage of the amount subscribed for qualifying investments.

For investments in **VCTs** and under the **EIS**, the percentage is **30%**. For investments under the **SEIS**, the percentage is **50%**. Further details are given later in this text.

If the individual is entitled to **more than one tax reducer** in relation to such investments, the **VCT reducer** is deducted **first, then** the **EIS reducer** and **finally** the **SEIS reducer**.

Question

During 2018/19 Peter, who lives in England, makes qualifying investments of £5,000 in a venture capital trust and of £2,000 under the seed enterprise investment scheme. Show his tax position for 2018/19 if his income consists of:

(a)   Trading profits of £50,875
(b)   Trading profits of £18,395.

Answer

	(a): High income Non-savings £	(b): Low income Non-savings £
Trading profits	50,875	18,395
Less personal allowance	(11,850)	(11,850)
Taxable income	39,025	6,545
Income tax		
	£	£
Non-savings income		
£34,500/£6,545 × 20%	6,900	1,309
£4,525/nil × 40%	1,810	
	8,710	1,309
Tax reducers		
VCT £5,000 × 30%	(1,500)	(1,309)
	7,210	0
SEIS £2,000 × 50%	(1,000)	–
Tax liability	6,210	0

The tax reducers cannot lead to repayments of tax, so in (b) the SEIS relief and some of the VCT relief is wasted if relief is taken in this tax year (see later in this Study Text for claim to use SEIS relief in previous tax year).

A spouse/civil partner can elect to transfer £1,190 of their personal allowance to the other spouse/civil partner if certain conditions are met. This is sometimes known as the marriage allowance.

Neither the spouse/civil partner making the transfer nor the spouse/civil partner receiving the transfer can be a higher rate or additional rate taxpayer.

The spouse/civil partner receiving the transfer does not have an increased personal allowance. **Instead, they are entitled to a tax reducer of £1,190 × 20% = £238.**

Question

Alec and Bertha are a married couple and live in Wales. In the tax year 2018/19, Alec has net income of £10,500 and Bertha has net income of £25,850. All their income is non-savings income. Alec has made an election to transfer part of his personal allowance to Bertha. Show Alec and Bertha's taxable income for 2018/19 and compute Bertha's income tax liability.

Alec

	Non-savings income £
Net income	10,500
Less personal allowance £(11,850 – 1,190)	(10,660)
Taxable income	0

Bertha

	Non-savings income £
Net income	25,850
Less personal allowance	(11,850)
Taxable income	14,000

	£
Income tax	
£14,000 × 20%	2,800
Less transferable personal allowance tax reducer £1,190 × 20%	(238)
Income tax liability	2,562

The election for the transferable personal allowance is made to HMRC online by the spouse/civil partner making the transfer. For the tax year 2018/19, if the election is made before 6 April 2019, it will have effect for 2018/19 and subsequent tax years unless it is cancelled by the transferor spouse/civil partner or circumstances change (eg divorce or a tax reduction is not actually obtained). **If the election for the tax year 2018/19 is made on or after 6 April 2019 it must be made within four years of the end of the tax year (ie by 5 April 2023) and will only apply for the tax year 2018/19. The couple, as a whole, will save tax through the election if the net income of the transferor is below £11,850.**

2.2 Income tax payable

FAST FORWARD ⟩⟩ From tax liability, deduct any income tax suffered at source to arrive at tax payable. Tax suffered at source can be repaid.

One of the competencies you require to fulfil Performance Objective 15 Tax computations and assessments of the PER is to prepare or contribute to the computation or assessment of tax computations for individuals. You can apply the knowledge you obtain from this section of the text to help to demonstrate this competence.

Step 1 **The first step in preparing a personal tax computation is to set up three columns**
One column for non-savings income, one for savings income and one for dividend income. Add up income from different sources. The sum of these is known as 'total income'. Deduct qualifying interest and trade losses to compute 'net income'. Deduct the personal allowance to compute 'taxable income'.

Step 2 **Deal with non-savings income first**
Any non-savings income up to the basic rate limit of £34,500 is taxed at 20%. Non-savings income between the basic rate limit and the higher rate limit of £150,000 is taxed at 40%. Any further non-savings income is taxed at 45%.

Step 3   **Now deal with savings income**

Savings income below the savings income starting rate limit of £5,000 is taxed at the savings income starting rate of 0%. Then tax savings income covered by the savings income nil rate band (for basic rate and higher rate taxpayers) at 0%. Savings income between the starting rate limit and the basic rate limit of £34,500, which is not covered by the savings income nil rate band, is taxed at 20%. Savings income between the basic rate limit and the higher rate limit of £150,000 is taxed at 40%. Any further savings income is taxed at 45%.

Step 4   **Lastly, tax dividend income**

The first £2,000 is within the dividend nil rate band and is taxed at 0%. Other dividend income below the basic rate limit of £34,500 is taxed at 7.5%. Dividend income between the basic rate limit and the higher rate limit of £150,000 is taxed at 32.5%. Any further dividend income is taxed at 38.1%.

Step 5   **Add the amounts of tax together.**

Step 6   Once tax has been computed, **deduct any available tax reducers** (eg EIS, transferable personal allowance).

Step 7   Calculate the amount of any **pension annual allowance charge** (see later in this text) add to the tax remaining after step 6. The resulting figure is the **income tax liability**.

Step 8   Finally **deduct the tax deducted at source from PAYE, savings income (if received net) and trust income (see later in this Study Text)**. These amounts can be repaid to the extent that they exceed the income tax liability.

Question   Calculation of income tax payable

In 2018/19, Jules, who lives in England, has employment income of £59,650 (PAYE deducted £5,800), corporate loan stock interest of £3,400 (net of 20% tax deducted at source) and dividends of £4,500. He pays qualifying interest of £3,000. Jules makes an investment of £5,000 under the Enterprise Investment Scheme. How much income tax is payable by Jules in 2018/19?

Answer

	Non-savings income £	Savings income £	Dividend income £	Total £
Employment income	59,650			
Loan stock interest £3,400 × 100/80		4,250		
Dividends			4,500	
Total income	59,650	4,250	4,500	
Less qualifying interest	(3,000)			
Net income	56,650	4,250	4,500	65,400
Less personal allowance	(11,850)			
Taxable income	44,800	4,250	4,500	53,550

	£
Non-savings income	
£34,500 × 20%	6,900
£10,300 (44,800 – 34,500) × 40%	4,120
	11,020
Savings income	
£500 × 0% (savings income nil rate band – higher rate taxpayer)	0
£3,750 (4,250 – 500) × 40%	1,500
Dividend income	
£2,000 × 0% (dividend nil rate band)	0
£2,500 (4,500 – 2,000) × 32.5%	812
Tax reducer	13,332
EIS £5,000 × 30%	(1,500)
Tax liability	11,832
Less: PAYE	(5,800)
tax suffered on company loan stock interest £4,250 × 20%	(850)
Tax payable	5,182

2.3 Calculating additional tax due

FAST FORWARD Calculating additional tax due, for example when a new source of income is acquired, can often be done by working at the margin.

Often a taxpayer is interested in looking at the after tax return from a particular investment or transaction. In each of the following examples we will **calculate the additional tax due as a result of acquiring a new source of income**. This is sometimes called 'working at the margin' as it relates to the marginal rate of tax which is the rate that the taxpayer has to pay on each additional pound of income received. Note how it is **not necessary here to use the full income tax proforma and therefore is a useful way of saving time in the exam**. This technique can also be used for other taxes such as capital gains tax and Class 4 national insurance contributions.

2.4 Examples: additional tax due

(a) Kate, who lives in England, has employment income each tax year of £70,000. Her grandfather dies leaving her a number of houses which are rented out to tenants. She has property business income of £25,000 during 2018/19. Kate's employment income uses up her personal allowance of £11,850 and the basic rate band of £34,500 (total £46,350) so the additional tax due as a result of receiving the property business income can be calculated simply as £25,000 × 40% = £10,000.

(b) Kate, who lives in England, has employment income each tax year of £45,350. Her grandfather dies leaving her a number of houses which are rented out to tenants. She has property business income of £25,000 during 2018/19. The additional tax due as a result of receiving the property business income can be calculated as follows:

Amount remaining below basic rate limit:
£34,500 – (£45,350 – £11,850) = £1,000

	£
£1,000 @ 20%	200
£24,000 (25,000 – 1,000) @ 40%	9,600
Additional tax due	9,800

(c) Kate, who lives in England, has employment income each tax year of £99,000. Her grandfather dies leaving her a number of houses which are rented out to tenants. She has property business income of £25,000 during 2018/19. Income tax on property business income is all at the higher rate. In addition, Kate will no longer be entitled to the personal allowance since her net income is £(99,000 + 25,000) = £124,000.

The additional tax due is therefore calculated as follows:

	£
Higher rate tax on property business income £25,000 @ 40%	10,000
Tax on income previously covered by personal allowance £11,850 @ 40%	4,740
Additional tax due	14,740

(d)   Kate, who lives in England, has employment income each tax year of £175,000. She has property business income of £25,000 during 2018/19. Kate's employment income uses up the basic rate band of £34,500 and the higher rate band of £115,500 (total £150,000) so the property business income will be taxed at the additional rate. Kate's existing income is of such a level that she is not entitled to the personal allowance, even before the property business income is received, and so there is no further impact on additional tax due. The additional tax due as a result of receiving the property business income therefore can be calculated simply as £25,000 × 45% = £11,250.

2.5 Income taxed as top slice of income

One type of income (covered later in this Study Text) is **taxed after dividend income**, so that dividend income is not always the top slice of income. This is the **taxable portions of partly exempt payments on the termination of employment**.

So someone with employment income of £26,350 (using the personal allowance of £11,850 and £14,500 of basic rate band), dividend income of £20,000 and a £50,000 termination payment will have the dividend income of £18,000, in excess of the £2,000 dividend nil rate band, taxed at 7.5%, instead of 32.5% as the dividend income will not exceed the basic rate limit. The termination payment will be wholly taxed at 40% since it is above the basic rate limit of £34,500.

2.6 The complete proforma

Here is a complete proforma computation. You can refer back to it as you work through this text. You will also see how losses fit into the proforma later in this text.

	Non-savings income £	Savings income £	Dividend income £	Total £
Trading income	X			
Employment income	X			
Property business income	X			
Bank/building society interest (received gross)		X		
Company loan stock interest (grossed up)		X		
Other interest (received gross)		X		
(as many lines as necessary)				
Dividends (received gross)			X	
Discretionary trust income	X			
Interest in possession trust income	X̲	X̲	X̲	
Total income	X	X	X	
Less qualifying interest	(X)	(X)	(X)	
Net income	X	X	X	X
Less personal allowance	(X)	(X)	(X)	
Taxable income	X̲	X̲	X̲	X

3 Families

FAST FORWARD

Spouses, civil partners and children are all separate taxpayers. There are special rules to prevent parents from exploiting a child's personal allowance.

One of the competencies you require to fulfil Performance Objective 17 Tax planning and advice of the PER is to review the situation of an individual or entity advising on any potential tax risks and/or additional tax minimisation measures. You can apply the knowledge you obtain from this section of the text to help to demonstrate this competence.

3.1 Spouses and civil partners

Spouses and civil partners are taxed as two separate people. Each spouse/civil partner is entitled to a personal allowance depending on their income.

Spouses and civil partners should ensure, where possible, that **each spouse/civil partner uses their savings income nil rate band and dividend nil rate band.**

Question — Tax planning for spouses/civil partners (1)

Liam and Joe are a married couple. In 2018/19, Liam has trading profits of £180,000 and receives building society interest of £300 and Joe has a salary of £88,000 and receives dividends of £8,000. Liam and Joe live in England.

Advise Liam and Joe how they can transfer assets to obtain the best use of their income nil rate bands.

Answer

Since Liam is an additional rate taxpayer, he is not entitled to the savings income nil rate band but he has not utilised his dividend nil rate band. Joe has not utilised his savings income nil rate band of £500 (higher rate taxpayer) and has exceeded his dividend nil rate band of £2,000.

Liam should therefore transfer his building society funds to Joe thus saving income tax of £300 × 45% = £135 and Joe should transfer shares producing £2,000 of dividends to Liam thus saving income tax of £2,000 × 32.5% = £650.

When spouses/civil partners jointly own income-generating property, it is assumed that they are entitled to equal shares of the income. This does not apply to income from shares held in close companies (see later in this text for an explanation of close companies).

If the spouses/civil partners are not entitled to equal shares in the income-generating property (other than shares in close companies), **they may make a joint declaration to HMRC, specifying the proportion to which each is entitled.** These proportions are used to tax each of them separately, in respect of income arising on or after the date of the declaration. For capital gains tax purposes it is always the underlying beneficial ownership that is taken into account.

Question — Tax planning for spouses/civil partners (2)

Brian is a higher rate taxpayer who owns a rental property producing £27,700 of property income on which he pays tax at 40%, giving him a tax liability of £11,080. His spouse, Mary, has no income. They live in England.

Advise Brian on the income tax saving if he transfers a 5% share of the property to Mary.

If Brian transfers a 5% share of property to Mary, they will be treated as jointly owning the property and will each be taxed on 50% of the income. Brian's tax liability on the property income will be reduced to £5,540.

Mary's liability is then calculated as follows:

	£
Net income	13,850
Less personal allowance	(11,850)
Taxable income	2,000
Tax on £2,000 × 20%	400

This gives an overall tax saving of £(5,540 − 400) = £5,140. This could alternatively be calculated as £11,850 × 40% = £4,740 plus £2,000 × 20% = £400 giving the total saving of £5,140.

3.2 Minor children

Income which is directly transferred by a parent to their minor child, or is derived from capital so transferred, remains income of the parent for tax purposes. This applies only to parents, however, and not to any other relatives. Even where a parent is involved, the child's income is not treated as the parent's if it does not exceed £100 (gross) a year.

Chapter roundup

- In a personal income tax computation, bring together income from all sources, splitting the sources into non-savings, savings and dividend income.

- Most savings income is received without deduction of tax. Dividends are also received gross. There are a number of sources of exempt income.

- Qualifying interest is deducted from total income to compute net income.

- All persons are entitled to a personal allowance. It is usually deducted from net income, first against non savings income, then against savings income and lastly against dividend income. The personal allowance is reduced by £1 for every £2 that adjusted net income exceeds £100,000 and can be reduced to nil.

- Income tax is worked out on taxable income. First tax non-savings income, then savings income and then dividend income. There are nil rate bands for savings income and dividend income.

- Qualifying interest and the personal allowance are usually set off first against non-savings income, then against savings income and then against dividend income. However, in some cases it is more beneficial to set these against dividend income in priority to savings income.

- Tax reducers reduce tax on income at a set rate of relief.

- From tax liability, deduct any income tax suffered at source to arrive at tax payable. The tax suffered at source can be repaid.

- Calculating additional tax due, for example when a new source of income is acquired, can often be done by working at the margin.

- Spouses, civil partners and children are all separate taxpayers. There are special rules to prevent parents from exploiting a child's personal allowance.

Quick quiz

1   At what rates is income tax charged on non-savings income?

2   Is UK rental income savings income?

3   What type of savings income is received by individuals net of 20% tax?

4   How is tax relief given on interest payable on a loan to invest in a partnership?

5   How is dividend income taxed?

6   What is the maximum tax saving obtained from the transferable personal allowance?

7   What is the amount below which a child's income deriving from a parental disposition (ie gift) is not taxed as the parents' income?

BPP
LEARNING MEDIA

Answers to quick quiz

1   Income tax on non-savings income is charged at 20% below the basic rate limit, at 40% between the basic rate limit and the higher rate limit and at 45% above the higher rate limit.

2   No. It is non-savings income.

3   Interest paid on company loan stock which is not listed on a recognised stock exchange.

4   Interest payable on a loan to invest in a partnership is deductible from total income to compute net income.

5   The first £2,000 of dividend income is within the dividend nil rate band and so taxable at 0%. Other dividend income below the basic rate limit is taxed at 7.5%. Dividend income between the basic rate limit and the higher rate limit is taxed at 32.5% and at 38.1% above the higher rate limit.

6   £1,190 × 20% = £238.

7   £100

Now try the question below from the Practice Question Bank

Number	Level	Marks	Time
Q1	Introductory	20	39 mins

1: Principles of income tax | Part A Income tax and national insurance contributions

Pensions and other tax efficient investment products

Topic list	Syllabus reference
1 Types of pension scheme and membership	A1(a)B7
2 Contributing to a pension scheme	A1(a)B7
3 Receiving benefits from pension arrangements	A1(a)B7
4 The enterprise investment scheme (EIS)	A1(g)(i)
5 The seed enterprise investment scheme (SEIS)	A1(g)(i)
6 Venture capital trusts (VCTs)	A1(g)(ii)

Introduction

In the previous chapter we looked at the basic income tax computation. We now look at some of the tax reliefs given to encourage individuals to invest in certain types of savings.

The most important type of saving is through pensions. Tax relief is given on contributions to pension schemes, and the schemes themselves can grow tax free. There are limits on the amounts that can be invested, and breach of these limits will incur tax charges. Failure to comply with the rules will also result in tax charges.

Investment in smaller companies is encouraged through the enterprise investment scheme, the seed enterprise investment scheme and venture capital trusts. We saw how relief is given as a tax reducer in the previous chapter, and here we will examine the conditions which must be satisfied by the investor before relief is available, how relief may be withdrawn and the capital gains tax implications of these investments.

In the next chapter, we will look at income from UK property and other investments.

Study guide

		Intellectual level
1	**Income and income tax liabilities in situations involving further overseas aspects and in relation to trusts, and the application of exemptions and reliefs**	
(a)	The contents of the Taxation - United Kingdom (TX – UK) study guide for income tax and national insurance, under heading:	2
•	B7 The use of exemptions and reliefs in deferring and minimising income tax liabilities	
(g)	The use of exemptions and reliefs in deferring and minimising income tax liabilities:	
(i)	Understand and apply the rules relating to investments in the seed enterprise investment scheme and the enterprise investment scheme	3
(ii)	Understand and apply the rules relating to investments in venture capital trusts	3

Exam guide

You may well come across pension contributions or investments under the EIS, under the SEIS, or in VCTs as part of a question. These investments all give tax relief for the amount invested, although the reliefs vary in amount. They are commonly used to mitigate tax liabilities, but you should note that they should be used for in-year tax planning, although there is carry back for EIS and SEIS reliefs.

Knowledge brought forward from earlier studies

This chapter builds upon the basic knowledge of tax relief for pension contributions necessary in Taxation (TX – UK). The examining team has identified essential underpinning knowledge from the Taxation (TX – UK) syllabus which is particularly important that you revise as part of your Advanced Taxation (ATX – UK) studies. In this chapter, the relevant topic is:

		Intellectual level
B7	**The use of exemptions and reliefs in deferring and minimising income tax liabilities**	
(a)	Explain and compute the relief given for contributions to personal pension schemes, and to occupational pension schemes	2

The only change in 2018/19 from the material you studied at Taxation (TX – UK) in 2017/18 is that the lifetime allowance has been increased to £1,030,000.

EIS, SEIS and VCTs are new topics.

One of the competencies you require to fulfil Performance Objective 17 Tax planning and advice of the PER is to review the situation of an individual or entity advising on any potential tax risks and/or additional tax minimisation measures. You can apply the knowledge you obtain from this chapter of the text to help to demonstrate this competence.

1 Types of pension scheme and membership

FAST FORWARD

An employee may be entitled to join their employer's occupational pension scheme. Both employees and the self employed can take out a 'personal pension' with a financial institution such as a bank or building society.

1.1 Types of pension provision

An individual is encouraged by the Government to make financial provision to cover their needs when they reach a certain age. There are state pension arrangements which provide some financial support, but the Government would like an individual not to rely on state provision but to make their own pension provision.

Under automatic enrolment employers must automatically enrol most employees into a workplace pension scheme (although employees can then opt out of the scheme). **There are minimum contributions to the workplace pension scheme required by law** (between April 2018 and April 2019 usually equal to 5% of earnings of which a minimum amount equal to 2% of earnings must be contributed by the employer).

Alternatively, individuals (employees, self-employed and those who are not working) may make their own pension provision through a personal pension provider such as an insurance company.

Tax relief is given for both employer pension provision and personal pension provision. This includes relief for contributions to a pension and an exemption from tax on income and gains arising in a pension fund.

1.2 Pension arrangements

An individual may make pension provision in a number of ways.

Key terms

> **Occupational pension schemes** are run by employers for their employees. **Personal pension schemes** are run by financial institutions: anyone may contribute to a personal pension.

Personal pension schemes and the majority of occupational pension schemes are **money purchase schemes**. These are also known as **defined contributions schemes**. The level of pension that the member can draw from such schemes will depend on the investment performance of the money invested.

Some occupational schemes are **final salary schemes**, where the pension depends on the period for which the individual has been a member of the scheme and their salary at the time of retirement. These are also known as **defined benefits schemes**, and are becoming less common due to the high level of contributions required.

An individual may make a number of different pension arrangements depending on their circumstances. For example, they may be a member of an occupational pension scheme and also make pension arrangements independently with a financial provider. If the individual has more than one pension arrangement, the rules we will be looking at in detail later apply to all the pension arrangements they make. For example, **there is a limit on the amount of contributions that the individual can make in a tax year. This limit applies to all the pension arrangements that they make, not each of them.**

2 Contributing to a pension scheme

FAST FORWARD

An individual can make tax relievable contributions to their pension arrangements up to the higher of their earnings and £3,600. Contributions to personal pensions are paid net of basic rate tax. Employers normally operate 'net pay' arrangements in respect of contributions to occupational schemes.

2.1 Contributions by a scheme member attracting tax relief 12/17, 6/18

An individual who is **under the age of 75 is entitled to tax relief on their contributions** to a registered pension scheme in a tax year.

The maximum gross contributions made by an individual in a tax year attracting tax relief is the higher of:

(a) **The individual's UK relevant earnings chargeable to income tax in the year; and**
(b) **The basic amount (set at £3,600 for 2018/19).**

Relevant UK earnings include employment income, trading income, and income from furnished holiday lettings (see later in this text). If the individual does not have any UK earnings in a tax year, the maximum contribution they can obtain tax relief on is £3,600.

Where an individual contributes to more than one pension scheme, the aggregate of their contributions will be used to give the total amount of tax relief.

There is an interaction between this provision and the annual allowance, which will be discussed later.

2.2 Methods of giving tax relief

2.2.1 Relief given at source

This method will be used where an individual makes a contribution to a pension scheme run by a personal pension provider such as an insurance company.

Relief is given at source by the contributions being deemed to be made net of basic rate tax. This applies whether the individual is an employee, self-employed or not employed at all and whether or not they have taxable income. HMRC then pay the basic rate tax to the pension provider.

Further tax relief is given if the individual is a higher rate or additional rate taxpayer. The relief is given by increasing the basic rate limit and the higher rate limit for the year by the gross amount of contributions for which the taxpayer is entitled to relief.

Question

Higher rate relief

Joe lives in England and has earnings of £65,000 in 2018/19. He pays a personal pension contribution of £7,200 (net). He has no other taxable income.

Show Joe's tax liability for 2018/19.

Answer

	Non-savings Income £
Earnings/Net income	65,000
Less personal allowance	(11,850)
Taxable income	53,150

Tax

	£
£	
43,500 (W) × 20%	8,700
9,650 × 40%	3,860
53,150	12,560

Working
Basic rate limit £34,500 + (£7,200 × 100/80) = <u>43,500</u>

2.2.2 Adjusted net income

Adjusted net income is net income less the gross amounts of personal pension contributions (and gift aid donations – these are not in your syllabus). **The restriction on the personal allowance is calculated in relation to adjusted net income.**

Question   Adjusted net income

Maria lives in England and earns a salary of £116,000 in 2018/19. In January 2019, she made a net personal pension contribution of £5,000.

Compute Maria's income tax liability for 2018/19.

Answer

		Non-savings income
		£
Salary/Net income		116,000
Less personal allowance (W)		(6,975)
Taxable income		109,025
Income tax	£	£
Basic rate £34,500 + (£5,000 × 100/80)	40,750 × 20%	8,150
Higher rate	68,275 × 40%	27,310
	109,025	35,460

Working	£
Net income	116,000
Less personal pension £5,000 × 100/80	(6,250)
Adjusted net income	109,750
Less income limit	(100,000)
Excess	9,750
Personal allowance	11,850
Less half excess £9,750 × ½	(4,875)
	6,975

Where an individual has an adjusted net income between £100,000 and £123,700, the rate of tax on the income between these two amounts will usually be 60%. This is calculated as 40% (the higher rate on income) plus 40% of half (ie 20%) of the excess adjusted net income over £100,000 used to restrict the personal allowance. The individual should consider **making personal pension contributions to reduce adjusted net income to below £100,000.**

2.2.3 Net pay arrangements

An occupational scheme will normally operate net pay arrangements.

In this case, the employer will deduct gross pension contributions from the individual's earnings before operating PAYE. The individual therefore obtains tax relief at their marginal rate of tax without having to make any claim.

Question | Net pay arrangements

Maxine lives in Northern Ireland and has taxable earnings of £65,000 in 2018/19. Her employer deducts a pension contribution of £9,000 from these earnings before operating PAYE. She has no other taxable income.

Show Maxine's tax liability for 2018/19.

Answer

	£
Earnings	65,000
Less pension contribution	(9,000)
Net income	56,000
Less personal allowance	(11,850)
Taxable income	44,150

Tax

£	£
34,500 × 20%	6,900
9,650 × 40%	3,860
44,150	10,760

This is the same result as Joe in the question earlier in this chapter. Joe had received basic rate tax relief of £(9,000 – 7,200) = £1,800 at source, so his overall tax position was £(12,560 – 1,800) = £10,760.

2.3 Contributions not attracting tax relief

An individual can also make contributions to their pension arrangements which do not attract tax relief, for example out of capital. The member must notify the scheme administrator if they make contributions in excess of the higher of their UK relevant earnings and the basic amount.

Such contributions do not count towards the annual allowance limit (discussed below) but will affect the value of the pension fund for the lifetime allowance.

2.4 Employer pension contributions 6/10, 12/17

FAST FORWARD

Employers may make contributions to pension schemes. In certain circumstances employers contributions are spread over a number of years.

2.4.1 Taxation consequences of employer pension contributions

Where the active scheme member is an employee, their **employer will often make contributions to their pension scheme** and under automatic enrolment are required by law to make at least minimum contributions to a workplace pension scheme. Employer pension contributions to any type of pension scheme are **exempt benefits** for the employee.

There is **no limit** on the amount of employer pension contributions that may be made but **such contributions always count towards the annual allowance and will also affect the value of the pension fund for the lifetime allowance** (see further below).

All contributions made by an employer are made gross and the employer will usually obtain tax relief for the contribution by deducting it as an expense in calculating trading profits for the period of account in which the payment is made.

2.4.2 Disallowance of employer pension contributions

HMRC may seek to disallow an employer pension contribution which it considers is not a revenue expense or is not made wholly and exclusively for the purposes of the trade.

2.4.3 Large employer pension contributions

There are 'spreading provisions' for large employer pension contributions, so that part of the contribution is treated as paid in a later period of account.

2.5 Annual allowance   12/15, 12/17, 6/18

FAST FORWARD
> The annual allowance is the limit on the amount that can be paid into a pension scheme each year. If this limit is exceeded there is an income tax charge on the excess contributions. The annual allowance is reduced if an individual has adjusted income in excess of £150,000. Unused annual allowance can be carried forward for up to three years.

2.5.1 Introduction

The **annual allowance** effectively restricts the amount of tax relievable contributions that can be paid into an individual's pension scheme each year. **The amount of the annual allowance is £40,000.**

Exam focus point

> These amounts will be shown in the Tax Rates and Allowances available in the exam. There were some complex transitional rules which meant that for 2015/16 the annual allowance could have been more than £40,000 for some individuals depending on when contributions were made in the year. These transitional rules were **not examinable** in Advanced Taxation (ATX – UK) and you should assume that in any exam question involving pensions the timing of the contributions means that only an annual allowance of £40,000 was available for 2015/16.

2.5.2 Reduced annual allowance

Individuals who have adjusted income in excess of £150,000 have a reduced annual allowance.

From the tax year 2016/17, the annual allowance is reduced by £1 for every £2 that the individual's adjusted income exceeds £150,000, subject to a **minimum annual allowance of £10,000**. The minimum annual allowance will apply where the individual has adjusted income of £210,000 or more since £(40,000 – [210,000 – 150,000]/2) = £10,000.

Adjusted income for the self-employed is the same as net income (ie total income less loss relief against general income and qualifying interest). This is because the individual will only have made pension contributions with tax relief by deduction at source (see Section 2.2.1) which does not affect the computation of net income. **Adjusted income for employees is net income plus pension contributions to occupational pension schemes under net pay arrangements** (as these will have been deducted in computing net income) **plus employer contributions to occupational pension schemes and/or personal pension schemes**. If the employee has made personal pension contributions with tax relief by deduction at source, these are not relevant in computing adjusted income.

The reduction in the annual allowance does not apply unless the individual's threshold income exceeds £110,000 (ie the £150,000 threshold less the full annual allowance). Threshold income is

usually **net income in the income tax computation less the individual's gross personal pension contributions.** Note that pension contributions by employees to occupational pension schemes under net pay arrangements (see Section 2.2.3) will already have been deducted in computing net income. The threshold income test ensures that individuals are not adversely affected by their employers making employer pension contributions which increase adjusted income so that it is over the £150,000 threshold.

Question   Reduced annual allowance

In the tax year 2018/19, Brian is an employee earning a salary of £138,000. This is Brian's only income for the tax year. During the tax year 2018/19, Brian has made pension contributions to his occupational pension scheme of £10,000 and his employer has made contributions of £20,000, in respect of Brian, to the occupational pension scheme. Brian has also made gross personal pension contributions of £6,000 in 2018/19.

What is Brian's annual allowance for 2018/19?

Answer

We start by working out Brian's net income.

	Non-savings income £
Salary	138,000
Less employee pension contributions	(10,000)
Employment income/net income	128,000

We now need to compute Brian's adjusted income.

	£
Net income	128,000
Add: employee pension contributions	10,000
employer pension contributions	20,000
Adjusted income	158,000

We also need to compute Brian's threshold income.

	£
Net income	128,000
Less gross personal pension contributions	(6,000)
Threshold income	122,000

Since Brian's adjusted income exceeds £150,000 and his threshold income exceeds £110,000, his annual allowance will be reduced as follows:

	£
Adjusted income	158,000
Less threshold	(150,000)
Excess	8,000

	£
Annual allowance	40,000
Less half excess £8,000 × ½	(4,000)
Reduced annual allowance	36,000

There is an **anti-avoidance provision** relating to **salary sacrifice and flexible remuneration arrangements** which prevent employees receiving reduced remuneration in exchange for larger employer pension contributions in order to ensure that threshold income is less than £110,000. This provision operates by **including in threshold income an amount which would otherwise have been employment income had the salary sacrifice or flexible remuneration arrangements not applied.**

2.5.3 Carry forward of unused annual allowance

Where **an individual is a member of a registered pension scheme** but **does not make contributions of at least the annual allowance in a tax year**, the individual can **carry forward the unused amount of the annual allowance for up to three years.**

The annual allowance in the current tax year is treated as being used first, then any unused annual allowance from earlier years, using the earliest tax year first. Where the annual allowance has been reduced as described in Section 2.5.2, the reduced amount will be carried forward to later years.

Carry forward of annual allowance

Ted is a sole trader. His gross contributions to his personal pension scheme have been as follows:

2015/16	£16,000
2016/17	£36,000
2017/18	£25,000

In 2018/19 Ted will have taxable trading profits of about £100,000 and wishes to make a large pension contribution in January 2019. He has no other sources of income.

(a) What is the maximum gross pension contribution Ted can make in January 2019 without incurring an annual allowance charge, taking into account any brought forward annual allowance?

(b) If Ted makes a gross personal pension contribution of £43,000 in January 2019, what are the unused annual allowances he can carry forward to 2019/20?

Answer

(a)

	£
Annual allowance 2018/19	40,000
Annual allowance unused in 2015/16 £(40,000 – 16,000)	24,000
Annual allowance unused in 2016/17 £(40,000 – 36,000)	4,000
Annual allowance unused in 2017/18 £(40,000 – 25,000)	15,000
Maximum gross pension contribution in 2018/19	83,000

(b)

	£
Annual allowance 2018/19 used in 2018/19	40,000
Annual allowance unused in 2015/16 used in 2018/19	3,000
Contribution in 2018/19	43,000

The remaining £(24,000 – 3,000) = £21,000 of the 2015/16 annual allowance cannot be carried forward to 2019/20 since this is more than three years after 2015/16. The unused annual allowances are therefore £4,000 from 2016/17 and £15,000 from 2017/18 and these are carried forward to 2019/20.

Exam focus point

> The use of annual allowances was tested in June 2013 Qu 3(a)(i) Shuttelle. The examining team commented that 'Many candidates were aware that there was a three-year rule in respect of the annual allowance, although many were not absolutely clear as to how the rule worked.'

2.5.4 Contributions in excess of annual allowance

FAST FORWARD

An annual allowance charge arises if tax-relievable contributions exceed the available annual allowance.

If tax-relievable pension contributions exceed the annual allowance, there is a charge to income tax based on the individual's taxable income. This will occur if the taxpayer has relevant earnings in excess of the available annual allowance and makes a contribution in excess of the available annual allowance (including any brought forward annual allowance).

The taxpayer is primarily liable for the tax on the excess contribution but in certain circumstances can give notice to the pension scheme for the charge to be payable from the taxpayer's pension benefits fund.

The annual allowance charge is calculated by taxing the excess contribution as an extra amount of income received by the taxpayer. The calculation therefore claws back the tax relief given on the pension contribution.

Question
Annual allowance charge

Jaida lives in Wales and had employment income of £240,000 in 2018/19. She made a gross personal pension contribution of £70,000 in 2018/19. She does not have any unused annual allowance brought forward. What is Jaida's income tax liability for 2018/19?

Answer

	Non-savings income £
Taxable income (no personal allowance available)	240,000
Tax	
	£
£104,500 (W1) × 20%	20,900
£115,500 × 40%	46,200
£220,000 (W2)	
£20,000 × 45%	9,000
£240,000	
£60,000 (W3) × 45%	27,000
Income tax liability	103,100

Workings

1   Basic rate limit £34,500 + £70,000 (gross contribution) = £104,500

2   Higher rate limit £150,000 + £70,000 (gross contribution) = £220,000

3   Excess pension contribution £(70,000 – 10,000 (minimum as adjusted income exceeds £210,000)) = £60,000

3 Receiving benefits from pension arrangements

PER alert

One of the competencies you require to fulfil Performance Objective 17 Tax planning and advice of the PER is to assess the tax implications of proposed activities or plans of an individual or entity with reference to relevant and up to date legislation. You can apply the knowledge you obtain from this section of the text to help to demonstrate this competence.

3.1 Pension benefits

FAST FORWARD

An individual can start to receive pension benefits from the age of 55. Under flexi-access drawdown, a tax-free lump sum of 25% of the pension fund can be taken and the remainder reinvested to give taxable pension income as required.

After reaching the minimum pension age of 55, an individual can start to receive pension benefits with complete flexibility to access their personal pensions.

There are a number of common ways in which an individual can receive benefits from personal pension schemes. One is **flexi-access drawdown** where the individual usually takes a **tax-free lump sum of 25%** of the pension fund. The **rest of the pension fund** is then reinvested to provide **taxable pension income** as required by the individual. Previously individuals usually had to buy an annuity with the balance (which is still an option).

Exam focus point

There is an anti-avoidance annual allowance limit which applies when an individual starts to receive pension benefits flexibly but is also entitled to make further contributions to the pension fund. This annual allowance limit is **not examinable** in Advanced Taxation (ATX – UK).

3.2 The lifetime allowance

12/15

FAST FORWARD

The maximum value that can be built up in a pension fund is known as the lifetime allowance.

An individual is not allowed to build up an indefinitely large pension fund. **There is a maximum value for a pension fund (for money purchase arrangements) or for the value of benefits (for defined benefits arrangements). This is called the lifetime allowance.** This allowance applies to the total funds built up in an individual's pension funds. The amount of the lifetime allowance in 2018/19 is £1,030,000.

The individual does not have to keep a running total of the value of their pension scheme. Instead, **the lifetime allowance limit is tested only when a benefit crystallisation event occurs. When a member takes a benefit from a pension scheme, there is usually a benefit crystallisation event so that the value of the pension fund has to be tested against the lifetime allowance for the year in which the event occurs.**

In many cases, the lifetime limit will not have been exceeded and there will be no income tax charge. **In some cases, the pension fund will exceed the lifetime allowance and this will give rise to an income tax charge on the excess value of the fund.** The rate of the charge depends on the type of benefit that will be taken from the excess funds.

Where funds are used to provide a lump sum, there will be a **charge to tax at 55% on the value of the lump sum. Where the excess funds are used to provide a pension income, the rate is 25%.**

3.3 Example: lifetime allowance exceeded

Amy attained the age of 55 on 1 July 2018 and decided to start taking her pension benefits on that date. She has a money purchase fund which was valued at £1,800,000 on 1 July 2018. Amy took the maximum tax-free lump sum of £1,030,000 × 25% = £257,500. The balance of the lifetime allowance is £(1,030,000 − 257,500) = £772,500 and this will be used to provide pension income by flexible access drawdown.

Amy also took the excess of the fund over the lifetime allowance as a lump sum ie £(1,800,000 − 1,030,000) = £770,000.

The tax charge is therefore £770,000 × 55% = £423,500.

4 The enterprise investment scheme (EIS) 12/13, 6/17

FAST FORWARD

> The enterprise investment scheme, seed enterprise investment scheme and venture capital trusts are designed to help unquoted trading companies raise finance.

Key term

> The **enterprise investment scheme (EIS)** is a scheme designed to promote enterprise and investment by helping high-risk, unlisted trading companies raise finance by the issue of shares to individual investors who are unconnected with that company.

4.1 Conditions for relief

Individuals who subscribe for EIS shares are entitled to both income tax and capital gains tax reliefs where certain conditions are satisfied.

4.1.1 The investor

The investor must **subscribe for shares wholly in cash in the company and must not be connected with it. Connection can broadly occur through employment or owning more than 30%** (including holdings of associates ie spouse/civil partner or child, but not a brother or sister) **of the issued ordinary share capital, issued share capital or voting power of the company or a subsidiary.** The investor must also qualify for the two years prior to and three years after the share issue date or if later, three years from the date trading commences.

There is a further requirement that the investor claiming relief cannot hold any other shares in the company at the time the investment is made. There is an exception to this requirement where existing holdings of shares are risk finance investments (eg EIS shares, SEIS shares).

4.1.2 The company

Exam focus point

> There are a number of conditions that need to be met by a company in order to qualify as an EIS company. Knowledge of these conditions are **excluded** from the Advanced Taxation (ATX – UK) syllabus.

4.1.3 The shares

Eligible shares are usually any new ordinary shares issued for bona fide commercial reasons which, throughout the period of three years beginning with the date on which they are issued, carry no preferential rights to assets on liquidation of the company. The shares may carry certain preferential rights to dividends but these are limited, for example, the rights to dividends cannot be cumulative.

The shares must be fully paid up at the time of issue and they cannot be redeemable.

4.2 Income tax relief 6/11

4.2.1 Tax reducer

Individuals can claim a **tax reducer** (see earlier in this text) **of the lower of:**

(a) **30% of the amount subscribed for qualifying investments;** and
(b) **The individual's tax liability for the year.**

A claim for EIS relief in respect of shares issued by a company in a tax year must be made by the fifth anniversary of the normal self-assessment filing date for the tax year (ie by 31 January 2025 for an investment made in 2018/19).

4.2.2 Limit for relief for investors

The annual maximum for EIS investments qualifying for income tax relief is **£1,000,000**, but individuals can invest in excess of this amount if they wish.

The investor may claim to have all or any of the shares treated as issued in the previous tax year. When carrying back relief, relief given in the previous year must not exceed overall EIS limit for that year.

4.2.3 Withdrawal of relief

Shares must be held by an investor for at least three years if the income tax relief is not to be withdrawn or reduced if the company was carrying on a qualifying trade at the time of issue. For companies which were preparing to trade at the time of issue, the minimum holding period ends when the company has been carrying on a qualifying trade for three years.

The main reason for the withdrawal of relief will be the sale of the shares by the investor within the three year period mentioned above. The consequences depend on whether the disposal is at arm's length or not:

(a)　If the disposal is not a bargain at arm's length the full amount of relief originally obtained is withdrawn.

(b)　If the disposal is a bargain at arm's length there is a withdrawal of relief on the consideration received. As the relief was originally given as a tax reduction, the withdrawal of relief must be made at the same rate of tax.

Question	Withdrawal of EIS relief

Ted lives in England and makes a £60,000 EIS investment in 2018/19. His income (all non-savings) for the year is £54,485. He does not make a claim to treat the investment as being made in the previous tax year since he had no taxable income in that tax year due to trading loss relief. In 2019/20, Ted sells the shares (an arm's length bargain) for £50,000. How much EIS relief is withdrawn as a result of the sale of the shares?

Answer

	£
2018/19	
Net income	54,485
Less personal allowance	(11,850)
Taxable income	42,635

	£
£34,500 × 20%	6,900
£8,135 × 40%	3,254
	10,154
Less EIS relief: £60,000 × 30% = £18,000, restricted to	(10,154)
Income tax liability	Nil

The effective rate of EIS relief is $\dfrac{10,154}{60,000} \times 100 = 16.92\%$

2019/20

The sale of the shares for £50,000 as a bargain at arm's length results in the withdrawal of income tax relief in 2018/19 of £8,460 (ie £50,000 × 16.92%).

June 2011 Question 4(b) Capstan concerned the sale of shares in respect of which EIS relief had been claimed. The examining team commented that 'Almost all candidates identified the claw back of the relief if the shares were sold within three years of the acquisition. However, many stated that the whole of the relief obtained would be withdrawn as opposed to a proportion of it.'

There are anti-avoidance rules to prevent an individual extracting money from the company without disposing of their shares. However, the rules do not apply where the amount is of an insignificant value (eg any amount of £1,000 or under) or if the receipt is returned without unreasonable delay.

4.3 CGT reliefs

Where shares qualify for income tax relief under the EIS there are also special rules that apply to those shares for capital gains purposes:

(a) Where shares are disposed of after the three year period any gain is exempt from CGT. If the shares are disposed of within three years any gain is computed in the normal way.

(b) If EIS shares are disposed of at a loss at any time, the loss is allowable but the acquisition cost of the shares is reduced by the amount of EIS relief attributable to the shares. The loss is eligible for relief against general income (see later in this text).

Question
Allowable losses

During 2017/18 Martin invested £35,000 in EIS shares and received relief against income tax of £35,000 × 30% = £10,500.

The shares are sold in February 2019 for £15,000. This will lead to a withdrawal of EIS relief of £15,000 × 30% = £4,500. What is the allowable loss for CGT purposes?

Answer

	£	£
Disposal proceeds		15,000
Less: cost	35,000	
EIS relief (10,500 – 4,500)	(6,000)	(29,000)
Allowable loss		(14,000)

If the shares had instead been sold outside the three year relevant period (ie so that there was no withdrawal of income tax relief), the allowable loss would instead be:

	£	£
Disposal proceeds		15,000
Less: cost	35,000	
EIS relief	(10,500)	(24,500)
Allowable loss		(9,500)

EIS reinvestment relief may be available to defer chargeable gains if an individual invests in EIS shares in the period commencing one year before and ending three years after the disposal of the asset (see later in this text).

5 The seed enterprise investment scheme (SEIS)

The **seed enterprise investment scheme (SEIS)** is a scheme similar to the EIS scheme but rewards investment in small, start-up unquoted trading companies with a more generous tax reducer.

5.1 Conditions for relief

Individuals who subscribe for SEIS shares are entitled to similar income tax relief (although at a more generous rate) **as subscribers for EIS shares** but the conditions that the company and investor must satisfy are slightly different.

5.1.1 The investor

The investor must not be an employee of the company, but can be a director. This condition must be satisfied during the period starting with the issue of the shares and ending on the third anniversary of the date on which the shares are issued.

The investor must not be connected with the company. Connection can broadly occur through employment or owning more than 30% (including holdings of associates ie spouse/civil partner or child, but not a brother or sister) **of the issued ordinary share capital, issued share capital or voting power of the company or a subsidiary.** This condition must be satisfied during the period starting with the incorporation of the company and ending on the third anniversary of the date on which the shares are issued.

5.1.2 The company

There are a number of conditions that need to be met by a company in order to qualify as a SEIS company. Knowledge of these conditions are **excluded** from the Advanced Taxation (ATX – UK) syllabus.

5.1.3 The shares

The share requirements are the same as for EIS investments, ie the investor must subscribe in cash for new ordinary shares for genuine commercial reasons, although shares with limited preferential rights to dividends can still be qualifying shares.

5.2 Income tax relief

5.2.1 Tax reducer

Individuals can claim a **tax reducer** (see earlier in this text) **of the lower of:**

(a)   **50% of the amount subscribed for qualifying investments**; and
(b)   **The individual's tax liability for the year.**

A claim for SEIS relief in respect of shares issued by a company in a tax year must be made by the fifth anniversary of the normal self-assessment filing date for the tax year (ie by 31 January 2025 for an investment made in 2018/19).

5.2.2 Limit for relief

The annual maximum SEIS investments qualifying for income tax relief is £100,000 (ie the maximum tax reducer is £50,000).

The investor may claim to have all or any of the shares treated as issued in the previous tax year. When carrying back relief, relief given in the previous year must not exceed overall SEIS limit for that year.

Question   EIS and SEIS

In 2018/19 Arthur, who lives in Wales, invested £40,000 in a qualifying EIS company, and £20,000 in a qualifying SEIS company. He had pension income of £130,000 in 2018/19. Calculate Arthur's income tax liability for 2018/19. He does not wish to treat any shares as issued in 2017/18.

	£
2018/19	
Taxable income (no personal allowance)	130,000
£34,500 × 20%	6,900
£95,500 × 40%	38,200
	45,100
Less EIS relief: £40,000 × 30%	(12,000)
Less SEIS relief: £20,000 × 50%	(10,000)
Income tax liability	23,100

Remember that if the individual is entitled to more than one investment tax reducer, the VCT reducer is deducted first, then the EIS reducer and finally the SEIS reducer (see earlier in this text).

5.2.3 Withdrawal of relief

As for EIS, **shares must be held by an investor for at least three years** if the income tax relief is not to be withdrawn. Where the disposal is a bargain at arm's length, the amount withdrawn will usually be 50% of the amount received for the shares (as for EIS relief it will be less if full relief was not given because the taxpayer's tax liability was less than the amount subscribed for). Where the disposal is not at arm's length, the whole of the relief given is withdrawn.

Exam focus point

> Although EIS and SEIS investments carry attractive tax reliefs remember that they are high risk investments.

5.3 CGT reliefs

Where shares qualify for income tax relief under the SEIS there are also special rules that apply to those shares for capital gains purposes in the same way as for EIS shares (see Section 4.3 above).

There is a SEIS reinvestment relief where an individual makes a gain in a tax year and also invests in SEIS shares in the same tax year. This relief is dealt with later in this text.

6 Venture capital trusts (VCTs)

Key term

> **Venture capital trusts (VCTs)** are listed companies which invest in unquoted trading companies and meet certain conditions.

6.1 Conditions for relief

Individuals who subscribe for VCT shares are entitled to both income tax and capital gains tax reliefs where certain conditions are satisfied.

6.1.1 The investor

The VCT scheme differs from EIS as the individual investor invests directly in a quoted VCT company that itself invests in higher risk unquoted companies. The investor therefore spreads their risk.

6.1.2 The company

Exam focus point

There are a number of conditions that need to be met by a company in order to qualify as a VCT. Knowledge of these conditions are **excluded** from the Advanced Taxation (ATX – UK) syllabus.

6.2 Tax reliefs

An individual investing in a VCT obtains the following tax benefits on a maximum qualifying investment of £200,000:

- **A tax reducer** (see earlier in this text) **of the lower of 30% of the amount invested and the individual's income tax liability for the year.**

- **Dividends received are tax-free income.**

- **Capital gains on the sale of shares in the VCT are exempt from CGT (and losses are not allowable).**

6.3 Withdrawal of relief

If the shares in the VCT are disposed of within five years of issue the following consequences ensue:

- **If the shares are not disposed of under a bargain made at arm's length, the tax reduction is withdrawn.**

- **If the shares are disposed of under a bargain made at arm's length, the tax reduction is withdrawn, up to the disposal proceeds × 30%.**

Note that there is no minimum holding period requirement for the benefits of tax-free dividends and CGT exemption.

Chapter roundup

- An employee may be entitled to join their employer's occupational pension scheme. Both employees and the self employed can take out a 'personal pension' with a financial institution such as a bank or building society.

- An individual can make tax relievable contributions to their pension arrangements up to the higher of their earnings and £3,600. Contributions to personal pensions are paid net of basic rate tax. Employers normally operate 'net pay' arrangements in respect of contributions to occupational schemes.

- Employers may make contributions to pension schemes. In certain circumstances employers contributions are spread over a number of years.

- The annual allowance is the limit on the amount that can be paid into a pension scheme each year. If this limit is exceeded there is an income tax charge on the excess contributions. The annual allowance is reduced if an individual has adjusted income in excess of £150,000. Unused annual allowance can be carried forward for up to three years.

- An annual allowance charge arises if tax-relievable contributions exceed the available annual allowance.

- An individual can start to receive pension benefits from the age of 55. Under flexi-access drawdown, a tax-free lump sum of 25% of the pension fund can be taken and the remainder reinvested to give taxable pension income as required.

- The maximum value that can be built up in a pension fund is known as the lifetime allowance.

- The enterprise investment scheme, seed enterprise investment scheme and venture capital trusts are designed to help unquoted trading companies raise finance.

Quick quiz

1 What are the two types of occupational pension scheme?

2 What is the maximum lump sum that can be taken on retirement (lifetime allowance not exceeded)?

3 What is the limit on contributions to an registered pension scheme?

4 What are the consequences of the total of employee and employer contributions exceeding the annual allowance?

5 Eileen is employed by Brad plc. In the tax year 2018/19, she has employment income of £161,500 after deducting a pension contribution made by her of £8,500 under net pay arrangements. Her employer does not make any contributions to the pension scheme. Eileen has no other income in 2018/19. What is Eileen's annual allowance for 2018/19?

6 What are the consequences of exceeding the lifetime allowance?

7 What income tax relief is available in respect of investments under the enterprise investment scheme for investments in 2018/19?

8 What is the maximum tax reducer available for investment by an individual under the seed enterprise investment scheme in 2018/19?

Answers to quick quiz

1 Occupational pension schemes may be defined contribution schemes or defined benefit schemes.

2 25% of the fund.

3 Higher of relevant earnings and the basic amount (£3,600).

4 The excess is subject to the annual allowance charge on the employee. (Any contributions by the employee which were not eligible for tax relief are ignored.)

5 Adjusted income is £(161,500 + 8,500) = £170,000.

   Reduced annual allowance is £(40,000 − [170,000 − 150,000]/2) = £30,000.

6 The excess is charged at 55% (if taken as a lump sum) or 25% (if taken as a pension).

7 EIS income tax relief is tax reducer up to 30% of amount subscribed up to £1,000,000.

8 £100,000 × 50% = £50,000.

Now try the question below from the Practice Question Bank

Number	Level	Marks	Time
Q2	Introductory	18	35 mins

Property and other investment income

Topic list	Syllabus reference
1 UK property business	A1(a)B4
2 Furnished holiday lettings	A1(a)B4
3 Rent a room relief	A1(a)B4
4 Trust income	A1(e)(iii)

Introduction

In the previous chapters we have covered the income tax computation, including tax reliefs on certain investments.

This chapter starts with the taxation of income arising from the letting of property in the UK. It looks at the basis of assessment of such income and at the computation of assessable profits and losses, and then covers the special rules for furnished holiday lettings and the rent a room relief.

Finally, this chapter deals with the taxation of trust income received by beneficiaries.

The following chapters will deal with income from employment and self-employment.

Study guide

		Intellectual level
1	**Income and income tax liabilities in situations involving further overseas aspects and in relation to trusts, and the application of exemptions and reliefs**	
(a)	The contents of the Taxation - United Kingdom (TX – UK) study guide for income tax and national insurance, under heading:	2
•	B4 Property and investment income	
(e)	Property and investment income:	3
(iii)	Income from trusts and settlements: Understand the income tax position of trust beneficiaries	

Exam guide

The computation of income from a UK property business is a generally straight forward matter, but you need to look out for the special areas of lease premiums, furnished holiday lettings and rent a room relief. The rules on finance costs are also highly examinable.

Although you are not required to know how to calculate the income tax liability of trustees, you need to know how the trust income is taxed in a beneficiary's hands.

Knowledge brought forward from earlier studies

Property income was dealt with in Taxation (TX – UK). The rest of the material in this chapter will be new to you in Advanced Taxation (ATX – UK) in 2018/19.

The changes in 2018/19 from 2017/18 in the material you have studied in Taxation (TX – UK) are that the cash basis applies to most individual taxpayers, tax relief on finance costs related to property business income is restricted to 50% and the other 50% is entitled to a tax reducer, and landlords can used fixed mileage rates. The accrued income scheme is not examinable in Advanced Taxation (ATX – UK).

1 UK property business

1.1 Profits of a UK property business

 PER alert One of the competencies you require to fulfil Performance Objective 15 of the PER is to prepare or contribute to the computation or assessment of tax computations for individuals. You can apply the knowledge you obtain from this section of the text to help to demonstrate this competence.

1.1.1 Taxation of UK property business income

FAST FORWARD Income from a UK property business is non-savings income.

Income from land and buildings in the UK, including caravans and houseboats which are not moved, is taxed as non-savings income.

1.1.2 Computing property business income

> Property business income is computed for tax years, usually on a cash basis. There is a special rule about finance costs for individuals.

A taxpayer (or a partnership) with UK rental income is treated as running a business, their 'UK property business'. All the rents and expenses for all properties are pooled, to give a single profit or loss.

The main taxable receipt for a property business is **rent paid by the tenant to the landlord taxpayer**, which is usually in the form of money. If the tenant is required to pay a **security deposit** to cover costs such as **unpaid rent, cleaning or making good damage by the tenant at the end of the tenancy**, this is **not treated as a receipt unless and until the landlord becomes legally entitled to use it under the terms of the deposit**.

Deductible expenses include **repairs** to the property, **agent's fees**, **insurance**, and **rent payable** where a landlord is renting the property which they in turn let to others. **Capital expenditure** (for example mortgage capital repayments, construction of an extension or boundary wall) **is not usually deductible**.

The **default basis for calculating property business income for individuals** is the **cash basis**. The property business profit under the cash basis is calculated as:

- **Rent received in the tax year; less**
- **Expenses paid in the tax year.**

Note that there is **automatic relief** for **irrecoverable rent** (to the extent not covered by a security deposit) since rent is only taxable on the cash basis in the tax year if it is actually received in that tax year.

Exam focus point

> The examining team has stated that in any examination question involving **property income for individuals and partnerships** (since the individual partners are taxed on their share of the partnership property business income), **it should be assumed** that the **cash basis is to be used** unless specifically stated to the contrary.

Property business income can alternatively be calculated on the accruals basis as rent receivable (rather than received) **and expenses payable** (rather than paid). This is in accordance with generally accepted accounting principles (GAAP) in the same way as most trading income (we deal with trading income later in this Study Text).

Where the **accruals basis** is used, relief is available for **irrecoverable rent** as an **impairment loss**.

The **accruals basis must be used in certain circumstances** including the following **three situations**:

- **If the property income cash basis receipts for the tax year exceed £150,000** (reduced proportionately if the property business is not carried on for a full tax year);
- **The property business is carried on by a company** (we deal with property business income for companies later in this Study Text);
- **An election is made for the accruals basis to apply.** The election must be made **by the 31 January which is 22 months from the end of the tax year concerned.** The election applies only for the tax year for which it is made.

A special rule was introduced from 2017/18 relating to **interest and other finance costs** (including incidental costs incurred in obtaining loans such as fees or commission payments) for **property businesses carried on by individuals** (not companies). The effect of the rule is to **restrict tax relief on these costs to the basic rate.** The tax liability of basic rate taxpayers will not be affected by the introduction of the rule but higher and additional rate taxpayers will have an increased tax liability.

The rule applies to **loans taken out for a residential property business**. It is not necessary for the loan to be for the purchase of the property, for example it could be taken out to pay for repairs to the property. Loans relating to commercial properties or for furnished holiday letting business (see later in this chapter) do not fall within the rule.

The rule is being phased in over four tax years. **In 2018/19, 50% of the finance costs are allowable** in the computation of property business income in the same way as other expenses. **The remaining 50%, multiplied by the basic rate of tax, is a tax reducer.**

Exam focus point

> **The 50% finance costs restriction** will be given to you in the Tax Rates and Allowances available in the exam.

Question

Finance costs

Millicent lets out a house throughout the tax year 2018/19 at a monthly rental of £1,500. She has a mortgage loan on the house and in 2018/19 she makes capital repayments of £1,000 and pays interest of £4,000. Millicent has other expenses (all allowable) of £2,500 for 2018/19. Millicent has other taxable income (after deduction of her personal allowance) of £60,000 in 2018/19.

Compute Millicent's income tax liability in respect of her property business income for the tax year 2018/19.

Answer

	£
Rental income £1,500 × 12	18,000
Less expenses	
finance costs £4,000 × 50%	(2,000)
other expenses	(2,500)
Property business income	13,500

Note that the mortgage capital repayments are not allowable.

Income tax on property business income	£
£13,500 × 40% (higher rate taxpayer)	5,400
Less property business finance costs tax reducer	
£4,000 × 50% × 20%	(400)
Property business income tax liability	5,000

A landlord may incur motoring expenses using their own transport, such as a car or van, in relation to their property business. **If the landlord is an individual, they can either deduct the actual motoring expenses or use the approved mileage allowances.** This applies to **both the cash basis and the accruals basis.**

Approved mileage allowances are calculated as the business mileage times the appropriate rate per mile. The relevant mileage rates for motor cars and vans are **45p per mile for the first 10,000 miles**, then **25p per mile thereafter.**

Exam focus point

> These rates are the **same as the approved mileage rates for employment income** given in the Tax Rates and Allowances available in the exam.

1.1.3 Replacement domestic items relief

FAST FORWARD

> If a residential property is let furnished, replacement of domestic items relief can be claimed.

No relief is given for the **initial cost** of providing domestic items. **Relief is given** if a domestic item is **replaced.** This applies to **both the cash basis and the accruals basis.**

Domestic items are defined as furniture, furnishings, household appliances and kitchenware. Examples include beds, televisions, fridges, freezers, washing machines, carpets and other floor coverings, curtains, crockery and cutlery. It does not include fixtures which become part of the property including boilers and radiators.

No relief is given for the **initial cost** of providing domestic items. **Relief is given** if a domestic item is **replaced**.

The amount of the relief is the expenditure on the new replacement asset less any proceeds from selling the old asset which has been replaced. If the new asset is not the same or substantially the same as the old asset, only the cost of an equivalent asset is given relief.

1.2 Losses of UK property business

A loss on a UK property business is carried forward to set against future profits from the UK property business.

A loss from a UK property business is carried forward to set against the first future profits from the UK property business. It may be carried forward until the UK property business ends, but it must be used as soon as possible. Generally, there is no difference between the treatment of a property business loss calculated under the cash basis or one calculated under the accruals basis.

Question   Property business income with replacement of domestic items relief

Peter purchased two properties in Manchester as 'buy to let' investments in 2017/18 and made a property business loss in that tax year of £300. He continued to let out these properties in 2018/19.

The first property, 5 Whitby Ave, was let out furnished at a rent of £500 per month payable on the first day of each month. The tenant had paid a security deposit of £1,500. The tenant left, with Peter's agreement, on 28 February 2019. The tenant had only paid her rent until 1 December 2018. Peter used £1,000 of the security deposit to cover the rent which should have been paid on 1 January and 1 February 2019 and a further £300 to repair damage made by the tenant. He returned the remaining £200 to the tenant. The property was then empty until 1 May 2019.

The second property, 17 Bolton Rd, was let furnished at a rent of £800 per month payable on the first day of each month.

Peter then purchased another property, 27 Turner Close, on 1 June 2018 which was empty whilst Peter redecorated it until 1 August 2018 when it was let unfurnished at a rent of £2,250 per quarter (three-month period), payable on 1 August, 1 November, 1 February and 1 May. Peter drove 200 miles in his own motor car in the period from 1 June 2018 to 5 April 2019 in respect of this property. He wishes to use approved mileage allowances to calculate his motoring expenses.

Peter's expenses paid during 2018/19 were:

	No 5 £	No 17 £	No 27 £
Insurance	250	250	200
Letting agency fees	–	–	100
Repairs	300	40	–
Redecoration	–	–	500
Curtains	130	–	–
Washer-dryer	–	600	–
Dining table and chairs	–	350	–

The insurance for No 5 and No 17 was for the tax year 2018/19 and for No 27 covered the period from 1 June 2018 to 31 May 2019.

The repairs for No 5 were those covered by the security deposit. No 27 was in a fit state to let when Peter bought it but he wanted to redecorate the property as he felt this would allow him to achieve a better rental income.

The new curtains for No 5 were replacements for old curtains. Peter sold the old curtains for £15.

The washer-dryer for No 17 was a replacement for a washing machine without a dryer. If Peter had bought a new washing machine without a dryer, similar to the old machine, it would have cost him £475. The old washing machine was scrapped with no proceeds. Peter had not previously provided a dining table and chairs in No 17.

What is Peter's taxable property income for 2018/19?

Answer

2018/19	No 5 £	No 17 £	No 27 £
Receipts (cash basis)			
8 × £500 (rent paid by tenant 1 May to 1 December)	4,000		
Security deposit retained £(1,000 + £300)	1,300		
12 × £800 (1 May to 1 April)		9,600	
3 × £2,250 (1 August, 1 November, 1 February)			6,750
Less: expenses paid (cash basis)			
approved mileage allowance 200 × £0.45			(90)
Insurance (no adjustment for No 27)	(250)	(250)	(200)
Letting agency fees			(100)
Repairs	(300)	(40)	
Redecoration (N)			(500)
Replacement domestic items relief			
Curtains £(130 – 15)	(115)		
Washer dryer (limited to cost of washing machine without dryer)		(475)	
Dining table and chairs (no relief for initial expenditure)		(0)	
Property business profit	4,635	8,835	5,860

	£
Total property business profit	19,330
Less loss b/fwd	(300)
Taxable property income for 2018/19	19,030

Note. The redecoration of No.27 is an allowable expense. This is an example of the application of the case of *Odeon Associated Theatres Ltd v Jones 1971* (covered in more detail later in this text) which showed that the cost of initial repairs to remedy normal wear and tear of a recently acquired asset was an allowable expense. This contrasts with the case of *Law Shipping v CIR 1923* where the cost of initial repairs to improve an asset recently acquired to make it fit to earn profits was disallowable capital expenditure. The key point in relation to No. 27 is that it was fit state to let when acquired.

1.3 Premiums on leases

FAST FORWARD

Part of the premium received on the grant of a short lease is taxed as rent.

When a premium or similar consideration is received on the grant (that is, by a landlord to a tenant) **of a short lease (50 years or less), part of the premium is treated as rent received (cash basis) or receivable (accruals basis) in the tax year of the grant.** A lease is considered to end on the date when it is most likely to terminate.

The premium taxed as rental income is the whole premium, less 2% of the premium for each complete year of the lease, except the first year. This applies to **both the cash basis and the accruals basis**. The formula is:

Formula to learn

Premium	P
Less 2% × (n–1) × P	(a)
Taxable as income	X̲

This rule does not apply on the **assignment** of a lease (ie one tenant selling their entire interest in the property to another).

1.4 Premiums paid by traders   12/15

Where a trader pays a premium for a lease, he may deduct an amount from his taxable trading profits in each year of the lease. The amount deductible is the figure treated as rent received by the landlord divided by the number of years of the lease.

1.5 Example: deduction for premium paid by trader

On 1 July 2018 Bryony, a trader, pays Scott, the landlord, a premium of £30,000 for a ten year lease on a shop. Bryony prepares accounts to 31 December each year.

Scott is taxable on property income in 2018/19 of £30,000 – (£30,000 × (10 – 1) × 2%) = £24,600.

Bryony can therefore deduct £24,600/10 = £2,460 in each of the ten years of the lease. She starts with the accounts year in which the lease starts (year ended 31 December 2018) and apportions the relief to the nearest month. Her deduction for the year ended 31 December 2018 (basis period for 2018/19) is therefore:

1 July 2018 to 31 December 2018: 6/12 × £2,460   £1,230̲

1.6 Real Estate Investment Trusts (REITs)

Property companies may operate as **real estate investment trusts** (RFITs).

REITs can elect for their property income (and gains) to be exempt from corporation tax and must withhold basic rate (20%) tax from distributions paid to shareholders (who cannot own more than 10% of a REIT's shares) out of these profits. These distributions are taxed as property income, not as dividends.

Distributions by REITs out of other income (ie not property income or gains) are taxed as dividends in the normal way.

2 Furnished holiday lettings   12/13, 6/14

FAST FORWARD

> Special rules apply to income from furnished holiday lettings. Whilst the income is taxed as normal as property business income, the letting is treated as if it were a trade. Finance costs are not restricted, capital expenses or capital allowances are available on the furniture and the income is relevant earnings for pension purposes. However, only carry forward trade loss relief is available.

PER alert

One of the competencies you require to fulfil Performance Objective 17 Tax planning and advice of the PER is to mitigate and/or defer tax liabilities through the use of standard reliefs, exemptions and incentives. You can apply the knowledge you obtain from this section of the text to help to demonstrate this competence.

Receipts and expenses of a furnished holiday letting (FHL) will usually be calculated using the **cash basis**, unless the taxpayer is required to use the accruals basis or has elected to do so.

A FHL is basically treated as if it were a trade. This means that, although the income is taxed as income from a property business, the provisions which apply to actual trades also apply to FHLs and so there are the **following differences between normal property businesses and FHLs:**

(a) **Finance costs for individuals are not restricted** (see earlier in this chapter).

(b) **Capital costs of furniture are deductible when paid if the cash basis is used** (or capital allowances are available on furniture if the accruals basis is used) **instead of replacement domestic items relief** (see earlier in this chapter).

(c) The income from a UK furnished holiday lettings business qualifies as **relevant earnings for pension relief** (see earlier in this text).

(d) Capital gains tax rollover relief, entrepreneurs' relief and relief for gifts of business assets are available (see later in this text).

However, losses from FHLs are not treated as trade losses for relief against general income, early years loss relief and terminal loss relief. If a loss arises on a FHL, the only trade loss relief available is carry forward loss relief by deduction from the first available future profits of the FHL. Trading loss reliefs are dealt with later in this text.

Note, however, that the basis period rules for trades do not apply, and the profits or losses must be computed for tax years.

A FHL must be situated in the UK or in another state within the European Economic Area. Separate computations must be made for a UK furnished holiday lettings business and an EEA furnished holiday lettings business (which consists of lettings in one or more EEA countries other than the UK).

Exam focus point

> The examining team has stated that any question in the exam would make it clear whether or not a property was situated in the EEA.

The letting must be of furnished accommodation made on a **commercial basis with a view to the realisation of profit**. The property must also satisfy the following three conditions.

(a) **The availability condition** – during the **relevant period**, the accommodation is available for **commercial let** as **holiday accommodation** to the **public** generally, for **at least 210 days**.

(b) **The letting condition** – during the **relevant period**, the accommodation is **commercially let** as holiday accommodation to members of the public **for at least 105 days** (the days let exclude any days that are longer term occupation as defined in condition (c) below).

If the **landlord has more than one FHL**, at least one of which satisfies the 105 day rule ('qualifying holiday accommodation') and at least one of which does not, ('the underused accommodation'), they may elect to **average the occupation of the qualifying holiday accommodation and any or all of the underused accommodation**. If the average of occupation is at least 105 days, the under-used accommodation will be treated as qualifying holiday accommodation.

Exam focus point

> It is possible to make an election so that a rental property continues to qualify as a furnished holiday letting for up to two years after the 105 day test ceases to be met. This election is **not examinable**.

(c) **The pattern of occupation condition** – during the **relevant period, not more that 155 days fall during periods of longer term occupation.** Longer term occupation is defined as a continuous period of more than 31 days during which the accommodation is in the same occupation unless there are abnormal circumstances.

If the taxpayer has a UK furnished holiday lettings business and other UK lettings, **draw up two income statements as if they had two separate property businesses.** This is so that the profits and losses can be identified for the special rules which apply to FHLs. The same rule also applies where someone has an EEA furnished holiday lettings business and other overseas lettings.

3 Rent a room relief

FAST FORWARD

> Up to £7,500 of rents received from letting a room or rooms in a main residence are tax free. If gross rents exceed £7,500, the taxpayer can elect to deduct £7,500 from rents received instead of actual expenses.

PER alert

One of the competencies you require to fulfil Performance Objective 17 Tax planning and advice of the PER is to mitigate and/or defer tax liabilities through the use of standard reliefs, exemptions and incentives. You can apply the knowledge you obtain from this section of the text to help to demonstrate this competence.

If an individual lets a room or rooms, furnished, in his or her main residence as living accommodation, a special exemption may apply.

The limit on the exemption is gross rents (before any expenses) of £7,500 a year. This limit is halved if any other person (including the first person's spouse/civil partner) also received income from renting accommodation in the property while the property was the first person's main residence. The receipts will usually be calculated using the cash basis, unless the taxpayer is required to use the accruals basis or has elected to do so.

If gross rents are not more than the limit, the rents are wholly exempt from income tax and expenses and capital allowances are ignored. However, the taxpayer may claim to ignore the exemption, for example to generate a loss by taking into account both rent and expenses.

If gross rents exceed the limit, the taxpayer will be taxed in the ordinary way, ignoring the rent a room scheme, unless he elects for the 'alternative basis'. If he so elects, he will be taxable on gross receipts less £7,500 (or £3,750 if the limit is halved), with no deductions for expenses. Again, the receipts and expenses will usually be calculated using the cash basis, unless the taxpayer is required to use the accruals basis or has elected to do so.

An election to ignore the exemption or an election for the alternative basis must be made by the 31 January which is 22 months from the end of the tax year concerned.

An election to ignore the exemption applies only for the tax year for which it is made, but an election for the alternative basis remains in force until it is withdrawn or until a year in which gross rents do not exceed the limit.

Exam focus point

Note the different elections carefully and the relevant time limits.

Question
Rent a room relief

Sylvia owns a house near the sea in Norfolk. She has a spare bedroom and during 2018/19 this was let to a chef working at a nearby restaurant for £150 per week which includes the cost of heating, lighting etc.

Sylvia estimates that each year her lodger costs her an extra £160 on gas, £75 on electricity and £50 on buildings insurance.

How much property income must Sylvia pay tax on?

Answer

Sylvia's gross rents are above the rent a room limit. Therefore she has the following choices:

(1)   Under the normal method (no election needed), she can be taxed on her actual profit:

	£
Rental income £150 × 52	7,800
Less expenses (160 + 75 + 50)	(285)
	7,515

(2)   Under the 'alternative basis' (elect for rent a room relief):

Total rental income of £150 × 52 = £7,800 exceeds £7,500 limit so taxable income is £300 (ie 7,800 – 7,500) if rent a room relief claimed.

Sylvia would be advised to claim the 'alternative basis'.

4 Trust income

FAST FORWARD

Income from trusts must be grossed up by either 100/55 (discretionary trusts) or by 100/80 or 100/92.5 (interest in possession trusts).

A trust is a vehicle in which assets are legally owned by the trustees for the benefit of the beneficiaries.

There are **two types of trust for income tax purposes**:

(a)   An **interest in possession trust** (a 'life interest' trust) where the income must be paid out to the beneficiary (often called the life tenant)

(b)   A **discretionary trust** where the income is distributed at the trustees' discretion

Income from discretionary trusts is received net of 45% tax. Gross it up in the income tax computation by multiplying by 100/55 and give credit for the tax already suffered when working out the final amount of tax payable. Such income is always treated as non-savings income.

If income from an interest in possession trust is paid out of the trust's non-savings income or savings income, it will be received by the beneficiary net of 20% tax and must be grossed up by multiplying by 100/80. If it is paid out of dividend income it **will be received by the beneficiary net of 7.5% tax** and must be grossed up by multiplying by 100/92.5. Each type of income is then taxed on the beneficiary under the normal rules.

Exam focus point

June 2010 Qu 2(iv) Poblano required an explanation of the income tax treatment of trusts. The examining team commented that 'There was the need to be specific and precise, as regards grossing up fractions and tax rates, rather than superficial and general in order to maximise the marks obtained.'

If a **minor beneficiary** receives income from a **trust set up by a parent**, then under the anti-avoidance rules the income is **taxed as the parent's income**. As we saw earlier, there is a £100 *de minimis* limit.

Question

Income from trusts

Victoria received the following income in 2018/19.

	£
Building society interest	7,750
Dividends	4,500
Income from discretionary trust	8,250
Income from life interest trust	2,280

The income from the life interest trust was paid out of the trust's property business income.

What income tax is repayable to Victoria?

Answer

	Non-savings income £	Savings income £	Dividend income £	Total £
Building society interest		7,750		
Dividends			4,500	
Income from discretionary trust (× 100/55)	15,000			
Income from life interest trust (× 100/80)	2,850			
Net income	17,850	7,750	4,500	30,100
Less personal allowance	(11,850)			
Taxable income	6,000	7,750	4,500	18,250

		£
Tax on non savings income	£6,000 × 20%	1,200
Tax on savings income	£1,000 × 0%	0
	£6,750 (7,750 – 1,000) × 20%	1,350
Tax on dividend income	£2,000 × 0%	0
	£2,500 (4,500 – 2,000) × 7.5%	187
Income tax liability		2,737
Less: Discretionary trust tax credit		(6,750)
Life interest trust tax credit		(570)
Income tax repayable		(4,583)

Exam focus point

Although you need to know the rate of tax deducted from income distributions from trusts, you do not need to know how to calculate the trustees' income tax liability.

Chapter roundup

- Income from a UK property business is non-savings income.

- Property business income is computed for tax years usually on a cash basis. There is a special rule about finance costs for individuals.

- If a residential property is let furnished, replacement of domestic items relief can be claimed.

- A loss on a UK property business is carried forward to set against future profits from the UK property business.

- Part of the premium received on the grant of a short lease is taxed as rent.

- Special rules apply to income from furnished holiday lettings. Whilst the income is taxed as normal as property business income, the letting is treated as if it were a trade. Finance costs are not restricted, capital expenses or capital allowances are available on the furniture and the income is relevant earnings for pension purposes. However, only carry forward trade loss relief is available.

- Up to £7,500 of gross rents received from letting a room or rooms in a main residence are tax free. If gross rents exceed £7,500, the taxpayer can elect to deduct £7,500 from rents received instead of actual expenses.

- Income from trusts must be grossed up by either 100/55 (discretionary trusts) or by 100/80 or 100/92.5 (interest in possession trusts).

Quick quiz

1 Describe replacement domestic items relief.

2 Frank lets out a residential property (not a furnished holiday letting) throughout the tax year 2018/19 and incurs finance costs in that year. How will these costs be given tax relief?

3 What are the conditions for a letting to be a furnished holiday letting?

4 Ferdinand owns a house which he occupies as his main residence. He wants to let out a furnished room in the house. What is the maximum monthly rent that Ferdinand can charge if the rent is to be wholly exempt from income tax in 2018/19?

5 Michela is a beneficiary of a discretionary trust. In 2018/19, she receives £495 income from a trust. How much does she enter as the gross amount in her tax return? Is it savings or non-savings income?

Answers to quick quiz

1   No relief for initial expenditure on domestic items. Relief for cost of replacement items, reduced by proceeds of old asset. Relief not given for cost of improving asset.

2   50% of the finance costs can be deducted in computing property business income and so will be given tax relief at Frank's marginal rate of tax. The remaining 50% of the finance costs will be given tax relief at the basic rate through a tax reducer.

3   FHL is – available for letting at least 210 days per tax year
        – actually let at least 105 days per tax year
        – not more than 155 days fall during periods of longer occupation (continuous period of more than 31 days).

4   £7,500/12 = £625 per month.

5   $£495 \times \dfrac{100}{55}$ = £900 gross. Non-savings income.

Now try the question below from the Practice Question Bank

Number	Level	Marks	Time
Q3	Introductory	15	29 mins

BPP LEARNING MEDIA

3: Property and other investment income | Part A Income tax and national insurance contributions

Employment income

Topic list	Syllabus reference
1 Employment income	A1(a)B2
2 Taxable benefits	A1(a)B2
3 Exempt benefits	A1(a)B2
4 Allowable deductions	A1(a)B2
5 National insurance for employers and employees	A1(a)B6
6 Personal service companies	A1(c)(iii), A4(b)(vi)

Introduction

In the previous chapters, we have looked at the basic income tax computation and the taxation of investments.

Most people have jobs, which pay them wages or salaries. They may also get other benefits from their employers and/or they may pay expenses connected with their employment. In this chapter, we see how to work out the basic employment income they must pay tax on.

We also look at national insurance contributions payable in respect of employees.

We conclude with a study of the rules for personal service companies, where the taxpayer is deemed to receive employment income even if he has routed his services through a company.

In the next chapter, we will look at share options and share incentives, and at lump sum receipts.

Study guide

		Intellectual level
1	**Income and income tax liabilities in situations involving further overseas aspects and in relation to trusts, and the application of exemptions and reliefs**	
(a)	The contents of the Taxation - United Kingdom (TX – UK) study guide for income tax and national insurance, under headings:	2
•	B2 Income from employment	
•	B6 National insurance contributions for employed and self-employed persons	2
(c)	Income from employment:	3
(iii)	Identify personal service companies and advise on the tax consequences of providing services via a personal service company	
4	**Corporation tax liabilities in situations involving further overseas and group aspects and in relation to special types of company, and the application of additional exemptions and reliefs**	
(b)	The scope of corporation tax:	3
(vi)	Identify personal service companies and advise on the tax consequences of services being provided via a personal service company	

Exam guide

In the exam, you may get a question which asks you to compare the after tax income from one benefit package with another, or the salary foregone in a salary sacrifice scheme. As well as calculating the marginal tax on the benefit provided or foregone, remember to take into account other costs. For example, an employee who chooses to receive a higher salary and use his own car for business will have to bear the running costs of the car as well as the capital depreciation. Don't forget national insurance!

> **Knowledge brought forward from earlier studies**

With the exception of the rules for personal service companies, this chapter is revision of your Taxation (TX – UK) studies. The examining team has identified essential underpinning knowledge from the Taxation (TX – UK) syllabus which is particularly important that you revise as part of your Advanced Taxation (ATX – UK) studies. In this chapter, the relevant topic is:

		Intellectual level
B2	**Income from employment**	
(g)	Explain and compute the amount of benefits assessable	2

The main changes in 2018/19 from the material covered in Taxation (TX – UK) in 2017/18 are as follows. The base percentage for car benefit for cars with CO_2 emissions of 95g/km has been increased to 20%. The three flat rate percentages for cars with CO_2 emissions less than 95g/km have been increased to 13%, 16% and 19%. The diesel addition has been increased to 4%. The fuel benefit base figure has increased to £23,400. The van benefit and fuel benefit for private use of vans have both increased to £3,350 and £633 respectively. For Class 1 NICs the employee's and employer's thresholds and the upper earnings limit have increased.

1 Employment income

1.1 Outline of the charge

One of the competencies you require to fulfil Performance Objective 17 Tax planning and advice of the PER is to review the situation of an individual or entity advising on any potential tax risks and/or additional tax minimisation measures. You can apply the knowledge you obtain from this section of the text to help to demonstrate this competence.

Employment income includes income arising from an employment under a contract of service (see below) and the income of office holders, such as directors. The term 'employee' is used in this text to mean anyone who receives employment income (ie both employees and directors).

There are two types of employment income:

(a)   **General earnings**; and
(b)   **Specific employment income.**

General earnings are an employee's earnings (see key term below) plus the 'cash equivalent' of any taxable non-monetary benefits.

Key term

'Earnings' means any salary, wage or fee, any gratuity or other profit or incidental benefit obtained by the employee if it is money or money's worth (something of direct monetary value or convertible into direct monetary value) or anything else which constitutes an emolument of the employment.

'Specific employment income' includes payments on termination of employment and share related income. This type of income is covered in the next chapter of this text.

The residence and domicile status of an employee determines whether earnings are taxable. If an employee is resident and domiciled in the UK, **taxable earnings from an employment in a tax year are the general earnings received in that tax year**. The rules relating to other employees are dealt with later in this text.

1.2 When are earnings received?

General earnings are taxed in the year of receipt. Money earnings are generally received on the earlier of the time payment is made and the time entitlement to payment arises. Non-money earnings are generally received when provided.

General earnings consisting of money are treated as received at the earlier of:

*   **The time when payment is made**
*   **The time when a person becomes entitled to payment of the earnings**.

If the employee is a **director** of a company, earnings from the company are received on the earliest of:

*   The earlier of the two alternatives given in the general rule (above)
*   The time when the amount is credited in the company's accounting records
*   The end of the company's period of account (if the amount was determined by then)
*   The time the amount is determined (if after the end of the company's period of account).

Taxable benefits are generally treated as received when they are provided to the employee.

The receipts basis does not apply to pension income or taxable social security benefits. These sources of income are taxed on the amount accruing in the tax year, whether or not it is received in that year.

Question

John is a director of X Corp Ltd. His earnings for 2018/19 are:

Salary	£60,000
Taxable benefits	£5,000

For the year ended 31 December 2018 the Board of Directors decide to pay John a bonus of £40,000. This is decided on 1 March 2019 at a board meeting and credited in the company accounts 7 days later. However John only received the bonus in his April pay on 30 April 2019.

What is John's employment income for 2018/19?

Answer

	£
Salary	60,000
Taxable benefits	5,000
Bonus (1.3.19)	40,000
Employment income	105,000

The salary and benefits were paid/made available during 2018/19 and so are taxable in 2018/19. The bonus was paid/made available on 30 April 2019 (2019/20) **but** was determined after the company's year end (31.12.18) by the board meeting on 1 March 2019 (2018/19) – and so is taxable in 2018/19 as this is the earliest of the relevant dates.

1.3 Net taxable earnings

Net taxable earnings of a tax year are total taxable earnings less total allowable deductions (see below). Deductions cannot usually create a loss: they can only reduce the net taxable earnings to nil.

1.4 Person liable for tax on employment income

The person liable to tax on employment income is generally the **person to whose employment the earnings relate**. However, if the tax relates to general earnings received after the death of the person to whose employment the earnings relate, the person's personal representatives are liable for the tax. The tax is a liability of the deceased person's estate.

1.5 Employment and self employment   9/15

FAST FORWARD

Employment involves a contract of service whereas self employment involves a contract for services.

1.5.1 Introduction

The distinction between employment (receipts taxable as earnings) and self employment (profits taxable as trading income) is not easy to determine. Employment involves a contract of service, whereas self employment involves a contract for services. Taxpayers tend to prefer self employment, because the rules on deductions for expenses are more generous. A worker's status also affects **national insurance**: the self-employed generally pay less than employees.

1.5.2 Factors indicating employment

- The **degree of control** exercised over the person doing the work (a high level of control indicates employment)
- Whether the worker must **accept further work if offered** (if yes, indicates employment)
- Whether the person who has offered work **must provide further work** (if yes, indicates employment)
- Whether the worker is entitled to **employment benefits** such as sick pay, holiday pay and pension facilities (entitlement indicates employment)
- Whether the worker works for **just one person or organisation** (such working indicates employment)

1.5.3 Factors indicating self-employment

- Whether the worker **provides his own equipment** (if yes, indicates self-employment)
- Whether the worker **hires his own helpers** (if yes, indicates self-employment)
- What degree of **financial risk** the worker takes (if high risk, indicates self-employment)
- What degree of **responsibility for investment and management** the worker has (if most of responsibility is the worker's, indicates self-employment)
- Whether the worker can profit from **sound management** (if can do so, indicates self-employment)
- Whether the worker can **work when he chooses** (if can do so, indicates self-employment)
- Whether the worker works for **a number of different persons or organisations** (such working indicates self-employment)

1.5.4 Wording of agreement

The **wording used in any agreement between the worker and the person for whom he performs work may also be taken into account.** For example, if the contract is described as a contract for services, this would suggest that the worker is self employed. However, **such wording is not conclusive** about the actual legal relationship and other factors may show that the contract is, in fact, a contract of service.

1.5.5 Case law

> Many of the tax rules have come about as a result of legal cases. In the exam you are not required to know the relevant cases. However we have included the case names in this Study Text for your information.

Relevant cases on the distinction between employment and self-employment include:

(a)   *Edwards v Clinch 1981*

A civil engineer acted occasionally as an inspector on temporary ad hoc appointments.

Held: there was no ongoing office which could be vacated by one person and held by another so the fees received were from self employment not employment.

(b)   *Hall v Lorimer 1994*

A vision mixer was engaged under a series of short-term contracts.

Held: the vision mixer was self employed, not because of any one detail of the case but because the overall picture was one of self-employment.

(c)   *Carmichael and Anor v National Power plc 1999*

Individuals engaged as visitor guides on a casual 'as required' basis were not employees. An exchange of correspondence between the company and the individuals was not a contract of employment as there was no provision as to the frequency of work and there was flexibility to accept work or turn it down as it arose. Sickness, holiday and pension arrangements did not apply and neither did grievance and disciplinary procedures.

2 Taxable benefits

12/13, 6/14, 6/15, 12/15

2.1 Introduction

> Employees are taxed on benefits under the benefits code. The amount of a taxable benefit is reduced by any amount paid by the employee to the employer (except private fuel) by 6 July following the end of the tax year.

Many employees receive non-cash benefits as part of their remuneration package. Under the benefits code, some of these benefits may be **fully taxable** and others may be **wholly or partly exempt (see later in this Chapter).**

In general, the amount taxable on the employee is reduced by any amount paid by the employee to the employer for providing the benefit (other than the provision of private fuel - see later in this Chapter) provided that the **payment by the employee is made on or before 6 July following the end of the tax year** for which the benefit is provided.

2.2 General business expenses

If business expenses, on such items as travel or hotel stays, are reimbursed by an employer, the basic rule is that the reimbursed amount is a taxable benefit for employees and, to avoid being taxed on this amount, **an employee must then make a claim to deduct it as an expense** under the rules set out below.

However, **such reimbursed expenses will be automatically treated as exempt, provided that the amount of the deduction is at least equal to the amount of the expense.** The exemption applies to actual expenses incurred and to flat rate payments such as allowances for travel or meals.

When an individual has to spend one or more nights away from home, their employer may reimburse expenses on items incidental to their absence (for example meals and private telephone calls). **Such incidental expenses are exempt** if:

(a)   The expenses of travelling to each place where the individual stays overnight, throughout the trip, are incurred necessarily in the performance of the duties of the employment (or would have been, if there had been any expenses).

(b)   The total (for the whole trip) of incidental expenses not deductible under the usual rules is no more than £5 for each night spent wholly in the UK and £10 for each other night. If this limit is exceeded, all of the expenses are taxable, not just the excess. The expenses include any VAT.

This incidental expenses exemption applies to expenses reimbursed, and to benefits obtained using credit tokens and non-cash vouchers.

2.3 Vouchers

If any employee:

(a)   Receives cash vouchers (vouchers exchangeable for cash);
(b)   Uses a credit token (such as a credit card) to obtain money, goods or services; or
(c)   Receives exchangeable vouchers (such as book tokens), also called non-cash vouchers

the employee is taxed on the cost to the employer of providing the voucher or the use of the credit token, less any amount paid by the employee to the employer.

Where a voucher is provided for a benefit which is exempt from income tax, the provision of the voucher itself is also exempt.

2.4 Accommodation

FAST FORWARD

The benefit in respect of accommodation is its annual value. There is an additional benefit if the property cost the employer over £75,000.

The taxable value of accommodation provided to an employee is the rent that would have been payable if the accommodation had been let at an amount equal to its annual value (generally taken to be its **rateable value**). **If the accommodation is rented** rather than owned by the employer, then **the taxable benefit is the higher of the rent actually paid and the annual value**. If accommodation does not have a rateable value, a value is estimated by HMRC.

If the accommodation cost the employer more than £75,000, an additional amount is chargeable:

Formula to learn

(Cost of providing the accommodation – £75,000) × the official rate of interest at the start of the tax year.

Thus with an official rate of 2.5%, the total benefit for accommodation costing £95,000 and with an annual value of £2,000 would be £2,000 + (£(95,000 – 75,000) × 2.5%) = £2,500.

The 'cost of providing' the accommodation is the aggregate of the cost of purchase and the cost of any improvements made before the start of the tax year for which the benefit is being computed. It is therefore not possible to avoid the charge by buying an inexpensive property requiring substantial repairs and improving it.

If the accommodation was acquired more than six years before first being provided to the employee, the market value when first provided plus the cost of subsequent improvements is used as the cost of providing it. However, unless the actual cost plus improvements to the start of the tax year in question exceeds £75,000, the additional charge cannot be imposed, however high the market value. In addition, the additional charge can only be imposed if the employer owns (rather than rents) the accommodation concerned.

Exam focus point

The 'official rate' of interest will be given to you in the Tax Rates and Allowances available.

There is no taxable benefit in respect of job related accommodation.

Key term

A person lives in **job-related accommodation** if:

(a) It **is necessary for the proper performance of the employee's duties** (as with a caretaker);

(b) It is provided **for the better performance of the employee's duties** and the employment is of a kind in which it is **customary for accommodation to be provided** (as with a policeman); or

(c) There is a **special threat to the employee's security**, and use of the accommodation is part of security arrangements

Directors can only claim exemptions (a) or (b) if:

*   They have no **material interest** ('material' means over 5%) in the company; and
*   Either they are **full time working directors** or the company is **non-profit making or is a charity**.

Any contribution paid by the employee is deducted from the annual value of the property and then from the additional benefit.

2.5 Expenses connected with living accommodation

In addition to the benefit of living accommodation itself, **employees are taxed on related expenses paid by the employer**, such as:

(a) **Heating, lighting or cleaning the premises;**
(b) **Repairing, maintaining or decorating the premises; and**
(c) **The provision of furniture (the annual value is 20% of the cost).**

Unless the accommodation qualifies as 'job related' (as defined above) **the full cost of these ancillary services** (excluding structural repairs) **is taxable. If the accommodation is 'job related'**, however, **taxable ancillary services are restricted to a maximum of 10% of the employee's 'net earnings'.**

For this purpose, net earnings are all earnings from the employment (excluding the ancillary benefits (a)–(c) above) less any allowable expenses, statutory mileage allowances, contributions to registered occupational pension schemes (but not personal pension schemes), and capital allowances.

If there are ancillary benefits other than those falling within (a)–(c) above (such as a telephone) they are taxable in full.

Question
Expenses connected with living accommodation

Quinton has a gross salary in 2018/19 of £28,850. He works as head of security for a company with a large office in London. He is required to live in a company house adjoining his employer's office, so that he can carry out his duties. The house cost £170,000 three years ago and its annual value is £650. In 2018/19 the company pays an electricity bill of £550, a gas bill of £400, a gardener's bill of £750 and redecoration costs of £1,800. Quinton makes a monthly contribution of £50 for his accommodation. He also pays £1,450 occupational pension contributions each year.

Calculate Quinton's employment income for 2018/19.

Answer

	£	£
Salary		28,850
Less occupational pension scheme contributions		(1,450)
Net earnings		27,400
Accommodation benefits		
Annual value: exempt (job related)		
Ancillary services		
Electricity	550	
Gas	400	
Gardener	750	
Redecorations	1,800	
	3,500	
Restricted to 10% of £27,400	2,740	
Less employee's contribution	(600)	
		2,140
Employment income		29,540

2.6 Cars
9/16, 12/17

FAST FORWARD

Employees who have a company car are taxed on a % of the car's list price which depends on the level of the car's CO_2 emissions. The same % multiplied by £23,400 determines the benefit where private fuel is also provided. Statutory approved mileage allowances can be paid tax free to employees who use their own vehicle for business journeys.

A car provided by reason of the employment to an employee, or member of his family or household, for private use gives rise to a taxable benefit. 'Private use' includes home to work travel.

(a) A tax charge arises whether the car is provided by the employer or by some other person. The benefit is computed as shown below, even if the car is taken as an alternative to another benefit of a different value.

(b) The starting point for calculating a car benefit is the list price of the car (plus accessories). **The percentage of the list price that is taxable depends on the car's CO_2 emissions**.

(c) The price of the car is the sum of the following items.

(i) The list price of the car for a single retail sale at the time of first registration, including charges for delivery and standard accessories. The manufacturer's, importer's or distributor's list price must be used, even if the retailer offered a discount. A notional list price is estimated if no list price was published.

(ii) The price (including fitting) of all optional accessories provided when the car was first provided to the employee, excluding equipment needed by a disabled employee. The extra cost of adapting or manufacturing a car to run on road fuel gases is not included.

(iii) The price (including fitting) of all optional accessories fitted later and costing at least £100 each, excluding equipment needed by a disabled employee. Such accessories affect the taxable benefit from and including the tax year in which they are fitted. However, accessories which are merely replacing existing accessories and are not superior to the ones replaced are ignored. Replacement accessories which **are** superior are taken into account, but the cost of the old accessory is then deducted.

(d) There is a special rule for classic cars. If the car is at least 15 years old (from the time of first registration) at the end of the tax year, and its market value at the end of the year (or, if earlier, when it ceased to be available to the employee) is over £15,000 and greater than the price found under (c), that market value is used instead of the price. The market value takes account of all accessories (except equipment needed by a disabled employee).

(e) Capital contributions are payments by the employee in respect of the price of the car or accessories. In any tax year, account is taken of deductible capital contributions up to £5,000; contributions beyond that total are ignored.

(f) For cars that emit CO_2 of 95 g/km (2018/19), the taxable benefit is 20% of the car's list price. This percentage Increases by 1% for every 5g/km (rounded down to the nearest multiple of 5) by which CO_2 emissions exceed 95g/km up to a maximum of 37%. Therefore the 20% rate also applies to cars with emissions between 96g/km and 99g/km as these are rounded down to 95g/km. Then, for cars with emissions between 100g/km and 104g/km, the relevant percentage will be $20 + ((100 - 95)/5) = 21\%$ etc.

Exam focus point

The CO_2 baseline figure of 95g/km will and the baseline percentage of 20% be given to you in the Tax Rates and Allowances available in the exam.

(g) **For cars that emit CO_2 between 76g/km and 94g/km, the taxable benefit is 19% of the car's list price. For cars that emit between 51g/km and 75g/km, the taxable benefit is 16% of the car's list price. For cars that emit 50 g/km or less, the taxable benefit is 13% of the car's list price.**

Exam focus point

The percentages for cars which emit CO_2 up to 94g/km will be given to you in the tax rates and allowance section of the exam.

(h) **Diesel cars have a supplement of 4% of the car's list price added to the taxable benefit.** The maximum percentage, however, remains 37% of the list price.

(i) **The benefit is reduced on a time basis where a car is first made available or ceases to be made available during the tax year** or is incapable of being used for a continuous period of not less than 30 days (for example because it is being repaired).

(j) **The benefit is reduced by any payment the user must make for the private use of the car** (as distinct from a capital contribution to the cost of the car). Payments for insuring the car do not count. The benefit cannot become negative to create a deduction from the employee's income.

(k) Pool cars are exempt. A car is a pool car if **all** the following conditions are satisfied.

    (i) It is used by more than one employee and is not ordinarily used by any one of them to the exclusion of the others;

    (ii) Any private use is merely incidental to business use; and

    (iii) It is not normally kept overnight at or near the residence of an employee.

There are many ancillary benefits associated with the provision of cars, such as insurance, repairs, vehicle licences and a parking space at or near work. No extra taxable benefit arises as a result of these, with the exception of the cost of providing a driver.

2.7 Fuel for cars

Where fuel is provided there may be a further benefit in addition to the car benefit.

No taxable benefit arises where either:

(a) **All the fuel provided was made available only for business travel; or**

(b) **The employee is required to make good, and has made good, the whole of the cost of any fuel provided for his private use.**

Unlike most benefits, **a reimbursement of only part of the cost of the fuel available for private use does not reduce the benefit.**

The taxable benefit is a percentage of a base figure. The base figure for 2018/19 is £23,400. The percentage is the same percentage as is used to calculate the car benefit (see above).

<table>
<tr><td>**Exam focus point**</td><td>The fuel base figure will be given to you in the Tax Rates and Allowances available in the exam.</td></tr>
</table>

The fuel benefit is reduced in the same way as the car benefit **if the car is not available for 30 days or more**.

The fuel benefit is also reduced if private fuel is not available for part of a tax year. However, if private fuel later becomes available in the same tax year, the reduction is not made. If, for example, fuel is provided from 6 April 2018 to 30 June 2018, then the fuel benefit for 2018/19 will be restricted to just three months. This is because the provision of fuel has permanently ceased. However, if fuel is provided from 6 April 2018 to 30 June 2018, and then again from 1 September 2018 to 5 April 2019, then the fuel benefit will not be reduced since the cessation was only temporary.

Question — Car and fuel benefit

An employee was provided with a new car costing £15,000 for the whole of 2018/19. The car emits 121g/km of CO_2. During the year, the employer spent £900 on insurance, repairs and a vehicle licence. The employer paid for all petrol, costing £1,500, without reimbursement. The employee paid the employer £270 for the private use of the car. Calculate the taxable benefit.

Answer

Round CO_2 emissions figure down to the nearest 5, ie 120 g/km.

Amount by which CO_2 emissions exceed the baseline:

$(120 - 95) = 25$ g/km

Divide by 5 = 5

Taxable percentage = 20% + 5% = 25%

	£
Car benefit £15,000 × 25%	3,750
Fuel benefit £23,400 × 25%	5,850
	9,600
Less contribution towards use of car	(270)
	9,330

If the contribution of £270 had been towards the petrol the benefit would have been £9,600. This is because partial reimbursement of private petrol does not reduce the fuel benefit.

2.8 Vans

If a van is made available for an employee's private use, there is an annual scale charge of £3,350. The scale charge covers ancillary benefits such as insurance and servicing. Paragraphs 2.6 (i) and (j) above apply to vans as they do to cars.

There is, however, **no taxable benefit where an employee takes a van home** (ie uses the van for home to work travel) but is not allowed any other private use.

If the employer provides **fuel for unrestricted private use**, an additional **fuel charge of £633** applies.

2.9 Statutory approved mileage allowances   6/17

A single approved mileage allowance for business journeys in an employee's own vehicle applies to all cars and vans. There is no income tax on payments up to this allowance and employers do not have to report mileage allowances up to this amount. The allowance for 2018/19 is 45p per mile on the first 10,000 miles in the tax year with each additional mile over 10,000 miles at 25p per mile. The approved mileage allowance for employees using their own motor cycle is 24p per mile. For employees using their own pedal cycle it is 20p per mile.

If employers pay less than the statutory allowance, employees can claim tax relief up to that level.

The statutory allowance does not prevent employers from paying higher rates, but any excess will be subject to income tax. There is a similar (but slightly different) system for NICs, covered later in this chapter.

Employers can make income tax and NIC free payments of up to 5p per mile for each fellow employee making the same business trip who is carried as a passenger. If the employer does not pay the employee for carrying business passengers, the employee cannot claim any tax relief.

Question	Mileage allowance

Sophie uses her own car for business travel. During 2018/19, Sophie drove 15,400 miles in the performance of her duties. Sophie's employer paid her a mileage allowance. How is the mileage allowance treated for tax purposes assuming that the rate paid is:

(a)   40p a mile; or

(b)   25p a mile?

Answer

(a)

	£
Mileage allowance received (15,400 × 40p)	6,160
Less tax free [(10,000 × 45p) + (5,400 × 25p)]	(5,850)
Taxable benefit	310

£5,850 is tax free and the excess amount received of £310 is a taxable benefit.

(b)

	£
Mileage allowance received (15,400 × 25p)	3,850
Less tax free amount [(10,000 × 45p) + (5,400 × 25p)]	(5,850)
Allowable deduction	(2,000)

There is no taxable benefit and Sophie can claim a deduction from her employment income of £2,000.

2.10 Beneficial loans

6/14, 9/16

Taxable cheap loans are charged to tax on the difference between the official rate of interest and any interest paid by the employee.

2.10.1 Introduction

Employment related loans to employees and their relatives give rise to a benefit equal to:

(a) **Any amounts written off** (unless the employee has died); and

(b) **The excess of the interest based on an official rate prescribed by the Treasury, over any interest actually charged (taxable cheap loan).** Interest payable during the tax year but paid after the end of the tax year is taken into account, but if the benefit is determined before such interest is paid a claim must be made to take it into account.

The following loans are normally not treated as taxable cheap loans for calculation of the interest benefits (but are taxable for the purposes of the charge on loans written off).

(a) A loan on normal commercial terms made in the ordinary course of the employer's money-lending business.

(b) A loan made by an individual in the ordinary course of the lender's domestic, family or personal arrangements.

2.10.2 Calculating the interest benefit

There are two alternative methods of calculating the taxable benefit. The simpler **'average' method** automatically applies unless the taxpayer or HMRC elect for the alternative **'strict' method**. (HMRC normally only make the election where it appears that the 'average' method is being deliberately exploited.) In both methods, the benefit is the interest at the official rate minus the interest payable.

The 'average' method averages the balances at the beginning and end of the tax year (or the dates on which the loan was made and discharged if it was not in existence throughout the tax year) and applies the official rate of interest to this average. If the loan was not in existence throughout the tax year only the number of complete tax months (from the 6th of the month) for which it existed are taken into account.

The 'strict' method is to compute interest at the official rate on the actual amount outstanding on a daily basis. However, for exam purposes, it is acceptable to work on a monthly basis.

Question

Loan benefit

At 6 April 2018 a taxable cheap loan of £40,000 was outstanding to an employee who repaid £18,000 on 6 December 2018. The remaining balance of £22,000 was outstanding at 5 April 2019. Interest paid during the year was £350. What was the benefit under both methods for 2018/19?

Average method

£

$$2.5\% \times \frac{40{,}000 + 22{,}000}{2}$$ 775

Less interest paid (350)

Benefit 425

Alternative method (strict method)

£

$£40{,}000 \times \dfrac{8}{12}$ (6 April – 5 December) × 2.5% 667

$£22{,}000 \times \dfrac{4}{12}$ (6 December – 5 April) × 2.5% 183

850

Less interest paid (350)

Benefit 500

HMRC could elect for the 'strict' method, although this is unlikely given the difference between the methods is relatively small and it does not appear that the 'average' method is being deliberately exploited.

2.10.3 The *de minimis* test

The benefit is not taxable if:

(a) The **total of all taxable cheap loans to the employee did not exceed £10,000** at any time in the tax year; or

(b) **The loan is not a qualifying loan and the total of all non-qualifying loans to the employee did not exceed £10,000** at any time in the tax year.

A qualifying loan is one on which all or part of any interest paid would qualify as qualifying interest.

When the £10,000 threshold is exceeded, a benefit arises on interest on the whole loan, not just on the excess of the loan over £10,000.

When a loan is written off and a benefit arises, there is no £10,000 threshold: writing off a loan of £1 gives rise to a £1 benefit.

2.10.4 Qualifying loans

If the whole of the interest payable on a qualifying loan is eligible for tax relief as qualifying interest, then no taxable benefit arises. If the interest is only partly eligible for tax relief, then the employee is treated as receiving earnings because the actual rate of interest is below the official rate. He is also treated as paying interest equal to those earnings. This **deemed interest paid may qualify as a business expense or as qualifying interest in addition to any interest actually paid.**

Question

Beneficial loans

Anna has an annual salary of £30,000, and two loans from her employer.

(a) A season ticket loan of £8,300 at no interest

(b) A loan, 90% of which was used to buy shares in her employee-controlled company, of £54,000 at 0.5% interest

What is Anna's tax liability for 2018/19?

Answer

	£
Salary	30,000
Season ticket loan (non-qualifying): not over £10,000	0
Loan to buy shares (qualifying): £54,000 × (2.5 − 0.5 = 2%)	1,080
Earnings	31,080
Less qualifying interest deemed to be paid (£54,000 × 2.5% × 90%)	(1,215)
	29,865
Less personal allowance	(11,850)
Taxable income	18,015
Income tax	
£18,015 × 20%	3,603

2.11 Other assets made available for private use

FAST FORWARD

20% of the value of assets made available for private use is taxable.

When assets are made available to employees or members of their family or household, the taxable benefit is the higher of 20% of the market value when first provided as a benefit to any employee and the rent paid by the employer. The 20% charge is time-apportioned when the asset is provided for only part of the year. The charge after any time apportionment is reduced by any payment made by the employee.

Certain assets, such as bicycles provided for journeys to work, are exempt. These are described later in this chapter.

If an asset made available is subsequently acquired by the employee, the taxable benefit on the acquisition is the greater of:

- The current market value minus the price paid by the employee; and
- The market value when first provided minus any amounts already taxed (ignoring contributions by the employee) minus the price paid by the employee.

This rule prevents tax free benefits arising on rapidly depreciating items through the employee purchasing them at their low second-hand value.

There is an exception to this rule for bicycles which have previously been provided as exempt benefits and for car benefit cars. The taxable benefit on acquisition is restricted to current market value, minus the price paid by the employee.

2.12 Example: assets made available for private use

A suit costing £400 is purchased by an employer for use by an employee on 6 April 2017. On 6 April 2018 the suit is purchased by the employee for £30, its market value then being £50.

The benefit in 2017/18 is £400 × 20%	£80

The benefit in 2018/19 is £290, being the **greater** of:

		£
(a)	Market value at acquisition by employee	50
	Less price paid	(30)
		20
(b)	Original market value	400
	Less taxed in respect of use	(80)
		320
	Less price paid	(30)
		290

Question

Rupert is provided with a new bicycle by his employer on 6 April 2018. The bicycle is available for private use as well as commuting to work. It cost the employer £1,500 when new. On 6 October 2018 the employer transfers ownership of the bicycle to Rupert when it is worth £800. Rupert does not pay anything for the bicycle.

What is the total taxable benefit on Rupert for 2018/19 in respect of the bicycle?

Answer

Use benefit	Exempt
Transfer benefit (use MV at acquisition by employee only)	
MV at transfer	<u>£800</u>

2.13 Scholarships

If scholarships are given to members an employee's family, the **employee is taxable on the cost** unless the scholarship fund's or scheme's payments by reason of people's employments are not more than 25% of its total payments.

2.14 Childcare   6/14

> **FAST FORWARD**
>
> Workplace childcare is an exempt benefit.

The cost of running a **workplace nursery or playscheme is an exempt benefit (without limit).**

Exam focus point

> A new tax-free childcare scheme for working families has been introduced to replace tax relief on childcare vouchers for employees, although some employees may continue to receive childcare vouchers under existing arrangements. Childcare vouchers and the new tax-free childcare scheme are **not examinable** in Advanced Taxation (ATX – UK).

2.15 Residual charge

> **FAST FORWARD**
>
> There is a residual charge for other benefits, usually equal to the cost of the benefits.

We have seen above how certain specific benefits are taxed. A 'residual charge' is made on the taxable value of other benefits. In general, the taxable value of a benefit is the cost of the benefit less any payment made by the employee to the persons providing the benefit.

The residual charge applies to any benefit provided for an employee or a member of the employee's family or household, by reason of the employment. There is an exception where the employer is an individual and the provision of the benefit is made in the normal course of the employer's domestic, family or personal relationships.

3 Exempt benefits

FAST FORWARD

Some benefits are exempt from tax such as removal expenses and the provision of sporting facilities (subject to certain limits).

Various benefits are exempt from tax. These include:

(a) **Reimbursed expenses** (see earlier in this chapter).

(b) **Entertainment provided to employees by genuine third parties** (eg seats at sporting/cultural events), even if it is provided by giving the employee a voucher.

(c) **Gifts of goods** (or vouchers exchangeable for goods) from third parties (ie not provided by the employer or a person connected to the employer) if the total cost (including VAT) of all gifts by the same donor to the same employee in the tax year is £250 or less. If the £250 limit is exceeded, the full amount is taxable, not just the excess.

(d) **Non-cash awards for long service** if the period of service was at least 20 years, no similar award was made to the employee in the past 10 years and the cost is not more than £50 per year of service.

(e) **Awards under staff suggestion schemes if:**

    (i) There is a formal scheme, open to all employees on equal terms.

    (ii) The suggestion is outside the scope of the employee's normal duties.

    (iii) Either the award is not more than £25, or the award is only made after a decision is taken to implement the suggestion.

    (iv) Awards over £25 reflect the financial importance of the suggestion to the business, and either do not exceed 50% of the expected net financial benefit during the first year of implementation or do not exceed 10% of the expected net financial benefit over a period of up to five years.

    (v) Awards of over £25 are shared on a reasonable basis between two or more employees putting forward the same suggestion.

If an award exceeds £5,000, the excess is always taxable.

(f) **The first £8,000 of removal expenses if:**

    (i) The employee does not already live within a reasonable daily travelling distance of the new place of employment, but will do so after moving.

    (ii) The expenses are incurred or the benefits provided by the end of the tax year following the tax year of the start of employment at the new location.

(g) **Workplace childcare** (see earlier in this chapter).

(h) **Sporting or recreational facilities available to employees generally and not to the general public,** unless they are provided on domestic premises, or they consist in an interest in or the use of any mechanically propelled vehicle or any overnight accommodation. Vouchers only exchangeable for such facilities are also exempt, but membership fees for sports clubs are taxable.

(i) **Assets or services used in performing the duties of employment** provided any private use of the item concerned is insignificant. This exempts, for example, the benefit arising on the private use of employer-provided tools.

(j) **Welfare counselling** and similar minor benefits if the benefit concerned is available to employees generally.

(k) **Bicycles or cycling safety equipment provided to enable employees to get to and from work or to travel between one workplace and another.** The equipment must be available to the employer's employees generally. Also, it must be used mainly for the aforementioned journeys.

(l)   **Workplace parking.**

(m)   **Up to £15,480 a year paid to an employee who is on a full-time course lasting at least a year**, with average full-time attendance of at least 20 weeks a year. If the £15,480 limit is exceeded, the whole amount is taxable.

(n)   **Work related training and related costs. This includes the costs of** training material and assets either made during training or incorporated into something so made.

(o)   **Air miles or car fuel coupons** obtained as a result of business expenditure but used for private purposes.

(p)   **The cost of work buses and minibuses or subsidies to public bus services.**

       A works bus must have a seating capacity of 12 or more and a works minibus a seating capacity of 9 or more but not more than 12 and be available generally to employees of the employer concerned. The bus or minibus must mainly be used by employees for journeys to and from work and for journeys between workplaces.

(q)   **Transport/overnight costs** where public transport is disrupted by industrial action, late night taxis and travel costs incurred where car sharing arrangements unavoidably breakdown.

(r)   The private use of one **mobile phone (which can be a smartphone)**. Top up vouchers for exempt mobile phones are also tax free. If more than one mobile phone is provided to an employee for private use only the second or subsequent phone is a taxable benefit.

(s)   **Employer provided uniforms** which employees must wear as part of their duties.

(t)   The cost of **staff parties** which are open to staff generally provided that the **cost per head per year (including VAT) is £150 or less**. The £150 limit may be split between several parties.

(u)   **Private medical insurance premiums paid to cover treatment when the employee is outside the UK in the performance of the employee's duties**. Other medical insurance premiums are taxable as is the cost of medical diagnosis and treatment except for routine check ups. Eye tests and glasses for employees using VDUs are exempt.

(v)   Cheap loans **that do not exceed £10,000** at any time in the tax year (see above).

(w)   **Job related accommodation** (see above).

(x)   **Employer contributions towards additional household costs incurred by an employee who works wholly or partly at home.** Payments up to £4 per week (or £18 per month for monthly paid employees) may be made without supporting evidence. Payments in excess of that amount require supporting evidence that the payment is wholly in respect of additional household expenses.

(y)   **Recommended medical treatment** costing up to £500 per employee per tax year paid for by an employer. The treatment must be recommended in writing by a health professional (eg doctor, nurse) and the purpose of the treatment must be to assist the employee to return to work after a period of injury or ill-health lasting at least 28 days. If the payments exceed £500, they are wholly taxable.

(z)   **Trivial benefits costing up to £50 per employee per tax year** provided these are not in the form of cash or a cash voucher. Examples of exempt trivial benefits include providing an employee with a Christmas or birthday present and sending flowers to an employee on the birth of a baby.

(aa)   **Pensions advice** up to £500 per employee per tax year under certain schemes open to the employer's employees generally. If the payments exceed £500 in a tax year, the first £500 is exempt.

Where a voucher is provided for a benefit which is exempt from income tax the provision of the voucher itself is also exempt.

4 Allowable deductions

To be deductible, expenses must be for qualifying travel or wholly, exclusively and necessarily incurred.

4.1 General principles

Certain expenditure is specifically deductible in computing net taxable earnings:

(a) **Contributions** (within certain limits) **to registered occupational pension schemes** (see earlier in this text)

(b) **Subscriptions to professional bodies** on the list of bodies issued by HMRC (which includes most UK professional bodies), if relevant to the duties of the employment

(c) Payments for certain **liabilities relating to the employment** and for insurance against them (see below)

(d) **Payments to charity made under the payroll deduction scheme** operated by an employer

(e) **Mileage allowance** relief (see above).

Otherwise, **allowable deductions are notoriously hard to obtain. They are limited to:**

- **Qualifying travel expenses** (see below)

- **Other expenses the employee is obliged to incur and pay as holder of the employment which are incurred wholly, exclusively and necessarily in the performance of the duties of the employment**

- **Capital allowances on plant and machinery (other than cars or other vehicles) necessarily provided for use in the performance of those duties.**

4.2 Liabilities and insurance

If a director or employee incurs a liability related to employment or pays for insurance against such a liability, the cost is a deductible expense. If the employer pays such amounts, there is no taxable benefit.

A liability relating to employment is one which is imposed in respect of the employee's acts or omissions as employee. Thus, for example, liability for negligence would be covered. Related costs, for example the costs of legal proceedings, are included.

For insurance premiums to qualify, the insurance policy must:

(a) Cover only liabilities relating to employment, vicarious liability in respect of liabilities of another person's employment, related costs and payments to the employee's own employees in respect of employment liabilities relating to employment and related costs; and

(b) It must not last for more than two years (although it may be renewed for up to two years at a time), and the insured person must not be not required to renew it.

4.3 Travel expenses

4.3.1 General principles

Tax relief is not available for an employee's normal commuting costs. This means relief is not available for any costs an employee incurs in getting from home to the employee's normal place of work. However **employees are entitled to relief for travel expenses which basically are the full costs that they are obliged to incur and pay as holder of the employment in travelling in the performance of their duties or travelling to or from a place which they have to attend in the performance of their duties (other than a permanent workplace).**

Question

Judi is an accountant who works in an office in Leeds. She often travels to meetings at the firm's offices in London, returning to her office in Leeds after the meetings. What tax relief is available for Judi's travel costs?

Answer

Tax relief is available for the full cost of these journeys as the travel is undertaken in the performance of Judi's duties.

Question

Zoe lives in Wycombe and normally works in Chiswick. Occasionally she visits a client in Wimbledon and travels direct from home. Distances are shown in the diagram below:

What tax relief is available for Zoe's travel costs?

Answer

Zoe is not entitled to tax relief for the costs incurred in travelling between Wycombe and Chiswick since these are normal commuting costs. However, relief is available for all costs that Zoe incurs when she travels from Wycombe to Wimbledon to visit her client.

To prevent manipulation of the basic rule, **normal commuting will not become a business journey just because the employee stops en-route to perform a business task** (eg make a 'phone call'). **Nor will relief be available if the journey is essentially the same as the employee's normal journey to work.**

Question

Jeffrey is based at an office in Birmingham city centre. One day he is required to attend a 9.00 am meeting with a client whose premises are near to his Birmingham office. Jeffrey travels from home directly to the meeting. What tax relief is available for Jeffrey's travel costs?

Answer

As the journey to the client is substantially the same as Jeffrey's ordinary journey to work, tax relief is not available for the cost of this journey.

4.3.2 Site based employees

Site based employees (eg construction workers, management consultants etc) who do not have a permanent workplace, are **entitled to relief for the costs of all journeys made from home to wherever they are working**. This is because these employees do not have an ordinary commuting journey or any normal commuting costs.

However this rule only applies if the employee does not spend more than 24 months of continuous work at any one site. Continuous work is defined as a period over which the duties of the employment are performed to a significant extent (40% or more of working time) at that place.

4.3.3 Temporary workplace

Tax relief is available for travel, accommodation and subsistence expenses incurred by an employee who is working at a temporary workplace on a secondment expected to last up to 24 months. If a secondment is initially expected not to exceed 24 months, but it is extended, relief ceases to be due from the date the employee becomes aware of the change. When looking at how long a secondment is expected to last, HMRC will consider not only the terms of the written contract but also any verbal agreement by the employer and other factors such as whether the employee buys a house etc.

Question
Temporary workplace

Philip works for Vastbank at its Newcastle city centre branch. Philip is sent to work full-time at another branch in Morpeth for 20 months at the end of which he will return to the Newcastle branch. Morpeth is about 20 miles north of Newcastle. What tax relief is available for Philip's travel costs?

Answer

Although Philip is spending all of his time at the Morpeth branch it will not be treated as his normal work place because his period of attendance will be less than 24 months. Thus Philip can claim tax relief in full for the costs of travel from his home to the Morpeth branch.

4.3.4 Travel expenses relating to overseas employment

There is also **tax relief for certain travel expenses relating to overseas employment**. These are dealt with later in this text.

4.4 Other expenses

The word 'exclusively' strictly implies that the expenditure must give no private benefit at all. If it does, none of it is deductible. In practice, HMRC may ignore a small element of private benefit or an apportionment between business and private use.

Whether an expense is 'necessary' is not determined by what the employer requires. The test is whether the duties of the employment could not be performed without the expense being incurred.

- *Sanderson v Durbridge 1955*

  The cost of evening meals taken when attending late meetings was not deductible because it was not incurred in the performance of the duties.

- *Blackwell v Mills 1945*

  As a condition of employment, an employee was required to attend evening classes. The cost of textbooks and travel was not deductible because it was not incurred in the performance of the duties.

- *Lupton v Potts 1969*

  Examination fees incurred by a trainee solicitor were not deductible because they were incurred neither wholly nor exclusively in the performance of the duties of the trainee's employment, but in furthering his ambition to become a solicitor.

- *Brown v Bullock 1961*

  The expense of joining a club that was virtually a requisite of an employment was not deductible because it would have been possible to carry on the employment without the club membership, so the expense was not necessary.

- *Elwood v Utitz 1965*

  A managing director's subscriptions to two residential London clubs were claimed by him as an expense on the grounds that they were cheaper than hotels.

  The expenditure was deductible as it was necessary in that it would be impossible for the employee to carry out his London duties without being provided with appropriate accommodation. The residential facilities (which were cheaper than hotel accommodation) were given to club members only.

- *Lucas v Cattell 1972*

  The cost of business telephone calls on a private telephone was deductible, but no part of the line or telephone rental charges was deductible.

- *Fitzpatrick v IRC 1994; Smith v Abbott 1994*

  Journalists could not claim a deduction for the cost of buying newspapers which they read to keep themselves informed, since they were merely preparing themselves to perform their duties.

The cost of clothes for work is generally not deductible, except that, for certain trades requiring uniforms or protective clothing such as overalls, protective gloves and boots, an expense may be claimed by the employee of either the actual cost incurred or a flat rate amount negotiated by HMRC with the relevant trade unions.

An employee required to work at home may be able to claim a deduction for an appropriate proportion of expenditure on lighting, heating and (if a room is used exclusively for work purposes) **the council tax.** Employers can pay up to £4 per week (or £18 per month to monthly paid employees). In certain circumstances, employers can reimburse expenses in excess of this limit if the employee submits evidence of their actual costs.

5 National insurance for employers and employees 6/14, 6/15, 6/16, 6/17, 12/17, 6/18

5.1 Classes of National Insurance contributions

> **FAST FORWARD**
>
> National insurance contributions are divided into four classes.

Four classes of national insurance contribution (NIC) exist, as set out below.

(a) **Class 1**. This is divided into:
  (i) **Employee's Class 1**, paid by employees
  (ii) **Employer's Class 1, Class 1A and Class 1B** paid by employers
(b) **Class 2**. Paid by the self-employed
(c) **Class 3**. Voluntary contributions (for example to maintain rights to certain state benefits)
(d) **Class 4**. Paid by the self-employed

Exam focus point

> Class 1B and Class 3 contributions are outside the scope of your syllabus.

In this section we focus on NIC for employees and their employers.

5.2 General principles

FAST FORWARD

Employees pay employee's Class 1 NICs. Employees pay the main employee's rate between the employee's threshold and upper earnings limit and the additional rate on earnings above the upper earnings limit. Employers pay employer's Class 1 NICs above the employer's threshold. For employers, there is no upper earnings limit.

5.2.1 Introduction

The National Insurance Contributions Office (NICO), which is part of HMRC, examines employers' records and procedures to ensure that the correct amounts of NICs are collected.

Both employees and employers pay Class 1 NICs related to the employee's earnings. NICs are not deductible from an employee's gross salary for income tax purposes. However, employers' contributions are deductible trade expenses.

5.2.2 What is 'earnings'?

'Earnings' broadly comprise gross pay, excluding benefits which cannot be turned into cash by surrender (eg holidays, cars, accommodation, use of employer's assets – these are subject to Class 1A contributions, see 5.3 below). It also includes mileage payments over the approved amount (see below) and readily convertible assets given to employees. No deduction is made for employee pension contributions.

An employer's contribution to a registered personal pension or a registered occupational pension is not 'earnings'. However, NICs are due on employer contributions to non-registered schemes.

In general income tax and NIC exemptions mirror one another. For example, payment of personal incidental expenses covered by the £5/£10 a night income tax *de minimis* exemption are excluded from NIC earnings. Relocation expenses of a type exempt from income tax are also excluded from NIC earnings but without the income tax £8,000 upper limit (although expenses exceeding £8,000 are subject to Class 1A NICs as described below). Similarly, the income tax rules for travel expenses are exactly mirrored for NIC treatment.

An expense with a business purpose is not treated as earnings. For example, if an employee is reimbursed for business travel or for staying in a hotel on the employer's business this is not normally 'earnings'. However, if an employee is reimbursed for their own home telephone charges the reimbursed cost of private calls (and all reimbursed rental) is earnings.

Where an employer reimburses an employee using their own car for business mileage, the earnings element is the excess of the mileage rate paid over HMRC's 'up to 10,000 business miles' 'approved mileage allowance payments' (AMAPs). This applies even where business mileage exceeds 10,000 pa.

In general, non cash vouchers are subject to NICs. However, the following are exempt:

- Childcare vouchers up to the amount exempt for income tax

- Vouchers for the use of sports and recreational facilities (where tax exempt)

- Vouchers for meals on the employer's premises

- Transport vouchers where the employee earns less than £8,500 a year

- Top up vouchers for pay as you go mobile phones where the provision of the phone itself is exempt from income tax

- Vouchers for eye tests and glasses for employees using VDUs

- Any other voucher which is exempt from income tax.

5.2.3 Rates

The rates of contribution for 2018/19, and the earnings bands to which they apply, are set out in the Rates and Allowances Tables in this text.

Employees pay main employee's contributions of 12% of earnings between the employee's threshold of £8,424 and the upper earnings limit of £46,350 or the equivalent monthly or weekly limit (see below). They also pay additional employee's contributions of 2% on earnings above the upper earnings limit.

Where the employee is aged 21 or over, employers pay employer's contributions of 13.8% on earnings above the employer's threshold of £8,424, or the equivalent monthly or weekly limit. There is no upper limit.

Exam focus point

> There are different rules for employer's contributions if the employee is aged under 21 and for apprentices aged under 25. These rules are **not examinable** in Advanced Taxation (ATX – UK). You should therefore assume that all employees are aged 25 or over in questions.

5.2.4 Earnings period

FAST FORWARD

> NICs are based on earnings periods.

NICs are calculated in relation to an earnings period. This is the period to which earnings paid to an employee are deemed to relate. Where earnings are paid at regular intervals, the earnings period will generally be equated with the payment interval, for example a week or a month. **Company directors have an annual earnings period, regardless of how they are paid.**

Exam focus point

> The examining team has stated that calculations of weekly or monthly contributions will not be examined. All calculations will be on an annualised basis.

Question   Class 1 contributions

Sally works for Red plc. She is paid £50,000 in 2018/19.

Show Sally's employee's contributions for 2018/19 and the employer's contributions paid by Red plc, before taking account of the employment allowance (see below).

Answer

Sally

	£
Employee's contributions	
£(46,350 – 8,424) = £37,926 × 12% (main)	4,551
£(50,000 – 46,350) = £3,650 × 2% (additional)	73
Total employee's contributions	4,624

Red plc

	£
Employer's contributions	
£(50,000 – 8,424) = £41,576 × 13.8%	5,737

5.2.5 Employment allowance

FAST FORWARD

> The employment allowance enables an employer to reduce its total Class 1 employer's contributions by up to £3,000 per tax year.

An **employer can make a claim** to **reduce its total Class 1 employer's contributions** by an **employment allowance equal to those contributions**, subject to a **maximum allowance of £3,000 per tax year**. The employment allowance is used against each payment of Class 1 employer's contributions in the tax year until the end of the tax year or until the £3,000 limit is reached. For example, if the Class 1 employer's contributions are £2,200 each month, £2,200 of the allowance will be used against the April liability and the remaining £800 against the May liability.

Some employers are **excluded employers** for the purposes of the employment allowance. These include **companies** where the **only employed earner for whom the company pays Class 1 employer's contributions is a director of the company**, employers who employ **employees for personal, household or domestic work**, **public authorities** and employers who **carry out functions either wholly or mainly of a public nature** such as provision of National Heath Service services.

The employment allowance cannot be used to reduce the Class 1 employer's contributions on deemed payments from Personal Service Companies (see later in this chapter).

5.3 Class 1A NIC

FAST FORWARD

Employers pay Class 1A NIC on most taxable benefits.

Employers must pay Class 1A NIC at 13.8% on most taxable benefits. However, benefits are exempt if they are:

- Within Class 1;
- Included in a PAYE settlement agreement; or
- Otherwise not required to be reported on P11Ds.

Class 1A contributions are usually collected annually in arrears. If the payment is made electronically, payment must reach HMRC's bank account no later than 22 July following the end of the tax year. Payment by cheque must reach HMRC no later than 19 July following the end of the tax year.

5.3.1 Example: Class 1A NICs

An employee is provided with benefits totaling £2,755 during 2018/19. The Class 1A contributions due from the employer are £2,755 @ 13.8% = £380.

6 Personal service companies   12/13, 3/16

FAST FORWARD

The IR35 provisions prevent avoidance of tax by providing services through a company.

6.1 Application and outline of computation

We looked at the distinction between employment and self employment earlier in this chapter. **Workers normally prefer to avoid being classified as employees as the tax and national insurance burden on the self-employed is lower**. However, there is a risk that workers claiming to be self employed will be classified by HMRC as employees, leading to increased taxation and liability to penalties, both for the workers and those who use their services.

One way to avoid this potential pitfall was for the **worker to set up a company (known as a personal service company or PSC) to provide services to a client**. The worker was **both the owner of the PSC** (usually as its sole shareholder) and **an employee of the PSC**. An employment relationship could not arise between the client and the worker because of the existence of the intermediary PSC and so payments by the client were not subject to PAYE and no NICs were payable.

In addition, it was **possible for the worker to arrange the affairs of the personal service company to obtain tax advantages in extracting profits from the PSC** as compared with the situation where the worker was self-employed. Thus the arrangement had advantages for both the client and the worker.

A typical arrangement is shown in the following diagram where a taxpayer called Ada used a PSC called Quality Ltd to provide computer services to a business client, Edward:

Quality Ltd invoiced Edward for the services provided. This **payment was made gross by Edward, rather than under PAYE** and there were **no national insurance contributions payable**.

Quality Ltd might then have paid Ada a salary (usually only a minimal amount to ensure that a small amount of national insurance contributions were payable which gave entitlement to state benefits such as Jobseeker's Allowance). **Quality Ltd paid corporation tax on its net income** after deduction of expenses wholly and exclusively incurred for the purposes of the trade (a more generous basis than the test for employment expenses), including Ada's salary and any employer national insurance contributions. The corporation tax charge (currently 19%) was substantially lower than the higher and additional rates of income tax.

Quality Ltd could then have distributed post-tax profits as dividends. Dividends are not subject to PAYE nor to national insurance contributions.

Such PSCs were so popular that the loss of tax and national insurance contributions as a result of their use caused serious concerns to HMRC. Consequently, there are now anti-avoidance rules which restrict the avoidance of tax and national insurance contributions by workers offering their services through an intermediary, such as a PSC. **These provisions are commonly known as the IR35 provisions.**

Broadly, the **IR35 provisions apply** where:

(a)   **An individual (the worker) performs, or has an obligation to perform, services for 'a client'**;

(b)   The **performance of those services is referable to arrangements involving a third party** (eg the personal service company), rather than referable to a contract between the client and the worker; and

(c)   **If the services were to be performed by the worker under a contract between the worker and the client, the worker would be regarded as employed by the client.**

In relation to the last condition, **the usual tests of whether an individual is employed or self-employed**, considered earlier in this chapter, **are used**.

If the intermediary is a **company**, the IR35 provisions will apply only if:

(a)   **The worker** (or the worker's associates) has a **material interest** in the company; or

(b)   The **payment or benefit arising** (other than employment income) from the work done for the client is **received or receivable directly from the intermediary** and can **reasonably be taken to represent remuneration for services provided by the worker to the client.**

Material interest is defined as being:

(a) **Beneficial ownership** of, or the ability to control, directly or indirectly **more than 5% of the ordinary share capital of the company**;

(b) **Possession** of, or entitlement to acquire, **rights to receive more than 5% of any distributions made by the company**; or

(c) Where the company is a **close company** (see later in this text), **possession** of, or entitlement to acquire, **rights to receive more than 5% of the assets available for distribution to participators in the event of a winding up of the company.**

6.2 Computation of deemed salary payment

If the IR35 provisions apply, then **a salary payment may be deemed to have been made to the worker at the end of the tax year.** The deemed payment is **subject to PAYE and NICs.**

The following steps should be followed to compute the amount of the deemed payment:

Step 1 **Take 95% of all payments and benefits received in respect of the relevant engagements by the third party.**

Step 2 **Add amounts received in respect of the relevant engagements by the worker otherwise than from the third party,** if they are not chargeable as employment income, but would have been so chargeable if the worker had been employed by the client.

Step 3 **Deduct expenses met by the third party** if those expenses would have been deductible had they been paid out of the taxable earnings of the employment by the worker. This also includes expenses paid by the worker and reimbursed by the third party. Mileage allowances up to the statutory amounts are also deductible where a vehicle is provided by the third party.

Step 4 **Deduct capital allowances on expenditure incurred by the third party** if the worker would have been able to deduct them had the worker incurred the expenditure and had the worker been employed by the client.

Step 5 **Deduct any registered pension contributions and employer's NICs paid by the third party** in respect of the worker.

Step 6 **Deduct amounts received by the worker from the third party** that are chargeable as employment income but were not deducted under Step 3.

Step 7 Find the amount that together with employer's NIC on it, is equal to the amount resulting from Step 6 above. This means that you should multiply the amount in Step 6 by 13.8/113.8 and deduct this amount from the amount in Step 6.

Step 8 The result is the amount of the deemed employment income.

6.3 Effect on company

The deemed employment income is an allowable trading expense for the personal service company and is treated as paid to the worker on the last day of the tax year. If dividends are paid out of this income, they are treated as exempt in order to avoid a double charge to tax on the same income.

The personal service company should consider having an accounting date of 5 April, or shortly thereafter.

For example, if accounts are prepared to 5 April the deemed employment income for 2018/19 is deductible in the company in the year to 5 April 2019, whereas with a 31 March year end the deemed payment would be deductible in the year to 31 March 2020.

6.4 Example: personal service company

Alison offers technical writing services through a company. During 2018/19 the company received income of £60,000 in respect of relevant engagements performed by Alison. The company paid Alison a salary of £30,000 plus employer's NIC of £2,977 (no employment allowance is available as this is a single employee/director company – see earlier in this chapter). The company also pays £4,000 into an occupational pension scheme in respect of Alison. Alison incurred travelling expenses of £400 in respect of the relevant engagements.

The deemed employment income taxed on Alison is:

	£
Income (£60,000 × 95%)	57,000
Less: travel	(400)
pension	(4,000)
salary	(30,000)
employer's NIC on actual salary	(2,977)
	19,623

Less employer's NIC on deemed payment

$$\frac{13.8}{113.8} \times £19,623 \qquad (2,380)$$

Deemed employment income	17,243

- General earnings are taxed in the year of receipt. Money earnings are generally received on the earlier of the time payment is made and the time entitlement to payment arises. Non-money earnings are generally received when provided.

- Employment involves a contract of service whereas self employment involves a contract for services.

- Employees are taxed on benefits under the benefits code. The amount of a taxable benefit is reduced by any amount paid by the employee to the employer (except private fuel) by 6 July following the end of the tax year.

- The benefit in respect of accommodation is its annual value. There is an additional benefit if the property cost the employer over £75,000.

- Employees who have a company car are taxed on a % of the car's list price which depends on the level of the car's CO_2 emissions. The same % multiplied by £23,400 determines the benefit where private fuel is also provided. Statutory approved mileage allowances can be paid tax free to employees who use their own vehicle for business journeys.

- Taxable cheap loans are charged to tax on the difference between the official rate of interest and any interest paid by the employee.

- 20% of the value of assets made available for private use is taxable.

- Workplace childcare is an exempt benefit.

- There is a residual charge for other benefits, usually equal to the cost of the benefits.

- Some benefits are exempt from tax such as removal expenses and the provision of sporting facilities (subject to certain limits).

- To be deductible, expenses must be for qualifying travel or wholly, exclusively and necessarily incurred.

- National Insurance contributions are divided into four classes.

- Employees pay employee's Class 1 NICs. Employees pay the main employee's rate between the employee's threshold and upper earnings limit and the additional rate on earnings above the upper earnings limit. Employers pay employer's Class 1 NICs above the employer's threshold. For employers, there is no upper earnings limit.

- NICs are based on earnings periods.

- The employment allowance enables an employer to reduce its total Class 1 employer's contributions by up to £3,000 per tax year.

- Employers pay Class 1A NIC on most taxable benefits.

- The IR35 provisions prevent avoidance of tax by providing services through a company.

1   Ben is employed by Crimson Ltd and paid £14,000 per annum. For the year ended 31 December 2018 he is paid a £5,000 bonus on 1 May 2019. He was paid a similar bonus of £3,000 on 1 May 2018 based on the year ended 31 December 2017 results. Ben is not a director of Crimson Ltd. How much is Ben's taxable income for 2018/19?

2   What accommodation does not give rise to a taxable benefit?

3   Josh was provided with a company car on 1 August 2018. It cost £25,000 and has a CO_2 emission of 100g/km. Josh uses the car 60% for business use as a sales representative. The company pays for Josh's private diesel for use in the car. What are Josh's benefits in respect of the car and the fuel?

4   When may an employee who is provided with a fuel by an employer avoid a fuel benefit?

5   To what extent are removal expenses paid for by an employer taxable?

6   When may travel expenses be deducted from the taxable earnings of an employee?

7   Lucy is provided with a mobile phone by her employer costing £350 per annum. What is taxable on Lucy?

8   What is the employment allowance?

9   On what and by whom are Class 1A NICs paid?

10   What are the IR35 provisions designed to prevent?

Answers to quick quiz

1   £17,000 (£14,000 + £3,000 bonus paid in 2018/19)

2   Job related accommodation

3   £8,067 (4,167 + 3,900)

   Car: $£25,000 \times (\left[\dfrac{100-95}{5}\right] + 20\% + 4\%)$ (diesel car)

   £25,000 × 25%

   £6,250 for 12 months

   £6,250 × 8/12 = 4,167

   Car: £4,167

   Fuel: £23,400 × 25% × 8/12 = £3,900

4   There is no fuel benefit if:

   (a)   All the fuel provided was made available only for business travel; or
   (b)   The full cost of any fuel provided for private use was completely reimbursed by the employee.

5   The first £8,000 of removal expenses are exempt. Any excess is taxable.

6   An employee can deduct travel costs incurred in travelling in the performance of their duties or in travelling to a place which they have to attend in the performance of their duties (other than the normal place of work).

7   Nothing. The provision of one mobile phone for private use is an exempt benefit.

8   The employment allowance is a reduction in an employer's Class 1 employer's contributions equal to those contributions, subject to a maximum of £3,000 per tax year.

9   Class 1A NICs are paid by employers on taxable benefits.

10 The provisions are designed to prevent workers avoiding tax and NIC by offering their services through an intermediary, such as a company.

Now try the questions below from the Practice Question Bank

Number	Level	Marks	Time
Q4	Introductory	13	25 mins
Q5	Introductory	10	20 mins

Employment income: additional aspects

Topic list	Syllabus reference
1 Shares and share options: general rules	A1(c)(i)
2 Tax advantaged share schemes	A1(c)(i)
3 Lump sum payments	A1(c)(ii)

Introduction

In the last chapter, we covered the general rules for employment income, including taxable and exempt benefits.

In this chapter, we first consider the general rules on the tax charges which may apply if an employer provides shares or share options to an employee. Then we look at the rules for tax advantaged share and share option schemes. Not only are these tax efficient means by which employees can be remunerated but they also provide a link between remuneration and the company's performance.

Finally, we look at the rules for lump sums paid to employees, usually on the termination of the employment.

In the next chapter, we will turn our attention to the self-employed.

Study guide

		Intellectual level
1	Income and income tax liabilities in situations involving further overseas aspects and in relation to trusts, and the application of exemptions and reliefs	
(c)	Income from employment:	3
(i)	Advise on the tax treatment of share option and share incentive schemes	
(ii)	Advise on the tax treatment of lump sum receipts	

Exam guide

Share incentives and share options may well feature in a question about employees. You may be required to advise the employer as to which incentive scheme would meet their needs. You need to know the different conditions for each scheme – you will not get any marks for recommending an enterprise management incentive scheme to a company whose gross assets exceed £30 million.

Lump sums are commonly paid on the termination of an employment. You may be required to discuss which elements of a termination package are tax free, and the consequences of the ongoing provision of a benefit.

Knowledge brought forward from earlier studies

None of the topics in this chapter were examinable in Taxation (TX – UK).

1 Shares and share options: general rules

FAST FORWARD

> Where shares or share options are provided to an employee, income tax and/or national insurance contributions may be payable.

One of the competencies you require to fulfil Performance Objective 17 Tax planning and advice of the PER is to mitigate and/or defer tax liabilities through the use of standard reliefs, exemptions and incentives. You can apply the knowledge you obtain from this section of the text to help to demonstrate this competence.

1.1 Introduction

An employer may include **shares and share options as part of an incentive package offered to employees**. Unless they fall within the special tax advantaged schemes which provide tax reliefs (see later in this chapter) tax charges may arise as described below.

1.2 Shares   12/17

1.2.1 Income tax

The ownership of shares in an employing company may lead to tax charges:

(a)   **If a director or an employee is given shares, or is sold shares for less than their market value, the director or employee is treated as receiving specific employment income of the difference between the market value and the amount (if any) which the director or employee pays for the shares.**

(b) If, while the director or employee still has a beneficial interest in the shares, a 'chargeable event' occurs, there is a charge on the increase in the value of the interest caused by the chargeable event as specific employment income.

A chargeable event is a change of rights or restrictions attaching to either the shares in question or to other shares which leads to the value of the shares in question increasing, and which takes place while the person concerned is a director or employee of the company within seven years of their ceasing to be one. However, where the change applies to all shares of the same class there is not, in general, a chargeable event.

(c) If an employee, having obtained shares by reason of being a director or employee, receives any special benefit because of owning the shares, he is taxable under on the benefit as specific employment income unless:

(i) The benefit is available to at least 90% of persons holding shares of the same class, and:

(1) The majority of the shares of the same class are not held by directors or employees, or

(2) The company is employee-controlled by virtue of holdings of the same class of shares.

(d) If an employee or director receives shares which may later be forfeited, there is no income tax charge when the shares are acquired. There is an income tax charge when the risk of forfeiture is lifted or when the shares are sold, if sooner. The amount of specific employment income will be the difference between the market value of the shares less the cost of the shares.

(e) If shares received as a result of employment are subsequently converted to shares of another class, there is an income tax charge on conversion on the difference between the market value and cost of the shares.

In the above situations, when the base cost of the shares is being calculated for capital gains tax purposes (see later in this text) any amount charged to income tax is added to the acquisition cost of the shares.

1.2.2 National insurance contributions

If there is an income tax charge in respect of acquiring shares, **Class 1 National insurance contributions (NIC) may also be due. An amount equal to that charged to income tax is treated as 'earnings' for NICs.** However, this treatment only applies if the shares are **'readily convertible assets' eg if they can be sold on a stock exchange.**

1.3 Share options

6/13

1.3.1 Income tax

(a) **If a director or an employee is granted an option to acquire shares (ie is given the right to buy shares at a future date at a price set now), then, in general, there is no income tax charge on the grant of the option.**

(b) On the exercise of the option **there is a charge as specific employment income on the market value of the shares at the date of exercise minus the sum of what (if anything) was paid for the option and what was paid for the shares.** If the taxpayer assigns or releases the option for money, or agrees (for money) not to exercise it or to grant someone else a right to acquire the shares, the taxpayer is likewise taxable on the amount received minus the amount paid for the option.

Question

Exercise of option

Simon was granted an option to buy 10,000 shares in his employer company in September 2015. The cost of the option was £1 per share. The price at which the option could be exercised was £5.

Simon exercised his option in August 2018, when the shares had a market value of £8.

What is the amount of specific employment income taxable in 2018/19?

	£
Market value at exercise 10,000 × £8	80,000
Less: price paid for option 10,000 × £1	(10,000)
price paid for shares 10,000 × £5	(50,000)
Chargeable on exercise	20,000

1.3.2 National insurance contributions

If there is an income tax charge in respect of shares options, **Class 1 National insurance contributions (NIC)** may also be due. **An amount equal to that charged to income tax is treated as 'earnings' for NICs.** However, this treatment only applies if the shares acquired on the exercise of the option are **'readily convertible assets'** (see above).

2 Tax advantaged share schemes

2.1 Introduction

FAST FORWARD

> There are a range of tax advantaged share schemes under which an employer may be able to give employees a stake in the business.

One of the competencies you require to fulfil Performance Objective 17 Tax planning and advice of the PER is to mitigate and/or defer tax liabilities through the use of standard reliefs, exemptions and incentives. You can apply the knowledge you obtain from this section of the text to help to demonstrate this competence.

Successive governments have recognised the need to encourage schemes that broaden share ownership among employees or reward personnel. **A number of tax advantaged schemes exist.** These are detailed in the following sections.

Exam focus point

If you are asked to recommend a tax advantaged scheme ensure that you select one which fits the employer's requirements.

There are four types of such share scheme:

- **Schedule 3 save as you earn (SAYE) share option schemes**
- **Schedule 4 company share option plans (CSOP)**
- **Schedule 5 enterprise management incentives (EMI)**
- **Schedule 2 share incentive plans (SIPs)**

The first three listed above involve share options, whereas SIPs involve employees being given shares. The schedule names refer to the relevant schedule in the Income Tax (Earnings and Pensions) Act (ITEPA) 2003.

There are many detailed rules governing these schemes, but in this chapter, the following aspects are considered for each scheme:

- **How the scheme operates.**

- **Taxation implications of grant and exercise of options** (where appropriate). These tax advantaged schemes generally allow options to be granted and exercised without income tax and national insurance charges.

- **Taxation implications of sale of shares.** Generally, the only tax charge is when the shares are sold at a gain and the charge is to capital gains tax (rather than income tax and national insurance).

- **Conditions for the scheme.** The conditions required by each scheme vary but may relate to the **company operating the scheme**, the **employees participating in the scheme**, the **shares being issued**, and the **price at which options can be exercised**. In some cases, certain **time limits** must be met eg shares/options must be held for a certain period.

- **Costs of setting up the scheme.** Deductions available for the operating company are considered.

SAYE, CSOP and SIP schemes must be registered and self-certified (a declaration made that the conditions are met) **by 6 July following the tax year in which the first option is granted or shares awarded**.

2.2 SAYE share option schemes

A Save As You Earn (SAYE) share option scheme allows employees to save regular monthly amounts for a fixed period and use the funds to take up options to buy shares free of income tax and NIC. Alternatively they can simply take the cash saved.

2.2.1 How the scheme operates

An employer can set up a scheme, which must be open to all employees (full-time or part-time) and full-time directors, under which employees can choose to make regular monthly investments in special bank or building society accounts called sharesave accounts. Employees can save a fixed monthly amount of between £5 and £500.

The investments are made for three or five years, and a tax-free bonus is then added to the account by way of interest.

At the withdrawal date, the employee may take the money in cash. The employee may alternatively use the money to buy ordinary shares in their employer company, or its holding company, under options granted when the employee started to save in the account.

The price of these shares is fixed by the option and must be at least 80% of the market value at the date the option was granted.

2.2.2 Tax implications of grant and exercise of options

There is no income tax or national insurance charge:

(a)   **When the options are granted** (ie when the employee starts saving in the scheme)

(b)   **While the employee saves money in the scheme**, in particular the bonus given by way of interest is tax-free

(c)   **When the options are exercised**

(d)   If the employee decides not to buy shares, but to **withdraw the money instead**.

2.2.3 Tax implications of sale of shares

There is no income tax or national insurance contributions payable on the sale of shares acquired under an SAYE scheme.

When the shares are sold, any gain is subject to CGT. The cost in the gain calculation is the price the employee paid for the shares.

2.2.4 Conditions for SAYE schemes

To qualify as an SAYE scheme, the scheme must be open to all employees and full-time directors, and on similar terms. Part-time directors may be included, but can be excluded. However, a minimum qualifying period of employment (of up to five years) may be imposed, and there may be differences based on remuneration or length of service.

2.2.5 Costs of setting up SAYE schemes

The costs of setting up an SAYE scheme incurred by a company are deductible in the accounting period in which they are incurred.

2.3 Company share option plans (CSOP)

12/14, 9/16

FAST FORWARD

> There is no income tax or NIC on the grant of a Company Share Option Plan (CSOP) option. There is also no income tax or NIC on an exercise taking place between three and ten years after the grant. Only CGT will apply to the profit on disposal of the shares.

2.3.1 How the scheme operates

Under a CSOP scheme, which can be restricted to selected employees and full-time directors, an employee is granted options to buy shares. Options must be exercised between three and ten years from grant to achieve the beneficial tax treatment (see below). An employee can be granted options over shares up to the value of £30,000 (at the date of grant).

2.3.2 Tax implications of grant and exercise of options

There is **no income tax** or national insurance on:

(a) **The grant of an option** under a CSOP; nor

(b) **On the profit arising from the exercise of an option under a CSOP between three and ten years after the grant.**

The tax exemption is lost in respect of an option if it is exercised earlier than three years or later than ten years after grant.

The three year waiting period does not apply when personal representatives exercise the options of a deceased employee within twelve months of death (but the ten year rule still applies).

If the options are exercised before three years after the grant, they will remain tax exempt if the exercise (and exit from the scheme) arises due to certain circumstances which include:

(a) Cessation of employment due to the injury, disability, redundancy or retirement of the employee

(b) A cash takeover of the company which results in a forced exercise of the options.

2.3.3 Tax implications of sale of shares

There are no income tax or national insurance consequences of the sale of shares acquired under a CSOP.

When the shares are sold, any gain is subject to CGT. The cost in the gain calculation is the option price paid by the employee to acquire the shares.

2.3.4 Conditions for CSOPs

To qualify as a CSOP, the scheme must satisfy the following **conditions:**

(a) The shares must be **fully paid ordinary shares.**

(b) The **price of the shares must not be less than their market value at the time of the grant of the option.**

(c) **Participation in the scheme must be limited to employees and full-time directors**, but the scheme need not be open to all employees and full-time directors.

(d) **No options may be granted which take the total market value of shares for which an employee holds options above £30,000.** Shares are valued as at the times when the options on them are granted. Options must not be transferable.

(e) If the issuing company has more than one class of shares, the **majority of shares in the class for which the scheme operates must be held other than by:**

    (i) **Persons acquiring them through their positions as directors or employees (unless the company is an employee controlled company)**

    (ii) **A holding company (unless the scheme shares are quoted)**

(f) **Anyone who has within the preceding 12 months held over 30% of the shares of a close company which is the company whose shares may be acquired under the scheme, or which controls that company either alone or as part of a consortium, must be excluded from the scheme.**

2.3.5 Costs of setting up CSOPs

The costs of setting up a CSOP incurred by a company are **deductible** in the accounting period in which they are incurred.

Exam focus point

> CSOPs were tested in December 2012 Qu 1(a). Flame plc group. The examining team commented that 'In order to do well, candidates needed to slow down for a moment and make sure that they were about to write about the correct scheme. They then needed to ensure that they addressed all of the issues set out in the question. The majority of candidates did both of these things and therefore scored well.'

2.4 Enterprise Management Incentives (EMI)   6/14, 12/17

FAST FORWARD

> No income tax or NIC is chargeable on either the grant or exercise of options under the enterprise management incentive (EMI) scheme provided the exercise takes place within 10 years of the grant and the exercise price is at least equal to the market value of the shares at the date of the grant.

2.4.1 How the scheme operates

The EMI scheme is intended to help smaller, higher risk companies recruit and retain employees who have the skills to help them grow and succeed. They are also a way of rewarding employees for taking a risk by investing their time and skills to help small companies achieve their potential. **Employees must spend a certain amount of time working for the company each week (see below) to be eligible to be given EMI options, but the company can choose to which of the eligible employees it grants such options. Therefore the EMI scheme is particularly useful if a company wishes to reward its key employees.**

EMIs are similar to CSOPs, as an employee is granted options to buy shares. Specific features of the EMI scheme include the following:

(a) **A qualifying company can grant each of its employees options over shares worth up to £250,000 at the time of grant, subject to a maximum of £3m in total.**

(b) **The company may set a target** to be achieved before an option can be exercised. The target must clearly be defined at the time the option is granted.

(c) **Options can be granted at a discount below the market value at the date of grant**, although there are tax consequences of this (see below).

Some of these features make the EMI a more attractive scheme than a CSOP, but there are restrictions, in particular regarding which companies can operate EMI schemes.

Exam focus point

> EMIs were tested in June 2010 Qu 4(a) Dokham. The examining team commented that 'A significant number of candidates confused the enterprise management incentive scheme with the enterprise investment scheme.'

2.4.2 Tax implications of grant and exercise of options

No income tax or national insurance is chargeable on either the grant or exercise of the options provided the exercise takes place within 10 years of the grant and the exercise price is at least equal to the market value of the shares at the date of the grant.

If the options were granted at a discount to the market value at the date of grant, there is an income tax charge (and possibly a national insurance contributions charge) when the options are exercised (not when they are granted) on the lower of:

(a) **The discount** (ie the difference between the market value of the shares at the date of grant and the price paid for the shares (the 'exercise' price)); and

(b) **The difference between the market value of the shares at the date of exercise and the exercise price.**

2.4.3 Tax implications of sale of shares

No income tax or national insurance is chargeable on the disposal of shares acquired under an EMI scheme.

When the shares are sold, any gain is subject to CGT. The cost in the gain calculation is the amount paid for the shares *plus* any discount taxed as earnings as described above.

Question

EMI shares

Melody is employed by Jez plc. In October 2018, J plc granted Melody options to purchase 25,000 shares at a price of £4.50 per share under the EMI scheme. The market value of the shares at the date of the grant was £4.75 per share. Melody intends to exercise her options in June 2020 (when the market value is estimated to be £5.50 per share) and sell the shares in December 2021, when she thinks they will be worth £6.50 per share.

What are the tax implications for Melody when she exercises her EMI share options and when she sell the shares? Assume that the tax rules in 2018/19 continue to apply for the foreseeable future.

Answer

In 2020/21, when Melody exercises the options and purchases shares in Jez plc, she will be liable to income tax and national insurance on the amount by which the value of the shares at the time the options were granted exceeded the price she pays for the shares, ie £6,250 (25,000 × (£4.75 − £4.50)). This is the amount taxed as it is lower than the difference between the market value at the time of exercise and the exercise price (ie 25,000 × (£5.50 − £4.50) = £25,000).

In 2021/22, when she sells the shares, she will have the following gain on sale:

	£	£
Sale proceeds 25,000 × £6.50		162,500
Less: price paid for shares 25,000 × £4.50	112,500	
discount taxed as earnings on exercise	6,250	
		(118,750)
Gain		43,750

Where an individual **acquires shares on the exercise of an EMI option** and disposes of those shares realising a chargeable gain, the gain is eligible for **entrepreneurs' relief where the option was granted at least one year before the date of disposal** (ie **the period of ownership of the option counts towards the one year ownership condition** for entrepreneurs' relief to apply). The individual must have been an **employee or officer for at least one year** ending with the disposal date, but **does not need to own at least 5% of the company's shares**, which is one of the usual conditions for entrepreneurs' relief to apply. We look at entrepreneurs' relief in detail later in this text.

2.4.4 Conditions for EMI schemes: qualifying company

The company, which can be listed on a stock exchange, must meet certain conditions when the options are granted. In particular, **the company's gross assets must not exceed £30m. The company must not be under the control of any other company.**

The company must carry on one of a number of qualifying trades. It must have a permanent establishment in the UK.

The company must have less than 250 full-time equivalent employees at the time the options are granted.

2.4.5 Conditions for EMI schemes: eligible employees

Employees must be employed by the company or group for at least 25 hours a week, or, if less, for at least 75% of their working time (including self-employment). **Employees who own 30% or more of the ordinary shares in the company** (disregarding unexercised options shares) **are excluded.**

2.4.6 Conditions for EMI schemes: qualifying shares

The share must be **fully paid up irredeemable ordinary shares.** The rules permit restrictions on sale, forfeiture conditions and performance conditions.

2.4.7 Conditions for EMI schemes: limit

At any one time, an employee may hold EMI options over shares with a value of up to £250,000 at the date of grant. Restrictions and conditions attaching to the shares may not be taken into account when valuing shares.

Where options are granted above the £250,000 limit, relief is given on options up to the limit. Once the employee has reached the limit, no more EMI options may be granted for 3 years ie the employee may not immediately top up with new options following the exercise of old options.

Any options granted under a CSOP reduce the £250,000 limit, but SAYE share options can be ignored.

2.4.8 Conditions for EMI schemes: disqualifying events

There are a number of disqualifying events including an employee ceasing to spend at least 75% of their working time with the company. There will be a tax charge on a subsequent exercise of the EMI option after a disqualifying event has occurred (unless the exercise takes place within 90 days of the event).

2.4.9 Costs of EMI schemes

The costs of setting up a scheme and on-going administration are deductible in computing profits.

2.4.10 Notification of grant of options in EMI schemes

HMRC must be notified online of the grant of options within 92 days. HMRC then has 12 months to check whether the grants satisfy the EMI rules.

2.5 Share Incentive Plans (SIPs)   12/14

FAST FORWARD

Employees may be given £3,600 of 'free' shares a year under a share incentive plan (SIP). In addition, they can purchase up to £1,800 worth of 'partnership' shares a year and employers can provide up to £3,600 worth of matching shares. Once the shares have been held for five years there is no income tax or NIC when shares are taken out of the plan.

2.5.1 How the scheme operates

SIPs differ from the other tax advantaged schemes, in that options are not granted to employees, but, instead, they are given shares which are held in the plan. All full and part-time employee of the company (subject to a minimum period of employment) must be eligible to participate in the plan.

There are **four ways that shares can be acquired by members of a SIP**:

(a) **Free shares: an employer can give up to £3,600 of free shares a year to an employee.** An employer offering free shares must offer a minimum amount to each employee on 'similar terms'. Between the minimum and the maximum of £3,600, the employer can offer shares in different amounts and on different bases to different employees. This means that the employer can reward either individual or team performance. The employer can set performance targets subject to the overriding requirement that a plan must not contain any features that concentrate rewards on directors and more highly paid employees.

(b) **Partnership shares: an employee can also purchase partnership shares at any time in the year.** These shares are funded through **deduction from the employee's pre-tax salary up to the lower of £1,800 and 10% of salary in any tax year.**

(c) **Matching shares: an employer can also award matching shares free to an employee who purchases partnership shares at a maximum ratio of 2:1.**

(d) **Dividend shares: dividends on shares in the plan are tax-free provided the dividends are used by the employee to acquire additional shares in the company, which are then held in the plan for three years.** The company may specify a percentage (which may be 100%) of dividends that may be used to acquire dividend shares and modify that percentage from time to time.

A plan may provide for free and matching shares to be forfeited if the employee leaves within three years, unless the employee leaves for specified reasons such as retirement or redundancy.

The plan must be operated through a UK resident trust. The trustees acquire the shares from the company or – if the plan incorporates partnership shares – from the employees. The existence of arrangements to enable employees to sell shares held in a new plan trust will not of itself make those shares readily convertible into cash and require employers, for example, to operate national insurance.

Stamp duty is not payable when an employee purchases shares from a SIP trust. The trust must pay stamp duty when it acquires the shares. No taxable benefit arises on an employee as a result of a SIP trust or an employer paying either stamp duty or the incidental costs of operating the plan.

2.5.2 Tax implications on giving shares and on withdrawal of shares from plan

There is no income tax or national insurance when shares are given to employees (and put in the plan) as described above.

Free and matching shares must normally be held in a plan for at least three years. **If shares are withdrawn within three years** (because the employee leaves) there is a **charge to income tax** (as specific employment income) **and NIC on the market value of the shares at the time of withdrawal. If shares are taken out of the plan after three years but before five years, there is charge to income tax and NIC based on the lower of the initial value of the shares and their value at the date of withdrawal**, so any increase in value is free of income tax and NIC. If one of the specified reasons applies, eg redundancy or retirement, there is no tax or NIC charge. **Once the shares have been held for five years, there is no income tax or national insurance when shares are taken out of the plan.**

Partnership shares can be taken out at any time. If the shares are held for less than three years, there is a charge to income tax and NIC on the market value at the time the shares are removed. If the shares are removed after three years but before five years, the charge to income tax and NIC is based on the lower of salary used to buy the shares and the market value at the date of removal. Once the shares have been held for five years, there is no income tax or national insurance when shares are taken out of the plan.

2.5.3 Tax implications of sale of shares

There is no charge to CGT on shares taken out of a plan and sold immediately. A charge to CGT will arise on sale to the extent that the shares increase in value after they are withdrawn from the plan.

2.5.4 Conditions for SIPs

Shares in the plan must be fully paid irredeemable ordinary shares in a company either:

(a) **Listed on a recognised stock exchange** (or in its subsidiary); or

(b) **Not controlled by another company.**

A plan established by a company that controls other companies, may be extended to any or all of these other companies. Such a plan is called a group plan.

A plan need not include all the components – it is possible to have a plan with only free shares.

Companies must offer all full and part-time employees the opportunity to participate in the plan. A minimum qualifying period of employment of up to 18 months may be specified. Any minimum period specified can be satisfied by working for any company within a group.

2.5.5 Costs of SIPs

A **deduction in computing profits** for the company is given for:

(a) The costs of setting up and administering the plan.

(b) The gross salary allocated by employees to buy partnership shares.

(c) The costs of providing shares to the extent that the costs exceed the employees contributions.

(d) The market value of free and matching shares when they are acquired by the trustees.

(e) Interest paid by the trustees on borrowing to acquire shares where the company meets the trustees' costs.

2.6 Tax advantaged share schemes summary

Scheme name	Gift/purchase/option scheme	Tax advantages	Employees
SAYE	Option scheme	• Tax free savings bonus • No income tax/NIC on exercise • CGT on sale of shares	All employees
CSOP	Option scheme	• No income tax/NIC on exercise • CGT on sale of shares	Selected employees
EMI	Option scheme	• No income/NIC tax on exercise (unless granted at a discount) • CGT on sale of shares	Key employees
SIP	Gift from employer and/or purchase by employee	• Favourable income tax charge if shares held ≥ 3yrs • No income tax/NIC if held ≥ 5 yrs • CGT on sale of shares	All employees

3 Lump sum payments

> Payments made on the termination of employment may be fully taxable, partially exempt or exempt. The first £30,000 of a genuinely *ex gratia* termination payment is normally exempt.

3.1 Payments on the termination of employment   6/14, 3/16, 6/17, 6/18

Termination payments may be entirely exempt, partly exempt or entirely chargeable.

3.1.1 Exempt termination payments

The following payments on the termination of employment are exempt.

- Payments on account of injury, disability or accidental death

- Lump sum payments from registered pension schemes

- Legal costs recovered by the employee from the employer following legal action to recover compensation for loss of employment, where the costs are ordered by the court or (for out-of-court settlements) are paid directly to the employee's solicitor as part of the settlement.

3.1.2 Fully taxable termination payments

Payments to which the employee is contractually entitled are, in general, taxable in full as general earnings. Payments for work already done (terminal bonuses) and for doing extra work during a period of notice are therefore taxable in full.

Payments in lieu of notice (PILONs) are made when an employment is terminated without notice but **payment is made of the earnings that the employee would have been entitled to if they had worked during the notice period. PILONs are taxable in full,** whether the employee is contractually entitled to them or not.

A **payment by one employer to induce an employee to take up employment with another employer** is also **taxable in full.**

An employee may, either on leaving an employment or at some other time, accept a limitation on their future conduct or activities in return for a payment. This is known as a restrictive covenant. **Such payments are taxable as general earnings.** However, a payment accepted in full and final settlement of any claims the employee may have against the employer is not automatically taxable under this rule.

3.1.3 Partly taxable termination payments

Other payments on termination (such as compensation for loss of office and statutory redundancy pay) and non-cash benefits such as the continued provision of a company car, which are not taxable under the general earnings rules because they are not in return for services, are nevertheless brought in as amounts which count as employment income. These are often called *ex gratia* payments. Such payments **are partly exempt from income: the first £30,000 is exempt; any excess is taxable as specific employment income.** The whole of the payment is **exempt from national insurance contributions,** not just the excess over £30,000.

Payments and other benefits provided in connection with termination of employment (or a change in terms of employment) **are taxable in the year in which they are received.** 'Received' in this case means when it is paid or the recipient becomes entitled to it (for cash payments) or when it is used or enjoyed (non-cash benefits).

All payments to an employee on termination, both cash and non-cash, should be considered. Non-cash benefits are taxed by reference to their cash equivalent (using the normal benefits rules). Thus if a company car continues to be made available to an ex-employee say for a further year after redundancy they will be taxed on the same benefit value as if they had remained in employment. The normal exemptions apply, so that the continued use of one mobile telephone and work related training would be exempt.

3.1.4 Special situations

HMRC regard payments notionally made as compensation for loss of office but which are made on retirement or death (other than accidental death) as **lump sum payments under non registered pension schemes, and therefore taxable in full**. Also, payments in circumstances which amount to unfair dismissal are treated as eligible for the £30,000 exemption.

3.1.5 National insurance contributions (NICs) on termination payments

3.1.6 Practical issues

If the termination package is a partially exempt one and exceeds £30,000 then the £30,000 exempt limit is allocated to earlier benefits and payments. In any particular year the exemption is allocated to cash payments before non-cash benefits.

Employers have an obligation to report termination settlements which include benefits to HMRC by 6 July following the tax year end. No report is required if the package consists wholly of cash. Employers must also notify HMRC by this date of settlements which (over their lifetime) may exceed £30,000.

3.2 Example: termination payment

Jonah is made redundant on 31 December 2018. He receives (not under a contractual obligation) the following termination payment:

- Total cash of £40,000 payable £20,000 in January 2019 and £20,000 in January 2020
- Use of company car for period to 5 April 2020 (benefit value per annum £5,000)

In 2018/19 Jonah receives as redundancy:

	£
Cash	20,000
Car (£5,000 × $^3/_{12}$)	1,250
	21,250

Wholly exempt (allocate £21,250 of £30,000 exemption to cash first then benefit).

In 2019/20 Jonah receives:

	£
Cash	20,000
Car	5,000
	25,000
Less exemption (remaining)	(8,750)
Taxable	16,250

£11,250 (£20,000 less £8,750) of the cash payment is taxable as specific employment income.

3.3 Other lump sum payments

Where lump sums are received otherwise than in connection with the termination of employment they will be taxable if they derive from the employment. Examples are:

(a) A golden hello, which is a one-off payment made to encourage someone to join a new employer. As it is effectively a reward for future services it is subject to both tax and NIC.

(b) A payment for a change in the terms of employment is also taxable.

Chapter roundup

- Where shares or share options are provided to an employee, income tax and/or national insurance contributions may be payable.

- There are a range of tax advantaged share schemes under which an employer may be able to give employees a stake in the business.

- A Save As You Earn (SAYE) share option scheme allows employees to save regular monthly amounts for a fixed period and use the funds to take up options to buy shares free of income tax and NIC. Alternatively they can simply take the cash saved.

- There is no income tax or NIC on the grant of a Company Share Option Plan (CSOP) option. There is also no income tax or NIC on an exercise taking place between three and ten years after the grant. Only CGT will apply to the profit on disposal of the shares.

- No income tax or NIC is chargeable on either the grant or exercise of options under the enterprise management incentive (EMI) scheme provided the exercise takes place within 10 years of the grant and the exercise price is at least equal to the market value of the shares at the date of the grant.

- Employees may be given £3,600 of free shares a year under a share incentive plan (SIP). In addition, they can purchase up to £1,800 worth of partnership shares a year and employers can provide up to £3,600 worth of matching shares. Once the shares have been held for five years there is no income tax or NIC when shares are taken out of the plan.

- Payments made on the termination of employment may be fully taxable, partially exempt or exempt. The first £30,000 of a genuinely *ex gratia* termination payment is normally exempt.

Quick quiz

1 Julia is employed by Z plc, a company whose shares are listed on the London Stock Exchange. In July 2018 she was sold 3,000 Z plc shares by the company for £1 each when they had a market value of £4. What Is are the income tax and national insurance consequences of this sale?

2 Which tax advantaged share option scheme allows employees to take a cash amount instead of exercising their options?

3 What Is the maximum amount of enterprise management incentive scheme options that an employee can hold?

4 How may 'free shares' can an employee receive under a share incentive plan?

5 How many matching shares can be given in respect of each partnership share purchased?

6 On what value is income tax charged if shares held within a share incentive plan are disposed of within three years?

7 Which termination payments are partly exempt?

8 Thomas was made redundant on 4 January 2019. His termination payment was:

Statutory redundancy pay	£12,000
Golden Goodbye	£40,000

The 'Golden Goodbye' was a payment made by the company to 'soften the blow' of redundancy to Thomas. It was not paid as part of his contract of employment. How much of the above (if any) is subject to income tax?

Answers to quick quiz

1 Julia is treated as receiving specific employment income of £(4 − 1) × 3,000 = £9,000 in 2018/19. She is also treated as receiving earnings of this amount for national insurance purposes as they are readily convertible assets.

2 SAYE share option scheme.

3 At any one time an employee may hold options over shares worth up to £250,000 at the date of grant.

4 Up to £3,600 worth of free shares.

5 Up to two.

6 Income tax is charged on the market value of the shares on the date of withdrawal.

7 The first £30,000 of genuinely *ex gratia* termination payments ie not in return for services.

8 £22,000.

	£
Statutory redundancy and Golden Goodbye £(12,000 + 40,000)	52,000
Less partial exemption	(30,000)
Subject to income tax as specific employment income	£22,000

Now try the question below from the Practice Question Bank

Number	Level	Marks	Time
Q6	Introductory	20	39 mins

Trade profits

Topic list	Syllabus reference
1 The badges of trade	A1(a)B3
2 The computation of trade profits	A1(a)B3
3 Basis periods	A1(a)B3
4 Change of accounting date	A1(d)(i)
5 National insurance	A1(a)B6

Introduction

In previous chapters, we have looked at the income tax computation, property and investment income and employment income. We are now going to look at the taxation of unincorporated businesses. We work out a business's profit as if it were a separate entity (the separate entity concept familiar to you from basic bookkeeping) but as an unincorporated business has no legal existence apart from its proprietor, we cannot tax it separately. We have to feed its profit into the proprietor's personal tax computation.

In this chapter, we look at the computation and taxation of profits. Standard rules on the computation of profits are used instead of individual traders' accounting policies, so as to ensure fairness. We also need special rules, the basis period rules, to link the profits of periods of account to the personal computations of tax years.

Finally, we see how national insurance contributions apply to the self-employed.

In the next chapters, we study the allowances available for capital expenditure and then we look at losses and partnerships.

Study guide

		Intellectual level
1	**Income and income tax liabilities in situations involving further overseas aspects and in relation to trusts, and the application of exemptions and reliefs**	
(a)	The contents of the Taxation - United Kingdom (TX – UK) study guide for income tax and national insurance, under heading:	2
•	B3 Income from self employment	
•	B6 National insurance contributions for employed and self-employed persons	
(d)	Income from self employment:	3
(i)	Advise on a change of accounting date	

Exam guide

Rather than being asked to calculate taxable trade profits you are more likely to be asked about the effect on after tax income of a business action such as taking on an additional contract. This will involve calculating the incremental profits, deducting tax payable, and taking any other costs (and their possible tax savings) into account. This will normally include VAT considerations. To be able to do this you need a full understanding of the rules for calculating taxable trade profits and allocating them to tax years.

Knowledge brought forward from earlier studies

Most of this chapter is revision from Taxation (TX – UK). The examining team has identified essential underpinning knowledge from the Taxation (TX – UK) syllabus which is particularly important that you revise as part of your Advanced Taxation (ATX – UK) studies. In this chapter, the relevant topic is:

		Intellectual level
B3	**Income from self-employment**	
(f)	Compute the assessable profits on commencement and on cessation	2

Change of accounting date is a new topic in Advanced Taxation (ATX – UK). The changes in 2018/19 from 2017/18 in the material covered in Taxation (TX – UK) are the change in the threshold for restriction on leasing costs for high emission cars from 130 g/km to 110 g/km, the Class 2 amount and small profits threshold, and the Class 4 NIC lower and upper limits.

1 The badges of trade

> The badges of trade can be used to decide whether or not a trade exists.

1.1 Introduction

Before a tax charge can be imposed it is necessary to establish the existence of a trade.

Key terms

A **trade** is defined in the legislation only in an unhelpful manner as including any venture in the nature of trade. It has therefore been left to the courts to provide guidance. This guidance is often summarised in a collection of principles known as the **'badges of trade'**. These are set out below. **Profits from professions and vocations are taxed in the same way as profits from a trade.**

1.2 The subject matter

Whether a person is trading or not may sometimes be decided by examining the subject matter of the transaction. Some assets are commonly held as investments for their intrinsic value: an individual buying some shares or a painting may do so in order to enjoy the income from the shares or to enjoy the work of art. A subsequent disposal may produce a gain of a capital nature rather than a trade profit. But **where the subject matter of a transaction is such as would not be held as an investment** (for example, 34,000,000 yards of aircraft linen (*Martin v Lowry 1927*) or 1,000,000 rolls of toilet paper (*Rutledge v CIR 1929*)), **it is presumed that any profit on resale is a trade profit.**

1.3 The frequency of transactions

Transactions which may, in isolation, be of a capital nature will be interpreted as trading transactions where their **frequency indicates the carrying on of a trade**. It was decided that whereas normally the purchase of a mill-owning company and the subsequent stripping of its assets might be a capital transaction, where the taxpayer was embarking on the same exercise for the fourth time they must be carrying on a trade *(Pickford v Quirke 1927)*.

1.4 Existence of similar trading transactions or interests

If there is an **existing trade**, then a **similarity to the transaction which is being considered** may point to that transaction having a trading character. For example, a builder who builds and sells a number of houses may be held to be trading even if they retain one or more houses for longer than usual and claims that they were held as an investment (*Harvey v Caulcott 1952*).

1.5 The length of ownership

The courts may infer adventures in the nature of trade where items purchased are sold soon afterwards.

1.6 The organisation of the activity as a trade

The courts may infer that a trade is being carried on if the transactions are **carried out in the same manner as someone who is unquestionably trading**. For example, an individual who bought a consignment of whiskey and then sold it through an agent, in the same way as others who were carrying on a trade, was also held to be trading (*CIR v Fraser 1942*). On the other hand, if an asset has to be sold in order to raise funds in an emergency, this is less likely to be treated as trading.

1.7 Supplementary work and marketing

When work is done to make an asset more marketable, or steps are taken to find purchasers, the courts will be more ready to ascribe a trading motive. When a group of accountants bought, blended and recasked a quantity of brandy they were held to be taxable on a trade profit when the brandy was later sold *(Cape Brandy Syndicate v CIR 1921)*.

1.8 A profit motive

The absence of a profit motive will not necessarily preclude a tax charge as trading income, but its presence is a strong indication that a person is trading. The purchase and resale of £20,000 worth of silver bullion by the comedian Norman Wisdom, as a hedge against devaluation, was held to be a trading transaction *(Wisdom v Chamberlain 1969)*.

1.9 The way in which the asset sold was acquired

If goods are acquired deliberately, trading may be indicated. If goods are acquired unintentionally, for example by gift or inheritance, their later sale is unlikely to be trading.

1.10 Method of finance

If the **purchaser has to borrow money to buy an asset such that they have to sell that asset quickly to repay the loan**, it may be inferred that trading was taking place. This was a factor in the *Wisdom v Chamberlain* case as Mr Wisdom financed his purchases by loans at a high rate of interest. It was clear that he had to sell the silver bullion quickly in order to repay the loan and prevent the interest charges becoming too onerous. On the other hand, taking out a long term loan to buy an asset (such as a mortgage on a house) would not usually indicate that trading is being carried on.

1.11 The taxpayer's intentions

Where a transaction is clearly trading on objective criteria, **the taxpayer's intentions are irrelevant**. If, however, a transaction has (objectively) a dual purpose, the taxpayer's intentions may be taken into account. An example of a transaction with a dual purpose is the acquisition of a site partly as premises from which to conduct another trade, and partly with a view to the possible development and resale of the site. This test is not one of the traditional badges of trade, but it may be just as important.

Exam focus point

> If on applying the badges of trade HMRC do not conclude that income is 'trade income' then they can potentially treat it as other income or a capital gain. Remember that capital gains are taxable at a maximum rate of 28% whereas income is subject to income tax at a maximum rate of 45% and also to Class 2 and Class 4 national insurance contributions. HMRC will therefore be looking very carefully to see if a transaction really results in a capital gain or whether it is really a trade receipt.

2 The computation of trade profits

FAST FORWARD

> The accounts profits need to be adjusted in order to establish the taxable trade profits.

> One of the competencies you require to fulfil Performance Objective 15 Tax computations and assessments of the PER is to extract and analyse data from financial records and filing information relevant to the preparation of tax computations and related supporting documents. You can apply the knowledge you obtain from this section of the text to help to demonstrate this competence.

2.1 The adjustment of profits

The net profit shown in the statement of profit or loss is the starting point in computing the taxable trade profits. Many adjustments may be required to calculate the taxable amount.

> Only International Accounting Standard terminology is used when presenting accounting information contained within an examination question. This applies for companies, sole traders and partnerships.

Here is an illustrative adjustment of a statement of profit or loss:

		£	£
Net profit			140,000
Add:	expenditure charged in the accounts which is not deductible from trading profits	50,000	
	income taxable as trading profits which has not been included in the accounts	30,000	
			80,000
			220,000
Less:	profits included in the accounts but which are not taxable trading profits	40,000	
	expenditure which is deductible from trading profits but has not been charged in the accounts	20,000	
			(60,000)
Adjusted taxable trading profit			160,000

You may refer to deductible and non-deductible expenditure as allowable and disallowable expenditure respectively. The two sets of terms are interchangeable.

2.2 Accounting policies

The fundamental concept is that the profits of the business must be calculated in accordance with generally accepted accounting principles. These profits are subject to any adjustment specifically required for income tax purposes. **The accounting method usually applies the accruals concept of accounting for income and expenditure as it accrues or is incurred, but some small unincorporated businesses can use a cash basis of accounting instead.** The adjustment rules described below relate to the accruals method. The cash basis of accounting mainly uses the same rules of adjustment but has some differences, particularly in relation to capital expenditure .We will look at the cash basis in detail later in this chapter.

2.3 Capital allowances

Under the Capital Allowances Act 2001 (CAA 2001) **capital allowances are treated as trade expenses and balancing charges are treated as trade receipts** (see later in this text).

2.4 Non-deductible expenditure

Certain expenses are specifically disallowed by the legislation. These are covered in paragraphs 2.4.1-2.4.10. If however a deduction is specifically permitted this overrides the disallowance.

2.4.1 Capital expenditure

Income tax is a tax solely on income so capital expenditure is not deductible. This denies a deduction for depreciation or amortisation (although there are special rules for companies in relation to intangible assets – see later in this text). **The most contentious items of expenditure will often be repairs** (revenue expenditure) **and improvements** (capital expenditure).

- The cost of restoration of an asset by, for instance, replacing a subsidiary part of the asset is revenue expenditure. Expenditure on a new factory chimney replacement was allowable since the chimney was a subsidiary part of the factory (*Samuel Jones & Co (Devondale) Ltd v CIR 1951*).

However, in another case a football club demolished a spectators' stand and replaced it with a modern equivalent. This was held not to be repair, since repair is the restoration by renewal or replacement of subsidiary parts of a larger entity, and the stand formed a distinct and *separate* part of the club (*Brown v Burnley Football and Athletic Co Ltd 1980*).

- The cost of initial repairs to improve an asset recently acquired to make it fit to earn profits is disallowable capital expenditure. In *Law Shipping Co Ltd v CIR 1923* the taxpayer failed to obtain relief for expenditure on making a newly bought ship seaworthy prior to using it.

- The cost of initial repairs to remedy normal wear and tear of recently acquired assets is allowable. *Odeon Associated Theatres Ltd v Jones 1971* can be contrasted with the *Law Shipping* judgement. Odeon were allowed to charge expenditure incurred on improving the state of recently acquired cinemas.

Other examples to note include:

- A one-off payment made by a hotel owner to terminate an agreement for the management of a hotel was held to be revenue rather than capital expenditure in *Croydon Hotel & Leisure Co v Bowen 1996*. The payment did not affect the whole structure of the taxpayer's business; it merely enabled it to be run more efficiently.

- A one-off payment to remove a threat to the taxpayer's business was also held to be revenue rather than capital expenditure in *Lawson v Johnson Matthey plc 1992*.

- An initial payment for a franchise (as opposed to regular fees) is capital and not deductible.

2.4.2 Expenditure not wholly and exclusively for the purposes of the trade

Expenditure is not deductible if it is not for trade purposes (the remoteness test), or if it reflects more than one purpose (the duality test). The private proportion of payments for motoring expenses, rent, heat and light and telephone expenses of a proprietor is not deductible. If an exact apportionment is possible relief is given on the business element. Fixed rate expenses, as prescribed in the legislation, can also be claimed in certain cases where there is a private element of expenditure (see later in this chapter). Where the payments are to or on behalf of employees, the full amounts are deductible but the employees are taxed under the benefits code (see earlier in this text).

The remoteness test is illustrated by the following cases:

- *Strong & Co of Romsey Ltd v Woodifield 1906*

  A customer injured by a falling chimney when sleeping in an inn owned by a brewery claimed compensation from the company. The compensation was not deductible: 'the loss sustained by the appellant was not really incidental to their trade as innkeepers and fell upon them in their character not of innkeepers but of householders'.

- *Bamford v ATA Advertising Ltd 1972*

  A director misappropriated £15,000. The loss was not allowable: 'the loss is not, as in the case of a dishonest shop assistant, an incident of the company's trading activities. It arises altogether outside such activities'.

- Expenditure which is wholly and exclusively to benefit the trades of several companies (for example, in a group) but is not wholly and exclusively to benefit the trade of one specific company is not deductible (*Vodafone Cellular Ltd and others v Shaw 1995*).

- *McKnight (HMIT) v Sheppard (1999)* concerned expenses incurred by a stockbroker in defending allegations of infringements of Stock Exchange regulations. It was found that the expenditure was incurred to prevent the destruction of the taxpayer's business and that as the expenditure was incurred for business purposes it was deductible. It was also found that although the expenditure had the effect of preserving the taxpayer's reputation, that was not its purpose, so there was no duality of purpose.

The **duality test** is illustrated by the following cases:

- *Caillebotte v Quinn 1975*

    A self-employed carpenter spent an average of 40p per day when obliged to buy lunch away from home but just 10p when he lunched at home. He claimed the excess 30p. It was decided that the payment had a dual purpose and was not deductible: a taxpayer 'must eat to live not eat to work'.

- *Mallalieu v Drummond 1983*

    Expenditure by a lady barrister on black clothing to be worn in court (and on its cleaning and repair) was not deductible. The expenditure was for the dual purpose of enabling the barrister to be warmly and properly clad as well as meeting her professional requirements.

- *McLaren v Mumford 1996*

    A publican traded from a public house which had residential accommodation above it. He was obliged to live at the public house but he also had another house which he visited regularly. It was held that the private element of the expenditure incurred at the public house on electricity, rent, gas, etc was not incurred for the purpose of earning profits, but for serving the non-business purpose of satisfying the publican's ordinary human needs. The expenditure, therefore had a dual purpose and was disallowed.

However, the cost of overnight accommodation when on a business trip may be deductible and reasonable expenditure on an evening meal and breakfast in conjunction with such accommodation is then also deductible.

2.4.3 Impairment losses (bad debts)

Only impairment losses where the liability was incurred wholly and exclusively for the purposes of the trade are deductible for taxation purposes. For example, **loans to employees written off are not deductible** unless the business is that of making loans, or it can be shown that the writing-off of the loan was earnings paid out for the benefit of the trade.

Under generally accepted accounting principles, a review of all trade receivables should be carried out to assess their fair value at the balance sheet date and any impairment losses written off. **The tax treatment follows the accounting treatment so no adjustment is required for tax purposes.** General provisions (ie those calculated as a percentage of total trade receivables, without reference to specific receivables) will now rarely be seen. In the event that they do arise, increases or decreases in a general provision are not allowable /taxable and an adjustment will need to be made.

If an impairment loss which has been deducted for tax purposes is later recovered, the recovery is taxable so no adjustment is required to the amount of the recovery shown in the statement of profit or loss.

2.4.4 Unpaid remuneration

If earnings for employees are charged in the accounts but are not paid within nine months of the end of the period of account, the cost is only deductible for the period of account in which the earnings are paid. When a tax computation is made within the nine month period, it is initially assumed that unpaid earnings will not be paid within that period. The computation is adjusted if they are so paid.

Earnings are treated as paid at the same time as they are treated as received for employment income purposes.

2.4.5 Entertaining and gifts

The general rule is that expenditure on entertaining and gifts is non-deductible. This applies to amounts reimbursed to employees for specific entertaining expenses and gifts, and to round sum allowances which are exclusively for meeting such expenses. There is no distinction between UK and overseas customer entertaining for income tax and corporation tax purposes (a different rule applies for value added tax).

There are specific exceptions to the general rule:

- **Entertaining for and gifts to employees are normally deductible** although where gifts are made, or the entertainment is excessive, a charge to tax may arise on the employee under the benefits legislation.

- **Gifts to customers not costing more than £50 per donee per year are allowed if they carry a conspicuous advertisement for the business and are not food, drink, tobacco or vouchers exchangeable for goods.**

- Gifts to charities may also be allowed although many will fall foul of the 'wholly and exclusively' rule above. If a gift aid declaration is made by an individual in respect of a gift, tax relief will be given under the gift aid scheme, not as a trading expense. If a qualifying charitable donation is made by a company, it will be given tax relief by deduction from total profits (see later in this text).

2.4.6 Lease charges for cars with CO_2 emissions exceeding 110g/km

There is a restriction on the leasing costs of a car with CO_2 emissions exceeding 110 g/km. 15% of the leasing costs will be disallowed in the calculation of taxable profits.

2.4.7 Interest payments

Interest which is allowed as deductible interest (see earlier in this text) is not also allowed as a trading expense.

2.4.8 National Insurance contributions

No deduction is allowed for any National Insurance contributions **except for employer's contributions**. For the purpose of your exam, these are Class 1 employer's contributions and Class 1A contributions (Class 1B contributions are not examinable). National Insurance contributions for self employed individuals are dealt with later in this chapter.

2.4.9 Penalties and interest on tax

Penalties and interest on late paid tax are not allowed as a trading expense. Tax includes income tax, capital gains tax, VAT and stamp duty land tax.

2.4.10 Crime related payments

A payment is not deductible if making it constitutes an offence by the payer. This covers protection money paid to terrorists, bribes and similar payments made overseas which would be criminal payments if they were made in the UK. Statute also prevents any deduction for payments made in response to blackmail or extortion.

2.5 Deductible expenditure

Most expenses will be deductible under the general rule that expenses incurred wholly and exclusively for the purpose of the trade are not disallowed. Some expenses which might otherwise be disallowed under the 'wholly or exclusively' rule, or under one or other of the specific rules discussed above are, however, specifically allowed by the legislation. These are covered in paragraphs 2.5.1–2.5.11.

2.5.1 Pre-trading expenditure

Expenditure incurred before the commencement of trade is deductible, if it is incurred within seven years of the start of trade and it is of a type that would have been deductible had the trade already started. **It is treated as a trading expense incurred on the first day of trading.**

2.5.2 Incidental costs of obtaining finance

Incidental costs of obtaining loan finance, or of attempting to obtain or redeeming it, are deductible other than a discount on issue or a premium on redemption (which are really alternatives to paying interest). This deduction for incidental costs does not apply to companies because they obtain a deduction for the costs of borrowing in a different way. We will look at companies later in this text.

2.5.3 Short leases

A trader may deduct an annual sum in respect of the amount liable to income tax on a lease premium which they paid to their landlord (see earlier in this text). Normally, the amortisation of the lease will have been deducted in the accounts (and must be added back as capital expenditure).

2.5.4 Renewals

Where a tool is replaced or altered then the cost of the renewal or alteration may be deducted as an expense in certain instances. These are that:

- A deduction would only be prohibited because the expenditure is capital expenditure; and

- No deduction can be given under any other provisions, such as under the capital allowances legislation.

2.5.5 Restrictive covenants

When an employee leaves their employment they may accept a limitation on their future activities in return for a payment. **Provided the employee is taxed on the payment as employment income** (see earlier in this text) **the payment is a deductible trading expense.**

2.5.6 Secondments

The **costs of seconding employees to charities or educational establishments are deductible**.

2.5.7 Contributions to agent's expenses

Many employers run payroll giving schemes for their employees. **Any payments made to the agent who administers the scheme towards running expenses are deductible.**

2.5.8 Counselling and retraining expenses

Expenditure on providing counselling and retraining for leaving employees is allowable.

2.5.9 Redundancy

Redundancy payments made when a trade ends are deductible on the earlier of the day of payment and the last day of trading. If the trade does not end, they can be deducted as soon as they are provided for, so long as the redundancy was decided on within the period of account, the provision is accurately calculated and the payments are made within nine months of the end of the period of account. **The deduction extends to additional payments of up to three times the amount of the redundancy pay on cessation of trade.**

2.5.10 Personal security expenses

If there is a particular security threat to the trader because of the nature of the trade, **expenditure on their personal security is allowable.**

2.5.11 Patents, trade marks and copyrights

The costs of **registering patents and trade marks** are deductible for trades only (not professions or vocations). Copyright arises automatically and so does not have to be registered. **Patent royalties and copyright royalties paid in connection with a trade are deductible as trading expenses.**

2.6 Trade income

There are also statutory rules governing whether certain receipts are taxable or not. These are discussed in 2.6.1–2.6.5.

2.6.1 Capital receipts

As may be expected, capital receipts are not included in trade income. They may, of course, be taken into account in the capital allowances computation, or as a capital gain.

However, compensation received in one lump sum for the loss of income is likely to be treated as income (*Donald Fisher (Ealing) Ltd v Spencer 1989*).

In some trades, (eg petrol stations and public houses), a wholesaler may pay a lump sum to a retailer in return for the retailer only supplying that wholesaler's products for several years (an **exclusivity agreement**). If the payment must be used for a specific capital purpose, it is a capital receipt. If that is not the case, it is an income receipt. If the sum is repayable to the wholesaler but the requirement to repay is waived in tranches over the term of the agreement, each tranche is a separate income receipt when the requirement is waived.

2.6.2 Debts released

If the trader incurs a deductible expense but does not settle the amount due to the supplier, then if the creditor releases the debt other than under a statutory arrangement, the amount released must be brought into account as trade income.

2.6.3 Takeover of trade

If a trader takes over a trade from a previous owner, then if they receive any amounts from that trade which related to a period before the takeover they must be brought into account unless the previous owner has already done so.

2.6.4 Insurance receipts

Insurance receipts which are revenue in nature, such as for loss of profits, are trading receipts. Otherwise the receipt must be brought in as trade income if, and to the extent that, any deduction has been claimed for the expense that the receipt is intended to cover.

2.6.5 Gifts of trading stock to educational establishments or schools

When a business makes a gift of equipment manufactured, sold or used in the course of its trade to an educational establishment or for a charitable purpose, nothing need be brought into account as a trading receipt or (if capital allowances had been obtained on the asset) as disposal proceeds, so full relief is obtained for the cost.

2.7 Excluded income

Although the accounts may include other income, such as interest, such income is not trade income. It will instead be taxed under the specific rules for that type of income, such as the rules for savings income. It is therefore excluded from trade profits.

Certain types of income are specifically exempt from tax, and should be excluded from trade profits.

2.8 Application of general rules

These general rules can be applied to particular types of expenditure and income that you are likely to come across.

2.8.1 Appropriations

Salary or interest on capital paid to the trader are not deductible.

2.8.2 Subscriptions and donations

The general 'wholly and exclusively' rule determines the deductibility of expenses. Subscriptions and donations are not deductible unless the expenditure is for the benefit of the trade. The following are the main types of subscriptions and donations you may meet and their correct treatments:

(a) Trade subscriptions (such as to a professional or trade association) are generally deductible.

(b) Charitable donations are deductible only if they are small and to local charities. Tax relief may be available for donations under the gift aid scheme. In the latter case they are not a deductible trading expense.

(c) Political subscriptions and donations are generally not deductible.

(d) Where a donation represents the most effective commercial way of disposing of stock (for example, where it would not be commercially effective to sell surplus perishable food), the donation can be treated as for the benefit of the trade and the disposal proceeds taken as £Nil. In other cases, the amount credited to the accounts in respect of a donation of stock should be its market value.

2.8.3 Legal and professional charges

Legal and professional charges relating to capital or non-trade items are not deductible. These include charges incurred in acquiring new capital assets or legal rights, issuing shares, drawing up partnership agreements and litigating disputes over the terms of a partnership agreement.

Charges are deductible if they relate directly to trading. Deductible items include:

- Legal and professional charges incurred defending the taxpayer's title to fixed assets
- Charges connected with an action for breach of contract
- Expenses of the **renewal** (not the original grant) of a lease for less than 50 years
- Charges for trade debt collection
- Normal charges for preparing accounts/assisting with the self assessment of tax liabilities

Accountancy expenses arising out of an enquiry into the accounts information in a particular year's return are not allowed where the enquiry reveals discrepancies and additional liabilities for the year of enquiry, or any earlier year, which arise as a result of negligent or fraudulent conduct.

Where, however, the enquiry results in no addition to profits, or an adjustment to the profits for the year of enquiry only and that assessment does not arise as a result of negligent or fraudulent conduct, the additional accountancy expenses are allowable.

2.8.4 Goods for own use

The usual example is when a trader takes goods for their own use. In such circumstances the selling price of the goods if sold in open market is added to the accounting profit. If the trader pays anything for the goods, this is left out of account. In other words, the trader is treated for tax purposes as having made a sale to themselves. This rule does not apply to supplies of services, which are treated as sold for the amount (if any) actually paid (but the cost of services to the trader or their household is not deductible).

2.8.5 Other items

Here is a list of various other items that you may meet.

Item	Treatment	Comment
Educational courses for staff	Allow	
Educational courses for trader	Allow	If to update existing knowledge or skills, not if to acquire new knowledge or skills

Item	Treatment	Comment
Removal expenses (to new business premises)	Allow	Only if not an expansionary move
Travelling expenses to the trader's place of business	Disallow	*Ricketts v Colquhoun 1925*: unless an itinerant trader (*Horton v Young 1971*)
Compensation for loss of office and ex gratia payments	Allow	If for benefit of trade: *Mitchell v B W Noble Ltd 1927*
Pension contributions (to schemes for employees and company directors)	Allow	Special contributions may be spread over the year of payment and future years
Parking fines	Allow	For employees using their employer's cars on business
	Disallow	For proprietors/directors
Damages paid	Allow	If not too remote from trade: *Strong and Co v Woodifield 1906*
Preparation and restoration of waste disposal sites	Allow	Spread preparation expenditure over period of use of site. Pre-trading expenditure is treated as incurred on the first day of trading. Allow restoration expenditure in period of expenditure
Rental income from letting part of premises	Deduct	Taxed as income of a UK property business unless it is the letting of surplus business accommodation

2.9 Rounding

Where an individual, a partnership or a single company (not a group of companies) has an annual turnover of at least £5,000,000, and prepares its accounts with figures rounded to at least the nearest £1,000, figures in computations of adjusted profits (including, for companies, non-trade profits but excluding capital gains) may generally be rounded to the nearest £1,000.

2.10 Cash basis of accounting for small businesses   6/16

2.10.1 Introduction

FAST FORWARD

An individual who is carrying on a trade may elect for the profits of the trade to be calculated on the cash basis (instead of in accordance with generally accepted accounting principles) in certain circumstances.

Usually, **businesses prepare accounts using generally accepted accounting principles for tax purposes.** In particular, this means that **income and expenses are dealt with on an accruals basis.** This is referred to as **'accruals accounting'** in this section.

Certain small unincorporated businesses may elect to use cash accounting (known as 'the cash basis') rather than accruals accounting for the purposes of calculating their taxable trading income.

Exam focus point

The detailed cash basis rules are quite complex. These **more complex aspects are not examinable in Advanced Taxation (ATX – UK).** In any examination question involving an unincorporated business, **it should be assumed that the cash basis is not relevant unless it is specifically mentioned.**

2.10.2 Which businesses can use the cash basis?

Unincorporated businesses (sole traders and partnerships) **can make an election to use the cash basis if their receipts for the tax year do not exceed £150,000** (this limit is given in the Tax Rates and Allowances available in the exam).

The election is generally effective for the tax year for which it is made and all subsequent tax years.

However, **a business must cease to use the cash basis** if:

(a)   (i)   **Receipts in the previous tax year exceeded twice the limit (ie £300,000);** and

       (ii)   **Receipts for the current year exceed £150,000**; or

(b)   Its 'commercial circumstances' change such that the cash basis is no longer appropriate and an election is made to use accruals accounting.

2.10.3 Calculation of taxable profits under the cash basis

The taxable trading profits under the cash basis are calculated as:

(a)   **Cash receipts; less**
(b)   **Deductible business expenses actually paid in the period.**

Cash receipts include all amounts received relating to the business including cash and card receipts. They include **amounts received from the sale of plant and machinery, other than on the sale of motor cars.** We look at the definition of plant and machinery when we look at capital allowances later in this text.

Receipts from the sale of motor cars and capital assets which are not classed as plant and machinery (eg land) are not taxable receipts.

Under the cash basis, business expenses are deductible when they are paid. Business expenses for the cash basis of accounting include capital expenditure on plant and machinery (except motor cars). Other capital expenses are not business expenses eg purchase of land and buildings, motor cars, and legal fees on such purchases.

The majority of the specific tax rules covered earlier in this chapter concerning the deductibility of business expenses also apply when the cash basis is used. It should be remembered, in particular, that only **business** expenses are tax deductible so that any private element must be disallowed. **Fixed rate expenses** for private use of motor cars and business premises used for private purposes may be used instead (see further below).

2.10.4 Basis of assessment

A trader using the cash basis can, like any other trader, prepare his accounts to any date in the year. The basis of assessment rules, which determine in which tax year the profits of an accounting period are taxed, apply in the same way for accruals accounting and cash basis traders (see later in this chapter).

2.10.5 Losses

A net cash deficit (ie a loss) can normally only be relieved against future cash surpluses (ie future trading profits). Cash basis traders cannot offset a loss against other income or gains. Trading losses for the accruals accounting traders are dealt with in detail later in this text.

2.10.6 Fixed rate expenses

FAST FORWARD

Fixed rate expenses can be used in relation to expenditure on motor cars and business premises partly used as the trader's home.

Exam focus point

Although the **use of fixed rate expenses is optional,** in **any examination question involving the cash basis,** it should be assumed that, where relevant, **expenses are claimed on this basis.**

The option of claiming expenses on a flat rate basis is also available to unincorporated businesses generally, but it will **only be examined in Advanced Taxation (ATX – UK) within the context of the cash basis.**

Where a business elects to use the cash basis, for Advanced Taxation (ATX – UK) purposes, it will be assumed to use fixed rate expenses rather than make deductions on the usual basis of actual expenditure incurred.

For Advanced Taxation (ATX – UK) purposes, fixed rate expenses relate to:

(a) **Expenditure on motor cars**; and
(b) **Business premises partly used as the trader's home.**

The **fixed rate mileage (FRM) expense** can be claimed in respect of **motor cars which are owned or leased by the business** and **which are used for business purposes by the sole trader/partner or an employee of the business.**

The FRM expense is calculated as the business mileage times the appropriate rate per mile. The appropriate mileage rates for motor cars are 45p per mile for the first 10,000 miles, then 25p per mile thereafter.

A **fixed rate monthly adjustment can be made where a sole trader/partner uses part of the business premises as his home** eg where a sole trader runs a small hotel or guesthouse and also lives in it. The adjustment is deducted from the actual allowable business premises costs to reflect the private portion of household costs, including food, and utilities (eg heat and light). It does not include mortgage interest, rent, council tax or rates: apportionment of these expenses must be made based on the extent of the private occupation of the premises.

The deductible fixed rate amount depends on **how many people use the business premises each month as a private home**:

Number relevant occupants	Non-business use amount
1	£350
2	£500
3 or more	£650

2.11 Example

Larry started trading as an interior designer on 6 April 2018. The following information is relevant for the year to 5 April 2019.

- Revenue was £65,000 of which £8,000 was owed as receivables at 5 April 2019.

- A motor car was acquired on 6 April 2018 for £15,000. Larry drove 10,000 miles in the car during the year to 5 April 2019 of which 3,000 miles were for private journeys. The car qualifies for a capital allowance of £1,890, after taking account of private use. The motoring costs were £2,000. The fixed rate mileage expense for motoring is 45p per mile for the first 10,000 miles, then 25p per mile after that.

- Machinery was acquired on 1 May 2018 for £4,000. The machinery qualifies for a capital allowance of £4,000.

- Other allowable expenses were £12,000 of which £1,000 was owed as payables at 5 April 2019.

If Larry uses the accruals accounting basis and does not use fixed rate expenses, his trading profit will be calculated as follows:

	£	£
Revenue (accruals)		65,000
Less: capital allowance on motor car	1,890	
business motoring expenses £2,000 × 7/10	1,400	
capital allowance on machinery	4,000	
other allowable expenses (accruals)	12,000	
		(19,290)
Taxable trading profit		45,710

If Larry uses the cash basis of accounting and fixed rate expenses, his trading profit will be calculated as follows:

	£	£
Revenue (cash received £65,000 – £8,000)		57,000
Less: FRM on car 7,000 × 45p	3,150	
cost of machinery	4,000	
other allowable expenses (cash paid £12,000 – £1,000)	11,000	
		(18,150)
Taxable trading profit		38,850

2.12 The cessation of trades

2.12.1 Post cessation receipts and expenses

Post-cessation receipts (including any releases of debts incurred by the trader) **are chargeable to income tax as miscellaneous income**.

If they are received in the tax year of cessation or the next six tax years, the trader can elect that they be treated as received on the day of cessation. The time limit for electing is the 31 January which is 22 months after the end of the tax year of receipt.

Certain post cessation expenses paid within seven years of discontinuance may be relieved against other income. The expenses must relate to costs of remedying defective work or goods, or legal expenses of or insurance against defective work claims. Relief is also available for trade receivable that subsequently prove to be impaired.

2.12.2 Valuing trading stock on cessation

When a trade ceases, the closing stock must be valued. The higher the value, the higher the profit for the final period of trading.

If the stock is sold to a UK trader who will deduct its cost in computing their taxable profits, it is valued under the following rules.

(a) If the seller and the buyer are unconnected, take the actual price.

(b) If the seller and the buyer are connected (see below), take what would have been the price in an arm's length sale.

(c) However, if the seller and the buyer are connected, the arm's length price exceeds both the original cost of the stock and the actual transfer price, and both the seller and the buyer make an election, then take the greater of the original cost of the stock and the transfer price. The time limit for election for unincorporated business is the 31 January which is 22 months after the end of the tax year of cessation (for companies, it is two years after the end of the accounting period of cessation).

In all cases covered above, the value used for the seller's computation of profit is also used as the buyer's cost.

An individual is **connected** (**connected person**) with their spouse (or civil partner), with the relatives (brothers, sisters, ancestors and lineal descendants) of themselves and their spouse (or civil partner), and with the spouses (or civil partners) of those relatives. In-laws and step family are included; uncles, aunts, nephews, nieces and cousins are not. He is also connected with their business partners (except in relation to bona fide commercial arrangements for the disposal of partnership assets), and with their spouses (or civil partners) and relatives (see diagram below). An individual is also connected with a company if he has control of that company (or if he and persons connected with him together have control of it). An individual is also connected with the trustees of a trust of which that individual is the settlor.

If the stock is not transferred to a UK trader who will be able to deduct its cost in computing their profits, then it is valued at its open market value as at the cessation of trade.

3 Basis periods
6/14, 9/15, 3/16

ACCA's article **Taxation of the unincorporated business – the new business,** written by a member of the Advanced Taxation (ATX – UK) examining team, looks at the issues relating to a new business including the choice of business vehicle and the first years of trading.

 FAST FORWARD

Basis periods are used to link periods of account to tax years.

3.1 Introduction

A tax year runs from 6 April to 5 April, but most businesses do not have periods of account ending on 5 April. **Thus there must be a link between a period of account of a business and a tax year.** The procedure is to **find a period to act as the basis period for a tax year. The profits for a basis period are taxed in the corresponding tax year**. If a basis period is not identical to a period of account, the profits of periods of account are time-apportioned as required on the assumption that profits accrue evenly over a period of account. We will apportion to the nearest month for exam purposes.

We will now look at the basis period rules that apply in the opening, continuing and closing years of a business when there is no change of accounting date. Special rules are needed when the trader changes their accounting date. We will look at these rules in the next section.

The first tax year is the year during which the trade commences. For example, if a trade commences on 1 June 2018 the first tax year is 2018/19.

3.2 The first tax year

In opening and closing years, special rules are applied so that a new trader can start to be taxed quickly, and a retiring trader need not be taxed long after their retirement.

The **basis period for the first tax year runs from the date the trade starts to the next 5 April** (or to the date of cessation if the trade does not last until the end of the tax year).

So continuing the above example a trader commencing in business on 1 June 2018 will be taxed on profits arising from 1 June 2018 to 5 April 2019 in 2018/19, the first tax year.

3.3 The second tax year

(a) **If the accounting date falling in the second tax year is at least 12 months after the start of trading, the basis period is the 12 months to that accounting date.**

(b) **If the accounting date falling in the second tax year is less than 12 months after the start of trading, the basis period is the first 12 months of trading.**

(c) **If there is no accounting date falling in the second tax year**, because the first period of account is a very long one which does not end until a date in the third tax year, **the basis period for the second tax year is the year itself (from 6 April to 5 April).**

The following flowchart may help you determine the basis period for the second tax year.

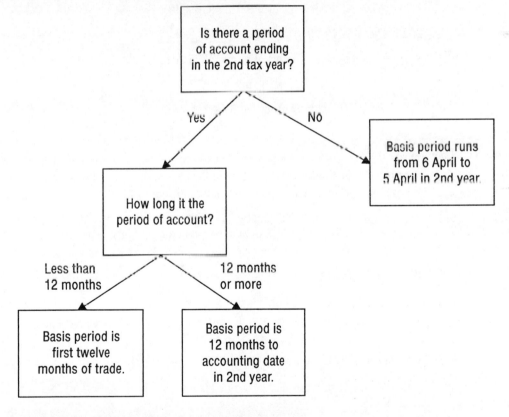

3.4 Examples: the first and second tax year

(a) John starts to trade on 1 January 2019 preparing accounts to 31 December 2019.

1st tax year: 2018/19 – tax profits 1.1.19–5.4.19

2nd tax year: 2019/20

- Is there a period of account ending in 2019/20?
- How long is the period of account?
  - 12 months or more ie 12 months (exactly) to 31.12.19.
- So in 2019/20 tax profits of 12 months to 31.12.19.

(b) Janet starts to trade on 1 January 2019 preparing accounts as follows:

- Six months to 30 June 2019
- 12 months to 30 June 2020

1st tax year: 2018/19 – tax profits 1.1.19–5.4.19

2nd tax year: 2019/20

- Is there a period of account ending in 2019/20?
- How long is the period of account?
  - Less than 12 months ie six months long.
- So in 2019/20 tax profits of first 12 months of trade ie 1.1.19–31.12.19, ie:
  - p.e. 30.6.19 profits; plus
  - 6/12 of y.e 30.6.20 profits

(c) Jodie starts to trade on 1 March 2019 preparing a 14 month set of accounts to 30 April 2020.

1st tax year: 2018/19 – tax profits 1.3.19–5.4.19

2nd tax year: 2019/20

- Is there a period of account ending in 2019/20?
  - No (p.e. 30.4.20 ends in 2020/21)
- So in 2019/20 tax profits of 6.4.19–5.4.20.

3.5 The third tax year

(a) **If there is an accounting date falling in the second tax year, the basis period for the third tax year is the period of account ending in the third tax year.**

(b) If there is no accounting date falling in the second tax year, the basis period for the third tax year is the 12 months to the accounting date falling in the third tax year.

3.6 Later tax years

For later tax years, except the year in which the trade ceases, **the basis period is the period of account ending in the tax year**. This is known as the **current year basis of assessment**.

3.7 The final year   9/16

(a) If a trade starts and ceases in the same tax year, the basis period for that year is the whole lifespan of the trade.

(b) If the final year is the second year, the basis period runs from 6 April at the start of the second year to the date of cessation. This rule overrides the rules that normally apply for the second year.

(c) If the final year is the third year or a later year, **the basis period runs from the end of the basis period for the previous year to the date of cessation**. This rule overrides the rules that normally apply in the third and later years.

This topic was tested in September 2016 question 2 Waverley. The examining team commented that 'An ability to identify the basis periods for taxation of a business in its opening and closing years, is a fundamental skill which candidates are expected to apply in Advanced Tax. Relatively few candidates were able to do this correctly in the case of the final tax year for this business. This is regarded as essential brought forward knowledge, and is tested on a regular basis.'

3.8 Overlap profits

Key term

Profits which have been taxed more than once are called **overlap profits**.

When a business starts, some profits may be taxed twice because the basis period for the second year includes some or all of the period of trading in the first year or because the basis period for the third year overlaps with that for the second year.

Overlap profits may be deducted on a change of accounting date (see below). Any overlap profits unrelieved when the trade ceases are deducted from the final year's taxable profits. Any deduction of overlap profits may create or increase a loss. The usual loss reliefs (covered later in this text) are then available.

3.9 Example: accounting date in 2nd year at least 12 months

Jenny trades from 1 July 2013 to 31 December 2018, with the following results.

Period	Profit £
1.7.13–31.8.14	7,000
1.9.14–31.8.15	12,000
1.9.15–31.8.16	15,000
1.9.16–31.8.17	21,000
1.9.17–31.8.18	18,000
1.9.18–31.12.18	5,600
	78,600

The profits to be taxed in each tax year from 2013/14 to 2018/19, and the total of these taxable profits are calculated as follows.

Year	Basis period	Working	Taxable profit £
2013/14	1.7.13–5.4.14	£7,000 × 9/14	4,500
2014/15	1.9.13–31.8.14	£7,000 × 12/14	6,000
2015/16	1.9.14–31.8.15		12,000
2016/17	1.9.15–31.8.16		15,000
2017/18	1.9.16–31.8.17		21,000
2018/19	1.9.17–31.12.18	£(18,000 + 5,600 – 3,500)	20,100
			78,600

The overlap profits are those in the period 1 September 2013 to 5 April 2014, a period of seven months. They are £7,000 × 7/14 = £3,500. Overlap profits are either relieved on a change of accounting date (see below) or are deducted from the final year's taxable profit when the business ceases. In this case the overlap profits are deducted when the business ceases. Over the life of the business, the total taxable profits equal the total actual profits.

Peter trades from 1 September 2013 to 30 June 2018, with the following results.

Period	Profit £
1.9.13–30.4.14	8,000
1.5.14–30.4.15	15,000
1.5.15–30.4.16	9,000
1.5.16–30.4.17	10,500
1.5.17–30.4.18	16,000
1.5.18–30.6.18	950
	59,450

Show the profits to be taxed in each year from 2013/14 to 2018/19, the total of these taxable profits and the overlap profits.

Answer

Year	Basis period	Working	Taxable profits £
2013/14	1.9.13–5.4.14	£8,000 × 7/8	7,000
2014/15	1.9.13–31.8.14	£8,000 + (£15,000 × 4/12)	13,000
2015/16	1.5.14–30.4.15		15,000
2016/17	1.5.15–30.4.16		9,000
2017/18	1.5.16–30.4.17		10,500
2018/19	1.5.17–30.6.18	£(16,000 + 950 – 12,000)	4,950
			59,450

The overlap profits are the profits from 1 September 2013 to 5 April 2014 (taxed in 2013/14 and in 2014/15) and those from 1 May 2014 to 31 August 2014 (taxed in 2014/15 and 2015/16).

	£
1.9.13–5.4.14 £8,000 × 7/8	7,000
1.5.14–31.8.14 £15,000 × 4/12	5,000
Total overlap profits	12,000

3.10 Example: no accounting date in the second year

Thelma starts to trade on 1 March 2017. Her first accounts, covering the 16 months to 30 June 2018, show a profit of £36,000. The taxable profits for the first three tax years and the overlap profits are as follows.

Year	Basis period	Working	Taxable profits £
2016/17	1.3.17–5.4.17	£36,000 × 1/16	2,250
2017/18	6.4.17–5.4.18	£36,000 × 12/16	27,000
2018/19	1.7.17–30.6.18	£36,000 × 12/16	27,000

The overlap profits are the profits from 1 July 2017 to 5 April 2018: £36,000 × 9/16 = £20,250.

3.11 The choice of an accounting date   12/14, 12/17

A new trader should consider which accounting date would be best. There are **a number of factors to consider** from the point of view of taxation.

- **If profits are expected to rise, a date early in the tax year** (such as 30 April) will delay the time when rising accounts profits feed through into rising taxable profits, whereas a date late in the tax year (such as 31 March) will accelerate the taxation of rising profits. This is because with an accounting date of 30 April, the taxable profits for each tax year are mainly the profits earned in the previous tax year. With an accounting date of 31 March the taxable profits are almost entirely profits earned in the current year.

- If the accounting date in the second tax year is less than 12 months after the start of trading, the taxable profits for that year will be the profits earned in the first 12 months. If the accounting date is at least 12 months from the start of trading, they will be the profits earned in the 12 months to that date. **Different profits may thus be taxed twice**, and if profits are fluctuating this can make a considerable difference to the taxable profits in the first few years.

- **The choice of an accounting date affects the profits shown in each set of accounts**, and this may affect the taxable profits.

- **An accounting date of 30 April gives the maximum interval between earning profits and paying the related tax liability.** For example if a trader prepares accounts to 30 April 2019, this falls into the tax year 2019/20 with payments on account being due on 31 January 2020 and 31 July 2020, and a balancing payment due on 31 January 2021 (details of payment of income tax are dealt with later in this text). If the trader prepares accounts to 31 March 2019, this falls in the tax year 2018/19 and the payments will be due one year earlier (ie on 31 January 2019, 31 July 2019 and 31 January 2020).

- **Knowing profits well in advance of the end of the tax year makes tax planning much easier.** For example, if a trader wants to make personal pension contributions and prepares accounts to 30 April 2019 (2019/20), they can make contributions up to 5 April 2020 based on those relevant earnings. If they prepare accounts to 31 March 2019, they will probably not know the amount of their relevant earnings until after the end of the tax year 2018/19, too late to adjust their pension contributions for 2018/19.

- **However, a 31 March or 5 April accounting date means that the application of the basis period rules is more straightforward and there will be no overlap profits.** This may be appropriate for small traders.

- **With an accounting date of 30 April, the assessment for the year of cessation could be based on up to 23 months of profits.** For example, if a trader who has prepared accounts to 30 April ceases trading on 31 March 2019 (2018/19), the basis period for 2018/19 will run from 1 May 2017 to 31 March 2019. This could lead to larger than normal trading profits being assessable in the year of cessation.

  However, this could be avoided by carrying on the trade for another month so that a cessation arises on 30 April 2019 so that the profits from 1 May 2017 to 30 April 2018 are taxable in 2018/19 and those from 1 May 2018 to 30 April 2019 are taxable in 2019/20. Each case must be looked at in relation to all relevant factors, such as other income which the taxpayer may have and loss relief – there is no one rule which applies in all cases.

Question   The choice of an accounting date

Christine starts to trade on 1 December 2016. Her monthly profits are £1,000 for the first seven months, and £2,000 thereafter. Show the taxable profits for the first three tax years with each of the following accounting dates (in all cases starting with a period of account of less than 12 months).

(a)   31 March
(b)   30 April
(c)   31 December

(a) *31 March*

Period of account	Working	Profits £
1.12.16–31.3.17	£1,000 × 4	4,000
1.4.17–31.3.18	£1,000 × 3 + £2,000 × 9	21,000
1.4.18–31.3.19	£2,000 × 12	24,000

Year	Basis period	Taxable profits £
2016/17	1.12.16–5.4.17	4,000
2017/18	1.4.17–31.3.18	21,000
2018/19	1.4.18–31.3.19	24,000

(b) *30 April*

Period of account	Working	Profits £
1.12.16–30.4.17	£1,000 × 5	5,000
1.5.17–30.4.18	£1,000 × 2 + £2,000 × 10	22,000

Year	Basis period	Working	Taxable profits £
2016/17	1.12.16–5.4.17	£5,000 × 4/5	4,000
2017/18	1.12.16–30.11.17	£5,000 + £22,000 × 7/12	17,833
2018/19	1.5.17–30.4.18		22,000

(c) *31 December*

Period of account	Working	Profits £
1.12.16–31.12.16	£1,000 × 1	1,000
1.1.17–31.12.17	£1,000 × 6 + £2,000 × 6	18,000
1.1.18–31.12.18	£2,000 × 12	24,000

Year	Basis period	Working	Taxable profits £
2016/17	1.12.16–5.4.17	£1,000 + £18,000 × 3/12	5,500
2017/18	1.1.17–31.12.17		18,000
2018/19	1.1.18–31.12.18		24,000

Exam focus point

December 2014 Qu 2(a) part (iii) Piquet required candidates to identify two advantages of using a 30 April year end as opposed to a year end of 28 February. The examining team commented that 'Many candidates were able to identify one advantage but few were able to come up with two. This was disappointing as the choice of year end is a basic aspect of tax planning for the unincorporated trader and one that candidates should be confident of.'

4 Change of accounting date   12/14, 12/17

Exam focus point

ACCA's article **Taxation of the unincorporated business – the existing business,** written by a member of the Advanced Taxation (ATX – UK) examining team, covers some of the issues relating to extraction of profits, change of accounting date and the final years of a business.

4.1 Introduction

A trader may change the date to which they prepare their annual accounts for a variety of reasons. For example, they may wish to move to a calendar year end or to fit in with seasonal variations of their trade. Special rules normally apply for fixing basis periods when a trader changes their accounting date.

On a change of accounting date there may be:

- One set of accounts covering a period of less than twelve months;
- One set of accounts covering a period of more than twelve months;
- No accounts; or
- Two sets of accounts

ending in a tax year. In each case, the basis period for the year relates to the new accounting date. We will look at each of the cases in turn.

4.2 One short period of account

When a change of accounting date results in one short period of account ending in a tax year, the basis period for that year is always the 12 months to the new accounting date.

4.3 Example: change of accounting date (1)

Sue prepares accounts to 31 December each year until she changes her accounting date to 30 June by preparing accounts for the six months to 30 June 2018.

There is one short period of account ending during 2018/19. This means the basis period for 2018/19 is the twelve months to 30 June 2018.

Sue's basis period for 2017/18 was the 12 months to 31 December 2017. This means the profits of the six months to 31 December 2017 are overlap profits that have been taxed twice. These overlap profits must be added to any overlap profits that arose when the business began. The total is either relieved when the business ceases or it is relieved on a subsequent change of accounting date.

4.4 One long period of account

When a change of accounting date results in one long period of account ending in a tax year, the basis period for that year ends on the new accounting date. It begins immediately after the basis period for the previous year ends. This means the basis period will exceed 12 months.

No overlap profits arise in this situation. However, more than 12 months worth of profits are taxed in one income tax year and to compensate for this, relief is available for brought forward overlap profits. The overlap relief must reduce the number of months' worth of profits taxed in the year to no more than twelve. So, if you have a fourteen month basis period you can give relief for up to two months worth of overlap profits.

4.5 Example: change of accounting date (2)

Zoe started trading on 1 October 2015 and prepared accounts to 30 September until she changed her accounting date by preparing accounts for the fifteen months to 31 December 2018. Her results were as follows.

Year to 30 September 2016	£24,000
Year to 30 September 2017	£48,000
Fifteen months to 31 December 2018	£75,000

Profits for the first three tax years of the business are:

2015/16 (1.10.15–5.4.16)	
6/12 × £24,000	£12,000
2016/17 (1.10.15–30.9.16)	£24,000
2017/18 (1.10.16–30.9.17)	£48,000

Overlap profits are £12,000. These arose in the six months to 5.4.16.

The change in accounting date results in one long period of account ending during 2018/19 which means the basis period for 2018/19 is the 15 months to 31 December 2018. Three months' worth of the brought forward overlap profits can be relieved.

	£
2018/19 (1.10.17–31.12.18)	75,000
Less overlap profits 3/6 × £12,000	(6,000)
	69,000

The unrelieved overlap profits of £6,000 (£12,000 – £6,000) are carried forward for relief either when the business ceases or on a further change of accounting date.

4.6 No accounting date ending in the year

If a change of accounting date results in there being no period of account ending in a tax year there is a potential problem because basis periods usually end on an accounting date. To get round this problem **you must manufacture a basis period by taking the new accounting date and deducting one year. The basis period is then the twelve months to this date.**

4.7 Example: change of accounting date (3)

Anne had always prepared accounts to 31 March. She then changed her accounting date by preparing accounts for the thirteen months to 30 April 2019.

There is no period of account ending during 2018/19 so the basis period for this year is the manufactured basis period of the twelve months to 30 April 2018.

You've probably spotted that this produces an overlap with the previous basis period. The overlap period is the eleven months from 1 May 2017 to 31 March 2018. The overlap profits arising in this period are added to any other unrelieved overlap profits and are carried forward for future relief.

4.8 Two accounting dates ending in the year

When two periods of account end in a tax year, the basis period for the year ends on the new accounting date. It begins immediately following the previous basis period. This means that the basis period will exceed 12 months and overlap relief can be allowed to ensure that only twelve months worth of profits are assessed in the tax year.

4.9 Example: change of accounting date (4)

Elizabeth prepared accounts to 30 September until 2019 when she changed her accounting date by preparing accounts for the six months to 31 March 2019.

The new accounting date is 31 March 2019. This is the end of the basis period for 2018/19. The basis period for 2017/18 ended on 30 September 2017. The 2018/19 basis period is therefore the 18-month period 1 October 2017 to 31 March 2019. Six months' worth of overlap profits can be relieved in this year.

4.10 Conditions

The above changes in basis period automatically occur if the trader changes their accounting date during the first three tax years of their business.

In other cases **the following conditions must be met before a change in basis periods can occur**:

- The trader must notify HMRC of the change by the 31 January, following the tax year in which the change is made (by 31 January 2020 for a change made during 2018/19).

- The period of account resulting from the change must not exceed 18 months.

- In general, there must have been no previous change of accounting date in the last 5 tax years. However, a second change can be made within this period if the later change is for genuine commercial reasons. If HMRC do not respond to a notification of a change of accounting date within 60 days of receiving it, the trader can assume that they are satisfied that the reasons for making the change are genuine commercial ones.

If the above conditions are not satisfied because the first period of account ending on the new date exceeds 18 months or the change of accounting date was not notified in time, but the 'five year gap or commercial reasons' condition is satisfied, then the basis period for the year of change is the 12 months to the **old** accounting date in the year of change. The basis period for the next year is then found using rules above as if it were the year of change.

If the 'five year gap or commercial reasons' test is not satisfied, the old accounting date remains in force for tax purposes (with the profits of accounts made up to the new date being time-apportioned as necessary) until there have been five consecutive tax years which were not years of change. The sixth tax year is then treated as the year of change to the new accounting date, and the rules above apply.

Exam focus point

December 2014 Qu 2(a) parts (i) and (ii) Piquet tested change of accounting date. The examining team commented that 'Unfortunately, most candidates who attempted this question did not know the rules, such that very few scored well on these parts of the question.' The examining team added that 'Candidates should recognise that change of accounting date is not part of the Taxation (TX – UK) syllabus and must therefore be regarded as an area that will be examined regularly in future Advanced Taxation (ATX – UK) exams.'

5 National insurance

5.1 National insurance contributions (NICs) for the self employed   6/17, 6/18

FAST FORWARD

The self employed pay Class 2 and Class 4 NICs. Class 4 NICs are based on the level of the individual's taxable profits. Class 2 NICs are paid at a weekly flat rate.

The self employed (sole traders and partners) **pay NICs in two ways.**

Class 2 contributions are payable at a flat rate. The Class 2 rate for 2018/19 is £2.95 a week. No Class 2 contributions are payable if the individual's taxable trading profits are less than the small profits threshold which is £6,205 for 2018/19.

Class 2 NICs are payable under the self assessment system but payments on account are not required. Therefore, for 2018/19, Class 2 NICs are payable by 31 January 2020.

Additionally, **the self employed pay Class 4 NICs, based on the level of the individual's trade profits.**

Main rate Class 4 NICs are calculated by applying a fixed percentage of 9% for 2018/19 to the individual's taxable trading profits between the lower limit, which is £8,424 for 2018/19, and the upper limit which is £46,350 for 2018/19. Additional rate contributions are 2% for 2018/19 on profits above that limit.

5.2 Example: Class 4 contributions

If a sole trader had profits of £17,089 for 2018/19 their Class 4 NIC liability would be as follows.

	£
Profits	17,089
Less lower limit	(8,424)
	8,665

Class 4 NICs = 9% × £8,665 = £780 (main only)

5.3 Example: additional Class 4 contributions

If an individual's profits were £52,000, additional Class 4 NICs are due on the excess over the upper limit. Thus the amount payable in 2018/19 is as follows.

	£
Profits (upper limit)	46,350
Less lower limit	(8,424)
	37,926
Main rate Class 4 NICs 9% × £37,926	3,413
Additional rate class 4 NICs £(52,000 – 46,350) = £5,650 × 2%	113
	3,526

Class 4 NICs are collected by HMRC through the self assessment system. They are paid **at the same time as the associated income tax liability and so are part of payments on account and balancing payments.** Interest is charged on overdue contributions.

5.4 Comparison of NICs for the employees and the self employed

The NIC burden on the self employed tends to be lower than that on employees, although the relative burdens vary with the level of income. The following example shows how a comparison may be made.

5.5 Example: employed and self employed NICs

Two single people, one employed and one self employed, each have annual gross income of £25,000. Show their national insurance contributions for 2018/19.

Solution

	Employed £	Self-employed £
NICs		
Class 1: £(25,000 – 8,424) × 12% (main only)	1,989	
Class 2: £2.95 × 52		153
Class 4: £(25,000 – 8,424) × 9%		1,492
	1,989	1,645

The self-employed person is better off by £(1,989 – 1,645) = £344 a year in NIC terms. However, that person will not be entitled to certain benefits such as job seekers allowance.

Chapter roundup

- The badges of trade can be used to decide whether or not a trade exists.

- The accounts profits need to be adjusted in order to establish the taxable trade profits.

- An individual who is carrying on a trade may elect for the profits of the trade to be calculated on the cash basis (instead of in accordance with generally accepted accounting principles) in certain circumstances.

- Fixed rate expenses can be used in relation to expenditure on motor cars and business premises partly used as the trader's home.

- Basis periods are used to link periods of account to tax years.

- In opening and closing years, special rules are applied so that a new trader can start to be taxed quickly, and a retiring trader need not be taxed long after their retirement.

- On a change of accounting date, special rules apply for fixing basis periods.

- The self employed pay Class 2 and Class 4 NICs. Class 4 NICs are based on the level of the individual's taxable profits. Class 2 NICs are paid at a weekly flat rate.

Quick quiz

1 List the six traditional badges of trade.

2 What are the remoteness test and the duality test?

3 What pre-trading expenditure is deductible?

4 In which period of account are earnings paid 12 months after the end of the period for which they are charged deductible?

5 What is the maximum allowable amount of redundancy pay on the cessation of a trade?

6 Which businesses can elect to use the cash basis of accounting?

7 What is the basis period for the tax year in which a trade commenced?

8 On what two occasions may overlap profits potentially be relieved?

9 How are Class 4 NICs calculated?

1   The subject matter
    The frequency of transactions
    The length of ownership
    Supplementary work and marketing
    A profit motive
    The way in which goods were acquired

2   Expenditure is not deductible if it is not for trade purposes (the remoteness test), or if it reflects more than one purpose (the duality test).

3   Pre-trading expenditure is deductible if it is incurred within seven years of the start of the trade and is of a type that would have been deductible if the trade had already started.

4   In the period in which they are paid.

5   3 × statutory amount

6   Unincorporated businesses (sole traders and partnerships) whose receipts for the tax year do not exceed £150,000 can use the cash basis of accounting.

7   Date of commencement to 5 April in that year.

8   On a change of accounting date where a basis period resulting from the change exceeds 12 months or on the cessation of a business.

9   The main rate is a fixed percentage of an individual's profits between the upper limit and lower limit. The additional rate applies above the upper limit.

Now try the question below from the Practice Question Bank

Number	Level	Marks	Time
Q7	Introductory	20	39 mins

7

Capital allowances

Topic list	Syllabus reference
1 Capital allowances in general	A1(a)B3
2 Plant and machinery – qualifying expenditure	A1(a)B3
3 The main pool	A1(a)B3, A1(d)(iii), (iv)
4 Special rate pool	A1(a)B3
5 Private use assets	A1(a)B3
6 Motor cars	A1(a)B3
7 Short-life assets	A1(a)B3
8 Hire purchase and leasing	A1(a)B3
9 Cessation and succession	A1(a)B3

Introduction

In the previous chapter, we saw how to adjust the accounting profit to find taxable trade profits and how to allocate those profits to tax years. The adjustments included adding back depreciation as a disallowable expenses and deducting capital allowances instead. In this chapter, we look at capital allowances on plant and machinery.

Our study of plant and machinery falls into three parts. First, we look at what qualifies for allowances: many business assets get no allowances at all. Second, we see how to compute the allowances and lastly, we look at special rules for assets with short lives, for private use assets, for assets which the taxpayer does not buy outright, and for transfers of whole businesses.

Study guide

		Intellectual level
1	**Income and income tax liabilities in situations involving further overseas aspects and in relation to trusts, and the application of exemptions and reliefs**	
(a)	The contents of the Taxation - United Kingdom (TX – UK) study guide for income tax and national insurance, under heading:	2
•	B3 Income from self employment	
(d)	Income from self employment:	
(iii)	Advise on the allocation of the annual investment allowance between related businesses	3
(iv)	Identify the enhanced capital allowances in respect of expenditure on green technologies	2

Exam guide

If you are asked to consider the tax costs of business strategies, whether for a sole trader or a company, you should always take capital allowances into account. This could apply when considering a particular contract, or when comparing the costs of different assets, or it could be in a buy or lease context.

Knowledge brought forward from earlier studies

This chapter is mainly revision from Taxation (TX – UK). The allocation of the annual investment allowance between related business and enhanced capital allowances are new.

The changes in the material you have studied in Taxation (TX – UK) are that for expenditure on or after 1 April 2018, the emission threshold for low emission cars qualifying for the 100% first year allowance has been reduced from 76 g/km to 50 g/km and for high emission cars qualifying for the 8% special rate has been reduced from 130g/km to 110 g/km.

1 Capital allowances in general

FAST FORWARD Capital allowances are available on plant and machinery.

 One of the competencies you require to fulfil Performance Objective 15 Tax computations and assessments of the PER is to prepare or contribute to the computation or assessment of tax computations for individuals. You can apply the knowledge you obtain from this section of the text to help to demonstrate this competence.

Capital expenditure cannot be deducted in computing taxable trade profits when using the accruals method of accounting, but it *may* attract capital allowances. Capital allowances are treated as a trading expense and are deducted in arriving at taxable trade profits. Balancing charges, effectively negative allowances, are added in arriving at those profits.

Capital expenditure on plant and machinery qualifies for capital allowances.

Both unincorporated businesses and companies are entitled to capital allowances. For completeness, in this chapter we will look at the rules for companies alongside those for unincorporated businesses. We will look at companies in more detail later in this text.

For unincorporated businesses, capital allowances are calculated for periods of account. These are simply the periods for which the trader chooses to make up accounts. For companies, capital allowances are calculated for accounting periods (see later in this text).

For capital allowances purposes, expenditure is generally deemed to be incurred when the obligation to pay becomes unconditional. This will often be the date of delivery, even if payment is actually required later than this date. For example, the sales contract may require payment to be made within four weeks of delivery but the obligation to pay still becomes unconditional on the delivery date. However, amounts due more than four months after the obligation becomes unconditional are deemed to be incurred when they fall due.

2 Plant and machinery – qualifying expenditure

2.1 Introduction

Capital expenditure on plant and machinery qualifies for capital allowances if the plant or machinery is used for a qualifying activity, such as a trade. 'Plant' is not defined by the legislation, although some specific exclusions and inclusions are given. The word 'machinery' may be taken to have its normal everyday meaning.

2.2 The statutory exclusions

FAST FORWARD

> Statutory rules generally exclude specified items from treatment as plant, rather than include specified items as plant.

2.2.1 Buildings

Expenditure on a building and on any asset which is incorporated in a building or is of a kind normally incorporated into buildings does not qualify as expenditure on plant. There are some exceptions to this rule (see Section 2.2.3 below). Also, certain 'integral features' (see section 2.2.5 below) are specifically treated as plant.

In addition to complete buildings, the following assets count as 'buildings', and are therefore not plant (except if they qualify as integral features).

- Walls, floors, ceilings, doors, gates, shutters, windows and stairs
- Mains services, and systems, of water, electricity and gas
- Waste disposal, sewerage and drainage systems
- Shafts or other structures for lifts etc.

2.2.2 Structures

Expenditure on structures and on works involving the alteration of land does not qualify as expenditure on plant, but see below for exceptions.

A 'structure' is a fixed structure of any kind, other than a building. An example is a bridge.

2.2.3 Exceptions

Over the years a large body of case law has been built up under which plant and machinery allowances have been given on certain types of expenditure which might be thought to be expenditure on a building or structure. Statute therefore gives a list of various assets which may still be plant. These include:

- Any machinery not within any other item in this list
- Gas and sewerage systems:
  - Provided mainly to meet the particular requirements of the trade; or
  - Provided mainly to serve particular machinery or plant used for the purposes of the trade

- Manufacturing or processing equipment, storage equipment, including cold rooms, display equipment, and counters, checkouts and similar equipment

- Cookers, washing machines, refrigeration or cooling equipment, sanitary ware and furniture and furnishings

- Hoists

- Sound insulation provided mainly to meet the particular requirements of the trade

- Computer, telecommunication and surveillance systems

- Refrigeration or cooling equipment

- Sprinkler equipment, fire alarm and burglar alarm systems

- Strong rooms in bank or building society premises, safes

- Partition walls, where movable and intended to be moved

- Decorative assets provided for the enjoyment of the public in the hotel, restaurant or similar trades, advertising hoardings

- Glasshouses which have, as an integral part of their structure, devices which control the plant growing environment automatically

- Swimming pools (including diving boards, slides) and structures for rides at amusement parks

- Caravans provided mainly for holiday lettings

- Movable buildings intended to be moved in the course of the trade

- Expenditure on altering land for the purpose only of installing machinery or plant

- Dry docks and jetties

- Pipelines, and also underground ducts or tunnels with a primary purpose of carrying utility conduits

- Silos provided for temporary storage and storage tanks, slurry pits and silage clamps

- Fish tanks, fish ponds and fixed zoo cages

- Rails, sleepers and ballast for a railway or tramway

Items falling within the above list of exceptions will only qualify as plant if they fall within the meaning of plant as established by case law. This is discussed below.

2.2.4 Land

Land or an interest in land does not qualify as plant and machinery. For this purpose 'land' excludes buildings, structures and assets which are installed or fixed to land in such a way as to become part of the land for general legal purposes.

2.2.5 Integral features

The following **integral features of a building or structure** qualify for capital allowances as plant (in the special rate pool, see later in this chapter):

- Electrical systems (including lighting systems)

- Cold water system

- Space or water heating system, a powered system of ventilation, air cooling or air purification, and any floor or ceiling comprised in such a system

- Lift, an escalator or a moving walkway

- External solar shading

When a building is sold, the vendor and purchaser can make a joint election to determine how the sale proceeds are apportioned between the building and its integral features.

2.3 The statutory inclusions

Certain expenditure is specifically deemed to be expenditure on plant.

The following are deemed to be plant.

- Expenditure incurred by a trader in complying with fire regulations for a building which they occupy

- Expenditure by a trader on thermal insulation of a building used for the trade

- Expenditure (by an individual or a partnership, not by a company) on security assets provided to meet a special threat to an individual's security that arises wholly or mainly due to the particular trade concerned. Cars, ships, aircraft and dwellings are specifically excluded from the definition of a security asset

On disposal, the sale proceeds for the above are deemed to be zero, so no balancing charge (see below) can arise.

Capital expenditure on computer software (both programs and data) **qualifies as expenditure on plant and machinery**:

(a)   Regardless of whether the software is supplied in a tangible form (such as a disk) or transmitted electronically; and

(b)   Regardless of whether the purchaser acquires the software or only a licence to use it.

Disposal proceeds are brought into account in the normal way, except that if the fee for the grant of a licence is taxed as income of the licensor, no disposal proceeds are taken into account in computing the licensee's capital allowances.

Where someone has incurred expenditure qualifying for capital allowances on computer software (or the right to use software), and receives a capital sum in exchange for allowing someone else to use the software, that sum is brought into account as disposal proceeds. However, the cumulative total of disposal proceeds is not allowed to exceed the original cost of the software, and any proceeds above this limit are ignored for capital allowances purposes (although they may lead to chargeable gains).

If software is expected to have a useful economic life of less than two years, its cost may be treated as revenue expenditure.

For companies the rules for computer software are overridden by the rules for intangible fixed assets unless the company elects otherwise.

2.4 Case law

FAST FORWARD

There are several cases on the definition of plant. To help you to absorb them, try to see the function/setting theme running through them.

Plant was originally defined to be apparatus used by taxpayers to carry on their businesses, other than inventory (*Yarmouth v France 1887*).

Subsequent cases have refined the original definition and have largely been concerned with the **distinction between plant actively used in the business (qualifying) and the setting in which the business is carried on (non-qualifying). This is the 'functional' test**. Some of the decisions have now been enacted as part of statute law, but they are still relevant as examples of the principles involved.

The whole cost of excavating and installing a swimming pool was allowed to the owners of a caravan park. *CIR v Barclay Curle & Co 1969* was followed: the pool performed **the function** of giving 'buoyancy and enjoyment' to the persons using the pool *(Cooke v Beach Station Caravans Ltd 1974)* (actual item now covered by statute).

A barrister succeeded in his claim for his law library *(Munby v Furlong 1977)*.

Office partitioning was allowed. Because it was movable it was not regarded as part of the setting in which the business was carried on *(Jarrold v John Good and Sons Ltd 1963)* (actual item now covered by statute).

A ship used as a floating restaurant was regarded as a structure in which the business was carried on (Buckley LJ). No capital allowances could be obtained *(Benson v Yard Arm Club 1979)*. The same decision was made in relation to a football club's spectator stand. The stand performed no function in the actual carrying out of the club's trade *(Brown v Burnley Football and Athletic Co Ltd 1980)*.

At a motorway service station, false ceilings contained conduits, ducts and lighting apparatus. **They did not qualify because they did not perform a function in the business. They were merely part of the setting in which the business was conducted** *(Hampton v Fortes Autogrill Ltd 1979)*.

Light fittings, decor and murals can be plant. A company carried on business as hoteliers and operators of licensed premises. The function of the items was the creation of an atmosphere conducive to the comfort and well being of its customers *(CIR v Scottish and Newcastle Breweries Ltd 1982)* (decorative assets used in hotels etc, now covered by statute).

On the other hand, it has been held that when an attractive floor is provided in a restaurant, the fact that the floor performs the function of making the restaurant attractive to customers is not enough to make it plant. It functions as premises, and the cost therefore does not qualify for capital allowances *(Wimpy International Ltd v Warland 1988)*.

General lighting in a department store was held not to be plant, as it was merely setting. Special display lighting, however, could be plant *(Cole Brothers Ltd v Phillips 1982)*. Note that changes in legislation mean that it is now possible to claim allowances on lighting as an integral feature (see earlier in this chapter), but the case is still a useful example of the distinction between setting and function.

Free-standing decorative screens installed in the windows of a branch of a building society qualified as plant. Their function was not to act a part of the setting in which the society's business was carried on; it was to attract local custom, and accordingly the screens formed part of the apparatus with which the society carried on its business *(Leeds Permanent Building Society v Proctor 1982)*.

In *Bradley v London Electricity plc 1996* an electricity substation was held not to be plant because it functioned as premises in which London Electricity carried on a trading activity rather than apparatus with which the activity was carried out.

3 The main pool

FAST FORWARD

> With capital allowances computations, the main thing is to get the layout right. Having done that, you will find that the figures tend to drop into place.

3.1 Main pool expenditure

Most expenditure on plant and machinery, including cars with CO_2 emissions of 110g/km or less, is put into a pool of expenditure (the main pool) on which capital allowances may be claimed. An addition increases the pool whilst a disposal decreases it.

Exceptionally the following items are not put into the main pool:

(a) Assets dealt with in the special rate pool
(b) Assets with private use by the trader
(c) Short life assets where an election has been made.

These exceptions are dealt with later in this chapter.

Expenditure on plant and machinery by a person about to begin a trade is treated as incurred on the first day of trading. Assets previously owned by a trader and then brought into the trade (at the start of trading or later) are treated as bought for their market values at the times when they are brought in.

3.2 Annual investment allowance

FAST FORWARD

Businesses are entitled to an annual investment allowance (AIA) of £200,000 for a 12 month period of account. Related businesses share one allowance between them.

3.2.1 Amount of annual investment allowance

Businesses can claim an **annual investment allowance (AIA) on the first £200,000 spent each year on plant or machinery**, including assets in the main pool, but not including motor cars. Expenditure on motorcycles does qualify for the AIA.

Where the period of account is more or less than a year, the maximum allowance is proportionately increased or reduced.

After claiming the AIA, the balance of expenditure on main pool assets after the AIA is transferred to the main pool immediately and is eligible for writing down allowances in the same period.

3.2.2 Allocation of annual investment allowance between related businesses

Related business are entitled to a single annual investment allowance between the businesses. The businesses may **allocate the allowance between them as they think fit.**

Business are related if they are carried on or controlled by the same individual or partnership and either:

- The businesses are **engaged in the same activity**; or
- The businesses **share the same premises**.

A business is **controlled by a person in a tax year** if it is controlled by the person **at the end of the chargeable period for that business ending in that tax year.**

The **nature of expenditure** by one business may be relevant when deciding how to allocate the allowance between the businesses. For example, it is **more tax efficient to set the annual investment allowance against special rate pool expenditure** because of the lower rate of subsequent writing down allowances on the special rate pool (8% pa) as opposed to the main pool (18% pa).

There are similar (but separate) rules relating to companies under common control and companies in a group. We will deal with these rules when we look at companies later in this text.

3.3 First year allowances and enhanced capital allowances

FAST FORWARD

A first year allowance (FYA) at the rate of 100% is available on new low emission cars. Enhanced capital allowances (ECAs) are available on green technologies. FYAs and ECAs are never pro-rated in short periods of account.

3.3.1 FYA on low emission cars

Key term

A **low emission car** is one which has CO_2 **emissions of 50g/km or less**. The threshold of 50g/km applies for expenditure incurred on or after 1 April 2018. The examining team has stated that **a question will not be set** involving the threshold that applied prior to this date.

A 100% first year allowance (FYA) is available for expenditure incurred on new low emission motor cars.

If the FYA is not claimed in full, the balance of expenditure is transferred to the main pool after any writing down allowance has been calculated on the main pool.

3.3.2 Enhanced capital allowances

Capital expenditure on new (ie not second hand) energy and water saving plant and machinery (green technologies) qualifies for 100% enhanced capital allowances (ECAs).

Companies can surrender ECAs for a tax credit of 12.67%. This is dealt with in more detail when we look at companies later in this text.

3.3.3 Short periods of account

FYAs and ECAs are not reduced pro-rata in a short period of account, unlike the AIA and writing down allowances.

3.4 Writing down allowances

Most expenditure on plant and machinery qualifies for a WDA at 18% every 12 months.

Key term

A **writing down allowance (WDA)** is given on main pool expenditure **at the rate of 18% a year** (on a reducing balance basis). The WDA is calculated on the tax written down value (TWDV) of pooled plant, after adding the current period's additions and taking out the current period's disposals.

When plant is sold, proceeds, **limited to a maximum of the original cost,** are taken out of the pool. Provided that the trade is still being carried on, the pool balance remaining is written down in the future by WDAs, even if there are no assets left.

3.5 Example: writing down allowances

Elizabeth has a tax written down value on her main pool of plant and machinery of £16,000 at 5 April 2018. In the year to 5 April 2019 she bought a car with CO_2 emissions of 90g/km for £8,000 (no non-business use) and she disposed of plant (which originally cost £4,000) for £6,000.

Calculate the maximum capital allowances claim for the year.

	Main pool £	Allowances £
Twdv b/f	16,000	
Addition (not qualifying for AIA or FYA)	8,000	
Less disposal (proceeds limited to cost)	(4,000)	
	20,000	
WDA @ 18%	(3,600)	3,600
TWDV c/f	16,400	
Maximum capital allowances claim		3,600

Question   Capital allowances

Julia is a sole trader preparing accounts to 5 April each year. At 5 April 2018, the tax written down value on her main pool is £12,500.

In the year to 5 April 2019, Julia bought the following assets:

1 June 2018	Machinery	£190,000
12 November 2018	Van	£17,500
10 February 2019	Car for salesperson (CO_2 emissions 100g/km)	£9,000

She disposed of plant on 15 December 2018 for £12,000 (original cost £16,000).

Calculate the maximum capital allowances claim that Julia can make for the year ended 5 April 2019.

	AIA £	Main pool £	Allowances £
y/e 5 April 2019			
TWDV b/f		12,500	
Additions qualifying for AIA			
1.6.18 Machinery	190,000		
12.11.18 Van	17,500		
	207,500		
AIA	(200,000)		200,000
	7,500		
Transfer balance to pool	(7,500)	7,500	
Additions not qualifying for AIA			
10.2.19 Car		9,000	
Disposal			
15.12.18 Plant		(12,000)	
		17,000	
WDA @ 18%		(3,060)	3,060
TWDV c/f		13,940	
Maximum capital allowances			203,060

3.6 Short and long periods of account

WDAs are 18% × number of months/12:

(a) For unincorporated businesses where the period of account is longer or shorter than 12 months

(b) For companies where the accounting period is shorter than 12 months (a company's accounting period for tax purposes is never longer than 12 months), or where the trade concerned started in the accounting period and was therefore carried on for fewer than 12 months. Remember that we will be studying companies in detail later in this text.

Question   Short period of account

Venus is a sole trader and has prepared accounts to 30 April each year. At 30 April 2018, the tax written down value of her main pool was £66,667. She decides to prepare her next set of accounts to 31 December 2018.

In the period to 31 December 2018, the following acquisitions were made:

1 May 2018	Plant	£146,666
10 July 2018	Car (CO_2 emissions 90 g/km)	£9,000
3 August 2018	Car (CO_2 emissions 45 g/km)	£11,000

Venus disposed of plant on 1 November 2018 for £20,000 (original cost £28,000).

Calculate the maximum capital allowances that Venus can claim for the period ending 31 December 2018.

	AIA £	FYA £	Main pool £	Allowances £
p/e 31 December 2018				
TWDV b/f			66,667	
Additions qualifying for AIA				
1.5.18 Plant	146,666			
AIA £200,000 × 8/12	(133,333)			133,333
	13,333			
Transfer balance to pool	(13,333)		13,333	
Additions qualifying for FYA				
3.8.18 Car (low emission)		11,000		
Less 100% FYA		(11,000)		11,000
Additions not qualifying for AIA nor FYA				
10.7.18 Car			9,000	
Disposals				
1.11.18 Plant			(20,000)	
			69,000	
WDA @ 18% × 8/12			(8,280)	8,280
TWDVs c/f			60,720	
Maximum allowances claim				152,613

Note that the annual investment allowance and the writing down allowance are reduced for the short period of account, but the first year allowance is given in full.

Question Long period of account

Oscar started trading on 1 July 2018 and prepared his first set of accounts to 31 December 2019. He bought the following assets:

1 July 2018	Plant	£250,000
10 October 2018	Car for business use only (CO₂ emissions 90g/km)	£11,000
12 February 2019	Plant	£115,000

Calculate the maximum capital allowances claim that Oscar can make for the period ended 31 December 2019. Assume the capital allowances rules in 2018/19 also apply in 2019/20.

Answer

	AIA £	Main pool £	Allowances £
p/e 31 December 2019			
Additions qualifying for AIA			
1.7.18 Plant	250,000		
12.2.19 Plant	115,000		
	365,000		
AIA £200,000 × 18/12	(300,000)		300,000
	65,000		
Transfer balance to main pool	(65,000)	65,000	
Additions not qualifying for AIA			
1.10.18 Car		11,000	
		76,000	
WDA @ 18% × 18/12		(20,520)	20,520
TWDV c/f		55,480	
Maximum capital allowances			320,520

Note that the AIA and the WDA are increased pro rata for the long period of account.

3.7 Small balance on main pool

A writing down allowance equal to unrelieved expenditure in the main pool (after adjusting for additions and disposals in the current period) can be claimed where this is **£1,000 or less for a 12 month period of account** (pro-rated for long or short period of account). If the maximum WDA is claimed, the main pool will then have a nil balance carried forward.

Question   Small balance on main pool

Alan has traded for many years, preparing accounts to 30 April each year. At 1 May 2018, the tax written down value of his main pool was £15,000.

On 1 October 2018, he sold some plant and machinery for £14,200 (original cost £16,000).

Calculate the maximum capital allowances claim that Alan can make for the year ending 30 April 2019. Assume the capital allowances rules in 2018/19 also apply in 2019/20.

Answer

	Main pool £	Allowances £
y/e 30 April 2019		
TWDV b/f	15,000	
Disposal	(14,200)	
	800	
WDA (small pool)	(800)	800
TWDV c/f	Nil	
Maximum capital allowances		800

Note the tax planning opportunities available. It may be important to buy plant just before an accounting date, so that allowances become available as soon as possible. Alternatively, it may be desirable to claim less than the maximum allowances to even out annual taxable profits and avoid a higher rate of tax in later years.

3.8 Balancing charges and allowances

Balancing charges occur when the disposal value deducted exceeds the balance remaining in the pool. The charge equals the excess and is effectively a negative capital allowance, increasing profits. Most commonly this happens when the trade ceases and the remaining assets are sold. It may also occur, however, whilst the trade is still in progress.

Balancing allowances on the main and special pools of expenditure arise only when the trade ceases. The balancing allowance is equal to the remaining unrelieved expenditure after deducting the disposal value of all the assets. Balancing allowances may also arise on single pool items (see below) whenever those items are disposed of.

4 Special rate pool

FAST FORWARD

The special rate pool contains expenditure on thermal insulation, long life assets, features integral to a building, solar panels, and cars with CO_2 emissions over 110g/km. The AIA can be used against such expenditure except cars. The WDA is 8% for a 12 month period.

4.1 Operation of the special rate pool

Expenditure on thermal insulation, long life assets, features integral to a building (see earlier in this chapter), **solar panels, and cars with CO_2 emissions over 110g/km, is not dealt with in the main pool but in a special rate pool.**

Exam focus point

The threshold of 110g/km applies for expenditure incurred on or after 1 April 2018. The examining team has stated that **a question will not be set** involving the threshold that applied prior to this date.

The annual investment allowance can apply to expenditure on such assets except on cars. The taxpayer can decide how to allocate the AIA. It will be more tax efficient to set the allowance against special rate pool expenditure in priority to main pool expenditure where there is expenditure on assets in both pools in the period.

The writing down allowance for the special rate pool is 8% for a twelve month period. As with the writing down allowance on the main pool, this is adjusted for short and long periods of account. Where the **unrelieved expenditure in the special rate pool** (after adjusting for additions and disposals in the current period) **is £1,000 or less for a 12 month period, a writing down allowance can be claimed of up to £1,000**. This amount is pro-rated for long and short periods. This is in addition to any similar claim in relation to the main pool (see earlier in this chapter).

4.2 Long life assets

Key term

Long life assets are assets with an expected working life of 25 years or more.

The **long life asset rules only apply to businesses whose total expenditure on assets with an expected working life of 25 years or more in a chargeable period is more than £100,000**. If the expenditure exceeds £100,000, the whole of the expenditure enters the special rate pool. For this purpose all expenditure incurred under a contract is treated as incurred in the first chargeable period to which that contract relates.

The £100,000 limit is reduced or increased proportionately in the case of a chargeable period of less or more than 12 months.

The following are **not** treated as long life assets:

(a) **Plant and machinery in dwelling houses, retail shops, showrooms, hotels and offices**

(b) **Cars**

4.3 Example: integral features

Lucy has been trading for many years, preparing accounts to 5 April each year. The tax written down value of her main pool at 5 April 2018 was £110,000. In the year to 5 April 2019, Lucy had the following expenditure:

10 June 2018	General plant costing £45,000
12 December 2018	Lighting system in shop £20,000
15 January 2019	Car for business use only (CO_2 emissions 125 g/km) £25,000
26 January 2019	Delivery van £15,000
4 March 2019	Lifts £182,500

The maximum capital allowances claim that Lucy can make for the year to 5 April 2019 is:

		AIA £	Main pool £	Special rate pool £	Allowances £
y/e 5 April 2019					
TWDV b/f			110,000		
Additions given AIA (best use)					
12.12.18	Lighting	20,000			
4.3.19	Lifts	182,500			
		202,500			
AIA		(200,000)			200,000
		2,500			
Transfer balance to special rate pool		(2,500)		2,500	
Additions not given AIA					
10.6.18	Plant		45,000		
26.1.19	Van		15,000		
Additions not qualifying for AIA					
15.1.19	Car			25,000	
			170,000	27,500	
WDA @ 18%			(30,600)		30,600
WDA @ 8%				(2,200)	2,200
TWDVs c/f			139,400	25,300	
Allowances					232,800

5 Private use assets

An asset which is used privately by a trader is dealt with in a single asset pool and the capital allowances are restricted.

An asset (for example, a car) which is used partly for private purposes by a sole trader or a partner is put into its own pool (single asset pool).

Capital allowances are calculated on the full cost. However, only the business use proportion of the allowances is allowed as a deduction from trading profits. This restriction applies to the AIA, FYAs, WDAs, balancing allowances and balancing charges.

An asset with some private use by an employee (not the owner of the business) suffers no such restriction. The employee may be taxed on an employment benefit (see earlier in this text) so the business receives capital allowances on the full cost of the asset.

Capital allowances on assets with some private use is a common exam topic. Check carefully whether the private use is by the owner of the business or by an employee.

Question

Capital allowances on private use asset

Jacinth has been in business as a sole trader for many years, preparing accounts to 31 March. On 1 November 2018 she bought computer equipment for £2,700 which she uses 75% in her business and 25% privately. She has already used the AIA against other expenditure in the year to 31 March 2019.

Calculate the maximum capital allowance that Jacinth can claim in respect to the computer equipment in the year to 31 March 2019.

Answer

	Computer equipment £	Allowances @ 75% £
y/e 31 March 2019		
Acquisition	2,700	
WDA @ 18%	(486)	365
TWDV c/f	2,214	
Maximum capital allowance on computer equipment		365

6 Motor cars

FAST FORWARD

Motor cars are generally dealt with in the special rate pool (cars emitting over 110g/km) or the main pool, unless there is private use by the trader.

As we have already seen, motor cars are categorised in accordance with their CO_2 emissions:

(a) **Cars emitting over 110g/km**: expenditure is added to the special rate pool,

(b) **Cars emitting between 51 and 110 g/km**: expenditure is added to the main pool,

(c) **Cars emitting 50 g/km or less**: expenditure eligible for 100% first year allowance, if allowance not claimed in full, excess added to main pool.

Cars with an element of private use are kept separate from the main and special pools and are dealt with in single asset pools. They are entitled to a WDA of 18% (car with CO_2 emissions between 51 and 110 g/km) or 8% (car with CO_2 emissions over 110 g/km).

Question

Capital allowances on private use car

Quodos started to trade on 1 July 2018, preparing accounts to 31 December 2018 and each 31 December thereafter. On 1 August 2018 he bought a car for £17,000 with CO_2 emissions of 90 g/km. The private use proportion is 10%. The car was sold in July 2020 for £4,000.

Calculate the capital allowances, assuming:

(a) The car was used by an employee; or
(b) The car was used by Quodos

and that the capital allowances rates in 2018/19 apply throughout.

(a)

	Main pool £	Allowances £
1.7.18–31.12.18		
Purchase price	17,000	
WDA 18% × 6/12 × £17,000	(1,530)	1,530
	15,470	
1.1.19–31.12.19		
WDA 18% × £15,470	(2,785)	2,785
	12,685	
1.1.20–31.12.20		
WDA 18% × £12,685	(2,283)	2,283
	10,402	
1.1.21–31.12.21		
Proceeds	(4,000)	
	6,402	
WDA 18% × £6,402	(1,152)	1,152
TWDV c/f	5,250	

The private use of the car by the employee has no effect on the capital allowances due to Quodos. The car will be placed in the main pool. No balancing allowance is available on the main pool until trade ceases even though the car has been sold.

(b)

	Car £	Allowances 90% £
1.7.18–31.12.18		
Purchase price	17,000	
WDA 18% × 6/12 × £17,000	(1,530)	1,377
	15,470	
1.1.19–31.12.19		
WDA 18% × £15,470	(2,785)	2,507
	12,685	
1.1.20–31.12.20		
WDA 18% × £12,685	(2,283)	2,055
	10,402	
1.1.21– 31.12.21		
Proceeds	(4,000)	
Balancing allowance	6,402	5,762

As the private use is by the proprietor, Quodos, only 90% of the WDAs and balancing allowance are available.

7 Short-life assets

Short life asset elections can bring forward the allowances due on an asset.

A trader can elect that specific items of plant, which are expected to have a short working life, be kept separately from the main pool.

Key term

> Any asset subject to this election is known as a **'short life asset'**, and the election is known as a 'de-pooling election'.

The election is irrevocable. For an unincorporated business, the time limit for electing is the 31 January which is 22 months after the end of the tax year in which the period of account of the expenditure ends. (For a company, it is two years after the end of the accounting period of the expenditure). **Short life asset treatment cannot be claimed for any motor cars, or plant used partly for non-trade purposes.**

The short life asset is kept in a single asset pool. Provided that the short life asset is disposed of **within eight years of the end of the accounting period** in which it was bought, a balancing charge or allowance arises on its disposal.

If the asset is not disposed of within this time period, its tax written down value is added to the main pool at the beginning of the next period of account (accounting period for companies). This will be after allowances have been claimed nine times on the asset; once in the period of acquisition and then each year for the following eight years. The election should therefore be made for assets likely to be sold for less than their tax written down values within eight years. It should not usually be made for assets likely to be sold within eight years for more than their tax written down values. There is no requirement to show from the outset that the asset will actually have a 'short life', so it is a matter of judgment whether the election should be made.

The Annual Investment Allowance can be set against short-life assets. The taxpayer can decide how to allocate the AIA. It will be more tax efficient to set the allowance against main pool expenditure in priority to short-life asset expenditure.

Question

Short life assets

Caithlin bought a machine for business use on 1 May 2018 for £9,000 and elected for de-pooling. She did not claim the AIA in respect of this asset. Her accounting year end is 30 April.

Calculate the capital allowances due if:

(a)   The asset is scrapped for £300 in August 2026
(b)   The asset is scrapped for £200 in August 2027

and assuming that the capital allowances rates in 2018/19 apply throughout.

(a) *Year to 30.4.19*   £
     Cost   9,000
       WDA 18%   (1,620)
                                                                                                      7,380

     Year to 30.4.20
       WDA 18%   (1,328)
                                                                                                      6,052

     Year to 30.4.21
       WDA 18%   (1,089)
                                                                                                      4,963

     Year to 30.4.22
       WDA 18%   (893)
                                                                                                      4,070

     Year to 30.4.23
       WDA 18%   (733)
                                                                                                      3,337

     Year to 30.4.24
       WDA 18%   (601)
                                                                                                      2,736

     Year to 30.4.25
       WDA 18%   (492)
                                                                                                      2,244

     Year to 30.4.26
       WDA 18%   (404)
                                                                                                      1,840

     Year to 30.4.27
       Disposal proceeds   (300)
       Balancing allowance   1,540

(b) If the asset is still in use at 30 April 2027, WDAs up to 30.4.26 will be as above. In the year to
     30.4.27, a WDA can be claimed of 18% × £1,840 = £331. The tax written down value of £1,840 −
     £331 = £1,509 will be added to the main pool at the beginning of the next period of account. The
     disposal proceeds of £200 will be deducted from the main pool in that period's capital allowances
     computation. No balancing allowance will arise and the main pool will continue.

8 Hire purchase and leasing

FAST FORWARD Capital allowances are available on assets acquired by hire purchase or long lease.

8.1 Assets on hire purchase or long term leases

**Any asset (including a car) bought on hire purchase (HP) is treated as if purchased outright for the
cash price.** Therefore:

(a) The buyer normally obtains **capital allowances on the cash price** when the agreement begins.
(b) He may write off the **finance charge as a trade expense** over the term of the HP contract.

Long term leases, (those with a term of 5 or more years), are treated in a similar way to HP transactions.

8.2 Other leases

If assets are leased and the term of the lease is less than 5 years, the lessee merely hires the asset over that period. The hire charge can normally be deducted in computing trade profits. If a car with emissions over 110g/km is leased, the maximum allowable deduction from trading profits for lease rentals is limited by 15% as described earlier in this text.

9 Cessation and succession

FAST FORWARD

Balancing adjustments usually apply when a business ceases.

9.1 Cessation of trade   12/13, 6/14, 9/16

Balancing adjustments arise on the cessation of a business. No **AIAs, FYAs or WDAs** are given **in the final period of account** (unincorporated businesses) or accounting period (companies – see later in this text).

Each asset is deemed to be disposed of on the date the trade ceased (usually at the then market value). Additions (if any) in the relevant period are brought in and then the disposal proceeds (limited to cost) are deducted from the balance of qualifying expenditure. **If the proceeds exceed the balance then a balancing charge arises. If the balance of qualifying expenditure exceeds the proceeds then a balancing allowance is given.**

9.2 Succession   9/16

FAST FORWARD

If a business is transferred to a connected person, the written down value of plant and machinery can be transferred thus avoiding a balancing charge.

Balancing charges may be avoided where the trade passes from one connected person to another. If a succession occurs both parties must elect if the avoidance of the balancing adjustments is required. **An election will result in the plant being transferred at its tax written down value for capital allowances purposes.** Even where a succession election is made, there is a cessation of trade so no allowances are available to the transferor in the final period in which the transfer of trade occurs.

If no election is made on a transfer of business to a connected person, usually assets are deemed to be sold at their market values if no proceeds are paid.

As we saw earlier, an individual is connected with their spouse, their, or their spouse's brothers, sisters, ancestors and lineal descendants, with their spouses, with business partners and their spouses and relatives, and with a company they control (either alone or in conjunction with persons connected with them). **'Spouses' includes civil partners.**

Where a person succeeds to a business under a will or on intestacy, then even if they were not connected with the deceased they may elect to take over the assets at the lower of their market value and their tax written down value.

For both connected persons transfers and transfers on death, where the elections are made, the limit on proceeds to be brought into account on a later sale of an asset is the original cost of the asset, not the deemed transfer price.

Exam focus point

Cessation and succession was tested in September 2016 question 3 Juanita. The examining team stated that 'The majority of candidates did not address the final part of the requirements relating to an explanation of the capital allowances available. There were two aspects to this; the first is the need to calculate a balancing adjustment in the final period, and explain why, in this case it is a balancing charge. The second relates to the 'beneficial election' which was referred to in this context in the requirements. This concerns the succession election to transfer assets at written down value when the business is transferred to her daughter. This is an important election, and one which Advanced Taxation (ATX – UK) candidates should always consider when a business is being transferred to a connected person.'

150   **7: Capital allowances** | Part A Income tax and national insurance contributions

BPP
LEARNING MEDIA

Chapter roundup

- Capital allowances are available on plant and machinery.

- Statutory rules generally exclude specified items from treatment as plant, rather than include specified items as plant.

- There are several cases on the definition of plant. To help you to absorb them, try to see the function/setting theme running through them.

- With capital allowances computations, the main thing is to get the layout right. Having done that, you will find that the figures tend to drop into place.

- Businesses are entitled to an annual investment allowance (AIA) of £200,000 for a 12 month period of account. Related businesses share one allowance between them.

- A first year allowance (FYA) at the rate of 100% is available on new low emission cars. Enhanced capital allowances (ECAs) are available on green technologies. FYAs and ECAs are never pro-rated in short periods of account.

- Most expenditure on plant and machinery qualifies for a WDA at 18% every 12 months.

- The special rate pool contains expenditure on thermal insulation, long life assets, features integral to a building, solar panels, and cars with CO_2 emissions over 110g/km. The AIA can be used against such expenditure. The WDA is 8% for a 12 month period.

- An asset which is used privately by a trader is dealt with in a single asset pool and the capital allowances are restricted.

- Motor cars are generally dealt with in the special rate pool (cars emitting over 110g/km) or the main pool, unless there is private use by the trader.

- Short life asset elections can bring forward the allowances due on an asset.

- Capital allowances are available on assets acquired by hire purchase or long lease.

- Balancing adjustments usually apply when a business ceases.

- If a business is transferred to a connected person, the written down value of plant and machinery can be transferred thus avoiding a balancing charge.

Quick quiz

1   For what periods are capital allowances for unincorporated businesses calculated?

2   Are writing down allowances pro-rated in a six month period of account?

3   Are first year allowances pro-rated in a six month period of account?

4   When may balancing allowances arise?

5   Within what period must an asset be disposed of if it is beneficial for it to be treated as a short life asset?

Answers to quick quiz

1   Periods of account

2   Yes. In a six month period, writing down allowance are pro-rated by multiplying by 6/12.

3   No. First year allowances are given in full in a short period of account.

4   Balancing allowances may arise in respect of pooled expenditure only when the trade ceases. Balancing allowances may arise on non-pooled items whenever those items are disposed of.

5   Within eight years of the end of the period of account (or accounting period) in which it was bought.

Now try the question below from the Practice Question Bank

Number	Level	Marks	Time
Q8	Introductory	10	20 mins

BPP
LEARNING MEDIA

8

Trading losses

Topic list	Syllabus reference
1 Losses – an overview	A1(a)B3
2 Carry forward trading loss relief	A1(a)B3
3 Trading loss relief against general income	A1(a)B3
4 Trade transferred to company	A1(d)(ii)
5 Early trading losses relief	A1(a)B3
6 Terminal trading loss relief	A1(a)B3
7 Share loss relief against general income	A2(f)(iv)

Introduction

In earlier chapters, we have seen how to compute taxable trading profits, after capital allowances, and allocate them to tax years.

Traders sometimes make losses rather than profits. In this chapter we consider the reliefs available for losses. A loss does not in itself lead to receiving tax back from HMRC. Relief is obtained by setting a loss against trading profits, against other income or against capital gains, so that tax need not be paid on them. There are restrictions on how much loss relief can be claimed in a tax year.

An important consideration is the choice between different reliefs. The aim is to use a loss to save as much tax as possible, as quickly as possible.

Finally, we consider how a loss on the disposal of shares in an unquoted trading company can be relieved against income in a similar fashion.

In the next chapter, we will see how individuals trading in partnership are taxed.

Study guide

		Intellectual level
1	**Income and income tax liabilities in situations involving further overseas aspects and in relation to trusts, and the application of exemptions and reliefs**	
(a)	The contents of the Taxation - United Kingdom (TX – UK) study guide for income tax and national insurance, under heading:	2
•	B3 Income from self employment	
(d)	Income from self employment:	3
(ii)	Advise on the relief available for trading losses following the transfer of a business to a company	
2	**Chargeable gains and capital gains tax liabilities in situations involving further overseas aspects and in relation to closely related persons and trusts together with the application of additional exemptions and reliefs**	
(f)	Gains and losses on the disposal of shares and securities:	
(iv)	Establish the relief for capital losses on shares in unquoted trading companies	3

Exam focus

There are various ways in which a trader can obtain relief for trading losses. You are likely to have to advise the most beneficial way of obtaining relief. This will involve considering the rate of tax relief, the potential waste of personal allowances, and how soon relief can be obtained. Read the question carefully to establish if the taxpayer has any particular requirements such as to obtain relief as soon as possible.

Knowledge brought forward from earlier studies

Trading losses have been covered in Taxation (TX – UK). The examining team has identified essential underpinning knowledge from the Taxation (TX – UK) syllabus which is particularly important that you revise as part of your Advanced Taxation (ATX – UK) studies. In this chapter, the relevant topics are:

		Intellectual level
B3	**Income from self-employment**	
(i)	Relief for trading losses	
(i)	Understand how trading losses can be carried forward	2
(ii)	Understand how trading losses can be claimed against total income and chargeable gains, and the restriction that can apply	2
(iii)	Explain and compute the relief for trading losses in the early years of a trade	1
(iv)	Explain and compute terminal loss relief	1
(v)	Recognise the factors that will influence the choice of loss relief claim	2

There are no changes in 2018/19 from 2017/18 in the material you have already studied at Taxation (TX – UK).

Loss relief on the transfer of a business to a company and share loss relief against general income is new in Advanced Taxation (ATX – UK).

1 Losses – an overview

FAST FORWARD

Trading losses may be relieved against future profits of the same trade, against general income and against capital gains.

1.1 Trading losses in general

This chapter considers how losses are calculated and how a loss-suffering taxpayer can use a loss to reduce their tax liability. Most of the chapter concerns losses in respect of trades, professions and vocations.

The rules in this chapter apply only to individuals, trading alone or in partnership. Loss reliefs for companies are completely different and are covered later in this text.

When computing taxable trading profits, profits may turn out to be negative, meaning a loss has been made in the basis period. **A loss is computed in exactly the same way as a profit**, making the same adjustments to the accounts profit or loss.

If there is a loss in a basis period, the taxable trading profits for the tax year based on that basis period are nil.

1.2 The computation of the loss

The trading loss for a tax year is the trading loss in the basis period for that tax year. However, **if basis periods overlap then a loss in the overlap period is a trading loss for the earlier tax year only**.

1.3 Example: computing the trading loss

Here is an example of a trader who starts to trade on 1 July 2018 and makes losses in opening years.

Period of account	Loss £
1.7.18 31.12.18	9,000
1.1.19–31.12.19	24,000

Tax year	Basis period	Working	Trading loss for the tax year £
2018/19	1.7.18–5.4.19	£9,000 + (£24,000 × 3/12)	15,000
2019/20	1.1.19–31.12.19	£24,000 – (£24,000 × 3/12)	18,000

1.4 Example: losses and profits

The same rule against using losses twice applies when losses are netted off against profits in the same basis period. Here is an example, again with a commencement on 1 July 2018 but with a different accounting date.

Period of account	(Loss)/profit £
1.7.18–30.4.19	(10,000)
1.5.19–30.4.20	24,000

Tax year	Basis period	Working	Trading (Loss)/Profit £
2018/19	1.7.18–5.4.19	£(10,000) × 9/10	(9,000)
2019/20	1.7.18–30.6.19	£(10,000) × 1/10 + £24,000 × 2/12	3,000

1.5 Other losses

Losses incurred in foreign trades are computed and relieved in a similar manner to those of UK trades and are discussed later in this text.

Losses from a UK property business have been discussed earlier, and losses on an overseas property business are relieved similarly. Losses on furnished holiday lettings can only be relieved using carry forward loss relief against future income from furnished holiday lettings. Losses on UK furnished holiday lettings and EEA furnished holiday lettings must be dealt with separately.

If a loss arises on a transaction which, if profitable, would give rise to taxable miscellaneous income (see earlier in this text), it can be set against any other similar income in the same year, and any excess carried forward for relief against miscellaneous income in future years.

1.6 Trading losses and Class 4 NIC

Trading losses can also be relieved against Class 4 NIC in the same way as for income tax. However, **relief can only be given against Class 4 NIC trading profits**. This may mean that losses are used differently for income tax and Class 4 NIC purposes where income tax loss relief is given against non-trading income.

2 Carry forward trading loss relief   12/14, 12/17

FAST FORWARD

A trading loss carried forward must be set against the first available profits of the same trade.

A trading loss not relieved in any other way must be **carried forward to set against the first available profits of the same trade** in the calculation of net trading income. Losses may be carried forward for any number of years.

2.1 Example: carrying forward losses

Ben has the following results.

Year ending	£
31 December 2016	(18,000)
31 December 2017	15,000
31 December 2018	33,000

Ben's net trading income, after carry forward loss relief, is:

	2016/17 £		2017/18 £		2018/19 £
Trading profits	0		15,000		33,000
Less carry forward loss relief	(0)	(i)	(15,000)	(ii)	(3,000)
Profits	0		0		30,000

Loss memorandum		
Trading loss 2016/17		18,000
Less: used in 2017/18	(i)	(15,000)
used in 2018/19 (balance of loss)	(ii)	(3,000)
		0

3 Trading loss relief against general income   12/14, 9/15, 12/17, 6/18

Where a loss relief claim is made, trading losses can be set against general income (and also gains if a further claim is made) in the current tax year and/or general income (and also gains if a further claim is made) in the preceding tax year.

3.1 Introduction

Instead of carrying a trading loss forward against future trading profits, it may be relieved against general income.

3.2 Relieving the loss

Relief is against the income of the tax year in which the loss arose. In addition or instead, relief may be claimed **against the income of the preceding year**.

If there are losses in two successive years, and relief is claimed against the first year's income both for the first year's loss and for the second year's loss, relief is given for the first year's loss before the second year's loss.

A claim for a loss must be made by the 31 January which is 22 months after the end of the tax year of the loss: so by 31 January 2021 for a loss in 2018/19.

The taxpayer **cannot choose the amount of loss to relieve**: so the loss may have to be set against income part of which would have been covered by the personal allowance or taxed at 0% in the savings income nil rate band or the dividend nil rate band. However, the taxpayer **can choose whether to claim full relief in the current year and then relief in the preceding year for any remaining loss**, or the **other way round**.

When calculating the income tax liability, the **loss is usually set against non-savings income, then against savings income and finally against dividend income**. However, as for deductible interest and the personal allowance, the loss should be **set against dividend income in priority to savings income in order to preserve the savings starting rate band and the savings income nil rate band.**

Relief is available by carry forward for any loss not relieved against general income.

Question	Loss relief against general income

Janet has a loss in her period of account ending 31 December 2018 of £36,000. Her other income is £30,000 dividend income, and she wishes to claim loss relief for the year of loss and then for the preceding year. Her trading income in the previous year was £nil. Show her taxable income for each year, and comment on the effectiveness of the loss relief. Assume that tax rates and allowances for 2018/19 have always applied.

Answer

The loss-making period ends in 2018/19, so the year of the loss is 2018/19.

	2017/18 £	2018/19 £
Dividend income	30,000	30,000
Less loss relief against general income	(6,000)	(30,000)
Net income	24,000	0
Less personal allowance	(11,850)	(11,850)
Taxable income	12,150	0

In 2018/19, £(2,000 + 11,850) = £13,850 of the loss has been wasted because that amount of income would have been covered by the personal allowance and the dividend nil rate band and the remainder of the loss will attract tax relief at the relatively low rate of 7.5%. If Janet claims loss relief against general income, there is nothing she can do about this inefficient use of loss relief.

3.3 Capital allowances

One of the competencies you require to fulfil Performance Objective 17 Tax planning and advice of the PER is to review the situation of an individual or entity advising on any potential tax risks and/or additional tax minimisation measures. You can apply the knowledge you obtain from this section of the text to help to demonstrate this competence.

The trader may adjust the size of the total loss relief claim by not claiming all the capital allowances they are entitled to: a reduced claim will increase the balance carried forward to the next year's capital allowances computation. This may be a useful **tax planning point where the effective rate of relief for capital allowances in future periods will be greater than the rate of tax relief for the loss relief.**

3.4 Trading losses relieved against capital gains

Where relief is claimed against general income of a given year, the taxpayer may include **a further claim to set the loss against their chargeable gains for the year** less any allowable capital losses for the same year or for previous years. This amount of net gains is computed ignoring the annual exempt amount (see later in this text).

The trading loss is first set against general income of the year of the claim, and only any excess of loss is set against capital gains. The taxpayer cannot specify the amount to be set against capital gains, so the annual exempt amount may be wasted. We include an example here for completeness. You will study chargeable gains later in this text and we suggest that you come back to this example at that point.

Question	Loss relief against income and gains

Sibyl had the following results for 2018/19.

	£
Loss available for loss relief against general income	27,000
Income	19,500
Capital gains less current year capital losses	11,400
Annual exempt amount for capital gains tax purposes	11,700
Capital losses brought forward	5,400

Show how the loss would be relieved against income and gains.

Answer

	£
Income	19,500
Less loss relief against general income	(19,500)
Net income	0
Capital gains	11,400
Less loss relief: lower of £(27,000 − 19,500) = £7,500 (note 1) and £(11,400 − 5,400) = £6,000 (note 2)	(6,000)
	5,400
Less annual exempt amount (restricted)	(5,400)
	0

Note 1. This equals the loss left after the loss relief against general income claim
Note 2. This equals the gains left after losses b/fwd but ignoring the annual exempt amount

A trading loss of £(7,500 – 6,000) = £1,500 is carried forward. Sibyl's personal allowance and £(11,700 – 5,400) = £6,300 of her capital gains tax annual exempt amount are wasted. Her capital losses brought forward of £5,400 are carried forward to 2019/20. Although we deducted this £5,400 in working out how much trading loss we were allowed to use in the claim, we do not actually use any of the £5,400 unless there are gains remaining in excess of the annual exempt amount.

3.5 Restrictions on trading loss relief against general income

3.5.1 Commercial basis

FAST FORWARD Loss relief cannot be claimed against general income unless the loss-making business is conducted on a commercial basis.

Relief cannot be claimed against general income unless the loss-making business is conducted on a commercial basis with a view to the realisation of profits throughout the basis period for the tax year.

3.5.2 Relief cap

FAST FORWARD An individual taxpayer can only deduct the greater of £50,000 and 25% of adjusted total income when making a claim for loss relief against general income.

There is a **restriction on certain deductions which may be made by an individual from total income for a tax year**. For Advanced Taxation (ATX – UK) purposes, the restricted deductions concern **trade loss relief against general income (whether claimed for the tax year of the loss or the previous year), early trading losses relief, share loss relief against general income** (these latter two reliefs are both dealt with later in this chapter), and **deduction of interest for qualifying purposes** (see earlier in this text).

The total deductions in a tax year cannot exceed the greater of:

(a)   **£50,000**; and

(b)   **25% of the taxpayer's adjusted total income for the tax year**.

Key term

> For the purposes of the Advanced Taxation (ATX – UK) examination, **adjusted total income** is total income less the gross amounts of personal pension contributions.

If a claim is made for relief against general income in the previous year, there is no restriction on the amount of loss that can be used against trading income (of the same trade). The restriction only applies to the other income in that year. Any loss which exceeds the maximum deduction can still be carried forward against future profits from the same trade.

The limits apply in each year for which relief is claimed. If a current year and a prior year claim are made, the relief in the current year is restricted to the greater of £50,000 and 25% of the adjusted total income in the current year. The relief in the prior year is restricted to the greater of £50,000 and 25% of the adjusted total income in the prior year.

The restriction only applies to relief against income, not if a claim is extended to capital gains.

 Question   Restriction on loss relief

Grace has been trading for many years, preparing accounts to 5 April each year. Her recent results have been as follows:

	Profit/(loss) £
Year to 5 April 2018	20,000
Year to 5 April 2019	(210,000)

Grace also owns a number of investment properties and her property business income is £130,000 in 2017/18 and £220,000 in 2018/19.

Show Grace's taxable income for the tax years 2017/18 and 2018/19 assuming that she claims relief for her trading loss against general income in both of those years and that the tax rates and allowances for 2018/19 have always applied.

Answer

	2017/18 £	2018/19 £
Trading income	20,000	0
Property business income	130,000	220,000
Total income	150,000	220,000
Less loss relief against general income	(70,000)	(55,000)
Net income	80,000	165,000
Less personal allowance	(11,850)	(0)
Taxable income	68,150	165,000

Loss relief for 2018/19 is capped at £(220,000 × 25%) = £55,000 since this is greater than £50,000. The personal allowance is not available as adjusted net income is at least £123,700.

In 2017/18 loss relief claim is not capped against the trading profit of £20,000. Relief against other income is capped at £50,000 since this is greater than £(150,000 × 25%) = £37,500. The total loss relief claim is therefore £(20,000 + 50,000) = £70,000. The balance of the loss is £(210,000 − 55,000 − 70,000) = £85,000 and is carried forward against future profits of the same trade.

Note that the restriction on loss relief means that the loss has been relieved at the additional rate in 2018/19 and at the higher rate in 2017/18. The personal allowance has also been restored for 2017/18.

3.6 The choice between loss reliefs

FAST FORWARD

It is important for a trader to choose the right loss relief, so as to save tax at the highest possible rate and so as to obtain relief reasonably quickly.

When a trader has a choice between loss reliefs, they should aim to obtain relief both quickly and at the highest possible tax rate. However, do consider that losses relieved against income which would otherwise be covered by the personal allowance are wasted.

Question

The choice between loss reliefs

Felicity's trading results are as follows.

Year ended 30 September	Trading profit/(loss) £
2016	5,500
2017	(21,000)
2018	15,100

Her other income (all non-savings income) is as follows.

	£
2016/17	4,900
2017/18	33,750
2018/19	16,750

Show the most efficient use of Felicity's trading loss. Assume that her personal allowance has been £11,850 throughout.

Relief could be claimed against general income for 2016/17 and/or 2017/18, with any unused loss being carried forward. Relief in 2016/17 would be against general income of £(5,500 + 4,900) = £10,400, all of which would be covered by the personal allowance anyway, so this claim should not be made. A loss relief claim against general income should be made for 2017/18 as this saves tax more quickly than carry forward loss relief in 2018/19 would. The final results will be as follows:

	2016/17 £	2017/18 £	2018/19 £
Trading income	5,500	0	15,100
Less carry forward loss relief	(0)	(0)	(0)
	5,500	0	15,100
Other income	4,900	33,750	16,750
	10,400	33,750	31,850
Less loss relief against general income	(0)	(21,000)	(0)
Net income	10,400	12,750	31,850
Less personal allowance	(11,850)	(11,850)	(11,850)
Taxable income	0	900	20,000

Exam focus point

Before recommending loss relief against general income consider whether it will result in the waste of the personal allowance, the nil rate bands for savings income and dividend income and any tax reducers. Such waste is to be avoided if at all possible.

Another consideration is that a trading loss cannot be set against the capital gains of a year unless relief is first claimed against general income of the same year. It may be worth making the claim against income and wasting the personal allowance in order to avoid a CGT liability. However, remember that using a loss against capital gains will only result in a maximum 28% tax saving, whereas setting losses against income can give a maximum 45% income tax saving and there may also be a saving of national insurance contributions.

Finally, it is important to consider how offsetting a loss against income will impact the taxation of any income which remains taxable. For example, setting a loss against non-savings income might mean that savings income becomes taxable at the starting rate, rather than the basic rate, or higher rate income becomes taxable at the basic rate.

3.7 Example

Luke has been in business as a sole trader for many years, preparing accounts to 31 December each year. In the year ended 31 December 2018, Luke made a profit of £23,850. He anticipates that he will make a loss of £(12,000) in the year ending 31 December 2019. In 2018/19, Luke received interest of £7,000. He will have no other income in 2019/20, so no claim can be made to set off the loss in that tax year. Before the loss relief claim, Luke's income tax liability in 2018/19 is as follows:

	Non-savings income £	Savings income £	Total £
Trading income	23,850		
Interest		7,000	
Total/net income	23,850	7,000	30,850
Less personal allowance	(11,850)		
Taxable income	12,000	7,000	19,000

	Non-savings income £	Savings income £	Total £
Tax			
Non-savings income			
£12,000 × 20%	2,400		
Savings income			
£1,000 × 0% (basic rate taxpayer)	0		
£6,000 (7,000 − 1,000) × 20%	1,200		
Income tax liability	3,600		

If loss relief is claimed against general income for 2018/19, Luke's income tax liability will be:

	Non-savings income	Savings Income	Total
Total income	23,850	7,000	30,850
Less carry back loss	(12,000)		
Net income	11,850	7,000	18,850
Less personal allowance	(11,850)		
Taxable income	0	7,000	7,000

Tax	
Savings income	
£5,000 × 0% (starting rate)	0
£1,000 × 0% (savings income nil rate – basic rate taxpayer)	0
£1,000 (7,000 − 5,000 − 1,000) × 20%	200
Income tax liability	200

The tax saved by making the loss relief claim is therefore £(3,600 − 200) = £3,400, which is 28.3% of the loss.

4 Trade transferred to company

FAST FORWARD

> If a business is transferred to a company, a loss of the unincorporated business can be set against income received from the company.

Although carry forward loss relief is restricted to future profits of the same business, this is extended to cover income received from a company to which the business is sold.

The amount carried forward is the total unrelieved trading losses of the business. The set-off must be made against the first available income from the company, including dividends, interest and salary.

Set-off the loss against non-savings income or savings income and then against dividend income.

The consideration for the transfer of the business must be wholly or mainly in the form of shares (at least 80%) which must be retained by the vendor throughout any tax year in which the loss is relieved.

5 Early trading losses relief   9/15, 6/17, 12/17, 6/18

FAST FORWARD

> In opening years, a special relief involving the carry back of losses against general income is available. Losses arising in the first four tax years of a trade may be set against general income in the three years preceding the loss making year, taking the earliest year first.

Early trading losses relief is available for **trading losses incurred in the first four tax years of a trade.**

Relief is obtained by **setting the allowable loss against general income in the three years preceding the year of loss**, applying the loss to the earliest year first. Thus a loss arising in 2018/19 may be set off against income in 2015/16, 2016/17 and 2017/18 in that order.

A claim for early trading losses relief applies to all three years automatically, provided that the loss is large enough. The taxpayer cannot choose to relieve the loss against just one or two of the years, or choose to relieve only part of the loss. However, the relief cap which was discussed earlier in this chapter, restricting loss relief against other income, also applies here. This means that losses may be restricted by the cap in earlier years (leaving some income left in charge) with the result that the remaining losses will be available for use in later years, again subject to the cap. Also, the taxpayer has some control as they could reduce the size of the loss by not claiming the full capital allowances available to them. This will result in higher capital allowances in future years.

Do not double count a loss. If basis periods overlap, a loss in the overlap period is treated as a loss for the earlier tax year only.

Claims for the relief must be made by the 31 January which is 22 months after the end of the tax year in which the loss is incurred.

The 'commercial basis' test is stricter for this loss relief. The trade must be carried on in such a way that profits could reasonably have been expected to be realised in the period of the loss or within a reasonable time thereafter.

Question   Early trade losses relief

Aran is employed as a refuse collector until 1 January 2017. On that date he starts up his own business as a scrap metal merchant, making up his accounts to 30 June each year. His earnings as a refuse collector are:

	£
2013/14	15,000
2014/15	18,000
2015/16	21,000
2016/17 (nine months)	18,000

His trading results as a scrap metal merchant are:

	Profit/(Loss) £
Six months to 30 June 2017	(9,000)
Year to 30 June 2018	(4,500)
Year to 30 June 2019	(3,600)

Assuming that loss relief is claimed as early as possible, show the final net income for each of the years 2013/14 to 2019/20 inclusive.

Answer

Since reliefs are to be claimed as early as possible, early trading losses relief is applied. The losses available for relief are as follows.

	£	£	Years against which relief is available
2016/17 (basis period 1.1.17–5.4.17)			
3 months to 5.4.17 £(9,000) × 3/6		(4,500)	2013/14 to 2015/16
2017/18 (basis period 1.1.17–31.12.17)			
6 months to 30.6.17			
(omit 1.1.17–5.4.17: overlap) £(9,000) × 3/6	(4,500)		
6 months to 31.12.17 £(4,500) × 6/12	(2,250)		
		(6,750)	2014/15 to 2016/17

			Years against which relief is available
	£	£	
2018/19 (basis period 1.7.17–30.6.18)			
12 months to 30.6.18			
(omit 1.7.17–31.12.17: overlap) £(4,500) × 6/12		(2,250)	2015/16 to 2017/18
2019/20 (basis period 1.7.18–30.6.19)			
12 months to 30.6.19		(3,600)	2016/17 to 2018/19

The net income is as follows.

		£	£
2013/14			
	Original	15,000	
	Less 2016/17 loss	(4,500)	
			10,500
2014/15			
	Original	18,000	
	Less 2017/18 loss	(6,750)	
			11,250
2015/16			
	Original	21,000	
	Less 2018/19 loss	(2,250)	
			18,750
2016/17			
	Original	18,000	
	Less 2019/20 loss	(3,600)	
			14,400

The taxable trading profits for 2016/17 to 2019/20 are zero. There were losses in the basis periods.

6 Terminal trading loss relief   6/15

FAST FORWARD

On the cessation of trade, a loss arising in the last 12 months of trading may be set against trading profits of the tax year of cessation and the previous 3 years, taking the last year first.

Loss relief against general income will often be insufficient on its own to deal with a loss incurred in the last months of trading. For this reason there is a special relief, **terminal trading loss relief, which allows a loss on cessation to be carried back for relief against taxable trading profits in previous years.**

6.1 Computing the terminal loss

A terminal loss is **the loss of the last 12 months of trading.**

It is built up as follows.

		£
(a)	The actual trading loss for the tax year of cessation (calculated from 6 April to the date of cessation)	X
(b)	The actual trading loss for the period from 12 months before cessation until the end of the penultimate tax year	X
	Total terminal loss	X

If either (a) or (b) above yields a profit rather than a loss, the profit is treated as zero.

Any unrelieved overlap profits are included within (a) above.

If any loss cannot be included in the terminal loss (eg because it is matched with a profit) it can be relieved instead by the loss relief against general income.

6.2 Relieving the terminal loss

Relief is given in the tax year of cessation and the three preceding years, later years first.

Question
Terminal loss relief

Set out below are the results of a business up to its cessation on 30 September 2018.

	Profit/(loss) £
Year to 31 December 2015	10,000
Year to 31 December 2016	8,000
Year to 31 December 2017	3,000
Nine months to 30 September 2018	(9,600)

Overlap profits on commencement were £4,500. These were all unrelieved on cessation.

Show the available terminal loss relief, and suggest an alternative claim if the trader had had other non-savings income of £26,200 in each of 2017/18 and 2018/19. Assume that 2018/19 tax rates and allowances apply to all years.

Answer

The terminal loss comes in the last 12 months, the period 1 October 2017 to 30 September 2018. This period is split as follows.

2017/18	Six months to 5 April 2018
2018/19	Six months to 30 September 2018

The terminal loss is made up as follows.

Unrelieved trading losses		£	£
2018/19			
6 months to 30.9.18	£(9,600) × 6/9		(6,400)
Overlap relief			(4,500)
2017/18			
3 months to 31.12.17	£3,000 × 3/12	750	
3 months to 5.4.18	£(9,600) × 3/9	(3,200)	
			(2,450)
			(13,350)

Taxable trading profits will be as follows.

Year	Basis period	Profits £	Terminal loss relief £	Final taxable profits £
2015/16	Y/e 31.12.15	10,000	2,350	7,650
2016/17	Y/e 31.12.16	8,000	8,000	0
2017/18	Y/e 31.12.17	3,000	3,000	0
2018/19	1.1.18–30.9.18	0	0	0
			13,350	

If the trader had had £26,200 of other income in 2017/18 and 2018/19 we could consider loss relief claims against general income for these two years, using the loss of £(9,600 + 4,500) = £14,100.

The final results would be as follows if a claim was made for 2017/18 (We could alternatively claim loss relief in 2018/19, but a claim in either year would save income tax at the same (basic) rate, so the preference is to save tax earlier rather than later).

	2015/16 £	2016/17 £	2017/18 £	2018/19 £
Trading profits	10,000	8,000	3,000	0
Other income	0	0	26,200	26,200
	10,000	8,000	29,200	26,200
Less loss relief against general income	0	0	(14,100)	0
Net income	10,000	8,000	15,100	26,200

Another option would be to make a loss relief claim against general income for the balance of the loss not relieved as a terminal loss of £(14,100 – 13,350) = £750 in either 2017/18 or 2018/19.

However, once the personal allowance has been deducted there is only taxable income in 2017/18 and 2018/19 so the full claim against general income is more tax efficient than the terminal loss relief claim.

7 Share loss relief against general income

FAST FORWARD

Capital losses arising on certain unquoted shares can be set against general income of the year of the loss and/or against general income of the preceding year.

Relief is available for capital losses on shares in unquoted trading companies (originally **subscribed for**) against general income of the taxpayer for the year **in which the loss arose and/or the preceding year.**

In summary, the relief is only available if the shares satisfy the conditions of the Enterprise Investment Scheme or the Seed Enterprise Investment Scheme (see earlier in this text). It is not, however, necessary for income tax relief to have been claimed on the shares.

A claim must be made by 31 January 22 months after the end of the year of the loss.

The relief cap, discussed earlier in this chapter, applies to this loss relief.

Chapter roundup

- Trading losses may be relieved against future profits of the same trade, against general income and against capital gains.

- A trading loss carried forward must be set against the first available profits of the same trade.

- Where a loss relief claim is made, trading losses can be set against general income (and also gains if a further claim is made) in the current tax year and/or general income (and also gains if a further claim is made) in the preceding tax year.

- Loss relief cannot be claimed against general income unless the loss-making business is conducted on a commercial basis.

- An individual taxpayer can only deduct the greater of £50,000 and 25% of adjusted total income when making a claim for loss relief against general income.

- It is important for a trader to choose the right loss relief, so as to save tax at the highest possible rate and so as to obtain relief reasonably quickly.

- If a business is transferred to a company, a loss of the unincorporated business can be set against income received from the company.

- In opening years, a special relief involving the carry back of losses against general income is available. Losses arising in the first four tax years of a trade may be set against general income in the three years preceding the loss making year, taking the earliest year first.

- On the cessation of trade, a loss arising in the last 12 months of trading may be set against trading profits of the tax year of cessation and the previous 3 years, taking the last year first.

- Capital losses arising on certain unquoted shares can be set against general income of the year of the loss and/or against general income of the preceding year.

Quick quiz

1   Against what income can trading losses carried forward be set off?

2   When a loss is to be relieved against total income, how are losses linked to particular tax years?

3   Against which years' total income may a loss be relieved against general income for a continuing business which has traded for many years?

4   Maggie has been trading as a decorator for many years. In 2017/18 she made a trading profit of £12,000. She has property business income of £6,000 each year. She makes no capital gains.

    Maggie makes a loss of £(30,000) in 2018/19 and expects to make either a loss or smaller profits in the foreseeable future. How can Maggie obtain loss relief?

5   For which losses is early years trading loss relief available?

6   In which years may relief for a terminal loss be given?

Answers to quick quiz

1   Against profits from the same trade.

2   The loss for a tax year is the loss in the basis period for that tax year. However, if basis periods overlap, a loss in the overlap period is a loss of the earlier tax year only.

3   The year in which the loss arose and/or the preceding year.

4   Maggie could make a claim to set the loss against general income of £6,000 in 2018/19, but should not do so, as this amount will be covered by the personal allowance. She can claim loss relief against general income of £(12,000 + 6,000) = £18,000 in 2017/18. The remaining £(30,000 − 18,000) = £12,000 will be carried forward and set against the first available trading profits of her decorating trade.

5   Losses incurred in the first four tax years of a trade.

6   In the year of cessation and then in the three preceding years, later years first.

Now try the question below from the Practice Question Bank

Number	Level	Marks	Time
Q9	Introductory	25	49 mins

Partnerships and limited liability partnerships

Topic list	Syllabus reference
1 Assessment of partnership to tax	A1(a)B3
2 Change in profit sharing ratios	A1(a)B3
3 Change in membership of partnership	A1(a)B3
4 Loss reliefs for partners	A1(a)B3

Introduction

In the previous chapters, we have dealt with the income tax rules for sole traders. We now see how those rules are adapted to deal with business partnerships.

On the one hand, a partnership is a single trading entity, making profits as a whole. On the other hand, each partner has a personal tax computation, so the profits must be apportioned to the partners. The general approach is to work out the profits of the partnership, then tax each partner as if they were a sole trader running a business equal to their slice of the partnership (for example 25% of the partnership).

This concludes our study of the different types of UK income to be included in an income tax computation. In the following chapter we will turn our attention to the overseas aspects of income tax.

Study guide

		Intellectual level
1	Income and income tax liabilities in situations involving further overseas aspects and in relation to trusts, and the application of exemptions and reliefs	
(a)	The contents of the Taxation - United Kingdom (TX – UK) study guide for income tax and national insurance, under heading:	2
•	B3 Income from self employment	

Exam guide

A question involving any aspect of unincorporated businesses may deal with a partnership rather than a sole trader. The principles are exactly the same, whether you are considering incremental income, possible claims for capital allowances or loss reliefs. Just remember that profits are apportioned to partners in the profit sharing ratio for the period of account after allocating interest on capital and/or salaries.

Knowledge brought forward from earlier studies

This chapter is revision of the partnership rules covered in Taxation (TX – UK).

There are no changes in 2018/19 from 2017/18 in the material you have already studied.

1 Assessment of partnership to tax

3/16

FAST FORWARD

A partnership is simply treated as a source of profits and losses for trades being carried on by the individual partners. Divide profits or losses between the partners according to the profit sharing ratio in the period of account concerned. If any of the partners are entitled to a salary or interest on capital, apportion this first, not forgetting to pro-rate in periods of less than 12 months.

1.1 Introduction

One of the competencies you require to fulfil Performance Objective 15 Tax computations and assessments of the PER is to prepare or contribute to the computation or assessment of tax computations for individuals. You can apply the knowledge you obtain from this section of the text to help to demonstrate this competence.

A partnership is **a group of individuals who are trading together.** They will agree amongst themselves how the business should be run and how profits and losses should be shared. A **partnership is not treated as a separate entity from the partners for tax purposes** (in contrast to a company where shareholders and directors are taxed separately from the company). Most partnerships have **unlimited liability** of the partners for the debts of the partnership.

It is possible to set up a **limited liability partnership** (LLP) where the **liability of the partners for debts of the partnership are limited**. A LLP is a legal person in its own right (similar to a company). However, **limited liability partnerships and their partners are generally taxed on the same basis as unlimited partnerships**, as described in the rest of this chapter.

1.2 Computing partnership profits

A partnership is treated like a sole trader when computing its profits. Partners' salaries and interest on capital are not deductible expenses and must be added back in computing profits, because they are a form of drawings.

Where the partners own assets (such as their cars) individually, a capital allowances computation must be prepared in respect of the assets the partners own (not forgetting any adjustment for private use). The capital allowances must go into the partnership's tax computation.

1.3 Allocating partnership profits between partners

Once the partnership's profits for a period of account have been computed, they are shared between the partners according to the profit sharing arrangements for that period of account.

Question — Allocating profits

Steve and Tanya have been in partnership for many years. For the year ended 31 October 2018, taxable trading profits were £70,000. Steve is allocated an annual salary of £12,000 and Tanya's salary is £28,000. The profit sharing ratio is 2:1.

Allocate the trade profit to each partner for the year ended 31 October 2018.

Answer

Allocate the profits for the year ended 31 October 2018.

	Total £	Steve £	Tanya £
Profit	70,000		
Salaries	40,000	12,000	28,000
Balance (2:1)	30,000	20,000	10,000
Total	70,000	32,000	38,000

1.4 Tax position of individual partners

Each partner is taxed like a sole trader who runs a business which:

- Starts when they join the partnership
- Finishes when they leave the partnership
- Has the same periods of account as the partnership (except that a partner who joins or leaves during a period will have a period which starts or ends part way through the partnership's period)
- Makes profits or losses equal to the partner's share of the partnership's profits or losses.

Exam focus point

Partners are effectively taxed in the same way as sole traders with just one difference. Before you tax the partner you need to take each set of accounts (as adjusted for tax purposes) and divide the trade profit (or loss) between each partner.

Then carry on as normal for a sole trader – each partner is treated as a sole trader in respect of their trade profits for each period of account.

2 Change in profit sharing ratios

The profits for a period of account are allocated between the partners according to the profit sharing agreement. If the salaries, interest on capital and profit sharing ratio change during the period of account the profits are time apportioned to the periods before and after the change and allocated accordingly. The constituent elements are then added together to give each partner's share of profits for the period of account.

Sue and Tim have been in partnership for many years. For the year ended 31 December 2018, taxable trading profits were £50,000. Sue is allocated an annual salary of £10,000 and Tim's salary is £15,000.

The profit sharing ratio was 1:1 until 31 August 2018 when it changed to 1:2 with no provision for salaries.

Allocate the trade profit to each partner for the year ended 31 December 2018.

Answer

Allocate the profits for the year ended 31 December 2018.

	Total £	Sue £	Tim £
Profit	50,000		
1 January–31 August (8 months)	33,333		
Salaries (8/12 × £10,000/£15,000)	16,667	6,667	10,000
Balance (1:1)	16,666	8,333	8,333
	33,333		
a	16,667		
Salaries	Nil	–	–
Balance (1:2)	16,667	5,556	11,111
	16,667		
Total	50,000	20,556	29,444

Note. Since the profit sharing arrangements changed part way through the period of account, the profits and salaries for the period of account must be pro-rated accordingly.

3 Change in membership of partnership   6/12, 6/18

FAST FORWARD

> The commencement and cessation rules apply to partners individually when they join or leave.

When a trade continues but partners join or leave (including cases when a sole trader takes in partners or a partnership breaks up leaving only one partner as a sole trader), **the special rules for basis periods in opening and closing years do not apply to the people who were carrying on the trade both before and after the change. They carry on using the period of account ending in each tax year as the basis period for the tax year ie the current year basis. The commencement rules only affect joiners, and the cessation rules only affect leavers.**

However, when no one same individual carries on the trade both before and after the change, as when a partnership transfers its trade to a completely new owner or set of owners, the cessation rules apply to the old owners and the commencement rules apply to the new owners.

 Question   Partner joining partnership

Daniel and Ashley have been in partnership for many years preparing accounts to 31 December each year and sharing profits in the ratio 2:1.

On 1 June 2018, Kate joined the partnership. From that date, profits were shared Daniel 50% and Ashley and Kate 25% each.

The partnership profits for the year ended 31 December 2018 were £72,000 and for the year ended 31 December 2019 were £90,000.

Compute the partnership profits taxable on Daniel, Ashley and Kate for 2018/19 and 2019/20 and the overlap profits for Kate on commencement.

Allocation of partnership profits

	Total £	Daniel £	Ashley £	Kate £
y/e 31.12.18				
1.1.18–31.5.18				
Profits (5/12) 2:1	30,000	20,000	10,000	n/a
1.6.18–31.12.18				
Profits (7/12) 50:25:25	42,000	21,000	10,500	10,500
Profit allocation	72,000	41,000	20,500	10,500
y/e 31.12.19				
Profits 50:25:25	90,000	45,000	22,500	22,500

Taxable partnership profits for 2018/19 and 2019/20

	Daniel £	Ashley £	Kate £
2018/19			
CYB y/e 31.12.18	41,000	20,500	
First year – actual basis			
1.6.18–31.12.18			10,500
1.1.19–5.4.19			
3/12 × £22,500			5,625
			16,125

	Daniel £	Ashley £	Kate £
2019/20			
CYB y/e 31.12.19	45,000	22,500	
Second year – 12 months to 31.12.19			22,500

Overlap profits

Kate has overlap profits for the period 1.1.19 to 5.4.19 of £5,625.

Maxwell, Laura and Wesley traded in partnership for many years, preparing accounts to 30 September.

Each partner was entitled to 5% interest per annum on capital introduced into the partnership. Each partner had introduced £60,000 of capital on the commencement of the partnership. From that date, profits were shared in the ratio 50% to Maxwell, 30% to Laura and 20% to Wesley.

On 1 May 2018, Wesley left the partnership. From that date profits were shared equally between the two remaining partners and no interest was paid on capital. The partnership taxable trading income for the year to 30 September 2018 was £120,000. Wesley had overlap profits on commencement of £5,000.

Compute the partnership profits taxable on Maxwell, Laura and Wesley for 2018/19.

Answer

Allocation of partnership profits

	Total £	Maxwell £	Laura £	Wesley £
1.10.17–30.4.18				
Interest 7/12 × £60,000 × 5% each	5,250	1,750	1,750	1,750
Profits (7/12) 50:30:20	64,750	32,375	19,425	12,950
	70,000	34,125	21,175	14,700

	Total £	Maxwell £	Laura £	Wesley £
1.5.18–30.9.18				
Profits (5/12) 1:1	50,000	25,000	25,000	n/a
Profits allocated for year	120,000	59,125	46,175	14,700

Taxable partnership profits for 2018/19

	Maxwell £	Laura £	Wesley £
2018/19			
CYB y/e 30.9.18	59,125	46,175	
Final year			
1.10.17– 30.4.18			14,700
Less overlap relief			(5,000)
			9,700

Exam focus point

The tax treatment of a new partner was tested in June 2012 Question 4(b) Tetra. The examining team commented that 'This question required knowledge of the opening year rules, the allocation of profits between partners and the calculation of national insurance. It was done well. Common errors included the treatment of the partner's salary as employment income rather than trading income and the failure to adjust the profit for the partners' salaries before splitting the remainder between the partners.'

4 Loss reliefs for partners   6/18

FAST FORWARD

Partners are entitled to the same loss reliefs as sole traders and make independent loss relief claims.

Partners are entitled to the same loss reliefs as sole traders. Partners may claim loss reliefs in different ways.

Partners are entitled to **early trade losses relief for losses in the four tax years starting with the year in which they are treated as starting to trade** and they are entitled to **terminal loss relief when they are treated as ceasing to trade**. This is so even if the partnership trades for many years before the partner joins or after they leave.

Loss relief against general income and carry forward loss relief is also available to partners.

When a **partnership business is transferred to a company**, each partner can **carry forward their share of any unrelieved losses against income from the company.**

Question   Partnership losses

Mary and Natalie have been trading for many years sharing profits equally. On 1 January 2019 Mary retired and Oliver joined the partnership. Natalie and Oliver share profits in the ratio of 2:1. Although the partnership had previously been profitable it made a loss of £24,000 for the year to 31 March 2019. The partnership is expected to be profitable in the future.

Calculate the loss accruing to each partner for 2018/19 and explain what reliefs are available.

We must first share the loss for the period of account between the partners.

	Total £	Mary £	Natalie £	Oliver £
y/e 31.3.19				
1.4.18–31.12.18				
Total £24,000 × 9/12	(18,000)	(9,000)	(9,000)	
1.1.19–31.3.18				
Total £24,000 × 3/12	(6,000)		(4,000)	(2,000)
Total for y/e 31.03.19	(24,000)	(9,000)	(13,000)	(2,000)

Mary

For 2018/19, Mary has a loss of £9,000. She may claim relief against general income of 2018/19 and/or 2017/18 and may extend the claim to capital gains.

Mary has ceased trading and may instead claim terminal loss relief. The terminal loss will be £9,000 (a profit arose in the period 1.1.18–31.3.18 which would be treated as zero) and this may be set against her taxable trade profits for 2018/19 (£nil), 2017/18, 2016/17 and 2015/16.

Natalie

For 2018/19, Natalie has a loss of £13,000. She may claim relief against general income of 2018/19 and/or 2017/18 and may extend the claim to capital gains. Any loss remaining unrelieved may be carried forward against future income from the same trade.

Oliver

Oliver's loss for 2018/19 is £2,000. He may claim relief for the loss against general income (and gains) of 2018/19 and/or 2017/18. As he has just started to trade he may claim relief for the loss against general income of 2015/16, 2016/17 and 2017/18. Any loss remaining unrelieved may be carried forward against future income from the same trade.

Chapter roundup

- A partnership is simply treated as a source of profits and losses for trades being carried on by the individual partners. Divide profits or losses between the partners according to the profit sharing ratio in the period of account concerned. If any of the partners are entitled to a salary or interest on capital, apportion this first, not forgetting to pro-rate in periods of less than 12 months.

- The commencement and cessation rules apply to partners individually when they join or leave.

- Partners are entitled to the same loss reliefs as sole traders and make independent loss relief claims.

Quick quiz

1   How are limited liability partnerships subject to tax?

2   How are partnership trading profits divided between the individual partners?

3   Janet and John are partners sharing profits 60:40. For the years ended 30 June 2018 and 2019 the partnership made profits of £100,000 and £150,000 respectively. What are John's taxable trading profits in 2018/19?

4   Pete and Doug have been partners for many years sharing profits equally. On 1 January 2018 Dave joins the partnership and it is agreed to share profits 40:40:20. For the year ended 30 June 2018 profits are £100,000. What is Doug's share of these profits?

5   What loss reliefs are partners entitled to?

Answers to quick quiz

1 In general, limited liability partnerships are taxed in the same way as unlimited partnerships.

2 Profits are divided in accordance with the profit sharing ratio that existed during the period of account in which the profits arose.

3 £40,000.

   2018/19: y/e 30 June 2018

   £100,000 × 40% = £40,000.

4 £45,000

	Pete £	Doug £	Dave £
Ye 30 June 2018			
1.7.17–31.12.17			
6m × 100,000			
£50,000 50:50	25,000	25,000	
1.1.18–30.6.18			
6m × £100,000			
£50,000 40:40:20	20,000	20,000	10,000
	45,000	45,000	10,000

5 Partners are entitled to the same loss reliefs as sole traders. These are loss relief against general income, early years trade loss relief, carry forward loss relief, terminal loss relief, and loss relief on transfer of a trade to a company.

Now try the question below from the Practice Question Bank

Number	Level	Marks	Time
Q10	Introductory	25	49 mins

10

Overseas aspects of income tax

Topic list	Syllabus reference
1 Residence and domicile	A1(a)B1,(b)(i),(iii)
2 Liability to UK income tax	A1(b)(i),(ii),(iv)
3 Double taxation relief (DTR)	A1(b)(v),(vi)

Introduction

In the previous chapters, we have studied most aspects of income tax. In this chapter we will look at the overseas aspects of income tax.

We start this chapter, by considering where taxpayers are resident and domiciled. We then consider how this affects their tax position. Finally, we look at the tax relief which can be available when income is taxed both overseas and in the UK.

In the next chapter, will we turn our attention to CGT. We will consider the administration of income tax when we have finished studying CGT as the personal tax return deals with both income and capital gains.

Study guide

		Intellectual level
1	**Income and income tax liabilities in situations involving further overseas aspects and in relation to trusts, and the application of exemptions and reliefs**	
(a)	The contents of the Taxation (TX – UK) study guide for income tax and national insurance contributions, under headings:	2
•	B1 The scope of income tax	
(b)	The scope of income tax:	3
(i)	Explain and apply the concepts of residence, domicile and deemed domicile and advise on the relevance to income tax	
(ii)	Advise on the availability of the remittance basis to UK resident individuals	2
(iii)	Advise on the tax position of individuals coming to and leaving the UK	
(iv)	Determine the income tax treatment of overseas income	
(v)	Understand the relevance of the OECD model double tax treaty to given situations	
(vi)	Calculate and advise on the double taxation relief available to individuals	

Exam guide

In an exam, question you may have to advise an individual how they will be taxed on their income from overseas. You may also need to advise an individual who has gone overseas how they will be taxed on their UK income, or how a taxpayer who is not domiciled in the UK is taxed on their non-UK income whilst they are resident in the UK. You must be sure that you can correctly determine an individual's residence and domicile status.

Knowledge brought forward from earlier studies

The topics covered in this chapter are mostly new in Advanced Taxation (ATX – UK), apart from the basic knowledge of the test of residence which is in the Taxation (TX – UK) syllabus.

Exam focus point

> **ACCA's article International aspects of personal taxation for Advanced Taxation (ATX – UK),** written by a member of the Advanced Taxation (ATX – UK) examining team, begins with some basic rules, an understanding of which enables the particular areas of tax affected by an individual coming to, or leaving, the UK to be identified. It then goes on to review those areas in some detail, and provides a clear set of questions to ask in order to determine an individual's liability to UK taxes. Finally, it deals briefly with the impact of double tax relief and treaties.

1 Residence and domicile

An individual may be both, or either of, resident and domiciled in the UK.

 PER alert

One of the competencies you require to fulfil Performance Objective 15 Tax computations and assessment of the PER is to explain the basis of tax calculations, and interpret the effect of current legislation and case law. You can apply the knowledge you obtain from this section of the text to help to demonstrate this competence.

1.1 Residence
12/14, 6/15, 9/16, 6/18, 6/19

1.1.1 Statutory residence test

FAST FORWARD

An individual will automatically not be UK resident if they meet any of the automatic overseas tests. An individual, who does not meet any of the automatic overseas tests, will automatically be UK resident if they meet any of the automatic UK tests. An individual who has not met any of the automatic overseas tests nor any of the automatic UK tests will be UK resident if they meet the sufficient ties test.

Statute sets out a test to determine whether or not an individual is UK resident in a tax year.

The **operation of the test** can be summarised as follows.

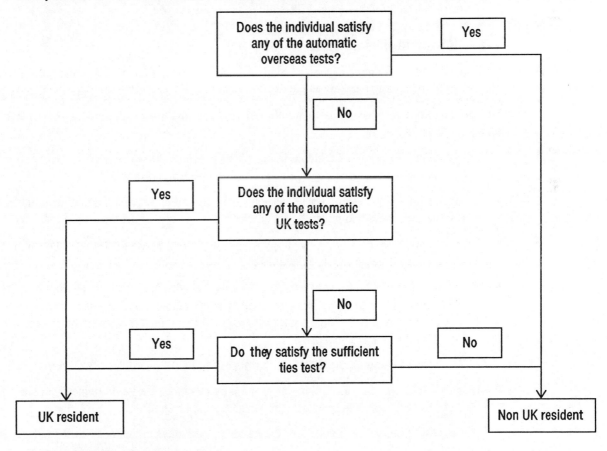

1.1.2 Automatic overseas tests

The automatic overseas tests must be considered first.

The automatic overseas tests treat an individual as not resident in the UK in a tax year if that individual:

*   **Spends less than 16 days in the UK in that tax year and was resident in the UK for one or more of the three previous tax years** (typically someone who is leaving the UK), or

- **Spends less than 46 days in the UK in that tax year and was not resident in the UK for any of the previous three tax years** (typically someone who is arriving in the UK), or

- **Works full-time overseas throughout that tax year**, without a significant break, and **spends less than 91 days in the UK during that tax year** and **there are less than 31 days in the tax year where the individual works in the UK for more than three hours a day.** A significant break from overseas work is any 31 day period in which there is no day that the individual works overseas for more than three hours or would have worked overseas for more than three hours but does not do so due to annual leave, sick leave or parenting leave.

1.1.3 Automatic UK tests

If none of the automatic overseas tests are met, then the automatic UK tests are considered.

The **automatic UK tests treat an individual as UK resident in a tax year** if that individual:

- **Spends 183 days or more in the UK** during that tax year, or

- During at least one period of 91 consecutive days, at least 30 days of which fall in the tax year, has a home in the UK in which the individual is present (no matter for how short a time) for at least 30 days in the tax year and either the individual has no home overseas or has an overseas home or homes in each of which the individual is present (again, no matter for how short a time) for fewer than 30 days in the tax year, or

- **Works full-time, without a significant break, in the UK during a 365-day period**, some of which falls within that tax year. A significant break from UK work is defined as for the third automatic overseas test, but in terms of UK, rather than overseas, work.

1.1.4 Sufficient UK ties tests

If the **individual meets none of the automatic overseas tests and none of the automatic UK tests**, the **'sufficient ties' test** must be considered.

The **sufficient ties test** compares the **number of days spent in the UK** and the **number of connection factors or 'ties' to the UK.**

An **individual who was not UK resident in any of the previous three tax years** (typically someone who is arriving in the UK) must determine whether any of the following ties apply:

- **UK resident close family** (eg spouse/civil partner, partner if living together as if married or in a civil partnership, child under the age of 18)

- **Substantive UK work** (employment or self-employment) where **40 days or more of working three hours a day is regarded as substantive**,

- **UK accommodation** (not necessarily owned by the individual) which is **available to that individual for a consecutive period of 91 days or more in the tax year** and in which the individual **spends one or more nights during the tax year** (16 or more nights if it is the home of a close relative such as a parent or an adult child)

- **More than 90 days spent in the UK in either or both of the previous two tax years.**

An **individual who was UK resident in any of the previous three tax years** (typically someone who is leaving the UK) must also determine whether an additional tie applies:

- **Present in the UK at midnight for the same or more days** in that tax year than in any other country.

The following table shows **how an individual's UK residence status is found** by comparing **the number of days in the UK** during a tax year and the **number of UK ties**:

Days in UK	Previously resident	Not previously resident
Less than 16	Automatically not UK resident	Automatically not UK resident
Between 16 and 45	Resident if 4 UK ties (or more)	Automatically not UK resident
Between 46 and 90	Resident if 3 UK ties (or more)	Resident if 4 UK ties
Between 91 and 120	Resident if 2 UK ties (or more)	Resident if 3 UK ties (or more)
Between 121 and 182	Resident if 1 UK tie (or more)	Resident if 2 UK ties (or more)
183 or more	Automatically UK resident	Automatically UK resident

Exam focus point

This table will be given in the Tax Rates and Allowances available in the exam.

1.1.5 Days spent in UK

Generally, **if a taxpayer is present in the UK at the end of a day (ie midnight)**, that **day counts as a day spent by the taxpayer in the UK**. However, they **do not need to count the first 60 days in a tax year that they spend in the UK due to circumstances beyond their control**, such as serious illness.

1.1.6 Examples

(a) James had not previously been resident in the UK before he arrived on 6 April 2018. He spent 40 days in the UK during the tax year 2018/19. James did not work during 2018/19.

James is arriving in the UK. He satisfies one of the automatic overseas tests since he spent less than 46 days in the UK in 2018/19 and was not resident in the UK for any of the previous three tax years. James is therefore not UK resident for the tax year 2018/19.

(b) Caroline had not previously been resident in the UK before she arrived on 6 April 2018. She spent 60 days in the UK during the tax year 2018/19. She did not work during 2018/19. Her only home during 2018/19, which she has throughout the whole year, is in the UK.

Caroline is arriving in the UK. She does not satisfy any of the automatic overseas tests since she spends 46 days or more in the UK and does not work overseas. She satisfies one of the automatic UK tests since there is a period of at least 91 days (the whole year) when she has a UK home in which she is present for 30 days or more in 2018/19, and she has no overseas home. Caroline is therefore UK resident for the tax year 2018/19.

(c) Miranda had always been resident in the UK before the tax year 2018/19 and has spent more than 90 days in the UK in every tax year before 2018/19. Miranda does not work during 2018/19. Miranda is married to Walter who is UK resident in 2018/19. They own a house in the UK which is available to them for the whole of 2018/19. On 6 April 2018, Miranda bought an overseas apartment where she spent 285 days during 2018/19. The remaining 80 days were spent in her UK house.

Miranda is leaving the UK. She does not satisfy any of the automatic overseas tests since she spends 16 days or more in the UK and does not work overseas. She does not satisfy any of the automatic UK tests since she spends less than 183 days in the UK, has an overseas home in which she is present for at least 30 days and does not work in the UK.

The 'sufficient ties' test is therefore relevant. Miranda has three UK ties:

(i) Close family in the UK (spouse)
(ii) Available accommodation in the UK in which she spent at least one night in the tax year
(iii) More than 90 days spent in the UK in both (ie at least one of) the previous two tax years.

Miranda spends between 46 and 90 days in the UK in 2018/19. These three ties are therefore sufficient to make her UK resident in 2018/19.

(d) Norman has not been resident in the UK in any tax year before 2018/19. He has not spent more than 90 days in the UK prior to 2018/19. On 6 April 2018, he arrived in the UK and went to stay at the home of his adult son for the first 160 days in the tax year 2018/19. Norman also has an overseas house in which he spent the remainder of the tax year 2018/19. Norman did not work in 2018/19 and his close family (which definition does not include his adult son) are not UK resident in 2018/19.

Norman is arriving in the UK. He does not satisfy any of the automatic overseas tests since he spends 46 days or more in the UK and does not work overseas. He does not satisfy any of the automatic UK tests as he spent less than 183 days in the UK, has an overseas home in which he is present for at least 30 days and does not work in the UK.

The 'sufficient ties' test is therefore relevant. Norman spends between 121 and 182 days in the UK during 2018/19 and so he would need two UK ties to be UK resident for that tax year. Since Norman has only one tie with the UK in 2018/19 (available accommodation with a close relative in which he spends at least 16 nights), he is therefore not UK resident for the tax year 2018/19.

Exam focus point

UK tax residence status was tested in June 2015 Question 1(a) Jodie. The examining team commented that this part of the question 'was generally answered well, with many candidates demonstrating a strong knowledge of these aspects of the syllabus. In particular, candidates knew how to determine the number of ties that needed to be satisfied and were able to describe the ties and relate them to the facts of the question.'

1.1.7 Splitting the tax year

FAST FORWARD

In general, an individual is either resident or non-resident for the whole of a tax year. However, in certain circumstances, the tax year may be split into UK and overseas parts.

Strictly, each tax year must be looked at as a whole. The general principle is that an individual is UK resident or non-UK resident either for a whole tax year or not at all.

However an individual may be able to **split a tax year into UK and overseas parts** in some circumstances. The split year treatment **can only apply for a year in which an individual is UK resident under the usual rules.** Where the tax year is split, the individual is **taxed as a UK resident for the UK part** and as a **non-UK resident for the overseas part.**

The **split year treatment** can be used by **an individual arriving in the UK** if that **individual is non-UK resident in the year prior to the split year** and if **one of the following circumstances applies:**

- The individual **comes to the UK, acquires a home in the UK,** and **does not have sufficient ties to the UK in order to be UK resident prior to acquiring the UK home** (the UK part starts when the individual acquires the UK home)

- The individual **comes to the UK** to **work full-time** for a **period of at least a year** and **does not have sufficient ties to the UK in order to be UK resident prior to starting that work** (the UK part starts when the individual starts the UK work)

- The individual **returns to the UK** following a **period where the individual has worked full-time overseas** (the UK part starts when the individual ceases working overseas); or

- The individual **returns to the UK** following a **period where the individual's partner** (spouse, civil partner or someone with whom the individual lives as spouse or civil partner) **has worked full-time overseas** (the UK part starts on the later of the individual's partner ceasing working overseas and the individual joining the partner in the UK).

The **split year treatment** can be used by **an individual leaving the UK** if that **individual is UK resident in the tax year prior to the spilt year** and **non-UK resident in tax year following the split year** and if **one of the following circumstances applies:**

- The individual **leaves the UK to begin full-time work overseas and meets similar, but modified, conditions in the third automatic overseas test above** (the overseas part starts when the individual starts the overseas work)

- The **individual's partner leaves the UK to begin full-time work overseas** and **the individual leaves the UK in order to continue living together with that partner** (the overseas part starts on the later of when the partner starts the overseas work and the individual joining the partner overseas); or

- The individual **leaves the UK in order to live overseas, ceases to have any UK home, spends a minimal amount of time in the UK**, and **establishes certain links with the overseas country** by, for example, becoming resident there (the overseas part starts when the individual ceases to have a home in the UK).

1.1.8 Examples

(a) Wolfgang has never been resident in the UK and has no UK ties before 1 July 2018 when he arrives in the UK from Germany. He rents out his flat in Germany on a two year lease from that date. He enters into a 12 month lease on a flat in London from 1 July 2018 when he starts living there. Wolfgang does not work.

Wolfgang is entitled to use split year treatment for 2018/19 since he is UK resident in 2018/19 (under the automatic UK tests as he spends more than 183 days in the UK), he was non-UK resident for 2017/18, he acquires a home in the UK during 2018/19, and spent no time in the UK between 6 April and 1 July 2018 so could not have been UK resident prior to acquiring the home (ie ties test irrelevant).

Wolfgang's overseas part of the tax year 2018/19 starts on 6 April 2018 and ends on 30 June 2018. The UK part of the tax year 2018/19 starts on 1 July 2018 (the day he acquires his home in the UK) and ends on 5 April 2019.

(b) Bruce has always been UK resident. He leaves the UK and begin a three year full-time contract overseas on 15 October 2018. He will not visit the UK during the period of the contract.

Bruce can split the tax year 2018/19 because he is UK resident in 2018/19 (spends more than 183 days in the UK), he was UK resident in 2017/18, he will be non-UK resident in 2019/20 (automatically because he works full-time overseas in that tax year and does not spend more than 90 days in the UK during that tax year), and he is leaving the UK to begin full-time work overseas.

The UK part of the tax year 2018/19 starts on 6 April 2018 and ends 14 October 2018. The overseas part of the tax year 2018/19 starts on 15 October 2018 and ends on 5 April 2019.

Exam focus point

> The detailed rules in the statutory residence test are quite complex, especially those in regard to what constitutes work and having a home in the UK, as well as details of the split year cases. These more complex aspects are **not examinable** in Advanced Taxation (ATX – UK).

1.2 Domicile and deemed domicile 12/10

1.2.1 Domicile

FAST FORWARD

> An individual is domiciled in the country which is the individual's permanent home.

Under general law, an individual is domiciled in the country which is the individual's permanent home. Domicile is distinct from nationality or residence. An individual may be resident in more than one country, but can be domiciled in only one country at a time.

Individuals acquire a domicile of origin at birth; this is normally the domicile of their father (or that of their mother if their father died before they were born or their parents were unmarried at their birth) and therefore not necessarily the country where they were born. **Individuals retain this domicile unless and**

until they acquire a different domicile of dependency (if, while they are under 16, their father's domicile changes) or domicile of choice. A domicile of choice can be acquired only by individuals aged 16 or over.

To acquire a domicile of choice individuals must sever their ties with the country of their former domicile and settle in another country with the clear intention of making their permanent home there. Long residence in another country is not in itself enough to prove that individuals have acquired a domicile of choice: there has to be evidence that they firmly intend to live there permanently.

1.2.2 Deemed domicile

New

FAST FORWARD

> An individual may be deemed to be UK domiciled for income tax and capital gains tax purposes.

An individual who is not UK domiciled under general law may be deemed to be UK domiciled in a tax year for income tax and capital gains tax purposes if they satisfy either one of two conditions. The first condition is relevant to **formerly UK domiciled residents** and the second condition is relevant to **long-term UK residents** (although it is possible for a particular individual to satisfy both conditions).

The first condition is that **the individual:**

- was **born in the UK;** and
- has a **UK domicile of origin;** and
- is **UK resident in the relevant tax year**.

The second condition is that **the individual has been UK resident for at least 15 of the 20 tax years immediately preceding the relevant tax year.** This condition does not apply if the individual is not UK resident in the relevant tax year and has not been UK resident in any tax year from 2017/18 onwards.

1.2.3 Examples

(a) Lin was born in the UK. Her parents were married and her father was domiciled in the UK so Lin had a UK domicile of origin. Lin acquired a domicile of dependency in Canada at the age of 15 when her father became domiciled there and so is not UK domiciled under general law. Lin is resident in the UK in the tax year 2018/19 under the statutory residence test (see earlier in this chapter).

   Lin is deemed UK domiciled in the UK under the first condition in the tax year 2018/19 because she satisfies all three parts of that condition.

(b) Simon was born in Australia. His father died before he was born. His mother was domiciled in the UK and so Simon had a UK domicile of origin. Simon acquired a domicile of choice in New Zealand in 2002. Simon became UK resident in the tax year 2012/13.

   Simon is not deemed domiciled in the UK in the tax year 2018/19 under the first condition because he only satisfies two of the three parts of that condition. He is not deemed domiciled in the UK in the tax year 2018/19 under the second condition because he has not been UK resident for at least 15 of the 20 tax years immediately preceding that tax year.

(c) Hanna does not have a UK domicile of origin so the first condition does not apply to her. She became UK resident in the tax year 1997/98. She was then resident in the UK up to and including the tax year 2006/07. She resumed being UK resident in the tax year 2013/14 and continues to be UK resident. This information can be displayed in the following table in relation to the tax year 2018/19:

20 tax years preceding 2018/19	UK resident tax years	Not UK resident tax years	Total tax years
1998/99 to 2006/07	9		9
2007/08 to 2012/13		6	6
2013/14 to 2017/18	5	–	5
Total	14	6	20

It will be seen that Hanna was only UK resident for 14 out of the 20 tax years immediately preceding the tax year 2018/19 and so is not deemed domiciled in the UK under the second condition in that tax year. Note that Hanna's UK residence in the tax year 1997/98 is not relevant as it was more than 20 tax years before 2018/19.

2 Liability to UK income tax 12/11

2.1 Overview

FAST FORWARD

Generally, a UK resident who is UK domiciled or deemed domiciled is liable to UK income tax on UK and overseas income as it arises. An individual who is UK resident but neither UK domiciled nor UK deemed domiciled is liable to UK income tax on income arising in the UK and may be entitled to be taxed on overseas income on the remittance basis. A non-UK resident is liable to UK income tax only on income arising in the UK.

Generally, a **UK resident individual who is UK domiciled or deemed domiciled is liable to UK income tax on both UK and overseas income as it arises (the arising basis).**

Under the remittance basis, **an individual who is UK resident but neither UK domiciled nor UK deemed domiciled is liable to UK income tax on overseas income only to the extent that it is brought (remitted) to the UK.** The individual may be subject to the Remittance Basis Charge (see later in this chapter). If the remittance basis does not apply (for example, if it is not claimed – see later in this chapter), overseas income is taxed on an arising basis.

An individual who is UK resident but not UK domiciled nor UK deemed domiciled is liable to UK income tax on UK income on an arising basis.

A **non-UK resident is liable to UK income tax only on income arising in the UK.**

The diagram below provides a broad **summary** of how an individual is taxed, based on the individual's residence and domicile (including deemed domicile) status.

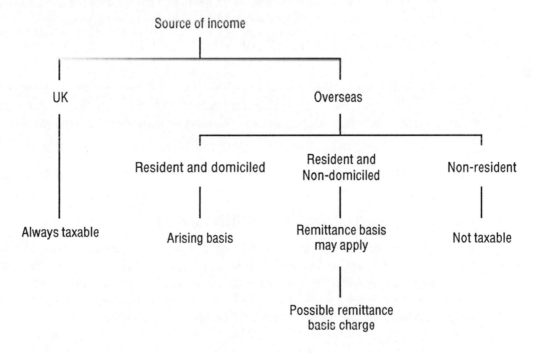

2.2 Individuals resident and domiciled in the UK

2.2.1 Overseas income: general principles

Individuals who are UK resident and UK domiciled or deemed domiciled (in most cases - see later in this chapter) **are taxable on their overseas income on an arising basis (ie it is irrelevant whether or not the income is remitted to the UK).** Double taxation relief may be available if the income is also taxed in the country in which it arises (see later in this chapter).

Overseas income is identified and taxed in broadly the same way as UK income, but the points set out below about overseas property business income should be noted.

Exam focus point

> The overseas aspects of income from employment are **not examinable** in Advanced Taxation (ATX – UK).

2.2.2 Overseas property business

An individual who receives rents and other income from property overseas is treated as carrying on an overseas property business. The income from the overseas property business is liable to income tax in the same way as income from a UK property business, and is calculated in the same way. If an individual has both a UK and an overseas property business, the profits must be calculated separately.

If a loss arises in an overseas property business, it may be carried forward and set against future income from the overseas property business, as soon as it arises.

The special treatment of furnished holiday lettings does not apply to overseas properties other than those in the European Economic Area.

2.3 Individuals resident but not domiciled in the UK   6/13, 12/14, 9/16

2.3.1 Remittance basis

An individual who is UK resident but neither UK domiciled nor UK deemed domiciled (but see further later in this section) **may be taxed on overseas income on the remittance basis.**

If the remittance basis does not apply, the individual is taxable in the same way as an individual who is UK resident and domiciled (ie on an arising basis on both UK and overseas income).

Where the remittance basis applies, all income from the relevant source is treated as non-savings income. The savings income nil rate band and the dividend nil rate band therefore do not apply. Overseas remittance basis income is taxed in the same way as other non-savings income ie at 20% in the basic rate band, 40% in the higher rate band and thereafter at 45%.

Exam focus point

> The rules of what constitutes a remittance are **not examinable** in Advanced Taxation (ATX – UK).

2.3.2 Automatic application of remittance basis

If an individual, who is entitled to be taxed on the remittance basis on overseas income, has unremitted non-UK income and gains of less than £2,000 arising in a tax year, the remittance basis will apply to that individual automatically without the need for a claim to be made.

Exam focus point

> The remittance basis was tested in June 2013 Question 3(b)(i) Lin, Nan and Yu. The examining team commented that 'One particular area of confusion related to the automatic applicability of the remittance basis where **unremitted** income and gains are less than £2,000; many candidates thought the rule related to the level of **remitted** income and gains.'

In deciding whether the individual can use the remittance basis for this purpose, the deemed domiciled rules do not apply. Therefore an individual who is not UK domiciled, but who is UK deemed domiciled, will only be liable to income tax on their overseas income on the arising basis if their unremitted non-UK income and gains exceed £2,000 in the tax year.

The individual can disapply the remittance basis for a tax year if they wish by giving HMRC notice in their self assessment tax return for that year. They will then be taxed on an arising basis on overseas income arising in that tax year.

The remittance basis will also apply automatically in a tax year if an individual:

- Is UK resident but is neither UK domiciled nor deemed domiciled in that year; and

- Has no UK income or gains other than taxed investment income not exceeding £100; and

- Does not remit income or gains to the UK in the year and

- Has been UK resident in not more than six out of the nine tax years immediately preceding that year or is under the age of 18 throughout the year

2.3.3 Claiming the remittance basis

In a particular tax year, any other individual who is entitled to be taxed on the remittance basis must make a claim if they wish for that basis to apply to their overseas income. The claim is made on the individual's self assessment tax return. If a claim is not made, the individual is taxed on their overseas income on an arising basis.

An individual who makes a claim for the remittance basis is not entitled to the personal allowance. This does not apply to an individual who is entitled to the remittance basis without a claim (see above). The savings income nil rate band and the dividend nil rate band will also not be available if the remittance basis applies (whether it is claimed or if it applies automatically) since the overseas remittance basis income is taxable as non-savings income.

An individual who makes a claim for the remittance basis is also not entitled to the annual exempt amount against chargeable gains. We deal with overseas aspects of Capital Gains Tax later in this text.

Question   Choosing the remittance basis (1)

Claudia has been UK resident for five years and lives in England, but is not domiciled nor deemed domiciled in the UK. In 2018/19, she has UK employment income of £30,000 and overseas dividend income of £7,000, of which she has remitted £3,000 to the UK.

You are required to state why Claudia is not entitled to the remittance basis automatically and advise her whether or not she should claim the remittance basis in 2018/19.

Answer

Claudia is not entitled to the remittance basis automatically because she has unremitted overseas income of £(7,000 – 3,000) = £4,000 which is in excess of the limit of £2,000.

Claudia should not make a claim for the remittance basis to apply to her overseas income in 2018/19. This is because she would lose her entitlement to the personal allowance of £11,850 and the use of the dividend nil rate band. She would pay less UK tax by having her overseas income taxed on the arising basis as shown below.

Remittance basis

	Non-savings Income £
UK employment income	30,000
Non-UK dividend income remitted	3,000
Taxable income (no personal allowance)	33,000

Her income tax liability will therefore be:

£33,000 × 20%	6,600

Arising basis

	Non-savings Income £	Dividend income £	Total £
UK employment income	30,000		
Non-UK dividend income		7,000	
Net income	30,000	7,000	37,000
Less personal allowance	(11,850)		
Taxable income	18,150	7,000	25,150

Her income tax liability will therefore be:

	£
Non-savings income	
£18,150 × 20%	3,630
Dividend income	
£2,000 × 0%	0
£5,000 (7,000 − 2,000) × 7.5%	375
	4,005

2.3.4 The remittance basis charge

FAST FORWARD

An individual who claims the remittance basis and is a long-term UK resident, but not yet UK deemed domiciled, is required to pay the Remittance Basis Charge on unremitted income and gains.

An individual is liable to the Remittance Basis Charge in a tax year if they:

- **claim the remittance basis for the tax year, and**
- **are aged 18 or over in the tax year, and**
- **have been UK resident for at least seven of the nine tax years immediately preceding that tax year.**

The **Remittance Basis Charge is a charge on non-UK income and gains not remitted to the UK.** The individual remains liable to UK tax on their UK source income and non-UK income remitted to the UK in the usual way. We deal with chargeable gains later in this text.

The amount of the **Remittance Basis Charge** in a tax year depends on the length of time the individual has been resident in the UK.

- An individual who has been resident for **12 of the 14 tax years** immediately preceding that tax year has a **Remittance Basis Charge of £60,000.**

- An individual who has been resident for **seven of the nine tax years** immediately preceding that tax year (but not yet 12 of the last 14 tax years) has a **Remittance Basis Charge of £30,000.**

The Remittance Basis Charge is treated as UK income tax or CGT paid on an arising basis and so should be available for double taxation relief, for example in the country in which the non-UK income or gains arises.

The individual is required to nominate unremitted non-UK income and gains on which the Remittance Basis Charge applies. If the unremitted income or gains are later remitted to the UK, that income or gains will not be taxed again. However, there are ordering rules which treat other untaxed income and gains as being remitted before nominated income and gains.

If the individual does not nominate sufficient non-UK income or gains to cover the relevant Remittance Basis Charge, there is an additional element added to ensure that the full tax charge is imposed.

2.3.5 Choosing whether or not to use the remittance basis

In each tax year, the individual can chose whether or not to claim the remittance basis, as has been discussed earlier in this chapter. This will be a particularly important decision if the individual would be liable to the Remittance Basis Charge and will depend on:

- The extent of their unremitted non-UK income and gains

- The effect of the loss of the personal allowance, the savings income nil rate band, the dividend nil rate band, and the annual exempt amount against chargeable gains.

Question   Choosing the remittance basis (2)

Nathan has been resident in the UK for tax purposes since 2009/10 but is not UK domiciled nor UK deemed domiciled. He lives in England.

In 2018/19, he has the following income:

UK trading income	£10,000
Non-UK trading income	£90,000

He remits £10,000 of his non-UK trading income into the UK.

You are required to advise Nathan whether or not he should claim the remittance basis in 2018/19.

Answer

Remittance basis

Nathan has been resident in the UK for nine tax years before 2018/19, so the Remittance Basis Charge is £30,000, if the remittance basis is claimed.

	Non-savings Income £
UK trading income	10,000
Non-UK trading income remitted	10,000
Taxable income (no personal allowance)	20,000

His income tax liability will therefore be:

	£
	£
£20,000 × 20%	4,000
Remittance Basis Charge	30,000
	34,000

Arising basis

	Non-savings Income £
UK trading income	10,000
Non-UK trading income	90,000
Net income	100,000
Less personal allowance	(11,850)
Taxable income	88,150

His income tax liability will therefore be:

	£
£34,500 × 20%	6,900
£53,650 × 40%	21,460
	28,360

Therefore Nathan should not claim the remittance basis for 2018/19.

2.4 Individuals not resident in the UK

6/15

2.4.1 Personal allowances for non-UK residents

In general, **non-UK residents are not entitled to personal allowances**. However, some individuals are entitled to allowances despite being non-UK resident including:

- Citizens of the European Economic Area
- Individuals resident in the Isle of Man and the Channel Islands.

2.4.2 Limit on income tax liability for non-UK residents

There is a limit on the income tax liability of an individual who is not resident in the UK (but not where the tax year is split as described above). The tax cannot exceed the tax liability if the individual was taxed on all income, apart from disregarded income, without a personal allowance.

Disregarded income includes **UK savings and dividend income**, but does not include non-savings income such as trading, employment or property income.

2.4.3 Free of Tax to Residents Abroad securities

Interest that arises on UK government 'Free of Tax to Residents Abroad' (FOTRA) securities (broadly UK Treasury Stock) **is not taxable** if received by **an individual who is not resident in the UK**.

3 Double taxation relief (DTR)

Double taxation relief may be available to reduce the burden of taxation. It is generally given by reducing the UK tax charged by the overseas tax suffered.

3.1 Introduction

As we have seen, **UK tax applies to the worldwide income of UK residents and the UK income of non-residents.**

When other countries adopt the same approach it is clear that some income may be taxed twice:

- Firstly in the country where it arises
- Secondly in the country where the taxpayer resides

Double taxation relief (DTR) as a result of international agreements may avoid the problem, or at least diminish its impact.

3.2 Double taxation agreements

Typical provisions of double taxation agreements based on the OECD Model are:

- Total exemption from tax is given in the country where income arises in the hands of, for example visiting diplomats and teachers on exchange programmes

- Preferential rates of withholding tax are applied to, for example, payments of rent, interest and dividends. The usual rate is frequently replaced by 15% or less

- DTR is given to taxpayers in their country of residence by way of a credit for tax suffered in the country where income arises. This may be in the form of relief for withholding tax only or, given a holding of specified size in a overseas company, for the underlying tax on the profits out of which dividends are paid

- There are exchanges of information clauses so that tax evaders can be chased internationally

- There are rules to determine a person's residence and to prevent dual residence (tie-breaker clauses)

- There are clauses which render certain profits taxable in only one rather than both of the contracting states

- There is a non-discrimination clause so that a country does not tax foreigners more heavily than its own nationals

3.3 Unilateral relief

If no relief is available under a double taxation agreement, UK legislation provides for unilateral relief. However, unilateral relief is not available if relief is specifically excluded under the terms of a double tax agreement.

Overseas income must be included gross (ie including overseas tax) in the UK tax computation. The overseas tax is deducted from the UK tax liability (this is credit relief) but the relief cannot exceed the UK tax on the overseas income so the taxpayer bears the higher of:

- The UK tax
- The overseas tax

The UK tax on the overseas income is the difference between:

- The UK tax before DTR on all income including the overseas income
- The UK tax on all income except the overseas income

In both cases, we take account of the savings income and dividend nil rate bands and tax reducers. If there is more than one source of overseas income, DTR is computed on a source by source basis treating the highest taxed source as the top slice of UK taxable income.

Double tax relief

Jim is a UK resident and domiciled individual who lives in Northern Ireland and who has the following income for 2018/19.

	£
UK employment income	40,350
Interest on overseas loan stock (before deduction of overseas tax of £250)	5,000
Overseas property business income (before deduction of overseas tax of £2,250)	3,750

Assuming that maximum DTR is claimed, show Jim's UK tax liability for 2018/19.

Answer

	Non-savings income £	Savings income £	Total £
UK employment income	40,350		
Overseas interest		5,000	
Overseas property business income	3,750		
Net income	44,100	5,000	49,100
Less personal allowance	(11,850)		
Taxable income	32,250	5,000	37,250

	£
Non-savings income	
£32,250 × 20%	6,450
Savings income	
£500 × 0% (higher rate taxpayer)	0
£1,750 (34,500 − 32,250 − 500) × 20%	350
£2,750 (5,000 − 500 − 1,750) × 40%	1,100
	7,900

Less: double taxation relief		
interest	250	
rents (see below)	1,400	
		(1,650)
UK tax liability		6,250

Since the rents are taxed more highly overseas, these should be regarded as the top slice of UK taxable income. Taxable income excluding the rents is £33,500 and the UK tax on this is:

	£
Non-savings income	
£28,500 × 20%	5,700
Savings income	
£1,000 × 0% (now basic rate taxpayer)	0
£4,000 (5,000 − 1,000) × 20%	800
	6,500

The UK tax on the rents is £1,400 (£7,900 − 6,500). Since overseas tax of £2,250 is greater, the DTR is the smaller figure of £1,400. The DTR on the overseas interest is the lower of the UK tax of £800 and the overseas tax of £250, so is £250.

Exam focus point

> It may be obvious that the overseas tax is the lower amount. In this case you can simply state that DTR is the amount of the overseas tax without needing to compute the UK tax on the overseas source.

Where there is no point in claiming this credit relief, perhaps because loss relief has eliminated any liability to UK tax, the taxpayer may elect for expense relief instead. No credit is given for overseas tax suffered, but only the income after overseas taxes is brought into the tax computation.

If overseas taxes are not relieved in the year in which the income is taxable in the UK, no relief can be obtained in any earlier or later year.

Taxpayers who have claimed relief against their UK tax bill for taxes paid overseas must notify HMRC in writing of any changes to the overseas liabilities if these changes result in the DTR claimed becoming excessive. This rule applies to all taxes not just income tax.

Chapter roundup

- An individual may be both, or either of, resident and domiciled in the UK.

- An individual will automatically not be UK resident if they meet any of the automatic overseas tests. An individual, who does not meet any of the automatic overseas tests, will automatically be UK resident if they meet any of the automatic UK tests. An individual who has not met any of the automatic overseas tests nor any of the automatic UK tests will be UK resident if they meet the sufficient ties test.

- In general, an individual is either resident or non-resident for the whole of a tax year. However, in certain circumstances, the tax year may be split into UK and overseas parts.

- An individual is domiciled in the country which is the individual's permanent home.

- An individual may be deemed to be UK domiciled for income tax and capital gains tax purposes.

- Generally, a UK resident who is UK domiciled or deemed domiciled is liable to UK income tax on UK and overseas income as it arises. An individual who is UK resident but neither UK domiciled nor UK deemed domiciled is liable to UK income tax on income arising in the UK and may be entitled to be taxed on overseas income on the remittance basis. A non-UK resident is liable to UK income tax only on income arising in the UK.

- An individual who claims the remittance basis and is a long-term UK resident, but not yet UK deemed domiciled, is required to pay the Remittance Basis Charge on unremitted income and gains.

- Double taxation relief may be available to reduce the burden of taxation. It is generally given by reducing the UK tax charged by the overseas tax suffered.

Quick quiz

1   What are the three automatic UK residence tests?

2   On what basis is a UK resident who is not domiciled in the UK taxed on overseas income?

3   On what basis is a UK resident who is deemed domiciled in the UK taxed on overseas income?

4   How will a overseas dividend of £10,000, of which £6,000 is remitted to the UK be taxed on an additional rate UK resident taxpayer if that taxpayer is:

    (a)   Domiciled or deemed domiciled in the UK: or
    (b)   Not domiciled nor deemed domiciled in the UK and makes a remittance basis claim?

5   How much is the Remittance Basis Charge?

6   What is the maximum amount of credit relief that can be given for overseas tax on overseas income?

Answers to quick quiz

1   (a)   The individual spends 183 days or more in the UK during a tax year.

    (b)   During at least one period of 91 consecutive days, at least 30 days of which fall in the tax year, the individual has a home in the UK in which the individual is present (no matter for how short a time) for at least 30 days in the tax year and either the individual has no home overseas or has an overseas home or homes in each of which the individual is present (again, no matter for how short a time) for fewer than 30 days in the tax year.

    (c)   The individual works full-time, without a significant break, in the UK during a 365-day period, some of which falls within that tax year. A significant break from UK work is defined as for the third automatic overseas test, but in terms of UK, rather than overseas, work.

2   On the remittance basis if a claim is made or automatically if the individual has unremitted income/gains not exceeding £2,000 in the tax year. Otherwise on the arising basis.

3   On the remittance basis automatically if the individual has unremitted income/gains not exceeding £2,000 in the tax year (ie a claim cannot be made for the remittance basis by these individuals). Otherwise on the arising basis.

4   (a)   £10,000 (arising basis) as dividend income liable to tax at 38.1%.
    (b)   £6,000 (remittance basis) as non-savings income liable to tax at 45%.

5   £30,000 if the individual has been resident in the UK for seven of the previous nine tax years, or £60,000 if the individual has been resident in the UK for 12 of the previous 14 tax years.

6   The lower of:

    (a)   UK tax on the overseas income, and
    (b)   The overseas tax on the overseas income

Now try the question below from the Practice Question Bank

Number	Level	Marks	Time
Q11	Introductory	20	39 mins

Capital gains tax

11

Chargeable gains: an outline

Topic list	Syllabus reference
1 Chargeable and exempt persons, disposals and assets	A2(a)C1, C2, (d)(ii)
2 Computing a gain or loss	A2(a)C2
3 CGT payable by individuals	A2(a)C5, (d)(iii)
4 Valuing assets	A2(a)C2
5 Connected persons	A2(d)(i)
6 Married couples and civil partners	A2(b)(i)
7 Business partnerships	A2(b)(vii)
8 Part disposals	A2(e)(i)

Introduction

Now that we have concluded our study of the income tax computation we can consider the capital gains tax computation. The two must be kept separate.

Capital gains arise when taxpayers dispose of assets, such as investments or capital assets used in the business. If, for example, you buy a picture for £10,000, hang it on your wall for 20 years and then sell it for £200,000, you will have a capital gain.

In this chapter, we see when a capital gain will be liable to tax and how to work out gains and losses.

We also look at some special cases where the rules are modified because of the relationship between the disposer and the acquirer of an asset; without such rules, people could do deals with their relatives to avoid tax.

We also look at how chargeable gains on partnership assets are dealt with.

In the following chapters, we will look at the special rules for certain types of assets and at what reliefs are available.

Study guide

		Intellectual level
2	**Chargeable gains and capital gains tax liabilities in situations involving further overseas aspects and in relation to closely related persons and trusts together with the application of additional exemptions and reliefs**	
(a)	The contents of the Taxation - United Kingdom (TX – UK) study guide for chargeable gains for individuals under headings:	2
•	C1 The scope of the taxation of capital gains	
•	C2 The basic principles of computing gains and losses	
•	C5 The computation of capital gains tax	
(b)	The scope of the taxation of capital gains:	3
(i)	Determine the tax implications of independent taxation and transfers between spouses	
(vii)	Identify the occasions when a capital gain would arise on a partner in a partnership on the disposal of a partnership asset	
(d)	The basic principles of computing gains and losses:	3
(i)	Identify connected persons for capital gains tax purposes and advise on the tax implications of transfers between connected persons	
(ii)	Advise on the impact of dates of disposal	
(iii)	Evaluate the use of capital losses in the year of death	
(e)	Gains and losses on the disposal of movable and immovable property:	3
(i)	Advise on the tax implications of a part disposal, including small part disposals of land	

Exam guide

Taxpayers normally plan major disposals of capital assets so you may get a question asking when would be the best time to make a disposal. You need to know the rules about the date of disposal, and then you need to be able to quantify any tax savings that might result from delaying or advancing a sale.

Knowledge brought forward from earlier studies

This chapter mainly revises topics covered in Taxation (TX – UK). The examining team has identified essential underpinning knowledge from the Taxation (TX – UK) syllabus which is particularly important that you revise as part of your Advanced Taxation (ATX – UK) studies. In this chapter, the relevant topics are:

		Intellectual level
C2	**The basic principles of computing gains and losses**	
(a)	Compute and explain the treatment of capital gains	2
(b)	Compute and explain the treatment of capital losses	2
C5	**The computation of capital gains tax**	
(a)	Compute the amount of capital gains tax payable	2

The new topics in this chapter include carry back losses in the year of death, business partnerships, and small disposals of land.

The only change in 2018/19 from the material studied in Taxation (TX – UK) in 2017/18 is the increase in the annual exempt amount to £11,700.

1 Chargeable and exempt persons, disposals and assets

FAST FORWARD

For CGT to apply, there needs to be a chargeable person, a chargeable disposal and a chargeable asset.

Exam focus point

For a chargeable gain to arise there must be:

- A chargeable person; and
- A chargeable disposal; and
- A chargeable asset

otherwise no charge to tax occurs.

1.1 Chargeable persons

The following are chargeable persons:

- Individuals
- Partnerships
- Companies
- Trustees

We will look at the taxation of chargeable gains on companies later in this text.

Persons who are not resident in the UK are usually exempt persons. We deal with overseas aspects of CGT later in this text.

1.2 Chargeable disposals

FAST FORWARD

A chargeable disposal usually occurs on the date of the contract. The date of disposal should be considered in relation to the use of capital losses, the annual exempt amount, the date for payment of tax and the availability of reliefs.

The following are chargeable disposals:

- Sales of assets or parts of assets
- Gifts of assets or parts of assets
- Receipts of capital sums following the surrender of rights to assets
- The loss or destruction of assets

A chargeable disposal occurs on the date of the contract (where there is one, whether written or oral). This may differ from the date of transfer of the asset. However, when a capital sum is received on a surrender of rights or the loss or destruction of an asset, the disposal takes place on the day the sum is received.

The timing of a disposal should be carefully considered. For example, an individual may wish to accelerate a gain into an earlier tax year to obtain earlier loss relief or to delay a gain until a later tax year when an unused annual exempt amount may be available and tax will be payable 12-months later. The availability of reliefs should also be taken into account, for example whether the taxpayer will have satisfied the conditions for entrepreneurs' relief at the date of disposal.

Where a disposal involves an acquisition by someone else, their date of acquisition is the same as the date of disposal.

Transfers of assets on death are exempt disposals. The heirs inherit assets as if they bought them at death for their then market values, but there is no capital gain or allowable loss on death. It is possible to vary or disclaim inherited assets. The CGT effect of such a variation or disclaimer is dealt with later in this text.

1.3 Chargeable assets

All forms of property, wherever in the world they are situated, are chargeable assets unless they are specifically designated as exempt.

The following are exempt assets (gains not taxable, losses not usually allowable losses, the few exceptions are explained in this text).

- **Motor vehicles** suitable for private use
- **National Savings and Investments certificates and premium bonds**
- Foreign currency bank accounts held by individuals, trustees and personal representatives
- Decorations awarded for bravery (unless purchased)
- Damages for personal or professional injury
- **Gilt-edged securities** (eg Treasury Stock)
- **Qualifying corporate bonds (QCBs)**
- **Certain chattels**
- Debts (except debts on a security)
- Investments held in individual savings accounts (ISAs)

There are also exemptions for enterprise investment scheme (EIS) shares, the seed enterprise investment scheme (SEIS), and venture capital trust (VCT) shares (see earlier in this text).

2 Computing a gain or loss

FAST FORWARD

A gain or loss is computed by taking the proceeds and deducting the cost. Incidental costs of acquisition and disposal are deducted together with any enhancement expenditure reflected in the state and nature of the asset at the date of disposal.

One of the competencies you require to fulfil Performance Objective 15 Tax computations and assessments of the PER is to prepare or contribute to the computation or assessment of tax computations for individuals. You can apply the knowledge you obtain from this section of the text to help to demonstrate this competence.

2.1 Basic calculation   3/16, 6/16, 12/17, 6/18

A gain (or an allowable loss) is generally calculated as follows.

	£
Disposal consideration	45,000
Less incidental costs of disposal	(400)
Net proceeds	44,600
Less allowable costs	(21,000)
Gain	23,600

Usually the disposal consideration is the proceeds of sale of the asset, but a disposal is deemed to take place at market value:

- Where the disposal is **not a bargain at arm's length**
- Where the disposal is made for a **consideration which cannot be valued**
- Where the disposal is by way of a **gift**

Special valuation rules apply for shares (see later in this text).

Incidental costs of disposal may include:

- Valuation fees
- Estate agency fees
- Advertising costs
- Legal costs

Allowable costs include:

- The original cost of acquisition
- Incidental costs of acquisition
- Capital expenditure incurred in enhancing the asset

Enhancement expenditure is capital expenditure which enhances the value of the asset and is reflected in the state or nature of the asset at the time of disposal, or expenditure incurred in establishing, preserving or defending title to, or a right over, the asset. Excluded from this category are:

- Costs of repairs and maintenance
- Costs of insurance
- Any expenditure deductible from trading profits
- Any expenditure met by public funds (for example council grants)

Question — Calculating the gain

Joanne bought a piece of land as an investment for £20,000. The legal costs of purchase were £250.

Joanne sold the land in December 2018 for £35,000. She incurred estate agency fees of £700 and legal costs of £500 on the sale.

Calculate Joanne's gain on sale.

Answer

	£
Proceeds of sale	35,000
Less costs of disposal £(700 + 500)	(1,200)
Net proceeds of sale	33,800
Less costs of acquisition £(20,000 + 250)	(20,250)
Gain	13,550

3 CGT payable by individuals 12/14, 3/16, 6/15, 9/16, 6/17, 12/17

FAST FORWARD

CGT is usually payable at the rate of 10% or 20% on most chargeable gains depending on the individual's taxable income. There are rates of 18% and 28% for residential property. Individuals are entitled to an annual exempt amount.

PER alert

One of the competencies you require to fulfil Performance Objective 15 Tax computations and assessments of the PER is to prepare or contribute to the computation or assessment of tax computations for individuals. You can apply the knowledge you obtain from this section of the text to help to demonstrate this competence.

3.1 Introduction

In general, individuals are liable to CGT on the disposal of assets situated anywhere in the world if, for any part of the tax year of disposal, they are resident in the UK. 'Residence' has the same meaning as for income tax purposes (see earlier in this text). Trustees also pay CGT on their gains.

An individual pays CGT on any taxable gains arising in the tax year. **Taxable gains are the net chargeable gains (gains minus losses) of the tax year reduced by unrelieved losses brought forward from previous years and the annual exempt amount.**

The annual exempt amount applies each tax year. For 2018/19 it is £11,700. It is the **last deduction** to be made in the calculation of taxable gains. **An individual who has gains taxable at more than one rate of tax may deduct any allowable losses and the annual exempt amount for that year in the way that produces the lowest possible tax charge.** We will look at this topic in detail later in this text when we consider gains on residential property and gains qualifying for entrepreneurs' relief.

3.2 Calculating CGT

3.2.1 CGT on most taxable gains

Taxable gains (other than those arising from residential property and those qualifying for entrepreneurs' relief) are chargeable to capital gains tax at the rate of 10% or 20% depending on the individual's taxable income for the tax year.

To work out which rate applies, follow these rules:

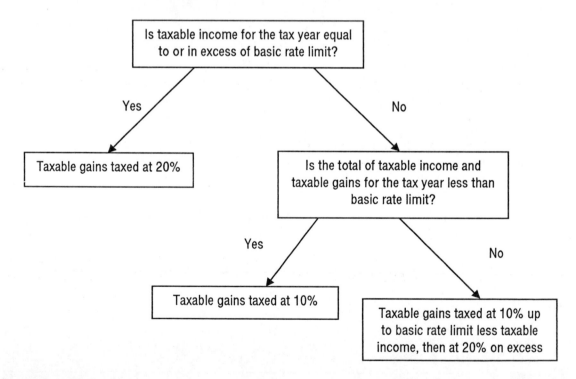

Remember that the basic rate band limit will usually be £34,500 for 2018/19 but the limit will be increased by the gross amount of personal pension contributions.

Question | Rates of CGT on most taxable gains

Mo has taxable income of £27,490 in 2018/19. He made personal pension contributions of £200 (net) per month during 2018/19. In December 2018, he makes a chargeable gain of £28,800 on the sale of some shares. Calculate the CGT payable by Mo for 2018/19.

	£
Chargeable gain	28,800
Less annual exempt amount	(11,700)
Taxable gain	17,100
Basic rate band limit	34,500
Add: personal pension contributions £(200 × 12) = £2,400 × 100/80	3,000
Increased basic rate limit	37,500

CGT

	£
£10,010 (37,500 – 27,490) (unused basic rate band) @ 10%	1,001
£7,090 (17,100 – 10,010) @ 20%	1,418
Total CGT payable	2,419

3.2.2 CGT on residential property gains

Residential property includes an interest in a dwelling such as a house or flat. It also includes an interest in a contract acquired 'off-plan' where the property has not yet been constructed.

Taxable gains on residential property which are not fully exempt under principal private residence relief (see later in this text) **are chargeable to capital gains tax at the rate of 18% or 28% depending on the individual's taxable income for the tax year.** Residential property gains within the basic rate band are taxed at 18% and those in excess of the basic rate limit (adjusted as described in the previous section) are taxed at 28%.

If an individual has a mixture of residential property gains and gains on other assets (other than those qualifying for entrepreneurs' relief – see later in this text), **the annual exempt amount and allowable losses should be deducted first from residential property gains and secondly from gains on other assets.**

Where the individual has unused basic rate band, it does not matter whether the residential property gains or the other gains are taxed first. This is because the differential between the rates in both cases is 10%.

Question   Rates of CGT on mixture of gains

Fran has taxable income of £25,500 in 2018/19. In August 2018, she makes a chargeable gain of £15,500 on the sale of some shares. In March 2019, she makes a chargeable gain of £19,600 on the disposal of a residential property which is not covered by principal private residence relief. Calculate the CGT payable by Fran for 2018/19.

Answer

	Other gain £	Residential property £
Shares	15,500	
Residential property		19,600
Less annual exempt amount (best use)		(11,700)
Taxable gains	15,500	7,900

	Other gain £	Residential property £
CGT		
If tax residential property gain first		
£7,900 @ 18%		1,422
£1,100 (34,500 – 25,500 – 7,900) @ 10%		110
£14,400 (15,500 – 1,100) @ 20%		2,880
Total CGT		4,412
If tax other gain first		
£9,000 (34,500 – 25,500) @ 10%		900
£6,500 (15,500 – 9,000) @ 20%		1,300
£7,900 @ 28%		2,212
Total CGT		4,412

3.2.3 CGT on entrepreneurs' relief gains

There is also a special 10% rate of tax for gains for which the taxpayer claims entrepreneurs' relief. We will look at this situation later in this text.

3.3 Allowable losses   6/16

Deduct allowable capital losses from chargeable gains in the tax year in which they arise. Any loss which cannot be set off is carried forward to set against future chargeable gains. Losses must be used as soon as possible (subject to the following paragraph). Losses may not normally be set against income (unless they arise on the disposal of certain unquoted trading company shares – see earlier in this text).

Allowable losses brought forward are only set off to reduce current year chargeable gains less current year allowable losses to the annual exempt amount. No set-off is made if net chargeable gains for the current year do not exceed the annual exempt amount.

3.4 Example: the use of losses

(a) George has chargeable gains for 2018/19 of £13,000 and allowable losses of £6,000. As the losses are **current year losses** they must be fully relieved against the £13,000 of gains to produce net gains of £7,000, despite the fact that net gains are below the annual exempt amount.

(b) Bob has gains of £15,600 for 2018/19 and allowable losses brought forward of £6,000. Bob restricts his loss relief to £3,900 so as to leave net gains of £(15,600 – 3,900) = £11,700, which will be exactly covered by his annual exempt amount for 2018/19. The remaining £2,100 of losses will be carried forward to 2019/20.

(c) Tom has chargeable gains of £11,500 for 2018/19 and losses brought forward from 2017/18 of £4,000. He will not use the losses in 2018/19 and will carry forward all of his losses to 2019/20. His gains of £11,500 are covered by his annual exempt amount for 2018/19.

3.5 Losses in the year of death   12/14

Losses arising in the tax year in which an individual dies can be carried back to the previous three tax years, later years first, and used so as to reduce gains for each of the years to an amount covered by the appropriate annual exempt amount. Only losses in excess of gains in the year of death can be carried back.

Joe dies on 1 January 2019. His chargeable gains and allowable loss have been as follows.

	Gain/(loss) £	Annual exempt amount £
2018/19	2,000	11,700
	(12,000)	
2017/18	11,500	11,300
2016/17	9,000	11,100
2015/16	28,000	11,100

How will the loss be set off?

Answer

The £10,000 net loss which arises in 2018/19 will be carried back. We must set off the loss against the 2018/19 gains first even though the gains are covered by the 2018/19 annual exempt amount.

£200 of the loss will be used in 2017/18. None of the loss will be used in 2016/17 (because the gains for that year are covered by the annual exempt amount), and so the remaining £9,800 will be used in 2015/16. Repayments of CGT will follow.

4 Valuing assets

FAST FORWARD

Market value must be used in certain capital gains computations. There are special rules for shares and securities.

4.1 General rules

Where market value is used in a chargeable gains computation (see Section 2 above), **the value to be used is the price which the assets in question might reasonably be expected to fetch on a sale in the open market.**

4.2 Shares and securities

The market value of quoted shares is the lower of the two prices shown in the Stock Exchange Daily Official List plus one-half of the difference between those two prices.

 Question

Calculation of CGT value

Shares in Abacus plc are quoted at 100–110p. What is the market value for CGT purposes?

Answer

The value is $100 + \frac{1}{2} \times (110 - 100) = 105p$.

Unquoted shares are harder to value than quoted shares. HMRC have a special office, Shares and Assets Valuation, to deal with the valuation of unquoted shares.

5 Connected persons

FAST FORWARD
> Disposals between connected persons are always deemed to take place for a consideration equal to market value. Any loss arising on a disposal to a connected person can be set only against a gain arising on a disposal to the same connected person.

5.1 Definition and effect   6/17

A transaction between 'connected persons' is treated as one between parties to a transaction otherwise than by way of a bargain made at arm's length. **This means that the acquisition and disposal are deemed to take place for a consideration equal to the market value of the asset, rather than the actual price paid.** In addition, if a loss results, it can be set only against gains arising in the same or future years from disposals to the same connected person and the loss can only be set off if he or she is still connected with the person sustaining the loss.

Key term

> **Connected person.** An individual is connected with:
>
> - Their spouse/civil partner
> - Their relatives (brothers, sisters, ancestors and lineal descendants)
> - The relatives of their spouse/civil partner
> - The spouses/civil partners of their and their spouse/civil partner's relatives
> - Their business partners, partners' spouses/civil partners and partners' relatives
> - The trustees of a trust of which the individual is the settlor

5.2 Assets disposed of in a series of transactions

A taxpayer might attempt to avoid tax by disposing of their property piecemeal to persons connected with them. For example, a majority holding of shares might be broken up into several minority holdings, each with a much lower value per share, and each of the shareholder's children could be given a minority holding.

To prevent the avoidance of tax in this way, **where a person disposes of assets to one or more persons, with whom they are connected, in a series of linked transactions, the disposal proceeds for each disposal will be a proportion of the value of the assets taken together**. Thus in the example of the shareholding, the value of the majority holding would be apportioned between the minority holdings. Transactions are linked if they occur within six years of each other.

6 Married couples and civil partners   12/13, 6/16

FAST FORWARD
> Spouses/civil partners are treated as separate people. Transfers of assets between spouses/civil partners give rise to neither a gain nor a loss.

Spouses/civil partners are taxed as two separate people. Each has an annual exempt amount, and losses of one spouse/civil partner cannot be set against gains of the other.

Disposals between spouses/civil partners who are living together give rise to no gain and no loss, whatever actual price (if any) **was charged by the person transferring the asset** to their spouse/civil partner. This means that there is no chargeable gain or allowance loss and the transferee takes over the transferor's cost.

Since transfers between spouses/civil partners are on a no gain no loss basis, it may be beneficial to transfer the whole or part of an asset to the spouse/civil partner with an unused annual exempt amount or with taxable income below the basic rate limit. The transferee spouse then makes a disposal to a third party, either alone (if the whole asset is transferred) or jointly with the transferor spouse (if only part of the asset is transferred). It is very important that the transferee spouse/civil partner does not have any arrangement to pay back their net proceeds of sale to the transferor spouse/civil partner. If such an arrangement is in place, HM Revenue & Customs may contend that the no gain no loss disposal was not valid and treat the transferor spouse as making the entire disposal.

Question — Inter spouse transfer

Harry has taxable income of £60,000 in 2018/19 and makes chargeable gains of £20,000 in 2018/19 on share disposals. His wife, Margaret, has taxable income of £6,990 in 2018/19 and has no chargeable assets. Harry bought a plot of land for £150,000 in 2014. He gave it to Margaret when it was worth £180,100 on 10 May 2018. Margaret sold it on 27 August 2018 for £188,800. The land is not residential property and does not qualify for entrepreneurs' relief.

Calculate any chargeable gains arising to Harry and Margaret in respect of the land and show the tax saving arising from the transfer between Harry and Margaret, followed by the disposal by Margaret, compared with Harry directly disposing of the land in August 2018.

Answer

The disposal from Harry to Margaret is a no gain no loss disposal. Harry has no chargeable gain, and the cost for Margaret is Harry's original cost.

The gain on the sale by Margaret is:

	£
Proceeds of sale	188,800
Less cost	(150,000)
Gain	38,800

Margaret's gain will be reduced by her annual exempt amount to £27,100 (£38,800 – £11,700). Margaret also has £(34,500 – 6,990) = £27,510 of her basic rate band remaining. She will therefore pay CGT at 10% on the taxable gain. In contrast, Harry would have paid CGT on £38,800 at 20%.

The tax saving is therefore:

	£
Tax saved on annual exempt amount £11,700 @ 20%	2,340
Tax saved at basic rate £27,100 @ (20 – 10)%	2,710
Tax saving on disposal by Margaret instead of Harry	5,050

This tax saving will only be obtained if Margaret does not have an agreement to pay back the net proceeds of sale to Harry.

7 Business partnerships

FAST FORWARD

> On the disposal of a partnership asset, the gain or loss is apportioned to partners in their capital profit sharing ratio.

When a business partnership disposes of an asset, any chargeable gain or allowable loss is apportioned to the partners in their capital profit sharing ratio.

8 Part disposals   12/14, 12/16

FAST FORWARD

> On a part disposal, the cost must usually be apportioned between the part disposed of and the part retained. On a small part disposal of land, there is no chargeable gain and the net proceeds of disposal are deducted from the cost of the land retained.

8.1 Basic rule

The disposal of part of a chargeable asset is a chargeable event. The chargeable gain (or allowable loss) is computed by deducting from the disposal value a fraction of the original cost of the whole asset.

Formula to learn

The fraction is:

$$\frac{A}{A+B} = \frac{\text{value of the part disposed of}}{\text{value of the part disposed of} + \text{market value of the remainder}}$$

In this fraction, A is the proceeds (for arm's length disposals) *before* deducting incidental costs of disposal.

The part disposal fraction should not be applied indiscriminately. Any expenditure incurred wholly in respect of a particular part of an asset should be treated as an allowable deduction in full for that part and not apportioned, such as incidental selling expenses, which are wholly attributable to the part disposed of.

Question

Part disposal

Henry owns a 4 hectare plot of land which originally cost him £150,000. He sold one hectare in July 2018 for £60,000. The incidental costs of sale were £3,000. The market value of the 3 hectares remaining is estimated to be £180,000. What is the gain on the sale of the one hectare?

Answer

The amount of the cost attributable to the part sold is $\frac{60,000}{60,000+180,000} \times £150,000 = £37,500$

	£
Proceeds	60,000
Less disposal costs	(3,000)
Net proceed of sale	57,000
Less cost (see above)	(37,500)
Gain	19,500

8.2 Land: small part disposal proceeds

Where the **consideration** for a part disposal of land **does not exceed 20% of the market value of the entire holding** of land prior to the part disposal, a chargeable disposal does not take place. The taxpayer must make a **claim** by the first anniversary of 31 January following the end of the tax year. The net disposal proceeds are deducted from allowable expenditure when computing a gain on a later disposal of the remaining land.

Question

Small part disposals of land

Bertha buys 10 acres of land for £20,000. She sells 1½ acres for £5,000 in July 2018 and disposal costs amount to £50. Market value of the land immediately prior to the disposal is £30,000. You are required to show Bertha's CGT position.

The consideration (£5,000) is less than 20% of market value (20% of £30,000 = £6,000). Bertha may therefore claim for the relief to apply. As a result, no chargeable disposal takes place in July 2018.

Allowable cost of the land retained is:

	£
Cost of 10 acres	20,000
Deduct: net proceeds of part disposal (£5,000 – £50)	(4,950)
Allowable expenditure of land retained	15,050

There are two further conditions to meet before this relief can apply:

- Proceeds from the part disposal do not exceed £20,000; and

- Aggregate proceeds from the part disposal and any other disposals of land (including buildings) in the same tax year do not exceed £20,000.

8.3 Example: proceeds exceeding £20,000

If, in the previous example, Bertha had made another disposal of land for £15,750 in 2018/19, the relief could not apply since proceeds for the tax year (ie £15,750 + £5,000 = £20,750) would exceed £20,000. The normal part disposal rules would apply.

Chapter roundup

- For CGT to apply, there needs to be a chargeable person, a chargeable disposal and a chargeable asset.

- A chargeable disposal usually occurs on the date of the contract. The date of disposal should be considered in relation to the use of capital losses, the annual exempt amount, the date for payment of tax and the availability of reliefs.

- A gain or loss is computed by taking the proceeds and deducting the cost. Incidental costs of acquisition and disposal are deducted together with any enhancement expenditure reflected in the state and nature of the asset at the date of disposal.

- CGT is usually payable at the rate of 10% or 20% on most chargeable gains depending on the individual's taxable income. There are rates of 18% and 28% for residential property. Individuals are entitled to an annual exempt amount.

- Market value must be used in certain capital gains computations. There are special rules for shares and securities.

- Disposals between connected persons are always deemed to take place for a consideration equal to market value. Any loss arising on a disposal to a connected person can be set only against a gain arising on a disposal to the same connected person.

- Spouses/civil partners are treated as separate people. Transfers of assets between spouses/civil partners give rise to neither a gain nor a loss.

- On the disposal of a partnership asset, the gain or loss is apportioned to partners in their capital profit sharing ratio.

- On a part disposal, the cost must usually be apportioned between the part disposed of and the part retained. On a small part disposal of land, there is no chargeable gain and the net proceeds of disposal are deducted from the cost of the land retained.

Quick quiz

1   Give some examples of chargeable disposals.

2   Are the following assets chargeable to CGT or exempt?

    (a)   Shares (not held in an ISA)
    (b)   Car
    (c)   Land
    (d)   Victoria Cross awarded to owner
    (e)   National Savings and Investments Certificates

3   Jed buys a house. He repairs the roof, installs central heating and builds an extension. The extension is blown down in a storm and not replaced. Which of these improvements is allowable as enhancement expenditure on a subsequent sale?

4   At what rates do individuals pay CGT on gains which are not residential property gains and do not qualify for entrepreneurs' relief?

5   To what extent must allowable losses be set against chargeable gains?

6   Shares in Abbey plc are quoted at 410 – 414p. What is the market value for CGT?

7   With whom is an individual connected?

8   Keith and Jonas have been in partnership for many years sharing income and capital profits in the ratio 3:2. In January 2019, the partnership sold its office building making a chargeable gain of £40,000. What are the gains assessable on Keith and Jonas on the sale?

9   10 acres of land are sold for £15,000, out of a plot of 25 acres. The original cost of the whole plot was £9,000 and costs of sale are £2,000. The rest of the land is valued at £30,000. What is the allowable expenditure?

Answers to quick quiz

1   Sales of assets or parts of assets
    Gifts of assets or parts of assets
    Receipts of capital sums following the surrender of rights to assets
    Loss or destruction of assets

2   (a)   Shares – Chargeable
    (b)   Car – Exempt as motor vehicle suitable for private use
    (c)   Land – Chargeable
    (d)   Victoria Cross – Exempt as medal for bravery not acquired by purchase
    (e)   National Savings and Investments Certificates – Exempt

3   Repairs to roof – not allowable as enhancement expenditure because not capital in nature
    Central heating – allowable as enhancement expenditure
    Extension – not allowable as not reflected in state of asset at time of disposal

4   10% and 20%

5   Current year losses must be set off against gains in full, even if this reduces gains below the annual
    exempt amount. Losses brought forward or carried back from year of death are set off to bring down
    gains to the level of the annual exempt amount.

6   410p + ½ (414 − 410) = 412p

7   An individual is connected with:

    (a)   Their spouse ('spouse' includes civil partners)
    (b)   Their relatives (brothers, sisters, ancestors and lineal descendants)
    (c)   The relatives of their spouse
    (d)   The spouses of their and their spouse's relatives
    (e)   Their business partners, partners' spouses/civil partners and partners' relatives
    (f)   Trustees of a trust of which they are the settlor

8   Keith £40,000 × 3/5 = £24,000

    Jonas £40,000 × 2/5 = £16,000

9   $\dfrac{15,000}{15,000 + 30,000} \times £9,000 = £3,000 + £2,000 \text{ (costs of disposal)} = £5,000$

Now try the question below from the Practice Question Bank

Number	Level	Marks	Time
Q12	Introductory	19	37 mins

12

Shares and securities

Topic list	Syllabus reference
1 The matching rules for individuals	A2(a)C4
2 The share pool	A2(a)C4
3 Alterations of share capital	A2(f)(I),(III)
4 Gilts and qualifying corporate bonds	A2(f)(ii)

Introduction

In the previous chapter, we have revised the basic computation of chargeable gains and how to calculate the CGT payable. In this chapter, we look at shares and securities held by individuals.

Shares and securities need special treatment because an investor may hold several shares or securities in the same company, bought at different times for different prices but otherwise identical.

The rules for shares and securities held by companies are different and are dealt with later in this text.

In the next chapter, we will consider CGT deferral reliefs and the CGT implications of varying a will.

Study guide

		Intellectual level
2	**Chargeable gains and capital gains tax liabilities in situations involving further overseas aspects and in relation to closely related persons and trusts together with the application of additional exemptions and reliefs**	
(a)	The contents of the Taxation - United Kingdom (TX – UK) study guide for chargeable gains for individuals under heading:	2
•	C4 Gains and losses on the disposal of shares and securities	
(f)	Gains and losses on the disposal of shares and securities:	3
(i)	Extend the explanation of the treatment of rights issues to include the small part disposal rules applicable to rights issues	
(ii)	Define a qualifying corporate bond (QCB), and understand what makes a corporate bond non-qualifying. Understand the capital gains tax implications of the disposal of QCBs in exchange for cash or shares	
(iii)	Apply the rules relating to reorganisations, reconstructions and amalgamations and advise on the most tax efficient options available in given circumstances	

Exam guide

Shares and securities are some of the more common assets held by individuals, and knowing how to compute the gain on their disposal is fundamental to an understanding of capital gains.

> **Knowledge brought forward from earlier studies**

This chapter revises the identification rules for individuals and the computation of gains on disposals that were covered in Taxation (TX – UK). It expands on the rules for rights issues, takeovers and reorganisations. There have been no changes to the rules in 2018/19 from 2017/18.

1 The matching rules for individuals

FAST FORWARD

> There are special rules for matching shares sold with shares purchased. Disposals are matched first with shares acquired on the same day, then within the following 30 days and finally with the share pool.

Quoted and unquoted shares and securities present special problems when attempting to compute gains or losses on disposal. For instance, suppose that an individual buys some quoted shares in X plc as follows.

Date	Number of shares	Cost £
5 May 2013	220	150
17 August 2018	100	375

On 15 August 2018, the individual sells 120 of the shares for £1,450. To determine the chargeable gain, we need to be able to work out which shares out of the two original holdings were actually sold.

We therefore need **matching rules**. These **allow us to decide which shares have been sold and so work out what the allowable cost on disposal should be.**

At any one time, we will only be concerned with shares or securities of the same class in the same company. If an individual owns both ordinary shares and preference shares in X plc, we will deal with the two classes of share entirely separately, because they are distinguishable.

Below 'shares' refers to both shares and securities.

For individuals, share disposals are matched with acquisitions in the following order.

(a) **Same day acquisitions**

(b) **Acquisitions within the following 30 days** (known as the 'bed and breakfast rule') if more than one acquisition on a 'first in, first out' (FIFO) basis

(c) **Any shares in the share pool** (see below)

The 'bed and breakfast' rule stops shares being sold to crystallise a capital gain or loss, usually to use the annual exempt amount and then being repurchased a day or so later. Without the rule a gain or loss would arise on the sale since it would be 'matched' to the original acquisition.

Exam focus point

Learn the 'matching rules' because a crucial first step to getting a shares question right is to correctly match the shares sold to the original shares purchased.

2 The share pool

One of the competencies you require to fulfil Performance Objective 15 Tax computations and assessments of the PER is to prepare or contribute to the computation or assessment of tax computations for individuals. You can apply the knowledge you obtain from this section of the text to help to demonstrate this competence.

2.1 Composition of pool

We treat any other shares acquired as a 'pool' which grows as new shares are acquired and shrinks as they are disposed.

In making computations which use the share pool, we must keep track of:

(a) The **number** of shares
(b) The **cost** of the shares

2.2 Disposals from the share pool

In the case of a disposal the cost attributable to the shares disposed of is deducted from the amounts within the share pool. The proportion of the cost to take out of the pool should be computed using the A/(A + B) fraction that is used for any other part disposal. However, we are not usually given the value of the remaining shares (B in the fraction). We just use numbers of shares.

Question   The share pool

In August 2006 Oliver acquired 4,000 shares in Twist plc at a cost of £10,000. Oliver sold 3,000 shares on 10 July 2018 for £17,000. Compute the gain and the value of the share pool following the disposal.

Answer

The gain is computed as follows:

	£
Proceeds	17,000
Less cost (working)	(7,500)
Gain	9,500

Working: share pool

	No of shares	Cost £
Acquisition – August 2006	4,000	10,000
Disposal – July 2018	(3,000)	
Cost $\frac{3,000}{4,000} \times £10,000$		(7,500)
	1,000	2,500

Question   Matching rules

Anita acquired shares in Kent Ltd as follows:

1 July 2000	1,000 shares for	£2,000
11 April 2005	2,500 shares for	£7,500
17 July 2018	500 shares for	£2,000
10 August 2018	400 shares for	£1,680

Anita sold 4,000 shares for £16,400 on 17 July 2018.

Calculate Anita's net gain on sale.

Answer

First match the disposal with the acquisition on the same day:

	£
Proceeds $\frac{500}{4,000} \times £16,400$	2,050
Less cost	(2,000)
Gain	50

Next match the disposal with the acquisition in the next 30 days:

	£
Proceeds $\frac{400}{4,000} \times £16,400$	1,640
Less cost	(1,680)
Loss	(40)

Finally, match the disposal with the shares in the share pool:

	£
Proceeds $\frac{3,100}{4,000} \times £16,400$	12,710
Less cost (working)	(8,414)
Gain	4,296

Net gain £(50 + 4,296 – 40)	4,306

Working

	No. of shares	Cost £
1.7.00 Acquisition	1,000	2,000
11.4.05 Acquisition	2,500	7,500
	3,500	9,500
17.7.18 Disposal	(3,100)	(8,414)
c/f	400	1,086

3 Alterations of share capital

> On an alteration of share capital, the general principle is only to tax gains immediately if cash is paid to the investors.

3.1 General principle

On a reorganisation we must apportion the original base cost of whatever the shareholder had beforehand between the elements of whatever the shareholder has afterwards.

3.2 Capital distributions

Normally a capital distribution is treated as a part disposal of an asset. If, however, the distribution is small (normally taken to mean not more than the higher of 5% of the value of the shares and £3,000) **then any gain can be deferred by treating the distribution as a deduction from the cost of the shares for the purposes of calculating any gains or losses on future disposals.**

If the taxpayer wants a part disposal (for example to use his annual exempt amount) HMRC will allow this even if the proceeds are small.

Question
Capital distributions

Barry holds 1,000 shares in Woodleigh plc which cost £4,000 in August 2003. The company is now in liquidation and in June 2017 the liquidator made a distribution of 35p per share. The market value of the shares after the distribution was £7,000. In November 2018 Barry received a final distribution of £7,200.

Show any chargeable gains arising, assuming that there is no part disposal in June 2017.

Answer

No gain arises in June 2017 as the distribution in June 2017 is not more than the higher of £3,000 and 5% of the value of the shares: £(350 + 7,000) × 5% = £368. The November 2018 distribution is treated as follows.

	Cost £
Proceeds	7,200
Less cost £(4,000 − 350)	(3,650)
Gain	3,550

3.3 Bonus issues (scrip issues)

When a company issues bonus shares all that happens is that the size of the original holding is increased. Since bonus shares are free shares, issued at no cost, there is no need to adjust the original cost. Instead the numbers purchased at particular times are increased by the bonus. The normal matching rules will then be applied.

3.4 Rights issues

The difference between a bonus issue and a rights issue is that in a rights issue the new shares are paid for and this results in an adjustment to the original cost.

In an **open offer**, shareholders have a right to subscribe for a minimum number of shares based on their existing holdings and may buy additional shares. Subscriptions up to the minimum entitlement are treated as a rights issue. Additional subscriptions are treated as new purchases of shares.

Question

Simon had the following transactions in Star Ltd.

1.10.06	Bought 10,000 shares for £15,000
1.2.12	Took up rights issue 1 for 2 at £2.75 per share
14.10.18	Sold 2,000 shares for £6,000

Compute the gain arising in October 2018.

Answer

Share pool

	No. of shares	Cost £
1.10.06 Acquisition	10,000	15,000
1.2.12 Rights issue	5,000	13,750
	15,000	28,750
14.10.18 Sale	(2,000)	(3,833)
c/f	13,000	24,917

Gain

	£
Proceeds	6,000
Less cost	(3,833)
Gain	2,167

3.5 Sales of rights nil paid

Where the shareholder does not take up his rights but sells them to a third party without paying the company for the rights shares, the proceeds are treated as a capital distribution (see above) **and will be dealt with either under the part disposal rules or, if not more than the higher of £3,000 and 5% of the value of the shareholding giving rise to the disposal, as a reduction of original cost** (unless the taxpayer chooses to use the part disposal treatment, for example if the gain would be covered by the annual exempt amount).

3.6 Reorganisations

A reorganisation takes place where new shares or a mixture of new shares and loan stock are issued in exchange for the original shareholdings. The new shares take the place of the old shares. The problem is how to apportion the original cost between the different types of capital issued on the reorganisation.

If the new shares and securities are quoted, then the cost is apportioned by reference to the market values of the new types of capital on the first day of quotation after the reorganisation.

Question

An original quoted shareholding of 3,000 shares is held in a share pool with a cost of £13,250.

In 2018, there is a reorganisation whereby each ordinary share is exchanged for two 'A' ordinary shares (quoted at £2 each) and one preference share (quoted at £1 each). Show how the original cost will be apportioned.

Share pool

	New holding	MV £	Cost £
Ords 2 new shares	6,000	12,000	10,600
Prefs 1 new shares	3,000	3,000	2,650
Total		15,000	13,250

Working

$^{12}/_{15} \times £13,250$ = cost of ordinary shares
$^{3}/_{15} \times £13,250$ = cost of preference shares

Where a reorganisation takes place and the new shares and securities are unquoted, the cost of the original holding is apportioned using the values of the new shares and securities when they come to be disposed of.

For both quoted and unquoted shares and securities, any incidental costs (such as professional fees) are treated as additional consideration for the new shares and securities.

3.7 Takeovers   12/13, 6/16

FAST FORWARD

> The special rules on takeovers only apply if the exchange is for bona fide commercial reasons and not for the avoidance of tax.

A chargeable gain does not arise on a 'paper for paper' takeover. The cost of the original holding is passed on to the new holding which takes the place of the original holding. If part of the takeover consideration is cash then a gain must be computed: the normal part disposal rules will apply.

If the cash received is not more than the higher of 5% of the total value on the takeover, and £3,000, then the small distribution rules apply and the cash received will be deducted from cost for the purpose of further disposals, unless the taxpayer chooses the part disposal treatment.

The takeover rules apply where the company issuing the new shares ends up with more than 25% of the ordinary share capital of the old company or the majority of the voting power in the old company, or the company issuing the new shares makes a general offer to shareholders in the other company which is initially made subject to a condition which, if satisfied, would give the first company control of the second company.

The exchange must take place for bona fide commercial reasons and must not have as its main purpose, or one of its main purposes, the avoidance of CGT or corporation tax.

Question   Takeover

Millie held 20,000 £1 shares in Drop plc out of a total number of issued shares of one million. They were bought in 2002 for £2 each. In 2018 the board of Drop plc agreed to a takeover bid by Stir plc under which shareholders in Drop plc received three ordinary Stir plc shares plus one preference share for every four shares held in Drop plc. Immediately following the takeover, the ordinary shares in Stir plc were quoted at £5 each and the preferences shares at 90p. Show the base costs of the ordinary shares and the preference shares.

Answer

The total value due to Millie on the takeover is as follows.

		£
Ordinary	20,000 × 3/4 × £5	75,000
Preference	20,000 × 1/4 × 90p	4,500
		79,500

Original cost of shares = 20,000 × £2 = £40,000

The base costs of the new holdings are therefore:

	£
Ordinary shares: 75,000/79,500 × £40,000	37,736
Preference shares: 4,500/79,500 × £40,000	2,264
	40,000

Part of the takeover consideration may include the right to receive deferred consideration in the form of shares or loan stock in the new company. The amount of the deferred consideration may be unascertainable at the date of the takeover, perhaps because it is dependent on the future profits of the company whose shares are acquired. The right is valued and treated as a security. This means the takeover rules apply and there is no need to calculate a gain in respect of the right. The issue of shares or loan stock as a result of the right is treated as a conversion of the right and, again, no gain arises.

3.8 Interaction with entrepreneurs' relief

Entrepreneurs' relief is discussed in Section 2 of Chapter 13. You may wish to read that first before studying this section.

There may be a problem if the rules on reorganisations and takeovers described above apply and the new shares do not qualify for entrepreneurs' relief when they are eventually disposed of (for example because the shareholder no longer works for the company or the level of shareholding is too low). In this case, without special rules, any entrepreneurs' relief accrued on the old shares will be lost.

In this case, **the legislation provides that the shareholder can elect to disapply the usual reorganisation or takeover treatment and can claim entrepreneurs' relief in the year of the reorganisation or takeover.** The shareholder will then make a chargeable disposal with proceeds of the shares acquired and costs apportioned as already described.

The election must be made by the same date as the claim for entrepreneurs' relief. So if the takeover occurs in 2018/19, the claim must be made by 31 January 2021.

4 Gilts and qualifying corporate bonds

Gilts and QCBs held by individuals are exempt from CGT.

4.1 Definitions and treatment

Gilts are British Government and Government guaranteed securities as shown on the Treasury list. Gilt strips (capital or interest entitlements sold separately) are also gilts. You may assume that the list of gilts includes all issues of Treasury Loan, Treasury Stock, Exchequer Loan, Exchequer Stock and War Loan.

Disposals of gilt edged securities (gilts) and qualifying corporate bonds by individuals and trusts are exempt from CGT. The rules for companies are different, and are explained later in this text.

Key term

> A **qualifying corporate bond (QCB)** is a security (whether or not secured on assets) which satisfies all of the following conditions:
>
> (a) Represents a **'normal commercial loan'**. This excludes any bonds which are convertible into shares (although bonds convertible into other bonds which would be QCBs are not excluded), or which carry the right to excessive interest or interest which depends on the results of the issuer's business;
>
> (b) Is **expressed in sterling** and for which no provision is made for conversion into or redemption in another currency;
>
> (c) Was **acquired** by the person now disposing of it **after 13 March 1984**; and
>
> (d) Does not have a redemption value which depends on a published index of share prices on a stock exchange.
>
> Permanent interest bearing shares issued by building societies which meet condition (b) above are also QCBs.

4.2 Reorganisations involving QCBs

FAST FORWARD

> If a reorganisation involves the acquisition of QCBs, a gain to the date of the takeover is computed but is 'frozen' until the disposal of the QCB.

Special rules apply when a reorganisation involves qualifying corporate bonds, either as the security in issue before the reorganisation (the 'old asset') or as a security issued on the reorganisation (a 'new asset').

Where QCBs are the old asset, the newly issued shares are treated as acquired at the time of the reorganisation, for the then market value of the old asset. This market value is reduced by any money paid to the security-holders, or increased by any money paid by them. If a company holds the QCBs, then the QCBs are treated as sold at the same time for their market value, so as to find the company's profit or loss.

Where QCBs are the new asset, the chargeable gain which would have accrued if the old asset had been sold at its market value at the time of the reorganisation must be computed and apportioned between the new assets issued. When the QCBs are disposed of, the part of that gain apportioned to them becomes chargeable. However, if that disposal is a no gain/no loss disposal to a spouse/civil partner, the gain does not become chargeable until a disposal outside the marriage. Furthermore, if the reorganisation is followed by the owner's death while he still owns the QCBs, the gain never becomes chargeable.

QCBs are often used in takeover situations instead of cash where for most shareholders the cash would not be a small capital distribution. This enables the shareholder to defer the gain until the QCBs are disposed of. This is often done over a period of time so as to use the annual exempt amount and any other reliefs available.

Question   Takeovers including QCBs

Zelda owned 10,000 shares in Red Ltd which she had acquired for £20,000. In July 2017, Red Ltd was taken over by Rainbow plc and Zelda received:

- 6,000 ordinary shares in Rainbow plc worth £2 per share; and

- £9,000 loan stock (which were qualifying corporate bonds) in Rainbow plc worth £4 for each £1 nominal value.

In August 2018 Zelda sold 2,000 shares in Rainbow plc for £2.40 per share, and £3,375 of the loan stock in Rainbow plc for £4.50 for each £1 nominal value.

Show the capital gains implications of the takeover and the subsequent sales.

Answer

July 2017

The total value due to Zelda on the takeover is as follows.

	£
Ordinary shares 6,000 × £2	12,000
Loan stock £9,000 × £4	36,000
Gain	48,000

The base costs of the new holdings are therefore:

	£
Ordinary shares: 12,000/48,000 × £20,000	5,000
Loan stock: 36,000/48,000 × £20,000	15,000
	20,000

On the takeover, there is no disposal for CGT on the exchange of Red Ltd shares for the Rainbow plc shares and the loan stock. However, the gain up to the date of the takeover on the loan stock is calculated as follows:

	£
Market value of loan stock received on takeover	36,000
Less cost	(15,000)
Gain	21,000

This gain is 'frozen'.

August 2018

On the disposal of the shares, a gain arises in the normal way:

	£
Proceeds 2,000 × £2.40	4,800
Less cost £5,000 × 2,000/6,000	(1,667)
Gain	3,133

Note that this gain includes the gain up to the date of the takeover and the gain from the date of the takeover.

On the disposal of the loan stock, part of the frozen gain becomes chargeable:

£21,000 × 3,375/9,000   £7,875

The gain on the loan stock sold is exempt from CGT because the loan stock itself are qualifying corporate bonds.

Exam focus point

> Takeover with corporate bonds were tested in June 2011 Question 4 Capstan. The examining team commented that 'there was often confusion as to the treatment of the sale of the corporate bonds. Many candidates who knew that corporate bonds are exempt from capital gains tax went on to calculate a gain on the sale and include it in the taxable capital gains for the year. Also, many candidates were not able to identify the gain on the original shares that was frozen at the time of the paper for paper exchange and then charged when the corporate bonds were sold.'

4.3 Interaction with entrepreneurs' relief

The situation in respect of entrepreneurs' relief available on the frozen gain on QCBs is similar to that involving shares. An election can be made for the gain not to be deferred but instead brought into charge at the time of the takeover, accompanied by a claim for entrepreneurs' relief (assuming the original shares met the relevant conditions). If no election is made and the gain is then deferred under the normal gains rules, the frozen gain will usually not qualify for entrepreneurs' relief when it comes back into charge on disposal.

Chapter roundup

- There are special rules for matching shares sold with shares purchased. Disposals are matched first with shares acquired on the same day, then within the following 30 days and finally with the share pool.

- On an alteration of share capital, the general principle is only to tax gains immediately if cash is paid to the investors.

- The special rules on takeovers only apply if the exchange is for bona fide commercial reasons and not for the avoidance of tax.

- Gilts and QCBs held by individuals are exempt from CGT.

- If a reorganisation involves the acquisition of QCBs, a gain to the date of the takeover is computed but is 'frozen' until the disposal of the QCB.

Quick quiz

1   In what order are acquisitions of shares matched with disposals for individuals?

2   In July 2006 Vince acquired 1,000 shares. He acquired 1,000 more shares on each of 15 January 2008 and 15 January 2019 in Xenon plc. He sells 1,800 shares on 10 January 2019. How are the shares matched on sale?

3   Sharon acquired 10,000 share in Zoom plc in 2006. She takes up a 1 for 2 rights offer in July 2018. How many shares does Sharon have in her share pool after the rights issue?

4   What is a qualifying corporate bond?

5   Why might a shareholder prefer to take a qualifying corporate bond instead of cash on a takeover?

Answers to quick quiz

1   The matching of shares sold is in the following order.

    (a)   Same day acquisitions
    (b)   Acquisitions within the following 30 days
    (c)   Shares in the shares pool

2   15 January 2019 1,000 shares (following 30 days)
    Share pool 800 shares

3   10,000 + 5,000 = 15,000 shares

4   A qualifying corporate bond is a security which:

- Represents a normal commercial loan
- Is expressed in sterling
- Was acquired after 13 March 1984
- Is not redeemable in relation to share prices on a stock exchange

5   The gain deferred on taking a qualifying corporate bond will be the same as if cash was taken but it is frozen until the bond is are disposed of which can over a period of time so as to use the annual exempt amount and any other reliefs available.

Now try the question below from the Practice Question Bank

Number	Level	Marks	Time
Q13	Introductory	15	29 mins

Chargeable gains: reliefs

Introduction

In the previous chapters, we have seen how to calculate chargeable gains. We now look at various reliefs relating to gains.

We first look at the gains people make on their homes which are usually exempt. This means there is no capital gains tax charge when people move home, but also means that there is no relief if their house is sold at a loss.

Entrepreneurs' relief is a very important relief. It applies on the disposal of a business and on the disposal of certain trading company shares. It applies a rate of 10% on all or part of the chargeable gains arising on such disposals, regardless of the level of the individual's taxable income. There is a similar investors' relief for external investors in a company.

In certain circumstances, it may be possible to defer a gain – that is to remove it from an immediate charge to CGT. However, it is important to realise the gain has not been exempted and it may become charged in the future.

Deferral reliefs operate in two ways. First, the gain may be deducted from the base cost of an asset (for example, rollover relief for replacement with non-depreciating business assets, incorporation relief, gift relief). Second, the gain may be 'frozen' until a certain event occurs (deferral relief for replacement with depreciating business assets, EIS deferral relief).

SEIS reinvestment relief operates in a different way as it exempts part of a gain made in a tax year if the individual subscribes for SEIS shares in the same tax year.

In the next chapter, we will look some further rules for gains and losses.

Study guide

		Intellectual level
2	**Chargeable gains and capital gains tax liabilities in situations involving further overseas aspects and in relation to closely related persons and trusts together with the application of additional exemptions and reliefs**	
(a)	The contents of the Taxation (TX – UK) study guide for chargeable gains for individuals under headings:	2
•	C3 Gains and losses on the disposal of movable and immovable property	
•	C5 The computation of capital gains tax	
•	C6 The use of exemptions and reliefs in deferring and minimising tax liabilities arising on the disposal of capital assets	
(g)	The use of exemptions and reliefs in deferring and minimising tax liabilities arising on the disposal of capital assets:	3
(i)	Understand and apply enterprise investment scheme reinvestment relief	
(ii)	Understand and apply seed enterprise investment scheme reinvestment relief	
(iii)	Advise on the availability of entrepreneurs' relief in relation to associated disposals	
(iv)	Understand and apply the relief that is available on the transfer of an unincorporated business to a limited company	

Exam guide

Minimising tax liabilities is likely to feature at some point in your exam. The reliefs in this chapter should be very familiar to you from your Taxation (TX – UK) studies.

Knowledge brought forward from earlier studies

This chapter revises principal private residence relief, entrepreneurs' relief, gift relief and rollover relief for the replacement of business assets, all of which you will have studied in Taxation (TX – UK). The examining team has identified essential underpinning knowledge from the Taxation (TX – UK) syllabus which is particularly important that you revise as part of your Advanced Taxation (ATX – UK) studies. In this chapter, the relevant topics are:

		Intellectual level
C3	**Gains and losses on the disposal of movable and immovable property**	
(c)	Calculate the chargeable gain when a principal private residence is disposed of	2
C5	**The computation of capital gains tax**	
(b)	Explain and apply entrepreneurs' relief	2
C6	**The use of exemptions and reliefs in deferring and minimising tax liabilities arising on the disposal of capital assets**	
(a)	Explain and apply capital gains tax reliefs:	
(i)	Rollover relief	2
(ii)	Holdover relief for the gift of business assets	2

The chapter extends your studies on entrepreneurs' relief, including investors' relief. Gift relief for gifts to trusts, incorporation relief, and EIS and SEIS reinvestment reliefs.

There are no changes in 2018/19 from the material studied in Taxation (TX – UK) in 2017/18.

1 Private residences   6/14, 6/15, 6/17

1.1 General principles

> There is an exemption for gains on principal private residences, but the exemption may be restricted because of periods of non-occupation or because of business use.

A gain arising on the sale of an individual's only or main private residence (his principal private residence or PPR) is exempt from CGT. The exemption covers total grounds, including the house, of up to half a hectare. The total grounds can exceed half a hectare if the house is large enough to warrant it, but if not, the gain on the excess grounds is taxable. If the grounds do not adjoin the house (for example when a road separates the two), they **may** still qualify but they may not; each case must be argued on its merits.

For the exemption to be available the taxpayer must have occupied the property as a residence rather than just as temporary accommodation.

There are special rules which apply if the residence is situated in a country other than one in which the individual (or his spouse/civil partner) is resident for tax purposes. These rules are discussed in the section on overseas aspects of capital gains tax later in this chapter.

1.2 Occupation

The gain is wholly exempt where the owner has occupied the whole of the residence throughout his period of ownership. Where occupation has been for only part of the period, a proportion of the gain is exempted.

Formula to learn

> The exempt proportion is:
>
> $$\text{Gain before relief} \times \frac{\text{Period of occupation}}{\text{Total period of ownership}}$$

The **last 18 months of ownership are always** treated as if it were **a period of occupation**, if at some time the residence has been the taxpayer's main residence, even if within those last 18 months the taxpayer also has another house which is his principal private residence.

1.3 Deemed occupation

The **period of occupation is also deemed to include certain periods of absence, provided the individual had no other exempt residence at the time and the period of absence was at some time both preceded by and followed by a period of actual occupation.** Deemed but non-actual occupation during the last 18 months of ownership does not count for this purpose.

These periods of **deemed occupation** are:

(a)   Any period (or periods taken together) of absence, for any reason, **up to three years**; and

(b)   **Any periods** during which the owner was **required by his employment (ie employed taxpayer) to live abroad**; and

(c)   Any period (or periods taken together) **up to four years** during which the owner was **required to live elsewhere due to his work** (ie both employed and self employed taxpayer) so that he could not occupy his private residence.

It does not matter if the residence is let during the absence.

Exempt periods of absence must normally be preceded and followed by periods of **actual occupation**. The reoccupation condition does not apply if an individual, who has been required to work abroad or elsewhere (ie the latter two categories mentioned above), is unable to resume residence in his home because the terms of his employment require him to work elsewhere.

Question	**Principal private residence relief**

Alan purchased a house in London on 1 April 1993 for £88,200. He lived in the house until 31 December 1994. He then worked abroad for two years before returning to the UK to live in the house again on 1 January 1997. He stayed in the house until 30 June 2013 before moving out to live with his mother in Scotland until the house was sold on 31 December 2018 for £520,000.

Calculate Alan's capital gains tax payable for 2018/19 assuming that this is the only disposal that he makes in the tax year and that he is a higher rate taxpayer.

Answer

	£
Proceeds	520,000
Less cost	(88,200)
Gain before PPR exemption	431,800
Less PPR exemption (working)	
$\frac{261}{309} \times £431,800$	(364,724)
Chargeable gain	67,076
Less annual exempt amount	(11,700)
Chargeable gain	55,376
CGT on £55,376 @ 28% (residential property higher rate)	15,505

Working

Exempt and chargeable periods

	Period	Total months	Exempt months	Chargeable months
(i)	April 1993–December 1994 (occupied)	21	21	0
(ii)	January 1995–December 1996 (working abroad)	24	24	0
(iii)	January 1997–June 2013 (occupied)	198	198	0
(iv)	July 2013–June 2017 (see below)	48	0	48
(v)	July 2017–December 2018 (last 18 months)	18	18	0
		309	261	48

No part of the period from July 2013 to June 2017 can be covered by the exemption for three years of absence for any reason because it is not followed at any time by actual occupation.

Exam focus point

> To help you to answer questions such as that above it is useful to draw up a table showing period of ownership, exempt months (real/deemed occupation) and chargeable months (non-occupation). You should also provide an explanation for any periods of deemed occupation.

1.4 Business use

Where part of a residence is used exclusively for business purposes throughout the period of ownership, the gain attributable to use of that part is taxable.

The 'last 18 months always exempt' rule does not apply to that part.

Question

Sameer purchased a property for £35,000 on 31 May 2012 and began operating a dental practice from that date in one quarter of the house. He closed the dental practice on 31 December 2018, selling the house on that date for £130,000. Compute the gain, if any, arising.

Answer

	£
Proceeds	130,000
Less cost	(35,000)
Gain before PPR exemption	95,000
Less PPR exemption 0.75 × £95,000	(71,250)
Gain	23,750

Exemption is lost on one quarter throughout the period of ownership (including the last 18 months) because of the use of that fraction for business purposes.

If part of a house was used for business purposes for part of the period of ownership, the gain is apportioned between chargeable and exempt parts in a just and reasonable manner. If the business part was **at some time** used as part of the only or main residence, the gain apportioned to that part **will** qualify for the last 18 months exemption.

1.5 More than one residence

1.5.1 The election for a residence to be treated as the main residence

Where a person has more than one residence (owned or rented), he may elect for one to be regarded as his main residence by notice to HMRC within two years of commencing occupation of the second residence. An election can have effect for any period beginning not more than two years prior to the date of election until it is varied by giving further notice. (The further notice may itself be backdated by up to two years.) In order for the election to be made, the individual must actually reside in both residences. Any period of ownership of a residence not nominated as the main residence will be a chargeable period for that residence.

There are further rules about electing for a UK property to be treated as the main residence where such a property is disposed of by a non-UK resident (see later in this chapter).

1.5.2 Job-related accommodation

The rule limiting people to only one main residence is relaxed for individuals living in job-related accommodation.

Such individuals will be treated as occupying any second dwelling house which they own if they intend in due course to occupy the dwelling house as their only or main residence. Thus it is not necessary to establish any actual residence in such cases. This rule extends to self-employed persons required to live in job-related accommodation (for example tenants of public houses).

Key term

> A person lives in **job-related accommodation** where:
>
> (a) It is necessary for the **proper performance of his duties**; or
>
> (b) It is provided for the **better performance of his duties** and his is one of the kinds of employment in which it is **customary** for employers to provide accommodation; or
>
> (c) There is a **special threat to the employee's security** and use of the accommodation is part of security arrangements.

1.6 Spouses/civil partners

Where a married couple/civil partners live together only one residence may qualify as the main residence for relief. If each owned one property before marriage/registration of the civil partnership, a new two year period for electing for which is to be treated as the main residence starts on marriage/registration.

Where a marriage/civil partnership has broken down and one spouse/civil partner owning or having an interest in the matrimonial home has ceased to occupy the house, by concession the departing spouse/civil partner will continue to be treated as resident for capital gains tax purposes provided that the other has continued to reside in the home and the departing spouse/civil partner has not elected that some other house should be treated as his or her main residence for this period. This only applies where one spouse disposes of his interest to the other spouse.

Where a house passes from one spouse/civil partner to the other (for example on death), the new owner also inherits the old owner's periods of ownership and occupation for PPR relief purposes.

1.7 Letting relief

FAST FORWARD

> There is also a relief for letting out a principal private residence if the gain arising during the letting would not be covered by the main relief.

The principal private residence exemption is extended to any gain accruing while the property is let, up to a certain limit. The two main circumstances in which the letting exemption applies are:

(a) When the owner is absent and lets the property, where the absence is not a deemed period of occupation.

(b) When the owner lets part of the property while still occupying the rest of it. The absence from the let part cannot be a deemed period of occupation, because the owner has another residence (the rest of the property). However, the let part will qualify for the last 18 months exemption **if** the let part has **at some time** been part of the only or main residence.

In both cases the letting must be for residential use. **The extra exemption is restricted to the lowest of:**

(a) The amount of the total **gain** which is already **exempt under the PPR provisions** (including the last 18 months exemption)

(b) The gain accruing during the letting period (the **letting part of the gain**)

(c) **£40,000**

The letting exemption cannot convert a gain into an allowable loss.

If a lodger lives as a member of the owner's family, sharing their living accommodation and eating with them, the whole property is regarded as the owner's main residence.

Question

Letting relief

Carole purchased a house on 1 April 2004 for £90,000. She sold it on 31 August 2018 for £340,000. In 2009 the house was redecorated and Carole began to live on the top floor renting out the balance of the house (constituting 60% of the total house) to tenants between 1 July 2009 and 31 December 2017. On 2 January 2018 Carole put the whole house on the market but continued to live only on the top floor until the house was sold. What is the chargeable gain?

	£
Proceeds	340,000
Less cost	(90,000)
Gain before PPR exemption	250,000
Less PPR exemption (working)	
$£250,000 \times \dfrac{117.8}{173}$	(170,231)
	79,769

Less letting exemption: Lowest of:

(a) Gain exempt under PPR rules: £170,231

(b) Gain attributable to letting: $£250,000 \times \dfrac{55.2}{173} = £79,769$

(c) £40,000 (maximum)		(40,000)
Gain		39,769

Working

Period	Notes	Total ownership months	Exempt months	Chargeable months
1.4.04–30.6.09	100% of house occupied	63	63	0
1.7.09–28.2.17	40% of house occupied	92	36.8	
	60% of house let			55.2
1.3.17–31.8.18	Last 18 months treated as 100% of house occupied	18	18	0
		173	117.8	55.2

Note. The gain on the 40% of the house always occupied by Carole is fully covered by PPR relief. The other 60% of the house has not always been occupied by Carole and thus any gain on this part of the house is taxable where it relates to periods of time when Carole was not actually (or deemed to be) living in it. Carole cannot claim exemption for the part of the period of letting under the three-year absence rule since during this time she has a main residence which qualifies for relief (ie the rest of the house). However, she can claim exemption for the whole of the house for the last 18 months since the let part was part of her only residence prior to the letting.

2 Entrepreneurs' relief   12/13, 6/14, 6/15, 9/15, 3/16, 6/17, 6/18

FAST FORWARD

Entrepreneurs' relief applies on the disposal of a business and certain trading company shares. The rate of tax on gains qualifying for entrepreneurs' relief is 10%.

One of the competencies you require to fulfil Performance Objective 17 Tax planning and advice of the PER is to assess the tax implications of proposed activities or plans of an individual or entity with reference to relevant and up to date legislation. You can apply the knowledge you obtain from this section of the text to help to demonstrate this competence.

2.1 Conditions for entrepreneurs' relief

Entrepreneurs' relief is available where there is a **material disposal of business assets. There are three categories of disposal, as explained below.**

2.1.1 Disposal of the whole or part of a business

The first category is a disposal of the **whole or part of a business. The business must have been owned by the individual** throughout the period of **one year** ending with the date of the disposal. It is important to note that there has to be a **disposal of the whole or part of the business as a going concern**, not just a disposal of individual assets in a continuing business.

The business must be a **trade, profession or vocation** conducted on a **commercial basis with a view to the realisation of profits**. It can be a sole trader business or one carried on as a partnership of which the individual is a partner.

Relief is only available on **relevant business assets**. These are assets **used for the purposes of the business** and **cannot include shares and securities** nor **assets held as investments.**

In certain circumstances, goodwill is not a relevant business asset. This restriction is discussed later in this chapter.

2.1.2 Disposal of assets used in a business which has ceased

The second category is a disposal of **one or more assets in use for the purposes of a business** at the time when the business **ceases to be carried on**. The following conditions must be satisfied:

(a)   The business has been owned by the individual throughout **the period of one year** ending with the date on which the business ceases to be carried on; and

(b)   The date of cessation is within **three years** before the date of the disposal.

As **for the first category**, relief is only available on **relevant business assets, not shares and securities** nor **assets held as investments**.

2.1.3 Disposal of shares or securities

The third category is a **disposal by an individual of shares or securities in a company**. The following conditions must be usually be satisfied:

(a)   The company is **the individual's personal company (see further below)**; and
(b)   The company is either a **trading company** or **holding company of a trading group**; and
(c)   The individual is an **officer or employee** of the company (or a group company).

These conditions must be satisfied either:

(a)   Throughout the period of **one year** ending with the date of the disposal; or

(b)   Throughout the period of **one year** ending with the date on which the company (or group) **ceases to be a trading company (or trading group)** and that date is within the period of **three years** ending with the date of the disposal.

A **personal company** in relation to an individual is one where:

(a)   The individual holds **at least 5% of the ordinary share capital**; and

(b)   The individual can exercise **at least 5% of the voting rights in the company** by virtue of that holding of shares.

If the **shares are qualifying Enterprise Management Incentive (EMI) shares**, the conditions are slightly different. The shares must have been **acquired under an option that had been granted at least one year prior to the date of disposal of the shares** and the **individual must have been an officer or an employee of the trading company (or one of the companies in the trading group) throughout that one year period.** There is no minimum ownership period for the shares themselves nor a minimum percentage shareholding.

2.2 The operation of the relief

Where there is a material disposal of business assets which results in both gains and losses, losses are netted off against gains to give a single chargeable gain on the disposal of the business assets.

The rate of tax on this chargeable gain is 10%, regardless of the level of the individual's taxable income.

An individual may use losses on assets not qualifying for entrepreneurs' relief and the annual exempt amount in the most beneficial way. This will be achieved if these amounts are **set off in the following order:**

(a) **Residential property gains**
(b) **Other gains not qualifying for entrepreneurs' relief**
(c) **Entrepreneurs' relief gains**

The chargeable gain qualifying for entrepreneurs' relief is always treated as the lowest part of the amount on which an individual is chargeable to capital gains tax. Although this does not affect the tax on the gain qualifying for entrepreneurs' relief (which is always at 10%), it may have an effect on the rate of tax on other taxable gains.

2.3 Example: entrepreneurs' relief

Riley sells his business, all the assets of which qualify for entrepreneurs' relief, in September 2018. The chargeable gain arising is £12,000.

Riley also made a chargeable gain of £24,600 in December 2018 on an asset which is not residential property and which did not qualify for entrepreneurs' relief.

Riley has taxable income of £20,500 in 2018/19.

The CGT payable for 2018/19 is calculated as follows:

	Gains £	CGT £
Gains qualifying for entrepreneurs' relief		
Taxable gain	12,000	
CGT @ 10%		1,200
Gains not qualifying for entrepreneurs' relief		
Gain	24,600	
Less annual exempt amount (best use)	(11,700)	
Taxable gain	12,900	
CGT on £2,000 (34,500 – 20,500 – 12,000) @ 10%		200
CGT on £10,900 (12,900 – 2,000) @ 20%		2,180
CGT 2018/19		3,580

Note that the £12,000 gain qualifying for entrepreneurs' relief is deducted from the basic rate limit for the purposes of computing the rate of tax on the gain not qualifying for entrepreneurs' relief.

2.4 Lifetime limit

There is a lifetime limit of £10 million of gains on which entrepreneurs' relief can be claimed.

Question   Limit on entrepreneurs' relief

Maureen sells a shareholding in January 2019, realising a gain of £9,300,000. The conditions for entrepreneurs' relief are satisfied for this disposal and Maureen makes a claim for the relief to apply. Maureen had already made a claim for entrepreneurs' relief in respect of gains totalling £900,000 in an earlier tax year. Maureen also makes an allowable loss of £(20,000) in 2018/19 on an asset not qualifying for entrepreneurs' relief. Her taxable income for 2018/19 is £200,000.

Calculate the CGT payable by Maureen for 2018/19.

	Gains £	CGT £
Gain qualifying for entrepreneurs' relief		
£(10,000,000 – 900,000)	9,100,000	
CGT @ 10% on £9,100,000		910,000
Gains not qualifying for entrepreneurs' relief		
£(9,300,000 – 9,100,000)	200,000	
Less allowable loss (best use)	(20,000)	
Net gain	180,000	
Less annual exempt amount (best use)	(11,700)	
Taxable gain	168,300	
CGT @ 20% on £168,300		33,660
Total CGT due		943,660

2.5 Goodwill: restriction

Goodwill is not usually a relevant business asset for entrepreneurs' relief if it is transferred directly or indirectly by a person to a close company, where the person is a related party to the close company. A close company is a company controlled by its shareholder-directors or by five or fewer shareholders. The person is a related party to the close company if he is, or is an associate of, a participator in the close company (see later in this text for further detail on these definitions, but broadly a participator is a shareholder of a company).

This situation typically occurs when an **unincorporated business** is incorporated by a sole trader or partnership by transferring assets to a company (to the extent that incorporation relief does not apply – see later in this chapter).

However, the **rule is relaxed** (so that goodwill will still be a relevant business asset for entrepreneurs' relief) where either:

(a) The individual (and connected persons) holds **less than 5% of the ordinary share capital or voting rights of the new company**; or

(b) The individual holds **5% or more of the ordinary share capital or voting rights of the new company**, sells the whole of the shareholding to another company (Company A) within 28 days and the individual (and connected persons) holds **less than 5% of the ordinary share capital or voting rights of Company A.** This relaxation is designed to cover the situation where an individual incorporates his business to facilitate the sale of the newly incorporated company.

If a partnership incorporates, any partner who leaves the business at that time is still a related party to the new company, as he is an associate of the other partners. However, a **specific exclusion exists** so that **this restriction on entrepreneurs' relief does not apply to a person who is a retiring partner.** A retiring partner is one who is not, and no arrangements exist under which he could become, a participator in the close company.

Question   Entrepreneurs' relief on incorporation

Edna, Frank and George have been trading in partnership for many years sharing profits equally. The chargeable assets of the partnership consist of a freehold building which was acquired for £60,000 and goodwill which has been built up since the partnership started business.

Edna has decided to retire from the partnership and Frank and George now wish to carry on the business through the medium of a company. Frank and George have therefore set up a new company, FG Ltd, in which they subscribed £100,000 each for 10,000 ordinary shares.

On 1 March 2019, Edna, Frank and George sold the partnership business to FG Ltd. The value of the building at that date was £105,000 and the goodwill was valued at £72,000. Edna was paid cash for her share of the partnership business and Frank and George's entitlements are held on loan accounts in FG Ltd. Frank and George still owned their shares in FG Ltd at the end of March 2019.

Show the CGT positions of Edna, Frank and George on the sale of the partnership business to FG Ltd. Assume they have no other chargeable assets and are higher rate taxpayers.

Answer

Edna

	Gains £	CGT £
Gains qualifying for entrepreneurs' relief		
Gain on building £(105,000 − 60,000) × 1/3	15,000	
Gain on goodwill £(72,000 − 0) × 1/3	24,000	
Less annual exempt amount	(11,700)	
Taxable gain	27,300	
CGT £27,300 @ 10%		2,730

Edna is a retiring partner so the restriction on goodwill does not apply to her.

Frank and George

	Gains £	CGT £
Gains qualifying for entrepreneurs' relief		
Gain on building £(105,000 − 60,000) × 1/3	15,000	
CGT @ 10%		1,500
Gains not qualifying for entrepreneurs' relief		
Gain on goodwill £(72,000 − 0) × 1/3	24,000	
Less annual exempt amount (best use)	(11,700)	
Taxable gain	12,300	
CGT on £12,300 @ 20%		2,460
CGT		3,960

Frank and George are related to FG Ltd as they are participators (shareholders). Therefore entrepreneurs' relief only applies to the gain on the building.

2.6 Associated disposals   12/12

Entrepreneurs' relief is also available on associated disposals.

An associated disposal asset is **an asset which is owned by an individual** and **used for at least one year for business purposes by a partnership of which he is a partner or by his personal trading company**.

An associated disposal is one which is associated with a material disposal of all or part of the individual's partnership interest or a disposal of shares in the company, as relevant. The disposal must be made as part of the **withdrawal from participation in the business of the partnership or the company by the individual.** There should also normally not be a significant time interval between the material disposal and the associated disposal.

If the individual charged rent to the partnership or company, entrepreneurs' relief will be restricted. If a full market rent was charged, there will be no entrepreneurs' relief. If less than a full market rent was charged, a just and reasonable proportion of gain will be eligible for entrepreneurs' relief. For example if the rental charged was 75% of the full market rent (100 − 75) = 25% of the gain will be eligible for entrepreneurs' relief.

The December 2012 exam required a statement of the conditions necessary for the disposal of an asset to be an associated disposal for the purposes of entrepreneurs' relief. The examining team commented that this was not well done. They went on to say that 'This is not an area of the syllabus that one would expect to see examined regularly and many candidates will have known immediately on reading the requirement that they did not know the answer. However, the sensible approach would then have been to write a very brief answer with some sensible comments on entrepreneurs' relief. It was pretty likely that this would then score one of the three marks available.'

2.7 Interaction with share reorganisations and takeovers

This topic was dealt in Chapter 12 Section 3.8 and you may wish to re-read this section now.

2.8 Claim

An individual must claim entrepreneurs' relief: it is not automatic.

The claim deadline is the first anniversary of 31 January following the end of the tax year of disposal. For a 2018/19 disposal, the taxpayer must claim by 31 January 2021.

2.9 Investors' relief

FAST FORWARD

Investors' relief will apply from 2019/20 for disposals of qualifying shares in unlisted trading companies of which the investor is not an officer or employee. The rate of tax on gains qualifying for investors' relief will be 10%.

Investors' relief is a similar relief to entrepreneurs' relief. It will apply to gains on qualifying shares from 2019/20.

Qualifying shares must satisfy the following conditions:

(a)   They must be **new ordinary shares** in an **unlisted trading company** (or unlisted holding company of a trading group) which have been **subscribed for** by the **individual making the disposal.**

(b)   The shares must have **been issued by the company on or after 17 March 2016 and held continuously** by that individual usually for **at least three years** from **the date of the issue of the shares** until **the date of disposal**. However, where the shares were issued between 17 March 2016 and 5 April 2016, the three year period is extended by the period between the issue of the shares and 5 April 2016.

There is **no minimum shareholding** requirement.

The individual normally must not be an officer or employee of the company (nor any connected company). There are limited exceptions for unremunerated officers and employees who subsequently join the company.

The rate of tax on investors' relief gains **will be 10%**. There will be a **£10 million lifetime limit of gains on which investors' relief can be claimed** separate from the limit for entrepreneurs' relief.

As a result of this three year holding period, investors' relief will not be available on disposals until the tax year 2019/20. You need to be aware of the tax advantages of investors' relief and the qualifying conditions. However, computational aspects will **not be examined** in Advanced Taxation (ATX – UK) until such time as the relief is available on disposals.

3 Gift relief (holdover relief)   12/13, 6/15, 3/16, 12/17, 6/18

3.1 The relief

Gift relief is available on both outright gifts and sales at an undervalue of business assets. Gift relief is also available on gifts which are immediately chargeable to inheritance tax.

One of the competencies you require to fulfil Performance Objective 17 Tax planning and advice of the PER is to mitigate and/or defer tax liabilities through the use of standard reliefs, exemptions and incentives. You can apply the knowledge you obtain from this section of the text to help to demonstrate this competence.

If an individual gives away a qualifying asset, the transferor and the transferee can jointly elect, or where a trust is the transferee, the transferor alone can elect, within four years after the end of the tax year of the transfer (by 5 April 2023 for a disposal in 2018/19), **that the transferor's gain be reduced, possibly to nil. The transferee is then deemed to acquire the asset for market value at the date of transfer less the transferor's deferred gain.**

If a disposal involves actual consideration rather than being an outright gift but is still not a bargain made at arm's length, the proceeds are deemed to be the market value of the asset **and any excess of actual consideration over allowable cost is chargeable immediately and only the balance of the gain is deferred.** The amount chargeable immediately is limited to the full gain.

Question   Gift relief

On 6 December 2018 Angelo sold to his son Michael a freehold shop valued at £200,000 for £50,000, and claimed gift relief. Angelo had originally purchased the shop from which he had run his business in July 2007 for £30,000. He continued to run his business from another shop. Michael decided to sell the shop in May 2019 for £195,000. Compute any chargeable gains arising. Assume the rules of CGT in 2018/19 continue to apply in May 2019.

Answer

(a)   *Angelo's CGT position (2018/19)*

	£
Proceeds (market value)	200,000
Less cost	(30,000)
Gain	170,000
Less gain deferred	(150,000)
Chargeable gain £(50,000 – 30,000)	20,000

(b)   *Michael's CGT position (2019/20)*

	£
Proceeds	195,000
Less cost £(200,000 – 150,000)	(50,000)
Gain	145,000

You may need to consider whether it would be more beneficial for an individual to claim entrepreneurs' relief or gift relief or both reliefs. Remember that entrepreneurs' relief is only available on the disposal of the whole or part of a business and not on individual business assets, so it is possible that only gift relief will apply to the disposal anyway.

An individual might wish to claim entrepreneurs' relief instead of gift relief if only a very small amount of gains are left in charge hand are taxable at the advantageous rate of 10%.

If both reliefs are claimed, gift relief will apply first and then entrepreneurs' relief will apply to the remaining gain. This may be relevant if there is actual consideration paid so that gift relief covers only part of the gain.

On 10 January 2019, Zack sold his business to his son, Darren. The only chargeable assets were goodwill which Zack had built up from the start of his business and a freehold shop which Zack had bought in September 2004 for £35,000. The goodwill was valued at £25,000 and the shop at £80,000. Darren paid Zack £10,000 for the goodwill and £60,000 for the shop.

Zack made a claim for entrepreneurs' relief and Zack and Darren made a claim for gift relief. Zack has no other chargeable assets.

Show the CGT positions of Zack and Darren.

Answer

(a)   Zack's CGT position

	£	£
Goodwill		
Market value	25,000	
Less cost	(nil)	
Gain	25,000	
Less gain deferred	(15,000)	
Chargeable gain £(10,000 – nil)		10,000
Shop		
Market value	80,000	
Less cost	(35,000)	
Gain	45,000	
Less gain deferred	(20,000)	
Chargeable gain £(60,000 – 35,000)		25,000
Gains left in charge after gift relief		35,000
Less annual exempt amount		(11,700)
Taxable gains		23,300
CGT @ 10%		2,330

(b)   Darren's CGT position

	£
Goodwill	
Market value	25,000
Less gain deferred	(15,000)
Cost for future disposal	10,000

	£
Shop	
Market value	80,000
Less gain deferred	(20,000)
Cost for future disposal	60,000

3.2 Qualifying assets

Gift relief can be claimed on gifts or sales at undervalue as follows.

(a)   Transfers of **business assets**

(i)   Trade assets

(ii)   Agricultural property (whether farmed by the owner or tenant – see further below)

(iii) Shares and securities (except where the transferee is a company)

(b)   Transfers of **any assets** subject to an immediate inheritance tax (IHT) charge. IHT is covered later in this text.

Transfers of business assets are transfers of assets:

(a)   **Used in a trade, profession or vocation** carried on:

(i)   By the donor

(ii)   If the donor is an individual, by a trading company which is his 'personal company' or a member of a trading group of which the holding company is his 'personal company' (a personal company is one in which the individual can exercise at least 5% of the voting rights).

(iii) If the donor is a trustee, by the trustee or by a beneficiary who has an interest in possession in the settled property (see later in this text)

If the asset was used for the purposes of the trade, profession or vocation for only part of its period of ownership, the gain to be held over is the gain otherwise eligible × period of such use/total period of ownership.

If the asset was a building or structure only partly used for trade, professional or vocational purposes, only the **part of the gain attributable to the part so used is eligible for gift relief**

(b)   **Agricultural property** which would attract inheritance tax agricultural property relief (see later in this text). The restrictions for periods of non-trade use and for partial trade use mentioned above do not apply.

(c)   **Shares and securities in trading companies**, or holding companies of trading groups, where:

(i)   The shares or securities are **not listed on a recognised stock exchange**; or

(ii)   If the donor is an individual, the company concerned is his **personal company** (defined as above); or

(iii) If the donor is a trustee, the trustee can exercise 25% or more of the voting rights.

If the company has chargeable non-business assets (ie investments) at the time of the gift, and either (ii) or (iii) applied at any time in the last 12 months, **the gain to be held over is the gain otherwise chargeable × the market value of the chargeable business assets/the market value of the chargeable assets.**

 Question   Gift of shares – CBA/CA restriction

Morris gifts shares in his personal company to his son Minor realising a gain of £100,000. The market values of the assets owned by the company at the date of the gift are:

	£
Freehold factory and offices	150,000
Leasehold warehouse	80,000
Investments	120,000
Current assets	200,000

You are required to show the gain qualifying for hold-over relief and the chargeable gain.

Gain qualifying for hold-over relief:

$$£100,000 \times \frac{\text{Chargeable business assets (CBA)}}{\text{Chargeable assets (CA)}} = £100,000 \times \frac{150+80}{150+80+120}$$

$$= £100,000 \times \frac{230}{350}$$

$$= \underline{£65,714}$$

The gain which is not held-over (ie chargeable in current year) is £100,000 − £65,714 = $\underline{£34,286}$

If relief is claimed on a transfer of business assets, and that transfer is (or later becomes) chargeable to inheritance tax, then when the transferee disposes of the assets his gain is reduced by the IHT finally payable (but not so as to create a loss).

Transfers subject to an immediate IHT charge include most gifts to trusts. A transfer will be regarded as chargeable to IHT even if it falls within the nil rate band of that tax or is covered by the IHT annual exemption. Gifts to settlor interested trusts, however, do not qualify for gift relief.

If a transfer of business assets could also be subject to an immediate charge to inheritance tax, the rules relating to the latter category apply and the restrictions related to period of use and to chargeable business assets therefore do not apply.

Remember that IHT is covered in detail later in this text. You should return to this section once you have studied the relevant chapters.

3.3 Anti-avoidance rules   6/15

The general rule is that gift relief is not available if the transferee is not resident in the UK at the time of the gift. However, gift relief is available if the asset is UK residential property (see later in this text).

If the transferee is an individual who becomes non-UK resident in any of the six tax years following the year of the transfer and before disposing of the asset transferred, then the gain held over is chargeable on him as if it arose immediately before he becomes not resident in the UK.

It is not possible to claim gift relief on transfers to a settlor-interested trust (see later in this text).

Exam focus point

> Gift relief is normally used whenever a business or business asset is gifted, but you should look out for the restriction for a non-resident donee.
>
> You should also consider whether retaining the asset until death so as to obtain the tax free uplift to probate value would be advantageous.

4 The replacement of business assets (rollover relief)

4.1 Conditions

FAST FORWARD 〉

> When assets falling within certain classes are sold and other such assets are bought, it is possible to defer gains on the assets sold by claiming rollover relief.

> One of the competencies you require to fulfil Performance Objective 17 Tax planning and advice of the PER is to mitigate and/or defer tax liabilities through the use of standard reliefs, exemptions and incentives. You can apply the knowledge you obtain from this section of the text to help to demonstrate this competence.

A gain may be 'rolled over' (deferred) where it arises on the disposal of a business asset which is replaced. This is **rollover relief**. A claim cannot specify that only part of a gain is to be rolled over. A claim for the relief must be made by the later of four years from the end of the tax year in which the disposal of the old asset takes place and four years from the end of the tax year in which the new asset is acquired. For example, if the old asset is disposed of in 2017/18 and the new asset is acquired in 2018/19, the time limit for a claim to roll-over relief is 5 April 2023 (four years from the end of the tax year in which the new asset is acquired).

All the following conditions must be met.

(a) **The old asset sold and the new asset bought are both used only in the trade** or trades carried on **by the person claiming rollover relief**. Where part of a building is in non-trade use for all or a substantial part of the period of ownership, the building (and the land on which it stands) can be treated as two separate assets, the trade part (qualifying) and the non-trade part (non-qualifying). This split cannot be made for other assets.

(b) **The old asset and the new asset both fall within one** (but not necessarily the same one) **of the following classes.**

   (i) Land and buildings (including parts of buildings) occupied, as well as used, only for the purpose of the trade

   (ii) Fixed (that is, immovable) plant and machinery

   (iii) Goodwill (not for companies)

(c) **Reinvestment of the proceeds of the old asset takes place in a period beginning one year before and ending three years after the date of the disposal.**

(d) **The new asset is brought into use in the trade on its acquisition** (not necessarily immediately, but not after any significant and unnecessary delay).

The new asset can be for use in a different trade from the old asset.

A rollover claim is not allowed when a taxpayer buys premises, sells part of the premises at a profit and then claims to roll over the gain into the part retained. However, a rollover claim is allowed (by concession) when the proceeds of the old asset are spent on improving a qualifying asset which the taxpayer already owns. The improved asset must already be in use for a trade, or be brought into trade use immediately the improvement work is finished.

4.2 Operation of relief

FAST FORWARD If an amount less than the proceeds of the old asset is invested in the new assets, a gain equal to the difference will be chargeable up to a maximum of the actual gain.

Deferral is obtained by deducting the chargeable gain from the cost of the new asset. For full relief, the whole of the consideration for the disposal must be reinvested. Where only part is reinvested, a part of the gain equal to the lower of the full gain and the amount not reinvested will be liable to tax immediately.

The new asset will have a base cost for chargeable gains purposes, of its purchase price less the gain rolled over into its acquisition.

Question   Rollover relief

A freehold factory was purchased by Zoë for business use in August 2005. It was sold in December 2018 for £70,000, giving rise to a gain of £17,950. A replacement factory was purchased in June 2019 for £60,000. Compute the base cost of the replacement factory, taking into account any possible rollover of the gain from the disposal in December 2018.

	£
Total gain	17,950
Less gain rolled over	(7,950)
Chargeable immediately (ie amount not reinvested: £(70,000 – 60,000))	10,000
Cost of new factory	60,000
Less rolled over gain	(7,950)
Base cost of new factory	52,050

You may need to consider whether an individual should claim rollover relief or entrepreneurs' relief or both reliefs. It will be relatively unusual for both reliefs to be available. This is because entrepreneurs' relief only applies on the disposal of a business or part of a business and rollover relief is typically relevant where there is the sale of an individual business asset and the individual continues to carry on the business.

However, if both reliefs can be claimed, consider whether it would better for the individual to claim entrepreneurs' relief instead of rollover relief if the individual is not a basic rate taxpayer and only a very small amount of gains are left in charge and are taxable at the advantageous rate of 10%.

If both reliefs are claimed, entrepreneurs' relief will apply to the gain left in charge after rollover relief has been applied. This will be relevant when there is an amount not reinvested so that rollover relief does not cover the whole of the gain.

4.3 Non-business use

Where the old asset has not been used in the trade for a fraction of its period of ownership, the amount of the gain that can be rolled over is reduced by the same fraction. If the proceeds are not fully reinvested the restriction on rollover by the amount not reinvested is also calculated by considering only the proportion of proceeds relating to the part of the asset used in the trade or the proportion relating to the period of trade use.

Question   Assets with non-business use

John bought a factory for £150,000 on 11 January 2014, for use in his business. From 11 January 2015, he let the factory out for a period of two years. He then used the factory for his own business again, until he sold it on 10 July 2018 for £225,000. On 13 January 2019, he purchased another factory for use in his business. This second factory cost £100,000.

Calculate the chargeable gain on the sale of the first factory and the base cost of the second factory.

Answer

Gain on first factory

	Non-business £	Business £
Proceeds of sale (24:30) (W1)	100,000	125,000
Less cost (24:30)	(66,667)	(83,333)
Gain before rollover relief	33,333	41,667
Less rollover relief		(16,667)
Gain (W2)	33,333	25,000

Base cost of second factory

	£
Cost	100,000
Less gain rolled over	(16,667)
Base cost c/f	83,333

Workings

1   *Use of factory*

Total ownership period:

11.1.14– 10.07.18 = 54 months

Attributable to non business use:

11.1.15– 10.1.17 = 24 months

Attributable to business use (remainder: 54m – 24m) = 30 months

2   *Proceeds not reinvested*

	£
Proceeds of business element	125,000
Less cost of new factory	(100,000)
Not reinvested	25,000

4.4 Depreciating assets

Where the replacement asset is a depreciating asset, the gain is not rolled over by reducing the cost of the replacement asset. Rather it is 'frozen', ie deferred, until it crystallises (ie becomes chargeable) on the earliest of:

(a)   The disposal of the replacement asset

(b)   The date the replacement asset ceases to be used in the trade (but the gain does not crystallise on the taxpayer's death)

(c)   Ten years after the acquisition of the replacement asset

Key term

> An asset is a **depreciating asset** if it is, or within the next 10 years will become, a wasting asset. So, any asset with an expected life of 60 years or less is covered by this definition. Plant and machinery is always treated as depreciating.

Question   Deferred gain on investment into depreciating asset

Norma bought a freehold shop for use in her business in June 2016 for £125,000. She sold it for £140,000 on 1 August 2017. On 10 July 2017, Norma bought some fixed plant and machinery to use in her business, costing £150,000. Norma makes a claim to defer the gain on the shop in relation to the acquisition of the plant and machinery. She then sells the plant and machinery for £167,000 on 19 November 2018. Show Norma's CGT position.

Gain deferred

	£
Proceeds of shop	140,000
Less cost	(125,000)
Gain	15,000

Sale of plant and machinery

	£
Proceeds	167,000
Less cost	(150,000)
Gain	17,000

Total gain chargeable on sale (gain on plant and machinery plus crystallised gain)

£(15,000 + 17,000)	£32,000

Where a gain on disposal is deferred on the purchase of a replacement depreciating asset it is possible to transfer the deferred, or 'frozen', gain to a non-depreciating asset provided the non-depreciating asset is bought before the deferred gain has crystallised.

4.5 Identifying availability of reliefs

It can be confusing to identify the availability of replacement of business assets (rollover) relief and/or gift relief and/or entrepreneurs' relief on a disposal because the conditions are similar. The following examples show whether these reliefs are available in a variety of circumstances. Remember that **all of these reliefs require a claim** so it is possible to choose which relief to claim and that **it may be possible to claim more than one relief** on a disposal.

4.6 Example: rollover relief, gift relief and entrepreneurs' relief

(a) Gary sold 10,000 ordinary shares in Nile Ltd for their market value of £20,000. Gary had acquired the shares four years previously when he also became an employee of Nile Ltd, but the shares are not EMI shares. Nile Ltd has always been a trading company. The shares represent 10% of the ordinary shares in Nile Ltd and carry the same percentage of voting rights in the company. Two months later, Gary acquired a 5% shareholding in Quin plc, another unquoted trading company, for £20,000.

Relief	Available	Comments
Rollover relief	No	Shares are not qualifying assets for replacement of business assets relief (neither as the old assets nor the new asset).
Gift relief	No	Sale at market value does not have an element of gift (must be either outright gift or sale at less than market value).
Entrepreneurs' relief	Yes	(a) Nile Ltd is Gary's personal company (at least 5% ordinary share capital and voting rights); and (b) Nile Ltd is a trading company; and (c) Gary is an employee of Nile Ltd and these conditions are satisfied throughout the period of one year ending with the date of the disposal.

(b)   Morton sold a freehold warehouse for £150,000 (market value) which he had occupied and used for five years in his sole trader business. The gain arising was £45,000. He had bought a freehold shop which he immediately occupied and started using in his trade for £130,000 eight months previously.

Relief	Available	Comments
Rollover relief	Yes – partially	(a) The old asset sold and the new asset bought are both used only in the trade or trades carried on by the person claiming rollover relief.
		(b) The old asset and the new asset both fall within one of the classes of assets (here both are land and buildings).
		(c) Reinvestment of the proceeds of the old asset takes place in a period beginning one year before and ending three years after the date of the disposal.
		(d) The new asset is brought into use in the trade on its acquisition.
		The excess proceeds not reinvested £(150,000 − 130,000) = £20,000 are chargeable immediately. The remainder of the gain £(45,000 − 20,000) = £25,000 is rolled over into the base cost of the new asset.
Gift relief	No	Sale at market value does not have an element of gift (must be either outright gift or sale at less than market value).
Entrepreneurs' relief	No	The disposal of individual assets in a continuing business does not qualify for entrepreneurs' relief.

(c)   Lynne had been in business as a sole trader for five years. She closed her business which had two assets, a freehold shop she had owned for three years and a freehold warehouse she had owned for six months. Immediately after cessation, she sold the warehouse to her son Steven at less than market value. The price paid by Steven was £9,000 more than Lynne had paid for the warehouse. Four months after cessation, she sold the shop to Joss at market value. The gain on the warehouse based on market value is £15,000.

Relief	Available	Comments
Rollover relief	No	There is no acquisition of replacement assets.
Gift relief	No – on shop	Sale at market value.
	Yes – partial on warehouse	Sale at undervalue of asset used in business by donor (there is no qualifying period). £9,000 of the gain is chargeable immediately. The remaining £(15,000 − 9,000) = £6,000 is available for gift relief.
Entrepreneurs' relief	Yes on both shop and warehouse	Disposal of one or more assets in use for the purposes of a business at the time at which the business ceases to be carried on since:
		(a) The business was owned by Lynne throughout the period of one year ending with the date on which the business ceased to be carried on; and
		(b) The date of cessation is within three years before the date of the disposal.
		The qualifying period applies to the **business**, not to individual assets and so entrepreneurs' relief is still available on the warehouse.

4.7 Example: gift relief and entrepreneurs' relief

Here we consider the availability of gift relief and entrepreneurs' relief on the gift of shares in a company. When considering reliefs in relation to shares, it is particularly important to look at the percentage shareholding represented by the shares, whether the company is quoted or not, and whether the individual is an employee or officer of the company.

These conditions are illustrated in the examples below where we have assumed that the shares have been owned for two years prior to the disposal (and are not EMI shares) and other circumstances relevant for entrepreneurs' relief (eg whether the company is a trading company, whether the shareholder is an officer or employee of the company) have existed throughout the period of ownership.

Trading company or holding company of trading group	Unquoted company	Percentage shareholding and voting rights	Officer or employee of company or group company	Gift relief available?	Entrepreneurs' relief available?
Yes	Yes	3%	No	Yes – any % of unquoted trading co. shares, no employment condition.	No – must be officer or employee
No	Yes	8%	Yes	No – must be trading company	No – must be trading company
Yes	Yes	4%	Yes	Yes – any % of unquoted trading co. shares	No – must be personal company (at least 5% ordinary share capital and voting rights)
Yes	No	8%	No	Yes – quoted company but personal company (at least 5% of the voting rights), no employment condition.	No – must be officer or employee
Yes	No	15%	Yes	Yes – personal company (at least 5% of the voting rights).	Yes – personal company (at least 5% ordinary share capital and voting rights) and officer or employee.

5 The transfer of a business to a company (incorporation relief)

5.1 The relief

FAST FORWARD

> When an individual transfers his unincorporated business to a company, the gain arising will be deducted from the cost of the shares received, unless the individual elects otherwise.

PER alert

One of the competencies you require to fulfil Performance Objective 17 Tax planning and advice of the PER is to mitigate and/or defer tax liabilities through the use of standard reliefs, exemptions and incentives. You can apply the knowledge you obtain from this section of the text to help to demonstrate this competence.

If an individual transfers his business to a company, he makes a disposal of the business assets for CGT purposes and realises net chargeable gains (chargeable gains less allowable losses) on those assets. It is, however, clearly undesirable to discourage traders from incorporating their businesses and so a relief is available.

The relief can also apply where an individual sells his unincorporated business to a company where the vendor and the company were not connected prior to the sale.

The relief (called incorporation relief) is automatic (so no claim need be made). **All or some of the gains are held over if all the following conditions are met.**

(a) The **business is transferred as a going concern**
(b) **All its assets** (or all its assets other than cash) **are transferred**
(c) **The consideration is wholly or partly in shares**

Formula to learn

> **The amount deferred is found by applying the fraction:**
> $$\frac{\text{Value of shares received from the company}}{\text{Total value of consideration from the company}} \times \text{gain before relief}$$

This amount is then deducted from the base cost of the shares received. The company is deemed to acquire the assets transferred at their market values.

Question

Incorporation relief

Petrie transferred his business to a company in July 2018, realising a gain of £240,000 on its only business asset (a factory). The consideration comprised cash of £150,000 and shares at a market value of £750,000.

(a) What is the gain on the transfer after incorporation relief but before any other reliefs?
(b) What is the base cost of the shares for any future disposal?

Answer

(a)

	£
Gain before incorporation relief	240,000
Less Incorporation relief: $\frac{750,000}{150,000 + 750,000} \times £240,000$	(200,000)
Gain after incorporation relief	40,000

(b)

	£
Market value	750,000
Less gain deferred	(200,000)
Base cost of shares	550,000

5.2 Election to disapply incorporation relief

An individual can elect not to receive incorporation relief. The election must usually be made by 31 January, 34 months after the end of the tax year of disposal. An election might be made if the taxpayer can set losses and/or the annual exempt amount against the gains which would otherwise be deferred under incorporation relief. The election therefore results in a higher base cost of the shares received on incorporation and so a lower gain on a future disposal of the shares.

Since incorporation usually involves the disposal of the whole or part of a business, entrepreneurs' relief can usually also be claimed on incorporation (except on goodwill – see earlier in this chapter). If the election is made to disapply incorporation relief, entrepreneurs' relief can then be claimed. This may be beneficial if the individual is not a basic rate taxpayer and only a small amount of gains are left in charge and are taxable at the advantageous rate of 10%.

Question — Disclaiming incorporation relief (1)

Willow transferred her business to Berry Ltd on 1 December 2018, comprising the following assets:

Asset	Market value £	Gain on disposal £
Freehold shop	150,000	8,000
Goodwill	20,000	20,000
Inventory	25,000	n/a
Cash	5,000	n/a

The consideration for the transfer was 200,000 £1 Berry Ltd ordinary shares. Berry Ltd is a close company and Willow is a participator of Berry Ltd.

Willow had losses brought forward from 2017/18 of £(7,000). She made no other disposals in 2018/19 and does not intend to make any disposals in the foreseeable future. She is a higher rate taxpayer.

Explain the capital gains tax implications if **either**:

(a) Incorporation relief applies on the transfer; **or**

(b) Willow makes an election to disapply incorporation relief and claims entrepreneurs' relief.

On the basis of these computations, what advice should be given to Willow?

Answer

(a) If incorporation relief applies on the transfer, the gains of £(8,000 + 20,000) = £28,000 are deferred (ie will not be chargeable in 2018/19). The gains are deducted from the base cost of the shares received. The base cost of the shares is £(200,000 – 28,000) = £172,000.

(b) If Willow makes an election to disapply incorporation relief, the gains of £28,000 will be chargeable in 2018/19. If she makes a claim for entrepreneurs' relief, her capital gains tax payable in 2018/19 will be as follows:

	Gains £	CGT £
Gains qualifying for entrepreneurs' relief		
Gain on shop	8,000	
CGT @ 10%		800
Gains not qualifying for entrepreneurs' relief		
Gain on goodwill	20,000	
Less losses b/f (best use)	(7,000)	

	Gains	CGT
Net gains	13,000	
Less annual exempt amount (best use)	(11,700)	
Taxable gain	1,300	
CGT on £1,300 @ 20%		260
CGT		1,060

The base cost of the shares will be £200,000.

On the basis of these computations, Willow should be advised to make an election to disapply incorporation relief and to claim entrepreneurs' relief. This will use her brought forward loss (which is unlikely to be utilised in the foreseeable future) and annual exempt amount for 2018/19 and results in only a relatively small amount of capital gains tax being payable. The base cost of the shares in Berry Ltd is increased by £28,000 which will result in a smaller gain on their eventual disposal.

Another situation where it may be beneficial to disapply incorporation relief and claim entrepreneurs' relief is where the shares received on incorporation will not qualify for entrepreneurs' relief and there are plans to dispose of them at a time when the individual will not be a basic rate taxpayer. It may be better to pay some capital gains tax on incorporation at 10% and have a higher base cost for the shares received, rather than deferring the gains on incorporation into the base cost of the shares and paying capital gains tax at 20% on their sale.

Question   Disclaiming incorporation relief (2)

Briony is a dentist who has run her dental practice as a sole trader since 2005. On 1 December 2018, Briony accepted an offer from a company, Brighter Smiles Ltd, to transfer her business to the company in exchange for 25,000 ordinary shares valued at £10 each. These shares represent a 2.5% shareholding in Brighter Smiles Ltd, which is an unquoted trading company. Brighter Smiles Ltd is not a close company. The gains on disposal of the assets of the sole trade on the transfer amounted to £120,000.

Briony also became an employee of Brighter Smiles Ltd at the time of the transfer of her business on fixed term contract until 30 November 2020. On that date she intends to sell her shareholding in Brighter Smiles Ltd. The value of shares in Brighter Smiles Ltd on 30 November 2020 can be taken to be £15 per share and the rates of capital gains tax in 2020/21 can be assumed to be the same as in 2018/19.

Briony makes disposals of quoted shares each year to exactly utilise her annual exempt amount. She is always a higher rate taxpayer.

Compute the total capital gains tax payable on the transfer of the business and the disposal of the shares in Brighter Smiles Ltd if **either**:

(a)   Incorporation relief applies on the transfer; **or**

(b)   Briony makes an election to disapply incorporation relief and claims entrepreneurs' relief on the transfer.

On the basis of these computations, what advice should be given to Briony?

Answer

(a)   If incorporation relief applies on the transfer, the gains of £120,000 will not be chargeable in 2018/19. The base cost of the shares in Brighter Smiles Ltd will therefore be £([25,000 × £10] − 120,000) = £130,000.

On the disposal of the Brighter Smiles Ltd shares in 2020/21, CGT will be payable as follows:

	£
Proceeds 25,000 × £15	375,000
Less cost	(130,000)
Taxable gains	245,000
Capital gains tax on £245,000 @ 20%	49,000

The conditions for entrepreneurs' relief are not satisfied on this disposal as Brighter Smiles Ltd is not Briony's personal company since she only owns a 2.5% shareholding (less than the 5% required).

The total capital gains tax payable is therefore £49,000.

(b) If Briony makes an election to disapply incorporation relief and claims entrepreneurs' relief, capital gains tax will be payable as follows:

	£
Taxable gains	120,000
Capital gains tax on £120,000 @ 10%	12,000

On the disposal of the Brighter Smiles Ltd shares in 2019/20, CGT will be payable as follows:

	£
Proceeds 25,000 × £15	375,000
Less cost 25,000 × £10	(250,000)
Taxable gains	125,000
Capital gains tax on £125,000 @ 20%	25,000

Again, conditions for entrepreneurs' relief are not satisfied on this disposal as Brighter Smiles Ltd is not Briony's personal company since she only owns a 2.5% shareholding.

The total capital gains tax payable is therefore £(12,000 + 25,000) = £37,000.

On the basis of these computations, Briony should be advised to make an election to disapply incorporation relief and claim entrepreneurs' relief as this will save capital gains tax of £(49,000 − 37,000) = £12,000. However, she must be made aware that £12,000 of the capital gains tax will be payable by 31 January 2020, with the balance of £25,000 payable by 31 January 2022, rather than the whole amount of £49,000 being payable by 31 January 2022 if incorporation relief applies.

5.3 Optimising the use of incorporation relief

Although the relief cannot be restricted to utilise losses brought forward, and the annual exempt amount, **it is possible to manipulate the amount of non-share consideration received** (whether in cash, loan stock, or left on loan account) **so that the gain remaining chargeable is equal to losses plus the annual exempt amount.**

Question   Optimising incorporation relief

Antonio transferred his business (market value £120,000) to a company on 16 August 2018, realising a gain of £90,000. He had capital losses brought forward of £6,300.

Advise Antonio how much of the consideration he should take as shares and how much he should leave on loan account.

Answer

Antonio should take shares worth £96,000 and leave the balance of £24,000 (£120,000 - £96,000) on loan account. These figures are found as follows:

	£
Gain before incorporation relief	90,000
Less incorporation relief (W)	(72,000)
Gain after incorporation relief	18,000
Less losses brought forward	(6,300)
	11,700
Less annual exempt amount	(11,700)
Taxable gain	nil

Working

Work backwards to calculate the incorporation relief required to defer sufficient gains to utilise annual exempt amount and losses:

	£
Annual exempt amount	11,700
Add losses	6,300
Gain covered by annual exempt amount/losses	18,000
Less total gain	(90,000)
Incorporation relief required	72,000

Once the incorporation relief figure is obtained, we can calculate the share consideration required:

$$\text{Total consideration} \times \frac{\text{Deferred gain}}{\text{Gain}}$$

$$£120,000 \times \frac{72,000}{90,000} \qquad\qquad £96,000$$

Exam focus point

When advising on the amount of share consideration to take on an incorporation, taking into account losses and the annual exempt amount, you may find it easier to work backwards from the annual exempt amount.

A claim for entrepreneurs' relief may usually be made where not all of the consideration is received in the form of shares. In this case, entrepreneurs' relief may apply to the gains left in charge after incorporation relief has been applied. If the gains left in charge include a part of a gain on goodwill which would not qualify for entrepreneurs' relief, the proportion of the gains not eligible for entrepreneurs' relief will be the same proportion as the gain on goodwill in relation to the total gains, before incorporation relief.

6 EIS deferral relief and SEIS reinvestment relief

FAST FORWARD

Gains can be deferred if an individual invests in shares in an EIS company and can be partially exempted if an individual invests in shares in a SEIS company.

6.1 EIS deferral relief   12/13, 6/17

6.1.1 Introduction

One of the competencies you require to fulfil Performance Objective 17 Tax planning and advice of the PER is to mitigate and/or defer tax liabilities through the use of standard reliefs, exemptions and incentives. You can apply the knowledge you obtain from this section of the text to help to demonstrate this competence.

An individual may defer a gain arising on the disposal of any type of asset if he invests in qualifying Enterprise Investment Scheme (EIS) shares (see earlier in this text). The 'frozen', or deferred, gain will usually become chargeable when the shares are disposed of (subject to a further claim for the relief being made).

It is not necessary for the shares acquired to qualify for the EIS income tax relief.

Where both EIS deferral relief and entrepreneurs' relief can be claimed on the gain, the individual must choose which relief to claim. However, where a gain exceeds the £10 million lifetime limit for entrepreneurs' relief an individual can claim entrepreneurs' relief on the gain up to that limit and then defer the gain above the limit under the EIS rules. Special rules provide that deferred EIS gains, where entrepreneurs' relief would have been available if deferral had not been claimed, do still qualify for entrepreneurs' relief when the gain comes back into charge (see later in this chapter).

6.1.2 Calculation of relief

The amount of the gain that can be deferred is the **lower of:**

(a)   **The amount subscribed by the investor for his shares,** which has not previously been matched under this relief; and

(b)   **The amount specified by the investor in the claim. This can take into account, for example the annual exempt amount and losses.**

Question

EIS deferral

Robert made a gain of £196,000 on the disposal of a property in 2018/19. He subscribed for some shares in a company which qualified under the EIS rules. What will the gain to defer be if:

(a)   The shares cost £200,000 and Robert wants to take the maximum deferral relief possible

(b)   The shares cost £170,000 and Robert wants to take the maximum deferral relief possible

(c)   The shares cost £200,000 and Robert, who has no other chargeable assets, wishes to utilise his annual exempt amount

Answer

(a)   £196,000. The qualifying expenditure on the shares exceeds the gain, so the whole gain can be deferred.

(b)   £170,000. The gain deferred is restricted to the qualifying expenditure. The remainder of the gain of £26,000 will remain in charge (subject to relief for any further investment).

(c)   A claim can be made to defer £184,300. This is calculated as follows:

	£
Gain before relief	196,000
Less EIS reinvestment relief (balancing figure)	(184,300)
Gain	11,700
Less annual exempt amount	(11,700)
Taxable gain	Nil

6.1.3 Conditions for the relief

The gain must either arise due to the disposal of an asset or on a gain coming back into charge under this relief.

The investor must be an individual who is UK resident at the time the gain to be deferred was made and at the time the investment was made in the shares.

The company must be a qualifying company under the EIS rules (see earlier in this text).

The shares must be qualifying shares under the EIS rules (see earlier in this text).

The shares must be issued to the investor within the period of one year before and three years after the gain to be deferred accrues (or such longer period as HMRC may allow). If the gain accrues after the issue of the shares, the shares must still be held by the investor at the time that the gain arises.

A claim for relief must be made within five years from 31 January following the end of the tax year in which the shares were issued ie by 31 January 2025 if the shares are issued in 2018/19.

6.1.4 Gain coming back into charge

The deferred gain will crystallise, ie come back into charge, on the following events:

(a) **The investor disposing of the shares except by an inter-spouse disposal.**

(b) The spouse/civil partner of an investor disposing of the shares, if the spouse/civil partner acquired the shares from the investor.

(c) **The investor becoming non resident, broadly within three years of the issue of the shares** (except if employed full time abroad for up to three years and retaining the shares until his return to the UK).

(d) The spouse/civil partner of an investor becoming non resident, broadly within three years of the issue of the shares (except if employed full time abroad for up to three years and retaining the shares until his return to the UK), if the spouse/civil partner acquired the shares from the investor.

(e) **The shares ceasing to be eligible shares,** eg the company ceases to be a qualifying company,

Note that the gain becomes chargeable in the year of the event, not the year when the original gain was made (if different). It will be charged on the holder of the shares at the date of the event, eg on the investor if he/she still holds the shares or the spouse/civil partner if the shares have been passed to her/him.

If the original gain would have been eligible for entrepreneurs' relief if it had not been deferred under EIS reinvestment relief, a claim can be made for entrepreneurs' relief to apply to the deferred gain when it comes back into charge. This claim must be made by the first anniversary of 31 January following the tax year in which the deferred gain comes back into charge.

6.1.5 Anti-avoidance

The same provisions that apply for EIS income tax relief apply here (see earlier in this text).

6.2 SEIS reinvestment relief

6.2.1 Calculation of relief

If an **individual makes a chargeable gain** and, **in the same year, subscribes for shares on which SEIS income tax relief is claimed, the gain can be matched with any amount of that SEIS expenditure,** as specified in a claim made by the individual. **50% of the amount of the gain matched with the SEIS expenditure is then treated as exempt.**

The relief is therefore the lower of:

* **50% of the amount of the gain reinvested in SEIS shares (maximum 50% of the £100,000 SEIS income tax limit);** and

* The **amount specified in the claim** for SEIS reinvestment relief.

Question   SEIS reinvestment relief

Raymond subscribed for shares worth £70,000 in an SEIS company on 14 May 2018. On 28 October 2018 he made a gain of £200,000 on the disposal of an investment property.

What is the maximum amount of SEIS reinvestment relief that Raymond can claim?

£70,000 of the gain can be matched with £70,000 of the SEIS subscription. 50% of this amount of the gain is treated as exempt. Therefore, the maximum SEIS reinvestment relief Raymond can claim in 2018/19 is £70,000 × 50% = £35,000.

The **time limit** for making the claim is **five years from 31 January following the end of the tax year in which the SEIS shares are issued** ie by 31 January 2025 if the shares are issued in 2018/19.

If a claim has been made, for income tax purposes, for all or some of the SEIS shares to be treated as issued in the previous tax year then, if a claim for SEIS reinvestment relief is made, it must also apply to gains made in that previous tax year.

6.2.2 Withdrawal of relief

If SEIS income tax relief is withdrawn or reduced on SEIS shares, for example if they are disposed of within three years of issue, **there is a corresponding withdrawal or reduction of SEIS reinvestment relief.**

SEIS income tax relief will be **withdrawn** if the disposal of the shares is **not at arm's length** such as a gift or a sale to a connected person. The **corresponding withdrawal of the SEIS reinvestment relief** is effected by a **chargeable gain** being treated as arising **in the tax year in which the shares were issued. This gain is equal to the amount of SEIS reinvestment relief attributable to those shares.**

SEIS income tax relief will be **reduced** if the disposal of the shares is **at arm's length**. The **corresponding reduction in the SEIS reinvestment relief** is effected by a **chargeable gain** being treated as arising **in the tax year in which the shares were issued.** This gain is equal to the **same proportion of the SEIS reinvestment relief gain as the reduction in the SEIS income tax relief.**

Question | SEIS reinvestment relief reduction

On 11 July 2018, Megan subscribed for 50,000 shares worth £75,000 in an SEIS company. Megan was entitled to SEIS income tax relief of £75,000 × 50% = £37,500 in 2018/19.

On 12 August 2018, Megan sold a painting and realised a chargeable gain of £48,000. She made the maximum SEIS reinvestment relief claim for 2018/19 of £48,000 × 50% = £24,000.

Megan sold all her SEIS shares on 12 December 2019 for £22,500 in an arm's length transaction. This resulted in a reduction of £22,500 × 50% = £11,250 in her SEIS income tax relief since the shares had not been held for 3 years.

What is gain chargeable on this disposal as a result of the reduction of Megan's SEIS reinvestment relief?

Answer

The percentage reduction in Megan's SEIS income tax relief is (11,250/37,500) × 100 = 30%.

The gain arising as a result of the reduction of Megan's SEIS reinvestment relief is therefore £24,000 × 30% = £7,200.

This gain is treated as arising in the year of issue of the shares (2018/19), not the year in which the sale was made (2019/20).

Chapter roundup

- There is an exemption for gains on principal private residences, but the exemption may be restricted because of periods of non-occupation or because of business use.

- There is also a relief for letting out a principal private residence if the gain arising during the letting would not be covered by the main relief.

- Entrepreneurs' relief applies on the disposal of a business and certain trading company shares. The rate of tax on gains qualifying for entrepreneurs' relief is 10%.

- Investors' relief will apply from 2019/20 for disposals of qualifying shares in unlisted trading companies of which the investor is not an officer or employee. The rate of tax on gains qualifying for investors' relief will be 10%.

- Gift relief is available on both outright gifts and sales at an undervalue of business assets. Gift relief is also available on gifts which are immediately chargeable to inheritance tax.

- When assets falling within certain classes are sold and other such assets are bought, it is possible to defer gains on the assets sold by claiming rollover relief.

- If an amount less than the proceeds of the old asset is invested in the new assets, a gain equal to the difference will be chargeable up to a maximum of the actual gain.

- When an individual transfers his unincorporated business to a company, the gain arising will be deducted from the cost of the shares received, unless the individual elects otherwise.

- Gains can be deferred if an individual invests in shares in an EIS company and can be partially exempted if an individual invests in shares in a SEIS company.

Quick quiz

1   For what periods may an individual be deemed to occupy his principal private residence?

2   What is the maximum letting exemption?

3   Peter sells his business as a going concern to another sole trader in August 2018, realising gains of £500,000. He has not made any previous disposals. Calculate Peter's CGT on the disposal.

4   Which disposals of shares qualify for gift relief?

5   What assets are eligible for rollover relief on the replacement of business assets by an individual?

6   What deferral of a gain is available when a business asset is replaced with a depreciating business asset?

7   What are the conditions for deferring gains on the incorporation of a business?

8   When is EIS deferral relief available?

9   When will a gain deferred using EIS deferral relief come back into charge?

10 Tamara sells an antique vase on 12 June 2018 for £120,000 realising a gain of £40,000. If she makes an investment of £50,000 in qualifying SEIS shares in September 2018, £25,000 of the gain will be deferred until the SEIS shares are sold. True/false?

1   Periods of deemed occupation are:

  •   Last 18 months of ownership;

  •   Any period of absence up to three years;

  •   Any period during which the owner was required by his employment to work abroad; and

  •   Any period up to four years during which the owner was required to live elsewhere due to his work (employed or self-employed) so that he could not occupy his private residence.

2   £40,000

3

	£
Gains	500,000
Less annual exempt amount	(11,700)
Taxable gain	488,300
CGT @ 10%	48,830

4   Shares which qualify for gift relief are those in trading companies which:

  •   Are not listed on a recognised stock exchange; or

  •   Where the donor is an individual, which are in that individual's personal company; or

  •   Where the donor is a trustee, where the trustee can exercise 25% or more of the voting rights in the company.

5   Assets eligible for rollover relief by an individual are:

  •   Land and buildings
  •   Fixed plant and machinery
  •   Goodwill

6   Where a depreciating asset is acquired, the gain is 'frozen', or deferred until it crystallises on the earliest of the disposal of the replacement asset, the date the replacement asset ceases to be used in the trade and ten years after the acquisition of the replacement asset.

7   The conditions for incorporation relief are:

  •   The business is transferred as a going concern
  •   All of its assets (or all assets other than cash) are transferred
  •   The consideration is wholly or partly in shares

8   EIS deferral relief is available where an individual makes a gain (on any type of asset) and invests in EIS shares within a certain time period.

9   A deferred gain will come back into charge where:

  •   Investor disposes of the shares (except inter-spouse/civil partner)

  •   Investor's civil partner/spouse disposes of shares (if acquired from investor)

  •   Investor (or investor's spouse/civil partner who acquires shares from investor) becomes non-resident within three years of issue of shares, unless employed full-time abroad for up to three years

  •   Shares cease to be eligible shares

10 **False**. The gain of £40,000 is matched with £40,000 of the subscription in the SEIS company. 50% of the amount of the gain matched with the SEIS expenditure is treated as exempt ie £20,000. In addition, this amount is exempt, not just deferred until the SEIS shares are sold.

Now try the question below from the Practice Question Bank

Number	Level	Marks	Time
Q14	Examination	12	23 mins

Chargeable gains: additional aspects

14

Topic list	Syllabus reference
1 Chattels, including wasting chattels	A2(a)C3,(e)(ii)
2 Other wasting assets	A2(e)(ii)
3 Leases	A2(e)(ii)
4 Loss, damage or destruction of an asset	A2(e)(iii),(iv)
5 Altering dispositions made on death	A2(g)(v)
6 CGT and trusts	A2(c)(i), (ii)
7 Overseas aspects of CGT	A2(a)C1,(b)(ii)-(vi)

Introduction

In the previous chapters, we have learnt how to calculate capital gains. We now look at some more of the rules for particular assets and particular situations.

First, we look at chattels, including wasting chattels. Unless capital allowances have been claimed there are special rules to ensure that the cost of the asset is restricted to reflect the fall in value of the asset over time. We then look the tax treatment of other wasting assets, such as options and copyrights.

Leases of land may also be wasting assets. They fall in value over their lives: a lease with 10 years left to run is worth less than a lease with 30 years left to run. The rules for wasting assets are modified to reflect the fact that the value of a lease falls more steeply the shorter it becomes.

We next look at the rules which apply when an asset is damaged or destroyed and the reliefs available where insurance proceeds are applied to restore or replace the asset.

Then we consider the CGT implications of varying a will.

Next, we consider how CGT applies when assets are transferred into trusts and finally we look at the overseas aspects of capital gains tax.

In the next chapter, we will study the administration of income tax and capital gains tax.

Study guide

		Intellectual level
2	**Chargeable gains and capital gains tax liabilities in situations involving further overseas aspects and in relation to closely related persons and trusts together with the application of additional exemptions and reliefs**	
(a)	The contents of the Taxation - United Kingdom (TX – UK) study guide for chargeable gains for individuals under headings:	2
•	C1 The scope of the taxation of capital gains	
•	C3 Gains and losses on the disposal of movable and immovable property	
(b)	The scope of the taxation of capital gains:	3
(ii)	Identify the concepts of residence, domicile and deemed domicile and determine their relevance to capital gains tax	
(iii)	Advise on the availability of the remittance basis to non-UK domiciled individuals	2
(iv)	Determine the UK taxation of foreign gains, including double taxation relief	
(v)	Conclude on the capital gains tax position of individuals coming to and leaving the UK	
(vi)	Advise on the UK taxation of gains on the disposal of UK residential property owned by non-residents	
(c)	Capital gains tax and trusts:	
(i)	Advise on the capital gains tax implications of transfers of property into trust	3
(ii)	Advise on the capital gains tax implications of property passing absolutely from a trust to a beneficiary	2
(e)	Gains and losses on the disposal of movable and immovable property:	3
(ii)	Determine the gain on the disposal of leases and wasting assets	
(iii)	Establish the tax effect of capital sums received in respect of the loss, damage or destruction of an asset	
(iv)	Advise on the tax effect of making negligible value claims	
(g)	The use of exemptions and reliefs in deferring and minimising tax liabilities arising on the disposal of capital assets:	3
(v)	Understand the capital gains tax implications of the variation of wills	

Exam guide

The rules for the damage or destruction of an asset are further rollover reliefs which can be used to defer capital gains. A negligible value claim can be used to crystallise a loss, and you must consider the time of the claim carefully to ensure the best possible use of the loss.

Do not be caught out by the overseas aspects. For CGT purposes the most useful exclusion is the fact that individuals who are not resident in the UK are not taxable on their UK gains, even on assets situated in the UK. An exception is the disposal of UK resident property by non-UK residents, for which there are specific rules.

The rules on chattels, wasting assets and the basic principles of the treatment of the loss, damage or destruction of an asset will be familiar from Taxation (TX – UK). The other topics in this chapter are new.

There are no changes in 2018/19 from the material studied in Taxation (TX – UK) in 2017/18.

1 Chattels, including wasting chattels

FAST FORWARD

Gains on most wasting chattels are exempt, and losses on them are not allowable. The CGT rules are modified for assets eligible for capital allowances.

1.1 Introduction

Key terms

A **chattel** is tangible movable property.

A **wasting asset** is an asset with an estimated remaining useful life of 50 years or less.

Special rules apply for wasting assets to prevent taxpayers from realising a capital loss simply due to the fall in value of a wasting asset over time. The rules are modified where capital allowances are available.

1.2 Chattels

Plant and machinery, whose predictable useful life is always deemed to be less than 50 years, is an example of a wasting chattel (unless it is immovable, in which case it will be wasting but not a chattel). Machinery includes, in addition to its ordinary meaning, motor vehicles (unless exempt as cars), railway and traction engines, engine-powered boats and clocks.

Wasting chattels are exempt (so that there are no chargeable gains and no allowable losses). There is one **exception** to this: assets used for the purpose of a trade, profession or vocation in respect of which **capital allowances** have been or could have been claimed. This means that items of plant and machinery used in a trade are not exempt merely on the ground that they are wasting. However, cars are always exempt.

If a chattel is not exempt under the wasting chattels rule, any gain arising on its disposal will still be exempt if the asset is sold for gross proceeds of £6,000 or less, even if capital allowances were claimed on it.

Exam focus point

The detailed calculations for non-wasting chattels where the cost or sale proceeds are less than £6,000, other than knowledge of the exemption where both cost and proceeds are less than £6,000, are excluded from the syllabus.

1.3 Chargeable gains and capital allowances   6/17

The wasting chattels exemption does not apply to chattels on which capital allowances have been claimed or could have been claimed, other than those sold for gross proceeds of £6,000 or less.

Where capital allowances have been obtained on any asset, and a loss would arise, the allowable cost for chargeable gains purposes must be reduced by the lower of the loss and the net amount of allowances (taking into account any balancing allowances or charges). The result is no gain and no loss.

If there is a gain, the cost is not adjusted for capital allowances.

2 Other wasting assets

Other wasting assets generally have their cost written down over time.

2.1 Introduction

A wasting asset is one which has an estimated remaining useful life of 50 years or less and whose original value will depreciate over time. **Freehold land is never a wasting asset**, and there are special rules for leases of land (see below).

Wasting chattels are exempt except for those on which capital allowances have been (or could have been) **claimed**.

2.2 Options

An option (for example an option to buy shares) is a right to buy or sell something at a specified price within a specified time. **An option is usually a wasting asset** because after a certain time it can no longer be exercised.

2.2.1 The grant of an option

The grant of an option is the disposal of an asset, namely the option itself, rather than a part disposal of the asset over which the option has been granted. The only allowable expenditure will be the incidental costs of the grant, such as legal fees. If the option is exercised the CGT treatment changes.

2.2.2 The exercise of an option

Where an option is exercised, the granting of the option and the subsequent disposal of the asset under the option are treated as a single transaction taking place when the option is exercised. Proceeds from the grant of the option plus the disposal of the asset are combined and become the disposal proceeds of the grantor and the allowable base cost of the grantee.

Where tax was paid on the original grant of the option it will usually be treated as a payment on account of the tax on the exercise.

2.2.3 Example: exercise of an option

Tom owns a plot of investment land which he bought for £10,000 in May 2012. He grants an option to Penelope for £1,000 in July 2012 whereby he will sell the land for £25,000 at any time nominated by Penelope before 30 June 2019. Penelope exercises her option in July 2018.

Tom's gain in 2018/19 will be:

	£
Proceeds (£1,000 + £25,000)	26,000
Less cost	(10,000)
Gain	16,000
Penelope's base cost will be: £1,000 + £25,000 =	26,000

The date of disposal is July 2018 (ie when the option is exercised).

2.2.4 Abandoned options

Where an option is abandoned, the position of the grantor and grantee are different. The grantor makes a chargeable disposal at the time when the option is granted. The grantee acquires a chargeable asset at the same time, but the abandonment of the option amounts to a disposal only where the option is:

(a)   A quoted option to subscribe for shares in a company
(b)   A traded option or financial option
(c)   An option to acquire assets for the purposes of a trade

2.2.5 Disposal of an option

The disposal (eg by sale to a third party) of an option (other than a quoted, traded or financial option) to buy or sell quoted shares or securities gives rise to a chargeable gain or allowable loss computed in accordance with the normal rules for wasting assets (see below). These options are assets which waste on a straight line basis.

2.3 Other wasting assets

The cost is written down on a straight line basis. So, if a taxpayer acquires such an asset with a remaining life of 40 years and disposes of it after 15 years (with 25 years remaining) only 25/40 of the cost is deducted from the disposal consideration.

Examples of such assets are **copyrights** (with 50 years or less to run) and **registered designs**.

Where the asset has an estimated residual value at the end of its predictable life, it is the cost less residual value which is written off on a straight line basis over the asset's life. Where additional expenditure is incurred on a wasting asset the additional cost is written off over the life remaining when it was incurred.

Assets eligible for capital allowances and used throughout the period of ownership in a trade, profession or vocation do not have their allowable expenditure written down.

3 Leases

FAST FORWARD

An ordinary disposal computation is made on the disposal of a lease with 50 years or more to run. For leases of land with less than 50 years to run, a special table of percentages is used.

3.1 Types of disposal

The gain that arises on the disposal of a lease will be chargeable according to the terms of the lease disposed of. We must consider:

(a)   The assignment of a lease or sub-lease with 50 years or more to run
(b)   The assignment of a lease or sub-lease with less than 50 years to run

There is an assignment when a lessee sells the whole of their interest. There is a grant when a new lease or sub-lease is created out of a freehold or existing leasehold, the grantor retaining an interest.

Exam focus point

The CGT rules for the **grant** of leases will not be examined.

The duration of the lease will normally be determined by the contract terms. The expiry date, however, will be taken as the first date on which the landlord has an option to terminate the lease or the date beyond which the lease is unlikely to continue because of, for example, the likelihood that the rent will be substantially increased at that date.

3.2 The assignment of a lease with 50 years or more to run

An **ordinary disposal computation** is made and the whole of any gain on disposal will be chargeable to CGT (subject to any private residence exemption, see below).

3.3 The assignment of a lease with less than 50 years less to run

In calculating the gain on the disposal of a lease with less than 50 years to run only a certain **proportion of the original expenditure counts as an allowable deduction**. This is because a lease is losing value anyway as its life runs out: only the cost related to the tail end of the lease being sold is deductible. The proportion is determined by a table of percentages.

Exam focus point

The appropriate lease percentages will be given in the exam question where relevant.

> **The allowable cost is given by:**
>
> $$\text{Original cost} \times \frac{X}{Y}$$
>
> where X is the percentage for the number of years left for the lease to run at the date of the assignment, and Y is the percentage for the number of years the lease had to run when first acquired by the seller.

The table only provides percentages for exact numbers of years. Where the duration is not an exact number of years the relevant percentage should be found by adding 1/12 of the difference between the two years on either side of the actual duration for each extra month. Fourteen or more days count as a month.

Question

The assignment of a short lease

Adrian acquired a 20-year lease on a block of flats on 1 August 2012 for £15,000. He assigned it on 2 August 2018 for £19,000. Compute the gain arising.

The percentage from the lease percentage table for 20 years is 72.770, for 14 years is 58.971 and for 6 years is 39.195.

Answer

	£
Proceeds	19,000
Less cost £15,000 × $\dfrac{\%14 \text{ years}: \ 58.971}{\%20 \text{ years}: 72.770}$	(12,156)
Gain	6,844

4 Loss, damage or destruction of an asset

FAST FORWARD

The gain which would otherwise arise on the receipt of insurance proceeds may, subject to certain conditions, be deferred.

4.1 Destroyed assets

If an asset is destroyed (compared to merely being damaged – see below) any compensation or insurance monies received will normally be brought into an ordinary CGT disposal computation as proceeds. The date of disposal is the date the insurance proceeds are received and not the date the asset is destroyed. If all the insurance proceeds from an asset are applied for the replacement of the asset within 12 months, any gain can be deducted from the cost of the replacement asset. The replacement asset should have a similar function to the destroyed asset and be a similar type of asset. If only part of the proceeds are used, the gain immediately chargeable can be limited to the amount not used. The rest of the gain is then deducted from the cost of the replacement. This is similar to rollover relief for replacement of business assets (see earlier in this text).

Question

Destroyed assets

Fiona bought a painting for £25,000 in June 2011. It was destroyed in March 2018. Insurance proceeds of £34,000 were received in September 2018, and Fiona spent £35,500 on a replacement painting. Compute the chargeable gain and the base cost of the new asset.

2018/19	£
Proceeds	34,000
Less cost	(25,000)
Gain (can be fully deferred as all insurance monies are spent on replacement)	9,000

The base cost of the new asset is £(35,500 – 9,000) = £26,500.

4.2 Damaged assets

3/16

If an asset is damaged and compensation or insurance money is received as a result, then **this will normally be treated as a part disposal.**

By election, however, the taxpayer can avoid a part disposal computation. **A capital sum received can be deducted from the cost of the asset rather than being treated as a part disposal if:**

(a)   **Any amount not spent in restoring the asset is small** (taken as the higher of 5% of the capital sum and £3,000); or

(b)   **The capital sum itself is small** (taken as the higher of 5% of the value of the asset and £3,000).

There are special restrictions if the asset is wasting (that is, it has a remaining useful life of 50 years or less).

(a)   The **whole** capital sum must be spent on restoration.

(b)   The capital sum can only be deducted from what would have been the allowable expenditure on a sale immediately after its application. If the asset is a wasting asset this will be less than the full cost of the asset, because the cost of a wasting asset is written down over its life.

If the amount not used in restoring the asset is not small, then the taxpayer can elect for the amount used in restoration to be deducted from the cost; the balance will continue to be treated as a part disposal.

Question

Asset damaged

Frank bought an investment property for £100,000 in May 2018. It was damaged two and a half months later. Insurance proceeds of £20,000 were received in November 2018, and Frank spent a total of £25,000 on restoring the property. Prior to restoration the property was worth £120,000. Compute the chargeable gain immediately chargeable, if any, and the base cost of the restored property assuming Frank elects for there to be no part disposal.

How would your answer differ if no election were made?

Answer

As all the proceeds have been applied in restoring the property Frank has elected to disregard the part disposal.

The base cost of the restored property is £(100,000 – 20,000 + 25,000) = £105,000.

If no election were made, the receipt of the proceeds would be a part disposal in November 2018. The gain would be:

	£
Proceeds	20,000
Less cost £100,000 × 20,000/(20,000 + 120,000)	(14,286)
Gain	5,714

The base cost of the restored asset is £(100,000 − 14,286 + 25,000) = £110,714.

Assuming this is Frank's only disposal in the tax year, the gain is covered by the annual exempt amount. It may therefore be preferable not to make the election.

4.3 Negligible value claims

12/14

If a chargeable asset's value becomes negligible a claim may be made to treat the asset as though it were sold, and then immediately reacquired at the value stated in the claim. This will usually give rise to an allowable loss.

The sale and reacquisition are treated as taking place when the claim is made, or at a specified earlier time. The earlier time can be any time up to two years before the start of the tax year in which the claim is made. (For companies, it can be as far back as the start of the earliest accounting period which ends within two years of the date of claim.) The asset must have been of negligible value at the specified earlier time.

On a subsequent actual disposal, any gain is computed using the negligible value as the acquisition cost.

Exam focus point

Since a negligible value claim can be backdated it can be used to generate an allowable loss to set against a gain that has already been realised.

5 Altering dispositions made on death

12/14

FAST FORWARD

A variation or disclaimer can be used to vary a will after death. This can have IHT and CGT consequences.

5.1 Variations and disclaimers

A **variation** or **disclaimer** can be used **to secure a fairer distribution of a deceased person's estate. They can also be used for tax planning.**

A variation of a will is usually made by rewriting the terms of the will so that the assets will pass in accordance with the variation, rather than the original will. For example, if Julius dies leaving an asset to his sister, Kathleen, Kathleen can make a variation which rewrites the will to pass the asset to someone else, such as her son, Luke.

If a beneficiary under a will makes a disclaimer, the disclaimed assets pass under the terms of the will to the beneficiary next entitled. Consider the situation where Petra dies and her will passes her house to her brother, Quayle and the residue of her estate to her sister, Ruby. If Quayle disclaims his entitlement under the will, the house will pass to Ruby as part of the residue of the estate. If this is not what Quayle wants to happen to the house, for example, if he wants it to pass to his daughter, Samantha, he should make a variation, rather than a disclaimer.

5.2 CGT implications of altering dispositions made on death

If, within two years of a death the terms of a will are changed, in writing, either by a variation of the terms of the will made by the persons who benefit or would benefit under the dispositions, or by a disclaimer, the change will not be a disposal for CGT purposes. The assets disposed of are taken by the new beneficiaries at their probate value (ie market value at death), rather than at the value at the date of the disclaimer or variation, as if the assets had been left directly to those persons by the deceased.

If the beneficiaries making a variation wish the relevant terms of the will to be treated as replaced by the terms of the variation for CGT purposes, it is necessary to state this in the variation. Where a disclaimer is made, the relevant terms in the will are *automatically* treated as replaced by the terms of the disclaimer for CGT purposes, regardless of whether this is stated in the disclaimer or not.

5.3 Example: passing on assets received on death

Trevor bought a 4% shareholding in an unquoted trading company in August 2007 for £10,000. He died in May 2018. In his will he left the shares, then worth £15,000 to Clive. You will remember from earlier in this text that transfers of assets on death are exempt disposals. Clive inherits the shares as if he had bought them at Trevor's death for their then market value of £15,000. There is no capital gain or allowable loss on Trevor's death.

In February 2019, Clive wishes to pass on the shares, now worth £28,000, to his daughter, Imogen. He can do this in either of two ways:

(a) Give the shares to Imogen. If Clive and Imogen make a joint gift relief claim (any shareholding in an unquoted trading company is a business asset for the purposes of gift relief), the gain between Trevor's death and the date of the gift of £(28,000 – 15,000) = £13,000 will be deducted from the Imogen's base cost, giving her a revised base cost of £(28,000 – 13,000) = £15,000. Clive has no CGT liability on the gift.

(b) Vary Trevor's will and include a statement for CGT that the shares are to be treated as passing in Trevor's will to Imogen. She takes them at the value at Trevor's death which is £15,000. The variation is not a CGT disposal by Clive.

The practical effect is the same for both methods – Imogen receives the shares with a base cost of £15,000 and Clive has no CGT liability when he passes the shares to Imogen.

Note that if the shares had been a 4% shareholding in a quoted trading company, gift relief would not be available since the company would not be Clive's personal company (requires at least 5% of the voting rights). In this case, only method (b) would pass the shares to Imogen at their value at Trevor's death.

5.4 IHT implications of altering dispositions made on death

Similar provisions apply for IHT purposes (see later in this text).

6 CGT and trusts

Exam focus point

ACCA's article **Trusts and tax for Advanced Taxation (ATX – UK),** written by a member of the Advanced Taxation (ATX – UK) examining team, sets out the rules that may be examined in Advanced Taxation (ATX – UK) and those areas where knowledge is not required. It considers the various types of trust and the capital gains tax and inheritance tax implications of transferring assets to a trust and property passing absolutely to beneficiaries.

FAST FORWARD

CGT may arise when assets are transferred into and out of trusts.

6.1 Assets being put into trusts

If a settlor puts an asset into any type of trust during his lifetime, they make a disposal for CGT purposes. It will be deemed to take place at market value and gift relief will be available (unless the trust is a settlor-interested trust – see below). This is because there is also an inheritance tax charge (see later in this text) when the assets enter the trust.

As there is no CGT on death, where a trust is created on death there is no deemed disposal. The trustees of a trust created under a will or on intestacy acquire the trust assets at their market value at death (ie probate value).

Exam focus point

Inheritance tax for trusts is covered later in this text. You should return to this section once you have completed your study of the relevant chapters.

6.2 Settlor-interested trusts

It is not possible to claim gift relief on transfers to a settlor-interested trust. This is a trust from which the settlor, or their spouse/civil partner or minor child (who is neither married nor in a civil partnership) can benefit.

6.3 Assets leaving trusts

When an asset leaves a trust, for example, when a beneficiary becomes entitled to trust property, the trustees make a disposal of the asset at market value. This may lead to a gain or loss.

If there is a gain, usually gift relief will be available because there will also be a charge to inheritance tax when property leaves a trust.

7 Overseas aspects of CGT   12/11, 6/13, 6/15, 6/16

FAST FORWARD

CGT applies primarily to individuals resident in the UK. Individuals who are neither UK domiciled nor deemed domiciled may be entitled to use the remittance basis.

7.1 Liability to CGT

7.1.1 UK resident and domiciled individuals

In general, individuals are subject to CGT on the disposal of assets situated anywhere in the world if they are resident and either domiciled or deemed domiciled in the UK in the tax year of the disposal.

Exam focus point

In certain circumstances, individuals who become UK deemed domiciled may elect to rebase the cost of their foreign assets held at 5 April 2017. This rebasing is **not examinable** in Advanced Taxation (ATX – UK).

7.1.2 Non-UK resident individuals

In general, an individual who is not UK resident in a tax year is not subject to CGT on the disposal of any assets, wherever situated, in that tax year. There is an exception where the individual is operating a business through a UK branch or agency: this exception is discussed later in this section. There are also special rules for disposals of interests in UK residential property by non-UK residents which are also discussed later in this section.

Exam focus point

It is important to note that a non-UK resident is not liable to CGT on investment assets, other than residential property, even if those assets are situated in the UK.

7.1.3 UK resident but not UK domiciled individuals

If an individual is resident in the UK but neither domiciled nor deemed domiciled in the UK, gains on the disposal of assets situated overseas are taxable only to the extent that the proceeds of the disposal are remitted to the UK if the individual has made a claim for the remittance basis or it applies automatically because their unremitted income and gains are less than £2,000 in the tax year. As explained earlier in this text, deemed domicile is ignored for the purpose of the automatic remittance test. Therefore an individual who is not UK domiciled, but who is UK deemed domiciled, will only be liable to capital gains tax on their overseas gains if their unremitted non-UK income and gains exceed £2,000 in the tax year.

An individual who claims the remittance basis is not entitled to an annual exempt amount against chargeable gains.

Some of the rules about where assets are situated are contained in legislation. Some of them are a matter of general law. Most of the rules are obvious, for example, land is situated where it actually is, chattels are situated where they are physically present. There are special rules relating to intangible assets, the most important of which are shares and securities in a company. **All shares and securities of a UK incorporated company are treated as situated in the UK, regardless of where the share certificate is kept.**

Exam focus point

June 2015 Question 5(c) Ravi concerned the capital gains tax position of an individual who was resident in the UK but domiciled overseas. The examining team commented that 'Although some candidates did reasonably well here, almost all candidates could have scored more marks if they had organised their thoughts before they began writing. There was a mark for making the point that Ravi was liable to UK capital gains tax because he was UK resident and a further mark for recognising that the remittance basis was available because he was domiciled overseas. In order to score these two marks, candidates had to make it clear that the liability to capital gains tax was due to his residence status and the remittance basis was due to his domicile status. Many candidates did not make these two points clearly, such that they only scored one of the two available marks.'

7.1.4 Split year treatment

If an individual is UK resident in a tax year, that individual may be entitled to split year treatment so that the tax year is split into a UK part and an overseas part. The availability of split year treatment is determined in the same way as for income tax (see earlier in this text).

If an individual makes **a disposal in the UK part of the tax year,** the individual will **be subject to CGT** on that disposal **as a UK resident.**

Conversely, if the individual makes a disposal in the overseas part of the tax year, the individual **will treated as non-UK resident and so will not be subject to CGT** on that disposal (unless the disposal is of UK residential property – see later in this chapter).

7.2 Losses on non-UK situated assets

7.2.1 UK resident and domiciled individuals

Losses are allowable losses if the individual is UK resident and either UK domiciled or deemed domiciled.

7.2.2 UK resident but not UK domiciled individuals

A UK resident individual who is neither UK domiciled nor deemed domiciled but has not claimed the remittance basis, for example because their income and gains are less than £2,000 in the tax year, is also automatically given relief for losses on assets situated outside the UK.

An individual who has claimed the remittance basis must make an irrevocable election to treat losses on assets situated outside the UK as allowable losses. The election must be made in relation to the first occasion when a non-UK individual claims remittance basis for a tax year.

If the individual does not make an election on that occasion, overseas losses of that tax year and all future years will not be allowable losses.

If the individual does make the election, there are special rules relating to the deduction to allowable losses where there are foreign chargeable gains. Broadly, losses cannot be set against non-UK gains arising in previous years and where losses are available for deduction, they are set first against non-UK gains arising and remitted in that year, then against other non-UK gains and lastly from UK gains arising in that year.

7.3 Non-UK residents operating through a UK branch or agency

The general rule is that an non-UK resident individual who makes a disposal of an asset situated in the UK is not liable to CGT on that disposal.

However, **there will be a liability to CGT where:**

- The individual is **carrying on a trade, profession or vocation in the UK** through **a branch or agency**; and

- There is a disposal of **an asset**, which has been:
    - Used in or for the **purposes of the trade, profession or vocation**; or
    - Used or held or acquired **for the purpose of the branch or agency**.

There will also be a deemed disposal at market value where an asset ceases to be a chargeable asset either by being removed from the UK or because the UK trade, profession or vocation ceases.

7.4 Disposals of UK residential property by non-UK residents   9/16, 6/17

One of the competencies you require to fulfil Performance Objective 17 Tax planning and advice of the PER is to identify when to refer matters to someone with more specialist knowledge. This section gives an outline of the rules on a complex area of tax which is sufficient for the Advanced Taxation (ATX – UK) exam, buts if you were required to deal with this area for a client you would probably need to refer the matter to someone with more specialist knowledge.

FAST FORWARD

From 6 April 2015, disposals of UK residential property by non-UK residents are subject to CGT. However, generally only the gain or loss accruing since 6 April 2015 is chargeable/allowable.

7.4.1 Non-resident CGT (NRCGT) disposals

From 6 April 2015, non-UK resident individuals are subject to capital gains tax on the disposal of interests in UK situated residential property.

In general **only the gain or loss accruing since 6 April 2015 is chargeable/allowable.** If the residential property was acquired before 6 April 2015 **the default method of calculating the gain or loss is:**

	£
Proceeds	X
Less: market value of residential property at 5 April 2015	(X)
enhancement expenditure incurred after 5 April 2015	(X)
Gain/loss	X/(X)

The individual can make an election to use either of the following methods of calculating the gain or loss:

(a)   **Straight line time apportionment of the gain/loss calculated under normal CGT rules** over the whole period of ownership with the part accruing after 5 April 2015 being chargeable/allowable; or

(b)   **Whole period gain/loss.** This method may be useful where there is a loss on the property since it was acquired as it will allow the whole of the loss, not just the part accruing since 5 April 2015.

 Question   NRCGT gain calculation

Lenny acquired a house in the UK on 1 October 2009 at a cost of £211,500. He disposed of it on 1 March 2019 for net disposal proceeds of £244,000. The house had a market value of £230,000 on 5 April 2015. Lenny is not UK resident in the tax year 2018/19. The house has never been used as Lenny's main residence. Advise Lenny whether he should make an election for the straight line time apportionment method of calculating his NRCGT gain.

First calculate the gain using the default method.

Default method

	£
Proceeds	244,000
Less market value at 5 April 2015	(230,000)
Gain	14,000

Next, calculate the gain using the straight line time apportionment method.

Straight line time apportionment method

	£
Proceeds	244,000
Less cost	(211,500)
Gain	32,500

Lenny owned the house from 1 October 2009 to 1 March 2019 (113 months). The period from 6 April 2015 to 1 March 2019 is 47 months.

Post 6 April gain 47/113 × £32,500	13,518

Lenny should therefore make an election to use the straight line time apportionment method.

An individual who has NRCGT gains is entitled to the annual exempt amount. The rate of CGT on NRCGT gains depends on the total of the individual's taxable UK income and gains.

7.4.2 Interaction with replacement of business assets relief

If the UK residential property is a business asset under normal rules (for example, furnished holiday accommodation) replacement of business assets relief is only available if the new asset is also a UK residential property.

7.4.3 Interaction with gift relief

If the UK property is a qualifying asset for gift relief (again an example is furnished holiday accommodation), then gift relief is available on a gift to a non-UK resident person. This is an exception to the usual rule that gift relief is available only if the donee is UK resident. The exception applies because the residential property remains within the charge to CGT in the hands of the non-UK resident donee.

7.4.4 Interaction with PPR relief

FAST FORWARD

PPR relief may be available on disposals of UK residential properties by non-UK resident individuals but is restricted for tax years where the individual is neither UK tax resident nor satisfies a 'day count test'. A similar restriction applies to UK residents who dispose of non-UK residential properties.

Where an individual has a NRCGT disposal of a main residence, principal private residence relief may be available for the period of ownership after 5 April 2015.

However, no period of actual occupation after 5 April 2015 is taken into account unless the individual (or their spouse/civil partner) was UK tax resident or satisfied the 'day count test' in the relevant tax year. The day count test is met if the individual (or their spouse/civil partner) stayed overnight at the property for at least 90 days in the tax year. If the property is owned for only part of a tax year, the day count test is scaled down in accordance with the period of ownership (eg if the property is owned for four months (one-third) of the tax year, then 90 days becomes 30 days).

The last 18 months of ownership are always treated as if it were a period of occupation, regardless of whether the individual satisfies the residence test or day count test during the tax year(s) for that period.

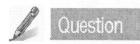
Michaela bought a UK house on 6 April 2012. She lived in the house until 5 April 2017 when she left the UK to live in Utopia in her sister's house and ceased to be UK tax resident on that date.

Michaela did not stay overnight in the house between leaving it and selling it on 5 April 2023. Her NRCGT gain on the sale was £126,000.

Calculate Michaela's taxable gain for 2022/23, assuming that the tax rules and allowances in 2018/19 continue to apply.

Answer

	£
Gain before PPR exemption	126,000
Less PPR exemption (working)	
$£126,000 \times \dfrac{42}{96}$	(55,125)
Chargeable gain	70,875
Less annual exempt amount	(11,700)
Gain	59,175

Working

Period	Period	Total ownership months	Exempt months	Chargeable months
6.4.15 – 5.4.17	Actual occupation, UK resident	24	24	0
6.4.17 – 5.10.21	Absent	54	0	54
6.10.21 – 5.4.23	Last 18 months	18	18	0
		96	42	54

Letting relief is available if the property is let out regardless of whether the individual satisfies the residence test or day count test during the letting period.

Similar PPR rules apply to UK resident individuals who dispose of a residential property situated in a country in which neither they nor their spouse/civil partner are tax resident nor in which they satisfy the day count test in a tax year.

7.5 Temporary non-residence

6/18

FAST FORWARD

Individuals who are temporarily non-UK resident are subject to CGT if they make disposals, during the non-UK resident period, of assets acquired before the individual became non-UK resident.

An individual who wishes to dispose of assets might decide **to become non-UK resident for a short period of time, make disposals during that non-UK resident period**, and then **become UK resident again**. There are **anti-avoidance rules** relating to **temporary non-UK residence**.

Temporary non-UK residents are subject to CGT whilst they are non-UK resident if:

(a) They were **UK resident in a tax year** (either a full tax year or a UK part of a split tax year) – this is referred to as Period A; and

(b) Immediately following that Period A, **one or more residence periods occur for which they are not UK resident**; and

(c) They were **UK resident for at least four out of the seven tax years immediately preceding the tax year of departure** (the tax year consisting of or including period A); and

(d) The **temporary period of non-residence is five years or less.**

Net gains realised in the tax year of departure (either the full tax year or the UK part of a split tax year) are subject to CGT under general principles.

Gains/ losses made by temporary non-UK residents in the non-UK resident period (including the overseas part of a split tax year) are chargeable/allowable in the period of return. This is the first residence period after period A for which the individual is UK resident (either for a full tax year or a UK part of a split tax year).

Gains on assets acquired in the non-UK resident period are not included in the above charge nor are gains which are already chargeable either because they arise on branch or agency assets or because they are NRCGT disposals (see earlier in this chapter).

Question

Sue had always been resident in the UK until (and including) the tax year 2018/19. She left the UK on 1 February 2019 to begin full-time work overseas.

Sue was then not resident in the UK for the tax years 2019/20, 2020/21, 2021/22 and 2022/23. Sue returned to the UK on 1 July 2023 when she ceased full-time work overseas. She was thereafter present in the UK so as to be UK resident.

Sue made the following disposals of shares:

Date of disposal	Proceeds £	Date of acquisition	Cost £
9 December 2018	29,000	11 June 2012	15,000
10 March 2019	150,000	15 May 2016	87,000
19 June 2021	80,000	10 August 2013	100,000
25 November 2022	60,000	11 June 2019	55,000

Explain how these disposals will be treated for CGT purposes and compute the amount of taxable gains. Assume 2018/19 tax rates and allowances continue to apply.

Answer

Sue was UK resident in the tax year 2018/19. She can split this tax year into UK and overseas parts since she left the UK to begin full time work overseas. Period A therefore ended on 31 January 2019 and the year of departure is 2018/19. Sue can also split the tax year 2023/24 into overseas and UK parts as she is returning to the UK following a period of full time work overseas.

The disposal in December 2018 is in the UK part of the split tax year 2018/19 and is therefore subject to CGT in that tax year.

December 2018 disposal

	£
Proceeds	29,000
Less cost	(15,000)
Gain	14,000
Less annual exempt amount	(11,700)
Taxable gain 2018/19	2,300

Sue is then non-UK resident from 1 February 2019 until 30 June 2023. Since this period of temporary non-UK residence is five years or less, she will be subject to CGT on the disposal of assets acquired before she became non-UK resident. The net gains will be chargeable in the period of return which starts on 1 July 2023.

March 2019 disposal

	£
Proceeds	150,000
Less cost	(87,000)
Gain	63,000

June 2021 disposal

	£
Proceeds	80,000
Cost	(100,000)
Loss	(20,000)

The disposal in November 2022 is not subject to CGT because the asset was acquired in the non-UK resident period.

Taxable gains 2023/24

	£
Gain	63,000
Less loss	(20,000)
	43,000
Less annual exempt amount	(11,700)
Taxable gains 2023/24	31,300

7.6 Double taxation relief 9/16

If a gain made on the disposal of an overseas asset suffers overseas taxation, relief will be available in the UK against any CGT on the same disposal.

7.7 Calculation of non-UK gains

If an asset is bought and/or sold for amounts in a foreign currency, each such amount is first translated into sterling (using the rate at the time of purchase or sale), and the gain or loss is computed using these sterling amounts.

7.8 Non-remittable proceeds

Tax on gains accruing on assets situated outside the UK may be deferred, until the gain becomes remittable, if:

- The taxpayer makes a claim;

- The gain could not be remitted to the UK because of the laws of the country where it arose, because of executive action of its government or because it was impossible to obtain foreign currency; and

- This was not because of any lack of reasonable endeavours on the taxpayer's part.

Chapter roundup

- Gains on most wasting chattels are exempt, and losses on them are not allowable. The CGT rules are modified for assets eligible for capital allowances.

- Other wasting assets generally have their cost written down over time.

- An ordinary disposal computation is made on the disposal of a lease with 50 years or more to run. For leases of land with less than 50 years to run, a special table of percentages is used.

- The gain which would otherwise arise on the receipt of insurance proceeds may, subject to certain conditions, be deferred.

- A variation or disclaimer can be used to vary a will after death. This can have IHT and CGT consequences.

- CGT may arise when assets are transferred into and out of trusts.

- CGT applies primarily to individuals resident in the UK. Individuals who are neither UK domiciled nor deemed domiciled may be entitled to use the remittance basis.

- From 6 April 2015, disposals of UK residential property by non-UK residents are subject to CGT. However, generally only the gain or loss accruing since 6 April 2015 is chargeable/allowable.

- PPR relief may be available on disposals of UK residential properties by non-UK resident individuals but is restricted for tax years where the individual is neither UK tax resident nor satisfies a 'day count test'. A similar restriction applies to UK residents who dispose of non-UK residential properties.

- Individuals who are temporarily non-UK resident are subject to CGT if they make disposals, during the non-UK resident period, of assets acquired before the individual became non-UK resident.

Quick quiz

1   What is the general treatment of intangible wasting assets (eg a copyright)?

2   When a lease with less than 50 years to run is assigned, what proportion of the cost is allowable?

3   Emma drops and destroys a vase. She receives compensation of £2,000 from her insurance company. How can she avoid a charge to CGT arising?

4   Joan dies on 10 September 2018. What is the latest date by which a variation of her will can be made if it is not to be treated as a CGT disposal?

5   Clive has always been UK resident. He acquires an asset in 2015. Clive becomes non-UK resident for the tax year 2018/19. He disposes of the asset in 2020, realising a gain of £50,000. Clive becomes UK-resident again in the tax year 2021/22. Clive is not entitled to split year treatment in any relevant year. How will the gain on the disposal in 2020 be taxed (if at all)?

Answers to quick quiz

1   The cost is written down on a straight line basis.

2   Allowable cost is original cost × X/Y where X is the % for the years left of the lease to run at assignment and Y is the % for the years the lease had to run when first acquired by the seller.

3   Emma can avoid a charge to CGT on receipt of the compensation by investing at least £2,000 in a replacement asset within 12 months.

4   9 September 2020 (two years from the date of death).

5   Clive is temporarily non-UK resident for five years or less (non-residence period from 6 April 2018 to 5 April 2021). He will be taxed on the gain made in 2020 in the period of return to UK residence which is the tax year 2021/22.

Now try the question below from the Practice Question Bank

Number	Level	Marks	Time
Q15	Introductory	21	41 mins

Tax administration for individuals

Self assessment for individuals and partnerships

Topic list	Syllabus reference
1 The administration of taxation	A6(b)A3
2 Notification of liability to income tax and capital gains tax	A6(b)A3
3 Tax returns and keeping records	A6(b)A3
4 Self-assessment and claims	A6(b)A4
5 Payment of income tax, national insurance contributions and capital gains tax	A6(b)A4
6 HMRC powers	A6(b)A5
7 Penalties	A6(b)A6,A6(b)(i)
8 Appeals	A6(h)A5
9 Tax offenders	A6(b)A6

Introduction

In the previous chapters, we have studied the comprehensive computation of income tax and capital gains tax liabilities.

In this chapter, we look at the overall system for the administration of tax. We then see how individuals and partnerships must 'self assess' their liability to income tax and capital gains tax. We deal with self assessment for companies later in this text.

In the next chapter, we will commence our study of inheritance tax.

Study guide

		Intellectual level
6	**Value added tax, tax administration and the UK tax system**	
(b)	The contents of the Taxation - United Kingdom (TX – UK) study guide for the UK tax system and its administration under headings:	2
•	A3 The systems for self assessment and the making of returns	
•	A4 The time limits for the submission of information, claims and payment of tax, including payments on account	
•	A5 The procedures relating to compliance checks, appeals and disputes	
•	A6 Penalties for non-compliance	
(i)	Advise on the increased penalties which apply in relation to offshore matters	2

Exam guide

In any tax advice question, you must consider the administrative requirements and time limits. You must know the taxpayer's responsibilities for making returns and paying tax, and the rules that HMRC can use to enforce compliance.

Knowledge brought forward from earlier studies

This chapter is mainly a revision of material studied in Taxation (TX – UK). The new topics are tax offenders and increased penalties which apply in relation to offshore matters.

The only change for 2018/19 in the rules which you studied in Taxation (TX – UK) in 2017/18 is that the rate of interest on underpaid tax has been increased from 2.75% to 3.00%. Standard penalties for errors are now shown in the Tax Rates and Allowances available in the exam.

1 The administration of taxation

FAST FORWARD

Taxes are administered by Her Majesty's Revenue & Customs.

The **Treasury** formally imposes and collects taxation. The management of the Treasury is the responsibility of the Chancellor of the Exchequer. **The administrative function for the collection of tax is undertaken by Her Majesty's Revenue & Customs (HMRC).** Rules on these administrative matters are contained in the **Taxes Management Act 1970 (TMA 1970).**

HMRC consists of the Commissioners for Her Majesty's Revenue & Customs and staff known **as Officers of Revenue and Customs** who are responsible for supervising the self-assessment system and agreeing tax liabilities.

Tax appeals are heard by the **Tax Tribunal** which is made up of **two tiers:**

(a) First Tier Tribunal; and
(b) Upper Tribunal.

The **First Tier Tribunal deals with most cases** other than complex cases. The **Upper Tribunal deals with complex cases** which either involve an important issue of tax law or a large financial sum. The Upper Tribunal **also hears appeals** against decisions of the First Tier Tribunal. We look at the appeals system in more detail later in this chapter.

Many taxpayers arrange for their accountants to prepare and submit their tax returns. The taxpayer remains responsible for submitting the return and for paying the tax; the accountant acts as the taxpayer's agent.

2 Notification of liability to income tax and capital gains tax

Individuals who do not receive a tax return or who have a new source of income or gains must notify their chargeability to income tax or CGT.

Individuals who have not received a notice to file a return, or who have a new source of income or gains in the tax year, are required to give notice of chargeability to HMRC within six months from the end of the year ie by 5 October 2019 for 2018/19.

A person who has no chargeable gains and who is not liable to higher rate tax does not have to give notice of chargeability if all their income:

(a)   Is taken into account under PAYE;

(b)   Is from a source of income not subject to tax under a self-assessment;

(c)   Has had (or is treated as having had) income tax deducted at source; or

(d)   Is savings income and/or dividend income falling within the savings income nil rate band and the dividend nil rate band.

A penalty is charged for late notification (see later in this chapter).

3 Tax returns and keeping records

Tax returns must usually be filed by 31 October (paper) or 31 January (electronic) following the end of the tax year.

3.1 Tax returns

HMRC usually issues a notice to the taxpayer requiring them to file a tax return. The tax return comprises a basic return form, together with supplementary pages for particular sources of income and chargeable gains. Taxpayers with simple tax affairs may be asked to complete a short tax return. The taxpayer may either file a **paper return** or an **electronic return** via the Internet. The taxpayer must make a declaration that the information given on the tax return and any supplementary pages is correct and complete to the best of the taxpayer's knowledge and belief and a statement that the taxpayer understands that they may have to pay financial penalties and face prosecution if they give false information.

Partnerships must file a separate return which includes a 'Partnership Statement' showing the firm's profits, losses, proceeds from the sale of assets, tax suffered, tax credits and the division of all these amounts between partners. A partnership return must include a declaration of the name and tax reference of each partner, as well as the usual declaration by the partner nominated to make the return that it is correct and complete to the best of the signatory's knowledge and belief. There is a warning on the form that if false information is given or any of the partnership's income or gains is concealed, the partners may be liable to financial penalties and/or HMRC may prosecute them. Each partner must then include their share of partnership profits on their personal tax return.

3.2 Time limit for submission of tax returns

The latest **filing date for a personal tax return** for a tax year (Year 1) is:

- 31 October in the next tax year (Year 2), for a non-electronic return (eg a paper return)
- 31 January in Year 2, for an electronic return (eg made via the internet)

There are **two exceptions to this general rule**.

The **first exception applies if the notice to file a tax return is issued by HMRC to the taxpayer after 31 July in Year 2, but on or before 31 October in Year 2**. In this case, the **latest filing date is**:

- **The end of 3 months following the notice, for a paper return**
- **31 January in Year 2, for an electronic return**

The second exception applies **if the notice to file the tax return is issued to the taxpayer after 31 October in Year 2**. In this case, **the latest filing date is the end of 3 months following the notice.**

Question   Submission of tax returns

Advise each of the following clients of the latest filing date for her personal tax return for 2018/19 if the return is:

(a)   Paper; or
(b)   Electronic.

Norma   Notice to file tax return issued by HMRC on 6 April 2019
Melanie   Notice to file tax return issued by HMRC on 10 August 2019
Olga   Notice to file tax return issued by HMRC on 12 December 2019

Answer

	Paper	Electronic
Norma	31 October 2019	31 January 2020
Melanie	9 November 2019	31 January 2020
Olga	11 March 2020	11 March 2020

A partnership return may be filed as a paper return or an electronic return. **The general rule and the exceptions to the general rule for personal returns apply also to partnership returns.**

3.3 Standard accounting information

The tax return requires trading results to be presented in a standard format. Although there is no requirement to submit accounts with the return, accounts may be filed. If accounts accompany the return, HMRC's power to raise a discovery assessment (see below) is restricted.

Only 'three line' accounts (ie income less expenses equals profit) need be included on the tax return of businesses with a turnover (or gross rents from property) of less than the threshold for VAT registration (£85,000). This is not as helpful as it might appear, as underlying records must still be kept for tax purposes (disallowable items etc) when producing three line accounts.

Large businesses with a turnover of at least £5 million which have used figures rounded to the nearest £1,000 in producing their published accounts can compute their profits to the nearest £1,000 for tax purposes.

3.4 Keeping of records

All taxpayers must retain all records required to enable them to make and deliver a correct tax return.

Records must be retained until the later of:

(a)   (i)   5 years after the 31 January following the tax year where the taxpayer is in business (as a sole trader or partner or letting property). Note that this applies to all of the records, not only the business records;

      (ii)   **1 year after the 31 January following the tax year otherwise; or**

(b)   Provided notice to deliver a return is given before the date in (a):

      (i)   **The time after which a compliance check enquiry by HMRC into the return can no longer be commenced;**

      (ii)   **The date any such a compliance check enquiry has been completed.**

HMRC can specify a shorter time limit for keeping records where the records are bulky and the information they contain can be provided in another way.

Where a person receives a notice to deliver a tax return after the normal record keeping period has expired, they must keep all records in their possession at that time until no compliance check enquiry can be started in respect of the return or until such a compliance check enquiry has been completed.

Taxpayers can keep 'information', rather than 'records', but must show that they have prepared a complete and correct tax return. The information must also be able to be provided in a legible form on request. Records can be kept in electronic format.

HMRC can inspect 'in-year' records, ie before a return is submitted, if they believe it is reasonably required to check a tax position.

4 Self-assessment and claims

One of the competencies you require to fulfil Performance Objective 16 Tax compliance and verification of the PER is to verify and question client submissions and ensure timely submission of all relevant information to the tax authorities by the due date. You can apply the knowledge you obtain from this section of the text to help to demonstrate this competence.

FAST FORWARD

If a paper return is filed the taxpayer can ask HMRC to compute the tax due. Electronic returns have tax calculated automatically.

4.1 Self-assessment

Key term

A **self-assessment** is a calculation of the amount of taxable income and gains after deducting reliefs and allowances, and a calculation of income tax and CGT payable after taking into account tax deducted at source.

If the taxpayer is filing a **paper return (other than a short tax return), they may make the tax calculation on their return or ask HMRC to do so on their behalf**. In either case, this is treated as a 'self-assessment' by the taxpayer.

If the taxpayer wishes HMRC to make the calculation for Year 1, a paper return must be filed:

- **On or before 31 October in Year 2; or**

- **If the notice to file the tax return is issued after 31 August in Year 2, within 2 months of the notice.**

If the taxpayer is filing an **electronic return, the calculation of tax liability is made automatically when the return is made online.**

4.2 Amending the self-assessment

The taxpayer may amend their return (including the tax calculation) for Year 1 within twelve months after the filing date. For this purpose the filing date means:

- **31 January of Year 2;** or

- **Where the notice to file a return was issued after 31 October in Year 2, the last day of the three month period starting with the issue.**

A return may be amended by the taxpayer at a time when a compliance check enquiry is in progress into the return. The amendment does not restrict the scope of a compliance check enquiry into the return but may be taken into account in that enquiry. If the amendment made during a compliance check enquiry is the amount of tax payable, the amendment does not take effect while the compliance check enquiry is in progress.

A return may be amended by HMRC to correct any obvious error or omission in the return (such as errors of principle and arithmetical mistakes) or anything else that an officer has reason to believe is incorrect in the light of information available. The correction must usually be made within nine months after the day on which the return was actually filed. The taxpayer can object to the correction but must do so within 30 days of receiving notice of it.

Similar rules apply to the amendment and correction of partnership returns.

4.3 Claims

All claims and elections which can be made in a tax return must be made in this manner if a return has been issued. A claim for any relief, allowance or repayment of tax must be quantified at the time it is made.

In general, the time limit for making a claim is four years from the end of tax year. Where different time limits apply these have been mentioned throughout this text.

4.4 Recovery of overpaid tax

If a taxpayer discovers that they have overpaid tax, for example because they have made an error in their tax return, they can make a claim to have the overpaid tax repaid to them. The claim must be made within four years of the end of the tax year to which the overpayment relates.

5 Payment of income tax, national insurance contributions and capital gains tax   12/14, 6/16

Two payments on account and a final balancing payment of income tax and Class 4 NICs are due. Class 2 NICs and CGT are payable at the same time as the balancing payment.

One of the competencies you require to fulfil Performance Objective 16 Tax compliance and verification of the PER is to determine the incidence (timing) of tax liabilities and their impact on cash flow/financing requirements. You can apply the knowledge you obtain from this section of the text to help to demonstrate this competence.

5.1 Payments on account and final payment

5.1.1 Introduction

The self-assessment system may result in the taxpayer making **three payments of income tax and Class 4 NICs.**

Date	Payment
31 January in the tax year	1st payment on account
31 July after the tax year	2nd payment on account
31 January after the tax year	Final payment to settle the remaining liability

Class 2 NICs and capital gains tax are payable on 31 January following the end of the tax year.

5.1.2 Payments on account

Key term

> **Payments on account** are usually required where the income tax and Class 4 NICs due in the previous year exceeded the amount of income tax deducted at source; this excess is known as **'the relevant amount'**. Income tax deducted at source includes tax suffered on company loan stock and PAYE deductions.

The payments on account are each equal to 50% of the relevant amount for the previous year.

Exam focus point

> Payments on account of Class 2 NICs and CGT are never required.

Question

Payments on account

Sue is a self employed writer who paid tax for 2018/19 as follows:

	£
Total amount of income tax charged	9,200
This included: Tax deducted on company loan stock	1,200
She also paid: Class 4 NIC	1,900

How much are the payments on account for income tax and Class 4 NIC for 2019/20 and by what dates are they due?

Answer

	£
Income tax:	
Total income tax charged for 2018/19	9,200
Less tax deducted at source on loan stock for 2018/19	(1,200)
	8,000
Class 4 NIC	1,900
'Relevant amount'	9,900
Payments on account for 2019/20:	
31 January 2020 £9,900 × 50%	4,950
31 July 2020 £9,900 × 50%	4,950

Payments on account are not required if the relevant amount falls below a *de minimis* limit of £1,000. Also, payments on account are not required from taxpayers who paid 80% or more of their tax liability for the previous year through PAYE or other deduction at source arrangements.

If the previous year's liability increases following an amendment to a self-assessment, or the raising of a discovery assessment, an adjustment is made to the payments on account due.

5.1.3 Reducing payments on account

Payments on account are normally fixed by reference to the previous year's tax liability but if a taxpayer expects their liability to be lower than this **they may claim to reduce their payments on account to:**

(a)   A stated amount; or
(b)   Nil.

The claim must state the reason why they believe their tax liability will be lower, or nil.

If the taxpayer's eventual liability is higher than they estimated they will have reduced the payments on account too far. Although the payments on account will not be adjusted, the taxpayer will suffer an interest charge on late payment.

A penalty of the difference between the reduced payment on account and the correct payment on account may be levied if the reduction was claimed fraudulently or negligently.

5.1.4 Balancing payment

The balance of any income tax and Class 4 NICs together with Class 2 NICs and CGT due for a year, is normally payable on or before the 31 January following the year.

Question	Payment of tax

Giles made payments on account for 2018/19 of £6,500 each on 31 January 2019 and 31 July 2019, based on his 2017/18 liability. He then calculates his total income tax and Class 4 NIC liability for 2018/19 at £15,250, none of which was collected at source. In addition he calculated that his CGT liability for disposals in 2018/19 is £5,120 and his Class 2 NIC liability is £153.

What is the final payment due for 2018/19?

Answer

Income tax and Class 4 NIC: £15,250 − £6,500 − £6,500 = £2,250. CGT = £5,120. Class 2 NIC = £153

Final payment due on 31 January 2020 for 2018/19 £2,250 + £5,120 + £153 = £7,523

In one case the due date for the final payment is later than 31 January following the end of the year. **If a taxpayer has notified chargeability by 5 October but the notice to file a tax return is not issued before 31 October, then the due date for the payment is three months after the issue of the notice.**

Tax charged in an amended self-assessment is usually payable on the later of:

(a)   The normal due date, generally 31 January following the end of the tax year; and
(b)   The day following 30 days after the making of the revised self-assessment.

Tax charged on a discovery assessment (see below) is due 30 days after the issue of the assessment.

5.2 Penalty for late payment of tax

One of the competencies you require to fulfil Performance Objective 16 Tax compliance and verification of the PER is to explain tax filing and payment requirements and the consequences of non-compliance to clients. You can apply the knowledge you obtain from this section of the text to help to demonstrate this competence.

A penalty is chargeable where tax is paid after the due date based on the amount of unpaid tax. Up to 15% of that amount is payable where the tax is more than 12 months late.

A penalty is chargeable where tax is paid after the penalty date. The penalty date is 30 days after the due date for the tax. Therefore no penalty arises if the tax is paid within 30 days of the due date.

The penalty chargeable is:

Date of payment	Penalty
Not more than 5 months after the penalty date	5% of tax which is unpaid at the penalty date.
More than 5 months after the penalty date but not more than 11 months after the penalty date	5% of tax which is unpaid at the end of the 5 month period. This is in addition to the 5% penalty above.
More than 11 months after the penalty date	5% of tax which is unpaid at the end of the 11 month period. This is in addition to the two 5% penalties above.

Penalties for late payment of tax apply to:

(a) **Balancing payments of income tax and Class 4 NICs and any CGT** under self-assessment or a determination

(b) Tax due on the amendment of a self-assessment

(c) Tax due on a discovery assessment

Penalties for late payment do not apply to late payments on account.

5.3 Interest on late paid tax

Interest is chargeable on late payment of both payments on account and balancing payments. Late payment interest is charged from the due date for payment until the date payment is made.

For the purpose of Advanced Taxation (ATX – UK) exams in June 2019, September 2019, December 2019, and March 2020, the assumed rate of interest on underpaid tax is 3.00%.

Exam focus point

The rate of interest will be given to you in the Tax Rates and Allowances available in the exam. You should work to the nearest month.

Interest is charged from 31 January following the tax year (or the normal due date for the balancing payment, in the rare event that this is later), even if this is before the due date for payment on:

(a) Tax payable following an amendment to a self-assessment;
(b) Tax payable in a discovery assessment; and
(c) Tax postponed under an appeal which becomes payable.

Since a determination (see below) is treated as if it were a self-assessment, interest runs from 31 January following the tax year.

If a taxpayer claims to reduce their payments on account and there is still a balancing payment to be made, interest is normally charged on the payments on account as if each of those payments had been the lower of:

(a) The reduced amount, plus 50% of the balancing payment; and
(b) The amount which would have been payable had no claim for reduction been made.

Herbert's payments on account for 2018/19 based on his income tax liability for 2017/18 were £4,500 each. However, when he submitted his 2017/18 income tax return in January 2019 he made a claim to reduce the payments on account for 2018/19 to £3,500 each. The first payment on account was made on 1 February 2019, and the second on 1 November 2019.

Herbert filed his 2018/19 tax return in December 2019. The return showed that his tax liabilities for 2018/19 (before deducting payments on account) were income tax and Class 4 NIC: £10,000, capital gains tax: £2,500. Herbert paid the balance of tax due of £5,500 on 1 April 2020.

For what periods (to the nearest month) and in respect of what amounts will Herbert be charged interest?

Answer

Herbert made an excessive claim to reduce his payments on account, and will therefore be charged interest on the reduction. The payments on account should have been £4,500 each based on the original 2017/18 liability (not £5,000 each based on the 2018/19 liability). Interest will be charged as follows:

(a)   First payment on account

    (i)   On £3,500 – nil as paid on time

    (ii)   On £1,000 from due date of 31 January 2019 to payment date, 1 April 2020 (14 months)

(b)   Second payment on account

    (i)   On £3,500 from due date of 31 July 2019 to payment date, 1 November 2019 (3 months)

    (ii)   On £1,000 from due date of 31 July 2019 to payment date, 1 April 2020 (8 months)

(c)   Balancing payment

    (i)   On £3,500 from due date of 31 January 2020 to payment date, 1 April 2020 (2 months)

Where interest has been charged on late payments on account but the final balancing settlement for the year produces a repayment, all or part of the original interest is repaid.

5.4 Repayment of tax and repayment supplement

Tax is repaid when claimed unless a greater payment of tax is due in the following 30 days, in which case it is set-off against that payment.

For the purpose of Advanced Taxation (ATX – UK) exams in June 2019, September 2019, December 2019, and March 2020, the assumed rate of interest on overpaid tax is 0.5%.

Exam focus point

> The rate of interest will be given to you in the Tax Rates and Allowances available in the exam. You should work to the nearest month.

Interest is paid on overpayments of:

(a)   Payments on account;

(b)   Final payments of income tax and Class 4 NICs, and CGT, including tax deducted at source or tax credits on dividends; and

(c)   Penalties.

Repayment supplement runs from the original date of payment (even if this was prior to the due date), until the day before the date the repayment is made. Income tax deducted at source and tax credits are treated as if they were paid on the 31 January following the tax year concerned.

Repayment supplement paid to individuals is tax free.

6 HMRC powers

6.1 Compliance check enquiries

FAST FORWARD

A compliance check enquiry into a return, claim or election can be started by an officer of HMRC within a limited period.

6.1.1 Starting a compliance check enquiry

HM Revenue & Customs has powers to make compliance check enquiries into returns, claims or elections which have already been submitted.

Some returns, claims or elections are **selected for a compliance check enquiry at random, others for a particular reason**, for example, if HM Revenue & Customs believes that there has been an **underpayment of tax** due to the taxpayer's failure to comply with tax legislation.

An officer of HM Revenue & Customs has a limited period within which to commence a compliance check enquiry on a return or amendment. **The officer must give written notice of their intention by:**

(a) **The first anniversary of the actual filing date, if the return was delivered on or before the due filing date**; or

(b) **The quarter day following the first anniversary of the actual filing date, if the return is filed after the due filing date. The quarter days are 31 January, 30 April, 31 July and 31 October.**

If the taxpayer amends the return after the due filing date, the compliance check enquiry 'window' extends to the quarter day following the first anniversary of the date the amendment was filed. Where the compliance check enquiry was not started within the limit which would have applied had no amendment been filed, the enquiry is restricted to matters contained in the amendment.

The officer does not have to have, or give, any reason for starting a compliance check enquiry. In particular, the taxpayer will not be advised whether they have been selected at random for an audit. Compliance check enquiries may be full enquiries, or may be limited to 'aspect' enquiries.

6.1.2 During the compliance check enquiry

In the course of the compliance check enquiry **the officer may require the taxpayer to produce documents, accounts or any other information required. The taxpayer can appeal to the Tax Tribunal against such a requirement.**

6.1.3 Completion of a compliance check enquiry

An officer must issue a notice that the compliance check enquiry is complete, state their conclusions and amend the individual's self-assessment, partnership statement, or claim accordingly.

The officer cannot then make a further compliance check enquiry into that return. HMRC may, in limited circumstances, raise a discovery assessment if they believe that there has been a loss of tax.

6.2 Determinations

If notice has been served on a taxpayer to submit a return but the return is not submitted by the due filing date, an officer of HMRC may make a determination of the amounts liable to income tax and CGT and of the tax due. Such a determination must be made to the best of the officer's information and belief, and is then treated as if it were a self-assessment. This enables the officer to seek payment of tax, including payments on account for the following year and to charge interest.

A determination must be made within four years following the end of the relevant tax year.

6.3 Discovery assessments

If an officer of HMRC discovers that profits have been omitted from assessment, that any assessment has become insufficient, or that any relief given is, or has become excessive, an assessment may be raised to recover the tax lost.

If the tax lost results from an error in the taxpayer's return but the return was made in accordance with prevailing practice at the time, no discovery assessment may be made.

A discovery assessment may only be raised where a return has been made if:

(a)   There has been **careless or deliberate understatement** by the taxpayer or their agent; or

(b)   At the time that compliance check enquiries on the return were completed, or could no longer be made, the officer **did not have information** to make them aware of the loss of tax.

Information is treated as available to an officer if it is contained in the taxpayer's return or claim for the year or either of the two preceding years, or it has been provided as a result of a compliance check enquiry covering those years, or it has been specifically provided.

The time limit for raising a discovery assessment is 4 years from the end of the tax year but this is extended to 6 years if there has been careless understatement and 20 years if there has been deliberate understatement. The taxpayer may appeal against a discovery assessment within 30 days of issue.

6.4 Dishonest conduct of tax agents

> **FAST FORWARD**
>
> HMRC can investigate dishonest conduct by a tax agent and issue a civil penalty of up to £50,000 where there has been dishonest conduct.

HMRC can investigate whether there has been dishonest conduct by a tax agent (ie an individual who, in the course of business, assists clients with their tax affairs). Dishonest conduct occurs when a tax agent does something dishonest with a view to bringing about a loss of tax.

HMRC can issue a civil penalty of up to £50,000 where there has been **dishonest conduct and the tax agent fails to supply the information or documents that HMRC has requested.**

7 Penalties

7.1 Penalties for errors

> **FAST FORWARD**
>
> There is a common penalty regime for errors in tax returns, including income tax, NICs, corporation tax and VAT. Penalties range from 30% to 100% of the Potential Lost Revenue. Penalties may be reduced.

A common penalty regime for errors in tax returns for income tax, national insurance contributions, corporation tax and value added tax.

A penalty may be imposed where **a taxpayer makes an inaccurate return** if they have:

- Been **careless** because they have not taken reasonable care in making the return or discover the error later but does not take reasonable steps to inform HMRC;

- Made a **deliberate error** but **does not make arrangements to conceal it**; or

- Made a **deliberate error** and **has attempted to conceal it** eg by submitting false evidence in support of an inaccurate figure.

Note that **an error which is made where the taxpayer has taken reasonable care** in making the return and which they **do not discover later, does not result in a penalty.**

In order for a penalty to be charged, the **inaccurate return must result in**:

- An **understatement of the taxpayer's tax liability**;
- A **false or increased loss for the taxpayer**; or
- A **false or increased repayment of tax to the taxpayer**.

If a return contains more than one error, a penalty can be charged for each error.

The rules also extend to **errors in claims for allowances and reliefs** and in **accounts submitted in relation to a tax liability**.

Penalties for error also apply where **HMRC has issued an assessment estimating a person's liability** where:

- A **return has been issued to that person and has not been returned**; or
- The taxpayer was **required to deliver a return to HMRC but has not delivered it**.

The taxpayer will be charged a penalty where:

- The **assessment understates the taxpayer's liability** to income tax, capital gains tax, corporation tax or VAT; and
- The taxpayer **fails to take reasonable steps within 30 days of the date of the assessment** to tell HMRC that there is an under-assessment.

The amount of **the penalty for error is based on the Potential Lost Revenue (PLR)** to HMRC as a result of the error. For example, if there is an understatement of tax, this understatement will be the PLR.

Exam focus point

> The percentages for penalties for errors will be given to you in the Tax Rates and Allowances available in the exam.

The maximum amount of the penalty for error depends on the type of error:

Type of error	Maximum penalty payable
Deliberate and concealed	100% of PLR
Deliberate but not concealed	70% of PLR
Careless	30% of PLR

Question   Penalty for error

Alexander is a sole trader. He files his tax return for 2018/19 on 10 January 2020. The return shows his trading income to be £60,000. In fact, due to carelessness, his trading income should have been stated to be £68,000.

State the maximum penalty that could be charged by HMRC on Alexander for his error.

Answer

The Potential Lost Revenue (PLR) as a result of Alexander's error is:

£(68,000 − 60,000) = £8,000 × [40% (income tax) + 2% (Class 4 NICs)]   £3,360

Alexander's error is careless so the maximum penalty for error is:

£3,360 × 30%   £1,008

A penalty for error may be reduced if the taxpayer tells HMRC about the error – this is called a disclosure. The reduction depends on the **circumstances of** the disclosure and the **help that the taxpayer gives to HMRC in relation to the disclosure**.

An **unprompted disclosure is one made at a time when the taxpayer has no reason to believe HMRC has discovered, or is about to discover, the error**. Otherwise, the disclosure will be a **prompted disclosure**.

The **minimum penalties** that can be imposed are as follows:

Type of error	Unprompted	Prompted
Deliberate and concealed	30% of PLR	50% of PLR
Deliberate but not concealed	20% of PLR	35% of PLR
Careless	0% of PLR	15% of PLR

Question — Reduction of penalty

Sofia is a sole trader. She files her tax return for 2018/19 on 31 January 2020. The return shows a trading loss for the year of £(40,000). In fact, Sofia has deliberately increased this loss by £(12,000) and has submitted false figures in support of her claim. HMRC initiate a review into Sofia's return and in reply Sofia then makes a disclosure of the error. Sofia is a higher rate taxpayer due to her substantial investment income and she has made a claim to set the loss against general income in 2018/19.

State the maximum and minimum penalties that could be charged by HMRC on Sofia for her error.

Answer

The potential lost revenue as a result of Sofia's error is:

£12,000 × 40%   £4,800

Sofia's error is deliberate and concealed so the maximum penalty for error is:

£4,800 × 100%   £4,800

Sofia has made a prompted disclosure so the minimum penalty for error is:

£4,800 × 50%   £2,400

The help that the taxpayer gives to HMRC relates to when, how and to what extent the taxpayer:

- **Tells HMRC about the error,** making full disclosure and explaining how the error was made; and
- **Gives reasonable help** to HMRC to enable it **to quantify the error**; and
- **Allows access to business and other records** and other relevant documents.

A taxpayer can appeal to the First Tier Tribunal against:

- The **penalty being charged**
- The **amount of the penalty**

7.2 Penalties for late notification of chargeability

FAST FORWARD

A common penalty regime also applies to late notification of chargeability.

A common penalty regime also applies to certain taxes for failure to notify chargeability to tax (or failure to register for value added tax) that results in a loss of tax. The taxes affected include income tax, NICs, PAYE, CGT, corporation tax and VAT. Penalties are behaviour related, increasing for more serious failures, and are based on the 'potential lost revenue'.

The minimum and maximum penalties as percentages of PLR are as follows:

Behaviour	Maximum penalty	Minimum penalty with unprompted disclosure		Minimum penalty with prompted disclosure	
Deliberate and concealed	100%	30%		50%	
Deliberate but not concealed	70%	20%		35%	
		>12m	<12m	>12m	<12m
Careless	30%	10%	0%	20%	10%

Note that there is no zero penalty for reasonable care (as there is for penalties for errors on returns – see above), although the penalty may be reduced to 0% if the failure is rectified within 12 months through unprompted disclosure. The penalties may also be reduced at HMRC's discretion in 'special circumstances'. However, inability to pay the penalty is not a 'special circumstance'.

The same penalties apply for failure to notify HMRC of a new taxable activity.

Where the taxpayer's failure is not classed as deliberate, there is no penalty if they can show they have a 'reasonable excuse'. Reasonable excuse does not include having insufficient money to pay the penalty. Taxpayers have a right of appeal against penalty decisions to the First Tier Tribunal, which may confirm, substitute or cancel the penalty.

7.3 Penalties for late filing of tax return

One of the competencies you require to fulfil Performance Objective 16 Tax compliance and verification of the PER is to explain tax filing and payment requirements and the consequences of non-compliance to clients. You can apply the knowledge you obtain from this section of the text to help to demonstrate this competence.

FAST FORWARD

A penalty can be charged for late filing of a tax return based on how late the return is and how much tax is payable.

An individual is liable to a penalty where a tax return is filed after the due filing date. The penalty date is the date on which the return will be overdue (ie the date after the due filing date).

The initial penalty for late filing of the return is £100.

If the failure continues after the end of the period of 3 months starting with the penalty date, HMRC may give the individual notice specifying that a daily penalty of £10 is payable for a maximum of 90 days. The daily penalty runs from a date specified in the notice which may be earlier than the date of the notice but cannot be earlier than the end of the 3-month period.

If the failure continues after the end of the period of 6 months starting with the penalty date, a further penalty is payable. This penalty is the greater of:

- **5% of the tax liability** which would have been shown in the return; and
- **£300.**

If the failure continues after the end of the period of 12 months starting with the penalty date, a further penalty is payable. This penalty is determined in accordance with the taxpayer's conduct in withholding information which would enable or assist HMRC in assessing the taxpayer's liability to tax.

The penalty is computed as follows:

Type of conduct	Penalty
Deliberate and concealed	Greater of: • 100% of tax liability which would have been shown on return; and • £300
Deliberate not concealed	Greater of: • 70% of tax liability which would have been shown on return; and • £300
Any other case (eg careless)	Greater of: • 5% of tax liability which would have been shown on return; and • £300

7.4 Penalties for offshore non-compliance

FAST FORWARD

There may be increased penalties for offshore non-compliance and an additional penalty where there is a relevant offshore asset move intended to prevent or delay HMRC from discovering a potential loss of revenue. Penalties may also be imposed on those who enable offshore non-compliance.

Offshore non-compliance relates to non-compliance involving an **offshore matter**.

Key term

An **offshore matter** relates to income arising from a source in a territory outside the UK; assets situated or held in a territory outside the UK; activities carried on wholly or mainly in a territory outside the UK; anything having effect as if it were income assets or activities of a similar kind.

The penalties for failure to notify chargeability to tax, late filing and errors may be increased where an offshore matter is involved. The rates of these increased penalties are linked to how much information the particular offshore territory shares with HMRC so that the more difficult it is for HMRC to obtain information, the higher the penalty.

There is an additional penalty where there is a relevant offshore asset move intended to prevent or delay HMRC from discovering a potential loss of revenue once a non-compliance penalty for deliberate failure has been imposed. A **relevant offshore asset move** includes where:

(a)   **An asset ceases to be situated or held in specified territory** (broadly one which automatically shares information with HMRC) and **becomes situated or held in a non-specified territory** (broadly one which does not automatically share information with HMRC); or

(b)   **The person who holds the asset ceases to be resident in a specified territory** and **becomes resident in a non-specified territory.**

A **penalty** may also be imposed on those who **enable offshore non-compliance to be carried out. HM Revenue & Customs** may **publish details** of such persons.

Exam focus point

The examining team has stated that candidates are expected to know that these additional penalties exist but do not need to know the precise amounts that may be charged nor the categorisation of particular territories.

BPP LEARNING MEDIA

7.5 Penalty for late payment of tax

This penalty was dealt with in Section 5.2 earlier in this chapter.

7.6 Penalties for failure to keep records

The maximum (mitigable) penalty for each failure to keep and retain records is £3,000 per tax year/accounting period.

8 Appeals

One of the competencies you require to fulfil Performance Objective 16 Tax compliance and verification of the PER is to identify available claims, or the need to object to/appeal an assessment, ensuring that they are submitted within the required time limits. You can apply the knowledge you obtain from this section of the text to help to demonstrate this competence.

FAST FORWARD

Disputes between taxpayers and HMRC can be dealt with by an HMRC internal review or by a Tribunal hearing.

8.1 Internal reviews

For direct taxes, appeals must first be made to HMRC, which will assign a 'caseworker'.

For indirect taxes, appeals must be sent directly to the Tribunal, although the taxpayer can continue to correspond with their caseworker where, for example, there is new information.

At this stage the taxpayer may be offered, or may ask for, an **'internal review'**, which will be made by an objective HMRC review officer not previously connected with the case. This is a less costly and more effective way to resolve disputes informally, without the need for a Tribunal hearing. An appeal to Tribunal cannot be made until any review has ended.

The taxpayer must either accept the review offer, or notify an appeal to the Tribunal within 30 days of being offered the review, otherwise the appeal will be treated as settled.

HMRC must usually carry out the review within 45 days, or any longer time as agreed with the taxpayer. The review officer may decide to uphold, vary or withdraw decisions.

After the review conclusion is notified, **the taxpayer has 30 days to appeal to the Tribunal.**

8.2 Tribunal hearings

If there is no internal review, or the taxpayer is unhappy with the result of an internal review, the case may be heard by the Tribunal. The person wishing to make an appeal (the appellant) must send a notice of appeal to the Tribunal. The Tribunal must then give notice of the appeal to the respondent (normally HMRC).

The Tribunal is made up of two 'tiers':

(a)   **A First Tier Tribunal; and**
(b)   **An Upper Tribunal.**

The case will be allocated to one of four case **'tracks':**

(a)   **Complex cases**, which the Tribunal considers will require lengthy or complex evidence or a lengthy hearing, or involve a complex or important principle or issue, or involves a large amount of money. Such cases will usually be heard by the Upper Tribunal;

(b)   **Standard cases, heard by the First Tier Tribunal**, which have detailed case management and are subject to a more formal procedure than basic cases;

(c) **Basic cases, also heard by the First Tier Tribunal**, which will usually be disposed of after a hearing, with minimal exchange of documents before the hearing; and

(d) **Paper cases, dealt with by the First Tier Tribunal**, which applies to straightforward matters such as fixed filing penalties and will usually be dealt with in writing, without a hearing.

A decision of the First Tier Tribunal may be appealed to the Upper Tribunal.

Decisions of the Upper Tribunal are binding on the Tribunals and any affected public authorities. A decision of the Upper Tribunal may be appealed to the Court of Appeal.

9 Tax offenders

FAST FORWARD

Deliberate tax defaulters whose actions result in a tax loss in excess of £25,000 may have their details published by HMRC on the internet.

9.1 'Naming and shaming' tax offenders

All deliberate tax defaulters (individuals and companies) whose actions result in a tax loss to HMRC in excess of £25,000 will have their names and details (such as address and profession) published on the internet by HMRC.

Names will not be published of those who make a full unprompted disclosure or a full prompted disclosure within the required time. Details will be published quarterly within one year of the penalty becoming final and will be removed from publication one year later.

9.2 Monitoring of serious tax offenders

Taxpayers who incur a penalty for deliberate evasion in respect of tax of £5,000 or more are required to submit returns for up to the following five years showing more detailed business accounts information and detailing the nature and value of any balancing adjustments within the accounts.

Chapter roundup

- Taxes are administered by Her Majesty's Revenue & Customs.

- Individuals who do not receive a tax return or who have a new source of income or gains must notify their chargeability to income tax or CGT.

- Tax returns must usually be filed by 31 October (paper) or 31 January (electronic) following the end of the tax year.

- If a paper return is filed the taxpayer can ask HMRC to compute the tax due. Electronic returns have tax calculated automatically.

- Two payments on account and a final balancing payment of income tax and Class 4 NICs are due. Class 2 NICs and CGT are payable at the same time as the balancing payment.

- A penalty is chargeable where tax is paid after the due date based on the amount of unpaid tax. Up to 15% of that amount is payable where the tax is more than 12 months late.

- A compliance check enquiry into a return, claim or election can be started by an officer of HMRC within a limited period.

- HMRC can investigate dishonest conduct by a tax agent and issue a civil penalty of up to £50,000 where there has been dishonest conduct.

- There is a common penalty regime for errors in tax returns, including income tax, NICs, corporation tax and VAT. Penalties range from 30% to 100% of the Potential Lost Revenue. Penalties may be reduced.

- A common penalty regime also applies to late notification of chargeability.

- A penalty can be charged for late filing of a tax return based on how late the return is and how much tax is payable.

- There may be increased penalties for offshore non-compliance and an additional penalty where there is a relevant offshore asset move intended to prevent or delay HMRC from discovering a potential loss of revenue. Penalties may also be imposed on those who enable offshore non-compliance.

- Disputes between taxpayers and HMRC can be dealt with by an HMRC internal review or by a Tribunal hearing.

- Deliberate tax defaulters whose actions result in a tax loss in excess of £25,000 may have their details published by HMRC on the internet.

Quick quiz

1   By when must a taxpayer who has a new source of income in 2018/19 give notice of their chargeability to income tax?

2   By when must a taxpayer file a paper tax return for 2018/19?

3   What are the normal payment dates for income tax?

4   What penalties are due in respect of income tax payments on account that are paid two months late?

5   Which body hears tax appeals?

Answers to quick quiz

1   Within six months of the end of the year, ie by 5 October 2019

2   By 31 October 2019 or, if the return is issued after 31 July 2019, by the end of 3 months following the issue of the notice to file the return

3   Two payments on account of income tax are due on 31 January in the tax year and on the 31 July following. A final balancing payment is due on 31 January following the tax year.

4   None. Penalties do not apply to late payment of payment on account.

5   The Tax Tribunal which consists of the First Tier Tribunal and the Upper Tribunal

Now try the question below from the Practice Question Bank

Number	Level	Marks	Time
Q16	Introductory	17	33 mins

Inheritance tax

An introduction to inheritance tax

Topic list	Syllabus reference
1 Scope of inheritance tax	A3(a)D1
2 Computing transfers of value	A3(a)D2,(b)(ii)
3 Exemptions	A3(a)D3,(c)(iii), f(i)
4 Excluded property	A3(b)(ii)
5 Calculation of tax on lifetime transfers	A3(a)D2,(d)(i),(ii)
6 Death estate: basic principles	A3(a)D2,(d)(iii)

Introduction

In this chapter, we move on to inheritance tax (IHT). IHT is primarily a tax on wealth left on death. It also applies to gifts within seven years of death and to certain lifetime transfers of wealth.

The tax is different from income tax and CGT, where the basic question is: how much has the taxpayer made? With IHT, the basic question is, how much have they given away? We tax the amount which the taxpayer has transferred – the amount by which they are worse off. If the taxpayer pays IHT on a lifetime gift, they are worse off by the amount of the gift plus the tax due, and we have to take that into account. Some transfers are, however, exempt from IHT.

We will see that the first £325,000 of transfers is taxed at 0% (the 'nil rate band'), and is therefore effectively tax-free. To stop people from avoiding IHT by, for example, giving away £1,625,000 in five lots of £325,000, we need to look back seven years every time a transfer is made to decide how much of the nil rate band is available to set against the current transfer.

Finally, we will see how to bring together all of a deceased person's assets at death, and compute the tax on the estate, including using the residence nil rate band.

In the next chapter, we will look at valuation, reliefs and further aspects of the death estate.

Study guide

		Intellectual level
3	**Inheritance tax in situations involving further aspects of the scope of the tax and the calculation of the liabilities arising, the principles of valuation and the reliefs available, transfers of property to and from trusts, overseas aspects and further aspects of administration**	
(a)	The contents of the Taxation - United Kingdom (TX – UK) study guide for inheritance tax under headings:	2
•	D1 The basic principles of computing transfers of value	
•	D2 The liabilities arising on chargeable lifetime transfers and on the death of an individual	
•	D3 The use of exemptions in deferring and minimising inheritance tax liabilities	
(b)	The scope of inheritance tax:	
(ii)	Identify excluded property	2
(c)	The basic principles of computing transfers of value:	
(iii)	Identify exempt transfers	2
(d)	The liabilities arising on chargeable lifetime transfers and the death of an individual:	3
(i)	Advise on the tax implications of chargeable lifetime transfers	
(ii)	Advise on the tax implications of transfers within seven years of death	
(iii)	Advise on the tax liability arising on a death estate	
(f)	The use of exemptions and reliefs in deferring and minimising inheritance tax liabilities:	3
(i)	Advise on the use of reliefs and exemptions to minimise inheritance tax liabilities, as mentioned in the sections above	

Exam guide

In the Advanced Taxation (ATX – UK) exam, you will be expected to deal with basic inheritance tax transfers and the death estate but also the more technical rules covered in this chapter such as excluded property and further exemptions. You will also be expected to use your knowledge of inheritance tax to advise clients about minimising inheritance tax liabilities.

This chapter revises the basic principles of inheritance tax covered in Taxation (TX – UK). The examining team has identified essential underpinning knowledge from the Taxation (TX – UK) syllabus which is particularly important that you revise as part of your Advanced Taxation (ATX – UK) studies. In this chapter, the relevant topics are:

		Intellectual level
D1	**The basic principles of computing transfers of value**	
(b)	Understand and apply the meaning of transfer of value, chargeable transfer and potentially exempt transfer.	2
(c)	Demonstrate the diminution in value principle.	2
(d)	Demonstrate the seven year accumulation principle taking into account changes in the level of the nil rate band.	2
D2	**The liabilities arising on chargeable lifetime transfers and on the death of an individual**	
(a)	Understand the tax implications of lifetime transfers and compute the relevant liabilities.	2
(b)	Understand and compute the tax liability on a death estate.	2

The only change in 2018/19 from 2017/18 in the material covered in Taxation (TX – UK) is the increase in the residence nil rate band on death to £125,000. Note that the nil rate band has remained at £325,000.

Exam focus point

> **ACCA's article Inheritance tax and capital gains tax for Advanced Taxation (ATX – UK),** written by a member of the Advanced Taxation (ATX – UK) examining team, considers the occasions where both capital gains and inheritance taxes are relevant to a transaction. It also features illustrations of some issues that need to be considered when giving advice in the context of the Advanced Taxation (ATX – UK) exam.

1 Scope of inheritance tax

> One of the competencies you require to fulfil Performance Objective 15 Tax computations and assessments of the PER is to prepare or contribute to the computation or assessment of tax computations for individuals. You can apply the knowledge you obtain from this section of the text to help to demonstrate this competence.

1.1 Transfers of value

IHT is a tax on gifts or '**transfers of value**' made by **chargeable persons of chargeable assets**. This generally involves a transaction as a result of which wealth is transferred by one person to another, either directly or via a trust.

1.2 Chargeable persons

Chargeable persons for IHT purposes are:

(a) Individuals; and
(b) Trustees of settled property.

Companies are not chargeable persons although if companies are used to transfer wealth an IHT liability can be charged on the shareholders (the details are outside the scope of your syllabus).

Spouses and civil partners are taxed separately although there is an exemption for transfers between the couple. There are also special valuation rules which are dealt with later.

1.3 Chargeable assets

All transfers of assets (worldwide ie both situated in the UK and outside the UK – see later in this text) **made by persons domiciled, or deemed domiciled, in the UK** (see later in this text) **whether during lifetime or on death are within the charge to IHT.**

For individuals not domiciled, nor deemed domiciled, in the UK, only transfers of UK assets are within the charge to IHT.

2 Computing transfers of value

2.1 Introduction

There are two main chargeable occasions for individuals:

(a)   Gifts made in the lifetime of the donor (**lifetime transfers**); and
(b)   Gifts made on death, for example when property is left in a will (**death estate**).

We will look in detail at lifetime transfers later in this chapter and at the death estate in the next chapter.

First, however, we start our study of IHT by looking at some general principles which apply to both chargeable occasions.

2.2 Transfers of value and chargeable transfers   6/18

FAST FORWARD IHT applies to transfers to trusts, transfers on death and transfers within the seven years before death.

IHT cannot arise unless there is a transfer of value. This is any gratuitous disposition (eg gift, sale at less than market value) made by a person which results in their being worse off, that is, they suffer a diminution (ie reduction) in the value of their estate.

The measure of a gift is always the loss to the transferor (the diminution in value of their estate), not the amount gained by the transferee.

2.3 Chargeable transfers

Inheritance tax arises on any **chargeable transfer. This is any transfer of value not covered by an exemption.**

Chargeable transfers made during the individual's lifetime are called **chargeable lifetime transfers (CLTs).**

On death, an individual is treated as if they had made a transfer of value of the property comprised in their estate. This, then, will be a chargeable transfer to the extent that it is not exempt.

2.4 Potentially exempt transfers

Key term

A **PET** is a **lifetime transfer made by an individual to another individual.** Any other lifetime transfer by an individual (eg gift to a trust) not covered by an exemption is a CLT.

A PET is exempt from IHT when made and will remain so if the transferor survives for at least seven years from making the gift. If the transferor dies within seven years of making the gift, it will become chargeable to IHT.

2.5 Diminution in value

In many cases the diminution in value of the transferor's estate will be the same as the increase in the value of the transferee's estate. However, sometimes the two will not be the same.

2.6 Example: diminution in value

Audrey holds 5,100 of the shares in an unquoted company which has an issued share capital of 10,000 shares. Currently Audrey's majority holding is valued at £15 per share.

Audrey wishes to give 200 shares to her son, Brian. However, to Brian the shares are worth only £2.50 each, since he will have only a small minority holding in the company. After the gift Audrey will hold 4,900 shares and these will be worth £10 each. The value per share to Audrey will fall from £15 to £10 per share since she will lose control of the company.

The diminution in value of Audrey's estate is £27,500, as follows.

	£
Before the gift: 5,100 shares × £15	76,500
After the gift: 4,900 shares × £10	(49,000)
Diminution in value	27,500

Brian has only been given shares with a market value of 200 × £2.50 = £500. Remember, a gift is also a deemed disposal at market value for CGT purposes, and it is this value that will be used in any CGT computation. IHT, however, uses the principle of diminution in value which can, as in this case, give a much greater value than the value of the asset transferred.

2.7 Exceptions to the IHT charge

The following are not chargeable to IHT:

(a) **Transfers where there is no gratuitous intent**: for example selling a painting for £1,000 which later turns out to be worth £100,000. The transaction must have been made at arm's length between unconnected persons

(b) **Transfers made in the course of a trade**: for example Christmas gifts to employees

(c) **Expenditure on family maintenance**: for example school fees paid for a child

(d) Waivers of remuneration

(e) Waivers of dividends provided the waiver is made within the 12 months before the dividend is declared

(f) Any transfer covered by a specific exemption (see further below)

(g) **Transfers of excluded property** (see below)

3 Exemptions

One of the competencies you require to fulfil Performance Objective 17 Tax planning and advice of the PER is to mitigate and/or defer tax liabilities through the use of standard reliefs, exemptions and incentives. You can apply the knowledge you obtain from this section of the text to help to demonstrate this competence.

FAST FORWARD

Exemptions may apply to make transfers or parts of transfers non-chargeable. Some exemptions only apply on lifetime transfers (annual, normal expenditure out of income, marriage/civil partnership), whilst some apply on both life and death transfers (eg spouses/civil partners, charities, political parties).

3.1 Introduction

There are various exemptions available to eliminate or reduce the chargeable amount of a lifetime transfer or property passing on an individual's death. Some exemptions apply to both lifetime transfers and property passing on death, whilst others apply only to lifetime transfers.

The lifetime exemptions apply to PETs as well as to CLTs. Only the balance of such gifts after the lifetime exemptions have been taken into account is then potentially exempt.

Exam focus point

> Where CLTs and PETS are made in the same year the CLTs should be made first to use any available exemptions. If used up against the PETs an exemption will be wasted if the PET never becomes chargeable.

3.2 Exemptions applying to lifetime transfers only

3.2.1 The small gifts exemptions   12/14, 12/15

Outright gifts to individuals totalling £250 or less per donee in any one tax year are exempt. If gifts total more than £250 the whole amount is chargeable. A donor can give up to £250 each year to each of as many donees as they wish. The small gifts exemption cannot apply to gifts into trusts.

3.2.2 The annual exemption (AE)   6/18

The first £3,000 of value transferred in a tax year is exempt from IHT. The annual exemption is used only after all other exemptions (such as for transfers to spouses/civil partners or charities (see below)). If several gifts are made in a year, the £3,000 exemption is applied to earlier gifts before later gifts. The annual exemption is used up by PETs as well as CLTs, even though the PETs might never become chargeable.

Any unused portion of the annual exemption is carried forward for one year only. Only use it the following year **after** that year's own annual exemption has been used.

Question   Annual exemptions

Frank has no unused annual exemption brought forward at 6 April 2017.

On 1 August 2017 he makes a transfer of £600 to Peter.
On 1 September 2017 he makes a transfer of £2,000 to Quentin.
On 1 July 2018 he makes a transfer of £3,300 to a trust for his grandchildren.
On 1 June 2019 he makes a transfer of £5,000 to Rowan.

Show the application of the annual exemptions.

Answer

2017/18	£
1.8.17 Gift to Peter	600
Less AE 2017/18	(600)
	0

	£
1.9.17 Gift to Quentin	2,000
Less AE 2017/18	(2,000)
	0

The unused annual exemption carried forward is £3,000 – £600 – £2,000 = £400.

2018/19	£	£
1.7.18 Gift to trust		3,300
Less: AE 2018/19	3,000	
AE 2017/18 b/f	300	
		(3,300)
		0

The unused annual exemption carried forward is zero because the 2018/19 exemption must be used before 2017/18 exemption brought forward. The balance of £100 of the 2017/18 exemption is lost, because it cannot be carried forward for more than one year.

2019/20	£
1.6.19 Gift to Rowan	5,000
Less AE 2019/20	(3,000)
	2,000

3.2.3 Normal expenditure out of income   12/15

Inheritance tax is a tax on transfers of capital, not income. A transfer of value is exempt if:

(a)   It is made as part of the normal expenditure of the transferor;
(b)   Taking one year with another, it was made out of income; and
(c)   It leaves the transferor with sufficient income to maintain their usual standard of living.

As well as covering such things as regular presents **this exemption can cover regular payments out of income such as a grandchild's school fees or the payment of life assurance premiums on a policy for someone else.**

3.2.4 Gifts in consideration of marriage/civil partnership

Gifts in consideration of marriage/civil partnership are exempt up to:

(a)   **£5,000 if from a parent of a party to the marriage/civil partnership**
(b)   **£2,500 if from a remoter ancestor or from one of the parties to the marriage/civil partnership**
(c)   **£1,000 if from any other person**

The limits apply to gifts from any one donor for any one marriage/civil partnership. The exemption is available only if the marriage/civil partnership actually takes place.

3.3 Exemptions applying to both lifetime transfers and transfers on death

3.3.1 Gifts between spouses/civil partners   6/16

Any transfers of value between spouses/civil partners are exempt provided the transferee is domiciled or deemed domiciled (see later in this text) in the UK at the time of transfer. The exemption covers lifetime gifts between them and property passing under a will or on intestacy.

If the transferor spouse/civil partner is domiciled or deemed domiciled in the UK but the transferee spouse/civil partner is not domiciled nor deemed domiciled in the UK, the exemption is limited to a cumulative total equal to the amount of the nil rate band at the date of the transfer ie £325,000 for 2018/19. If neither spouse/civil partner is domiciled nor deemed domiciled in the UK there is no limit on the exemption. An election may be made for a non-UK domiciled individual who is, or was, the spouse or civil partner of a UK domiciled individual, to be treated as UK domiciled for IHT purposes. We look at this election later in this text when we deal with overseas aspects of IHT.

A simple planning point follows from this exemption. Spouses/civil partners may avoid IHT, at least in the short term, if each makes a will leaving their property to the other.

Claims can also be made to transfer any unused nil rate band and the residence nil rate band from one spouse/civil partner to the surviving spouse/civil partner (see later in this text).

Question   Exemptions

Dale made a gift of £153,000 to her son on 17 October 2018 on the son's marriage. Dale gave £400,000 to her spouse on 1 January 2021. Dale gave £70,000 to her daughter on 11 May 2021. The only other gifts Dale made were birthday and Christmas presents of £100 each to her grandchildren.

Show what exemptions are available assuming:

(a)   Dale's spouse is domiciled in the UK; or

(b)   Dale's spouse is not domiciled in the UK.

Answer

(a)   *17 October 2018*

	£
Gift to Dale's son	153,000
Less: ME	(5,000)
AE 2018/19	(3,000)
AE 2017/18 b/f	(3,000)
PET	142,000

1 January 2021

	£
Gift to Dale's spouse	400,000
Less spouse exemption	(400,000)
	0

11 May 2021

	£
Gift to Dale's daughter	70,000
Less: AE 2021/22	(3,000)
AE 2020/21 b/f	(3,000)
PET	64,000

The gifts to the grandchildren are covered by the small gifts exemption.

(b)   *17 October 2018*

As in part (a)

1 January 2021

	£
Gift to Dale's spouse	400,000
Less spouse exemption (restricted)	(325,000)
Less: AE 2020/21	(3,000)
AE 2019/20 b/f	(3,000)
PET	69,000

Note that the annual exemption is available to set against the gift remaining after deducting the spouse exemption.

11 May 2021

	£
Gift to Dale's daughter	70,000
Less AE 2021/22	(3,000)
PET	67,000

3.3.2 Other exempt transfers

Transfers (whether outright or by settlement) **to UK charities are exempt** from inheritance tax.

Gifts to a qualifying political party are exempt. A political party qualifies if, at the general election preceding the transfer of value, either:

(a) At least two members were elected to the House of Commons; or

(b) One member was elected and the party polled at least 150,000 votes.

Gifts for national purposes are exempt. Eligible recipients include museums and art galleries.

4 Excluded property

FAST FORWARD

If excluded property is given away, there are no IHT consequences.

4.1 Types of excluded property

The following are examples of excluded property.

(a) A reversionary interest in settled property. A reversionary interest is a future interest in trust property. An example is when an income beneficiary (with the present interest) dies and the capital passes to the remainderman. A reversionary interest will not, however, be treated as excluded property if:

   (i)   It has been acquired at any time for consideration in money or money's worth; or

   (ii) Either the settlor or their spouse is or has been beneficially entitled to the interest at any time.

(b) Foreign assets owned by non-UK domiciled individuals (see later in this text).

5 Calculation of tax on lifetime transfers
12/13, 6/14, 6/15, 3/16, 6/16, 6/17, 12/17, 6/18

5.1 Basic principles

FAST FORWARD

Transfers are cumulated for seven years so that the nil rate band is not available in full on each of a series of transfers in rapid succession.

There are two aspects of the calculation of tax on lifetime transfers:

(a) Lifetime tax on CLTs; and

(b) Additional death tax on CLTs and on PETs where the transferor dies within seven years of making the transfer.

Exam focus point

You should always calculate the lifetime tax on any CLTs first, then move on to calculate the death tax on all CLTs and PETs made within seven years of death.

5.2 Lifetime tax

FAST FORWARD

IHT is charged on what a donor loses. If the donor pays the IHT on a lifetime gift they lose both the asset given away and the money with which they paid the tax due on it. Grossing up is required.

5.2.1 Transferee pays tax

When a CLT is made and the transferee (ie the trustees) pays the lifetime tax, follow these steps to work out the lifetime IHT on it:

Step 1   Look back seven years from the date of the transfer to see if any other CLTs have been made. If so, these transfers use up the nil rate band available for the current transfer. Work out the value of any nil rate band still available.

Step 2   Compute the gross value of the CLT. You may be given this in the question or you may have to work out the diminution of value, deduct reliefs (such as business property relief as described later in the text) or exemptions (such as the annual exemption described earlier in this chapter).

Step 3   Any part of the CLT covered by the nil rate band is taxed at 0%. Any part of the CLT not covered by the nil rate band is charged at 20%.

Exam focus point

> The life rate of 20%, the current nil rate band and those for previous years are given in the Tax Rates and Allowances available in the exam.

Question — Transferee pays the lifetime tax

Eric makes a gift of £336,000 to a trust on 10 July 2018. He has not used his annual exemption in 2018/19 nor in 2017/18. The trustees agree to pay the tax due.

Calculate the lifetime tax payable by the trustees if Eric has made:

(a)   A lifetime chargeable transfer of value of £100,000 in August 2010
(b)   A lifetime chargeable transfer of value of £100,000 in August 2011
(c)   A lifetime chargeable transfer of value of £350,000 in August 2011

Answer

(a)   **Step 1**   No lifetime transfers in seven years before 10 July 2018. Nil rate band of £325,000 available.

Step 2

	£
Gift	336,000
Less: AE 2018/19	(3,000)
AE 2017/18 b/f	(3,000)
Chargeable lifetime transfer	330,000

Step 3

	IHT
	£
£325,000 × 0%	0
£5,000 × 20%	1,000
£330,000	1,000

(b)   **Step 1**   Lifetime transfer of value of £100,000 in 7 years before 10 July 2018 (transfers after 10 July 2011). Nil rate band of £(325,000 – 100,000) = £225,000 available.

Step 2   Value of CLT is £330,000 (as before).

Step 3

	IHT
	£
£225,000 × 0%	0
£105,000 × 20%	21,000
£330,000	21,000

(c) **Step 1** Lifetime transfer of value of £350,000 in seven years before 10 July 2018 (transfers after 10 July 2011). No nil rate band available as all covered by previous transfer.

Step 2 Value of CLT is £330,000 (as before).

Step 3

	IHT £
£330,000 @ 20%	66,000

5.2.2 Transferor pays tax

Where IHT is payable on a CLT, the **primary liability to pay tax is on the transferor,** although the transferor may agree with the transferee (as in the above example) that the transferee is to pay the tax instead.

If the transferor pays the lifetime IHT due on a CLT, the total reduction in value of their estate is the transfer of value plus the IHT due on it. The transfer is therefore a net transfer and must be grossed up in order to find the gross value of the transfer. **We do this by working out the tax as follows.**

Formula to learn

Chargeable amount (ie not covered by nil rate band) $\times \dfrac{20\,(\text{rate of tax})}{80\,(100\,\text{minus the rate of tax})}$

When a CLT is made and the transferor pays the lifetime tax, follow these steps to work out the lifetime IHT on it:

Step 1 Look back seven years from the date of the transfer to see if any other CLTs have been made. If so, these transfers use up the nil rate band available for the current transfer. Work out the value of any nil rate band still available.

Step 2 Compute the net value of the CLT. You may be given this in the question or may have to work out the diminution of value, deduct reliefs (such as business property relief as described later in the text) or exemptions (such as the annual exemption discussed earlier in this chapter).

Step 3 Any part of the CLT covered by the nil rate band is taxed at 0%. Any part of the CLT not covered by the nil rate band is taxed at 20/80.

Step 4 Work out the gross transfer by adding the net transfer and the tax together. You can check your figure by working out the tax on the gross transfer.

Question Transferor pays the lifetime tax

James makes a gift of £336,000 to a trust on 10 July 2018. He has not used his annual exemption in 2018/19 nor in 2017/18. James will pay the tax due.

Calculate the lifetime tax payable, if James has made:

(a) A lifetime chargeable transfer of value of £100,000 in August 2010
(b) A lifetime chargeable transfer of value of £100,000 in August 2011
(c) A lifetime chargeable transfer of value of £350,000 in August 2011

(a) **Step 1** No lifetime transfers in seven years before 10 July 2018. Nil rate band of £325,000 available.

Step 2

	£
Gift	336,000
Less: AE 2018/19	(3,000)
AE 2017/18 b/f	(3,000)
Net CLT	330,000

Step 3

	IHT
	£
£325,000 × 0%	0
£5,000 × 20/80	1,250
£330,000	1,250

Step 4 Gross transfer is £(330,000 + 1,250) = £331,250. **Check:** Tax on the gross transfer would be:

	IHT
	£
£325,000 × 0%	0
£6,250 × 20%	1,250
£331,250	1,250

(b) **Step 1** Lifetime transfer of value of £100,000 in seven years before 10 July 2018 (transfers after 10 July 2011). Nil rate band of £(325,000 − 100,000) = £225,000 available.

Step 2 Net value of CLT is £325,000 (as before).

Step 3

	IHT
	£
£225,000 × 0%	0
£105,000 × 20/80	26,250
£330,000	26,250

Step 4 Gross transfer is £(330,000 + 26,250) = £356,250. **Check:** Tax on the gross transfer would be:

	IHT
	£
£225,000 × 0%	0
£131,250 × 20%	26,250
£356,250	26,250

(c) **Step 1** Lifetime transfer of value of £350,000 in seven years before 10 July 2018 (transfers after 10 July 2011). No nil rate band available as all covered by previous transfer.

Step 2 Net value of CLT is £330,000 (as before).

Step 3

	IHT
	£
£330,000 × 20/80	82,500

Step 4 Gross transfer is £(330,000 + 82,500) = £412,500. **Check:** Tax on the gross transfer would be:

	IHT
	£
£412,500 × 20%	82,500

5.3 Death tax

The longer the transferor survives after making a gift, the lower the death tax. This is because taper relief applies to lower the amount of death tax payable as follows:

Years between transfer and death	% reduction in death tax
3 years or less	0
More than 3 but less than 4	20
More than 4 but less than 5	40
More than 5 but less than 6	60
More than 6 but less than 7	80

Exam focus point

The rates of taper relief will be given in the rates and allowances section of the exam.

Death tax on a lifetime transfer is **always** payable by the transferee, so grossing up is not relevant.

Follow these steps to work out the death tax on a CLT:

Step 1 Look back seven years from the **date of the transfer** to see if any other chargeable transfers were made. If so, these transfers use up the nil rate band available for the current transfer. Work out the value of any nil rate band remaining.

Step 2 Compute the value of the CLT. This is the gross value of the transfer that you worked out for computing lifetime tax.

Step 3 Any part of the CLT covered by the nil rate band is taxed at 0%. Any part of the CLT not covered by the nil rate band is charged at 40%.

Step 4 Reduce the death tax by taper relief (if applicable).

Step 5 Deduct any lifetime tax paid. The death tax may be reduced to nil, but there is no repayment of lifetime tax.

Exam focus point

The death rate of 40%, the current nil rate band and those for previous years are given in the Tax Rates and Allowances available in the exam.

Question   Lifetime tax and death tax on CLTs

Trevor made a cash gift of £300,000 to a trust on 9 December 2006. This was his first transfer of value.

He then made a gift to another trust of shares worth £206,000 on 15 November 2013.

Trevor paid the lifetime tax due on the December 2006 transfer but the trustees paid the lifetime tax due on the November 2013 transfer.

Trevor died in August 2018.

Compute:

(a) The lifetime tax payable by Trevor on the lifetime transfer in December 2006;

(b) The lifetime tax payable by the trustees on the lifetime transfer in November 2013; and

(c) The death tax (if any) payable on the lifetime transfer in November 2013.

(a) Lifetime tax on December 2006 transfer

Step 1 No lifetime transfers in seven years before 9 December 2006. Nil rate band of £285,000 available (given in Tax Tables).

Step 2

	£
Gift	300,000
Less: AE 2006/07	(3,000)
AE 2005/06 b/f	(3,000)
Net CLT	294,000

Step 3

	IHT
	£
£285,000 × 0%	0
£9,000 × 20/80	2,250
£294,000	2,250

Step 4 Gross transfer is £(294,000 + 2,250) = £296,250. **Check:** Tax on the gross transfer would be:

	IHT
	£
£285,000 × 0%	0
£11,250 × 20%	2,250
£296,250	2,250

There will not be any additional inheritance tax on this transfer as the transferor survived seven years from making it. However, note that it is cumulated with the November 2013 to work out the inheritance tax on that later transfer.

(b) Lifetime tax on November 2013 transfer

Step 1 Lifetime transfer of value of £296,250 in 7 years before 15 November 2013 (transfers after 15 November 2006). Nil rate band of £(325,000 [nil rate band in 2013/14] − 296,250) = £28,750 available.

Step 2

	£
Gift	206,000
Less: AE 2013/14	(3,000)
AE 2012/13 b/f	(3,000)
	200,000

Step 3

	IHT
	£
£28,750 × 0%	0
£171,250 × 20%	34,250
£200,000	34,250

(c) Death tax on November 2013 transfer

Step 1 Lifetime transfer of value of £296,250 in 7 years before 15 November 2013 (transfers after 15 November 2006). Nil rate band of £(325,000 [nil rate band in 2018/19] – 296,250) = £28,750 available.

Step 2 Value of CLT is £200,000.

Step 3

	IHT £
£28,750 × 0%	0
£171,250 × 40%	68,500
£200,000	68,500

Step 4 Death more than 4 years but less than 5 years after transfer

	£
Death tax	68,500
Less taper relief @ 40%	(27,400)
Death tax left in charge	41,100

Step 5 Tax due £(41,100 – 34,250) | 6,850

5.4 Death tax on potentially exempt transfers

If the transferor dies within seven years of making a PET it will become chargeable to death tax in the same way as a CLT. There will be no lifetime tax paid, so Step 5 above will not apply.

Remember that the exemptions which apply to lifetime transfers only, such as the annual exemption and the marriage/civil partner exemption, are available to set against PETs. **You must apply them in chronological order**, so that if a PET is made before a CLT in the same tax year, the exemption is set against the PET. This may waste the exemption (unless the donor dies within seven years), and is disadvantageous in cash flow terms since lifetime tax is paid on CLTs but not on PETs.

We will now work through an example where there is both a PET and a CLT.

Question Lifetime tax and death tax on CLTs and PETs

Louise gave £346,000 to her son on 1 February 2015. This was the first transfer that Louise had made.

On 10 October 2018, Louise gave £376,000 to a trust. The trustees paid the lifetime IHT due.

On 11 January 2019, Louise died.

Compute:

(a) The lifetime tax payable by the trustees on the lifetime transfer made in 2018;
(b) The death tax payable on the lifetime transfer made in 2015; and
(c) The death tax payable on the lifetime transfer made in 2018.

(a) Lifetime tax – 2018 CLT

Step 1 There are no chargeable lifetime transfers in the seven years before 10 October 2018 because the 2015 transfer is a PET and therefore exempt during Louise's lifetime. Nil rate band of £325,000 available.

Step 2

		£
Gift		376,000
Less: AE 2018/19		(3,000)
AE 2017/18 b/f		(3,000)
CLT		370,000

Step 3

	IHT £
£325,000 × 0%	0
£45,000 × 20%	9,000
£370,000	9,000

(b) Death tax – 2015 PET becomes chargeable

Step 1 No lifetime transfers of value in seven years before 1 February 2015 (transfers after 1 February 2008). Nil rate band of £325,000 available.

Step 2

		£
Gift		346,000
Less: AE 2014/15		(3,000)
AE 2013/14 b/f		(3,000)
PET now chargeable		340,000

Step 3

	IHT £
£325,000 × 0%	0
£15,000 × 40%	6,000
£340,000	6,000

Step 4 Death more than 3 years but less than 4 years after transfer

	£
Death tax	6,000
Taper relief @ 20%	(1,200)
Death tax due	4,800

(c) *Death tax – 2018 CLT additional tax*

Step 1 Lifetime transfer of value of £340,000 in seven years before 10 October 2018 (transfers after 10 October 2011). Note that as the PET becomes chargeable on death, its value is now included in calculating the death tax on the CLT. No nil rate band available.

Step 2 Value of CLT is £370,000 as before.

Step 3

	IHT £
£370,000 @ 40%	148,000

Step 4 Death within 3 years of transfer so no taper relief.

Step 5 Tax due £(148,000 – 9,000) — 139,000

6 Death estate: basic principles 12/14, 9/15, 6/17

> When someone dies, we must bring together all their assets to find the value of their death estate and then charge inheritance tax on it (to the extent that it is not exempt), taking account of the available residence nil rate band and the available nil rate band after transfers made in the seven years before death.

6.1 Composition of death estate

6.1.1 General principles

An individual's death estate consists of all the property they owned immediately before death, with the exception of excluded property. The estate also includes anything acquired as a result of death, for example the proceeds of a life assurance policy.

The estate at death may include:

(a) Free estate (assets passing by will or intestacy).

(b) Property given subject to a reservation. This is property given away before death, but in which the deceased person retains a benefit (see later in this text). For example, someone might give away a house but continue to live in it rent-free.

The whole of the death estate will be chargeable to tax, subject to reliefs (such as BPR and APR – see later in this text) **and any exemptions which may be available on death. In particular, if property passes to the deceased person's spouse this will be an exempt transfer. A transfer to any other person eg children, will be chargeable to IHT, whether this is made outright or to any type of trust.**

6.1.2 Debts and funeral expenses

(a) **Debts incurred by the deceased can be deducted** if they can be **legally enforced** as they are either **imposed by law** or they are a debt for which the deceased received **consideration**. Specific examples of the application of these rules include:

    (i) **Taxes** – deductible as imposed by law

    (ii) **Electricity and gas bills** – deductible as incurred for consideration

    (iii) **Gambling debts** – deductible if relates to legal gambling (eg in a licenced casino or betting shop), not deductible if relates to illegal gambling or any gambling in Northern Ireland as not legally enforceable

    (iv) **Promise to pay an amount to a relative** – not deductible as no consideration received

    (v) **Oral agreement for purchase of interest in land** – not deductible as not legally enforceable since contracts for such purchases must be evidenced in writing

(b) **Debts incurred by the deceased but payable after the death may be deductible under the above rules,** but the amount should be discounted because of the future date of payment.

(c) **Rent and similar amounts which accrue day by day should be accrued up to the date of death.**

(d) **If a debt is charged on a specific property it is deductible primarily from that property.** For example, a mortgage secured on a house is deductible from the value of that house.

This does not include endowment mortgages as these are repaid upon death by the life assurance element of the mortgage.

Repayment mortgages and interest-only mortgages are deductible (although there may be separate life assurance policies which become payable at death and which will effectively cancel out the mortgage).

Reasonable funeral expenses may also be deducted:

(a) What is reasonable depends on the deceased's condition in life.
(b) Reasonable costs of mourning for the family are allowed.
(c) **The cost of a tombstone is deductible.**

Question

Zack died on 19 June 2018.

Zack's assets at the date of his death consisted of the following:
10,000 shares in A plc valued at £8,525
Cash in bank £9,280
House valued at £150,000 subject to a repayment mortgage of £45,000

Zack's debts due at the date of his death were as follows:

Electricity £150
Council tax £300

Zack had also told his daughter on 10 June 2018 that he would pay £1,000 towards the cost of her summer holiday and that he would pay her this amount on 1 July 2018.

Zack's executors paid reasonable funeral expenses of £2,000 (including the cost of a tombstone) on 1 September 2018.

Calculate Zack's net death estate for IHT purposes.

Answer

	£	£
A plc shares		8,525
Cash in bank		9,280
House	150,000	
Less repayment mortgage	(45,000)	
		105,000
Gross death estate		122,805
Less: debts and funeral expenses		
electricity (incurred for consideration)	150	
council tax (imposed by law)	300	
amount towards holiday for daughter (gratuitous promise)	0	
funeral expenses	2,000	
		(2,450)
Net death estate		120,355

6.2 Death tax on the death estate

6.2.1 Residence nil rate band

There is an **additional nil rate band on death** called the **residence nil rate band**. This is **used in computing IHT on the death estate** (but not death tax on lifetime transfers, unlike the nil rate band).

The **residence nil rate band** is used where:

- **The deceased person died on or after 6 April 2017**;
- **The deceased person owned a home** in which they lived (for Advanced Taxation (ATX – UK) purposes called 'the **main residence**') which is **part of their death estate** (which includes property subject to a reservation – see later in this text); and
- **The main residence passes** (eg under a will) to **one or more direct descendents** of the deceased person (eg children, grandchildren).

The **available residence nil rate band** is the **lower** of:

- **The maximum residence nil rate band** which is:
  - **£125,000** for 2018/19 (but subject to tapering as explained in Section 6.2.2) **plus**
  - Any transferred residence nil rate band from a spouse or civil partner (see later in this chapter); and
- **The value of the main residence passing to direct descendent(s)** after deducting any repayment mortgage or interest-only mortgage secured on the property.

Exam focus point

> The current residence nil rate band will be given in the Tax Rates and Allowances available in the exam.

If the **value of the main residence passing to direct descendent(s) is equal to or exceeds the maximum residence nil rate band, all of the maximum residence nil rate band is used up.** However, **if the value of the main residence passing to direct descendent(s) is less than the maximum residence nil rate band,** for example because the value of the main residence is the lower amount in computing the available residence nil rate band, or it passes to a spouse or civil partner, or even if there is no main residence, **the unused residence nil rate band may be transferred to the estate of a surviving spouse or civil partner** (see later in this chapter).

6.2.2 Residence nil rate band tapering

If the deceased's net estate, as calculated in Section 6.1 and before the deduction of agricultural property relief and business property relief (see later in this text) and any exemptions, **exceeds £2 million**, the residence nil rate band is tapered away. **Tapering is £1 for every £2 that the net estate exceeds £2 million.** Therefore, for a **death in 2018/19, the residence nil rate band of £125,000 will be tapered to nil if the net estate exceeds £2.25 million.**

Question   Residence nil rate band tapering

Edith died on 10 July 2018 leaving a main residence valued at £500,000, on which there was secured a repayment mortgage of £405,000, and quoted shares and cash valued at £2,015,000. The debts and funeral expenses of the estate amounted to £30,000. Edith left quoted shares valued at £600,000 to her husband and the remainder of her estate to her daughter.

What is the available residence nil rate band for computing IHT on Edith's death estate?

Answer

Edith's net estate is as follows:

	£	£
Quoted shares and cash		2,015,000
Main residence	500,000	
Less repayment mortgage	(405,000)	
		95,000
Gross estate		2,110,000
Less debts and funeral expenses		(30,000)
Net death estate		2,080,000

Tapering applies as the net estate (before taking into account the spouse exemption) exceeds £2 million.

	£
Net death estate	2,080,000
Less threshold	(2,000,000)
Excess	80,000

	£
Maximum residence nil rate band	125,000
Less half excess £80,000 × ½	(40,000)
Reduced maximum residence nil rate band	85,000

The available residence nil rate band is therefore the lower of £85,000 and the net value of the main residence of £95,000 and so is £85,000.

Exam focus point

There are **other aspects** to the residence nil rate band. **Neither of the following are examinable** in Advanced Taxation (ATX – UK):

- **Protection of the residence nil rate band** where an individual downsizes to a less valuable property or where a property is disposed of; and

- **Nominating which property should qualify** where there is more than one main residence.

6.2.3 Nil rate band

The **available nil rate band for the death estate** is:

- **The maximum nil rate band**, which is:

    - **£325,000** for 2018/19 **plus**
    - **Any transferred nil rate band from a spouse or civil partner** (see later in this chapter); **less**

- **Lifetime transfers in the seven years before death** (CLTs and PETs which have become chargeable).

6.2.4 Computing death tax on the death estate

Inheritance tax on the death estate is chargeable at two rates: 0% and 40%.

In order to calculate the tax on the death estate, use the following steps:

Step 1   Compute the value of the death estate.

Step 2   Deduct any amount covered by exemptions to leave the chargeable death estate.

Step 3   Calculate the amount of the available residence nil rate band (see Section 6.2.1).

Step 4   Calculate the amount of the available nil rate band (see Section 6.2.3)

Step 5   Charge the residence nil rate band found in Step 3 at 0%.

Step 6   Charge the nil rate band found in Step 4 at 0%.

Step 7   Charge the remainder of the chargeable death estate (ie the value in Step 2 less the nil rate bands in Steps 3 and 4) at 40%.

Question   Tax on death estate

Laura dies on 1 August 2018, leaving a net death estate valued at £480,000. In her will, Laura left cash of £80,000 to her husband and the remainder of her estate to her son which included her main residence valued at £150,000. Laura had made a gift of £171,000 to her sister on 11 September 2017.

Compute the tax payable on Laura's death estate.

Death tax

Note. There is no death tax on the September 2017 PET which becomes chargeable as a result of Laura's death, as it is within the nil rate band at her death. However, it will use up part of the nil rate band, as shown in Step 4.

Step 1   Value of death estate is £480,000.

Step 2   Chargeable death estate is £(480,000 – 80,000) = £400,000.

Step 3   Available residence nil rate band is the lower of £125,000 and the value of the main residence which is £150,000 and so is £125,000.

Step 4   Lifetime transfer of value of £171,000 less £3,000 (AE 2017/18) and £3,000 (AE 2016/17 b/f) = £165,000 in seven years before 1 August 2018 (transfers after 1 August 2011). Available nil rate band is £(325,000 – 165,000) = £160,000.

Steps 5–7

	IHT
	£
£125,000 × 0% (Step 5)	0
£160,000 × 0% (Step 6)	0
£115,000 × 40% (Step 7)	46,000
£400,000	46,000

Exam focus point

> **A question will make it clear if the residence nil rate band is available.** Therefore, you should assume that the **residence nil rate band is not available** if there is **no mention of a main residence**. Note that other residential property, such as buy-to-let property, does not qualify.

6.3 Transfer of unused nil rate bands

FAST FORWARD

> If one spouse or civil partner does not use up their whole nil rate bands on death, the excesses may be transferred to the surviving spouse/civil partner.

PER alert

> One of the competencies you require to fulfil Performance Objective 17 Tax planning and advice of the PER is to review the situation of an individual or entity advising on any potential tax risks and/or additional tax minimisation measures. You can apply the knowledge you obtain from this section of the text to help to demonstrate this competence.

6.3.1 Transfer of unused nil rate band

If:

- **An individual ('A') dies;** and

- **A had a spouse or civil partner ('B') and A and B were married or in a civil partnership immediately before B's death;** and

- **B had unused nil rate band (wholly or in part) on death;**

then **a claim may be made to increase the nil rate band maximum at the date of A's death by B's unused nil rate band** in order to calculate the IHT on A's death. **The revised nil rate band will apply to the calculation of additional death tax on CLTs made by A, PETs made by A and death tax on A's death estate.**

6.3.2 Example

Robert and Claudia were married for many years until the death of Robert on 10 April 2018 leaving an estate of £500,000.

In his will, Robert left cash of £100,000 to his sister and the remainder of his estate to Claudia. He had made no lifetime transfers.

Claudia died on 12 January 2019 leaving an estate (including the assets passed to her by Robert) of £850,000 to her brother, so the residence nil rate band is not relevant. Claudia had made a chargeable lifetime transfer of £50,000 in 2016.

The inheritance tax payable on the death of Claudia, assuming that a claim is made to transfer Robert's unused nil rate band, is calculated as follows:

Step 1 (a) Lifetime transfer of value of £50,000 in seven years before 12 January 2019 (transfers after 12 January 2012).

(b) Nil rate band at death is £325,000. Nil rate band is increased by claim to transfer Robert's unused nil rate band at death £(325,000 – 100,000) = £225,000. The maximum nil rate band at Claudia's death is therefore £(325,000 + 225,000) = £550,000 and the available nil rate band is £(550,000 – 50,000) = £500,000.

Step 2 Value of death estate is £850,000.

Step 3

	IHT £
£500,000 × 0%	0
£350,000 × 40%	140,000
£850,000	140,000

Step 4 Tax payable by personal representatives £140,000

Note that the legacy to Robert's sister was a chargeable death transfer but that the gift of the rest of the estate to Claudia was exempt under the spouse exemption.

6.3.3 Changes in nil rate band between deaths of spouses/civil partners

If the nil rate band increases between the death of B and the death of A, the amount of B's unused nil rate band must be scaled up so that it represents the same proportion of the nil rate band at A's death as it did at B's death.

For example, if the nil rate band at B's death was £300,000 and B had an unused nil rate band of £90,000, the unused proportion in percentage terms is therefore 90,000/300,000 × 100 = 30%. If A dies when the nil rate band has increased to £325,000, B's unused nil rate band is £325,000 × 30% = £97,500 and this amount is transferred to increase the nil rate band maximum available on A's death.

The increase in the nil rate band maximum cannot exceed the nil rate band maximum at the date of A's death eg if the nil rate band is £325,000, the increase cannot exceed £325,000, giving a total of £650,000.

Question   Transfer of nil rate band

Jenna and Rebecca were civil partners until the death of Jenna on 19 August 2007.

Jenna made no lifetime transfers. Her death estate was £440,000 and she left £200,000 to Rebecca and the remainder to her mother.

Rebecca died on 24 February 2019. Her death estate was £550,000 (including the assets passed to her by Jenna) and she left her entire estate to her nephews and niece, so the residence nil rate band is not relevant. She had made no lifetime transfers.

You are required to calculate the inheritance tax payable on the death of Rebecca, assuming that any beneficial claims are made.

Answer

Step 1 (a) No lifetime transfers of value in seven years before 24 February 2019.

(b) Nil rate band at death is £325,000. Nil rate band is increased by claim to transfer Jenna's unused nil rate band at death. The nil rate band at Jenna's death in August 2007 was £300,000. Unused proportion was £(300,000 – 240,000) = 60,000/300,000 × 100 = 20%. The adjusted unused proportion is therefore £325,000 x 20% = £65,000. The maximum nil rate band at Rebecca's death is therefore £(325,000 + 65,000) = £390,000 and this is also the available nil rate band.

Step 2 Value of death estate is £550,000.

Step 3

		IHT £
£390,000 × 0%		0
£160,000 × 40%		64,000
£550,000		64,000

Step 4 Tax payable by personal representatives £64,000

6.3.4 Transfer of unused residence nil rate band

The **unused residence nil rate band** can be **transferred to a spouse or civil partner**, in a similar way to the nil rate band, if **A dies on or after 6 April 2017**. It does not matter when B died nor if their estate included a main residence.

If the residence nil rate band increases between the death of B and the death of A, the amount of B's unused residence nil rate band must be scaled up, in the same way as for the nil rate band, **so that it represents the same proportion of the residence nil rate band at A's death as it did at B's death.** As for the nil rate band, the increase in the residence nil rate band maximum cannot exceed the residence nil rate band maximum at the date of A's death.

Tapering applies to B's residence nil rate band if their net estate exceeds £2 million.

Question
Transfer of nil rate bands

Daniel and Lucy were married for many years until the death of Lucy on 2 August 2017. Lucy made no lifetime transfers. In her will, Lucy left her main residence to her son which used 85% of her residence nil rate band, cash to her daughter which used 20% of her nil rate band and the remainder of her estate to Daniel.

Daniel died on 19 January 2019. His death estate consisted of his main residence valued at £170,000, on which there was secured an interest only mortgage of £40,000, and other assets valued at £720,000. In his will, Daniel left his entire estate to his daughter. Daniel had made no lifetime transfers.

Calculate the inheritance tax payable on the death of Daniel, assuming that any beneficial claims are made.

Step 1   Value of Daniel's death estate is £(170,000 – 40,000) = £130,000 + £720,000 = £850,000.

Step 2   Daniel's own maximum residence nil rate band is £125,000. The unused proportion of Lucy's residence nil rate band is £125,000 × (100 – 85)% = £18,750. The maximum residence nil rate band at Daniel's death is therefore £(125,000 + 18,750) = £143,750. The available residence nil rate band is the lower of £143,750 and the net value of the main residence which is £130,000 and so is £130,000.

Step 3   (a)   No lifetime transfers of value in seven years before 19 January 2019.

(b)   Nil rate band at Daniel's death is £325,000. Nil rate band is increased by claim to transfer the unused proportion of Lucy's nil rate band: £325,000 × (100 – 20)% = £260,000. Maximum nil rate band at Daniel's death is therefore £(325,000 + 260,000) = £585,000, all available as Daniel made no lifetime transfers.

Step 4

	IHT
	£
£130,000 × 0%	0
£585,000 × 0%	0
£135,000 × 40%	54,000
£850,000	54,000

If B died before 6 April 2017, they are **deemed to have had a residence nil rate band, all of which is available for transfer. This will therefore be £125,000 where A dies in 2018/19.**

6.3.5 Claims

Claims to transfer the unused nil rate bands are usually made by the personal representatives of A. The time limit for the claims is two years from the end of the month of A's death (or the period of three months after the personal representatives start to act, if later) or such longer period as an officer of HMRC may allow in a particular case.

If the personal representatives do not make a claim, a claim can be made by any other person liable to tax chargeable on A's death within such later period as an officer of HMRC may allow in a particular case.

Chapter roundup

- IHT applies to transfers to trusts, transfers on death and transfers within the seven years before death.

- Exemptions may apply to make transfers or parts of transfers non-chargeable. Some exemptions only apply on lifetime transfers (annual, normal expenditure out of income, marriage/civil partnership), whilst some apply on both life and death transfers (eg spouses/civil partners, charities, political parties).

- If excluded property is given away, there are no IHT consequences.

- Transfers are cumulated for seven years so that the nil rate band is not available in full on each of a series of transfers in rapid succession.

- IHT is charged on what a donor loses. If the donor pays the IHT on a lifetime gift they lose both the asset given away and the money with which they paid the tax due on it. Grossing up is required.

- When someone dies, we must bring together all their assets to find the value of their death estate and then charge inheritance tax on it (to the extent that it is not exempt), taking account of the available residence nil rate band and the available nil rate band after transfers made in the seven years before death.

- If one spouse or civil partner does not use up their whole nil rate bands on death, the excesses may be transferred to the surviving spouse/civil partner.

Quick quiz

1   What is a transfer of value?

2   Who is chargeable to inheritance tax?

3   What is the effect of property being excluded property?

4   What types of transfer by an individual are potentially exempt transfers?

5   To what extent may unused annual exemption be carried forward?

6   Don gives some money to his daughter on her marriage. What marriage exemption is applicable?

7   Which lifetime transfers may lead to tax being charged on death of the transferor?

8   Why must some lifetime transfers be grossed up?

9   What is taper relief?

10 Sonia dies leaving the following debts:

    (a)   Grocery bill
    (b)   HM Revenue & Customs – income tax to death
    (c)   Repayment mortgage on house
    (d)   Debt from illegal gambling

    Which are deductible against her death estate and why?

11 Mark and Hilary had been married for many years. Mark died on 11 May 2016 leaving his estate worth £800,000 to Hilary. He had made a chargeable lifetime transfer of £160,000 in July 2014. The nil rate band in 2016/17 was £325,000. Hilary dies in February 2019 leaving her estate worth £1,000,000 (including her main residence worth £500,000) to her son. What are the maximum nil rate bands on her death, assuming any beneficial claims are made?

Answers to quick quiz

1. A transfer of value is any gratuitous disposition by a person resulting in a diminution of the value of their estate.

2. Individuals and trustees

3. Excluded property is ignored for IHT purposes.

4. A potentially exempt transfer is a lifetime transfer made by an individual to another individual.

5. An unused annual exemption can be carried forward one tax year.

6. The marriage exemption for a gift to the transferor's child is £5,000.

7. An IHT charge on death arises on PETs and CLTs made within seven years of the transferor's death.

8. Where the donor pays the lifetime tax due it must be grossed up to calculate the total reduction in value of the estate.

9. Taper relief reduces death tax where a transfer is made between three and seven years before death.

10.
    (a) Grocery bill – deductible as incurred for full consideration
    (b) Income tax to death – deductible as imposed by law
    (c) Repayment mortgage – deductible, will be set against value of house primarily
    (d) Debt from illegal gambling – not deductible as not legally enforceable

11. Hilary's own residence nil rate band is £125,000. Mark's unused residence nil rate band is £125,000 as it was all unused since Mark died before 6 April 2017. The maximum residence nil rate band on Hilary's death is therefore £250,000.

    Hilary's own nil rate band is £325,000. Mark's unused nil rate band is £(325,000 – 160,000) = £165,000. The maximum nil rate band on Hilary's death is therefore £490,000.

> Now try the question below from the Practice Question Bank

Number	Level	Marks	Time
Q17	Introductory	16	31 mins
Q39	Examination	18	35 mins

Question 39 has been analysed to show you how to approach Advanced Taxation (ATX – UK) exams.

Inheritance tax: valuation, reliefs and the death estate

Topic list	Syllabus reference
1 Relief for the fall in value of lifetime gifts	A3(d)(iv)
2 The valuation of assets for IHT purposes	A3(c)(i)
3 Business property relief (BPR)	A3(c)(ii), (f)(i)
4 Agricultural property relief (APR)	A3(c)(ii), (f)(i)
5 Death estate: further aspects	A3(d)(iii)
6 Quick succession relief (QSR)	A3(d)(v)

Introduction

We started our study of IHT in the previous chapter with a look at which transfers are exempt from IHT and the charge to IHT on lifetime transfers which are, or become, chargeable.

This chapter opens with a relief for the fall in value of lifetime gifts which ensures that IHT is payable on the lower of the value of value of the gifted asset when the gift was made and its value on the donor's death.

We then have a section on how assets are valued. Pay particular attention to the related property rules, which prevent one way of avoiding IHT.

Two of the reliefs described in this chapter, business property relief and agricultural property relief, are very generous. If the conditions are satisfied, assets can be exempted from IHT without any limit on the value of the assets.

We then deal with some additional rules on the calculation of IHT on the death estate such as the reduced rate where there are gifts to charity.

Finally, we look at quick succession relief where there are transfers within five years of each other.

In the next chapter, we turn our attention to some additional aspects of IHT including the overseas aspects and administration rules.

Study guide

		Intellectual level
3	Inheritance tax in situations involving further aspects of the scope of the tax and the calculation of the liabilities arising, the principles of valuation and the reliefs available, transfers of property to and from trusts, overseas aspects and further aspects of administration	
(c)	The basic principles of computing transfers of value:	
(i)	Advise on the principles of valuation	3
(ii)	Advise on the availability of business property relief and agricultural property relief	3
(d)	The liabilities arising on chargeable lifetime transfers and on the death of an individual:	3
(iii)	Advise on the tax liability arising on a death estate	
(iv)	Advise on the relief for the fall in value of lifetime gifts	
(v)	Advise on the operation of quick succession relief	
(f)	The use of exemptions and reliefs in deferring and minimising inheritance tax liabilities:	3
(i)	Advise on the use of reliefs and exemptions to minimise inheritance tax liabilities, as mentioned in the sections above	

Exam guide

In the Advanced Taxation (ATX – UK) exam, you may be required to deal with advanced aspects of inheritance tax such as valuing overseas property and quick succession relief. These are covered in this chapter.

Business and agricultural property reliefs are a new topic for Advanced Taxation (ATX – UK). They are extremely valuable reliefs as they enable assets to be passed on tax free, and they are therefore likely to feature in IHT planning. You should note the withdrawal of the relief on lifetime transfers if the donee sells the property or ceases to use if for business or agricultural purposes. There is no such limitation for gifts on death. Another new topic is the reduced rate of IHT on the death estate where at least 10% of the net estate passes to charity.

Knowledge brought forward from earlier studies

The basic principles of valuation of assets for inheritance tax were covered in the Taxation (TX – UK) syllabus. The valuation of quoted shares is new in Advanced Taxation (ATX – UK). The remaining topics in this chapter are new at Advanced Taxation (ATX – UK).

There are no changes in 2018/19 in the topics covered at Taxation (TX – UK) in 2017/18.

1 Relief for the fall in value of lifetime gifts 12/14

FAST FORWARD

> If an asset falls in value between a lifetime gift and death, fall in value relief reduces the death tax payable. The relief affects the tax on the transfer concerned. It does not reduce the value of the gross chargeable transfer for the purpose of computing later IHT.

Where a PET or CLT becomes chargeable to IHT on death and the value of the gift has fallen between the date of the gift and the death of the transferor (or the sale of the property if this precedes death) **fall in value relief may be claimed. Relief is available only if the transferee** (or his spouse/civil partner) **still holds the property at the date of death, or it has been sold in an arm's length transaction** to an unconnected person.

Only the tax on the transfer is reduced by the relief. It does not affect the value of the gross chargeable transfer when considering how much of the nil rate band is used by the gift.

Question The fall in value of lifetime gifts

Horace transferred a house worth £335,000 to his son on 1 June 2015. Horace then gave £205,000 cash to his daughter on 20 August 2017. Shortly before Horace's death his son sold the house on the open market for £270,000. Horace died on 14 July 2018. Calculate the IHT liabilities arising.

Answer

1 June 2015

There is no IHT liability when the gift is made because it is a PET.

	£
Gift	335,000
Less: AE 2015/16	(3,000)
AE 2014/15 b/f	(3,000)
PET	329,000

The PET becomes chargeable as a result of death within seven years. The value of the chargeable transfer is reduced by the fall in value of the house:

Death tax	Chargeable transfer £
PET	329,000
Less relief for fall in value £(335,000 − 270,000)	(65,000)
	264,000

This is within the nil rate band so the IHT payable by the son is £Nil.

20 August 2017

There is no IHT liability when the gift is made because it is a PET.

	£
Gift	205,000
Less: AE 2017/18	(3,000)
AE 2016/17 b/f	(3,000)
PET	199,000

Gross chargeable transfers in the seven years prior to the gift total £329,000 (**not £264,000**), so none of the nil rate band remains available to use when calculating IHT on the PET to the daughter. The IHT payable by her is, therefore, £199,000 × 40% = £79,600. No taper relief applies as gift was within three years of death.

2 The valuation of assets for IHT purposes

FAST FORWARD

> There are special rules for valuing particular kinds of assets, such as quoted shares and securities. The related property rules prevent artificial reductions in value.

2.1 The general principle

The value of any property for the purposes of IHT is the price which the property might reasonably be expected to fetch if sold in the open market at the time of the transfer.

Two or more assets can be valued jointly if disposal as one unit is the course that a prudent hypothetical vendor would have adopted in order to obtain the most favourable price: *Gray v IRC 1994*.

2.2 Quoted shares and securities   12/13

The valuation of quoted shares and securities is easy: the stock exchange daily official list gives the closing bid and offer prices of all quoted securities. **Inheritance tax valuations are done by taking the lower of:**

(a)   The value on the quarter up basis (bid price plus 1/4 of the difference between the bid and offer prices)

(b)   The average of the highest and lowest marked bargains for the day, ignoring those marked at special prices

Exam focus point

> Note the difference between the valuation of quoted shares for capital gains tax purposes and inheritance tax purposes.

The transfer may take place on a day on which the stock exchange is closed, in which case the valuation is done on the basis of the prices marked on the last previous day of business or the first following day of business. The lowest of, in this case, the four alternatives will be taken.

Valuations for transfers on death must be cum dividend or cum interest, including the value of the right to the next dividend or interest payment. However, if the question gives an **ex dividend** or an ex interest price and the transfer is on death then the valuation is done on the basis of **adding the whole of the impending dividend**, or the whole of the impending interest payment.

For lifetime transfers, the stock exchange list prices are used without adjustment, whether they are cum or ex dividend or interest.

2.3 Unquoted shares and securities

There is no easily identifiable open market value for shares in an unquoted company. Shares and Assets Valuation at HMRC is the body with which the taxpayer must negotiate. If agreement cannot be reached, an appeal can be made to the Tax Tribunal.

2.4 Unit trusts

Units in authorised unit trusts are valued at the managers' bid price (**the lower of the two published prices**).

2.5 Life assurance policies

Where a person's estate includes a life policy which matures on his death, the proceeds payable to his personal representatives must be included in his estate for IHT purposes. But where a person's estate includes a life policy which matures on the death of someone else, the open market value must be included in his estate.

If an individual writes a policy in trust, or assigns a policy, or makes a subsequent declaration of trust, the policy proceeds will not be paid to his estate but to the assignee or to the trustees for the trust beneficiaries. The proceeds will, therefore, not be included as part of his free estate at death. It is common to write policies in trust for the benefit of dependants to avoid IHT. If the individual continues to pay the premiums on such policies, each premium constitutes a separate transfer of value. However, in many cases these transfers will be exempted as normal expenditure out of income.

2.6 Overseas property 6/17

The basis of valuation is the same as for UK property. The value is converted into sterling at the exchange rate (the 'buy' or 'sell' rate) which will give the lower sterling equivalent. Overseas debts are deductible.

If the property passes on death, the costs of administering and realising overseas property are deductible up to a maximum of 5% of the gross value of the property, so far as those expenses are attributable to the property's location overseas. **Capital taxes paid overseas which are the foreign equivalent of IHT may give rise to double taxation relief** (see later in this text). Such taxes are given as a credit against the IHT payable; they do not reduce the value of the asset.

2.7 Related property 9/16

Related property must be valued as a proportion of the value of the whole of the related property if this produces a higher value than the stand alone value.

Key term

Property is related to that in a person's estate (**related property**) if:

(a)   It is included in the estate of his spouse/civil partner; or

(b)   It has been given to a charity, political party, national public body or housing association as an exempt transfer by either spouse or civil partner and still is, or within the preceding five years has been, the property of the body it was given to.

To reduce the value transferred individuals might fragment an asset into several parts which are collectively worth less than the whole. This way of reducing the value of an asset or set of assets is normally prevented using the diminution in value principle. However, this application of the principle could be thwarted by use of exempt inter-spouse/civil partner transfers. To deter this method of avoiding IHT, there are provisions under which related property is taken into account.

Property which is related to other property must be valued as a proportion of the value of the whole of the related property but only if, by so doing, a higher value is produced. For example, where a husband and wife each hold 40% of the issued shares of a company, the husband's holding will normally be valued as a proportion (one half) of the price which an 80% shareholding would fetch, as an 80% interest would normally be more valuable than two 40% interests.

2.8 Example: related property

Lenny has a leasehold interest in a property. The value of his interest is £25,000. His wife Mandy holds the freehold reversion of the property, which has a market value of £40,000. The value of the freehold not subject to the lease (that is the value of the freehold reversion plus the lease) is £80,000. If Lenny wishes to transfer his interest to their daughter Sarah the value transferred will be the greater of:

(a)   The value of the interest by itself, £25,000; and

(b)   The value of his part of the total related property, which is

$$\frac{\text{The value of the property transferred at its } \textbf{unrelated} \text{ value}}{\text{The value of the property transferred at its } \textbf{unrelated} \text{ value} + \text{The value of any related property at its } \textbf{unrelated} \text{ value}} \times \text{The value of the whole property}$$

$$\frac{25,000}{25,000 + 40,000} \times £80,000 = £30,769.$$

The higher value is £30,769. This is therefore the value transferred by Lenny.

If the property in question is shares, then in arriving at the fraction set out above, the numbers of shares held are used instead of unrelated values.

Question
Valuation of shares

Shares in an unquoted company are held as follows.

	Number of shares
Husband (H)	4,000
Wife (W)	2,000
Son (S)	750
Shares given by H to a charity by an exempt transfer eight years ago (and still owned by the charity)	3,250
	10,000

Estimated values for different sizes of shareholding are as follows.

Number of shares	*Pence per share*	£
750	60	450
2,000	90	1,800
4,000	130	5,200
7,250	200	14,500
9,250	250	23,125

What is the value of H's holding, taking into account related property?

Answer

There are three related holdings.

	Shares
H	4,000
W	2,000
Charity	3,250
	9,250

The value of H's 4,000 shares is $\dfrac{4,000}{9,250} \times £23,125 = £10,000$ (ie 250 pence × 4,000 shares).

If in the above exercise H gives away half of his holding to his son, the transfer of value is as follows.

	£
Holding before transfer (as above)	10,000
Less holding after transfer	
$\dfrac{2,000}{7,250} \times £14,500$	(4,000)
Transfer of value	6,000

If H transferred all his shares the value transferred would be £10,000 (no holding after, so no value in the calculation performed above).

3 Business property relief (BPR)

One of the competencies you require to fulfil Performance Objective 17 Tax planning and advice of the PER is to mitigate and/or defer tax liabilities through the use of standard reliefs, exemptions and incentives. You can apply the knowledge you obtain from this section of the text to help to demonstrate this competence.

FAST FORWARD

BPR can reduce the values of assets by 100% or 50%. However, there are strict conditions, which are largely intended to prevent people near death from obtaining the reliefs by investing substantial sums in businesses.

3.1 Business property

BPR is applied to the value of relevant business property transferred, to prevent large tax liabilities arising on transfers of businesses.

Relevant business property is:

(a) Property consisting of a business or an interest (such as a partnership share) in a business

(b) Securities of a company which are unquoted and which (alone or with other securities or unquoted shares) gave the transferor control of the company immediately before the transfer (control may be achieved by taking into account related property)

(c) Any unquoted shares (not securities) in a company

(d) Shares in or securities of a company which are quoted and which (alone or with other such shares or securities) gave the transferor control of the company immediately before the transfer (control may be achieved by taking into account related property)

(e) Any land or building, machinery or plant which, immediately before the transfer, was used wholly or mainly for the purposes of a business carried on by a company of which the transferor then had control, or by a partnership of which he was then a partner

Shares or securities listed on the AIM sub-market of the London Stock Exchange count as unquoted

The reliefs available are percentage reductions in the value transferred: 100% for assets within Paragraph (a), (b) or (c) above, and 50% for assets within Paragraph (d) or (e) above.

3.2 Conditions for BPR

BPR is only available if the relevant business property:

(a) Was owned by the transferor for at least the two years preceding the transfer; or

(b) Replaced other relevant business property (which includes agricultural property used in a farming business) where the combined period of ownership of both sets of property was at least two out of the last five years. In this situation relief is given on the lower of the values of the two sets of property.

If the property was inherited, it is deemed to have been owned from the date of the death unless it was inherited from the transferor's spouse or civil partner, in which case the transferor is deemed to have owned it for the period the spouse or civil partner owned it.

BPR is still available even if the transferor cannot fulfil either of the two year ownership criteria if when he acquired the property it was eligible for BPR and either the previous or this current transfer was made on death.

3.3 Additional conditions for BPR on lifetime transfers

If, as a result of the donor's death within seven years of a gift, a PET becomes chargeable or additional tax is due on a CLT, two further conditions must be fulfilled for BPR to be available.

(a) The donee must still own the original property at the date of the donor's death, or the donee's death if earlier.

(b) The original property must still qualify as relevant business property at the date of the donor's death, or the donee's death if earlier.

These conditions are fulfilled if the donee disposed of the original property but reinvested **all** of the disposal proceeds in replacement property within three years of the disposal.

3.4 Non-qualifying businesses

BPR is not available if the business consists wholly or mainly of:

(a) Dealing in securities, stocks and shares (except for discount houses and market makers on the stock exchange or on LIFFE)

(b) Dealing in land or buildings

(c) Making or holding investments (including land which is let)

Shares in holding companies, where the subsidiaries have activities which would qualify shares in them for BPR, are eligible for relief.

3.5 Excepted assets

Relevant business property excludes assets which were neither used wholly or mainly for the purposes of the business in the two years preceding the transfer nor required at the time of the transfer for future use in the business.

Formula to learn

> **For shares or securities in a company, the value which we compute BPR on (at 100% or 50%) is:**
>
> $$\text{Total value} \times \frac{\text{the company's relevant business property}}{\text{the company's total assets before deducting liabilities}}$$

3.6 Contracts for sale

BPR is not available if at the date of transfer there is a binding contract for the sale of a business or an interest in a business, unless the sale is to a company which will continue the business and the consideration is wholly or mainly shares or securities in the company.

BPR is not available if at the date of the transfer there is a binding contract for the sale of shares or securities of a company unless the sale is for the purpose of reconstruction or amalgamation.

If any other relevant business property is subject to a binding contract for sale, BPR is not available on it at all.

Partnership agreements often contain a buy/sell clause under which surviving partners must buy a deceased partner's share in the partnership. HMRC regard such a clause as a binding contract for sale which disentitles the deceased partner to BPR. However, neither an accruer clause whereby the deceased partner's share accrues to the surviving partners, nor an option for the surviving partners to buy the deceased partner's share is regarded as binding contract for sale. This means that from a tax planning point of view the latter types of arrangement should be used.

Question

On 31 July 2018 relevant business property valued at £16,800 is transferred to a trust. Assuming that the 2017/18 and 2018/19 annual exemptions have not been used what will the chargeable transfer be if:

(a) The property consists of unquoted shares?
(b) The property consists of land used by a company in which the transferor has a controlling interest?
(c) The property consists of quoted shares which formed part of a 20% interest before the transfer?

Answer

	(a) £	(b) £	(c) £
Value transferred	16,800	16,800	16,800
Less BPR	(16,800)	(8,400)	0
	0	8,400	16,800
Less: AE 2018/19		(3,000)	(3,000)
2017/18 b/f		(3,000)	(3,000)
Chargeable transfer	0	2,400	10,800

Question

Jeremy had shares in a quoted trading company, Jazzy plc. The shares in the company were held as follows.

	%
Jeremy	40
Kathy, Jeremy's wife	30
Other unconnected persons	30
	100

The shareholdings have been unchanged since 2002. On 1 May 2018 Jeremy gave a 30% holding to his son, Felix. The values of the shares in May 2018 were agreed as follows.

	£
70% holding	1,600,000
40% holding	900,000
30% holding	840,000
10% holding	200,000

Jeremy, who had made a previous chargeable lifetime transfer of £350,000 in 2012, died in January 2019.

Calculate the IHT arising on the gift of the shares if:

(a) Felix still holds the shares in January 2019
(b) Felix sells the shares in June 2018 and retains the cash proceeds

Answer

No IHT arises when the gift was made, because it was a PET. It becomes chargeable as a result of Jeremy's death within seven years as follows.

(a)   If Felix still holds the shares, BPR at 50% is available to reduce the chargeable transfer:

£

914,286

Before: $\dfrac{40\%}{40\% + 30\%} \times £1,600,000$

After: $\dfrac{10\%}{10\% + 30\%} \times £900,000$

(225,000)

689,286

Less BPR at 50% (control (with related property of Kathy) of quoted company)   (344,643)

344,643

Less: AE 2018/19   (3,000)

AE 2017/18 b/f   (3,000)

Chargeable transfer   338,643

Gross chargeable transfers in the seven years before May 2018 amount to £350,000. This means none of the nil rate band remains and IHT payable on death amounts to:

IHT at 40% = £135,457

(b)   If Felix does not hold the shares on Jeremy's death, BPR is not available to reduce the value of the chargeable transfer:

£

Transfer (see above)   689,286

Less: AE 2018/19   (3,000)

AE 2017/18   (3,000)

Chargeable transfer   683,286

IHT @ 40% = £273,314

4 Agricultural property relief (APR)   3/16, 12/17

One of the competencies you require to fulfil Performance Objective 17 Tax planning and advice of the PER is to mitigate and/or defer tax liabilities through the use of standard reliefs, exemptions and incentives. You can apply the knowledge you obtain from this section of the text to help to demonstrate this competence.

APR usually reduces a transfer of agricultural property by 100% of agricultural value.

4.1 Agricultural property

APR is available on the agricultural value of agricultural property.

Agricultural property is agricultural land or pasture (including short rotation coppice) situated in the UK, the Channel Islands, the Isle of Man or a country other than the UK which is in the European Economic Area at the time of the transfer. It includes woodland and any building used in connection with the intensive rearing of livestock or fish where the occupation of the woodland or building is ancillary to that of the land or pasture. It also includes cottages, farm buildings and farm houses of a character appropriate to the property.

The agricultural value will be given to you in the exam.

APR works like BPR in reducing the value being transferred by a certain percentage before any exemptions. APR is given before BPR and double relief cannot be obtained on the agricultural value. If the non-agricultural part of the value of the property meets the relevant business property conditions, however, BPR will be available on that value. **The percentage reduction in agricultural value is, in general, 100%** (it is 50% on some land held under pre-September 1995 tenancies).

4.2 Conditions for relief

For relief to apply the transferor must either:

(a)   Own the property and have occupied it themselves for the purpose of agriculture for the two years before the transfer (ie they farm the land themselves); or

(b)   Own the property for at least the seven years before the transfer, during which it must have been occupied for the purposes of agriculture by either the transferor or a tenant (ie the property is or has been let out).

If a company controlled by the transferor occupies the property the transferor is treated as occupying it. A farmhouse which is being redecorated, renovated or altered is not treated as though it is occupied for agricultural purposes.

If the property transferred replaces other agricultural property, the condition will be satisfied provided that:

(a)   The transferor has occupied the properties for the purposes of agriculture for at least two out of the last five years; or

(b)   The transferor has owned the properties (and somebody has occupied them for agricultural purposes) for at least seven out of the last ten years.

If agricultural properties have been replaced the APR will apply only to the lowest of the values of the various properties considered.

If the property transferred was acquired on the death of the transferor's spouse or civil partner then the period of ownership or occupation of the first spouse or civil partner can count towards the seven years or the two years required. If the property transferred was acquired on the death of somebody else the transferor will be deemed to own it from the date of death and if he subsequently occupies it, to have occupied it from the date of death.

APR is still available even if the transferor cannot fulfil any of the two or seven year ownership criteria if when he acquired the property it was eligible for APR and either the previous or this current transfer was made on death.

4.3 Additional conditions for lifetime transfers

If, as a result of the donor's death within seven years of a gift, a PET becomes chargeable or additional tax is due on a CLT, two further conditions must be fulfilled for APR to be available.

(a)   The donee must still own the original property at the date of the donor's death, or the donee's death if earlier.

(b)   The original property must still qualify as agricultural property immediately prior to the date of the donor's death, or the donee's death if earlier, and must have been occupied as such since the original transfer.

These conditions are fulfilled if the donee disposed of the original property but reinvested **all** of the disposal proceeds in replacement property within three years of the disposal.

4.4 Shares in companies owning agricultural property

If a company owns agricultural property and satisfies the occupation or ownership conditions above then APR is available in respect of the agricultural value that can be attributed to shares or securities transferred by an individual who controls the company. The shares or securities must have been held by the transferor for the relevant period (two years or seven years).

Question
Farming companies

On 13 June 2018 Kevin gives his shares in Farm Ltd to his son. Kevin owns 65% of the shares in issue, with an agreed value of £400,000. Kevin has owned the shares for nine years. The company has owned and occupied farmland (for agricultural purposes) for the last eight years. The agricultural value of this land represents 20% of the total value of the company's net assets.

Calculate the chargeable transfer assuming that Kevin dies on 14 July 2019 and the son still holds the shares at the date of his father's death.

Answer

	£
Unquoted trading company shares	
Value of holding	400,000
Less: APR 100% × 20% × £400,000 (on agricultural value)	(80,000)
BPR 100% × 80% × £400,000 (on balance)	(320,000)
Chargeable transfer	0

4.5 Contracts for sale

No APR is available if, at the time of the transfer, a binding contract for sale of the agricultural property exists unless the sale is to a company (the consideration being wholly or mainly shares or securities which will give the transferor control), or is to enable a reorganisation or reconstruction of a farming company.

5 Death estate: further aspects
12/14, 9/15, 12/17

5.1 Reduced rate on death estate

FAST FORWARD

The rate of inheritance tax on a death estate is reduced to 36% if at least 10% of the estate is left to charity.

We saw earlier in this text that gifts to charities are exempt. To encourage more people to leave gifts to charity on their death, there is also **a reduced rate of inheritance tax (36%**, rather than 40%) available **on the remaining death estate** if an individual **leaves at least 10% of his net estate to charity**.

There are therefore two benefits of leaving such a legacy – the donated part of the estate is exempt and the remainder is charged at a lower rate of IHT.

For the purpose of determining whether the 10% condition is met, **the net estate** is calculated as the **assets owned at death as reduced by liabilities, exemptions, reliefs and the available nil rate band (but not the residence nil rate band), but before the charitable legacy itself is deducted**. However the inheritance tax itself is then charged (at 36%) on the usual death estate (ie after the legacy has been deducted).

Question

Margie died on 1 September 2018. The assets in her estate were valued at £380,000, and she had made a gross chargeable transfer of £100,000 in 2013. In her will she left £20,000 to charity and the rest of her estate to a trust for her children. Calculate the inheritance tax payable on her death estate.

Answer

First, work out whether the reduced rate of IHT applies, as follows.

	£
Death estate (before deduction of charitable legacy)	380,000
Less available nil rate band £(325,000 – 100,000)	(225,000)
Net estate	155,000

10% of £155,000 is £15,500, so the legacy of £20,000 is at least 10% of the net estate and therefore the reduced rate of 36% applies.

	£
Death estate	380,000
Less charitable legacy	(20,000)
Chargeable estate	360,000

IHT

£225,000 × 0%	0
£135,000 × 36%	48,600
£360,000	
IHT payable on death estate	48,600

Exam focus point

> The calculation can become complicated where there are assets owned jointly with other people or assets held on trust but the examining team has stated that the reduced rate will only be examined where all of the assets are 100% owned by the deceased.

A variation of the will (see later in this text) may be entered into after the death of an individual in order to increase the amount given to charity, such that the estate then qualifies for the reduced rate. Although the gross value of the remaining estate is then lower for the other beneficiaries of the will, the reduced rate of IHT on this lower amount may outweigh the cost of the increased gift to charity and increase the net assets passing to other beneficiaries.

5.2 Example

Barry died on 1 July 2018 leaving a gross chargeable estate valued at £860,000. In his will, he left a donation of £60,000 to charity and the rest of his estate to his son, Trig. Barry's available nil rate band at his death was £170,000.

Barry's net estate for the purposes of working out whether the reduced rate applies is £(860,000 – 170,000) = £690,000. Therefore at least 10% × £690,000 = £69,000 must be left to charity for the reduced rate of IHT to apply to the death estate.

The reduced rate is not available because Barry's charitable donation is less than £69,000. The inheritance tax on Barry's death estate is therefore £(860,000 – 60,000 – 170,000) = £630,000 × 40% = £252,000. Trig will received net assets of £(860,000 – 60,000 – 252,000) = £548,000.

However, a variation of the will could be used to increase the charitable donation by £9,000 to £69,000. This would reduce the inheritance tax liability to £(860,000 – 69,000 – 170,000) × 36% = £223,560. This is a saving of £252,000 – £223,560 = £28,440 which is greater than the additional charitable donation. Trig will receive net assets of £(860,000 – 69,000 – 223,560) = £567,440.

FAST FORWARD ▶▶ Gross up specific gifts on death if the residue of the estate is left to an exempt recipient.

We saw that grossing up applies to CLTs when the donor pays the IHT. **We must also gross up on a death when there is a specific legacy (ie gift on death) of UK property, and the residue of the estate (ie what's left of the estate after specific gifts have been paid out) is exempt. This can happen when the residue is left to a spouse/ civil partner or charity.**

The reason for this is that the recipients of specific gifts of UK property do not pay the tax on the gift (unless this is specifically stated). Instead this must be borne by the residue of the estate – which is exempt. Specific gifts of foreign property, on the other hand, do bear their own tax (ie the recipient must pay any IHT) and do not need to be grossed up.

Do not gross up specific gifts if the whole estate is chargeable. In such cases, work out IHT as normal.

Specific gifts of UK property are given to the heirs in full (unless there is not enough residue to pay the IHT), and the IHT on those gifts comes out of the residue. In this case, the formula used to calculate the tax is as follows.

Formula to learn

$$\text{Chargeable amount (in excess of the nil rate band)} \times \frac{40}{60} \text{ ie } \frac{\text{rate of tax}}{100 \text{ minus the rate of tax}}$$

Question — Specific gifts and exempt residue

Rory dies on 29 May 2018 leaving an estate valued at £490,000. Included in this is a commercial property in Manchester valued at £400,000 which he leaves to his son, Ian. He leaves the residue of the estate to his wife, Sonya.

Calculate the IHT liability arising on death assuming Rory has made no lifetime transfers.

Answer

There is an exempt residue and a specific gift of a UK asset. Therefore the specific gift must be grossed up:

	IHT
	£
£325,000 @ 0%	0
£75,000 @ 40/60	50,000
£400,000	50,000

The gross transfer is £(400,000 + 50,000) = £450,000.

Check tax £(450,000 – 325,000) = £125,000 @ 40% = £50,000.

Ian receives £400,000, HMRC receives £50,000.

The residue available to Sonya is £490,000 – £450,000 = £40,000.

This calculation would not have applied if:

(a) The residue of the estate had been chargeable rather than exempt, in which case IHT would have been calculated on a gross chargeable estate of £490,000 in the normal way; or

(b) The will had left a specific gift of £90,000 to Sonya and the residue to Ian. In that case, Ian would have received £400,000 less tax of £(400,000 – 325,000) × 40% = £30,000, giving him a net amount of £370,000 and Sonya would have received £90,000. This would be a tax saving of £20,000.

6 Quick succession relief (QSR)

FAST FORWARD

> Quick succession relief applies where there are two charges to IHT within five years.

If a person dies shortly after receiving property by way of a chargeable transfer the same property will be taxed twice within a short space of time: it will be taxed as the original chargeable transfer and it will be taxed again as part of the estate of the deceased transferee. QSR reduces the tax on the estate.

The tax on the estate is calculated normally. A credit is then given as follows.

Formula to learn

$$\text{Tax paid on first transfer} \times \frac{\text{net transfer}}{\text{gross transfer}} \times \text{percentage}$$

The percentage to use is as follows.

Period between the transfer and the death of the transferee	Relief
	%
1 year or less	100
1–2 years	80
2–3 years	60
3–4 years	40
4–5 years	20
Over 5 years	0

If the period is precisely 2 years, 80% relief is given, and so on.

The relief applies even where the asset has been disposed of before death.

Question

QSR

Oscar died on 29 September 2018 leaving an estate valued at £385,000 to his son. Oscar had received £28,000 gross in July 2014 from his uncle's estate. IHT of £4,200 had been payable by Oscar on this legacy.

Calculate the IHT payable on Oscar's estate, assuming he has made no lifetime transfers.

Answer

	£
IHT on £385,000 (£325,000 @ 0% + £60,000 @ 40%)	24,000
Less QSR: £4,200 × (23,800/28,000) × 20% (4-5 years)	(714)
IHT payable on Oscar's estate	23,286

Chapter roundup

- If an asset falls in value between a lifetime gift and death, fall in value relief reduces the death tax payable. The relief affects the tax on the transfer concerned. It does not reduce the value of the gross chargeable transfer for the purpose of computing later IHT.

- There are special rules for valuing particular kinds of assets, such as quoted shares and securities. The related property rules prevent artificial reductions in value.

- Related property must be valued as a proportion of the value of the whole of the related property if this produces a higher value than the stand alone value.

- BPR can reduce the values of assets by 100% or 50%. However, there are strict conditions, which are largely intended to prevent people near death from obtaining the reliefs by investing substantial sums in businesses.

- APR usually reduces a transfer of agricultural property by 100% of agricultural value.

- The rate of inheritance tax on a death estate is reduced to 36% if at least 10% of the estate is left to charity.

- Gross up specific gifts on death if the residue of the estate is left to an exempt recipient.

- Quick succession relief applies where there are two charges to IHT within five years.

Quick quiz

1 How are quoted securities valued?

2 What is related property?

3 What rate of BPR is given on a controlling shareholding in:

    (a) A quoted trading company; and
    (b) An unquoted trading company?

4 What periods of ownership or occupation are required to obtain agricultural property relief?

5 Richard died on 2 August 2018. He had used up his nil rate band with lifetime transfers. The assets in his estate were valued at £900,000. In his will Richard left £100,000 to charity and the rest of his estate to his sister. What is the inheritance tax payable on his death estate?

6 How is quick succession relief calculated?

Answers to quick quiz

1   The value is the lower of:

- The value on the quarter up basis (bid price plus 1/4 of the difference between the bid and offer prices)

- The average of highest and lowest marked bargains for the day (ignoring special price bargains)

2   Related property is property:

- Comprised in the estate of the transferor's spouse; or

- Which has been given to a charity, political party, national public body or housing association as an exempt transfer by either spouse and still is, or has been within the past five years, been the property of the body it was given to.

3   (a)   50%
    (b)   100%

4   For APR the transferor must have either:

- Owned and farmed the land themselves for two years before the transfer; or

- Owned the property for at least seven years before the transfer during which time it was farmed either by the transferor or a tenant.

5   The charitable legacy is at least 10% of the net estate of £900,000 and therefore the reduced rate of 36% applies. £(900,000 – 100,000) = £800,000 × 36% = £288,000.

6   QSR is calculated as:

$$\text{Tax paid on first transfer} \times \frac{\text{net transfer}}{\text{gross transfer}} \times \%$$

Now try the question below from the Practice Question Bank

Number	Level	Marks	Time
Q18	Examination	25	49 mins

17: Inheritance tax: valuation, reliefs and the death estate | Part D Inheritance tax

Inheritance tax: additional aspects

Topic list	Syllabus reference
1 Overseas aspects	A3(b)(i), (b)(iii), (d)(vi)
2 Gifts with reservation	A3(b)(iv)
3 Altering dispositions made on death	A3(d)(vii)
4 Trusts	A3(e)(i)–(v)
5 The administration of IHT	A3(a)D4, (g)(i), (ii)

Introduction

In the previous two chapters, we have studied the charge to IHT both on lifetime transfers and on death, and have looked at some exemptions and reliefs.

In this chapter, we look at overseas aspects, including relief where property is subject both to IHT and to a similar tax abroad.

We also look at an important anti-avoidance provision. The rules on gifts with reservation prevent people from avoiding IHT by claiming to give property away before death while in fact retaining rights over it.

We also consider how a will can be altered.

We review the IHT charge on gifts into discretionary trusts and the subsequent impact of IHT on those trusts. Trusts have historically been used in estate planning as they allow the settlor to direct how the assets should be dealt with even after they have been given away. Even though there are periodic and exit charges, discretionary trusts can still be used for tax mitigation.

Finally, we look at the administration and payment of IHT. This concludes our study of IHT.

In the next chapter, we look at stamp taxes.

Study guide

		Intellectual level
3	**Inheritance tax in situations involving further aspects of the scope of the tax and the calculation of the liabilities arising, the principles of valuation and the reliefs available, transfers of property to and from trusts, overseas aspects and further aspects of administration**	
(a)	The contents of the Taxation - United Kingdom (TX – UK) study guide for inheritance tax under headings:	2
•	D4 Payment of inheritance tax	
(b)	The scope of inheritance tax:	
(i)	Explain the concepts of domicile and deemed domicile and understand the application of these concepts to inheritance tax	2
(iii)	Identify and advise on the tax implications of the location of assets	3
(iv)	Identify and advise on gifts with reservation of benefit	3
(d)	The liabilities arising on chargeable lifetime transfers and on the death of an individual:	3
(vi)	Advise on the operation of double tax relief for inheritance tax	
(vii)	Advise on the inheritance tax effects and advantages of the variation of wills	
(e)	The liabilities arising in respect of transfers to and from trusts and on property within trusts:	
(i)	Define a trust	2
(ii)	Distinguish between different types of trust	3
(iii)	Advise on the inheritance tax implications of transfers of property into trust	3
(iv)	Advise on the inheritance tax implications of property passing absolutely from a trust to a beneficiary	2
(v)	Identify the occasions on which inheritance tax is payable by trustees	3
(g)	The system by which inheritance tax is administered, including the instalment option for the payment of tax:	
(i)	Identify the occasions on which inheritance tax may be paid by instalments	2
(ii)	Advise on the due dates, interest and penalties for inheritance tax purposes	3

Exam guide

The topics covered in this chapter are mainly new in Advanced Taxation (ATX – UK) and are important for tax planning questions. The anti-avoidance rule for gifts with reservation is designed to ensure that individuals are taxed on what they have effectively given away entirely. The rules for foreign assets are beneficial to non-domiciliaries. Note, however, that you have to take positive action to change your domicile, and that the deemed domicile rules mean that it takes at least three years to escape the UK IHT net.

Trusts are useful in tax planning. The trustees retain control over assets until they deem a beneficiary to be sufficiently capable of looking after them. Be aware of the IHT implications for trusts.

The topic of inheritance tax administration was covered in the Taxation (TX – UK) syllabus and is included in this chapter. A new aspect covered in this chapter is the payment of tax by instalments. There are no changes in 2018/19 from the material studied in Taxation (TX – UK) for 2017/18. The other topics in this chapter are new.

1 Overseas aspects   6/14, 6/15, 9/16, 6/17

1.1 Domicile

1.1.1 UK domicile

FAST FORWARD

A UK domiciled, or deemed UK domiciled, individual is subject to inheritance tax on transfers of all assets, wherever situated.

If an individual is **UK domiciled**, or deemed UK domiciled (see below), **transfers of all assets, wherever situated, are subject to IHT.**

Domicile for IHT has the same meaning as in general law, namely **the country of one's permanent home**.

Also, an individual is **deemed to be domiciled in the UK for IHT purposes at a relevant time** (eg the time a transfer of value is made) **if they satisfy any one of three conditions**.

The first condition is that the **individual was domiciled in the UK within the 3 years immediately preceding that time**. This covers individuals who leave the UK and acquire a non-UK domicile. It is unique to inheritance tax.

The second condition is that the **individual is a formerly UK domiciled individual**. This is an individual who:

(a)   was **born in the UK**; and
(b)   has a **UK domicile of origin**; and
(c)   is **UK resident in the relevant tax year** (ie the tax year in which the relevant time falls); and
(d)   was **UK resident in at least 1 of the 2 tax years immediately before the relevant tax year.**

The term 'residence' has the same meaning as for income tax and capital gains tax (see earlier in this text).

The first three of these requirements are the same as for formerly UK domiciled individuals for income tax and capital gains tax (see earlier in this text). This means that for those taxes the individual will become UK deemed domiciled in the first year they become UK resident. The additional fourth condition means that an individual will not become deemed domiciled for inheritance tax purposes until the second tax year that they are UK resident.

The third condition is that **the individual is UK resident**:

(a)   **for at least 15 of the 20 tax years immediately preceding the relevant tax year**; and
(b)   **for at least 1 of the 4 tax years ending with the relevant tax year.**

Again, the first requirement is the same as for long-term residents for income tax and capital gains tax (see earlier in this text). However, for these taxes deemed domicile will only be relevant if the individual is also UK resident in the tax year. For inheritance tax purposes the requirement can be satisfied if the individual is UK resident in the relevant tax year but also if they are non-UK resident in that tax year but were UK resident in any one of the three preceding tax years.

Exam focus point

These deemed domicile rules are similar to those for income tax and capital gains tax but not quite the same! Make sure you know the differences between them and apply the correct rules to the relevant tax.

An election may be made for a non-UK domiciled individual who is, or was, the spouse or civil partner of a UK domiciled individual, to be treated as UK domiciled for IHT purposes.

An individual who is:

(a)   **Not UK domiciled, nor deemed UK domiciled; and**

(b)   **is the spouse or civil partner of a UK domiciled individual**

may make an irrevocable election to be treated as UK domiciled for IHT purposes only.

The **effect of the election** is that **transfers by the UK domiciled spouse/civil partner to the non-UK domiciled individual are wholly exempt** and not subject to the restriction for transfers to a non-domiciled spouse/civil partner detailed earlier in this text. However, the election also has the effect of **bringing the non-UK domiciled individual's assets situated outside the UK within the charge to IHT.** It is therefore important to consider both these aspects before the election is made.

An election is called a **'lifetime election'** if it is **made by the non-UK domiciled spouse/civil partner** in the **lifetime of the UK domiciled spouse/civil partner.**

An election is called a **'death election'** if it is **made after the death of the UK domiciled spouse/civil partner**, where that death was on or after 6 April 2013. That **deceased spouse/civil partner** must have been **UK domiciled within the period of seven years ending with the date of death.** A death election can be made by the non-UK domiciled spouse/civil partner or his personal representatives. A death election must be made within two years of the death of the UK domiciled spouse/civil partner, or such longer period as an officer of HMRC may allow.

UK domicile is treated as taking effect on a date specified in the election. This date **cannot be prior to 6 April 2013.** Subject to this, **the specified date can be within seven years before the date of the election** (for a lifetime election) or **within seven years before the UK domiciled spouse/civil partner's death** (for a death election).

A lifetime or death election cannot be revoked. However, **if the individual who made the election is not resident in the United Kingdom for the purposes of income tax for a period of four successive tax years**, beginning at any time after the election is made, **the election ceases to have effect at the end of that period.**

Exam focus point

> This topic was tested in September 2016 question 2 Waverley. The examining team commented that this was not well done with 'many candidates not recognising the relevance of the concept of deemed domicile, and of the location of the asset being gifted. The definition and relevance of an individual's residence and domicile for the purposes of both capital taxes is a frequently tested area in Advanced Taxation (ATX – UK), and candidates should ensure that they are confident with applying these in context.'

1.1.2 Non-UK domicile

Non-UK assets of individuals not domiciled in the UK are not subject to IHT.

For individuals **not domiciled, nor deemed domiciled, in the UK, only transfers of UK assets are within the charge to IHT**, and even some assets within the UK are excluded property.

1.2 The location of assets

For someone not domiciled, nor deemed domiciled, in the UK, the location of assets is clearly important:

(a)   **Land and buildings**, freehold or leasehold, are in the country in which they are **physically situated**.

(b)   **A debt** is in the **country of residence of the debtor** unless it is a debt evidenced by a deed, when the debt is where the deed is. Judgement debts are situated wherever the judgement is recorded.

(c)   **Life policies** are in the **country where the proceeds are payable.**

(d) **Registered shares and securities** are in the **country where they are registered**, or where they would normally be dealt with in the ordinary course of business.

(e) **Bearer securities** are **where the certificate of title is located** at the time of transfer.

(f) **Bank accounts** are at the **branch** where the account is kept.

(g) **An interest in a partnership** is where the partnership **business is carried on**.

(h) **Goodwill** is where the **business** to which it is attached is **carried on**.

(i) **Tangible property** is at its **physical location**.

(j) Property held in trust follows the above rules regardless of the rules of the trust or residence of the trustees.

1.3 Excluded property

As we saw earlier, foreign property of an individual who is not domiciled, nor deemed domiciled, in the UK is excluded property so is ignored for IHT purposes. The following are also excluded property.

(a) Foreign assets in a trust established when the settlor was non-UK domiciled for IHT purposes. No IHT is due on the trust assets even if the settlor becomes UK domiciled at a later date.

(b) Certain British Government securities whose terms of issue provide that they shall be exempt from taxation so long as they are owned by non-resident individuals.

(c) The following savings if held by persons domiciled in the Channel Islands or the Isle of Man (the extended IHT definition of deemed domicile above does not apply):

   (i) National Savings and Investments certificates
   (ii) Premium savings bonds
   (iii) Deposits in National Savings and Investments accounts
   (iv) Schedule 3 save as you earn (SAYE) share option schemes (see earlier in this text)

(d) Unit trust units or shares in open ended investment companies (OEICs) held by non-UK domiciliaries.

In addition, if someone dies when neither domiciled nor resident in the UK, a foreign currency account held at a UK bank is ignored in computing his death estate.

1.4 Double taxation relief (DTR)

 FAST FORWARD

Double taxation relief may reduce the IHT on assets also taxed overseas.

DTR applies to transfers (during lifetime and on death) of assets situated overseas which suffer tax overseas as well as IHT in the UK. Relief may be given under a treaty, but if not then the following rules apply.

DTR is given as a tax credit against the IHT payable on the overseas asset. The amount available as a tax credit is the lower of the foreign tax liability and the IHT (at the average rate) on the asset.

Question DTR

Peter died on 15 October 2018 leaving a chargeable estate of £282,000. Included in this total is a foreign asset valued at £80,000 in respect of which foreign taxes of £20,000 were paid.

Calculate the IHT payable on the estate assuming that Peter made a gross chargeable lifetime transfer of £187,000 one year before his death.

	£
IHT on chargeable estate of £282,000	
(available nil rate band £(325,000 − 187,000) = £138,000 @ 0%, £144,000 @ 40%	57,600
(Average rate: 57,600/282,000 = 20.42553%)	
Less DTR: lower of:	
(a) £20,000	
(b) £80,000 × 20.42553% = £16,340	(16,340)
IHT payable on the estate	41,260

2 Gifts with reservation

12/13

The rules on gifts with reservation ensure that gifts which are effectively made on death or within the seven years before death, even though apparently made earlier, are taxed.

One of the competencies you require to fulfil Performance Objective 17 Tax planning and advice of the PER is to assess the tax implications of proposed activities or plans of an individual or entity with reference to relevant and up to date legislation. You can apply the knowledge you obtain from this section of the text to help to demonstrate this competence.

2.1 Introduction

There are rules to prevent the avoidance of IHT by the making of gifts while reserving some benefit. Without these rules, incomplete lifetime gifts would escape IHT by being PETs but would also reduce the individual's estate at death. The value of the assets could thus escape tax entirely, despite the original owner deriving some benefit from them up to his death.

The obvious example is a gift of a home to the donor's children but with the donor continuing to live in it rent free. Another example is a gift of income-producing assets, for example shares, but with the income continuing to be received by the donor.

Key term

Property given subject to a reservation (**gifts with reservation**) is property where:

(a) Such property is not enjoyed virtually to the entire exclusion of the donor (in the case of land only, also the donor's spouse or civil partner); or

(b) Possession and enjoyment of the property transferred is not *bona fide* assumed by the donee.

'Virtually to the entire exclusion' would, for example, allow a donor occasional brief stays in a house he had given away without creating a reservation, but spending most weekends in the house would create a reservation.

2.2 IHT consequences

Where a gift with reservation is made, it is treated in the same way as any other gift at the time it is made (as a PET or a CLT, as appropriate). **However, special rules apply on the death of the donor.**

(a) **If the reservation still exists at the date of the donor's death, the asset is included in the donor's estate at its value at that time** (not its value at the date the gift was made) and **can qualify for the residence nil rate band**.

(b) **If the reservation ceases within the seven years before death, then the gift is treated as a PET made at the time the reservation ceased.** The charge is based on its value at that time. The annual exemption cannot be used against such a PET.

If the gift could be taxed as a PET or CLT when made, as well as taxed under (a) or (b) above, it will be taxed either under (a) or (b), or as a PET or CLT when made (but not both), whichever gives the higher total tax.

2.3 Exceptions

There are **exceptions to the gifts with reservation rules** as follows.

(a) A gift will not be treated as being with reservation if **full consideration is given** for any right of occupation or enjoyment retained or assumed by the donor (or his spouse or civil partner, in the case of land), and the property is land or chattels. For example, an individual might give away his house and continue to live in it, but pay a full market rent for doing so.

(b) A gift will not be treated as being with reservation if the circumstances of the donor change in a way that was unforeseen at the time of the original gift and the benefit provided by the donee to the donor only represents reasonable provision for the **care and maintenance of the donor, being an elderly or infirm relative**. This exception only applies to interests in land.

Exam focus point

Gifts with reservation of benefit were tested in December 2011 Question 2 Mirtoon. The examining team commented that 'the vast majority of candidates knew all about gifts with reservation and answered this part of the question well'.

3 Altering dispositions made on death 12/14, 6/17

FAST FORWARD

A variation or disclaimer can be used to vary a will after death. This can have IHT and CGT consequences.

3.1 Introduction

One of the competencies you require to fulfil Performance Objective 17 Tax planning and advice of the PER is to review the situation of an individual or entity advising on any potential tax risks and/or additional tax minimisation measures. You can apply the knowledge you obtain from this section of the text to help to demonstrate this competence.

There are **two main ways in which dispositions on death may be altered: by application to the courts, and by means of a voluntary variation or a disclaimer** of a legacy. Application to the courts may be made if the family and dependants of the deceased feel that the will has not made adequate provision for them. Any changes to the will made in this way will be treated for IHT purposes as if made by the deceased when writing his will.

A variation or disclaimer may be of benefit in reducing tax or in securing a fairer distribution of the deceased's estate or both.

3.2 IHT consequences

Within two years of a death the terms of a will can be changed in writing, either by a variation of the terms of the will made by the persons who benefit or would benefit under the dispositions, or by a disclaimer, with the change being effective for IHT purposes. The variation or disclaimer will not be treated as a transfer of value. Inheritance tax will be calculated as if the terms contained in the variation replaced those in the will. If a legacy is disclaimed, it will pass under the terms of the will (or possibly under the intestacy rules) to some other person, usually the residuary legatee, and tax will apply as if the will originally directed the legacy to that new recipient.

There is a similar provision for CGT. **This was covered in Chapter 13**.

If the beneficiaries making the variation wish the relevant terms of the will to be treated as replaced by the terms of the variation, it is necessary to state this in the variation. The statement can apply for inheritance tax or capital gains tax or both. **Where a disclaimer is made, the relevant terms in the will are *automatically* treated as replaced by the terms of the disclaimer for both IHT and CGT purposes,** regardless of whether this is stated in the disclaimer or not.

Question
Altering disposition made on death

Monty died on 13 May 2018, leaving his entire estate of £450,000 in his will to his sister, Dora. The inheritance tax payable on his estate was £50,000. It is now November 2018 and Dora wishes to pass the net assets (after payment of inheritance tax) of £400,000 from the estate to her son, Jack. Dora has not made any lifetime transfers of value. She is not in good health and may not survive until November 2025.

Show the inheritance tax consequences if **either**:

(a)   Dora makes a potentially exempt transfer to Jack in November 2018, of the net assets of £400,000 from Monty's estate, and Dora dies in May 2024; **or**

(b)   Dora makes a variation of her entitlement to Monty's estate in November 2018, such that Monty's will is treated as leaving the entire estate to Jack, and Dora dies in May 2024.

Assume that the nil rate band and the rates of inheritance tax in 2018/19 also apply in 2024/25.

Answer

(a)   *Potentially exempt transfer November 2018*

	£
Gift	400,000
Less: AE 2018/19	(3,000)
AE 2017/18 b/f	(3,000)
PET now chargeable	394,000

	IHT
	£
£325,000 × 0%	0
£69,000 × 40%	27,600
£394,000	27,600
Less taper relief @ 60% (death within 5–6 years)	(16,560)
Death tax due	11,040

(b)   *Variation November 2018*

The assets from Monty's estate are treated as passing directly to Jack from Monty. Dora does not make a transfer of value of the assets when she makes the variation and so there is no charge to inheritance tax on her death in respect of these assets.

3.3 Other points

These provisions do not apply where the variation or disclaimer is made for consideration.

Property which is deemed to be included in an estate at the date of death because the deceased made a previous gift with reservation cannot be redirected by a deed of variation in a way which is effective for IHT purposes.

Variations or disclaimers can be made in respect of property passing under the intestacy rules in the same way as for property passing under a will, and with the same IHT and CGT consequences.

4 Trusts

Exam focus point

> **ACCA's article Trusts and tax for Advanced Taxation (ATX – UK),** written by a member of the Advanced Taxation (ATX – UK) examining team, sets out the rules that may be examined in Advanced Taxation (ATX – UK) and those areas where knowledge is not required. It considers the various types of trust and the capital gains tax and inheritance tax implications of transferring assets to a trust and property passing absolutely to beneficiaries.

4.1 What is a trust?

FAST FORWARD

> A trust is an arrangement under which a person, the settlor, transfers property to another person, the trustee or trustees, who is required to deal with the trust property on behalf of certain specified persons, the beneficiaries.

A trust may be created during the **lifetime of the settlor**, in which case the terms of the trust will be contained in the trust deed. Alternatively a trust may arise on the **death of the settlor**, in which case the terms of the trust will be laid down in the will, or by the statutory provisions which apply on an intestacy.

The first trustee will normally be specified in the trust deed or will. Trustees may retire and new trustees may be appointed, but for tax purposes they are regarded as a single continuing body of persons. The beneficiaries will also be specified in the trust deed or will. They may be separately named, 'my daughter Ann', or may be members of a particular class of persons, 'my children'. The trust property will comprise the original property settled (or property replacing it), plus any property added to the trust, plus income accumulated as an addition to capital, less any amounts advanced to beneficiaries.

4.2 Example of a discretionary trust

A discretionary trust for a family may have the following provisions:

(a)   Settlor: James Brown.

(b)   Trustees: John Brown (son) and Jean White (daughter).

(c)   Beneficiaries: the children and remoter issue of the settlor, and their spouses/civil partners.

(d)   Trust property: £100,000 originally settled and any property deriving from that property.

(e)   Income may be accumulated for up to 21 years from the date of the settlement; subject to which it is to be distributed to the beneficiaries at the trustees' discretion.

(f)   Capital may be advanced to beneficiaries at the trustees' discretion. Any capital remaining undistributed on the 80th anniversary of the date of settlement is to be distributed to the settlor's grandchildren then living, failing which to Oxfam.

This gives the trustees complete discretion over income and capital.

4.3 Example of an interest in possession trust

An interest in possession trust may have the following provisions:

(a)   Settlor: Alice
(b)   Trustees: Margaret and Crispin (solicitors)
(c)   Trust property: 10,000 T plc shares, £5,000 cash
(d)   Beneficiaries: Ruth (daughter), Lawrence (grandson)
(e)   Income: payable to Ruth during her lifetime
(f)   Capital: distributed to Lawrence on the death of Ruth

In this trust, the trustees have no discretion over the payment of either income or capital: both must be dealt with in accordance with the terms of the trust. Ruth has an **interest in possession** in the trust because she is entitled to the income of the trust now. She might also be called the life tenant of the trust because her right to income lasts for her lifetime. Lawrence has **reversionary interest** in the trust because he is only entitled to the capital after Ruth's interest has come to an end. He may be called the **remainderman**.

4.4 Charges to inheritance tax on trusts

FAST FORWARD

There is a CLT when a trust is set up. The trust suffers the IHT principal charge once every ten years and the exit charge when property leaves the trust.

4.4.1 IHT on creation of a trust

As we saw earlier in this text, **when an individual makes a gift to a trust it is a CLT for IHT purposes**. If the gift is made on death, IHT is charged on the death estate in the normal way before the assets enter the trust.

Exam focus point

There are special rules where a trust is created on the death of the settlor giving an immediate interest in possession (immediate post-death interest). These rules are **not examinable** in Advanced Taxation (ATX – UK).

4.4.2 IHT charges on a trust

The property in the trust is known as 'relevant property'. So long as it remains relevant property it is subject to the **principal charge** on every tenth anniversary from the start of the trust.

If property leaves the trust (and so ceases to be relevant property) an **exit charge** arises. An example would be where the trustees advance capital to a beneficiary.

Exit charge before first principal charge

The amount subject to the exit charge is the amount distributed from the trust. The rate of IHT is 30% of the (lifetime) rate that would apply to a notional (ie pretend) transfer of the initial value of the trust, assuming cumulative transfers by the trust equal to those made by the settlor in the seven years prior to the setting up of the trust. Once the rate of IHT has been established, it is then further reduced by multiplying by x/40 where x is the number of complete successive quarters that have elapsed since the trust commenced.

The principal charge

IHT is charged on the value of the property in the trust at each tenth anniversary of the trust. The rate is 30% of the (lifetime) rate that would apply to a transfer of the property in the trust at the tenth anniversary, assuming cumulative transfers equal to the gross amount of any capital paid out of the trust in the previous ten years **plus** the settlor's transfers in the seven years prior to the creation of the trust.

Exit charge after a principal charge

Use the rate that applied at the last tenth anniversary, reduced by multiplying by a fraction that reflects the time elapsed since the tenth anniversary. The fraction is x/40, where x is the number of complete quarters since the last tenth anniversary. If there has been a change in the nil rate band, the rate applied at the last tenth anniversary is recomputed using the new nil rate band.

Exam focus point

Although you must have an awareness of these exit and principal charges, you will not be expected to perform a computation in the exam.

4.5 Reasons to use trusts

Trusts help preserve family wealth while maintaining flexibility over who should benefit.

PER alert

One of the competencies you require to fulfil Performance Objective 17 Tax planning and advice of the PER is to mitigate and/or defer tax liabilities through the use of standard reliefs, exemptions and incentives. You can apply the knowledge you obtain from this section of the text to help to demonstrate this competence.

4.5.1 Introduction

Trusts are useful vehicles for non-tax reasons such as to preserve family wealth, to provide for those who are deemed to be incapable (minors, and the disabled) or unsuitable (due to youth or poor business sense) to hold assets directly.

4.5.2 Will trusts

A discretionary trust may be set up by will. The rate of inheritance tax on principal charges and exit charges within the trust will then depend on the settlor's cumulative transfers in the seven years before his death and the value of the trust property. The discretionary trust allows the transferee flexibility about who is to benefit from the trust and to what extent. This can be useful if there are beneficiaries of differing ages and whose financial circumstances may differ.

4.5.3 Lifetime trusts

Although gifts to trusts during lifetime can lead to an IHT charge (a CLT), there can be tax benefits from setting up trusts during the settlor's lifetime. As long as the cumulative total of CLTs in any seven year period does not exceed the nil rate band there will be no lifetime IHT to pay on creation of the trust. The trust will be subject to IHT at 0% on the ten year anniversary and later advances, unless the value of the trust property grows faster than the nil rate band.

If a discretionary trust is used, the settlor can preserve the maximum flexibility in the class of beneficiaries and how income and capital should be dealt with.

If the settlor is included as a beneficiary of the trust the gift will be treated as a gift with reservation.

5 The administration of IHT

IHT is administered by HMRC Inheritance Tax. The due date for payment depends on the type of event giving rise to the charge to tax.

5.1 Accounts

IHT is administrated by HMRC Inheritance Tax.

There is no system of regular returns as for income tax, corporation tax and capital gains tax. **Instead, any person who is liable for IHT on a transfer is required to deliver an account giving details of the relevant assets and their value. An account delivered by the personal representatives (PRs) of a deceased person has to provide full details of the assets in the death estate. The PRs also have to include in their account details of any chargeable transfers made by the deceased person in the seven years before his death.**

PRs must deliver an account within 12 months following the end of the month in which death occurred or, if later, three months following the date when they become PRs. **Where no tax is due, and certain other conditions are satisfied, it is not necessary to submit an account. Estates where no account needs to be submitted are called excepted estates.**

A person responsible for the delivery of an account in relation to a PET that has become chargeable by reason of death, must do so within 12 months following the end of the month in which death occurred unless already reported by the PRs.

Any other account (such as for a chargeable lifetime transfer) must be delivered within 12 months of the end of the month in which the transfer was made or, if later, within three months from the date liability to tax arose.

If a person has delivered an account and then discovers a material defect in it, he must deliver a corrective account within six months.

5.2 Power to call for documents

HMRC may require any person to provide any information, documents, etc needed for the purposes of IHT. There is a right of appeal against such an information notice.

5.3 Determinations and appeals

HMRC issue a written notice of determination where, for example, they do not agree a value of transfer or where payment of tax has not been made. It may be made on the basis of a submitted account or to the best of the inspector's judgement.

An appeal against a notice of determination may be made to the Tax Chamber of the Tribunal within 30 days of its being served. Questions of land valuation are dealt with by the Lands Tribunal.

HMRC cannot take legal proceedings to recover tax charged by a notice of determination while an appeal is pending.

5.4 Liability for IHT

FAST FORWARD
The liability to pay IHT depends on the type of transfer and whether it was made on death.

On death, liability for payment is as follows.

(a)   **Tax on the free estate is paid by the PRs** out of estate assets, with the burden generally falling on the residuary legatee (ie the recipient of the assets in the residue).

(b)   **Tax on property** not in the possession of the personal representatives, having been transferred by the donor **subject to a reservation, is payable by the person in possession of the property.**

(c)   **Tax on PETs that have become chargeable is paid and borne by donees.**

(d)   **Additional liabilities on CLTs must be paid and borne by the donees.**

HMRC can look beyond the person primarily responsible. Most significantly a PR may become liable where the tax remains unpaid. This overall liability is limited to the value of estate assets in his possession. HMRC will not pursue the PR for tax if lifetime transfers are later discovered and the PR has made the fullest reasonably practicable enquiries to discover lifetime transfers and has obtained a certificate of discharge before distributing the estate.

If the PRs do not pay IHT due on an estate, HMRC may collect the tax from beneficiaries under the will to the extent they receive assets under the will.

The donor is primarily liable for the tax due on chargeable lifetime transfers.

5.5 Due dates

One of the competencies you require to fulfil Performance Objective 16 Tax compliance and verification of the PER is to determine the incidence (timing) of tax liabilities and their impact on cash flow/financing requirements. You can apply the knowledge you obtain from this section of the text to help to demonstrate this competence.

(a) **For chargeable lifetime transfers the due date is the later of:**
  (i) **30 April just after the end of the tax year of the transfer**
  (ii) **Six months after the end of the month of the transfer**

  Interest (not tax deductible) is payable from the due date to the day before the day on which payment is made (inclusive).

(b) **Tax arising on the free estate at death (and on gifts with reservation if the reservation still existed at death) is payable by the PRs on delivery of their account.** The time limit for this is 12 months from the end of the month in which the death occurred. However, most PRs deliver their account before the twelve month deadline as it needs to be submitted to obtain a grant of representation (probate or letters of administration). Interest runs from six months after the end of the month when death occurred.

(c) **Tax arising on death in respect of PETs and CLTs with additional tax is payable within six months from the end of the month of death and interest runs from this due date.**

Interest (not taxable) is paid on repayments of tax from the date of payment to the date of repayment.

Question

Interest on IHT

Walter died on 10 March 2018. IHT of £375,000 on his estate was paid on 1 November 2018. Calculate the interest payable on the late paid IHT, assuming an interest rate of 3.00%.

Answer

Interest runs from 30 September 2018 until 31 October 2018 (inclusive).

Interest = £375,000 × 3.00% × 1/12 = £937

5.6 The instalment option

IHT on certain property can be paid by ten equal annual instalments on CLTs where tax is borne by the donee, or on the transfer of a person's death estate.

The instalment option may also be used for IHT payable due to the death of the donor within seven years of making a PET. In this case, the donee must have kept the property (or replacement property qualifying for business or agricultural property relief) until the donor's death (or his own, if earlier), and if the property qualifies under (c) or (d) below the shares must remain unquoted until the earlier of the two deaths.

The first instalment is due for payment:

(a) On transfers on death and liabilities arising as a result of death, six months after the end of the month of death

(b) On chargeable lifetime transfers, on the normal due date

The instalment option applies to:

(a) **Land and buildings**

(b) **Shares or securities in a company controlled by the transferor** immediately before the transfer

(c) **Other holdings in unquoted companies** where the tax on them together with that on other instalment property represents **at least 20% of the total liability** on the estate on a death, **or where the tax cannot all be paid at once without undue hardship**

(d) **Shares in an unquoted company (including an AIM listed company) representing at least 10%** of the nominal value of the issued share capital and **valued for IHT purposes at not less than £20,000**

(e) **A business or an interest in a business**

If the property is sold, all outstanding tax must then be paid.

Chapter roundup

- A UK domiciled, or deemed UK domiciled, individual is subject to inheritance tax on transfers of all assets, wherever situated.

- An election may be made for a non-UK domiciled individual who is, or was, the spouse or civil partner of a UK domiciled individual, to be treated as UK domiciled for IHT purposes.

- Non-UK assets of individuals not domiciled in the UK are not subject to IHT.

- Double taxation relief may reduce the IHT on assets also taxed overseas.

- The rules on gifts with reservation ensure that gifts which are effectively made on death or within the seven years before death, even though apparently made earlier, are taxed.

- A variation or disclaimer can be used to vary a will after death. This can have IHT and CGT consequences.

- A trust is an arrangement under which a person, the settlor, transfers property to another person, the trustee or trustees, who is required to deal with the trust property on behalf of certain specified persons, the beneficiaries.

- There is a CLT when a trust is set up. The trust suffers the IHT principal charge once every ten years and the exit charge when property leaves the trust.

- Trusts help preserve family wealth while maintaining flexibility over who should benefit.

- IHT is administered by HMRC Inheritance Tax. The due date for payment depends on the type of event giving rise to the charge to tax.

- The liability to pay IHT depends on the type of transfer and whether it was made on death.

Quick quiz

1   How is domicile defined for IHT purposes?

2   How is double taxation relief given?

3   Within what time limit must a variation of a will be made?

4   What is the IHT principal charge?

5   What are the IHT consequences of advancing capital from a trust to a beneficiary 20 months after the tenth anniversary?

6   When is lifetime inheritance tax on a chargeable lifetime transfer due for payment?

Answers to quick quiz

1 Domicile for IHT is:

   - Domicile under the general law (permanent home); and
   - Deemed domicile in the UK if domiciled in the UK within immediately preceding 3 years; and
   - Deemed domicile in the UK if a formerly UK domiciled individual (born and domicile of origin in UK, UK resident in tax year and at least 1 of 2 immediately preceding tax years); and
   - Deemed domicile in the UK if UK resident at least 15 of the 20 tax years immediately preceding the relevant tax year and for at least 1 of the 4 tax years ending with the relevant tax year.

2 DTR is given as a tax credit against IHT payable on the overseas asset to the extent of the lower of foreign tax and the IHT (at average rate) on it.

3 A variation of a will must be made within two years of death.

4 The principal charge is a charge on relevant property held in trust at each ten year anniversary of the trust.

5 If capital is advanced from a trust there is an exit charge. This is calculated using the rate of tax that applied on the 10 year anniversary × 6/40 as between 6 and 7 quarters have elapsed since then.

6 The due date for lifetime tax on a chargeable lifetime transfer is the later of:

   (a) 30 April just after the end of the tax year of the transfer; and
   (b) 6 months after the end of the month of transfer.

Now try the question below from the Practice Question Bank

Number	Level	Marks	Time
Q19	Introductory	11	21 mins

Stamp taxes

Stamp taxes

Topic list	Syllabus reference
1 Stamp duty	A5(a)(i), A5(b)(i)
2 Stamp duty reserve tax (SDRT)	A5(a)(i), A5(b)(i)
3 Stamp duty land tax (SDLT)	A5(a)(i), A5(b)(ii)
4 Exemptions and reliefs relating to stamp taxes	A5(c)(i), (ii)

Introduction

In this chapter we look at stamp taxes.

Stamp duty is a charge on transfers of shares and securities by stock transfer form of 0.5% of the consideration for the sale.

The same rate of duty applies for stamp duty reserve tax which applies where shares and securities are transferred in a paperless transaction.

Stamp duty land tax is charged on transfers of land in England and Northern Ireland.

In the next chapter, we will turn our attention to corporation tax.

Study guide

		Intellectual level
5	**Stamp taxes (stamp duty, stamp duty reserve tax, and stamp duty land tax)**	
(a)	The scope of stamp taxes:	3
(i)	Identify the property in respect of which stamp taxes are payable	
(b)	Identify and advise on the liabilities arising on transfers:	3
(i)	Advise on the stamp taxes payable on transfers of shares and securities	
(ii)	Advise on the stamp taxes payable on transfers of land	
(c)	The use of exemptions and reliefs in deferring and minimising stamp taxes:	3
(i)	Identify transfers involving no consideration	
(ii)	Advise on group transactions	

Exam guide

Stamp taxes will be a minor part of a question, but must not be overlooked as they can be a significant cost in many transactions.

> Knowledge brought forward from earlier studies

The topics in this chapter are new.

1 Stamp duty

 FAST FORWARD

> Stamp duty applies to transfers of shares and securities transferred by a stock transfer form.

⚠ **PER alert**
Two of the competencies you require to fulfil Performance Objective 15 Tax computations and assessments of the PER are to prepare or contribute to the computation or assessment of tax computations for individuals and to prepare or contribute to the computation or assessment of tax computations for single companies, groups or other entities. You can apply the knowledge you obtain from this section of the text to help to demonstrate these competences.

Stamp duty applies to **transfers of shares and securities** which are effected by a paper **stock transfer form.** It is **payable** by the **purchaser.**

Stamp duty applies at the **rate** of **0.5%** of the **consideration** unless the transfer falls within one of the **specific exemptions** (see Section 4). The duty is rounded up to the nearest £5.

2 Stamp duty reserve tax (SDRT)

 FAST FORWARD

> Stamp duty reserve tax (SDRT) applies to electronic transfers of shares and securities.

⚠ **PER alert**
Two of the competencies you require to fulfil Performance Objective 15 Tax computations and assessments of the PER are to prepare or contribute to the computation or assessment of tax computations for individuals and to prepare or contribute to the computation or assessment of tax computations for single companies, groups or other entities. You can apply the knowledge you obtain from this section of the text to help to demonstrate these competences.

Stamp duty reserve tax (SDRT) is applicable to **transfers of shares and securities** which are effected by an **electronic paperless transaction.** It is **payable** by the **purchaser.**

Most of these transactions are made through **an electronic system** called **CREST.** Some shares are held outside CREST ('Off Market') but may still be transferred electronically, for example if they are held by a nominee such as a bank.

SDRT applies at the **rate** of **0.5%** of the **consideration** unless the transfer falls within one of the **specific exemptions** (see Section 4).

3 Stamp duty land tax (SDLT) 12/17

3.1 Land transactions

FAST FORWARD

Stamp duty land tax (SDLT) applies to the sale of land, or of rights over land, in England and Northern Ireland.

Two of the competencies you require to fulfil Performance Objective 15 Tax computations and assessments of the PER are to prepare or contribute to the computation or assessment of tax computations for individuals and to prepare or contribute to the computation or assessment of tax computations for single companies, groups or other entities. You can apply the knowledge you obtain from this section of the text to help to demonstrate these competences.

Stamp duty land tax (SDLT) applies to **land transactions in England and Northern Ireland.**

Exam focus point

There are similar taxes called Land and Buildings Transaction Tax (LBTT) on land transactions in Scotland and Land Transaction Tax (LTT) on land transactions in Wales. LBTT and LTT are **excluded** from the Advanced Taxation (ATX – UK) syllabus.

A land transaction is a **transfer of land** or an **interest in**, or **right over**, land. **SDLT is** generally **payable** based on the **consideration for the land transaction.** It is **payable** by the **purchaser.** The **amount of the charge to SDLT** depends on whether the land is **residential** (eg houses, flats) or **non-residential** (eg shops, warehouses, factories).

Exam focus point

The charge to stamp duty land tax on residential property and the treatment of leases are **excluded** from the Advanced Taxation (ATX – UK) syllabus.

3.2 Non-residential property

The following rates of SDLT apply to non-residential property:

Non-residential	Rate (%)
Up to £150,000	0
£150,001 – £250,000	2
£250,001 and above	5

Exam focus point

The thresholds and rates of stamp duty land tax for non-residential property will be shown in the Tax Rates and Allowances available in the exam.

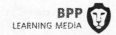

3.3 Examples: non-residential property

(a) Raymond buys a freehold shop in England in November 2018 for £145,000. His stamp duty land tax is £145,000 × 0% = £0.

(b) Klear plc buys a freehold factory in Northern Ireland in August 2018 for £350,000. Its stamp duty land tax is:

	£
£150,000 × 0%	0
£100,000 (£250,000 – 150,000) × 2%	2,000
£100,000 (£350,000 – 250,000) × 5%	5,000
£350,000	7,000

4 Exemptions and reliefs relating to stamp taxes

> There are exemptions and reliefs for stamp taxes, for example on transfers of securities traded on growth markets, when the transfer does not involve payment of consideration, such as a gift, and on transfers between group companies.

4.1 Transfers of securities traded on a recognised growth market

Stamp duty and stamp duty reserve tax is not chargeable on transfers of securities (eg shares) which are traded on a recognised growth market such as the AIM sub-market of the London Stock Exchange.

4.2 Transfers with no consideration

Stamp taxes are charged on the **consideration** passing under the document or transaction. If there is **no consideration**, there is **an exemption from stamp taxes**. Examples include:

- **Gifts** (except a gift of land to a connected company)
- A **transfer on divorce**, annulment of marriage or judicial separation
- **Variations** of a **will** or **intestacy** made within two years of death for no consideration
- Transfers to **charities** if the shares or land is to be used for charitable purposes

If **land is transferred** to a **company**, for example on **incorporation**, SDLT is payable on the **market value** of land.

4.3 Company transactions   6/15, 6/17, 12/17

Relief from **stamp duty** and **SDLT** is given for **transfers of assets** between **companies within a stamp taxes group**. There is no direct relief for stamp duty reserve tax so the transaction must be made by using a stock transfer form and a claim made for stamp duty relief.

There are **two conditions** which must be met to attract the relief, namely that:

- Effect must be to transfer the **beneficial interest** in property from one company to another; and
- **One company must be the parent of the other company** or **both companies must have a common parent company.**

One company is regarded as the parent of another if:

- The company has **beneficial ownership** of at least **75% of the ordinary share capital**, ie if all the issued share capital of a company, other than fixed rate preference shares; and
- The company has at least a **75% interest in dividends** and **assets in a winding up**; and
- There are no 'arrangements' for a non-group person to acquire control of the transferee company but not the transferor company.

For indirect holdings, it is necessary to reduce the degree of ownership at each level to the appropriate fraction in determining whether the 75% test is met (as for corporation tax group relief).

Question

Allegri Ltd owns 90% of the ordinary share capital of Byrd Ltd, which in turn owns 85% of the ordinary share capital of Corelli Ltd. Shares are transferred from Corelli Ltd to Allegri Ltd under an instrument executed on 1 June 2018. Is stamp duty relief available?

Answer

Relief is available, since Allegri Ltd owns indirectly 76½ % (ie 90% × 85%) of the ordinary share capital of Corelli Ltd.

SDLT relief is withdrawn where **land has been transferred from one group company to another** and **within three years of the transfer** the **transferee company leaves the group** whilst still owning the land. Note that the **transferor** company leaving the group does not cause the SDLT relief to be withdrawn as the land is still held by the transferee company and so it is still within the group.

Exam focus point

Stamp duty land tax on groups was tested in June 2015 Question 2(a) Helm Ltd group. The examining team commented that 'the stamp duty land tax aspects of the question were not handled well with very few candidates recognising that the inter group exemption that was available when the trade and assets of Aero Ltd were transferred to Bar Ltd would be withdrawn due to the sale of Bar Ltd within three years'.

Chapter roundup

- Stamp duty applies to transfers of shares and securities transferred by a stock transfer form.

- Stamp duty reserve tax (SDRT) applies to electronic transfers of shares and securities.

- Stamp duty land tax (SDLT) applies to the sale of land, or of rights over land, in England and Northern Ireland.

- There are exemptions and reliefs for stamp taxes, for example on transfers of securities traded on growth markets, when the transfer does not involve payment of consideration, such as a gift, and on transfers between group companies.

Quick quiz

1   What is the stamp duty on a share transfer form if the consideration for sale was £50,000?

2   When is stamp duty reserve tax charged?

3   On 6 October 2018, Way Ltd buys a freehold factory in England for £800,000. What is the SDLT payable by Way Ltd?

4   In order for a variation of a will to be exempt from stamp duties, it must be made within ___ years of the date of death. Fill in the blank.

5   Stamp duty land tax group relief will be withdrawn where land has been transferred from one group company to another and within ___ years of the transfer the transferee company leaves the group whilst still owning the land. Fill in the blank.

Answers to quick quiz

1   £50,000 × 0.5% = £250

2   Stamp duty reserve tax (SDRT) applies to electronic share transactions.

3

		£
£150,000 × 0%		0
£100,000 (£250,000 – 150,000) × 2%		2,000
£550,000 (£800,000 – 250,000) × 5%		27,500
£800,000		29,500

4   In order for a variation of a will to be exempt from stamp duties, it must be made within **two** years of the date of death.

5   Stamp duty land tax group relief will be withdrawn where land has been transferred from one group company to another and within **three** years of the transfer the transferee company leaves the group whilst still owning the land.

Now try the question below from the Practice Question Bank

Number	Level	Marks	Time
Q20	Introductory	3	6 mins

19: Stamp taxes | Part E Stamp taxes

Corporation tax

Corporation tax computation

Topic list	Syllabus reference
1 Scope of corporation tax	A4(a)E1
2 Charge to corporation tax	A4(a)E4
3 Taxable total profits	A4(a)E2,E6
4 Loan relationships	A4(a)E2
5 Intangible fixed assets	A4(c)(iv)
6 Transfer pricing	A4(c)(v)
7 Research and development (R&D)	A4(c)(i)
8 Enhanced capital allowances (ECAs)	A4(c)(ii)

Introduction

At this point in our studies we turn to corporation tax, covering the basic corporation tax rules in this chapter.

We start by looking at accounting periods, which are the periods for which companies pay corporation tax. Next we look at the charge to corporation tax based on financial years. We then see in more detail how to bring together all of a company's profits in a corporation tax computation and discuss the special rules for certain types of income that apply to companies.

In the next chapter, we will deal with the rules on chargeable gains for companies.

Study guide

		Intellectual level
4	**Corporation tax liabilities in situations involving overseas and further group aspects and in relation to special types of company, and the application of additional exemptions and reliefs**	
(a)	The contents of the Taxation - United Kingdom (TX – UK) study guide, for corporation tax, under headings:	2
•	E1 The scope of corporation tax	
•	E2 Taxable total profits	
•	E4 The comprehensive computation of the corporation tax liability	
•	E6 The use of exemptions and reliefs in deferring and minimising corporation tax liabilities	
(c)	Taxable total profits:	3
(i)	Identify qualifying research and development expenditure, both capital and revenue, and determine the reliefs available by reference to the size of the individual company/group	
(ii)	Identify the enhanced capital allowances available in respect of expenditure in respect of expenditure on green technologies, including the tax credit available in the case of a loss making company	
(iv)	Recognise the alternative tax treatments of intangible assets and conclude on the best treatment for a given company	
(v)	Advise on the impact of the transfer pricing and thin capitalisation rules on companies	

Exam guide

Although you are unlikely simply to be asked to calculate the corporation tax payable for an accounting period, you may have to be able to work out tax savings or additional tax costs when giving advice about using losses, new projects, etc. You may be asked to comment on how certain types of income would be included in the taxable total profits computation where there are special rules, such as for loan relationships, intangible fixed assets and research and development expenditure. You may also be asked to discuss how the transfer pricing rules work.

Knowledge brought forward from earlier studies

This chapter revises the scope of corporation tax, the computation of corporation tax payable and the basic computation of taxable total profits. The examining team has identified essential underpinning knowledge from the Taxation (TX – UK) syllabus which is particularly important that you revise as part of your Advanced Taxation (ATX – UK) studies. In this chapter, the relevant topic is:

E2	**Taxable total profits**	
(h)	Recognise and apply the treatment of interest paid and received under the loan relationship rules	1
E4	**The comprehensive computation of the corporation tax liability**	
(a)	Compute the corporation tax liability	2

There are no changes for Advanced Taxation (ATX – UK) exams in Financial Year 2018 from the material studied for Taxation (TX – UK) for exams in Financial Year 2017.

There are two new topics: intangible fixed assets and research and development.

1 Scope of corporation tax

ACCA's article Corporation tax for Advanced Taxation (ATX – UK), written by a member of the Advanced Taxation (ATX – UK) examining team, considers the taxation of a company as it begins trading, acquires an additional business, and eventually invests overseas. It sets out the commercial decisions taken by the company and its shareholders at the different stages in the company's development and summarises the tax implications of those decisions.

1.1 Introduction

Companies pay corporation tax on their taxable total profits of each accounting period.

Corporation tax is paid by companies. It is charged on the taxable total profits of each accounting period. For the purposes of the Advanced Taxation (ATX – UK) exam, corporation tax is not charged on dividends received from UK resident or non-resident companies.

A 'company' is any corporate body (limited or unlimited) or unincorporated association eg sports clubs.

1.2 The residence of companies

A company incorporated in the UK is resident in the UK. A company incorporated abroad is resident in the UK if its central management and control are exercised here.

1.3 Accounting periods

An accounting period cannot exceed 12 months in length. A long period of account must be split into 2 accounting periods, the first of which is 12 months long.

Corporation tax is chargeable in respect of accounting periods. It is important to understand the difference between an accounting period and a period of account. A period of account is any period for which a company prepares accounts; usually this will be 12 months in length but it may be longer or shorter than this. An accounting period starts when a company starts to trade, or otherwise becomes liable to corporation tax, or immediately after the previous accounting period finishes. An accounting period finishes on the earliest of:

- 12 months after its start
- The end of the company's period of account
- The company starting or ceasing to trade
- The company entering/ceasing to be in administration (see later in this text)
- The commencement of a company's winding up (see later in this text)
- The company ceasing to be resident in the UK
- The company ceasing to be liable to corporation tax

In many cases, the company will have a period of account of 12 months and an accounting period of 12 months. We will deal with long periods of account (exceeding 12 months) later in this chapter.

2 Charge to corporation tax

2.1 Financial years

Tax rates are set for financial years.

The rates of corporation tax are fixed for financial years. A financial year runs from 1 April to the following 31 March and is identified by the calendar year in which it begins. For example, the year ended 31 March 2019 is the Financial Year 2018 (FY 2018). This should not be confused with a tax year, which runs from 6 April to the following 5 April.

2.2 Computing the corporation tax liability   6/16

There is a single rate of corporation tax which is applied to a company's taxable total profits to compute the corporation tax liability.

For financial year 2018, there is a single rate of corporation tax (the main rate) which is 19%. This rate is applied to the company's taxable total profits to compute the corporation tax liability. The rate of corporation tax for financial year 2017 was 19% and for financial year 2016 was 20%.

Exam focus point

The rates of corporation tax will be given in the Tax Rates and Allowances available in the exam.

2.3 Accounting period in more than one financial year

An accounting period **may fall within more than one financial year. If the rates for corporation tax are the same in both financial years, tax can be computed for the accounting period as if it fell within one financial year.**

However, **if the rates for corporation tax are different in the financial years, taxable total profits are time apportioned between the financial years**. The rate of corporation tax in the financial year 2016 was 20% so if the accounting period spans 31 March 2017, apportionment will be needed.

Question   Corporation tax liability

Wentworth Ltd makes up its accounts to 31 December each year. For the year to 31 December 2017, it has taxable total profits of £480,000. Compute Wentworth Ltd's corporation tax liability.

Answer

	£
FY 2016 (1.1.17 to 31.3.17 – 3 months)	
£480,000 × 3/12 = 120,000 × 20%	24,000
FY 2017 (1.4.17 to 31.12.17 – 9 months)	
£480,000 × 9/12 = 360,000 × 19%	68,400
Corporation tax liability for year to 31 December 2017	92,400

3 Taxable total profits

FAST FORWARD

> Taxable total profits are the total profits (income and gains) less some losses and qualifying charitable donations.

PER alert

> One of the competencies you require to fulfil Performance Objective 15 Tax computations and assessments of the PER is to prepare or contribute to the computation or assessment of tax computations for single companies, groups or other entities. You can apply the knowledge you obtain from this section of the text to help to demonstrate this competence.

3.1 Introduction

The corporation tax computation draws together all of the company's income and gains from various sources. The income from each different type of source must be computed separately because different computational rules apply.

The taxable total profits for an accounting period are derived as follows.

	£
Trading income	X
Property business income	X
Interest income from non-trading loan relationships	X
Miscellaneous income	X
Chargeable gains	X
Total profits	X
Less losses relieved by deduction from total profits	(X)
Less qualifying charitable donations	(X)
Taxable total profits for an accounting period	X

Each of the above items is dealt with in further detail later in this text.

Exam focus point

> You should be familiar with this proforma from your Taxation (TX – UK) studies. The calculation of taxable total profits may also be required in the Advanced Taxation (ATX – UK) exam, so you must understand how different types of income and gains are dealt with.

Dividends received from both UK and non-UK resident companies are usually exempt and so not included in taxable total profits.

Exam focus point

> The examining team has stated that dividends which are taxable in the hands of the recipient company are **not examinable** in the Advanced Taxation (ATX – UK) exam.

3.2 Trading income

The trading income of companies is derived from the profit before taxation shown in the accounts. The adjustments that need to be made to the accounts are broadly the same for companies as they are for income tax purposes (companies cannot use the cash basis) (see Chapter 6). Companies may also claim relief for the expenses of managing their investments (see Chapter 25). Where shares in UK companies are held as trading assets, and not as investments, any dividends on those shares will be treated for tax purposes as trading profits.

Qualifying charitable donations are added back in the calculation of adjusted profit. They are instead deducted from total profits (see below).

Interest received on a trading loan relationship (see later in this chapter) is included within trading profits on an accruals basis. Similarly, interest paid on a trading loan relationship is deducted at arriving at trading profits.

When adjusting profits as supplied in a statement of profit or loss confusion can arise as regards to whether the figures are net or gross. Properly drawn up company accounts should normally include all income gross. However, some examination questions include items 'net'. Read the question carefully.

Pre-trading expenditure incurred by the company within the seven years before trade commences is treated as an allowable expense incurred on the first day of trading provided it would have been allowable had the company been trading when the expense was actually incurred.

Trading income also includes post cessation receipts arising from a trade which would not otherwise be chargeable to tax.

The calculation of capital allowances follows income tax principles. However, for companies, there is never any restriction of allowances to take account of any private use of an asset. The director or employee suffers a taxable benefit instead.

3.3 Property business income   9/15

The taxation of UK property business income, in particular the deductibility of property expenses, generally **follows similar rules to those for income tax (see earlier in this text). The accruals basis always applies to companies.** In summary:

(a)   All UK rental activities are treated as a single source of income calculated in the same way as trading profits.

(b)   Capital allowances on plant and machinery (but not furniture) are taken into account when computing property income or losses.

However, **interest paid by a company on a loan to buy or improve property is not a property income expense. The loan relationship rules apply instead** (see later in this chapter). The restriction on finance costs is not relevant to companies.

3.4 Interest income

UK companies normally receive interest gross. Interest relating to non-trading loan relationships is taxed separately as interest income on an accruals basis (see later in this chapter for the loan relationship rules).

3.5 Miscellaneous income

Income and expenditure relating to intellectual property, which is not used in the trade nor in a property business, are dealt with as miscellaneous income. We consider intellectual property in more detail later in this chapter.

3.6 Chargeable gains

Companies do not pay capital gains tax. Instead their chargeable gains are included in the taxable total profits. We look at companies' chargeable gains in the next chapter.

3.7 Qualifying charitable donations

Qualifying charitable donations are deductible from total profits when computing taxable total profits.

Almost all donations of money to charity by a company can be qualifying charitable donations whether they are single donations or regular donations. There is no need for a claim to be made in order for a payment to be treated as a qualifying charitable donation (compare with gift aid donations where a declaration is required).

Donations to local charities which are incurred wholly and exclusively for the purposes of a trade are deducted in the calculation of the tax adjusted trading profits.

The following is a summary of the statement of profit or loss of Acre Ltd for the year to 31 March 2019.

	£	£
Gross profit		180,000
Other income		
Treasury stock interest (non-trading investment)		700
Dividends from UK companies		3,600
Loan interest from UK company (non-trading investment)		4,000
Building society interest received (non-trading investment)		292
Expenses		
Trade expenses (all allowable)	62,000	
Qualifying charitable donation paid	1,100	
		(63,100)
Profit before taxation		125,492

The capital allowances for the period total £5,500. There was also a chargeable gain of £13,867. Compute the taxable total profits.

Answer

	£	£
Profit before taxation		125,492
Less: treasury stock interest	700	
dividends received	3,600	
building society interest	292	
loan interest received	4,000	
		(8,592)
		116,900
Add qualifying charitable donation		1,100
		118,000
Less capital allowances		(5,500)
Trading income		112,500
Interest income £(700 + 292 + 4,000)		4,992
Chargeable gain		13,867
Total profits		131,359
Less qualifying charitable donation		(1,100)
Taxable total profits		130,259

3.8 Long periods of account

If a company has a long period of account, exceeding 12 months, it is split into two accounting periods: the first 12 months and the remainder.

Where the period of account differs from the corporation tax accounting periods, profits are **allocated to the relevant periods** as follows:

- **Trading income** before capital allowances and property income are apportioned on a **time basis**.

- **Capital allowances** and balancing charges are **calculated for each accounting period.**

- **Other income is allocated to the period to which it relates** (eg interest to the period when accrued). Miscellaneous income, however, is apportioned on a time basis.

- **Chargeable gains and losses** are allocated to the **period in which they are realised.**

- **Qualifying charitable donations** are deducted in the accounting **period in which they are paid.**

Question

Xenon Ltd prepares an 18 month set of accounts to 30 June 2019 with the following results.

	£
Trading profits	180,000
Interest income	
18 months @ £500 accruing per month	9,000
Capital gain (1 May 2019 disposal)	250,000
Less qualifying charitable donation (paid 31 December 2018)	(50,000)
	389,000

What are the taxable total profits for each of the accounting periods?

Answer

The 18 month period of account is divided into:

Year ending 31 December 2018
6 months to 30 June 2019

Results are allocated:

	Y/e 31.12.18 £	6m to 30.6.19 £
Trading profits 12:6	120,000	60,000
Interest income		
12 × £500	6,000	
6 × £500		3,000
Capital gain (1.5.19)		250,000
Total profits	126,000	313,000
Less qualifying charitable donation (31.12.18)	(50,000)	
Taxable total profits	76,000	313,000

Exam focus point

Question 2(a) Sprint Ltd in the September 2015 exam required a calculation of the corporation tax payable for a company in respect of a 16-month set of accounts. The examining team commented that 'it was surprising, and indeed disappointing, to see that the majority of candidates calculated the corporation tax payable for the 16-month period as a whole, rather than recognising the need to split this into two separate accounting periods, the first covering the first 12 months and the second covering the remaining four months. This led to the loss of a number of what should have been easy marks. Candidates are reminded that a good level of familiarity with the Taxation (TX – UK) syllabus is required for Advanced Taxation (ATX – UK); it is not enough to just focus on the new areas, candidates must ensure that they are also confident in dealing with more basic issues.'

4 Loan relationships

6/15

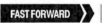 **FAST FORWARD**

A loan relationship arises when a company lends or borrows money. Trading loan relationships are dealt with as trading income. Non-trading loan relationships are dealt with as interest income.

4.1 Introduction

If a company borrows or lends money, including issuing or investing in loan stock or buying gilts, it has a loan relationship. This can be a creditor relationship (where the company lends or invests money) or a debtor relationship (where the company borrows money or issues securities). The loan relationship rules apply to both revenue and capital items.

4.2 Trading loan relationships

If the company is a party to a **loan relationship for trade purposes, any debits, ie interest payable or other debt costs, charged through its accounts are allowed as a trading expense** and are therefore deductible in computing trading profits.

Loans taken out by a company for trade purposes include loans used to:

- **Purchase plant and machinery**
- **Provide working capital**
- **Purchase property used for trading purposes** such as an office, warehouse or factory

Similarly **if any credits, ie interest income or other debt returns, arise on a trading loan these are treated as a trading receipt and are taxable as part of trading profit**. This is not likely to arise unless the trade is one of money lending so will usually fall within the rules for non-trading loan relationships (below).

4.3 Non-trading loan relationships

If a **loan relationship is not for trade purposes, any debits or credits** (eg interest paid or received) **must be pooled. A net credit on the pool is chargeable as interest income. Relief is available if there is a net 'deficit' (ie loss)** (see later in this text).

Loans taken out by a company for non-trade purposes include loans used to:

- **Purchase property which is then let out**
- **Acquire the share capital of another company**

Creditor non-trading loan relationships include:

- **Depositing cash on deposit at a bank**
- **Investing in loan stock or gilts**

Interest charged on underpaid tax is a debit and interest received on overpaid tax is a credit under the rules for non-trading loan relationships.

4.4 Example: loan relationships

During its year ended 31 December 2018 Jello Ltd received bank interest of £13,500 and loan stock interest from Wobble Ltd of £45,400. It also paid loan stock interest of £40,000 to Shaker Ltd on a loan of £1,000,000. The loan stock was issued to Shaker Ltd in May 2017 to raise £700,000 for the purchase of a factory to use in the trade and £250,000 for the purchase of an investment property. The balance was used as working capital. All figures are stated gross and are the amounts shown in the accounts.

The loan stock interest payable to Shaker Ltd was used partly for trade purposes, and partly for non trade purposes and must be apportioned:

	£
Non-trade purposes 250,000 × £40,000/1,000,000	10,000
Trade purposes (700,000 + 50,000 (bal)) = 750,000 × 40,000/1,000,000	30,000
Total interest payable	40,000

The £30,000 of interest paid for trade purposes is deducted in the computation of trading profits.

The £10,000 of interest paid for non-trade purposes is deducted from non-trading interest received. The amount taxable as a non-trading loan relationship credit is:

	£
Bank interest (received gross)	13,500
Debenture interest receivable from Wobble Ltd	45,400
	58,900
Non-trade loan stock interest paid to Shaker Ltd	(10,000)
Non-trading loan relationship credit	48,900

4.5 Incidental costs of loan finance

Under the loan relationship rules expenses ('debits') are allowed if incurred directly:

- Bringing a loan relationship into existence (eg loan arrangement fees);
- Entering into or giving effect to any related transactions;
- Making payment under a loan relationship or related transactions; or
- Taking steps to ensure the receipt of payments under the loan relationship or related transaction.

A related transaction means 'any disposal or acquisition (in whole or in part) of rights or liabilities under the relationship, including any arising from a security issue in relation to the money debt in question'.

The above categories of incidental costs are also allowable even if the company does not enter into the loan relationship (ie abortive costs). Cost directly incurred in varying the terms of a loan relationship are also allowed.

4.6 Other matters

It is not only the interest costs of borrowing that are allowable or taxable. The capital costs are treated similarly.

Relief for pre-trading expenditure extends to expenses incurred on trading loan relationships in accounting periods ending within seven years of the company starting to trade. An expense that would have been a trading debit if it was incurred after the trade had commenced, is treated as a trading debit of the first trading period. An election has to be made within two years of the end of the first trading period.

Interest charged on underpaid tax is deductible and interest received on overpaid tax is assessable under the loan relationship rules as interest income.

5 Intangible fixed assets   3/16, 6/17

5.1 Definition

Intangible fixed assets are defined for taxation purposes in the same way as for accounting purposes. Examples include:

- (a) **Intellectual property** (eg patents, copyrights)
- (b) **Goodwill**
- (c) **Marketing-related intangible assets** (eg registered trademarks, internet domain names)
- (d) **Customer-related intangible assets** (eg customer lists, customer relationships)

5.2 Tax treatment of most intangible fixed assets

> **FAST FORWARD** 〉〉 Gains/losses arising on most intangible fixed assets are recognised for tax purposes on the same basis as they are recognised in the accounts.

5.2.1 Introduction

Patents and most other intangible fixed assets (except for goodwill and customer-related intangible assets dealt with in Section 4.3 later in this chapter) **are treated for tax purposes in a similar manner**.

5.2.2 Intangible fixed assets used for trading purposes

If the intangible fixed asset is used for trading purposes, any income or expenditure (including depreciation or amortisation) associated with **intangible fixed assets is taxable/deductible as trading income**. Provided the accounts have been prepared using generally accepted accounting practice, this means that no adjustment will be needed to the profit before taxation for tax purposes.

There is one exception to this. **Instead of deducting the depreciation or amortisation as shown in the accounts the company may claim a writing down allowance of 4%.** Such a claim might be made if, for example, the company did not charge amortisation on the intangible fixed asset.

As for loan relationships, **the rules apply to capital debits and credits as well as revenue items**. For example, on the **disposal of the intangible fixed asset**, a **taxable credit or allowable debit arises** which is the **difference between the proceeds received and the tax written down value of the intangible fixed asset.** The tax written down value will be the same as the accounts value (except where the 4% writing down allowance has been claimed) ie the tax treatment on disposal follows the accounting treatment.

| Question | Disposal of patent |

Moon Ltd prepares accounts to 31 December each year. It sold a patent to an unrelated company on 1 December 2018 for £28,000. Moon Ltd had acquired the patent for use in its trade on 1 December 2016 for £25,000. The patent is being written off in Moon Ltd's accounts on a straight-line basis over a ten-year period. What are the corporation tax implications of the sale of the patent?

Answer

The patent is an intangible fixed asset. On a disposal of the patent, the sales proceeds will be compared with the amortised cost.

	£	£
Proceeds		28,000
Cost	25,000	
Less amortisation £25,000 × 10% × 2	(5,000)	
		(20,000)
Profit on sale		8,000

The profit on sale is a credit which will be included as part of Moon Ltd's trading income because the patent was purchased for the purposes of the trade.

5.2.3 Intangible fixed assets used for non-trading purposes

If the **intangible fixed asset is used for non-trade purposes, credits and debits are netted off. A net credit** is taxable as **miscellaneous income. A claim can be made for the whole or part of a net debit to be set off against total profits in the accounting period** or a claim can be made for **group relief**. Any **remaining debit** is **carried forward** to the next accounting period as a non-trading debit of that period.

5.3 Tax treatment of goodwill

FAST FORWARD

No debits (amortisation or impairment) on goodwill are allowable for tax purposes except on disposal. On a disposal of goodwill, a credit is taxable as trading income but a debit is a non-trading debit.

Exam focus point

The following tax treatment applies to goodwill acquired on or after 8 July 2015. Only these rules **are examinable** in Advanced Taxation (ATX – UK).

In relation to goodwill, **no debits (eg amortisation) are brought into account for tax purposes.** Where **amortisation has been deducted in the accounts**, this must be **added back in calculating the tax-adjusted trading profit** (as for unincorporated businesses).

On a disposal of goodwill, a credit or debit must be calculated which is the **difference between the proceeds received and the original cost of the goodwill. A credit is taxable as trading income. A debit is a non-trading debit** which can be **relieved as explained in Section 5.2.3 above.**

Customer-related intangible assets are treated for tax purposes in a similar way to goodwill.

Star Ltd prepares accounts to 31 March each year. Star Ltd had purchased goodwill from an unrelated company on 1 August 2017 for £80,000. The goodwill has not been amortised in the company's accounts. Star Ltd sold the goodwill to an unrelated company on 1 March 2019. In the year to 31 March 2019 Star Ltd had trading profits (before taking account of the sale of goodwill) of £15,000 and a chargeable gain of £3,000.

What are Star Ltd's taxable total profits for the year to 31 March 2019 if the sale proceeds of the goodwill are:

(a) £100,000; or
(b) £55,000?

Assume that Star Ltd claims relief for debits as soon as possible. Briefly explain how any remaining debit at 31 March 2019 will be dealt with.

Answer

(a) *Proceeds of £100,000*

	£
Trading profit before sale of goodwill	15,000
Trading credit on sale of goodwill £(100,000 – 80,000)	20,000
Trading income	35,000
Chargeable gain	3,000
Total profits/taxable total profits	38,000

(b) *Proceeds of £55,000*

	£
Trading profit before sale of goodwill	15,000
Chargeable gain	3,000
Total profits	18,000
Less non-trading debit on sale of goodwill £(55,000 – 80,000) = £(25,000) restricted to total profits	(18,000)
Taxable total profits	0

The remaining debit of £(18,000 – 25,000) = £(7,000) is carried forward to the next accounting period as a non-trading debit of that period.

5.4 Replacement of business assets relief

When an intangible fixed asset is disposed of, a claim for replacement of business assets relief may be made similar to that for chargeable gains. Details are covered when we look at rollover relief for chargeable gains in companies.

6 Transfer pricing   12/13, 9/16, 6/17

FAST FORWARD

The transfer pricing legislation prevents manipulation of profits between members of a group which can occur when a company chooses to buy and sell goods at a price which is not a market price.

6.1 General rules

Companies under common control can structure their transactions in such a way that they can shift profit (or losses) from one company to another. For example consider a company which wishes to sell goods valued at £20,000 to an independent third party.

Selling company ———— Goods invoice value: £20,000 ————→ Buying company

In this case all the profit on the sale arises to the selling company. Alternatively the sale could be rearranged:

Selling company ———— Goods invoice value: £16,000 ——→ Subsidiary company ———— Goods invoice value: £20,000 ——→ Buying company

In this case £4,000 of the profit has been diverted to the subsidiary.

This technique could be used to direct profits to a company where they can be sheltered by losses brought forward, or even to an overseas company paying tax at a lower rate. This is a 'tax advantage' and there is **anti avoidance legislation** which **requires the profit to be computed as if the transactions had been carried out at arm's length and not at the prices actually used.** This is called a **transfer pricing adjustment**.

The transfer pricing rules apply to transactions between two persons if either:

(a)   One person directly or indirectly participates in the management, control or capital of the other; or

(b)   A third party directly or indirectly participates in the management, control or capital of both.

Where a **transfer pricing adjustment is required to the tax computation of a company subject to UK corporation tax** and **the other person to the transaction (who is disadvantaged) is within the charge to UK tax, a claim can be made to amend the tax computation of the disadvantaged person to arm's length basis,** in place of the actual price used. The claim must be made within two years from the date of the return which includes the transfer adjustment.

6.2 Exemption for small and medium sized enterprises

Small and medium-sized enterprises (SMEs) are normally exempt from the transfer pricing requirements.

The definition of SMEs for the purposes of the transfer pricing rules are that the number of staff must be less than, and either the turnover or the balance sheet total not more than, the limits in the table below:

	Staff	Turnover	Balance sheet
Small	50	€10m (about £9m)	€10m (about £9m)
Medium	250	€50m (about £44m)	€43m (about £38m)

The exemption does not apply to transactions with parties which are resident in a non-qualifying territory. This includes most foreign countries which do not have a double tax treaty with the UK, and certain other designated countries.

HMRC may direct that a medium sized enterprise should be brought within the scope of the legislation.

6.3 Transactions affected

The rules apply to all types of transactions. This includes not only the simple cases of sales of goods or provision of services, but also **loans**. A transfer pricing adjustment may be required if the loan would not have been made between the companies had there not been a relationship between them, or if a different amount would have been lent, or if the interest rate would have been different. Thus an adjustment to the interest charged in the accounts would be needed if the loan was sufficiently large that in an arm's length situation the lending company would have required equity, ie shares, instead of the loan. This situation is referred to as '**thin capitalisation**'.

6.4 Tax implications

Companies must self-assess their liability to tax under the transfer pricing rules and pay any corporation tax due. A statutory procedure exists for advance pricing arrangements (APAs) whereby a company can agree in advance that its transfer pricing policy is acceptable to HMRC ie not requiring a self-assessment adjustment. The APA facility is voluntary but companies may feel the need to use the facility as it provides necessary advance confirmation that their approach to transfer pricing in their self-assessment is acceptable.

7 Research and development (R&D)   9/15, 12/17, 6/18

FAST FORWARD

> Companies can claim a deduction for the actual amount of revenue and capital expenditure on research and development. SMEs can obtain 230% relief for qualifying research and development expenditure. There is an 'above the line' tax credit for large companies.

7.1 General rules

Research and development expenditure of a revenue nature may be deducted as allowable expenditure if it is related to the company's trade and the activity is undertaken by the company or on its behalf.

'Research and development' covers any activities that would be described as such under generally accepted accounting practice. It is related to the trade if it will lead to an extension of the trade or is directed towards the medical welfare of workers employed in the trade. The definition does not cover expenditure incurred on acquiring rights arising from research and development.

Expenditure of a capital nature on research and development related to the company's trade is also wholly allowable as a deduction ie 100% allowances are available. This covers capital expenditure on the provision of laboratories and research equipment. Note, however, that no allowance is available for expenditure on land. If any proceeds are received from the disposal of the capital assets, that receipt is taxable as trading income.

7.2 R&D relief: SMEs

A **small or medium sized enterprise** which incurs research and development expenditure of a specific nature may claim R&D tax relief.

The general definition of an SME for R&D purposes is the same as for the transfer pricing rules (see above). The definition of SME has also been extended to companies ('larger SMEs') with fewer than 500 employees, an annual turnover not exceeding €100 million and/or an annual balance sheet not exceeding €86 million. An SME must not be owned as to 25% or more by a non-SME.

Exam focus point

It will be stated whether or not a company is a SME for R&D purposes in examination questions.

Research and development expenditure which **qualifies for the relief** is revenue expenditure on:

(a)   **Staff costs**, ie salaries (but not benefits), pension contributions and employer's Class 1 NICs;

(b)   **Software and consumable items**, including fuel, power and water;

(c)   Subcontracted expenditure of the same nature; and

(d)   Expenditure on externally related workers. Unless the workers are provided by a connected company this is limited to 65% of the amounts paid in respect of these workers.

R&D relief for SMEs is given by allowing the company to claim 230% of the expenditure as a deduction instead of the actual cost.

7.3 R&D tax credits

A company qualifying for SME R&D relief may claim a tax credit if it has a surrenderable loss.

The surrenderable loss is the lower of:

(a)   **The company's unrelieved trading loss;** and
(b)   **230% of qualifying R&D expenditure.**

The unrelieved trading loss is defined as the **company's trading current period loss less any current period loss relief claim that could be made** (whether or not such a claim is actually made) **and any actual carry back claim and group relief claim** (see later in this text).

The credit is 14.5% (FY 2018) of the surrenderable loss. The tax credit will be paid to the company by HMRC or set against any corporation tax liability.

The **trading loss then carried forward** is reduced by the **amount of the loss surrendered**.

Question   R&D expenditure for small enterprise

Saturn Ltd is a small enterprise for the purposes of research and development. It was incorporated and started trading on 1 April 2018. During the year to 31 March 2019, it made a tax adjusted trading loss of £(100,000) before taking into account research and development expenditure of £30,000. It has no other income or gains.

Explain the tax deductions and/or credits available in the year ending 31 March 2019 in respect of the R&D expenditure and comment on any choices available to Saturn Ltd.

Answer

Since Saturn Ltd is a small enterprise for the purposes of research and development, the expenditure of £30,000 will result in a tax deduction of £30,000 × 230% = £69,000. This will result in an increase in the loss of £69,000 which it must carry forward against future profits of the same trade since it has no other income or gains in the current period (and has no previous accounting periods since this is its first accounting period).

Saturn Ltd can choose to claim tax credit of 14.5% of the lower of its surrenderable loss, which is the lower of the trading loss (£169,000) and £69,000, as an alternative to carrying the loss forward. This is therefore 14.5% × £69,000 = £10,005.

Saturn Ltd should consider claiming the 14.5% tax credit if cash flow is its main priority. Alternatively, if the company wishes to maximise the tax saved in respect of the expenditure, it should carry the loss forward. It will then save tax at 19% (provided it succeeds in becoming profitable).

7.4 R&D relief: Above the line (ATL) tax credit for large companies

An 'above the line' (ATL) tax credit for large company research and development (R&D) investment can be claimed.

The company must elect for the ATL tax credit within two years of the end of the accounting period

The credit is 12% (from 1 January 2018) of R&D expenditure. It is a taxable receipt but is also a credit against the company's corporation tax liability.

For **companies with no corporation tax liability**:

(a) The tax credit is **paid net of corporation tax**

(b) The amount of **tax credit it can receive is limited to the PAYE/NIC liabilities of the company's R&D staff**

Any amount above this PAYE/NIC cap is carried forward and treated as a tax credit of the following accounting period. Alternatively the company can claim to offset the excess against the corporation tax liabilities of other accounting periods or of other group companies.

Question	R&D expenditure for large companies

Innovative plc, a large company, spends £100,000 on qualifying R&D expenditure during the year to 31 March 2019. The company has taxable total profits of £2,135,000 before any deduction is taken for the R&D expenditure.

Calculate the company's corporation tax liability for the year to 31 March 2019.

Answer

	£
Taxable total profit before R&D expenditure	2,135,000
Add ATL credit £100,000 × 12%	12,000
Less R&D expenditure	(100,000)
Taxable total profit	2,047,000
Corporation tax £2,047,000 × 19%	388,930
Less ATL credit £100,000 × 12%	(12,000)
Corporation tax payable	376,930

Note. The tax saving using the ATL credit is as follows:

	£
Corporation tax on additional income £12,000 × 19%	2,280
Less ATL credit deducted from CT liability £100,000 × 12%	(12,000)
Corporation tax saving (9.72% of R&D expenditure)	9,720

8 Enhanced capital allowances (ECAs)

ECAs are available on energy-saving and water-saving plant and machinery. A company may surrender tax losses attributable to ECAs for a first year tax credit of 12.67% of the loss surrendered.

8.1 Availability of ECAs

As was described earlier in this text, expenditure on energy saving or water saving plant and machinery qualifies for enhanced capital allowances of 100%.

8.2 Surrender of ECAs

Companies are able to surrender tax losses attributable to ECAs for a cash payment called a first-year tax credit.

The first-year tax credit is the applicable percentage of the loss surrendered. The applicable percentage is two-thirds of the rate of corporation tax for the accounting period (or the average of rates for the period if more than one) **rounded up to the nearest second decimal place** (ie for financial year 2018 it is 19% × 2/3 = 12.67%).

The first-year tax credit is subject to an upper limit which is the greater of:

- The total of the company's PAYE and NICs liabilities for the period for which the loss is surrendered; or

- £250,000.

Where the loss could be used by the company against its taxable profits in the same period or surrendered as group relief, then it cannot be surrendered for a first-year tax credit. Any losses available to carry forward are reduced by the amount of the loss that has been surrendered.

The company must claim first-year tax credits in its corporation tax return for the relevant accounting period.

There will be a claw-back of the relief if the ECA qualifying plant and machinery is sold within four years after the end of the period for which the tax credit was paid. If this happens, the surrendered loss will become available for relief again.

Chapter roundup

- Companies pay corporation tax on their taxable total profits of each accounting period.

- An accounting period cannot exceed 12 months in length. A long period of account must be split into 2 accounting periods, the first of which is 12 months long.

- Tax rates are set for financial years.

- There is a single rate of corporation tax which is applied to a company's taxable total profits to compute the corporation tax liability.

- Taxable total profits are the total profits (income and gains) less some losses and qualifying charitable donations.

- A loan relationship arises when a company lends or borrows money. Trading loan relationships are dealt with as trading income. Non-trading loan relationships are dealt with as interest income.

- Gains/losses arising on most intangible fixed assets are recognised for tax purposes on the same basis as they are recognised in the accounts.

- No debits (amortisation or impairment) on goodwill are allowable for tax purposes except on disposal. On a disposal of goodwill, a credit is taxable as trading income but a debit is a non-trading debit.

- The transfer pricing legislation prevents manipulation of profits between members of a group which can occur when a company chooses to buy and sell goods at a price which is not a market price.

- Companies can claim a deduction for the actual amount of revenue and capital expenditure on research and development. SMEs can obtain 230% relief for qualifying research and development expenditure. There is an 'above the line' tax credit for large companies.

- ECAs are available on energy-saving and water-saving plant and machinery. A company may surrender tax losses attributable to ECAs for a first year tax credit of 12.67% of the loss surrendered.

Quick quiz

1   When does an accounting period end?

2   How are trading profits (before capital allowances) of a long period of account divided between accounting periods?

3   Does a company pay loan stock interest to another UK company gross or net of tax?

4   How is interest arising on a non-trading loan relationship taxed?

5   What steps can be taken against the use of artificial transfer prices?

6   A small or medium sized company can claim ....% relief for qualifying research and development expenditure. Fill in the blank.

7   X plc spends £100,000 on energy saving plant and machinery in the year to 31 March 2019. X plc has a trading loss of £500,000 for the year including the enhanced capital allowance on the energy saving plant and machinery. What first year tax credit can it claim?

Study guide

		Intellectual level
4	**Corporation tax liabilities in situations involving further overseas and group aspects and in relation to special types of company, and the application of additional exemptions and reliefs**	
(a)	The contents of the Taxation - United Kingdom (TX – UK) study guide, for corporation tax, under heading:	2
•	E3 Chargeable gains for companies	
(f)	The use of exemptions and reliefs in deferring and minimising corporation tax liabilities:	3
(i)	Determine the application of the substantial shareholdings exemption	

Exam guide

You may well be asked to compute chargeable gains or losses for a company as part of a tax planning question so you must know the rules in this chapter very well.

> **Knowledge brought forward from earlier studies**

This chapter mainly revises topics you should be familiar with from Taxation (TX – UK). The technical change for Advanced Taxation (ATX – UK) exams in Financial Year 2018 from the material studied for Taxation (TX – UK) for exams in Financial Year 2017 is that the indexation allowance has been frozen at December 2017 and that you will be given indexation factors where relevant in a question rather than having to compute them from RPIs.

The new topic is the substantial shareholdings exemption which has often been examined in Advanced Taxation (ATX – UK).

1 Corporation tax on chargeable gains

> **FAST FORWARD**
>
> Chargeable gains for companies are computed in broadly the same way as for individuals, but indexation allowance applies and there is no annual exempt amount.

> **PER alert**
>
> One of the competencies you require to fulfil Performance Objective 15 Tax computations and assessments of the PER is to prepare or contribute to the computation or assessment of tax computations for single companies, groups or other entities. You can apply the knowledge you obtain from this section of the text to help to demonstrate this competence.

Companies do not pay capital gains tax. Instead their chargeable gains are included in taxable total profits.

A company's capital gains or allowable losses are computed in a similar way to individuals but with a few major differences:

- There is relief for inflation called the **indexation allowance** (but which is frozen at December 2017)
- **No annual exempt amount** is available
- **Different matching rules for shares** apply if the shareholder is a company.

1   An accounting period ends on the earliest of:

    (a)   12 months after its start
    (b)   The end of the company's period of account
    (c)   The company starting or ceasing to trade
    (d)   The company entering/ceasing to be in administration
    (e)   The commencement of the company's winding up
    (f)   The company ceasing to be resident in the UK
    (g)   The company ceasing to be liable to corporation tax

2   Trading income (before capital allowances) is apportioned on a time basis.

3   Gross

4   Interest on a non-trading loan relationship is aggregated with all other income and gains from non-trading loans. From this is deducted interest paid on and losses on non-trading loans. The resulting net amount is taxed as interest income.

5   Although a company may buy and sell goods at any price it wishes, the transfer pricing anti-avoidance legislation requires profit to be computed as if the transactions had been carried out at arm's length, in certain circumstances.

6   A small or medium sized company can claim **230%** relief for qualifying research and development expenditure.

7   £100,000 × 100% × 12.67% = £12,670 (less than upper limit of £250,000)

> Now try the question below from the Practice Question Bank

Number	Level	Marks	Time
Q21	Introductory	15	29 mins

Chargeable gains for companies

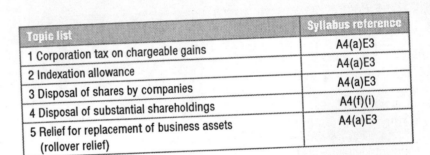

Topic list	Syllabus reference
1 Corporation tax on chargeable gains	A4(a)E3
2 Indexation allowance	A4(a)E3
3 Disposal of shares by companies	A4(a)E3
4 Disposal of substantial shareholdings	A4(f)(i)
5 Relief for replacement of business assets (rollover relief)	A4(a)E3

Introduction

We studied chargeable gains for individuals earlier in this text. In this chapter, we will consider the treatment of chargeable gains for companies.

Companies pay corporation tax on their chargeable gains, rather than capital gains tax. The computation of gains for companies is slightly more complicated than for individuals because companies are entitled to indexation allowance.

We also consider the matching rules for companies which dispose of shares in other companies. Again, these rules are slightly more complicated than for individuals. We also consider the relief for substantial shareholdings.

Finally, we look at how the relief for replacement of business assets applies to companies.

In the next chapter, we look at the administration of corporation tax.

A non-UK resident company which disposes of a residential property may be liable to UK tax on the gain in a similar way to a non-UK individual. However, the disposal by a company of a residential property is **excluded** from the Advanced Taxation (ATX – UK) syllabus.

2 Indexation allowance

9/15

FAST FORWARD

The indexation allowance gives relief for the inflation element of a gain but is frozen at December 2017.

The purpose of having an indexation allowance is to remove the inflation element of a gain from taxation. However, the indexation allowance is frozen at December 2017 so that the inflation element of a gain beyond that date will be taxable.

Companies are entitled to indexation allowance on an asset from the date of its acquisition until the earlier of the date of disposal of the asset and December 2017. It is based on the movement in the Retail Price Index (RPI) between those two dates.

For example, if Jones Ltd bought a painting on 2 January 2005 and sold it on 19 November 2018, the indexation allowance is available from January 2005 until December 2017 (the earlier of December 2017 and November 2018).

If an asset is acquired on or after 1 January 2018 there will be no indexation allowance on the disposal of the asset.

Exam formula

The indexation factor is:

$$\frac{\text{RPI for month of disposal / December 2017} - \text{RPI for month of acquisition}}{\text{RPI for month of acquisition}}$$

The calculation is expressed as a decimal and is rounded to three decimal places.

Exam focus point

The examining team will always give the indexation factor in the question. You will not have to calculate the indexation factor using RPIs.

Indexation allowance is available on the allowable cost of the asset from the date of acquisition (including incidental costs of acquisition). It is also available on enhancement expenditure from the month in which such expenditure becomes due and payable (for expenditure before January 2018). Indexation allowance is not available on the costs of disposal.

Question

The indexation allowance

An asset is acquired by Lenny Ltd on 15 February 2003 at a cost of £5,000. Enhancement expenditure of £2,000 is incurred on 10 April 2004 and further enhancement expenditure of £4,000 is incurred on 18 May 2018. The asset is sold for £30,500 on 20 August 2018. Incidental costs of sale are £500. The indexation factor between February 2003 and December 2017 is 0.551 and between April 2004 and December 2017 is 0.498. Calculate the chargeable gain arising.

Answer

The indexation allowance is computed as follows:

	£
0.551 × £5,000	2,755
0.498 × £2,000	996
Indexation allowance	3,751

There is no indexation on the enhancement in May 2018 since it is incurred after December 2017.

The computation of the chargeable gain is as follows:

	£
Proceeds	30,500
Less incidental costs of sale	(500)
Net proceeds	30,000
Less allowable costs £(5,000 + 2,000 + 4,000)	(11,000)
Unindexed gain	19,000
Less indexation allowance (see above)	(3,751)
Indexed gain	15,249

Exam focus point

> In an exam question you may be **given the indexation factor to the date of disposal** (if later than December 2017) **as well as the indexation factor to December 2017. This is to test that you know the rule that indexation is frozen to December 2017. Make sure you use the factor to December 2017!**

Indexation allowance cannot create or increase an allowable loss. If there is a gain before the indexation allowance, the allowance can reduce that gain to zero but no further. If there is a loss before the indexation allowance, there is no indexation allowance.

If the indexation allowance calculation gives a negative figure, treat the indexation as nil: do not add to the indexed gain.

3 Disposal of shares by companies   12/13

FAST FORWARD

> There are special rules for matching shares sold by a company with shares purchased. Disposals are matched with acquisitions on the same day, the previous nine days and the FA 1985 share pool.

3.1 The matching rules

We have discussed the share matching rules for individuals earlier in this text. We also need special rules for companies.

For companies the matching of shares sold is in the following order:

(a)   Shares acquired on the **same day**

(b)   Shares acquired in the **previous nine days**, if more than one acquisition on a 'first in, first out' (FIFO) basis

(c)   Shares from the **FA 1985 pool**

The composition of the FA 1985 pool in relation to companies which are shareholders is explained below.

Exam focus point

> Learn the 'matching rules' because a crucial first step to getting a shares question right is to correctly match the shares sold to the original shares purchased.

3.2 Example: share matching rules for companies

Nor Ltd acquired the following shares in Last plc:

Date of acquisition	No of shares
9.11.02	15,000
15.12.04	15,000
11.7.18	5,000
15.7.18	5,000

Nor Ltd disposed of 20,000 of the shares on 15 July 2018.

We match the shares as follows:

(a)   Acquisition on same day: 5,000 shares acquired 15 July 2018.

(b)   Acquisitions in previous 9 days: 5,000 shares acquired 11 July 2018.

(c)   FA 1985 share pool: 10,000 shares out of 30,000 shares in FA 1985 share pool (9.11.02 and 15.12.04).

3.3 The FA 1985 share pool

Exam focus point

> The examining team has stated that a detailed question will not be set on the pooling provisions. However, work through the examples below as you are expected to understand how the pool works.

The FA 1985 pool comprises the following shares of the same class in the same company.

- **Shares held by a company on 1 April 1985 and acquired by that company on or after 1 April 1982.**

- **Shares acquired by that company on or after 1 April 1985.**

We must keep track of:

(a)   The **number** of shares
(b)   The **cost** of the shares ignoring indexation
(c)   The **indexed cost** of the shares

The first step in constructing the FA 1985 share pool is to calculate the value of the pool at 1 April 1985 by indexing the cost of each acquisition before that date up to April 1985.

3.4 Example: the FA 1985 share pool

Oliver Ltd bought 1,000 shares in Judith plc for £2,750 in August 1984 and another 1,000 for £3,250 in December 1984. The indexation factor from August 1984 to April 1985 is 0.055 and from December 1984 to April 1985 is 0.043. The FA 1985 pool at 1 April 1985 is as follows:

	No of shares	Cost £	Indexed Cost £
August 1984 (a)	1,000	2,750	2,750
December 1984 (b)	1,000	3,250	3,250
	2,000	6,000	6,000
Indexation allowance			
0.055 × £2,750			151
0.043 × £3,250			140
Indexed cost of the pool at 1 April 1985			6,291

Disposals and acquisitions of shares which affect the indexed value of the FA 1985 pool are termed **'operative events'. Prior to reflecting each such operative event within the FA 1985 share pool, a further indexation allowance (an 'indexed rise') must be computed from the date of the last such operative event** (or from the later of the first acquisition and April 1985 if the operative event in question is the first one) **up to the earlier of the date of the operative event concerned and December 2017.** If the last operative event was in December 2017 or later, no further indexed rises will be calculated.

Exam focus point

> Legislation provides that **indexation calculations within the FA 1985 pool** (after its April 1985 value has been calculated) **are not rounded to three decimal places.** However, the examining team has stated that **for the purposes of the Advanced Taxation (ATX – UK) exam you should use the indexation factor(s) rounded to three decimal places provided in the question to compute indexed rises within the share pool.**

Following on from the above example, assume that Oliver Ltd acquired 2,000 more shares on 10 July 1986 at a cost of £4,000. Recalculate the value of the FA 1985 pool on 10 July 1986 following the acquisition. The indexation factor from April 1985 to July 1986 is 0.028.

Answer

	No of shares	Cost £	Indexed cost £
Value at 1.4.85 b/f	2,000	6,000	6,291
Indexed rise 0.028 × £6,291			176
	2,000	6,000	6,467
Acquisition	2,000	4,000	4,000
Value at 10.7.86	4,000	10,000	10,467

In the case of a disposal, following the calculation of the indexed rise to earlier of the date of disposal and December 2017, the cost and the indexed cost attributable to the shares disposed of are deducted from the amounts within the FA 1985 pool. The proportions of the cost and indexed cost to take out of the pool should be computed by using the proportion that the shares disposed of bear to the total number of shares held.

The indexation allowance is the indexed cost taken out of the pool minus the cost taken out. As usual, the indexation allowance cannot create or increase a loss.

Continuing the above exercise, suppose that Oliver Ltd sold 3,000 shares on 10 July 2018 for £24,500. Compute the gain, and the value of the FA 1985 pool following the disposal. The indexation factor from July 1986 to December 2017 is 1.852 and from July 1986 to July 2018 is 1.887.

Answer

	No of shares	Cost £	Indexed cost £
Value at 10.7.86	4,000	10,000	10,467
Indexed rise to 12.17			
1.852 × £10,467			19,385
	4,000	10,000	29,852
Disposal	(3,000)		
Cost and indexed cost $\frac{3,000}{4,000}$ × £10,000 and £29,852		(7,500)	(22,389)
Value at 10.7.18	1,000	2,500	7,463

Did you remember to use the indexation factor to December 2017?

The gain is computed as follows:

	£
Proceeds	24,500
Less cost	(7,500)
Unindexed gain	17,000
Less indexation allowance £(22,389 – 7,500)	(14,889)
Indexed gain	2,111

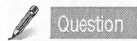
Continuing the above exercise, suppose that Oliver Ltd sold 200 shares on 18 November 2018 for £1,800. Compute the gain, and the value of the FA 1985 pool following the disposal.

Answer

	No of shares	Cost £	Indexed cost £
Value at 10.7.18	1,000	2,500	7,463
Disposal	(200)		
Cost and indexed cost $\frac{200}{1,000}$ × £2,500 and £7,463		(500)	(1,493)
Value at 18.11.18	800	2,000	5,970

The gain is computed as follows:

	£
Proceeds	1,800
Less cost	(500)
Unindexed gain	1,300
Less indexation allowance £(1,493 – 500)	(993)
Indexed gain	307

3.5 Bonus and rights issues

When **bonus issue shares are issued**, all that happens is that **the size of the original holding is increased**. Since bonus issue shares are issued at no cost there is **no need to adjust the original cost** and there is **no operative event for the FA 1985 pool** (so no indexation allowance needs to be calculated).

When **rights issue shares are issued**, the **size of the original holding is increased** in the same way as for a bonus issue. So if the original shareholding was part of the FA 1985 pool, the rights issue shares are added to that pool. This might be important for the matching rules if a shareholding containing the rights issue shares is sold shortly after the rights issue.

However, in the case of a rights issue, the **new shares are paid for and this results in an adjustment to the original cost**. For the purpose of **calculating the indexation allowance, expenditure on a rights issue is taken as being incurred on the date of the issue** and not the date of the original holding.

3.6 Example: bonus and rights issue

Star Ltd bought 10,000 shares in Turn plc in May 2000 at a cost of £45,000. There was a 2 for 1 bonus issue in October 2002. There was a 1 for 3 rights issue in June 2006 at a cost of £4 per share. Star Ltd took up all of its rights entitlement. Star Ltd sold 20,000 shares in Turn plc for £120,000 in January 2019.

Indexation factors:

May 2000 – October 2002 = 0.042
October 2002 – June 2006 = 0.116
May 2000 – June 2006 = 0.163
June 2006 – December 2017 = 0.401

FA 1985 share pool

		No of shares	Cost £	Indexed cost £
5.00	Acquisition	10,000	45,000	45,000
10.02	Bonus 2:1	20,000		
		30,000		
6.06	Indexed rise			
	0.163 × £45,000			7,335
	Rights 1:3	10,000	40,000	40,000
		40,000	85,000	92,335
1.19	Index rise to 12.17			
	0.401 × £92,335			37,026
				129,361
	Disposal	(20,000)	(42,500)	(64,681)
c/f		20,000	42,500	64,680

The gain is:

	£
Proceeds	120,000
Less cost	(42,500)
Unindexed gain	77,500
Less indexation allowance (£64,681 − 42,500)	(22,181)
Indexed gain	55,319

3.7 Re-organisations and takeovers

The rules on re-organisation and takeovers apply in a similar way for company shareholders as they do for individuals.

In the case of a **re-organisation, the new shares or securities take the place of the original shares. The original cost and the indexed cost of the original shares is apportioned between the different types of capital issued on the re-organisation.**

Where there is a takeover of shares which qualifies for the 'paper for paper' treatment, the cost and indexed cost of the original holding is passed onto the new holding which take the place of the original holding.

Question — Takeover

Jojoba Ltd acquired 20,000 shares in Grape Ltd in August 1990 at a cost of £40,000. It acquired a further 5,000 shares in December 2006 at a cost of £30,000.

In September 2017, Grape Ltd was taken over by Kiwi plc and Jojoba Ltd received one ordinary share and two preference shares in K plc for each one share held in Grape Ltd. Immediately following the takeover, the ordinary shares in Kiwi plc were worth £4 per share and the preference shares in Kiwi plc were worth £1 per share.

The indexation factor from August 1990 to December 2006 is 0.582, from December 2006 to December 2017 is 0.372, from December 2006 to September 2017 is 0.357 and from September 2017 to December 2017 is 0.011.

(a) Show Jojoba Ltd's cost and indexed cost of the ordinary shares and the preference shares in Kiwi plc.

(b) Calculate the gain arising if Jojoba Ltd sells 10,000 of its ordinary shares in Kiwi plc for £45,000 in February 2019.

(a)   *Grape Ltd FA 1985 share pool*

		No. of shares	Cost £	Indexed cost £
8.90	Acquisition	20,000	40,000	40,000
12.06	Indexed rise			
	0.582 × £40,000			23,280
	Acquisition	5,000	30,000	30,000
Pool at takeover		25,000	70,000	93,280

Note that the takeover is not an operative event because the pool of cost is not increased or decreased and so it is not necessary to calculate an indexed rise.

Apportionment of cost/indexed cost to Kiwi plc shares

	No. of shares	MV £	Cost £	Indexed cost £
Ords × 1	25,000	100,000	46,667	62,187
Prefs × 2	50,000	50,000	23,333	31,093
Totals		150,000	70,000	93,280

(b)   *Kiwi plc ordinary shares FA 1985 share pool*

		No. of shares	Cost £	Indexed cost £
12.06	Acquisition (deemed)	25,000	46,667	62,187
2.19	Indexed rise to 12.17			
	0.372 × £62,187			23,134
				85,321
	Disposal	(10,000)	(18,667)	(34,128)
		15,000	28,000	51,193

Note that the indexation allowance on the ordinary shares is calculated from December 2006, not from the date of the takeover.

The gain is:

	£
Proceeds	45,000
Less cost	(18,667)
Unindexed gain	26,333
Less indexation allowance £(34,128 – 18,667)	(15,461)
Indexed gain	10,872

4 Disposal of substantial shareholdings

6/14, 6/15, 9/15, 6/16, 6/17, 12/17

4.1 Principles

FAST FORWARD

Where a company owns shares in a trading company, there is an exemption on disposal if 10% or more of the shares are held.

One of the competencies you require to fulfil Performance Objective 17 Tax planning and advice of the PER is to mitigate and/or defer tax liabilities through the use of standard reliefs, exemptions and incentives. You can apply the knowledge you obtain from this section of the text to help to demonstrate this competence.

There is an exemption from corporation tax for any gain arising when a **company disposes of the whole or any part of a substantial shareholding in a trading company** (or in the holding company of a trading group or sub-group). Usually it is **not necessary for the company to continue to be a trading company** after the disposal.

Exam focus point

There are special rules which apply for institutional investors. These rules are **not examinable** in Advanced Taxation (ATX – UK).

Key term

A **substantial shareholding** is one where the investing company holds at least 10% of ordinary share capital and is beneficially entitled to at least 10% of the

(a)   profits available for distribution to equity holders, and
(b)   assets of the company available for distribution to equity holders on a winding up.

To meet the 10% test shares owned by members of a chargeable gains group (see later in this text) may be amalgamated. **The 10% test must have been met for a continuous 12 month period during the six years preceding the disposal.**

The 12 month period condition can also be satisfied by including a period during which assets, which are being used in its trade by the company whose shares are being disposed of (Company A), were being used in the trade of another group company (Company B) and then transferred to Company A before the sale of the Company A shares. This enables the exemption to apply in the situation where an existing trade carried on by one group company is transferred to a new group company before that new company is sold outside the group. This may be preferred to selling the original company carrying on the trade, for example if it also has contingent liabilities.

The exemption is given automatically and cannot be disclaimed. This means that as well as exempting gains, it denies relief for losses.

The exemption applies to the disposal of part of a substantial holding. This means that if A Ltd owns 10% of the ordinary share capital in B Ltd, and disposes of 1% of that share capital, any gain will be exempt. In addition, the disposal of the remaining 9% may result in an exempt gain.

4.2 Example: disposal of substantial shareholding

On 1 December 2012 SD Ltd bought 20% of the shares in AM Ltd. The shareholding qualifies for the substantial shareholding exemption. During its accounting period to 31 March 2019, SD Ltd made the following disposals:

(a)   On 30 June 2018 it disposed of a 15% holding in AM Ltd.
(b)   On 30 December 2018 it disposed of the remaining 5% holding in AM Ltd.

Both of these shareholdings qualify for the substantial shareholdings exemption. Clearly the first disposal is of at least a 10% holding which was held for 12 months prior to disposal. The second disposal also qualifies despite being only a 5% holding, because SD Ltd owned a 10% holding throughout a 12 month period in the six years prior to this second disposal.

The substantial shareholding exemption was tested in the September 2015 examination in Question 3(b) Cinnabar Ltd. The examining team commented that: 'In any question regarding the sale of shares in one company by another, candidates should automatically consider the application of the substantial shareholding exemption (SSE). This is an area where it is very important to know the precise conditions, to be able to state definitively whether or not the exemption applies, and the reasons why, or why not. In this case the timing of the disposal was critical; bringing the date of disposal forward would mean that the requirement to hold at least 10% of the shares for a continuous 12 month period in the [six] years prior to sale would be satisfied, whereas this would not be the case if the disposal was delayed. An ability to advise on the timing of transactions in respect of all taxes is an important skill at Advanced Taxation (ATX – UK).'

5 Relief for replacement of business assets (rollover relief)
6/15, 9/16, 12/17

FAST FORWARD

Relief for replacement of business assets is available to companies to defer gains arising on the disposal of business assets.

5.1 Conditions for relief

As for individuals, a gain may be rolled over by a company where the proceeds on the disposal of a business asset are spent on a replacement business asset under rollover relief.

A claim for the relief must be made by the later of four years of the end of the accounting period in which the disposal of the old asset takes place and four years of the end of the accounting period in which the new asset is acquired. For example, if a disposal is made by a company in its accounting period to 30 June 2018 and a claim for roll-over relief is made in respect of a new asset acquired in the accounting period to 30 June 2019 the time limit for a claim is 30 June 2023 (four years after the end of the accounting period in which the disposal of the old asset was made).

The conditions for the relief to apply to company disposals are:

(a)   The old assets sold and the new asset bought are both used only in the trade of the company (apportionment into business and non-business parts available for buildings).

(b)   The old asset and the new asset both fall within one (but not necessarily the same one) of the following classes:

(i)   **Land and buildings** (including parts of buildings) occupied as well as used only for the purposes of the trade

(ii)   **Fixed plant and machinery**

(c)   Reinvestment of the proceeds received on the disposal of the old asset takes place in a period beginning one year before and ending three years after the date of the disposal.

(d)   The new asset is brought into use in the trade on its acquisition.

Note that goodwill is not a qualifying asset for the purposes of corporation tax.

5.2 Operation of relief

Deferral is obtained by deducting the indexed gain from the cost of the new asset. For full relief, the whole of the proceeds must be reinvested. If only part is reinvested, a gain equal to the amount not invested, or the full gain, if lower, will be chargeable to tax immediately.

The new asset will have a base cost for chargeable gains purposes of its purchase price less the gain rollover over.

Question

Dream Ltd acquired a factory in April 2000 at a cost of £120,000. It used the factory in its trade throughout the period of its ownership.

In August 2018, Dream Ltd sold the factory for £250,000. The indexation factor between April 2000 and December 2017 is 0.635. In November 2018, it acquired another factory at a cost of £220,000.

Calculate the gain chargeable on the sale of the first factory and the base cost of the second factory.

Answer

Chargeable gain on sale of first factory

	£
Proceeds	250,000
Less cost	(120,000)
Unindexed gain	130,000
0.635 × £120,000	(76,200)
Indexed gain	53,800
Less rollover relief (balancing figure)	(23,800)
Chargeable gain: amount not reinvested £(250,000 – 220,000)	30,000

Base cost of second factory

	£
Cost of second factory	220,000
Less rolled over gain	(23,800)
Base cost	196,200

5.3 Depreciating assets   12/15

The relief for investment into depreciating assets works in the same way for companies as it does for individuals.

The indexed gain is calculated on the old asset and is deferred until the gain crystallises on the earliest of:

(a) The disposal of the replacement asset
(b) The date the replacement asset ceases to be used in the trade
(c) Ten years after the acquisition of the replacement asset.

5.4 Intangible fixed assets

 FAST FORWARD

There is a similar replacement of business assets relief for replacement of intangible fixed assets. However, relief is restricted to the gain based on original cost, not on the written down cost.

As we have seen earlier in this text, **gains on the disposal of intangible fixed assets are taxable as trading income rather than as chargeable gains.** However, there is a form of **relief for replacement of intangible business assets for companies which is very similar to that for chargeable gains** and so it is convenient to consider it in this section.

A profit on the disposal of an intangible fixed asset can be rolled over by the acquisition of a replacement asset within the period beginning one year before and ending three years after the date of the disposal. Relief is given by rolling over the gain into the base cost of the replacement asset.

The maximum profit which can be rolled over is the profit comparing proceeds with original cost, not with the written down cost. Therefore, if the intangible fixed asset has been written down, the gain relating to the amount written down will be chargeable as trading income.

If the expenditure on the new intangible fixed asset equals or exceeds the proceeds of the old intangible fixed asset, then relief is available to roll over the whole of the gain based on the original cost.

If expenditure on the new intangible fixed asset is less than the proceeds of the old intangible fixed asset, the relief is restricted to the excess of the amount invested in the new intangible fixed asset over the original cost of the old asset.

Question   Intangible fixed assets

In August 2018, Turnbull Ltd disposed of patents acquired in 2015 for use in its trade. The patents had cost £150,000 but had been written down to £110,000 by the date of sale. The sale realised £200,000 and the company acquired further patents two months later. Calculate how much of the profit could be rolled over, any amount remaining taxable as trading income and the base cost of the new asset, if the new patents were acquired for (a) £280,000, or (b) £180,000.

Answer

(a)   **New investment £280,000 (ie all proceeds invested in new asset)**

Accounting profit on old patents £200,000 – £110,000	£90,000
Profit for potential rollover £200,000 – £150,000	£50,000
Profit which cannot be rolled over taxable as trading income £90,000 – £50,000	£40,000
Base cost of replacement asset (new patents) £280,000 – £50,000	£230,000

(b)   **New investment £180,000 (ie partial investment in new asset)**

Accounting profit (as above)	£90,000
Profit for potential rollover £180,000 – £150,000	£30,000
Profit which cannot be rolled over taxable as trading income £90,000 – £30,000	£60,000
Base cost of replacement new asset £180,000 – £30,000	£150,000

Chapter roundup

- Chargeable gains for companies are computed in broadly the same way as for individuals, but indexation allowance applies and there is no annual exempt amount.

- The indexation allowance gives relief for the inflation element of a gain but is frozen at December 2017.

- There are special rules for matching shares sold by a company with shares purchased. Disposals are matched with acquisitions on the same day, the previous nine days and the FA 1985 share pool.

- Where a company owns shares in a trading company, there is an exemption on disposal if 10% or more of the shares are held.

- Relief for replacement of business assets is available to companies to defer gains arising on the disposal of business assets.

- There is a similar replacement of business assets relief for intangible fixed assets. However, relief is restricted to the gain based on original cost, not on the written down cost.

Quick quiz

1   A company is entitled to an annual exempt amount against its chargeable gains. TRUE/FALSE?

2   Indexation allowance runs from the date of __ to the earlier of the date of __ and __. Fill in the blanks.

3   What are the share matching rules for company shareholders?

4   Axel Ltd, a trading company, has a long standing 15% shareholding in Bearing Ltd, an investment company. Does the substantial shareholding exemption apply on a disposal of an 8% holding by Axel Ltd?

5   Horace Ltd sells a warehouse for £400,000. The warehouse cost £220,000 and the indexation allowance available is £40,000. The company acquires another warehouse ten months later for £375,000. What is the amount of rollover relief?

Answers to quick quiz

1   FALSE. A company is not entitled to an annual exempt amount against its chargeable gains.

2   Indexation allowance runs from the date of acquisition to the earlier of the date of disposal and December 2017.

3   The matching rules for shares disposed of by a company shareholder are:

   (a)   Shares acquired on the same day
   (b)   Shares acquired in the previous nine days
   (c)   Shares from the FA 1985 pool

4   No. Bearing Ltd is an investment company, not a trading company.

5   The gain on the sale of first warehouse is:

	£
Proceeds	400,000
Less cost	(220,000)
Unindexed gain	180,000
Less indexation allowance	(40,000)
Indexed gain	140,000
Less rollover relief (balancing figure)	(115,000)
Chargeable gain: amount not reinvested £(400,000 – 375,000)	25,000

Now try the question below from the Practice Question Bank

Number	Level	Marks	Time
Q22	Introductory	10	20 mins

Corporation tax administration

22

Topic list	Syllabus reference
1 Returns, records, compliance checks, assessments and claims	A6(b)A3-5
2 Payment of corporation tax and interest	A6(b)A4, A6

Introduction

In this chapter, we look at the administration of corporation tax, including payment of corporation tax in instalments.

In the next chapter, we will consider the rules for winding up companies and for companies purchasing their own shares.

Study guide

		Intellectual level
6	**Value added tax, tax administration and the UK tax system**	
(b)	The contents of the Taxation - United Kingdom (TX – UK) study guide for the UK tax system and its administration under headings:	2
•	A3 The systems for self assessment and the making of returns	
•	A4 The time limits for the submission of information, claims and payment of tax, including payments on account	
•	A5 The procedures relating to compliance checks, appeals and disputes	
•	A6 Penalties for non-compliance	

Exam guide

You must know the rules regarding administration as the company's obligations could form a part of any question.

Knowledge brought forward from earlier studies

This chapter revises the rules for corporation tax administration. The main technical change for Advanced Taxation (ATX – UK) exams in Financial Year 2018 from the material studied for Taxation (TX – UK) for exams in Financial Year 2017 is the increase in the rate of interest on underpaid tax from 2.75% to 3.00%.

1 Returns, records, compliance checks, assessments and claims

1.1 Notification to HMRC

FAST FORWARD A company must notify HMRC within three months of starting to trade.

A company must notify HMRC of the beginning of its first accounting period (ie usually when it starts to trade) and the beginning of any subsequent period that does not immediately follow the end of a previous accounting period. The notice must be in the prescribed form and submitted within three months of the relevant date.

A company which is chargeable to tax for an accounting period and has not received a notice to file a tax return must give notice of chargeability within 12 months of the end of the accounting period. The common penalty regime for failing to notify applies (see earlier in this text).

1.2 Returns   12/14, 12/17

 One of the competencies you require to fulfil Performance Objective 16 Tax compliance and verification of the PER is to verify and question client submissions and ensure timely submission of all relevant information to the tax authorities by the due date. You can apply the knowledge you obtain from this section of the text to help to demonstrate this competence.

FAST FORWARD Corporation tax returns must usually be filed within 12 months of the end of an accounting period.

A company's tax return must be filed electronically and must include a self assessment of any tax payable. Limited companies are also required to file electronically a copy of their accounts. The filing of accounts must be done in inLine eXtensible Business Reporting Language (iXBRL).

iXBRL is a standard for reporting business information in an electronic form which uses tags which can be read by computers. HMRC supplies software which can be used by small companies with simple accounts. This software automatically produces accounts and tax computations in the correct format. Other companies can use:

(a)   other software that automatically produces iXBRL accounts and computations; or

(b)   a tagging service which will apply the appropriate tags to accounts and computations; or

(c)   software that enables the appropriate tags to be added to accounts and computations.

The tags used are contained in dictionaries known as taxonomies, with different taxonomies for different purposes. The tagging of tax computations is based on the corporation tax computational taxonomy, which includes over 1,200 relevant tags.

An obligation to file a return arises only when the company receives a notice requiring a return. A return is required for each accounting period ending during or at the end of the period specified in the notice requiring a return. A company also has to file a return for certain other periods which are not accounting periods (eg for a period when the company is dormant).

A company that does not receive a notice requiring a return must, if it is chargeable to tax, notify HMRC within twelve months of the end of the accounting period. Failure to do so results in a maximum penalty equal to the tax unpaid 12 months after the end of the accounting period. Tax for this purpose includes corporation tax and notional tax on loans to participators of close companies (see later in this text).

A notice to file a return may also require other information, accounts and reports. For a UK resident company the requirement to deliver accounts normally extends only to the accounts required under the Companies Act.

A return is due on or before the filing date. This is the later of:

(a)   **12 months after the end of the period to which the return relates**

(b)   **If the relevant period of account is not more than 18 months long, 12 months from the end of the period of account**

(c)   **If the relevant period of account is more than 18 months long, 30 months from the start of the period of account**

(d)   **Three months from the date on which the notice requiring the return was made.**

The relevant period of account is that in which the accounting period to which the return relates ends.

Question

Filing date

Ark Ltd prepares accounts for the 18 months to 30 June 2018. A notice requiring a return for the period ended 30 June 2018 was issued to Ark Ltd on 1 September 2018. State the periods for which Ark Ltd must file a tax return and the filing dates.

Answer

The company must file a return for the two accounting periods ending in the period specified in the notice requiring a return. The first accounting period is the 12 months to 31 December 2017 and the second is the six months to 30 June 2018. The filing date is 12 months after the end of the relevant period of account, 30 June 2019.

One of the competencies you require to fulfil Performance Objective 16 Tax compliance and verification of the PER is to explain tax filing and payment requirements and the consequences of non-compliance to clients. You can apply the knowledge you obtain from this section of the text to help to demonstrate this competence.

There is a £100 penalty for a failure to submit a return on time, rising to £200 if the delay exceeds three months. These penalties become £500 and £1,000 respectively when a return was late (or never submitted) for each of the preceding two accounting periods.

An additional tax geared penalty is applied if a return is more than six months late. The penalty is 10% of the tax unpaid six months after the return was due if the total delay is up to 12 months, and 20% of that tax if the return is over 12 months late.

The common penalty regime for making errors in tax returns discussed earlier in this text in relation to individuals also applies to companies.

HMRC may amend a return to correct obvious errors, or anything else that an officer has reason to believe is incorrect in the light of information available, within nine months of the day the return was filed, or if the correction is to an amended return, within nine months of the filing of an amendment. The company may amend its return so as to reject the correction. If the time limit for amendments has expired, the company may reject the correction by giving notice within three months.

Exam focus point

Sample question September/December 2017 question 3(b) Damiana tested filing dates for a long period of account and penalties for late filing. The examining team commented that 'Surprisingly, this was not done at all well. Most candidates recognised that the long period would be split into two accounting periods for tax purposes, but fewer were able to state the correct split of the long period. Fewer still correctly identified the filing dates, with the most common error being to state the payment dates instead. The implications for a company in respect of late filing of returns elicited a number of answers stating that 'penalties will arise' but candidates must be precise as to the nature and amounts of such penalties in order to gain marks in this type of question.'

1.3 Records

Companies must keep records until the latest of:

(a) Six years from the end of the accounting period
(b) The date any compliance checks are completed
(c) The date after which compliance checks may not be commenced.

All business records and accounts, including contracts and receipts, must be kept, or information showing that the company has prepared a complete and correct tax return.

If a return is demanded more than six years after the end of the accounting period, any records which the company still has must be kept until the later of the end of any compliance check and the expiry of the right to start a compliance check.

Failure to keep records can lead to a penalty of up to £3,000 for each accounting period affected. However, this penalty does not apply when the only records which have not been kept are ones which could only have been needed for the purposes of claims, elections or notices not included in the return.

1.4 Compliance checks

 A compliance check enquiry into a return, claim or election can be started by an officer of HMRC within a limited period.

1.4.1 Starting a compliance check enquiry

HMRC may decide to conduct a compliance check enquiry on a return, claim or election that has been submitted by a company, in the same way as for individuals.

The officer of HMRC must give written notice of his intention to conduct a compliance check enquiry. The notice must be given by the later of:

(a)   **The first anniversary of the due filing date** (most group companies) or **the actual filing date** (other companies), **if the return was delivered on or before the due filing date,** or

(b)   **The quarter day following the first anniversary of the actual filing date, if the return is filed after the due filing date. The quarter days are 31 January, 30 April, 31 July and 31 October.**

If the company amends the return after the due filing date, the compliance check enquiry 'window' extends to the quarter day following the first anniversary of the date the amendment was filed. Where the compliance check enquiry was not started within the limit which would have applied had no amendment been filed, the enquiry is restricted to matters contained in the amendment.

1.4.2 Conduct of compliance check enquiry

The procedure for the conduct of compliance check enquiries relating to individuals, discussed earlier in this text, also applies to companies.

1.5 Determinations

The rules about determinations relating to individuals, discussed earlier in this text, also applies to companies.

1.6 Discovery assessments

The rules about discovery assessments relating to individuals, discussed earlier in this text, also applies to companies.

1.7 Appeals

The procedure for HMRC internal reviews and appeals relating to individuals, discussed earlier in this text, also applies to companies.

2 Payment of corporation tax and interest   6/18

One of the competencies you require to fulfil Performance Objective 16 Tax compliance and verification of the PER is to determine the incidence (timing) of tax liabilities and their impact on cash flow/financing requirements. You can apply the knowledge you obtain from this section of the text to help to demonstrate this competence.

FAST FORWARD

Large companies pay their corporation tax in quarterly instalments. Other companies pay their tax nine months and one day after the end of an accounting period.

2.1 Companies which are not large companies

Corporation tax is due for payment by **companies which are not large companies** (see below), **nine months and one day after the end of the accounting period.** For example, if a company, which is not a large company, has an accounting period ending on 31 December 2018, the corporation tax for the period is payable on 1 October 2019.

2.2 Large companies

2.2.1 Payment in instalments

Large companies must pay their corporation tax in instalments.

2.2.2 What is a large company?

A large company is one whose profits exceed the profit threshold.

For this purpose profits (which may be referred to as **augmented profits**) **are the taxable total profits of the company plus dividends received from other companies.**

The exception to this rule is that any dividends received from a 51% subsidiary company (sometimes called 'group dividends') **are ignored and so are not included.**

Key term

> A company (company B) is a **51% subsidiary** of company A if more than 50% of company B's ordinary shares are owned directly or indirectly by company A.

Question
Profits

Queen plc had the following results for the year ended 31 March 2019.

	£
Taxable total profits	1,142,000
Dividend received 1 May 2018 from company in which Queen plc has 40% shareholding	278,000
Dividend received 1 August 2018 from company in which Queen plc has 90% shareholding	378,000

What are Queen plc's profits for determining whether it is a large company?

Answer

	£
Taxable total profits	1,142,000
Dividend from company in which Queen plc has 40% shareholding	278,000
Profits	1,420,000

The dividend from the company in which Queen plc has 90% shareholding is ignored because this is from a company which is a '51% subsidiary'.

The profit threshold is £1,500,000 for a 12-month accounting period.

Exam focus point

> The profit threshold will be given in the Tax Rates and Allowances in the exam.

The profit threshold is reduced in two circumstances.

The first is where the company has a **short accounting period where the threshold is scaled down.** For example, if a company has a three month accounting period, the threshold is (£1,500,000 × 3/12) = £375,000.

The second is where the company has **related 51% group companies at the end of the immediately preceding accounting period.** The threshold is **divided by that number of related 51% group companies,** including the company itself.

A company (company B) is a **related 51% group company** of another company (company A) if company A is a 51% subsidiary of company B or company B is a 51% subsidiary of company A or both company A and company B are 51% subsidiaries of another company. Non-UK resident company may be included as related 51% group companies. Companies which do not carry on a trade (dormant companies) are not related 51% group companies.

Question   Related 51% group companies

Yew Ltd prepares accounts to 31 March each year. At 31 March 2018, Yew Ltd had three wholly owned subsidiary companies, Wych Ltd, Sycamore Ltd and Rowan Ltd, and owned 45% of the ordinary shares of Holly Ltd. Sycamore Ltd did not carry on any trade or business during the year to 31 March 2018. Rowan Ltd is not resident in the UK.

Yew Ltd acquired 75% of the ordinary shares of Larch Ltd on 1 July 2018.

What is the profit threshold for Yew Ltd for determining corporation tax payment dates for the year ending 31 March 2019?

Answer

Wych Ltd and Rowan Ltd (residence not relevant) are related 51% group companies with Yew Ltd so there are three related 51% group companies in total.

Sycamore Ltd is not a related 51% group company because it is dormant.

Holly Ltd is not a related 51% group company because it is not a 51% subsidiary of Yew Ltd.

Larch Ltd was not a related 51% group company at the end of the previous accounting period and so does not reduce the profit threshold of Yew Ltd in respect of the year ending 31 March 2019.

The profit threshold for Yew Ltd for the year ending 31 March 2019 is therefore £(1,500,000/3) = £500,000.

2.2.3 Due dates for instalments

Instalments are due on the 14th day of the month, starting in the seventh month of the accounting period. Provided that the accounting period is 12 months long subsequent instalments are due in the tenth month during the accounting period and in the first and fourth months after the end of the accounting period. If an accounting period is less than 12 months long subsequent instalments are due at three monthly intervals but with the final payment being due in the fourth month of the next accounting period.

Question   Instalment due dates

Dahlia Ltd is a large company which has a 12 month accounting period which ends on 31 December 2018. What are the due dates for payment of Dahlia Ltd's instalments of corporation tax for this accounting period?

Answer

14 July 2018, 14 October 2018, 14 January 2019 and 14 April 2019.

2.2.4 Calculating the instalments

Instalments are based on the estimated corporation tax liability for the **current period** (not the previous period). **A company is therefore required to estimate its corporation tax liability before the end of the accounting period, and must revise its estimate each quarter.** It is extremely important for companies to forecast their tax liabilities accurately. Large companies whose directors are poor at estimating may find their companies incurring significant interest charges. **Companies can have instalments repaid if they later conclude the instalments ought not to have been paid.**

The amount of each instalment is computed by:

(a) **Working out 3 × CT/n** where CT is the amount of the estimated corporation tax liability payable in instalments for the period and n is the number of months in the period

(b) **Allocating the smaller of that amount and the total estimated corporation tax liability to the first instalment**

(c) **Repeating the process for later instalments until the amount allocated is equal to the corporation tax liability**

If the company has an accounting period of 12 months, there will be four instalments and each instalment should be 25% of the estimated amount due.

Question — Instalments for 12 month accounting period

Brook Ltd is a large company which has a corporation tax liability of £440,000 for the year ended 31 March 2019. Show when the corporation tax liability is due for payment.

Answer

Due date	Amount £
14 October 2018	110,000
14 January 2019	110,000
14 April 2019	110,000
14 July 2019	110,000
	440,000

The position is slightly more complicated if the company has an accounting period of less than 12 months, as is shown in the following question.

Question — Instalments for short accounting period

Kept plc is a large company which has a corporation tax liability of £880,000 for the eight-month accounting period to 30 September 2018. Show when the corporation tax liability is due for payment.

Answer

£880,000 must be paid in instalments.

The amount of each instalment is $3 \times \dfrac{£880,000}{8} = £330,000$

The due dates and the amounts payable are:

	£
14 August 2018	330,000
14 November 2018	330,000
14 January 2019	220,000 (balance)

2.2.5 Exceptions

A company is not required to pay instalments in the first period that it is a large company, unless its profits exceed £10 million. The £10 million threshold is reduced proportionately by the number of related 51% group companies (including the company in question) at the end of the previous accounting period.

Any company whose corporation tax liability does not exceed £10,000 need not pay by instalments.

2.3 Interest on late or overpaid tax

Interest runs from the due date on over/underpaid instalments. The position is looked at cumulatively after the due date for each instalment. HMRC calculate the interest position after the company submits its corporation tax return.

Companies which do not pay by instalments are charged interest if they pay their corporation tax after the due date, and will receive interest if they overpay their tax or pay it early.

Interest paid/received on late payments or over payments of corporation tax is dealt with as investment income as interest paid/received on a non-trading loan relationship. For the purpose of the exam sittings in June 2019, September 2019, December 2019 and March 2020, the assumed rate of interest on underpaid tax is 3.00% and the assumed rate of interest on overpaid tax is 0.5%.

2.4 Group payment arrangements

Where more than one company in a group is liable to pay their tax by instalments, arrangements may be made for the instalments to be paid by one company (the nominated company), and allocated amongst the group. These provisions were introduced because groups often have uncertainties over the tax liabilities of individual group members until all relevant group reliefs and claims are decided upon following the end of the accounting period.

Chapter roundup

- A company must notify HMRC within three months of starting to trade.
- Corporation tax returns must usually be filed within 12 months of the end of an accounting period.
- A compliance check enquiry into a return, claim or election can be started by an officer of HMRC within a limited period.
- Large companies pay their corporation tax in quarterly instalments. Other companies pay their tax nine months and one day after the end of an accounting period.

Quick quiz

1   Youngs Ltd makes up a 12 month set of accounts to 31 December 2018. When must the company file its CT return based on these accounts?

2   When must HMRC give notice that they are going to start a compliance check enquiry if a return was filed on time by a company not in a group?

3   Which companies must pay quarterly instalments of their corporation tax liability?

4   State the due dates for the payment of quarterly instalments of corporation tax for a 12-month accounting period.

5   Freeman Ltd changes its accounting date and makes up accounts for the ten months to 31 December 2018. The company is large and is due to pay tax by instalments. Outline when the tax is due.

6   In question 5, if the CT liability is £1,000,000 for the ten month period what amount is due at each date?

Answers to quick quiz

1   By 31 December 2019.

2   Notice must be given by one year after the actual filing date.

3   'Large' companies which are broadly those with profits exceeding £1,500,000

4   14th day of:

    (a)   7th month in AP
    (b)   10th month in AP
    (c)   1st month after AP ends
    (d)   4th month after AP ends

5   Due dates are:

    14 September 2018
    14 December 2018
    14 April 2019

6   £300,000, £300,000 and finally £400,000.

Now try the questions below from the Practice Question Bank

Number	Level	Marks	Time
Q23	Introductory	6	12 mins
Q24	Introductory	10	20 mins

23

Administration, winding up, purchase of own shares

Topic list	Syllabus reference
1 Winding up	A4(b)(iii),(iv)
2 The purchase by a company of its own shares	A4(b)(v)

Introduction

In this chapter, we look at some of the consequences of placing a company into administration or liquidation.

We also consider the tax consequences which accrue when a company purchases its own shares.

In the next chapters, we will consider further aspects of corporation tax, starting with losses.

Study guide

		Intellectual level
4	**Corporation tax liabilities in situations involving further overseas and group aspects and in relation to special types of company, and the application of additional exemptions and reliefs**	
(b)	The scope of corporation tax:	3
(iii)	Identify and evaluate the significance of accounting periods on administration or winding up	
(iv)	Conclude on the tax treatment of returns to shareholders after winding up has commenced	
(v)	Advise on the tax implications of a purchase by a company of its own shares	

Exam guide

If the exam includes a question which includes the purchase by a company of its own shares you must be careful to consider whether the capital treatment will apply, and if so, whether it is beneficial. You must be prepared to advise whether any variation to a suggested purchase would be beneficial.

> **Knowledge brought forward from earlier studies**

The topics in this chapter are new.

1 Winding up

9/16

FAST FORWARD

> A new accounting period (AP) begins when a winding up commences. Thereafter APs are for 12 months until the winding up is complete. Distributions made during a winding up are capital. There are special rules in respect of accounting periods when companies go into administration.

1.1 Liquidation

A company **in liquidation is chargeable to corporation tax on the profits arising during the winding up.**

An accounting period ends and a new one begins when a winding up commences. Thereafter, accounting periods end **only** on each anniversary of the commencement of winding up, until the final period which ends when the winding up is completed. A cessation of trade after a winding up has commenced will not bring an accounting period to an end.

1.2 Example: accounting periods on a winding up

Totterdown Ltd, a company with a 31 December year end, ceased trading on 10 June 2017. The members passed a resolution to wind up the company on 12 September 2017 and the winding up was completed on 15 January 2019. From 1 January 2017 the accounting periods will be:

1.1.17–10.6.17	To the date trade ceased.
11.6.17–11.9.17	The commencement of a winding up brings an AP to an end.
12.9.17–11.9.18	Anniversary of commencement of winding up.
12.9.18–15.1.19	Final AP ends when winding up complete.

1.3 Administration

The Enterprise Act 2002 provides for companies to go from liquidation to administration and for assets to be distributed without a formal liquidation. Alternatively, a company may be placed in administration in an effort to avoid liquidation. In such cases, the following rules apply relating to when an accounting period will be deemed to end.

A new accounting period begins when a company goes into administration. An accounting period ends when a company ceases to be in administration and a new accounting period begins when a company moves out of liquidation into administration.

In contrast to the position in liquidation, where the corporation tax accounting periods are then annual from the date of appointment of the liquidator, there is no requirement to change the accounting reference date of the company. Therefore, future accounting periods in administration follow the original accounting dates.

1.4 Example: accounting periods in administration

Pine Ltd has a normal accounting date of 31 December annually. An administrator is appointed on 17 August 2018. As a result, for corporation tax purposes the company's accounting periods will be 1 January to 16 August 2018 before administration and 17 August to 31 December 2018 after the appointment of the administrator. Accounting periods will then be 31 December annually while the company remains in administration.

When an administration ceases, a new accounting period must start for tax purposes, whether the company comes out of administration and recommences to trade normally or goes from administration into winding up.

1.5 Example: administration to liquidation

Pine Ltd remains in administration for 14 months and a liquidator is appointed on 10 October 2019.

The accounting period in administration will therefore be 1 January 2019 to 9 October 2019. The next accounting period will be the first liquidation accounting period, 10 October 2019 to 9 October 2020. Accounting periods will then be annually to 9 October until the company ceases to be in liquidation (either by striking off or returning to administration).

When a company comes out of liquidation into administration, a new accounting period must start. This permits proper computation of the tax due as an expense of liquidation or administration as appropriate.

1.6 Example: liquidation to administration

Following the above example, Pine Ltd remains in liquidation for only three months, and a court order appointing a new administrator is granted on 14 January 2020.

The accounting periods are therefore 10 October 2019 to 13 January 2020 in liquidation, then 14 January to (presumably) 31 December 2020 in administration.

If the company had been in liquidation for some time, so that liquidation accounts had been prepared to 9 October for a number of years, the post-liquidation accounting periods would end on 9 October annually unless the administrator changed the accounting reference date.

1.7 Significance of accounting periods

The date on which an accounting period ends will affect the accounting periods into which income and capital profits and losses fall. This may prevent relief being obtained in the most beneficial way. For example trading losses of the current year or carried back can be set against other income or gains, whilst trading losses carried forward can only be set against trading profits in certain circumstances, for example if the company's business has become small or negligible in the loss making period. Capital gains may therefore be taxable if made after trade ceases even though there may be unrelieved trading losses.

1.8 Distributions

One of the competencies you require to fulfil Performance Objective 17 Tax planning and advice of the PER is to assess the tax implications of proposed activities or plans of an individual or entity with reference to relevant and up to date legislation. You can apply the knowledge you obtain from this section of the text to help to demonstrate this competence.

1.8.1 Distributions during a liquidation

Distributions made after the liquidation has started are capital and treated as a part disposal of shares in the hands of the shareholder. This is the position even if the distributions include accumulated net profits of the company out of which dividends could be paid.

Where a company has distributable profits, it may be preferable to pay these out as a dividend before the liquidation starts. Any such distribution will be chargeable to income tax on a shareholder who is an individual.

Assets distributed in specie (ie in their existing form rather than sold and distributed as cash) by the liquidator are deemed to be disposed of at market value. Where the assets are chargeable assets, any chargeable gain arising is charged to corporation tax in accordance with the normal rules. Consequently there is double taxation on assets distributed to shareholders in the liquidation since the asset distribution will also be treated as a capital distribution in the hands of the shareholders.

1.8.2 Distributions outside a formal winding up

Ordinarily, assets distributed outside a formal winding up represent an income distribution. This might occur prior to an application to strike the company off the Companies Register which is a cheaper way of ending a company's existence than a formal liquidation.

However, under limited circumstances, distributions made in anticipation of such an application to strike off a company, are treated as capital receipts of the shareholders for the purpose of calculating any chargeable gains arising to them on the disposal of their shares. This may or may not be advantageous to the shareholders.

The conditions that have to be met for this treatment to apply are:

- At the time of the distribution, the company intends to secure (or has secured) **payment of any sums due to it**, and intends to satisfy (or has satisfied) any **debts or liabilities of the company**

- The amount of the distribution (or total amount of distributions if there is more than one) **does not exceed £25,000**

If the company has not been dissolved **two years** after making the distribution, or has failed to secure payment of all sums due to it, or to satisfy all its debts and liabilities, then the capital treatment does not apply.

An alternative method for distributing assets outside a formal winding up is to use the provisions of Companies Act 2006 to reduce the capital of the company prior to striking off. A distribution made as a result of such a capital reduction will automatically be a capital distribution and so the above conditions for the capital treatment do not have to be met.

1.9 Other points

The appointment of a receiver, a manager or administrator has no tax consequences, apart from determining accounting periods as discussed above.

When a company is put into liquidation, it loses beneficial ownership of its assets. If the company to be liquidated is a parent company, it will therefore lose its group relationship with its former subsidiaries. No group relief (see later in this text) will be available to any of the companies in the former group. By contrast, a group continues to exist for chargeable gains purposes (see later in this text), notwithstanding the commencement of liquidation.

2 The purchase by a company of its own shares

FAST FORWARD

A purchase of a company's own shares may be taxable on the vendor shareholder as the receipt of an income distribution or (if certain conditions are satisfied) as capital proceeds.

> One of the competencies you require to fulfil Performance Objective 17 Tax planning and advice of the PER is to review the situation of an individual or entity advising on any potential tax risks and/or additional tax minimisation measures. You can apply the knowledge you obtain from this section of the text to help to demonstrate this competence.

2.1 Tax treatment for vendor shareholder

2.1.1 Income treatment

If a company buys its own shares for more than the amount originally subscribed, general tax rules state that there is an income distribution of the excess of the amount received over the subscription. This is called the **income treatment.**

Recipients of such distributions are treated in the same way as recipients of ordinary dividends. This means that the individual must pay income tax on the distribution if it is not covered by the dividend nil rate band.

The remainder of the proceeds (ie those not treated as income) will be a capital receipt. Thus there will also be a disposal of the shares by the vendor shareholder for capital gains tax. If the vendor shareholder originally subscribed for the shares, there will be no gain or loss, since the shareholder is merely getting back the subscription cost as the disposal proceeds. If, however, the vendor shareholder acquired the shares other than by subscription (for example by purchase), a gain or, more usually, a loss may arise. The proceeds for the disposal is equal to the original subscription cost, since this is the capital amount received by the shareholder on the purchase of the shares by the company.

2.1.2 Example

Jess bought 5,000 shares in Pink Ltd in July 2016 for £3 per share. The original subscription cost for these shares was £1 per share. Pink Ltd has agreed to repurchase these shares from Jess for £10 each in December 2018.

If the income treatment applies, Jess will receive a distribution from Pink Ltd as follows:

	£
Cash received £10 × 5,000	50,000
Less subscription price (capital) £1 × 5,000	(5,000)
Net distribution subject to income tax	45,000

Jess will also have a capital gains tax allowable loss on his disposal of Pink Ltd shares as follows:

	£
Proceeds: return of subscription £1 × 5,000	5,000
Less cost of shares for Jess £3 × 5,000	(15,000)
Allowable loss	(10,000)

2.1.3 Capital treatment

When an unquoted trading company (or the unquoted parent of a trading group) **buys back its own shares in order to benefit its trade, and certain other conditions are satisfied (see Section 2.2), the capital treatment *automatically* applies. This means that the distribution is treated as a capital receipt for the disposal of the shares by the shareholder rather than as an income distribution.**

Under the current CGT rules, the capital treatment may result in less tax being payable, particularly if the disposal qualifies for entrepreneurs' relief, than if the income treatment applies.

Question

Walter subscribed for 1,000 shares in BB Ltd, an unquoted trading company, at £1 per share. BB Ltd has agreed to repurchase Walter's shares for £15 each in March 2019.

Walter has taxable income of £40,000 in 2018/19, none of which is dividend income. He has made no other gains in 2018/19.

Show the tax payable by Walter if:

(a)   The income treatment applies.

(b)   The capital treatment applies and **either**:
   (i)   a claim is made for entrepreneurs' relief; **or**
   (ii)   a claim is not made for entrepreneurs' relief.

Answer

(a)   If the income treatment applies, Walter will have a net distribution as follows:

	£
Cash received £15 × 1,000	15,000
Less subscription price (return of capital) £1 × 1,000	(1,000)
Distribution	14,000
Income tax	
£2,000 × 0%	0
£12,000 (14,000 – 2,000) × 32.5%	3,900
	£3,900

For capital gains tax, there will be no gain or loss:

	£
Proceeds: return of subscription £1 × 1,000	1,000
Less cost £1 × 1,000	(1,000)
	0

(b)   If the capital treatment applies, the gain will be as follows:

	£
Cash received £15 × 1,000	15,000
Less cost £1 × 1,000	(1,000)
Gain	14,000
Less annual exempt amount	(11,700)
Taxable gain	2,300
Capital gains tax	
(i) If claim made for entrepreneurs' relief £2,300 × 10%	230
(ii) If claim not made for entrepreneurs' relief £2,300 × 20%	460

2.2 Conditions for capital treatment to apply

The company purchasing its own shares must be an unquoted trading company (or the unquoted parent of a trading group). The trade must not consist of dealing in shares, securities, land or futures.

The **'benefit to the trade' test** will be satisfied where:

•   A **dissident and disruptive shareholder** is bought out

•   The **proprietor wishes to retire** to make way for new management

- An **outside investor** who provided equity wishes to **withdraw his investment**
- A **shareholder dies** and his personal representatives do not wish to retain his shares.

The **conditions to be satisfied by the vendor shareholder** are as follows:

(a) **The shareholder must be resident in the UK** when the purchase is made

(b) **The shares must have been owned by the vendor or his spouse/civil partner throughout the five years preceding the purchase**. This is reduced to three years if the vendor is the personal representative or the heir of a deceased member and previous ownership by the deceased will count towards the qualifying period.

Exam focus point

> The period of ownership will often be an essential point in an exam question. For example, you may be given a scenario where the purchase can be timed either before the five year deadline, or after it, and asked to show the taxation consequences in each case.

(c) **The vendor and his associates must as a result of the purchase have their interest in the company's share capital reduced to 75% or less of their interest before the disposal.** Associates include spouses/civil partners, minor children, controlled companies, trustees and beneficiaries. Where a company is a member of a group the whole group is effectively considered as one for this test.

(d) **The vendor must not be connected with the company or any company in the same 51% group after the transaction.** A person is connected with a company if he can control more than 30% of the ordinary share capital, the issued share capital and loan capital or the voting rights in the company.

Question   The reduction of a shareholding

Henry holds 300 of Hay Ltd's 1,000 issued ordinary shares.

Will the capital treatment apply if the company buys 80 shares back from him?

Answer

	Total shares	Held by Henry
Initially	1,000	300
Less repurchased (and cancelled)	(80)	(80)
	920	220

Henry originally had a 30% interest. This is reduced to 220/920 = 23.9%, a reduction to 23.9/30 – 79.7% of his original interest. For a capital gain to arise, he must sell at least 97 shares back to Hay Ltd, thus reducing his percentage holding below 30% × 75% = 22.5%.

2.3 Other points

The capital gains treatment is not given if a main objective is tax avoidance.

As seen in the above example, any shares repurchased by the company must usually be cancelled.

The capital treatment is also available where a company purchases shares to enable the vendor to pay any inheritance tax arising on a death (the 'benefit to the trade' test and the other conditions in Section 2.2 do not then apply).

Companies considering the purchase of their own shares may seek HMRC clearance to ensure that the capital treatment applies.

Chapter roundup

- A new accounting period (AP) begins when a winding up commences. Thereafter APs are for 12 months until the winding up is complete. Distributions made during a winding up are capital. There are special rules in respect of accounting periods when companies go into administration.

- A purchase of a company's own shares may be taxable on the vendor shareholder as the receipt of an income distribution or (if certain conditions are satisfied) as capital proceeds.

Quick quiz

1   Inca Ltd makes up accounts to 31 March. The company goes into liquidation on 1 November 2018 and cease to trade on 31 December 2018. The company is finally wound up on 31 July 2019. What are the accounting periods from 1 April 2017?

2   Does the appointment of an administrator affect a company's accounting periods?

3   What is the impact (if any) on a company accounting period when a company moves out of liquidation into administration?

4   Are distributions made during a liquidation treated as capital or income distributions?

5   A company is about to make an application to be struck off the Companies Register. It has secured payments of sums due to it and satisfied its debts and liabilities. The company has surplus cash of £20,000 to distribute to its shareholders. How will the distribution be treated for tax purposes in relation to the shareholders?

6   When a company buys its own shares, what potential tax consequences may occur for the shareholder whose shares are being bought?

Answers to quick quiz

1   1 April 2017–31 March 2018
       1 April 2018–31 October 2018
       1 November 2018– 31 July 2019

2   Yes. A new accounting period begins when a company goes into administration. An accounting period ends when a company ceases to be in administration.

3   A new accounting period begins when a company moves status from liquidation into administration.

4   Distributions are capital distributions and are treated as a part disposal of the shares in the hands of the shareholder.

5   The distribution will be treated as a capital receipt for the shareholders as the conditions for payments and debts have been satisfied and the amount of the distribution does not exceed £25,000.

6   If a company buys its own shares from a shareholder and pays more than the amount originally subscribed, the general tax rules treat the excess amount paid as a distribution (taxed in the same way as an ordinary dividend) made by the company to the shareholder. Income tax applies to the shareholder recipient of the distribution. There will also be a disposal of the shares for capital gains tax purposes: the proceeds will be the original subscription for the shares.

       If certain conditions are met, however, the full amount paid by the company for a purchase of own shares will be treated as capital proceeds for the shareholder and capital gains tax will be due on the gain. A claim may be made for entrepreneurs' relief on the disposal.

Now try the question below from the Practice Question Bank

Number	Level	Marks	Time
Q25	Introductory	10	20 mins

Losses and deficits on non-trading loan relationships

Topic list	Syllabus reference
1 Reliefs for losses – overview	A4(a) E2,E6
2 Trading losses	A4(a) E2,E6
3 Reliefs for deficits on non-trading loan relationships	A4(c)(iii)
4 Restriction on loss relief	A4(c)(vi)
5 Choosing loss reliefs	A4(a) E2,E6

Introduction

We now see how a company may obtain relief for trading losses and also for deficits on non trading loan relationships. Then we consider a restriction on the use of loss relief where there has been a change in ownership of the company. We look at the factors to take into account when deciding which loss relief to choose.

In the next chapter, we will look at close companies and investment companies, and then we will turn to groups and consortia.

Study guide

		Intellectual level
4	**Corporation tax liabilities in situations involving further overseas and group aspects and in relation to special types of company, and the application of additional exemptions and reliefs**	
(a)	The contents of the Taxation - United Kingdom (TX – UK) study guide for corporation tax, under headings:	
•	E2 Taxable total profits	2
•	E6 The use of exemptions and reliefs in deferring and minimising corporation tax liabilities.	2
(c)	Taxable total profits:	3
(iii)	Determine the tax treatment of non trading deficits on loan relationships	
(vi)	Advise on the restriction on the use of losses on a change in ownership of a company	

Exam guide

You are likely to come across company losses at some point in the exam, although the question may include group relief. Always look to see if any requirements are specified in the question, such as to claim relief as early as possible, and then consider how to optimise the relief.

Knowledge brought forward from earlier studies

This chapter revises the treatment of trading losses which should be familiar from your Taxation (TX – UK) studies. The examining team has identified essential underpinning knowledge from the Taxation (TX – UK) syllabus which is particularly important that you revise as part of your Advanced Taxation (ATX – UK) studies. In this chapter, the relevant topics are:

		Intellectual level
E2	**Taxable total profits**	
(d)	Compute property business profits and understand how relief for a property business loss is given	2
(e)	Understand how trading losses can be carried forward	2
(f)	Understand how trading losses can be claimed against income of the current or previous accounting periods	2
(g)	Recognise the factors that will influence the choice of loss relief claim	2

The technical change for Advanced Taxation (ATX – UK) exams in Financial Year 2018 from the material studied for Taxation (TX – UK) for exams in Financial Year 2017 is that carry forward trading losses may now be set against total profits in most cases, not just against trading profits of the same trade.

The relief for deficits on non-trading loan relationships and the restriction on the use of losses are new to you.

1 Reliefs for losses – overview

1.1 Trading losses

Trading losses may be relieved by deduction from current period total profits, total profits of earlier periods or total profits of future periods. Deficits on non-trading loan relationships can be used in a similar way to trading losses.

In summary, the following reliefs are available for trading losses incurred by a company:

- **Claim to deduct the loss from current period total profits** (current period relief)
- **Claim to deduct the loss from earlier period total profits** (carry back relief)
- **Claim to deduct the loss usually from future period total profits** (carry forward relief)

These reliefs may be used in combination. The options open to the company are:

(a)   Current period relief only
(b)   Current period relief, then carry back relief
(c)   Current period relief, then carry forward relief
(d)   Current period relief, then carry back relief, then carry forward relief
(e)   Carry forward relief only.

These reliefs are explained in further detail later in this chapter.

1.2 Non-trading deficits

Non-trading deficits on loan relationships can be relieved in similar ways to trading losses, but against different profits in the case of carry back relief (see later in this chapter).

1.3 Capital losses

Capital losses can only be set against capital gains in the current or future accounting periods.

Capital losses can only be set against capital gains in the same or future accounting periods, never against income. **Capital losses must be set against the first available gains to the fullest extent possible** (ie in the current period first and then any excess loss carried forward and relieved in the next accounting period and so on unless the loss has been fully relieved). No claims are made as the relief is automatic. Note that capital losses are relieved in the computation of total profits, rather than by deduction from total profits to compute taxable total profits. **Capital losses cannot be carried back.**

1.4 Property income losses

Property business losses must be set off first against total profits in the current accounting period and then a carry forward loss relief claim can be made to set unrelieved losses against future total profits.

A company must deduct a property business loss incurred in an accounting period from its total profits of the same accounting period to the fullest extent possible. Note that this treatment is different from trading loss relief because it does not depend on a claim being made and there is no carry back property business loss relief.

A property business loss which has not been relieved in the current period (nor subject to group relief – see later in this text), **is automatically carried forward to the next accounting period. The company can then make a claim to deduct the whole or part of the loss from its total profits of the next accounting period** (and then subsequent accounting periods if there is any unrelieved loss). The company can restrict its claim for the amount of the loss which is to be relieved so preventing qualifying charitable donations becoming unrelieved.

Claims for carry forward loss relief must be made within two years of the end of the accounting period in which the loss is relieved.

2 Trading losses

2.1 Current period and carry back trading loss relief

Current period trading loss relief and carry back trading loss relief are optional but if claimed must be taken to the fullest extent possible against total profits and so qualifying charitable donations may become unrelieved.

2.1.1 Current period relief

A company may claim to deduct a trading loss incurred in an accounting period from its total profits of the same accounting period. The company cannot chose the amount of loss to relieve – current period loss relief must be taken to the fullest extent possible. This may make qualifying charitable donations unrelieved because such donations are deducted from total profits after this loss relief to compute taxable total profits.

2.1.2 Carry back relief

After current period loss relief has been taken, any remaining loss may then be carried back and deducted from total profits of an accounting period falling wholly or partly within the 12 months prior to the start of the period in which the loss was incurred. Again, the company cannot chose the amount of loss to relieve – carry back loss relief must be taken to the fullest extent possible so this may cause qualifying charitable donations to be unrelieved.

Any carry back is to more recent periods before earlier periods. Relief for earlier losses is given before relief for later losses.

2.1.3 The claim

A claim for relief against current or prior period profits must be made within two years of the end of the accounting period in which the loss arose.

Question	Current period and carry back loss relief

Helix Ltd has the following results.

	Y/e 30.11.17 £	y/e 30.11.18 £
Trading profit/(loss)	22,500	(19,500)
Bank interest	500	500
Chargeable gains	0	4,000
Qualifying charitable donation	250	250

Show the taxable total profits for both periods affected assuming that current period and carry back loss relief is claimed.

The loss of the year to 30 November 2018 is relieved by deduction from current year total profits and from total profits of the previous 12 months.

	y/e 30.11.17 £	y/e 30.11.18 £
Trading profit	22,500	0
Investment income	500	500
Chargeable gains	0	4,000
Total profits	23,000	4,500
Less current period loss relief	0	(4,500)
	23,000	0
Less carry back loss relief	(15,000)	(0)
	8,000	0
Less qualifying charitable donation	(250)	0
Taxable total profits	7,750	0
Unrelieved qualifying charitable donation		250

Loss memorandum

Loss incurred in y/e 30.11.18		19,500
Less used:	y/e 30.11.18	(4,500)
	y/e 30.11.17	(15,000)
Loss available to carry forward		0

2.1.4 Periods of account which are not 12 months in length

If a period falls partly outside the 12 months, loss relief is limited to the proportion of the period's profits (before qualifying charitable donations) equal to the proportion of the period which falls within the 12 months.

Question   Short accounting period and loss relief

Tallis Ltd had the following results for the three accounting periods to 31 December 2018.

	Y/e 30.9.17 £	3 months to 31.12.17 £	Y/e 31.12.18 £
Trading profit (loss)	20,000	12,000	(39,000)
Building society interest	1,000	400	1,800
Qualifying charitable donations	600	500	0

Show the taxable total profits for all periods assuming that current period and carry back loss relief is claimed.

	Y/e 30.9.17 £	3 months to 31.12.17 £	Y/e 31.12.18 £
Trading profit	20,000	12,000	0
Interest income	1,000	400	1,800
Total profits	21,000	12,400	1,800
Less current period loss relief			(1,800)
	21,000	12,400	0
Less carry back loss relief	(15,750)	(12,400)	
	5,250	0	0
Less qualifying charitable donations	(600)		0
Taxable total profits	4,650	0	0
Unrelieved qualifying charitable donations	0	500	0

Loss memorandum	£
Loss incurred in y/e 31.12.18	39,000
Less used y/e 31.12.18	(1,800)
Less used p/e 31.12.17	(12,400)
Less used y/e 30.9.17 £21,000 × 9/12 (max)	(15,750)
C/f	9,050

Notes

1. The loss can be carried back to be deducted from profits of the previous 12 months. This means profits in the y/e 30.9.17 must be time apportioned by multiplying by 9/12.

2. Losses remaining after the loss relief claims by deduction from total profits are carried forward to be deducted from future trading profits.

2.1.5 Terminal loss relief

9/16

FAST FORWARD

Trading losses in the last 12 months of trading can be carried back and deducted from profits of the previous 36 months.

For trading losses incurred in the 12 months up to the cessation of trade the carry back period is extended from 12 months to 3 years, later years first.

Question — Terminal losses

Brazil Ltd had the following results for the accounting periods up to the cessation of trade on 30 September 2018.

	Y/e 30.9.15 £	Y/e 30.9.16 £	Y/e 30.9.17 £	Y/e 30.9.18 £
Trading profits	60,000	40,000	15,000	(180,000)
Gains	0	10,000	0	6,000
Property income	12,000	12,000	12,000	12,000

You are required to show how the losses are relieved assuming that current period and carry back loss relief is claimed.

Answer

	Y/e 30.9.15 £	Y/e 30.9.16 £	Y/e 30.9.17 £	Y/e 30.9.18 £
Trading profits	60,000	40,000	15,000	0
Property income	12,000	12,000	12,000	12,000
Gains	0	10,000	0	6,000
Total profits	72,000	62,000	27,000	18,000
Less current period loss relief				(18,000)
Less carry back loss relief	(72,000)	(62,000)	(27,000)	
Taxable total profits	0	0	0	0

Loss memorandum

	£
Loss in y/e 30.9.18	180,000
Less used y/e 30.9.18	(18,000)
Loss of y/e 30.9.18 available for 36 months carry back	162,000
Less used y/e 30.9.17	(27,000)
	135,000
Less used y/e 30.9.16	(62,000)
	73,000
Less used y/e 30.9.15	(72,000)
Loss remaining unrelieved	1,000

Exam focus point

In September 2016 question 5 Cresco Ltd, candidates were required to show how a company could relieve trading losses incurred in its last few periods of account. This involved consideration of loss relief in an ongoing company, in addition to the availability of terminal loss relief. The examining team commented that: 'It is important in any question dealing with relief for losses that a well-considered and chronological approach is taken. Precise explanations of the reliefs are required in these sorts of questions. Well-prepared candidates were able to deal correctly with the earlier losses in accounting periods prior to the final period, and were aware that, on cessation, an extended three-year carry back is available, but almost all neglected to correctly calculate the loss which was available for this terminal loss relief. Nevertheless, those who adopted a sensible, logical approach scored well on this question part.'

2.2 Carry forward trading loss relief   New

FAST FORWARD

Unrelieved trading losses are carried forward and claims may be made to set them against total profits of future accounting periods. The claim may restrict the amount of loss that is relieved to prevent qualifying charitable donations becoming unrelieved.

Exam focus point

Carried forward losses arising prior to 1 April 2017 **are not examinable** in Advanced Taxation (ATX – UK) as different rules apply to such losses.

2.2.1 Carry forward trading loss relief against total profits

A trading loss, which has not been relieved under a current period claim or carry back claim (nor subject to group relief – see later in this text), **is automatically carried forward to the next accounting period. The company can then make a claim to deduct the whole or part of the loss from its total profits of that accounting period.** Claims for carry forward loss relief must be made within two years of the end of the accounting period in which the loss is relieved.

Note that, unlike current period and carry back claims, **under carry forward loss relief the company can restrict its claim for the amount of the loss which is to be relieved so preventing qualifying charitable donations becoming unrelieved.**

If the loss is not completely relieved in the next accounting period, it is automatically carried forward to the following accounting period and the company may make a further claim to deduct the whole or part of the remaining loss from total profits. This procedure is repeated until the loss is completely relieved.

A company is entitled to a **deductions allowance of £5 million** for a 12-month accounting period. Carried forward losses can be **relieved in full up to the amount of deductions allowance plus 50% of the company's profits in excess of the deductions allowance** (ie after deduction of current period reliefs (including group relief) and the deductions allowance).

Exam focus point

> You are only required to **have an awareness** of this restriction in Advanced Taxation (ATX – UK). You will not be expected to apply this knowledge to a particular situation in an exam question.

Question
Carry forward loss relief

Warnock Ltd commenced trading on 1 April 2017. The company's results for its first two accounting periods are as follows:

	y/e 31.3.18 £	y/e 31.3.19 £
Trading profit/(loss)	(18,000)	7,500
Chargeable gains	3,750	4,500
Qualifying charitable donations	500	1,000

Calculate the company's taxable total profits for the years ended 31 March 2018 and 2019, assuming that it makes a current period loss relief claim and the most beneficial carry forward loss relief claim, and identify any unrelieved qualifying charitable donations and the amount of any unrelieved trading loss at 31 March 2019.

Answer

	y/e 31.3.18 £	y/e 31.3.19 £
Trading profit	0	7,500
Chargeable gains	3,750	4,500
Total profits	3,750	12,000
Less: current period relief	(3,750)	
Less: carried forward relief		(11,000)
Less: QCD	(0)	(1,000)
Taxable total profits	0	0
Unrelieved QCDs	500	0

Loss memorandum

	£
Loss in y/e 31.3.18	18,000
Less used y/e 31.3.18	(3,750)
Less used y/e 31.3.19	
£(12,000 – 1,000) restricted to relieve QCD	(11,000)
Unrelieved loss at 31.3.19	3,250

2.2.2 Carry forward trading loss relief against trading profits

If a company's trade has become small or negligible in an accounting period, it can only set carried forward trading losses from that period against trading profits of the same trade.

A claim to use trading losses against total profits of the company in a later accounting period cannot be made if the company's trade has become small or negligible in the period in which the loss was made (or in a period from which a loss is carried forward).

In this case, if the company continues to carry on the trade in the next accounting period, the loss will automatically be set against profits of the same trade in that period, unless the company makes a claim for the whole or part of the loss not to be so relieved. It is not possible to set such a loss against total income even if the trade revives.

If the company ceases to trade, trading losses cannot be carried forward against other types of income.

Exam focus point

You are **not expected to have knowledge** of the effect which a company's trade becoming small or negligible has on any other types of losses carried forward in Advanced Taxation (ATX – UK).

3 Reliefs for deficits on non-trading loan relationships

6/15

Deficits on non-trading loan relationships can be relieved by deduction from current period total profits, carried back against non-trading credits of the previous 12 months or carried forward against total profits.

3.1 Current period relief

A claim can be made for a deficit on a non-trading loan relationships to be set (in whole or in part) against total profits of the same accounting period. The claim must be made within two years of the deficit period.

Relief is given before a trading loss of the current period or carried back, any deficit carried back, and current period property business loss relief. There is no reduction for brought forward trading losses.

A deficit is also eligible for group relief (see later in this text).

Question   Relief for deficit on non-trading loan relationship

Witherspoon Ltd has the following results for the two years ended 31 March 2019:

	2018 £	2019 £
Trading profit/(loss)	50,000	(42,000)
Bank interest receivable	2,000	
Interest payable on a loan for non-trading purposes	(11,000)	

Show how relief may be given for the deficit on the non-trading loan relationship in the year ended 31 March 2018.

Answer

Y/e 31.3.18	£
Trading income	50,000
Less non-trading deficit £(11,000 – 2,000)	(9,000)
	41,000
Losses carried back	(41,000)
Total taxable profits	0

Loss memorandum	£
Incurred in y/e 31.3.19	42,000
Less used: y/e 31.3.18	(41,000)
Available to carry forward	1,000

3.2 Carry back relief

A company can claim to set (in whole or in part) any deficit remaining after current period relief against non-trading loan relationships credits arising in the previous 12 months. Unlike trading losses, it is not necessary to make a current period claim first before making a carry back claim. The claim must be made within two years of the deficit period.

Relief is given after any current period deficit, any brought forward deficit, qualifying charitable donations and trading losses of the current period or carried forward.

3.3 Carry forward relief

Any deficit unrelieved, after claiming current period and carry back relief and group relief, is automatically carried forward to the next accounting period.

The company can usually then make a claim to deduct the whole or part of the deficit from its total profits of that accounting period and then from total profits in subsequent accounting periods until the deficit is wholly relieved. Claims must be made within two years of the period in which the deficit is relieved.

4 Restriction on loss relief   12/14, 3/16

If there is a change in ownership of a company, the carry forward of losses is restricted if there is also a major change in the nature or conduct of the trade within a five year period beginning no earlier than three years before the change in ownership.

Trading losses may be restricted where there is both a change in ownership of a company and there is:

(a)   A major change in the nature or conduct of the trade within any period of five years (beginning no later than the change in ownership and no earlier than three years before the change in ownership), or

(b)   After the change in ownership there is a considerable revival of the company's trading activities which at the time of the change had become small or negligible.

Exam focus point

These rules apply where there is **both** a change in ownership **and** a major change in the business of a company on or after 1 April 2017. Changes occurring prior to 1 April 2017 are **not examinable** in Advanced Taxation (ATX – UK).

If the restriction applies:

- **Any losses incurred before the change in ownership cannot be carried forward against post-acquisition profits.**

- **Any losses incurred after the change in ownership cannot be carried back against profits arising before the date of the change of ownership.**

For example, if a company changes its ownership on 1 July 2020 and there is a major change in the nature or conduct of its trade between 1 July 2017 and 30 June 2025 the carry back and carry forward of losses is restricted.

Examples of a major change in the nature or conduct of a trade include changes in:

- The **type of property dealt in** (for example a company operating a dealership in saloon cars switching to a dealership in tractors)

- The **services or facilities provided** (for example a company operating a public house changing to operating a discotheque)

- **Customers, outlets or markets**

However, **changes to keep up to date with technology or to rationalise existing ranges of products are unlikely to be regarded as major**.

5 Choosing loss reliefs

FAST FORWARD

When selecting a loss relief, consider the timing of the relief and whether relief for qualifying charitable donations may be lost.

PER alert

One of the competencies you require to fulfil Performance Objective 17 Tax planning and advice of the PER is to mitigate and/or defer tax liabilities through the use of standard reliefs, exemptions and incentives. You can apply the knowledge you obtain from this section of the text to help to demonstrate this competence.

Several alternative loss reliefs may be available. In making a choice consider:

- **Timing of relief**: current period and carry back loss reliefs give relief for the loss more quickly than carry forward loss relief and so it is generally preferable to carrying forward the loss for cash flow reasons. It also has the advantage of enabling a carry back of the loss to a prior accounting period, potentially saving tax at a higher rate if the rate of corporation tax in later years is lower than those in earlier years.

- **The extent to which relief for qualifying charitable donations might be lost** for example by not claiming current period or carry back relief and by restricting carry forward claims to keep an amount of total profits in charge after loss relief to match donations.

Monster Ltd has the following results.

	Year ended 31 March			
	2017	2018	2019	2020
	£	£	£	£
Trading profit/(loss)	2,000	(500,000)	100,000	120,000
Chargeable gains	35,000	250,000	30,000	45,000
Qualifying charitable donations	30,000	20,000	20,000	20,000

Recommend appropriate loss relief claims, stating by when the claims should be made, and compute the corporation tax for all years based on your recommendations, showing any unrelieved qualifying charitable donations. Assume the rate of corporation tax is 20% in financial year 2016 and 19% in financial years 2017, 2018 and 2019.

Answer

A current period loss relief claim for the year ended 31 March 2018 will be against total profits of £250,000 and obtain relief quickly. This is outweighs the fact that the claim will waste the qualifying charitable donations of £20,000 so a current period claim should be made by 31 March 2020 (two years from the end of the loss making period).

If a current period loss relief claim is made, a carry back relief claim can also be made for the year ended 31 March 2017. This will be against total profits of (£35,000 + £2,000) = £37,000. This claim will waste qualifying charitable donations of £30,000 and so would use £37,000 of loss to save tax at 20% on £7,000 (£35,000 + £2,000 – £30,000). A carry back claim should therefore not be made.

A carry forward relief claim will obtain relief in the year ended 31 March 2019 against total profits. The claim should be restricted to (£100,000 + £30,000 – £20,000) = £110,000 to keep £20,000 of total profit in charge to match the qualifying charitable donation. The remaining £(500,000 – 250,000 – 110,000) = £140,000 of the loss will be carried forward to the year ended 31 March 2020 to be set against total profits. This claim should be made in full, as it will not result in any qualifying charitable donations becoming unrelieved. These claims should be made by 31 March 2021 and 31 March 2022 respectively (two years from the end of the period in which the loss is relieved).

The corporation tax computations are as follows:

	Year ended 31 March			
	2017	2018	2019	2020
	£	£	£	£
Trading income	2,000	0	100,000	120,000
Chargeable gains	35,000	250,000	30,000	45,000
Total profits	37,000	250,000	130,000	165,000
Less current period loss relief		(250,000)		
Less carry forward loss relief			(110,000)	(140,000)
Less qualifying charitable donations	(30,000)	0	(20,000)	(20,000)
Taxable total profits	7,000	0	0	5,000
CT at 20%/19%	1,400	0	0	950
Unrelieved qualifying charitable donations	0	20,000	0	0

Chapter roundup

- Trading losses may be relieved by deduction from current period total profits, total profits of earlier periods or total profits of future periods. Deficits on non-trading loan relationships can be used in a similar way to trading losses.

- Capital losses can only be set against capital gains in the current or future accounting periods.

- Property business losses must be set off first against total profits in the current accounting period and then a carry forward loss relief claim can be made to set unrelieved losses against future total profits.

- Current period trading loss relief and carry back trading loss relief are optional but if claimed must be taken to the fullest extent possible against total profits and so qualifying charitable donations may become unrelieved.

- A claim for current period loss relief can be made without a claim for carry back. However, if a loss is to be carried back a claim for current period relief must have been made first.

- Trading losses in the last 12 months of trading can be carried back and deducted from profits of the previous 36 months.

- Unrelieved trading losses are carried forward and claims may be made to set them against total profits of future accounting periods. The claim may restrict the amount of loss that is relieved to prevent qualifying charitable donations becoming unrelieved.

- If a company's trade has become small or negligible in an accounting period, it can only set carried forward trading losses from that period against trading profits of the same trade.

- Deficits on non-trading loan relationships can be relieved by deduction from current period total profits, carried back against non-trading credits of the previous 12 months or carried forward against total profits.

- If there is a change in ownership of a company, the carry forward of losses is restricted if there is also a major change in the nature or conduct of the trade within a five year period beginning no earlier than three years before the change in ownership.

- When selecting a loss relief, consider the timing of the relief and whether relief for qualifying charitable donations may be lost.

Quick quiz

1   What loss reliefs are available to a company, which is not in a group, that has a property business loss?

2   To what extent may losses in a continuing trade be carried back?

3   In what circumstances may a company not be able to set carried forward trading losses against total profits and how will the loss then be relieved?

4   What relief is available in the current accounting period for a non-trading deficit?

5   What are the two key factors in choosing which loss relief claim to make?

Answers to quick quiz

1   Deduct from the company's total profits of the current accounting period. Excess carried forward to the next accounting period and a claim can be made to set all or part of the loss against total profits.

2   A loss may be carried back and deducted from total profits (before deducting qualifying charitable donations) of the prior 12 months. The loss carried back is the trading loss left unrelieved after a claim against total profits (before deducting qualifying charitable donations) of the loss making accounting period has been made.

3   If the company's trade has become small or negligible in the period in which the trading loss was made (or in a period from which a loss is carried forward). The company may make a claim to set the loss against profits of the same trade in future accounting periods.

4   A claim can be made for a deficit on a non-trading loan relationship to be set (in whole or in part) against total profits of the same accounting period. The deficit is also eligible for group relief.

5   •   How quickly relief will be obtained.
    •   The extent to which relief for qualifying charitable donations might be lost.

Now try the question below from the Practice Question Bank

Number	Level	Marks	Time
Q26	Introductory	16	31 mins
Q27	Introductory	16	31 mins

BPP
LEARNING MEDIA

Close companies and investment companies

Topic list	Syllabus reference
1 Companies with investment business	A4(b)(i)
2 Close companies	A4(b)(ii)

Introduction

Having looked at the general rules for companies, we now look at the specific rules for investment companies and close companies.

Companies with investment business are any companies that make investments, for example in shares, and collect the income from them. Expenses of managing those investments are generally deductible for corporation tax purposes.

A close company may have any type of business, but it needs special tax treatment because it is under the control of a few people who might try to take profits out of it in non-taxable forms.

In the next chapter, we will go on to look at groups and consortia.

Study guide

		Intellectual level
4	**Corporation tax liabilities in situations involving further overseas and group aspects and in relation to special types of company, and the application of additional exemptions and reliefs**	
(b)	The scope of corporation tax:	3
(i)	Identify and calculate corporation tax for companies with investment business.	
(ii)	Close companies: • Apply the definition of a close company to given situations • Conclude on the tax implications of a company being a close company or a close investment holding company	

Exam guide

You may be asked about how a company with investment business can deduct management expenses. Questions involving planning for families may include a consideration of close companies. The rules for treating benefits as distributions are fairly straightforward, but you must be careful not to overlook the disallowance of the expenses in the corporation tax computation. The tax charge for loans to participators is a significant cost of making any such loan, even though it is recovered when the loan is repaid or written off.

> **Knowledge brought forward from earlier studies**

The topics in this chapter are new.

1 Companies with investment business

FAST FORWARD

> A company that generates income from investments can usually deduct the expenses of managing their investments for corporation tax purposes.

A company with investment business is any company whose **business consists wholly or partly in making investments.**

The principal overhead of the investment business will be the costs of running the business which are called management expenses. These are generally deductible from total profits. A claim can be made to deduct whole or part of any excess management expenses in the next accounting period as if they were management expenses deductible for that accounting period. **The claim must be made within two years after the end of the next accounting period.**

Excessive directors' remuneration is not deductible for tax purposes. Capital expenditure is excluded from deduction as a management expense and HMRC may also refuse a deduction for any amounts which are not in fact expenses of management. Capital allowances on plant and machinery used for the investment business are allowed as a management expense if they cannot be relieved in any other way.

Non-trading loan relationships expenses and losses are dealt with under the loan relationship rules, not as a management expense.

Question

TC Ltd, a non-close company with wholly investment business, has the following results for the year ended 31 March 2019.

	£
Rental income	150,000
Building society interest	8,000
Chargeable gains	100,000
Management expenses	
Property management	40,000
General	50,000
Capital allowances	
On property	800
General	1,000
Qualifying charitable donations	47,000

Unrelieved management expenses carried forward at 1 April 2018 amounted to £60,500. TC Ltd wishes to make a claim wholly to relieve these in the current accounting period.

Compute the corporation tax payable.

Answer

	£	£
Rents		150,000
Less: capital allowances	800	
property management expenses	40,000	
		(40,800)
Property income		109,200
Interest income		8,000
Chargeable gains		100,000
Total profits		217,200
Less: general management expenses	50,000	
general capital allowances	1,000	
management expenses brought forward	60,500	
		(111,500)
		105,700
Less qualifying charitable donations		(47,000)
Taxable total profits		58,700
Corporation tax payable £58,700 × 19%		£11,153

2 Close companies

12/13, 6/14, 6/15, 9/16

2.1 Close company definitions

Owner-managed and family-owned companies could easily be used for tax avoidance. **Special rules apply to these 'close' companies** to counteract this. Broadly, **a close company is one that is under the control of either five or fewer shareholders or any number of its shareholding directors.** Shareholders and shareholding directors are known as 'participators'.

Direct relatives, business partners and certain trusts set up by the participator (or their direct relatives or business partners) are known as 'associates'. The rights and powers of associates are attributed to participators when determining control.

Thus if the five largest shareholders of Wye Ltd own 9% of the shares each, and they have no associates, the company will not be close. If, however, the wife and son of Darren, one of the five largest shareholders, each hold 3% the company will be close as Darren is deemed to hold (9 + 3 + 3) = 15%, so that the holdings of the five largest shareholders is (4 × 9 + 15) = 51%.

A company which is controlled by a close company will also itself be a close company. A company which is not resident in the UK cannot be a close company. A **close investment-holding company** is a close company which is not a trading company and is not a member of a trading group.

2.2 Loans to participators

> **FAST FORWARD**
>
> The rules on loans and benefits from close companies are intended to deter shareholders from using the obvious ways of extracting value from their company without paying tax.

When a close company makes a loan to one of its participators or an associate it must make a tax payment to HMRC equal to 32.5% of the loan for loans made on or after 6 April 2016. This may be referred to as 'penalty tax'. If the loan is repaid, HMRC will repay this tax charge.

For companies which are not large, the tax charge is due for payment nine months and one day after the end of the accounting period. The tax charge is subject to the quarterly payments on account regime if the company is large. If the loan is repaid before the tax charge is due to be paid then the requirement to pay the penalty tax charge is cancelled. Interest runs from the due date until the earlier of payment of the tax and repayment of the loan. The loan must be notified on the company's tax return.

A loan for these purposes includes:

- A debt owed to the company
- A debt incurred by a participator or his associate and assigned to the company
- An advance of money
- A director's overdrawn current account

Certain loans are excluded from these provisions. These are:

- Money owed for goods or services supplied in the ordinary course of the company's trade unless the credit period exceeds:

    - Six months, or, if less
    - The normal credit period given to the company's other customers.

- Loans to directors and employees providing they do not exceed £15,000 in total per borrower and:

    - The borrower works full-time for the close company
    - He does not have a material interest (entitlement to over 5% of the assets available for distribution on a winding up) in the close company.

If at the time a loan was made the borrower did not have a material interest but he later acquires one, the company is regarded as making a loan to him at that date.

When all or part of the loan is repaid by the participator to the company, or the company writes off all or part of the loan, then the company can reclaim all or a corresponding part of the tax charge paid over to HMRC. If the loan is repaid or written of on or after the due date for paying the tax charge, the tax is not repayable until nine months and one day after the end of the accounting period of repayment or write off of the loan.

HMRC pay interest up to the time they repay the tax. If the loan is repaid/written off before nine months from the end of the accounting period in which the loan is made, interest runs from the end of those nine months. Otherwise, it runs from the date when the tax is repayable.

<table>
<tr><td>Exam focus point</td><td>If a loan made during an accounting period is to be repaid during the next accounting period, repayment before the due date for payment of the corporation tax will avoid the need for the penalty tax charge to be paid. Later repayment will defer the refund date for a year.</td></tr>
</table>

Although tax is charged on the company when a loan is made to a participator, the loan is not at that stage treated as the participator's income. If the loan is later written off:

(a) **The amount written off is treated as the participator's income** and is included within his total income. It is taxed **as if it were a dividend** received by him

(b) If the participator is a director or employee, there is no taxable benefit because the above tax charge applies instead

Question
Close company loan

Cinnamon Ltd, a close company which prepares accounts to 31 July each year, lends £50,000 to a shareholder in July 2018. Cinnamon Ltd is required to account for a tax charge of £16,250 to HMRC. In July 2019 the shareholder repays £20,000. In January 2019 Cinnamon Ltd writes off the remaining £30,000. Compute the amount of penalty tax recovered by Cinnamon Ltd following the repayment in July 2019 and the write off in January 2020.

Answer

(a) The penalty tax recovered after the repayment is $\frac{20,000}{50,000} \times £16,250 = £6,500$.

(b) The penalty tax recovered after the write off is £9,750.

2.3 Benefits treated as distributions

Benefits given by a close company to participators and their associates and which are not taxable earnings, for example where the participator does not work for the company, **are treated as distributions.** The amount of the deemed distribution is the amount that would otherwise be taxed as earnings. The actual cost is a disallowable expense for corporation tax purposes and no capital allowances can be claimed by the company on the provision of assets which are treated as distributions.

Question
Benefits

Olive Ltd provides a new car for Liam, who is a participator but not a director or employee of Olive Ltd, in May 2018. The taxable benefit in 2018/19 under the income tax legislation would be valued at £3,500. No fuel is provided. What are the tax consequences?

Answer

Liam is taxed as if he had received a dividend of £3,500 in 2018/19. Olive Ltd cannot deduct capital allowances on the car or any running costs in computing its taxable profits.

Chapter roundup

- A company that generates income from investments can usually deduct the expenses of managing their investments for corporation tax purposes.

- The rules on loans and benefits from close companies are intended to deter shareholders from using the obvious ways of extracting value from their company without paying tax.

Quick quiz

1   How may a company obtain relief for management expenses?

2   What is a close company?

3   What are the immediate consequences of a loan by a close company to a participator?

4   What are the tax consequences of the repayment by a participator of the whole of a loan made by a close company?

5   What items are treated as distributions by close companies?

Answers to quick quiz

1   Management expenses are deductible when computing taxable total profits A claim can be made to deduct whole or part of any excess management expenses in the next accounting period as if they were management expenses deductible for that accounting period.

2   A close company is one that is under the control of either five or fewer shareholders or any number of shareholding directors.

3   When a close company makes a loan to one of its participators it must make a payment to HMRC equal to 32.5% of the loan.

4   When all of a loan is repaid by the participator, the close company can reclaim all of the tax charge paid over to HMRC.

5   Benefits given to participators or their associates which are not taxed under the benefits legislation.

Now try the questions below from the Practice Question Bank

Number	Level	Marks	Time
Q28	Introductory	15	29 mins
Q38	Examination	25	49 mins

Question 38 has been analysed to show you how to approach Advanced Taxation (ATX–UK) exams.

Groups and consortia

26

Topic list	Syllabus reference
1 Types of group	A4(a)E5
2 Annual investment allowance	A4(e)(i)
3 Group relief	A4(a)E5,(e)(iv),(v),(viii)
4 Chargeable gains group	A4(a)E5,(e)(ii),(vi),(vii)
5 Succession to trade	A4(e)(iii)

Introduction

So far we have studied the corporation tax rules for single companies. In this chapter we consider the extent to which tax law recognises group relationships between companies.

Companies in a group are still separate entities with their own tax liabilities but tax law recognises the close relationship between group companies. They can, if they meet certain conditions, share their losses and pass assets between each other without chargeable gains.

Consortium companies are companies which are controlled by several companies. They can also share their losses, but the rules are restricted to recognise the ownership shares of the controlling companies.

In the next chapter, we will complete our study of corporation tax by looking at overseas aspects.

Study guide

		Intellectual level
4	**Corporation tax liabilities in situations involving further overseas and group aspects and in relation to special types of company, and the application of additional exemptions and reliefs**	
(a)	The contents of the Taxation - United Kingdom (TX – UK) study guide, for corporation tax, under heading:	2
•	E5 The effect of a group corporate structure for corporation tax purposes	
(e)	The effect of a group structure for corporation tax purposes:	3
(i)	Advise on the allocation of the annual investment allowance between group or related companies	
(ii)	Advise on the tax consequences of a transfer of intangible assets	
(iii)	Advise on the tax consequences of a transfer of a trade and assets where there is common control	
(iv)	Understand the meaning of consortium owned company and consortium member	2
(v)	Advise on the operation of consortium relief	
(vi)	Determine pre-entry losses and understand their tax treatment	
(vii)	Determine the degrouping charge where a company leaves a group within six years of receiving an asset by way of a no gain/no loss transfer	
(viii)	Determine the effects of the anti-avoidance provisions, where arrangements exist for a company to leave a group	

Exam guide

Groups and consortia are likely to be examined at most sittings. You must understand the difference between the definitions of a 75% group for group relief and a chargeable gains group, and understand the definition of a consortium. The question is likely to require a consideration of the various reliefs specifically available in group situations, with a view to minimising the group's tax liability.

Knowledge brought forward from earlier studies

This chapter revises the rules for group relief and for the transfer of capital assets between group companies and extends these to cover intangible fixed assets. It introduces the rules on allocation of the annual investment allowance between companies, consortium relief, and examines the anti-avoidance rules specifically applicable to groups.

The technical changes for Advanced Taxation (ATX – UK) exams in Financial Year 2018 from the material studied for Taxation (TX – UK) for exams in Financial Year 2017 involve the availability of carry forward group relief.

1 Types of group

A group exists for taxation purposes where one company is a subsidiary of another. The percentage shareholding involved determines the taxation consequences of the fact that there is a group.

The types of relationship for tax purposes covered in this chapter are:

- **Groups for annual investment allowance purposes**
- **Loss relief**
- **Consortia**
- **Chargeable gains groups**

2 Annual investment allowance

A group of companies is only entitled to a single annual investment allowance (AIA) which can be allocated between the companies as they think fit. A similar rule applies to companies under common control.

One of the competencies you require to fulfil Performance Objective 15 Tax computations and assessments of the PER is to prepare or contribute to the computation or assessment of tax computations for single companies, groups or other entities. You can apply the knowledge you obtain from this section of the text to help to demonstrate this competence.

2.1 Allocation of AIA between group companies   12/14, 9/15

A group of companies is entitled to a single annual investment allowance (AIA) between the group companies. The companies may allocate the allowance between them as they think fit. The relevant AIA qualifying expenditure is that incurred by the group companies in their chargeable periods ending in the financial year being considered.

A group for these purposes is defined in relation to a 'parent undertaking' in a financial year. A company is a parent undertaking of another company (the subsidiary undertaking) if:

- **It holds a majority of the voting rights in the undertaking**

- **It is a member of the undertaking and has the right to appoint or remove a majority of its board of directors**

- **It has the right to exercise a dominant influence over the undertaking** by virtue of a provision in the articles or under a control contract

- **It is a member of the undertaking and controls alone,** pursuant to an agreement with other shareholders or members, **a majority of the voting rights in the undertaking**

The parent undertaking company must satisfy one of these conditions at the end of the subsidiary company's chargeable period of account ending in the financial year being considered.

The following factors may be relevant when considering how to allocate the annual investment allowance:

- **Nature of expenditure**, for example main pool or special rate pool (more tax efficient to set against special rate pool because of lower subsequent WDA)

- **If the company is making a loss, how that loss can be relieved** (the AIA will create or increase a loss)

- **Lowering augmented profits** so they fall below the level where a company is required to pay corporation tax by instalments thus improving cash flow within the group.

2.2 Allocation of AIA between companies under common control

Companies under common control are entitled to a single annual investment allowance between them and the companies may allocate the allowance between them as they think fit.

Companies are under common control if:

- **They are controlled by the same person,** and
- **They are related to one another**

'Control' means that a person has power to secure that the affairs of a company are conducted in accordance with the wishes of that person. This could be by the holding of shares or voting rights or as the result of any powers in the company's constitution or that of another body.

Companies are related to one another if either they share premises or carry on similar activities.

Similar considerations apply to the consideration of how to allocate the annual investment allowance between companies under common control as to companies within a group.

3 Group relief   6/14, 9/15, 9/16, 12/17, 6/18

Exam focus point

> **ACCA's article Corporation tax – group relief for Advanced Taxation (ATX – UK),** written by a member of the Advanced Taxation (ATX – UK) examining team, considers a number of group relief tax planning issues that could be introduced in an exam question.

> One of the competencies you require to fulfil Performance Objective 17 Tax planning and advice of the PER is to mitigate and/or defer tax liabilities through the use of standard reliefs, exemptions and incentives. You can apply the knowledge you obtain from this section of the text to help to demonstrate this competence.

3.1 Definitions

> Group relief is available where the existence of a group or consortium is established through companies resident anywhere in the world.

The group relief provisions enable companies within a 75% group to transfer trading losses and certain other losses to other profit making companies within the group, in order to reduce the group's overall corporation tax liability.

Key term

> For one company to be a **75% subsidiary** of another, the holding company must have:
>
> - At least 75% of the ordinary share capital of the subsidiary
> - A right to at least 75% of the distributable income of the subsidiary, and
> - A right to at least 75% of the net assets of the subsidiary were it to be wound up.
>
> Two companies are members of a group for group relief purposes where one is a 75% subsidiary of the other, or both are 75% subsidiaries of a third company. Ordinary share capital is any share capital other than most preference shares.

Two companies are in a group only if there is a 75% effective interest. Thus an 80% subsidiary (T) of an 80% subsidiary (S) is not in a group with the holding company (H), because the effective interest is only 80% × 80% = 64%. However, S and T are in a group and can claim group relief from each other. S **cannot** claim group relief from T and pass it on to H; it can only claim group relief for its own use.

A group relief group may include non-UK resident companies. However, losses may generally only be surrendered between companies within the charge to corporation tax (UK resident companies and overseas resident companies with a UK permanent establishment).

3.2 Example

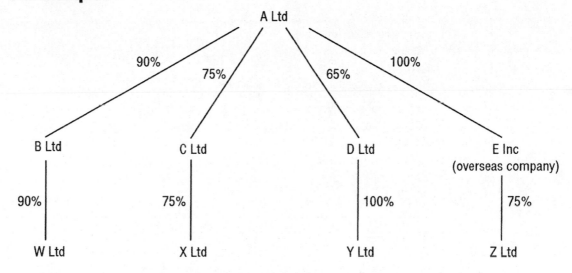

The companies in the group for group relief purposes are:

A Ltd
B Ltd
W Ltd (81% effective holding by A)
C Ltd
E Inc
Z Ltd (75% effective holding by A)

In addition C Ltd and X Ltd and also D Ltd and Y Ltd form their own separate mini-groups.

3.3 Current period group relief

FAST FORWARD

A surrendering company can surrender any amount of its current period trading loss but a claimant company can only claim an amount up to its available taxable total profits.

3.3.1 Operation of current period group relief

A company which has made a current period loss (the surrendering company) may transfer all or part of this loss to another member of the 75% group (the claimant company).

A **claimant company** is assumed to use its own current period losses or losses brought forward in working out the profits against which it may claim group relief, even if it does not in fact claim loss relief against total income for those losses. Furthermore, **group relief is against profits after all other reliefs for the current period or brought forward from earlier periods**, including non-trading deficits on loan relationships and qualifying charitable donations. Group relief is given before relief for any amounts brought back from later periods.

A surrendering company may group relieve a current period loss before setting it against its own profits for the period of the loss, and may specify any amount to be surrendered. Any amount of trading losses and non-trading loan relationships deficits may be surrendered: they need not first be used by the loss-making company.

Qualifying charitable donations, property business losses, management expenses and non-trading losses on intangible fixed assets can be surrendered as group relief only to the extent that they exceed the surrendering company's other profits of the accounting period, ignoring any losses of the current period or any other period. Other profits include any amounts apportioned from controlled foreign companies.

Where a surrendering company has more than one of these types of loss available for surrender, the order of surrender is:

- Qualifying charitable donations
- Property business losses
- Management expenses
- Non-trading losses on intangible fixed assets.

The legislation does not specify the order of surrender of trade losses, excess capital allowances or non-trading loan relationship deficits. The surrendering company is free to choose which of these it surrenders in what order.

Question

Group relief

Kit plc has one 75% subsidiary, Lion plc. The results for the group for the year ended 31 March 2019 are as follows:

	Kit plc £	Lion plc £
Trading (loss)	(4,000)	(20,700)
Non-trading loan relationship income	10,000	2,900
Chargeable gain	15,000	0
Qualifying charitable donations	(2,000)	(3,200)

What is the maximum current period group relief that Kit plc can claim from Lion plc?

Answer

Lion plc can surrender losses under group relief as follows:

	£
Current period trading loss	20,700
Excess qualifying charitable donations £(3,200 – 2,900)	300
Total losses available for current period group relief	21,000

Kit plc has the following available taxable total profits:

	£
Non-trading loan relationship income	10,000
Chargeable gain	15,000
	25,000
Less current period trading loss	(4,000)
	21,000
Less qualifying charitable donations	(2,000)
Available taxable total profits	19,000

Maximum group relief that Kit plc can claim from Lion Ltd (lower of £21,000 and £19,000)	19,000

Kit plc must take account of its current period trading loss in working out available taxable total profits even if it does not actually make a claim for current period relief.

3.3.2 Corresponding accounting periods

Losses surrendered under current period group relief must be set against profits of a corresponding accounting period. If the accounting periods of a surrendering company and a claimant company are not the same this means that both the profits and losses must be apportioned so that only the results of the period of overlap may be set off. Apportionment is on a time basis.

However, if the corresponding accounting periods are relevant because a company joins or leaves a group, an alternative method may be used if the result given by time-apportionment would be unjust or unreasonable.

Question — Corresponding accounting periods

	£
Silver Ltd incurs a trading loss for the year to 30 September 2018	(150,000)
Gold Ltd makes taxable profits:	
for the year to 31 December 2017	200,000
for the year to 31 December 2018	100,000

What current period group relief can Gold Ltd claim from Silver Ltd?

Answer

Gold Ltd can claim current period group relief as follows.

	£
For the year ended 31 December 2017 profits of the corresponding accounting period (1.10.17 – 31.12.17) are £200,000 × 3/12	50,000
Losses of the corresponding accounting period are £150,000 × 3/12	37,500
A claim for £37,500 of current period group relief may be made against Gold Ltd's profits	
For the year ended 31 December 2018 profits of the corresponding accounting period (1.1.18 – 30.9.18) are £100,000 × 9/12	75,000
Losses of the corresponding accounting period are £150,000 × 9/12	112,500
A claim for £75,000 of current period group relief may be made against Gold Ltd's profits	

If a claimant company claims relief for losses surrendered by more than one company, the total relief that may be claimed for a period of overlap is limited to the proportion of the claimant's profits attributable to that period. Similarly, if a company surrenders losses to more than one claimant, the total losses that may be surrendered in a period of overlap is limited to the proportion of the surrendering company's losses attributable to that period.

3.4 Carry forward group relief   New

FAST FORWARD Carried forward losses may also be surrendered under group relief.

Exam focus point

A question **will not be set** in Advanced Taxation (ATX – UK). involving carried forward losses arising prior to 1 April 2017 (nor in a period straddling 1 April 2017) since carry forward group relief is not available for pre-1 April 2017 losses.

3.4.1 Operation of carry forward group relief

A company which has a loss carried forward (the surrendering company) may transfer all or part of this loss to another member of the 75% group (the claimant company).

The surrendering company may surrender carried forward trading losses, property business income losses, non-trading loan relationships deficits, management expenses and non-trading losses on intangible fixed assets to other group companies under carry forward group relief. Unlike current period group relief, **a surrendering company can only surrender carried forward losses that it cannot deduct from its own total profits for the current period.** The company may specify an amount less than the maximum amount to be surrendered.

The claimant company must use its own losses to the fullest extent possible in working out the available taxable total profits against which it may claim carry forward group relief. Carry forward group relief is set against taxable total profits after all other reliefs for the current period but before relief for any amounts carried back from later periods.

Broom plc has one 75% subsidiary, Sweep Ltd. The results for the group for the year ended 31 March 2019 are as follows:

	Broom plc £	Sweep Ltd £
Trading profit	50,000	60,000
Trading loss carried forward at 1 April 2018	(6,500)	(120,000)
Non-trading loan relationship income	2,000	3,000
Non-trading loan relationship debit brought forward at 1 April 2018	(300)	(4,400)
Chargeable gain	9,000	2,000

What is the maximum carry forward group relief that Broom plc can claim from Sweep Ltd?

Answer

Sweep Ltd can surrender its carried forward trading loss and its non-trading loan relationship debit under carry forward group relief as follows:

	£
Carried forward trading loss	120,000
Carried forward non-trading loan relationship debit	4,400
Less: could be used against own current period total profits £(60,000 + 3,000 + 2,000)	(65,000)
Loss available for carry forward group relief	59,400

Broom plc has the following available taxable total profits:

	£
Trading income	50,000
Non-trading loan relationship income	2,000
Chargeable gain	9,000
	61,000
Less carried forward trading loss	(6,500)
carried forward non-trading loan relationship debit	(300)
Available taxable total profits	54,200

Maximum carry forward group relief that Broom plc can claim from Sweep plc (lower of £59,400 and £54,200)	54,200

3.4.2 Overlapping periods

Losses surrendered under carry forward group relief must be set against profits of an overlapping accounting period. This is similar to the rules about corresponding accounting periods discussed earlier in this chapter.

The **overlapping period** is the period which **falls within both of the following**:

- The accounting period to which the **surrendering company has carried forward the loss**; and
- The accounting period in which the **claimant company will offset the loss**.

3.4.3 Restriction on carry forward group relief following change of ownership

There is a restriction on the use of carry forward group relief where there has been **a change in ownership of a company** (Company A) **such that Company A joins a group relief group.**

Company A's carried forward losses arising before it joined the group cannot be surrendered to other group companies, broadly for five years following the change in ownership.

Note that there is generally **no restriction on other group companies surrendering losses to Company A.**

3.5 Group relief claims

A claim for group relief is normally made on the claimant company's tax return. It is ineffective unless a notice of consent is also given by the surrendering company. Where the surrendering company is also claiming loss relief against its own profits the group relief surrender must be made first.

Any payment by the claimant company for group relief, up to the amount of the loss surrendered, is ignored for all corporation tax purposes.

3.6 Arrangements to leave a group

Group relief is not available for any period during which there are arrangements in force for either the surrendering company or the claimant company to leave the group. If necessary, profits and losses are apportioned on a time basis.

The term 'arrangements' is not defined, but HMRC normally accept that negotiations to sell a company are not arrangements until an offer is accepted, even if it is then subject to contract or is conditional. If shareholder approval is required for the sale, arrangements do not exist until approval has been given.

3.7 Consortium relief   9/15

FAST FORWARD
Within a consortium there is some scope for loss relief.

The definition of a consortium is given below.

Key term

> A company is owned by a consortium (and is known **as a consortium-owned company**) if.
>
> - 75% or more of its ordinary share capital is owned by companies (the members of the consortium), none of which has a holding of less than 5%, and
> - Each member of the consortium is entitled to at least 5% of any profits available for distribution to equity holders of the company and at least 5% of any assets so available on a winding up.

Illustration of a consortium

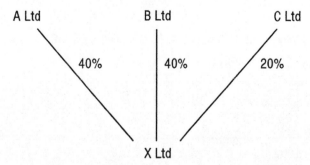

X Ltd is the consortium-owned company A Ltd, B Ltd and C Ltd are the consortium members.

Consortium relief is a loss relief which is available:

(a)   Where the surrendering company is a trading company owned by a consortium and is not a 75% subsidiary of any one company and the claimant company belongs to the consortium

(b)   Where the surrendering company is a trading company which is a 90% subsidiary of a holding company which is owned by a consortium and is not a 75% subsidiary of any one company and the claimant company is a member of the consortium

(c)   Where the surrendering company is a holding company owned by a consortium and is not a 75% subsidiary of any one company and the claimant company is a member of the consortium.

A **trading company** is one whose business consists wholly or mainly in carrying on a trade. A holding company is one whose business consists wholly or mainly in holding shares in companies which are trading companies.

A consortium-owned company can surrender losses in proportion to the stakes of the members of the consortium. Thus if a member holds 20% of the shares in the company, up to 20% of the company's losses can be surrendered to that member. **Current period losses are available for current period consortium relief and they must be set against profits of a corresponding accounting period. Consortium relief is given by the company receiving the loss deducting it from total profits.**

Consortium relief can also flow downwards. **A consortium member may surrender its losses to set against its share of the consortium-owned company's profits.** So, a member with a 25% stake in the consortium-owned company can surrender losses to cover up to 25% of the company's profits.

Whereas normally a surrendering company can surrender current period group relief without having to consider any possible current period loss relief claim, **a loss made by a consortium-owned company must be reduced by any potential loss relief claims against current period profits** (not profits of previous periods) **before it may be surrendered as current period consortium relief.**

Carried forward losses can also be surrendered under consortium relief.

Although a consortium can be established with non-UK resident companies, losses cannot, in general, be surrendered to/from a non-UK resident.

Question	Consortium relief of losses

Cranberry Ltd is owned 60% by Apple Ltd, 30% by Banana Ltd and 10% by an overseas company Kiwi Inc. Results for the year ended 31 March 2019 are as follows:

	Apple Ltd	Banana Ltd	Cranberry Ltd
	£	£	£
Trading profit/(loss)	200,000	75,000	(50,000)
Property income	0	0	12,000

Compute the corporation tax liabilities of all three companies, assuming that all possible current period consortium relief claims are made but that Cranberry Ltd does not claim current period loss relief.

Answer

Apple Ltd may claim £(50,000 – 12,000) × 60% = £22,800.

Banana Ltd may claim £(50,000 – 12,000) × 30% = £11,400.

Apple Ltd's corporation tax liability is:
£(200,000 – 22,800) = £177,200 × 19%   £33,668

Banana Ltd's corporation tax liability is:
£(75,000 – 11,400) = £63,600 × 19%   £12,084

Cranberry Ltd's corporation tax liability is:
£12,000 × 19%   £2,280

3.8 Alternative loss reliefs

Several alternative loss reliefs may be available, including group relief and/or consortium relief. In making a choice consider:

- **How quickly relief will be obtained**: obtaining loss relief by using current period group relief or consortium relief is quicker than a company using its own carry forward loss relief and so generally preferable to carrying forward the loss.

- **The extent to which relief for qualifying charitable donations might be lost**: group relief is deducted after qualifying charitable donations in the claimant company, so relief for these donations is not lost. By contrast, if the loss-making company claims relief for the loss against its own current year total profits, relief for qualifying charitable donations in that company may be wasted.

3.9 Payment of corporation tax and group relief   9/16

Companies whose augmented profits exceed the profit threshold may be required to pay corporation tax in instalments. **Group relief can be used to even out profits across a group and thus provide a cash flow advantage by minimising the amount of corporation tax payable in instalments.**

| Question | Payment of corporation tax and group relief |

The Jar plc group consists of Jar plc and its 100% subsidiary Klip plc and its 80% subsidiary Mat plc. All companies are UK resident and prepare accounts to 31 March each year. In the year to 31 March 2018 all of the companies in the Jar plc group paid corporation tax in instalments. In the year to 31 March 2019 the Jar plc group companies had the following results:

	Jar plc	Klip plc	Mat plc
	£	£	£
Trading profit/(loss)	400,000	450,000	(100,000)
Dividends received from non-group companies	30,000	75,000	0

Compute the overall corporation tax liability of the Jar plc group and state the due date of payment, assuming that any claims are made which defer payment of tax.

Answer

The Jar plc group is a group relief group and the companies are also 51% related group companies.

The profit threshold for paying corporation tax by instalments is therefore £1,500,000/3 = £500,000.

Jar plc's augmented profits are £(400,000 + 30,000) = £430,000 which is below the profit threshold so it will not pay corporation tax in instalments.

Klip plc has augmented profits of £(450,000 + 75,000) = £525,000. A group relief claim should therefore be made to reduce these to £500,000 or less so that Klip plc does not have to pay corporation tax in instalments. (The following computation assumes that the excess loss of £25,000 is also claimed by Klip plc but it could also be claimed by Jar plc without affecting the overall corporation tax payable by the Jar plc group nor affecting the date of payment.)

Jar plc's corporation tax liability is:
£400,000 × 19%   £76,000

Klip plc's corporation tax liability is:
£(450,000 – 100,000) = £350,000 × 19%   £66,500

The total corporation tax liability of the Jar plc group (due date 1 January 2020) is:
£(76,000 + 66,500)   £142,500

4 Chargeable gains group   9/15, 6/16, 9/16, 6/17, 12/17, 6/18

ACCA's article **Corporation tax – groups and chargeable gains for Advanced Taxation (ATX – UK)**, written by a member of the Advanced Taxation (ATX – UK) examining team, considers various issues relating to capital gains groups that could be introduced in an exam question.

4.1 Definition

Companies are in a chargeable gains group if:

(a)   At each level, there is a 75% holding
(b)   The top company has an effective interest of over 50% in the group companies.

If A holds 75% of B, B holds 75% of C and C holds 75% of D, then A, B and C are in such a group, but D is outside the group because A's interest in D is only 75% × 75% × 75% = 42.1875%. Furthermore, D is not in a group with C, because the group must include the top company (A). This is illustrated in the diagram below.

4.2 Example

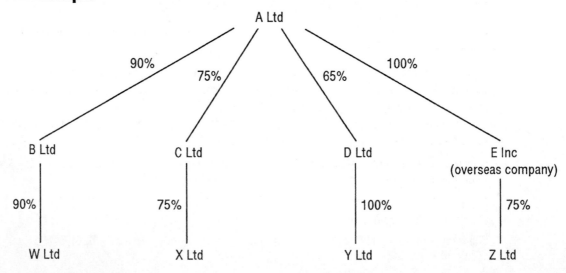

The companies in a chargeable gains group are:

A Ltd
B Ltd
W Ltd
C Ltd
X Ltd (75% subsidiary of 75% subsidiary, effective interest over 50%)
E Inc
Z Ltd

There is a separate chargeable gains group of D Ltd and Y Ltd.

4.3 Intra-group transfers   6/17

FAST FORWARD

Within a chargeable gains group, assets are automatically transferred at no gain/no loss.

Companies in a group make intra-group transfers of chargeable assets without a chargeable gain or an allowable loss arising. No election is needed, as this relief is compulsory. The assets are deemed to be transferred at such a price as will give the transferor no gain and no loss. Similarly, intangible assets can be transferred between members of a chargeable gains group without a trading profit or loss arising (see earlier in this text).

Non-UK resident companies are included as members of a chargeable gains group. Provided the assets transferred do not result in a potential leakage of UK corporation tax, no gain/no loss transfers are possible within a worldwide (global) group of companies. This means that it may be possible to make no gain/no loss transfers to non-UK resident companies with a branch or agency in the UK.

4.4 Degrouping charge on company leaving the group
12/13, 6/15, 6/16, 12/17

FAST FORWARD

A degrouping charge arises if a company leaves a group within six years of acquiring an asset from another group member.

A charge arises if a company leaves a group while it owns one or more assets transferred to it by another group member within the previous six years under the provisions described above. The departing company is treated as though it had, at the time of its acquisition of such assets, sold and immediately re-acquired them at their then market values. The consequent gain or loss (computed using indexation allowance up to the date of the no gain/no loss transfer or December 2017 if earlier) is sometimes referred to as a degrouping charge. This gain is added to (or if a loss, deducted from) the consideration received by the selling company when calculating the gain or loss on the disposal of shares of the departing company.

Any exemption or relief that may apply to the share disposal, such as the substantial shareholding exemption (dealt with earlier in this text), also applies to the element of a gain on the share disposal relating to the degrouping charge.

Exam focus point

Be careful when deciding whether the degrouping charge applies. It applies where there is a **sale of the shares in the company** as a result of which the company leaves the group. It does **not apply where a company simply sells its assets** to another company.

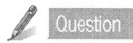
In May 2018, Top Ltd, a trading company, sold the whole of the share capital of Bottom Ltd, a 100% subsidiary, to Take plc for £600,000. Bottom Ltd is an investment company and had been owned by Top Ltd since July 2006 when Top Ltd acquired the entire share capital for £50,000. The indexation allowance to December 2017 is £20,050.

Included in Bottom Ltd's assets is a warehouse acquired by Side Ltd in January 2008 for £96,000. Side Ltd is also a 100% subsidiary of Top Ltd. The warehouse was transferred by Side Ltd to Bottom Ltd in August 2012 for £100,000. Its market value at the date of transfer was £310,000. The indexation allowance on a sale in August 2012 would have been £15,168.

What is the effect of Bottom Ltd leaving the group? Compute Top Ltd's corporation tax for the year ended 31 March 2019 if it has trading income of £2,000,000. How would your answer be different if Bottom Ltd was a trading company?

Answer

Bottom Ltd leaves the group within six years of acquiring the warehouse from Side Ltd. Bottom Ltd will be treated as if it had sold the warehouse at its market value in August 2012 and then immediately reacquired it.

	£	£
Proceeds (ie MV in August 2012)		310,000
Less cost: cost to Side Ltd	96,000	
indexation allowance to August 2012	15,168	
		(111,168)
Chargeable gain		198,832

Top Ltd's gain on the sale of the shares in Bottom Ltd is as follows.

	£	£
Proceeds received from Take plc		600,000
Degrouping charge gain		198,832
		798,832
Less cost: original cost	50,000	
indexation allowance to December 2017	20,050	
		(70,050)
Chargeable gain		728,782

Top Ltd's corporation tax for the year to 31.3.19 is as follows:

	£
Trading profits	2,000,000
Chargeable gain on sale of Bottom Ltd shares	728,782
Taxable total profits	2,728,782
Corporation tax £2,728,782 × 19%	£518,469

If Bottom Ltd was a trading company, Top Ltd will not have a chargeable gain on the sale of its shares in Bottom Ltd, due to the substantial shareholdings exemption applying to the sale of the subsidiary. This will include the element relating to the degrouping charge. The corporation tax liability of Top Ltd for the year to 31.3.19 will therefore be £2,000,000 × 19% = £380,000.

The degrouping charge was tested in December 2012 Question 1 Flame plc group. The examining team commented that: 'The degrouping charge was done well on the whole. Those candidates who did not do so well were divided into two groups. The first group missed the degrouping charge altogether. The second group of candidates knew that there would be a degrouping charge somewhere in the answer and earned most of the marks available for saying why and for calculating it. However, they did not know which of the two possible transactions (a sale of a group company's shares or a sale of its assets) would give rise to the charge and either put it into the wrong section of the report or put it into both sections. This was not particularly costly, but would have been in a different question which was only concerned with one of these two transactions. Candidates must know their stuff; degrouping charges only occur on the sale of a company, ie on the sale of shares, and not on the sale of assets.'

4.5 Transfer of gains and losses within group   6/15, 6/17, 6/18

FAST FORWARD

Gains and losses can be transferred between group companies.

One of the competencies you require to fulfil Performance Objective 17 Tax planning and advice of the PER is to mitigate and/or defer tax liabilities through the use of standard reliefs, exemptions and incentives. You can apply the knowledge you obtain from this section of the text to help to demonstrate this competence.

Two members of a chargeable gains group can elect to transfer a chargeable gain or allowable loss, or any part of a gain or loss, between them. Both companies must be members of the group at the time that the gain or loss arose. The election must be made within two years of the end of the accounting period in which the gain or loss accrues in the company which is making the transfer.

From a tax planning point of view, election(s) should be made to match gains and losses. **Intra-group transfers can be used in a similar way to group relief to ensure that payment of corporation tax by instalments is minimised.**

4.6 Rollover relief   12/14, 12/17

FAST FORWARD

Rollover relief is available in a chargeable gains group.

If a member of a chargeable gains group disposes of an asset eligible for chargeable gains rollover relief it may treat all of the group companies as a single unit for the purpose of claiming such relief. Acquisitions by other group members within the qualifying period of one year before the disposal to three years afterwards may **be matched with the disposal.** However, both the disposing company and the acquiring company must make the claim. If an asset is transferred at no gain and no loss between group members, that transfer does not count as the acquisition of an asset for rollover relief purpose. Claims may also be made by non-trading group members which hold assets used for other group members' trades.

Try to remember the following summary – it will be of great help in the exam.
Parent Co owns ≥ 75% of subsidiary and has indirect holding of ≥ 75% of sub-subsidiaries

- Surrender trading losses, excess property income losses, excess qualifying charitable donations, loan deficits, excess management expenses to companies with some taxable total profits for same time period

Parent Co owns ≥ 75% of subsidiary and has indirect holding of > 50% of sub-subsidiaries (but must be ≥ 75% at each level)

- Transfer assets between companies automatically at no gain/no loss
- Chargeable gains and losses can be matched between group member companies
- All companies treated as one for rollover relief purposes.

4.7 Intangible fixed assets

Similar rules apply to intangible fixed assets held within a chargeable gains group, although with some differences particularly regarding degrouping. The rules are:

(a) **Rollover relief** can be claimed where an intangible fixed asset used for trade purposes is sold where the reinvestment is made by another member of the chargeable gains group, and also where the reinvestment is in the shares of another company

(b) **Transfers of intangible assets between members of a chargeable gains group are on a tax neutral basis** (ie no disposal by transferee company, no acquisition by transferor company but the transferor company is treated as having held the asset throughout so that the transferee company 'stands in the shoes' of the transferor company)

(c) Where a company leaves a chargeable gains group holding an intangible asset transferred to it in the previous six years the gain or loss that would have arisen on the date of the transfer is realised and included (in the computation of the departing company) in trading profits (if the asset is used for the trade), the profits of a UK property letting business (if the asset is used for letting), or miscellaneous income (if the asset is an investment)

(d) The degrouping charge may be transferred from the company leaving the group to another (old) group company

(e) Either the company leaving the chargeable gains group or a continuing member can claim to rollover any profit arising. The departing company can claim relief if it retains the profit and acquires a new asset. The continuing company can claim relief if the profit has been transferred to it and it acquires a new intangible asset

4.8 Pre-entry losses

4.8.1 Pre-entry capital losses

FAST FORWARD

Restrictions apply to the use of pre-entry losses within chargeable gains groups.

A chargeable gains group might acquire a company that has capital losses brought forward. The use of such 'pre-entry' capital losses is restricted.

If a company (Company A) joins a chargeable gains group, Company A's pre-entry (capital) losses are losses made on disposals before Company A joined the group.

Company A's pre-entry losses may (subject to the usual rule against not carrying back capital losses to previous accounting periods) be set against gains on assets which:

- Company A disposed of before joining the group

- Company A already owned when it joined the group

- Company A acquired after joining the group from someone outside the group and which have, since acquisition, not been used except for the purposes of any trade or business which Company A was carrying on immediately before joining the group and either continued to carry on or was carried on by another group member until the disposals giving rise to the gains.

In any one accounting period, pre-entry losses (whether of the current period or brought forward) are used (so far as possible) before other losses.

4.8.2 Pre-entry losses set against total profits

A chargeable gains group might acquire a company that has losses brought forward such as trading losses which could be set against total profits. The use of such 'pre-entry' losses is restricted.

The **restriction applies** where:

- There has been a **change in ownership of a company (Company A);** and

- A chargeable gain is transferred to Company A by another chargeable gains group company (either by transfer of the asset on a no gain, no loss basis which is then disposed of by Company A realising a gain or by an election being made to transfer a gain to Company A).

If the gain is treated as accruing to Company A within five years of the date of the change of ownership, Company A cannot relieve the gain by using its own losses carried forward at the date of the change in ownership.

There is a **similar provision** which applies to **transfers of intangible assets on a tax-neutral basis**.

There is a **similar provision** preventing the **use of carried forward losses** being transferred to Company A under **group relief** to relieve gains transferred to that company.

5 Succession to trade 6/17

FAST FORWARD

A succession occurs when a trade carried on by one company is transferred to another company in substantially the same ownership. In this case losses may be carried forward, subject to certain restrictions, and balancing adjustments do not arise for capital allowances purposes.

5.1 General principles

Generally, if a trade is transferred from one company (Company A) to another (Company B), that is treated as a cessation of the trade by Company A and a commencement of the trade by Company B. Any trading losses brought forward by Company A are extinguished and cannot be utilised by the Company B. In addition, balancing adjustments may arise on assets qualifying for capital allowances.

If however the **transfer of the trade amounts to a 'succession'**, it is **treated as continuing** for certain specific purposes.

Key term

> A **'succession to trade'** occurs if a trade carried on by one company (the 'predecessor' ie Company A) is transferred to another company (the 'successor' ie Company B) in **substantially the same ownership**.

The above test is met if the same persons hold an interest of at least 75% in the trade **both:**

(a)   At some time during the 12 months prior to transfer, and
(b)   At some time during the 24 months following the transfer

and throughout those periods the trade is carried on by a company chargeable to tax in respect of it.

The transfer of a trade from a company to its 75% subsidiary will generally qualify as a succession. Such a transfer is often referred to as a 'hive down'.

Other circumstances where a succession takes place include a transfer from a 75% subsidiary to its parent and a transfer of trade between two companies with a common 75% parent (or indeed owned to the extent of at least 75% by the same individual). There is no stipulation that the companies have to be UK resident, so the provisions can apply to UK branches of non-resident companies.

When a trade is transferred in this way:

(a) An **accounting period ends** on the date of transfer

(b) Company A may claim **capital allowances** in the final accounting period as if no transfer had taken place. Company B automatically takes over the unrelieved expenditure and is entitled to capital allowances thereon in the period in which the transfer takes place.

(c) Company B is entitled to relief for **carried forward trading losses** not utilised by Company A (subject to the restrictions explained in the next section).

The following are **not** transferred and remain with Company A:

(a) Capital losses
(b) Deficits on non-trading loan relationships

These provisions do **not** enable a trading loss incurred by the Company B to be carried back against profits realised by Company A. Also, Company A's cessation of trade does not qualify it for a three year carry back of losses.

5.2 Restrictions on use of transferred losses

There is a **restriction on the use of transferred losses if**:

(a) There has been a **change in ownership of a company (Company A)**, and

(b) **Company A transferred its trade to another company (Company B) within a period of eight years beginning three years before the change in ownership** (and therefore ending five years after the change in ownership).

For a **period of five years starting with the change in ownership, Company B cannot use Company A's transferred losses for carry forward loss relief against total profits** (only against profits of the transferred trade) and **cannot surrender them under group relief to another company.**

Chapter roundup

- A group of companies is only entitled to a single annual investment allowance (AIA) which can be allocated between the companies as they think fit. A similar rule applies to companies under common control.

- Group relief is available where the existence of a group or consortium is established through companies resident anywhere in the world.

- A surrendering company can surrender any amount of its current period trading loss but a claimant company can only claim an amount up to its available taxable total profits.

- Carried forward losses may also be surrendered under group relief.

- Within a consortium there is some scope for loss relief.

- Within a chargeable gains group, assets are automatically transferred at no gain/no loss.

- A degrouping charge arises if a company leaves a group within six years of acquiring an asset from another group member.

- Gains and losses can be transferred between group companies.

- Rollover relief is available in a chargeable gains group.

- Restrictions apply to the use of pre-entry losses within chargeable gains groups.

- A succession occurs when a trade carried on by one company is transferred to another company in substantially the same ownership. In this case losses may be carried forward, subject to certain restrictions, and balancing adjustments do not arise for capital allowances purposes.

Quick quiz

1   Under what circumstance may companies be entitled to a single annual investment allowance between them?

2   List the losses which may be current period group relieved.

3   List the losses which may be carry forward group relieved.

4   What is the definition of a consortium?

5   When may assets be transferred intra-group at no gain and no loss?

6   How can gains and losses within a chargeable gains group be matched with each other?

7   What is the restriction for pre-entry losses which could be set against total income where a company joins a chargeable gains group?

8   What are the benefits of a transfer of trade between companies being treated as a succession?

Answers to quick quiz

1   Companies are entitled to a single annual investment allowance between them either if they are in a group with a parent undertaking and a subsidiary undertaking or if the companies are under common control (controlled by a person and either sharing premises or carrying on similar activities).

2   Trading losses, excess UK property business losses, non-trading deficits on loan relationships, excess qualifying charitable donations, excess management expenses and excess non-trading losses on intangible fixed assets.

3   Carried forward trading losses, property business income losses, non-trading deficits on loan relationships, management expenses and non-trading losses on intangible fixed assets.

4   A company is owned by a consortium if 75% or more of its ordinary share capital is owned by companies none of which have a holding of less than 5%.

    Each consortium member (ie company shareholders) must have at least a 5% stake in profits and assets on a winding up in the consortium company.

5   No gain no loss asset transfers are automatic between companies in a chargeable gains group.

6   Two members of a chargeable gains group can elect to transfer all or part of gains and losses between them.

7   A gain transferred to a company joining a group which arises within five years of the date the company joined the group cannot be relieved by the company using its own losses which could be set against total income carried forward at the date of the change in ownership.

8   The predecessor company's losses may be carried forward and used by the successor company, subject to certain restrictions, and capital allowances balancing adjustments do not arise for the predecessor company.

Now try the question below from the Practice Question Bank

Number	Level	Marks	Time
Q29	Introductory	20	39 mins

Overseas aspects of corporate tax

Topic list	Syllabus reference
1 Company residence	A4(d)
2 Double taxation relief (DTR)	A4(d)(i),(v)
3 Groups of companies	A4(e)(ix)
4 Controlled foreign companies	A4(d)(iii)
5 Permanent establishment (PE) or subsidiary abroad	A4(d)(ii),(e)(ix)
6 Non-UK resident companies	A4(d)(iv)

Introduction

We have nearly completed our study of corporation tax, except for the consideration of overseas aspects.

This chapter starts by considering which country a company 'lives' in. We then see how relief may be given for overseas taxes suffered, how overseas companies may impact a group and how UK companies are taxed on the profits of certain overseas subsidiaries.

Finally, we look at UK companies trading abroad, and some miscellaneous points on overseas companies trading in the UK.

In the next chapter we will turn our attention to VAT.

Study guide

		Intellectual level
4	**Corporation tax liabilities in situations involving further overseas and group aspects and in relation to special types of company, and the application of additional exemptions and reliefs**	
(d)	The comprehensive calculation of corporation tax liability:	3
(i)	Assess the impact of the OECD model double tax treaty on corporation tax	
(ii)	Evaluate the meaning and implications of a permanent establishment	
(iii)	Identify and advise on the tax implications of controlled foreign companies	
(iv)	Advise on the tax position of overseas companies trading in the UK	
(v)	Calculate double taxation relief	
(e)	The effect of a group structure for corporation tax purposes:	3
(ix)	Advise on the tax treatment of an overseas branch	

Exam guide

A question on the overseas aspects of corporation tax could require you to advise on the tax consequences of relationships with overseas companies. This could involve a discussion of the merits of trading through a permanent establishment (eg a branch) or subsidiary, and could extend to the anti-avoidance controlled foreign company rules where the subsidiary is resident overseas but controlled by UK shareholders. Double tax relief is an important consideration; the relief is the lower of the UK corporation tax and the foreign tax paid.

Knowledge brought forward from earlier studies

The topics in this chapter are new.

1 Company residence

FAST FORWARD

Company residence is important in determining whether its profits are subject to UK tax.

1.1 Introduction

A company is resident in the UK if it is incorporated in the UK or if its central management and control are exercised in the UK. Central management and control are usually treated as exercised where the board of directors meets.

A UK resident company is subject to corporation tax on its worldwide profits.

1.2 Non-UK resident companies trading in the UK

A non-UK resident company will be chargeable to corporation tax if it carries on a trade in the UK through a permanent establishment (PE).

The profits of such a company which are chargeable to corporation tax, whether or not they arise in the UK, are:

- Any trading income arising directly or indirectly from the PE
- Any income from property or rights used by, or held by or for, the PE (other than dividends from UK companies)
- Any chargeable gains arising from the disposal of assets situated in the UK.

Key term

> A **permanent establishment** is a fixed place of business through which the business of the enterprise is wholly or partly carried on. It includes a branch, office, factory, workshop, mine, oil or gas well, quarry and construction project lasting more than twelve months. It does not include use of storage facilities, maintenance of a stock of goods and delivery of them or a fixed place of business used solely for purchasing goods or any ancillary activity.

1.3 UK resident companies with overseas income

If a UK resident company makes investments overseas it will be liable to corporation tax on the profits made, the taxable amount being before the deduction of any foreign taxes. The profits may be any of the following.

(a) Trading income: profits of an overseas permanent establishment controlled from the UK (unless an election for the exemption of profits and losses from overseas permanent establishments is made (see later in this chapter))

(b) Interest income: income from overseas securities, for example loan stock in overseas companies

(c) Overseas income: income from other overseas possessions including:

   (i) Dividends from overseas subsidiaries
   (ii) Profits of an overseas branch or agency controlled abroad

(d) Chargeable gains on disposals of overseas assets

A UK resident company may receive dividends from an overseas subsidiary. Most dividends received by a UK resident company from a non-UK resident company are exempt from corporation tax.

Exam focus point

> Taxable overseas dividends will not be examined in Advanced Taxation (ATX – UK).

A company may be subject to overseas tax as well as to UK corporation tax on the same profits usually if it has a PE in that overseas country. Double taxation relief (see below) is available in respect of the overseas tax suffered.

2 Double taxation relief (DTR)   12/13

FAST FORWARD

> A company may obtain DTR for overseas withholding tax. The allocation of qualifying charitable donations and losses can affect the relief.

2.1 General principles

In the UK relief for overseas tax suffered by a company may be currently available in one of three ways.

(1) **Treaty relief**
Under a treaty entered into between the UK and the overseas country, a treaty may exempt certain profits from taxation in one of the countries involved, thus completely avoiding double taxation. More usually treaties provide for credit to be given for tax suffered in one of the countries against the tax liability in the other.

(2)   **Unilateral credit relief**
      Where no treaty relief is available, unilateral relief may be available in the UK giving credit for the overseas tax against the UK tax.

(3)   **Unilateral expense relief**
      Not examined in your syllabus.

2.2 Treaty relief

A tax treaty based on the OECD Model Agreement may use either the exemption method or the credit method to give relief for tax suffered on income from a business in country B by a resident of country R.

(a)   Under the **exemption method**, the income is not taxed at all in country R, or if it is dividends or interest (which the treaty allows to be taxed in country R) credit is given for any country B tax against the country R tax

(b)   Under the **credit method**, the income is taxed in country R, but credit is given for any country B tax against the country R tax.

Under either method, any credit given is limited to the country B tax attributable to the income.

2.3 Unilateral credit relief

FAST FORWARD

Double tax relief (DTR) is the lower of the UK tax on overseas profits and the overseas tax on overseas profits.

Relief is available for overseas tax suffered on PE profits, interest and royalties, up to the amount of the UK corporation tax attributable to that income. The tax that is deducted overseas is usually called withholding tax. The gross income including the withholding tax is included within the taxable total profits. It is not relevant whether those profits are remitted back to the UK or not.

The amount of double tax relief (DTR) is the lower of:

(a)   **The UK tax on overseas profits;**
(b)   **The overseas tax on overseas profits.**

Question   Unilateral credit relief

AS plc has UK trading income of £2,000,000 in the year to 31 March 2019. In that year, AS plc also operated an overseas branch. The profits of the branch were £85,000, after deduction of 15% withholding tax. Compute the corporation tax payable, assuming that no election has been made to exempt the branch profits.

Answer

	Total	UK	Overseas
	£	£	£
Trading income	2,000,000	2,000,000	
Overseas trading profit (W1)	100,000		100,000
Taxable total profits	2,100,000	2,000,000	100,000
Corporation tax at 19%	399,000	380,000	19,000
Less DTR (W2)	(15,000)		(15,000)
	384,000	380,000	4,000

Working:

1   £85,000 × 100/(100 − 15) = £100,000.

2   DTR is lower of:

   (i)   UK tax on overseas profit £100,000 × 19% = £19,000
   (i)   Overseas tax on overseas profit £100,000 × 15% = £15,000

A company may allocate its qualifying charitable donations and losses relieved against total profits in whatever manner it likes for the purpose of computing double taxation relief. It should set the maximum amount against any UK profits, thereby maximising the corporation tax attributable to the overseas profits and hence maximising the double taxation relief available.

If a company has several sources of overseas profits, then deficits, qualifying charitable donations and losses should be allocated first to UK profits, and then to overseas sources which have suffered the **lowest** rates of overseas taxation.

A company with a choice of loss reliefs should consider the effect of its choice on double taxation relief. For example, a loss relief claim might lead to there being no UK tax liability, or a very small liability, so that overseas tax would go unrelieved. Carry forward loss relief might avoid this problem and still leave very little UK tax to pay for the period of the loss.

Exam focus point

> Double tax relief may be reduced where losses have been group relieved. This reduction is **not examinable** in Advanced Taxation (ATX – UK).

Companies that have claimed DTR must notify HMRC if the amount of overseas tax they have paid is adjusted and this has resulted in the DTR claim becoming excessive. The notification must be in writing within one year of any adjustment to the overseas tax.

Question   Allocation of qualifying charitable donations

Kairo plc is a UK resident company with five UK resident subsidiaries and two overseas branches, one in Atlantis and one in Utopia. The company produced the following results for the year to 31 March 2019.

	£
UK trading profits	10,000
Profits from overseas branch in Atlantis (before overseas tax of £6,000)	40,000
Profits from overseas branch in Utopia (before overseas tax of £110,000)	250,000
Qualifying charitable donations	(15,000)

Compute the UK corporation tax liability, assuming an election has not been made to exempt the profits of overseas PEs.

Answer

Kairo plc – corporation tax year to 31 March 2019

	Total £	UK £	Atlantis £	Utopia £
Total profits	300,000	10,000	40,000	250,000
Less: qualifying charitable donations (W)	(15,000)	(10,000)	(5,000)	–
Taxable total profits	285,000	Nil	35,000	250,000
Corporation tax @ 19%	54,150	–	6,650	47,500
Less DTR (W)	(53,500)	–	(6,000)	(47,500)
Corporation tax	650	–	650	–

Working

The DTR is the lower of:

Atlantis: UK tax £6,650
    Overseas tax £6,000 (Rate of overseas tax = 15%), ie £6,000

Utopia: UK tax £47,500
    Overseas tax £110,000 (Rate of overseas tax = 44%), ie £47,500

Note. The Atlantis branch profits suffer the lower rate of overseas tax so the qualifying charitable donations remaining after offset against the UK income are allocated against the Atlantis branch income in preference to the Utopia branch income.

Exam focus point

If there are several sources of overseas income it is important to keep them separate and to calculate double tax relief on each source of income separately. Get into the habit of setting out a working with a separate column for UK income and for each source of overseas income. You should then find arriving at the right answer straightforward.

3 Groups of companies

FAST FORWARD

The group relief rules allow groups and consortia to be established through companies resident anywhere in the world.

3.1 Introduction

Groups and consortia can be established through companies resident anywhere in the world.

However, group relief is normally only available to, and may only be claimed from, companies which are within the charge to corporation tax. Group relief therefore applies to companies which are:

(a) **Resident in the UK**
(b) **Resident overseas but operating through a permanent establishment in the UK**

If the company is operating through a permanent establishment in the UK, it can only usually surrender losses made by that permanent establishment.

Similarly, a consortium may exist for relief purposes where one or more of the members is not resident in the UK but relief cannot be passed to or from a company which is not within the charge to corporation tax.

3.2 Example

Joshua Inc
(US resident company)

100%   80%   75%

Aim Ltd   Blade Ltd   Clear Ltd

Aim Ltd, Blade Ltd and Clear Ltd are all UK resident companies. As the three UK companies share a common parent they will be treated as part of a group relief group despite the fact that the parent company is not UK resident. The UK companies may surrender losses to each other (but not normally to or from the overseas parent company).

3.3 Permanent establishments (PEs) of companies

UK PEs of EEA resident companies can **surrender UK losses** under group relief to **UK group members**, if those losses have not been relieved against profits in the overseas country.

UK PEs of companies resident in non-EEA countries can also surrender UK losses to UK group members, but only if **those losses are not available for use against profits in the overseas country** (regardless of whether the losses have actually been relieved overseas).

Losses incurred by overseas PEs of UK companies can be surrendered as group relief only if they not available for relief against profits in the overseas country.

<table>
<tr><td>Exam focus point</td><td>The use of losses in terms of overseas operations is complex and is simplified here for the purpose of the Advanced Taxation (ATX – UK) examination.</td></tr>
</table>

3.4 The global group concept

The 'global group concept' means that instead of looking at the residence of a company one needs to look at whether the company is subject to UK corporation tax on any of its chargeable gains. Provided the assets transferred do not result in a potential leakage of UK corporation tax, no gain/no loss transfers will be possible within a worldwide (global) group of companies.

The global group concept applies to the transfer of the whole or part of a trade and extends to certain intra-group transfers of assets and to transfers of assets where one company disposes of the whole or part of its business to another company as part of a scheme of reconstruction or amalgamation.

4 Controlled foreign companies   12/14, 6/18

FAST FORWARD

Chargeable profits of a controlled foreign company (CFC) are apportioned to UK resident companies entitled to at least 25% of those profits, and are subject to a CFC charge.

4.1 Introduction

The controlled foreign company (CFC) rules focus on the artificial diversion of income profits (ie not chargeable gains) from the UK.

Where a **CFC has 'chargeable profits'** and the **CFC is not covered by one of the exemptions**, those **chargeable profits are apportioned to the CFC's UK corporate shareholders.**

Any **UK resident company with at least a 25% holding in the CFC** will be required to **self-access a CFC charge, in respect of the apportioned profits.** Any **overseas tax** attributable to the apportioned profits can be **credited against the CFC charge.**

4.2 What is a CFC?

<table>
<tr><td>Key term</td><td>A controlled foreign company is a company which is not resident in the UK but is controlled by persons resident in the UK.</td></tr>
</table>

A **company is controlled by persons resident in the UK** if:

(a)   A **UK person, or persons, controls the company** (ie more than 50%, or control as a matter of fact)

(b)   It is **at least 40% held by a UK resident** and **at least 40% but no more than 55% by a non-UK resident.**

Alpha AG is resident in Germany and is owned as follows:

Orange Ltd	⎤	35%
Lemon Ltd	⎬ UK resident companies	15%
Lime Ltd	⎦	25%
Pomegranate Ltd (Resident in the Bahamas)		25%
		100%

Beta Ltd is resident in Ireland and is owned as follows:

Apple GmbH (resident in Switzerland, 80% owned by Orchard plc which is UK resident)	60%
Pear SpA (resident in Italy)	40%
	100%

Gamma Ltd is resident in Jersey and is owned as follows:

Tiny SA (also resident in Jersey)	56%
Big plc (UK resident)	42%
Arnold (resident in Guernsey)	2%
	100%

Explain which of the companies are CFCs.

Answer

Alpha AG is a CFC because it is 75% owned by UK resident persons.

Beta Ltd is a CFC because, although Orchard plc only has a 48% 'effective' interest, Orchard plc can control it as a matter of fact. This is because it controls Apple GmbH, which in turn controls Beta Ltd.

Gamma Ltd is not a CFC. This is because although there is a UK shareholder (Big plc) with a shareholding of at least 40%, and also a non-UK shareholder with a shareholding of at least 40% (Tiny SA), the non-UK shareholder has a holding of more than 55%.

Note that if Tiny SA's shareholding had been 55% or less, Gamma Ltd would be a CFC under the 40% test.

4.3 Chargeable profits

Chargeable profits are those income profits (not chargeable gains) of the CFC, calculated using UK tax rules, **which have been artificially diverted from the UK.**

Profits are chargeable profits unless a company meets at least one of the following conditions:

(a)   The **company has not been a party to arrangements**, one of the main purposes of which is to **reduce or eliminate a charge to UK or overseas tax** at any time in the accounting period.

(b)   **None of the company's assets or risks are managed or controlled from the UK to any significant extent** at any time in the accounting period.

(c)   If the company does have assets or risks that are managed or controlled from the UK, it has the **commercial capability to ensure that the company's business could continue if the UK managed assets and risks were no longer being managed from the UK.** This is intended as a test of how reliant the CFC is on UK management.

Exam focus point

> There are further rules in relation to, among other things, finance companies, and companies in the financial services industry. These rules are **not examinable** in Advanced Taxation (ATX – UK).

4.4 Exemptions

Even if a CFC has chargeable profits, there is **no CFC charge if one of the following exemptions applies**.

4.4.1 Exempt period

This is intended to **give companies coming within the UK CFC rules time to restructure** so that they are not subject to a charge.

An exempt period ends 12 months after a company comes under the control of UK residents. An accounting period ending within the exempt period is exempt (with periods falling partly within the exempt period being partly exempt). To qualify for exemption, the company must be within the scope of the CFC rules (ie still be a CFC) in its first accounting period after the end of the exempt period, but with none of its profits in that subsequent accounting period subject to an apportionment (ie not be subject to a CFC charge).

4.4.2 Excluded territories

HMRC issues regulations **setting out a list of 'good' territories, where a company's profits are not generally subject to a low rate of tax.**

A company which is resident and fully taxable in a listed territory will not generally be subject to a CFC charge.

4.4.3 Low profits

A company is exempt from an apportionment (and so a CFC charge) **where its profits are**:

(a)   **No more than £50,000**
(b)   **No more than £500,000, of which no more than £50,000 is non-trading profits**

Profits can be determined on either a tax or accounts basis, and the limits are scaled down for accounting periods of less than 12 months.

4.4.4 Low profit margin

A company is exempt from an apportionment if its **accounting profits are no more than 10% of its relevant operating expenditure.**

4.4.5 Tax exemption

A company is exempt from an apportionment if its **tax paid in its territory of residence is at least 75% of the UK corporation tax which would have been payable if it had been resident in the UK.**

The local tax must be adjusted for items which are taxed locally but not in the UK, and expenditure which is allowed locally but is not allowed in the UK computation.

4.5 The CFC charge

UK companies which own at least 25% of a CFC will be **taxed at the usual rate of corporation tax on their share of the CFC's profits which represent its chargeable profits. UK losses** and **surplus management expenses cannot be set against the CFC charge**. The UK company is responsible for **self-assessing** the CFC charge.

The CFC charge is reduced by 'creditable tax' which is the aggregate of:

(a) **Any DTR which would be available if the CFC's chargeable profits were chargeable to UK corporation tax under normal rules**, ie the lower of the UK corporation tax payable and actual foreign corporation tax paid

(b) **Any income tax deducted at source on income received by the CFC**

(c) **Corporation tax payable in the UK on any CFC income taxable in this country.**

Question
CFC charge

Ribbon Inc is owned 75% by Jenkins Ltd and 25% by Jack. Both Jenkins Ltd and Jack are UK resident. Ribbon Inc is a non UK resident company such that it is a controlled foreign company. None of the CFC exemptions apply to Ribbon Inc.

In the year to 31 March 2019, Ribbon Inc had chargeable profits of £650,000. It paid income tax in its own country at the rate of 8%.

Show how the profits of Ribbon Inc will be apportioned to Jenkins Ltd and the CFC charge on Jenkins Ltd.

Answer

	£
Chargeable profits of Ribbon inc	650,000
Apportioned to Jenkins Ltd (75%)	487,500

Jenkins Ltd's CFC charge

Tax on apportioned profits	
£487,500 × 19%	92,625
Less creditable tax (8% × £650,000) × 75%	(39,000)
CFC charge	53,625

4.6 Clearance procedure

There is a **clearance procedure** whereby HMRC will confirm how the rules will apply in a company's particular circumstances.

5 Permanent establishment (PE) or subsidiary abroad
6/11, 12/13

FAST FORWARD

A UK resident company intending to do business abroad must choose between a permanent establishment and a subsidiary.

PER alert

One of the competencies you require to fulfil Performance Objective 17 Tax planning and advice of the PER is to assess the tax implications of proposed activities or plans of an individual or entity with reference to relevant and up to date legislation. You can apply the knowledge you obtain from this section of the text to help to demonstrate this competence.

5.1 General principles

Where a overseas country has a lower rate of company taxation than the UK, it can be beneficial for the UK company to conduct its overseas activities through a **non-UK resident subsidiary** if profits are anticipated (assuming that the CFC rules (see above) do not apply), or through a **PE, if losses are likely to arise**.

The general rule is that the **profits of a overseas PE** are treated as part of the profits of the UK company and are normally included in its computation of trading profits. If, however, the operations of the overseas PE amount to a separate trade which is wholly carried on overseas, the profits are assessed as separate overseas trading income.

The losses of an overseas PE are normally netted off against the UK company's trading income and the usual loss reliefs are available, subject to the restriction on group relief mentioned earlier in this chapter. Any such overseas income trading loss can be carried forward to set against future profits of the same trade.

The profits of a non-resident **overseas subsidiary** are not liable to UK tax when remitted to the UK, for example in the form of dividends.

5.2 Election to exempt overseas PE profits and losses

FAST FORWARD

An irrevocable election can be made to exempt profits and losses of all overseas PEs from UK corporation tax.

A UK company may make an **election to exempt the profits and losses of all its overseas PEs from UK corporation tax**. Note that the election will **disallow loss relief** for overseas PEs against UK profits and that the **election must apply to all of the UK company's PEs** – it is not possible to exclude, for example, a loss making PE from the election. The election also means that **no capital allowances** can be claimed by the UK parent company in respect of past or current future capital expenditure by exempt overseas PEs.

The election **takes effect from the start of the accounting period after the one in which the election is made**. The election is **irrevocable** and so it is important to consider the effect of making the election for all future accounting periods, in particular whether any of the PEs is likely to make a loss.

Double taxation relief should also be taken into account when deciding whether or not to make the election. If the **operation of DTR means that there is little or no UK corporation tax payable** on overseas profits, it may be **better not to make the election**. This means that **loss relief will be available** in future accounting periods.

Question   Election to exempt PE profits

Brown Ltd is a UK resident company with two overseas PEs. It prepares accounts to 31 March each year. In the year to 31 March 2019, Brown Ltd made a UK trading profit of £210,000, the first overseas PE made a trading profit of £40,000 (overseas tax payable £6,000), and the second overseas PE made a trading loss of £25,000. Compute the UK corporation tax payable for the year to 31 March 2019 by Brown Ltd if:

(a)   No election has been made to exempt the profits and losses of the overseas PEs; or
(b)   An election was made prior to 1 April 2018 to exempt the profits and losses of the overseas PEs.

(a) **No election made**

	£
UK trading profit	210,000
First overseas PE trading profit	40,000
Second overseas PE trading loss	(25,000)
Taxable total profits	225,000
Corporation tax at 19%	42,750
Less double taxation relief (W)	(6,000)
UK corporation tax payable by Brown Ltd	36,750

Working

DTR is lower of:

(i) UK tax on overseas profit £40,000 × 19% = £7,600
(ii) Overseas tax on overseas profit £6,000

(b) **Election made**

	£
UK trading profit/Taxable total profits	210,000
UK corporation tax at 19% payable by Brown Ltd	39,900

The election was therefore not beneficial.

Exam focus point

> The rules regarding the exemption of overseas PE profits are complex, especially where small companies are concerned. The examining team has stated that these more complex aspects are not examinable. In any examination question, **it should therefore be assumed that the exemption option is available for all overseas PEs.**

5.3 Incorporating an overseas PE

5.3.1 The decision to incorporate

Where a overseas operation is likely to show a loss in the early years, it may be worthwhile to trade through an overseas PE whilst losses arise (these are usually then automatically netted off against the company's UK profits).

If the **PE then becomes profitable,** consideration should be given to either **making the election to exempt all branch profits and losses** or **converting the PE into a non-UK resident subsidiary company (so that profits can be accumulated at potentially lower rates of overseas tax).**

Both of these methods mean that the overseas profits will not be subject to UK corporation tax (provided the subsidiary does not become a controlled foreign company). However, they also both mean that any future overseas losses cannot be relieved against UK profits and capital allowances are not available.

It is important to remember that the **election to exempt PE profits and losses is irrevocable** and **applies to all the PEs** operated by the UK company. It may therefore be better to incorporate profitable PEs and maintain a **mixture of PEs and subsidiaries** which may give more flexibility.

If it is decided to convert a overseas PE into a non-UK resident subsidiary, there are important tax implications both in the UK and the overseas country.

5.3.2 Issue of shares/loan stock by non-UK company

It is illegal for a UK resident company to cause or permit a non-UK resident company over which it has control to create or issue any shares or loan stock. It is also illegal for a UK resident company to transfer to any person, or cause or permit to be transferred to any person, any shares or loan stock of a non-UK resident company over which it has control.

However, there are a number of situations which are excluded from these rules, for example where the transaction is intra-group or full consideration is given.

Where the transaction has a value of more than £100m, the transaction must be reported to HMRC within six months, subject to certain exclusions, for example where the transaction is carried out in the ordinary course of a trade.

5.3.3 Postponement of gains

The conversion will constitute a disposal of the assets of the PE giving rise to a chargeable gain or loss in the hands of the UK company. A chargeable gain can be postponed where:

(a)   The trade of the overseas PE is transferred to the non-UK resident company with all the assets used for that trade except cash

(b)   The consideration for the transfer is wholly or partly securities (shares or shares and loan stock)

(c)   The transferring company owns at least 25% of the ordinary share capital of the non-resident company

(d)   A claim for relief is made.

There is full postponement of the net gains arising on the transfer where the consideration is wholly securities. Where part of the consideration is in a form other than securities, eg cash, that proportion of the net gains is chargeable immediately.

The postponement is indefinite. The gain becomes chargeable only when:

(a)   The transferor company at any time disposes of any of the securities received on the transfer

(b)   The non-UK resident company within six years of the transfer disposes of any of the assets on which a gain arose at the time of the transfer.

The 'global group' concept applies to certain intra-group transfers of assets and also where one company disposes of the whole of part of its business to another company as part of a reconstruction or amalgamation scheme. Such asset transfers are on a no gain/no loss basis provided the assets transferred do not result in a potential leakage of UK corporation tax.

5.4 European Union companies

If all or part of a trade carried on in the UK by a company resident in one EU state is transferred to a company resident in another EU state, then the transfer is deemed to be at a price giving no gain and no loss, if all the following conditions are fulfilled:

(a)   The transfer is wholly in exchange for shares or securities

(b)   The company receiving the trade would be subject to UK corporation tax on any gains arising on later disposals of the assets transferred

(c)   Both parties claim this special treatment

(d)   The transfer is for bona fide commercial reasons. Advance clearance that this condition is satisfied may be obtained.

6 Non-UK resident companies

A non resident company is liable to UK corporation tax if it carries on trade in the UK through a permanent establishment.

6.1 Corporation tax charge

A non resident company is liable to tax in the UK if it carries on a trade in the UK through a permanent establishment (defined as above).

The PE has **the profits it would have made if it were a distinct and separate establishment engaged in the same or similar activities in the same or similar conditions, dealing wholly independently with the non resident company attributed to it.** Deductions are available for allowable expenses incurred for the purposes of the PE including executive and general administrative expenses whether in the UK or elsewhere. The term 'allowable expenses' has the same meaning as for a UK resident company. Relief is available for the expenses of managing investments for all companies whether or not they qualify as 'investment companies'.

Transactions between the PE and the non resident company are treated as taking place at **arm's length prices.**

For the purposes of collection of tax a PE will be treated as the UK representative through which the non resident company carries on a trade in the UK.

These rules align with the normal provision in tax treaties (based on the OECD Model Agreement) **that a overseas trader is taxable on his trading profits in the UK if he has a permanent establishment in the UK.**

6.2 Tax charge on income

Income charged to corporation tax comprises:

(a) Trading income arising directly or indirectly through or from the permanent establishment

(b) Any income, wherever arising, from property or rights used by, held by or held for the permanent establishment.

Annual interest and other annual payments are received under deduction of income tax. Provided that the income is charged to corporation tax, the company can offset the income tax suffered against its corporation tax liability and, in appropriate circumstances, obtain repayment in the same manner as a resident company.

Income from sources within the UK which is not subject to corporation tax is subject to income tax. This could arise, for example, if a non-resident company carries on a trade in the UK without having a permanent establishment, or receives letting income from a UK property.

6.3 Tax charge on capital gains

Capital gains are charged to corporation tax where the company carries on a trade in the UK through a permanent establishment if they arise on:

(a) Assets situated in the UK used in or for the purposes of the trade at or before the time when the gain accrued

(b) Assets situated in the UK held or used for the purposes of the permanent establishment at or before the time when the gain accrued.

As it would be possible to avoid gains being chargeable by, for example, ceasing to trade in the UK through a permanent establishment prior to selling the asset or exporting the asset, there are two further charging provisions:

(1) Where a non-UK resident company ceases to trade through a permanent establishment in the UK, a charge will arise. Any chargeable asset which would otherwise become non-chargeable shall be deemed to be disposed of and reacquired at market value immediately before it ceases to trade.

(2) Where a non-UK resident company trading through a UK permanent establishment exports a chargeable asset, so that it becomes non-chargeable, the gain will crystallise immediately before it is exported.

6.4 Tax planning

An overseas resident company may have to decide **whether to trade in the UK through a PE or via a UK subsidiary**. A PE may be favoured because if the subsidiary makes losses the overseas company may be restricted in the relief it can claim. The overseas company would also need to consider the repatriation of profits and the provision of finance.

Chapter roundup

- Company residence is important in determining whether its profits are subject to UK tax.

- A company may obtain DTR for overseas withholding tax. The allocation of qualifying charitable donations and losses can affect the relief.

- Double tax relief (DTR) is the lower of the UK tax on overseas profits and the overseas tax on overseas profits.

- The group relief rules allow groups and consortia to be established through companies resident anywhere in the world.

- Chargeable profits of a controlled foreign company (CFC) are apportioned to UK resident companies entitled to at least 25% of those profits, and are subject to a CFC charge.

- A UK resident company intending to do business abroad must choose between a permanent establishment and a subsidiary.

- An irrevocable election can be made to exempt profits and losses of all overseas branches from UK corporation tax.

- A non resident company is liable to UK corporation tax if it carries on trade in the UK through a permanent establishment.

Quick quiz

1   When is a company UK resident?

2   How best should qualifying charitable donations be allocated in computing credit relief for overseas tax?

3   What is the definition of a CFC?

4   What is the CFC charge?

5   A UK company is planning to set up a new operation in Australia that will initially be loss making. Should it set up as a permanent establishment or a subsidiary of the UK company?

BPP
LEARNING MEDIA

Answers to quick quiz

1   A company is resident in the UK if it is incorporated in the UK or if its central management and control are exercised in the UK.

2   Qualifying charitable donations should be set-off firstly from any UK profits, then from overseas income sources suffering the lowest rates of overseas taxation before those suffering at the higher rates.

3   A CFC is a non-UK resident company that is controlled by UK resident companies and/or individuals.

4   UK companies which own at least 25% of a CFC are taxed at the usual rate of corporation tax on their share of the CFC's profits which represent its chargeable profits.

5   If losses are expected then a PE is best since losses of a overseas PE can be used by the UK company whereas losses of an Australian subsidiary cannot be group relieved.

Now try the question below from the Practice Question Bank

Number	Level	Marks	Time
Q30	Introductory	15	29 mins

Value added tax

Value added tax 1

Topic list	Syllabus reference
1 Basic principles	A6(a)F2
2 Scope of VAT	A6(a)F2
3 Taxable and exempt supplies	A6(a)F2
4 Registration	A6(a)F1
5 Deduction of input tax	A6(a)F2
6 Transfer of going concern	A6(a)F2
7 Accounting for VAT	A6(a)F2
8 Valuation of supplies	A6(a)F2
9 Administration	A6(a)F2
10 Penalties	A6(a)F2
11 Imports, exports, acquisitions and dispatches	A6(a)F2
12 Special schemes	A6(a)F3

Introduction

In this and the next chapter, we study value added tax (VAT). VAT is a tax on turnover rather than on profits.

As the name of the tax suggests, it is charged on the value added. If someone in a chain of manufacture or distribution buys goods for £1,000 and sells them for £1,200 they have increased their value by £200. (They may have painted them, packed them or distributed them to shops to justify their mark-up, or they may simply be good at making deals to buy cheaply and sell dearly.) Because they have added value of £200, they collect VAT of £200 × 20% = £40 (assuming a standard rate of 20%) and pays this over to the government. The VAT is collected bit by bit along the chain and finally hits the consumer who does not add value, but uses up the goods.

VAT is a tax with simple computations but many detailed rules to ensure its enforcement. You may find it easier to absorb the detail if you ask yourself, in relation to each rule, exactly how it helps to enforce the tax.

All of the topics in this chapter are revision from Taxation (TX – UK) but are very important in your understanding of VAT.

In the next chapter, we will look at the rules which are new in Advanced Taxation (ATX – UK).

Study guide

		Intellectual level
6	**Value added tax, tax administration and the UK tax system:**	
(a)	The contents of the Taxation - United Kingdom (TX – UK) study guide for value added tax (VAT) under headings:	2
•	F1 The VAT registration requirements	
•	F2 The computation of VAT liabilities	
•	F3 The effect of special schemes	

Exam guide

VAT is a very important tax for businesses as there are few small enough not to be registerable. You may be required to advise on almost any aspect, such as registration, including group registration.

Knowledge brought forward from earlier studies

This chapter revises your knowledge of topics tested in Taxation (TX – UK). The examining team has identified essential underpinning knowledge from the Taxation (TX – UK) syllabus which is particularly important that you revise as part of your Advanced Taxation (ATX – UK) studies. In this chapter, the relevant topics are:

		Intellectual level
F1	**The VAT registration requirements**	
(a)	Recognise the circumstances in which a person must register or deregister for VAT (compulsory) and when a person may register or deregister for VAT (voluntary)	2
(c)	Explain the conditions that must be met for two or more companies to be treated as a group for VAT purposes, and the consequences of being so treated	1
F2	**The computation of VAT liabilities**	
(j)	Explain the treatment of imports, exports and trade within the European Union	2
F3	**The effect of special schemes**	
(a)	Understand the operation of, and when it will be advantageous to use, the VAT special schemes:	
(i)	Cash accounting scheme	2
(ii)	Annual accounting scheme	2
(iii)	Flat rate scheme	2

There are no changes in 2018/19 from 2017/18 in the material you have previously studied at Taxation (TX – UK) level. In particular, note that the registration and deregistration limits have not changed.

1 Basic principles

VAT is charged on turnover at each stage in a production process, but in such a way that the burden is borne by the final consumer.

PER alert

One of the competencies you require to fulfil Performance Objective 15 Tax computations and assessments of the PER is to prepare or contribute to computations or assessments of indirect tax liabilities. You can apply the knowledge you obtain from this section of the text to help to demonstrate this competence.

1.1 Introduction

Value Added Tax (VAT) is a tax on turnover, not on profits. The basic principle is that the VAT should be borne by the final consumer. Registered traders may deduct the tax which they suffer on supplies to them (input tax) from the tax which they charge to their customers (output tax) at the time this is paid to HM Revenue & Customs (HMRC). So, at each stage of the manufacturing or service process, the net VAT paid is on the value added at that stage.

1.2 Example: the VAT charge

During 2018 a forester sells wood to a furniture maker for £100 plus VAT. The furniture maker uses this wood to make a table and sells the table to a shop for £150 plus VAT of 20%. The shop then sells the table to the final consumer for £300 plus VAT. VAT will be accounted for to HMRC as follows:

	Cost £	Input tax 20% £	Net sale price £	Output tax 20% £	Payable to HMRC £
Forester	0	0	100	20.00	20.00
Furniture maker	100	20.00	150	30.00	10.00
Shop	150	30.00	300	60.00	30.00
					60.00

Because the traders involved account to HMRC for VAT charged less VAT suffered, their profits for income tax or corporation tax purposes are based on sales and purchases net of VAT.

2 Scope of VAT

FAST FORWARD

VAT is charged on taxable supplies of goods and services made by a taxable person in their business.

2.1 General principles

VAT is charged on taxable supplies of goods and services made in the UK by a taxable person in the course or furtherance of any business carried on by them. It is also chargeable on the import of goods into the UK (whether they are imported for business purposes or not, and whether the importer is a taxable person or not), and on certain services received from abroad if a taxable person receives them for business purposes.

Special rules for trade with the European Union (the EU) are covered later.

Key term

A **taxable supply** is a supply of goods or services made in the UK, other than an exempt supply.

A taxable supply is either standard-rated or zero-rated. The standard rate is usually 20%.

Certain supplies, which fall within the classification of taxable supplies, are charged at a reduced rate of 5%. An example is the supply of domestic fuel.

2.2 Supplies of goods

Goods are supplied if exclusive ownership of the goods passes to another person.

The following are treated as supplies of goods.

- The supply of any form of power, heat, refrigeration or ventilation, or of water

- The grant, assignment or surrender of a major interest (the freehold or a lease for over 21 years) in land

- Taking goods permanently out of the business for the non-business use of a taxable person or for other private purposes including the supply of goods by an employer to an employee for their private use

- Transfers under an agreement contemplating a transfer of ownership, such as a hire purchase agreement

Gifts of goods are normally treated as sales at cost (so VAT is due). **However, business gifts are not supplies of goods if:**

(a) **The total cost of gifts made to the same person does not exceed £50 in any 12 month period.** If the £50 limit is exceeded, output tax will be due in full on the total of gifts made. Once the limit has been exceeded a new £50 limit and new 12 month period begins

(b) **The gift is a sample** (unlimited number of samples allowed)

2.3 Supplies of services

Apart from a few specific exceptions, **any supply which is not a supply of goods and which is done for a consideration is a supply of services.** Consideration is any form of payment in money or in kind, including anything which is itself a supply.

A supply of services also takes place if:

- Goods are lent to someone for use outside the business
- Goods are hired to someone
- Services bought for business purposes are used for private purposes

The European Court of Justice has ruled that restaurants supply services rather than goods.

2.4 Taxable persons

The term 'person' includes individuals, partnerships (which are treated as single entities, ignoring the individual partners), **companies, clubs, associations and charities. If a person is in business making taxable supplies, then the value of these supplies is called the taxable turnover. If a person's taxable turnover exceeds the registration limit then they are a taxable person and should be registered for VAT.**

3 Taxable and exempt supplies   6/17

FAST FORWARD

Some supplies are taxable at standard-rate, reduced-rate or zero-rate. Others are exempt.

One of the competencies you require to fulfil Performance Objective 15 Tax computations and assessments of the PER is to prepare or contribute to computations or assessments of indirect tax liabilities. You can apply the knowledge you obtain from this section of the text to help to demonstrate this competence.

3.1 Types of supply

Zero-rated supplies are taxable at 0%. A taxable supplier whose outputs are zero-rated but whose inputs are standard-rated will obtain repayments of the VAT paid on purchases.

4.3 Intending trader registration

Providing that a trader satisfies HMRC that they are carrying on a business, and intends to make taxable supplies, they are entitled to be registered if they choose. But, once registered, they are obliged to notify HMRC within 30 days if they no longer intend to make taxable supplies.

4.4 Exemption from registration

If a person makes only zero-rated supplies, they may request exemption from registration. The trader is obliged to notify HMRC of any material change in the nature of their supplies.

HMRC may also allow exemption from registration if only a small proportion of supplies are standard-rated, provided that the trader would normally receive repayments of VAT if registered.

4.5 Group registration

9/15, 9/16

Companies under common control may apply for group registration. The effects and advantages of group registration are as follows:

- Each VAT group must appoint a representative member which must **account for the group's output tax and input tax, thus simplifying VAT accounting** and allowing payments and repayments of VAT to be netted off. However, all members of the group are jointly and severally liable for any VAT due from the representative member.

- Any supply of goods or services by a member of the group to another member of the group is, in general, disregarded for VAT purposes, reducing the VAT accounting required.

- Any other supply of goods or services by or to a group member is in general treated as a supply by or to the representative member.

- Any VAT payable on the import of goods by a group member is payable by the representative member.

Two or more companies are eligible to be treated as members of a group provided each of them is either established in the UK or has a fixed establishment in the UK, and:

- **One of them controls each of the others**
- **One person** (which could be an individual or a holding company) **controls all of them**
- **Two or more persons carrying on a business in partnership control all of them**

Anti-avoidance rules prevent a company from belonging to a VAT group where it would otherwise be eligible but it is in fact run for the benefit of an external third party.

An application to create, terminate, add to or remove a company from a VAT group may be made at any time. Applications may be refused when it appears to HMRC to be necessary to do so for the protection of the revenue. However, if a company is no longer eligible to belong to a VAT group because the common control test is failed, the company must leave the VAT group even if revenue might not be lost.

A group registration, or any change to it, will take effect from the date the application is received by HMRC although applications may have an earlier or later effect. Therefore it is possible to apply in advance for group changes and it is also possible to apply for changes having a retrospective effect. However, HMRC have 90 days to refuse an application.

Individual companies which are within a group for company law purposes may still register separately and stay outside the VAT group. This may be done to ensure that a company making exempt supplies does not restrict the input tax recovery of the group as a whole (see the partial exemption rules in the next chapter).

It is not possible for a company to be in two VAT groups at the same time.

A person making exempt supplies is unable to recover VAT on inputs (in exactly the same way as for a non-registered person). An exempt supplier has to shoulder the burden of VAT. They may increase their prices to pass on the charge, but they cannot issue a VAT invoice which would enable a taxable customer to obtain a credit for VAT, since no VAT is chargeable on their supplies.

3.2 Example: standard-rated, zero-rated and exempt supplies

Here are figures for three traders, the first with standard-rated outputs, the second with zero-rated outputs and the third with exempt outputs. All their inputs are standard-rated at 20%.

	Standard-rated £	Zero-rated £	Exempt £
Inputs	20,000	20,000	20,000
VAT	4,000	4,000	4,000
	24,000	24,000	24,000
Outputs	30,000	30,000	30,000
VAT	6,000	0	0
	36,000	30,000	30,000
Pay/(reclaim)	2,000	(4,000)	0
Net profit	10,000	10,000	6,000

VAT legislation lists zero-rated, reduced-rate and exempt supplies. There is no list of standard-rated supplies.

If a trader makes a supply you need to categorise that supply for VAT as follows:

Step 1 Consider if it is a zero-rated supply. If not:

Step 2 Consider if it is exempt. If not:

Step 3 Consider if it is reduced-rated supply. If not:

Step 4 The supply is standard-rated.

3.3 Zero-rated supplies

The following are some common items on the **zero-rated list**.

(a) Human and animal food

(b) Printed matter used for reading (eg books, newspapers)

(c) Construction work on new homes or the sale of the freehold, or a lease over 21 years (at least 20 years in Scotland), of new homes by builders

(d) Exports of goods to outside the EU

(e) Clothing and footwear for young children and certain protective clothing eg motor cyclists' crash helmets

3.4 Exempt supplies

The following are some common items on the **exempt** list:

(a) Sales of freeholds of buildings (other than commercial buildings within three years from completion) and leaseholds of land and buildings of any age including a surrender of a lease

(b) Financial services

(c) Insurance

3.5 Reduced rate of VAT

Certain supplies are charged at **5%. The supplies are still taxable supplies.**

The main supplies are:

(a) Supplies of fuel for domestic use, and

(b) Supplies of the services of installing energy saving materials to homes

3.6 Exceptions to the general rule

There are many exceptions to the general rule.

For example the zero-rated list states human food is zero-rated. However, the legislation then states that food supplied in the course of catering (eg restaurant meals, hot takeaways) is not zero-rated. Luxury items of food (eg crisps, peanuts, chocolate covered biscuits) are also not zero-rated.

In the exempt list we are told that financial services are exempt. However the legislation then goes on to state that this does not include credit management, except if the credit management is by the person who also granted the credit.

Great care must be taken when categorising goods or services as zero-rated, exempt or standard-rated. It is not as straightforward as it may first appear.

3.7 Standard-rated supplies

There is no list of standard-rated supplies. If a supply is not zero-rated, is not exempt and is not reduced-rated then it is treated as standard-rated. The standard rate of VAT is 20%.

4 Registration   12/14, 9/15

FAST FORWARD

A trader becomes liable to register for VAT if the value of taxable supplies in any period up to 12 months exceeds £85,000 or if there are reasonable grounds for believing that the value of the taxable supplies will exceed £85,000 in the next 30 days. A trader may also register voluntarily.

4.1 Compulsory registration   6/17

At the end of every month a trader must calculate their cumulative turnover of taxable supplies to date. However this cumulative period does not extend beyond the previous 12 months. **The trader becomes liable to register for VAT if the value of their cumulative taxable supplies** (excluding VAT) **exceeds £85,000.** The person is required to notify HMRC within 30 days of the end of the month in which the £85,000 limit is exceeded. HMRC will then register the person with effect from the end of the month following the month in which the £85,000 was exceeded, or from an earlier date if they and the trader agree.

Registration under this rule is not required if HMRC are satisfied that the value of the trader's taxable supplies (excluding VAT) in the year then starting will not exceed £83,000.

A person is also liable to register at any time if there are reasonable grounds for believing that their taxable supplies (excluding VAT) in the following 30 days will exceed £85,000. Only taxable turnover of that 30 day period is considered **not** cumulative turnover. HMRC must be notified by the end of the 30 day period and registration will be with effect from the beginning of that period.

When determining the value of a person's taxable supplies for the purposes of registration, supplies of goods and services that are *capital assets* **of the business are to be disregarded,** except for non zero-rated taxable supplies of interests in land.

If a business makes taxable supplies in the UK but has no establishment here, it has to register for VAT, whatever the value of its taxable supplies ie even if this is below the VAT registration threshold.

Unless factors in the question indicate otherwise, assume the business does have an establishment in the UK when determining whether to register for VAT.

Question   VAT registration

Fred started to trade in cutlery on 1 January 2018. Sales (excluding VAT) were £8,000 a month for the first nine months and £8,500 a month thereafter. From what date should Fred be registered for VAT?

Answer

	£	
Sales to 31 October 2018	80,500	
Sales to 30 November 2018	89,000	(exceeds £85,000)

Fred must notify his liability to register by 30 December 2018 (not 31 December) and will be registered from 1 January 2019 or from an agreed earlier date.

When a person is liable to register in respect of a past period, it is their responsibility to pay VAT. If they are unable to collect it from those to whom they made taxable supplies, the VAT burden will fall on them. A person must start keeping VAT records and charging VAT to customers as soon as it is known that they are required to register. However, VAT should not be shown separately on any invoices until the registration number is known. The invoice should show the VAT inclusive price and customers should be informed that VAT invoices will be forwarded once the registration number is known. Formal VAT invoices should then be sent to such customers within 30 days of receiving the registration number.

Notification of liability to register must be made on form VAT 1. This can be downloaded from the HMRC website, can be requested by telephone, or an application to register can be made online through the website. Simply writing to, or telephoning, a local VAT office is not enough. On registration the VAT office will provide the trader with a certificate of registration. This shows the VAT registration number, the date of registration, the end of the first VAT period and the length of later VAT periods.

If a trader makes a supply before becoming liable to register, but gets paid after registration, VAT is not due on that supply.

4.2 Voluntary registration   6/16

A person may decide to become registered even though his taxable turnover falls below the registration limit. Unless a person is registered they cannot recover the input tax they pay on purchases.

Voluntary registration is advantageous where a person wishes to recover input tax on purchases. For example, consider a trader who has one input during the year which cost £1,000 plus £200 VAT; they work on the input which becomes their sole output for the year and they decide to make a profit of £1,000.

(a) If they are not registered they will charge £2,200 and their customer will obtain no relief for any VAT.

(b) If they are registered they will charge £2,000 plus VAT of £400. Their customer will have input tax of £400 which they will be able to recover if they, too, are registered.

If the customer is a non-taxable person they will prefer (a) as the cost to them is £2,200. If they are taxable they will prefer (b) as the net cost is £2,000. Thus, a decision whether or not to register voluntarily may depend upon the status of customers. It may also depend on the status of the outputs and the image of their business the trader wishes to project (registration may give the impression of a substantial business). The administrative burden of registration should also be considered.

This topic was tested in September 2016 Question 1 Hahn Ltd group related to the consideration of specific matters relating to the group of companies when deciding which companies should be included in a group registration for value added tax (VAT) purposes. The examining team commented that 'Despite the requirement stating that candidates were to refer only to the specific matters within the memorandum provided, a significant number wrote in detail about the general advantages and disadvantages of registering as a group, which was not relevant, and so wasted time. However, many candidates did identify the specific issues – one of the companies being partially exempt, and another using the annual accounting scheme and the cash accounting scheme – but then discussed what this meant for the relevant companies themselves, rather than the implications of including that company within a group registration. Unfortunately though, having identified the issues, they didn't go on to score as many marks as they could have done by answering the precise requirement.'

4.6 Deregistration   6/15, 9/16

4.6.1 Voluntary deregistration

A person is eligible for voluntary deregistration if HMRC are satisfied that the value of their taxable supplies (net of VAT and excluding supplies of capital assets) **in the following one year period will not exceed £83,000.** However, voluntary deregistration will not be allowed if the reason for the expected fall in value of taxable supplies is the cessation of taxable supplies or the suspension of taxable supplies for a period of 30 days or more in that following year.

HMRC will cancel a person's registration from the date the request is made or from an agreed later date.

4.6.2 Compulsory deregistration   6/15

Traders may be compulsorily deregistered. Failure to notify a requirement to deregister within 30 days may lead to a penalty. Compulsory deregistration may also lead to HMRC reclaiming input tax which has been wrongly recovered by the trader since the date on which they should have deregistered.

Other points to note are:

- If HMRC are misled into granting registration then the registration is treated as void from the start.

- A person may be compulsorily deregistered if HMRC are satisfied that they are no longer making nor intending to make taxable supplies.

- Changes in legal status also require cancellation of registration. For example:

    - A sole trader becoming a partnership
    - A partnership reverting to a sole trader
    - A business being incorporated
    - A company being replaced by an unincorporated business

4.6.3 The consequences of deregistration

On deregistration, VAT is chargeable on all inventory and capital assets in a business on which input tax was claimed, since the registered trader is in effect making a taxable supply to himself as a newly unregistered trader. If the VAT chargeable does not exceed £1,000, it need not be paid.

This special VAT charge does not apply if the business (or a separately viable part of it) **is sold as a going concern to another taxable person** (or a person who immediately becomes a taxable person as a result of the transfer). **Such transfers are outside the scope of VAT** (except for certain buildings being transferred which are 'new' or opted buildings and the transferee does not make an election to waive exemption – refer to the section on land in the next chapter).

If the original owner ceases to be taxable, the new owner of the business may also take over the existing VAT number. If they do so, they take over the rights and liabilities of the transferor as at the date of transfer.

4.7 Pre-registration input tax

> **FAST FORWARD**
>
> VAT incurred on goods and services before registration can be treated as input tax and recovered from HMRC subject to certain conditions.

VAT incurred before registration can be treated as input tax and recovered from HMRC subject to certain conditions.

If the claim is for input tax suffered on goods purchased prior to registration then the following conditions must be satisfied.

(a) The goods were acquired for the purpose of the business which either was carried on or was to be carried on by them at the time of supply.

(b) The goods have not been supplied onwards or consumed before the date of registration (although they may have been used to make other goods which are still held).

(c) The VAT must have been incurred in the four years prior to the effective date of registration.

If the claim is for input tax suffered on the supply of services prior to registration then the following conditions must be satisfied.

(a) The services were supplied for the purposes of a business which either was carried on or was to be carried on by them at the time of supply.

(b) The services were supplied within the six months prior to the date of registration.

Input tax attributable to supplies made before registration is not deductible even if the input tax concerned is treated as having been incurred after registration.

5 Deduction of input tax

> **FAST FORWARD**
>
> Not all input VAT is deductible, eg VAT on most motor cars.

5.1 Introduction

Input tax is deductible for supplies to a taxable person in the course of their business.

5.2 Capital items

There is no distinction between capital and revenue expenditure for VAT. So a manufacturer paying VAT on the purchase of plant to make taxable supplies will be able to obtain a credit for all the VAT immediately (see below for the capital goods scheme).

5.3 Non-deductible input tax

The following input tax is not deductible.

(a) **VAT on purchased motor cars** not used wholly for business purposes. VAT on cars is never reclaimable unless the car is acquired new for resale or is acquired for use in or leasing to a taxi business, a self-drive car hire business or a driving school (see below for treatment of motor expenses). **If VAT is not recoverable on a car because it is not used wholly for business purposes, then VAT is not charged if the car is subsequently sold.**

(b) **50% of the VAT on leased motor cars which are 'qualifying cars'.** The 50% restriction covers any private use of the car. A qualifying car is one on which input tax has not already been irrecoverable.

(c) **VAT on business entertaining** where the cost of the entertaining is not a tax deductible trading expense unless the entertainment is of overseas customers in which case the input tax is deductible.

(d)   **VAT on expenses incurred on domestic accommodation for directors or proprietors of a business.**

(e)   **VAT on non-business items passed through the business accounts.** If goods are bought partly for business use the purchaser may:

    (i)   Deduct all the input tax, and account for output tax in respect of the private use, or
    (ii)   Deduct only the business proportion of the input tax.

5.4 Irrecoverable VAT

Where input tax on a purchase is not deductible that input **VAT is included in the cost for income tax, corporation tax, capital allowance or capital gains purposes.**

Deductible VAT is omitted from costs, so that only net amounts are included in accounts. Similarly, sales (and proceeds in chargeable gains computations) **are shown net of VAT**, because the VAT is paid over to HMRC.

5.5 Motoring expenses

5.5.1 Accessories and maintenance costs

Input VAT can be reclaimed if accessories for business use are fitted after the original purchase of a car and a separate invoice is raised.

If a car is used for any business purposes (even if it is also used for private purposes) then any VAT charged on repair and maintenance costs can be treated as input tax.

5.5.2 Fuel

FAST FORWARD

> If fuel is supplied for private purposes all input VAT incurred on the fuel is allowed and the business will normally account for output VAT using a set of scale charges.

If a business pays for fuel which is only used for business purposes, it can claim all the input tax paid on that fuel. However, many businesses will pay for fuel which is used for private motoring by employees.

If a business does provide fuel for private and business use to an employee but the employee reimburses the business the full cost of the private fuel, there is an actual taxable supply by the business valued at the amount received from that employee. The business can claim its input tax on all fuel, but then must account for output tax on the amount paid by the employee. HMRC will accept that the full cost of all private fuel has been reimbursed where a log is kept recording private miles and the employee pays a fuel-only mileage rate that covers the average fuel cost (on its website, HM Revenue and Customs publish a set of such rates for different sizes of engine).

If a business provides fuel to its employees for private use without charge or at a charge below the full cost, there is a deemed taxable supply. The business then has the following options for how to account for VAT on fuel:

(i)   **Not to claim any input tax in respect of fuel** purchased by the business. **No output tax is charged.** In effect, the fuel is not brought into the VAT system at all.

(ii)   **Claim input VAT only on the fuel purchased for business journeys.** This requires the business to keep detailed mileage records of business and private use. **No output tax is charged in respect of private use.** In effect, the private fuel is not brought into the VAT system.

(iii)   **Claim input tax on all fuel purchased and charge output tax based either on the full cost of the private fuel supplied** (again, this requires detailed mileage records to be kept) **or the fuel scale charge which reflects the deemed output in respect of private use. The fuel scale charge is based on the CO_2 emissions of the car.**

In the Advanced Taxation (ATX – UK) exam, questions on the treatment of private use fuel will normally involve the use of the fuel scale charge.

The above rules apply **even where employees pay for the fuel themselves and the business reimburses them**: as long as the business obtains VAT invoices for the fuel, it can treat the fuel as its own purchase/input.

Question
Fuel scale charge

Iain is an employee of ABC Ltd. He has the use of a car with CO_2 emissions of 176 g/km for one month and a car with CO_2 emissions of 208 g/km for two months during the quarter ended 31 August 2018.

ABC Ltd pays all the petrol costs in respect of both cars without requiring Iain to make any reimbursement in respect of private fuel. Total petrol costs for the quarter amount to £390 (including VAT). ABC Ltd wishes to use the fuel scale charge as detailed records of private mileage have not been kept.

What is the VAT effect of the above on ABC Ltd?

VAT scale rates (VAT inclusive) for three month periods

CO_2 emissions	£
175	351
205	436

Answer

Value added tax for the quarter:

	£
Car 1	
£351 × 1/3 =	117
Car 2	
£436 × 2/3 =	291
	408
Output tax:	
1/6 × £408	£68
Input tax	
1/6 × £390	£65

5.6 Relief for impairment losses (bad debts)

FAST FORWARD

Relief for VAT on impairment losses (bad debts) is available if the VAT has been accounted for, the debt is over six months old (measured from when the payment is due) and has been written off in the trader's accounts.

A trader may claim a refund of VAT on amounts unpaid by debtors if:

(a) They have accounted for VAT
(b) The debt is over six months old
(c) The debt has been written off in the creditor's accounts.

If the debtor later pays all (or part) of the amount owed, the corresponding amount of VAT repaid must be paid back to HMRC.

Impairment loss relief claims must be made within four years of the time the impairment loss became eligible for relief (in other words, within four years and six months from when the payment was due).

6 Transfer of going concern

The transfer of a business as a going concern is outside the scope of VAT provided certain conditions are satisfied.

The transfer of assets will not be treated as a supply for VAT purposes (a transfer of going concern (TOGC)) if all of the following conditions are satisfied.

(a) The **assets are to be used by the transferee in the same kind of business** (whether or not as part of an existing business) as that carried on by the transferor, the **business being transferred as a going concern**

(b) If only part of the business is transferred, that part is capable of separate operation

(c) If the transferor is a taxable person, **transferee is also a taxable person** when the transfer takes place or immediately becomes one as a result of the transfer

(d) There must be **no significant break in the normal trading pattern** before or immediately after the transfer

(e) In the case of **land and buildings**, the **transferee makes an election to tax** if the transferor has done so (the election to tax is explained later in this text)

(f) In the case of **'new' buildings the transferee makes an election to tax**.

Note. For the last two points if the election to tax is not made by the transferee the supply of land or buildings is standard rated. All the other business assets can be transferred outside the scope of VAT under the TOGC rules.

7 Accounting for VAT

7.1 VAT periods

VAT is accounted for on regular returns which are usually filed online within one month plus seven days of the end of the VAT period. Extensive records must be kept.

The VAT period (also known as the tax period) is the period covered by a VAT return. It is usually three calendar months. The return shows the total input and output tax for the tax period.

HMRC allocate VAT periods according to the class of trade carried on (ending in June, September, December and March; July, October, January and April; or August, November, February and May), to spread the flow of VAT returns evenly over the year. When applying for registration a trader can ask for VAT periods which fit in with their own accounting year. It is also possible to have VAT periods to cover accounting systems not based on calendar months.

A registered person whose input tax will regularly exceed their output tax can elect for a one month VAT period, but will have to balance the inconvenience of making 12 returns a year against the advantage of obtaining more rapid repayments of VAT.

Certain small businesses may submit an annual VAT return (see later in this text).

7.2 The VAT return

The regular VAT return to HMRC is made on form VAT 100.

Input and output tax figures must be supported by the original or copy tax invoices, and records must be maintained for six years.

7.3 Electronic filing

Nearly all VAT registered businesses must file their VAT returns online and make payments electronically.

The time limit for submission and payment is one month plus seven days after the end of the VAT period. For example, a business which has a VAT quarter ending 31 March 2019 must file its VAT return and pay the VAT due by 7 May 2019.

7.4 Substantial traders

Once a trader's total VAT liability for the 12 months or less to the end of a VAT period exceeds £2,300,000, the trader must start making payments on account of each quarter's VAT liability during each quarter.

Two payments on account of each quarter's VAT liability must usually be made. The first is due one month before the end of the quarter and the second is due at the end of the month which is the final month of the quarter. The amount of each payment on account made during the quarter is 1/24 of the trader's annual VAT liability in the period in which the threshold is exceeded. For the purposes of calculating the payments on account (but not for the purposes of the £2,300,000 threshold for entry into the scheme), a trader's VAT due on imports from outside the EU is ignored.

If the VAT liability for the quarter exceeds the total of the payments on account, a balancing payment is due one month after the end of the quarter to bring the total payments for that quarter to the amount of the VAT liability. If the VAT liability for the quarter is less than the total of the payments on account, HMRC will make a repayment to the trader.

Payments must be made and the quarterly VAT return submitted by the last day of the relevant month ie there is no additional seven days. **Payments must be made electronically.**

The default surcharge (see later in this chapter) applies to late payments.

Question	Substantial traders

Large Ltd is liable to make payments on account calculated at £250,000 each for the quarter ended 31 December 2018.

What payments/repayment are due if Large Ltd's VAT liability for the quarter is calculated as:

(a) £680,000?
(b) £480,000?

Answer

(a)

Date	Payment
30 November 2018	Payment on account of £250,000
31 December 2018	Payment on account of £250,000
31 January 2019	Balancing payment of £(6 – 250,000 – 250,000) = £180,000 with submission of VAT return for quarter

(b)

Date	Payment/repayment
30 November 2018	Payment on account of £250,000
31 December 2018	Payment on account of £250,000
31 January 2019	Repayment by HMRC of £(480,000 – 250,000 – 250,000) = £(20,000) on submission of VAT return for quarter

Once a trader is in the scheme, the payments on account are reviewed annually at a set time. However, **the trader can apply to reduce payments on account at any time if the total VAT liability for the latest four returns is less than 80% of the total on which the payments on account are currently based**, ie the VAT liability decreases by 20% or more. **Conversely, HMRC may increase the payments on account in between annual reviews if the trader's total 12 month VAT liability increases by 20% or more**, ie the VAT for the last four periods is at least 120% of the amount on which the payments on account are currently based. **A trader can apply to leave the scheme if their 12 month VAT liability is below £1,800,000. A trader whose VAT liability at the annual review was below £2,300,000 will be automatically removed from the scheme six months later.**

A trader may elect to pay their actual VAT liability monthly instead of making payments on account. For example, the actual liability for January would be due at the end of February. The trader can continue to submit quarterly returns as long as HMRC is satisfied the trader is paying sufficient monthly amounts.

7.5 Refunds of VAT

There is a four year time limit on the right to reclaim overpaid VAT. This time limit does not apply to input tax which a business could not have reclaimed earlier because the supplier only recently invoiced the VAT, even though it related to a purchase made some time ago. Nor does it apply to overpaid VAT penalties.

If a taxpayer has overpaid VAT and has overclaimed input tax by reason of the same mistake, HMRC can set off any tax, penalty, interest or surcharge due to them against any repayment due to the taxpayer and repay only the net amount. In such cases the normal four year time limit for recovering VAT, penalties, interest, etc by assessment does not apply.

HMRC can refuse to make any repayment which would unjustly enrich the claimant. They can also refuse a repayment of VAT where all or part of the tax has, for practical purposes, been borne by a person other than the taxpayer (eg by a customer of the taxpayer) except to the extent that the taxpayer can show loss or damage to any of their businesses as a result of mistaken assumptions about VAT.

7.6 Records

Every VAT registered trader must keep records for six years, although HMRC may sometimes grant permission for their earlier destruction. They may be kept on paper, on microfilm or microfiche or on computer. However, there must be adequate facilities for HMRC to inspect records.

All records must be kept up to date and in a way which allows:

- The calculation of VAT due
- Officers of HMRC to check the figures on VAT returns

The following records are needed:

- Copies of VAT invoices, credit notes and debit notes issued

- A summary of supplies made

- VAT invoices, credit notes and debit notes received

- A summary of supplies received

- Records of goods received from and sent to other EU member states

- Documents relating to imports from and exports to countries outside the EU

- A VAT account

- Order and delivery notes, correspondence, appointment books, job books, purchases and sales books, cash books, account books, records of takings (such as till rolls), bank paying-in slips, bank statements and annual accounts

- Records of zero-rated and exempt supplies, gifts or loans of goods, taxable self-supplies and any goods taken for non-business use

8 Valuation of supplies

VAT is charged on the VAT-exclusive price. Where a discount is offered for prompt payment, VAT is chargeable on the actual amount received for the supply.

One of the competencies you require to fulfil Performance Objective 15 Tax computations and assessments of the PER is to prepare or contribute to computations or assessments of indirect tax liabilities. You can apply the knowledge you obtain from this section of the text to help to demonstrate this competence.

8.1 General principles

The value of a supply is the VAT-exclusive price on which VAT is charged. The consideration for a supply is the amount paid in money or money's worth. Thus with a standard rate of 20%:

Value + VAT = consideration
£100 + £20 = £120

and the VAT fraction is

$$\frac{\text{rate of tax}}{100 + \text{rate of tax}} = \frac{20}{100 + 20} = \frac{1}{6}$$

Provided the consideration for a bargain made at arm's length is paid in money, the value for VAT purposes is the VAT-exclusive price charged by the trader. If it is paid in something other than money, as in a barter of some goods or services for others, it must be valued and VAT will be due on the value.

If the price of goods is effectively reduced with money off coupons, the value of the supply is the amount actually received by the taxpayer.

8.2 Mixed supplies and composite supplies

Different goods and services are sometimes invoiced together at an inclusive price (a 'mixed supply'). Some items may be chargeable at the standard rate and some at the zero-rate. **The supplier must account for VAT separately on the standard rated and zero rated elements by splitting the total amount payable in a fair proportion between the different elements and charging VAT on each at the appropriate rate.** There is no single way of doing this: one method is to split the amount according to the cost to the supplier of each element, and another is to use the open market value of each element. Mixed supplies are also known as 'multiple supplies'.

If a supply cannot be split into components, there is a 'composite' supply, to which one VAT rate must be applied. The rate depends on the nature of the supply as a whole. Composite supplies are also known as 'compound supplies'.

A supply of air transport including an in-flight meal has been held to be a single, composite supply of transport (zero-rated) rather than a supply of transport (zero-rated) and a supply of a meal (standard-rated). Contrast this with catering included in the price of leisure travel – there are two separate supplies: standard-rated catering and zero-rated passenger transport.

Broadly, a composite supply occurs when one element of the supply is merely incidental to the main element. A mixed supply occurs where different elements of the supply are the subject of separate negotiation and customer choice giving rise to identifiable obligations on the supplier.

8.3 Discounts

If the trader offers a discount for prompt payment, output VAT is charged on the actual amount received for the supply. The trader must either provide details of the discount on the sales invoice or must issue an invoice for the full amount and then issue a credit note if the discount is taken up.

8.4 Miscellaneous

For goods supplied under a hire purchase agreement VAT is chargeable on the cash selling price at the start of the contract.

If a trader charges different prices to customers paying with credit cards and those paying by other means, the VAT due in respect of each standard-rated sale is the full amount paid by the customer × the VAT fraction.

When goods are permanently taken from a business for non-business purposes VAT must be accounted for on their market value. Where business goods are put to a private or non-business use, the value of the resulting supply of services is the cost to the taxable person of providing the services. If services bought for business purposes are used for non-business purposes (without charge), then VAT must be accounted for on their cost, but the VAT to be accounted for is not allowed to exceed the input tax deductible on the purchase of the services.

9 Administration

FAST FORWARD VAT is administered by HMRC and the Tax Tribunal hears appeals.

9.1 Introduction

The administration of VAT is dealt with by HM Revenue and Customs (HMRC).

9.2 Local offices

Local offices are responsible for the local administration of VAT and for providing advice to registered persons whose principal place of business is in their area. They are controlled by regional collectors.

From time to time a registered person will be visited by HMRC staff from a local office to ensure that the law is understood and is being applied properly. If a trader disagrees with any decision as to the application of VAT given by HMRC they can ask their local office to reconsider the decision. It is not necessary to appeal formally while a case is being reviewed in this way. Where an appeal can be settled by agreement, a written settlement has the same force as a decision decided through the normal appeals process (see below). A trader can ask for a reconsideration even if they have already appealed to the Tax Tribunal.

HMRC may issue assessments of VAT due to the best of their judgement if they believe that a trader has failed to make returns or if they believe those returns to be incorrect or incomplete. The time limit for making assessments is normally four years after the end of a VAT period, but this is extended to 20 years in the case of fraud, dishonest conduct, certain registration irregularities and the unauthorised issue of VAT invoices.

HMRC sometimes write to traders, setting out their calculations, before issuing assessments. The traders can then query the calculations.

9.3 Appeals

A trader may appeal to the Tax Tribunal in the same way as an appeal may be made for income tax and corporation tax (see earlier in this text). VAT returns and payments shown thereon must have been made before an appeal can be heard.

The Tribunal can waive the requirement to pay all VAT shown on returns before an appeal is heard in cases of hardship. It cannot allow an appeal against a purely administrative matter such as HMRC's refusal to apply an extra statutory concession.

There may be a dispute over the deductibility of input tax which hinges on the purposes for which goods or services were used, or on whether they were used to make taxable supplies. The trader must show that HMRC acted unreasonably in refusing a deduction, if the goods or services are luxuries, amusements or entertainment.

9.4 Tax avoidance and evasion

Significant resources are deployed to tackle fraud, tax evasion and avoidance.

Avoidance is also countered by the requirement for traders to disclose to HMRC any use of a notifiable VAT avoidance scheme (see later in this text).

10 Penalties

A default occurs when a trader either submits their VAT return late, or submits the return on time but pays the VAT late. A default surcharge is applied if there is a default involving late payment during a default surcharge period.

10.1 The default surcharge

A default occurs when a trader either submits their VAT return late, or submits the return on time but pays the VAT late. It also occurs when a payment on account from a substantial trader is late. **If a trader defaults, HMRC will serve a surcharge liability notice on the trader. The notice specifies a surcharge period running from the date of the notice to the anniversary of the end of the period for which the trader is in default.**

If a further default occurs in respect of a return period ending during the specified surcharge period, the original surcharge period will be extended to the anniversary of the end of the period to which the new default relates. In addition, if the default involves the late payment of VAT (as opposed to simply a late return) **a surcharge is levied.**

The surcharge depends on the number of defaults involving late payment of VAT which have occurred in respect of periods ending in the surcharge period, as follows:

Default involving late payment of VAT in the surcharge period	Surcharge as a percentage of the VAT outstanding at the due date
First	2%
Second	5%
Third	10%
Fourth or more	15%

Surcharges at the 2% and 5% rates are not normally demanded unless the amount due would be at least £400 but for surcharges calculated using the 10% or 15% rates there is a minimum amount of £30 payable.

If a substantial trader is late with more than one payment (on account or final) for a return period, this only counts as one default. The total VAT paid late is the total of late payments on account plus the late final payment.

Question

Default surcharge

Peter has an annual turnover of around £300,000. His VAT return for the quarter to 31.12.18 is late. He then submits returns for the quarters to 30.9.19 and 31.3.20 late as well as making late payment of the tax due of £12,000 and £500 respectively.

Peter's VAT return to 31.3.21 is also late and the VAT due of £1,100 is also paid late. All other VAT returns and VAT payments are made on time. Outline Peter's exposure to default surcharge.

A surcharge liability notice will be issued after the late filing on the 31.12.18 return outlining a surcharge period extending to 31.12.19.

The late 30.9.19 return is in the surcharge period so the period is extended to 30.9.20. The late VAT payment triggers a 2% penalty. 2% × £12,000 = £240. Since £240 is less than the £400 *de minimis* limit it is not collected by HMRC.

The late 31.3.20 return is in the surcharge period so the period is now extended to 31.3.21. The late payment triggers a 5% penalty. 5% × £500 = £25. Since £25 is less than the £400 *de minimis* limit it is not collected by HMRC.

The late 31.03.21 return is in the surcharge period. The period is extended to 31.03.22. The late payment triggers a 10% penalty. 10% × £1,100 = £110. This is collected by HMRC since the £400 *de minimis* does not apply to penalties calculated at the 10% (and 15%) rate.

Peter will have to submit all four quarterly VAT returns to 31.3.22 on time and pay the VAT on time to 'escape' the default surcharge regime.

A trader must submit one year's returns on time and pay the VAT shown on them on time in order to break out of the surcharge liability period and the escalation of surcharge percentages.

A default will be ignored for all default surcharge purposes if the trader can show that the return or payment was sent at such a time, and in such a manner, that it was reasonable to expect that HMRC would receive it by the due date. Posting the return and payment first class the day before the due date is generally accepted as meeting this requirement. A default will also be ignored if the trader can demonstrate a reasonable excuse for the late submission or payment.

The application of the default surcharge regime to small businesses is modified. A small business is one with a turnover below £150,000. When a small business is late submitting a VAT return or paying VAT **it will first receive a letter from HMRC offering help.** No penalty will be charged. If **a further default occurs within 12 months of the letter** then a surcharge liability notice is issued, and the surcharge system formally begins as described above. Subsequent defaults then lead to surcharges of 2%, 5%, 10% and 15% if the VAT payment is late as described above, with the surcharge period extended each time. Effectively a small business is allowed an extra chance to default (and receive a help letter first) before the usual default surcharge system begins.

10.2 Penalties for errors

FAST FORWARD

There is a common penalty regime for errors in tax returns, including VAT. Errors in a VAT return up to certain amounts may be corrected in the next return.

10.2.1 Common penalty regime

The common penalty regime for making errors in tax returns discussed earlier in this text applies for value added tax.

10.2.2 Errors corrected in next return

Errors on previous VAT returns not exceeding the greater of:

- £10,000 (net under-declaration minus over-declaration); or
- 1% × net VAT turnover for return period (subject to an upper limit for the 1% amount of £50,000);

may be **corrected in the next return**.

Other errors should be notified to HMRC on form VAT652 or by letter.

In both cases, a penalty for error may be imposed. Correction of an error on a later return is not, of itself, an unprompted disclosure of the error and fuller disclosure is required for the penalty to be reduced. Default interest (see below) on the unpaid VAT as a result of the error is only charged where the limit is exceeded for the error to be corrected on the next VAT return.

10.3 Interest on unpaid VAT

FAST FORWARD

Default interest is charged on unpaid VAT if HMRC raise an assessment of VAT or the trader makes a voluntary payment before the assessment is raised. It runs from the date the VAT should have been paid to the actual date of payment but cannot run for more than three years before the assessment or voluntary payment.

Interest (not deductible in computing taxable profits) **is charged on VAT which is the subject of an assessment** (where returns were not made or were incorrect), **or which could have been the subject of an assessment but was paid before the assessment was raised. It runs from the reckonable date until the date of payment.** This interest is sometimes called 'default interest'.

The reckonable date is when the VAT should have been paid (one month and seven days from the end of the return period), or in the case of VAT repayments, seven days from the issue of the repayment order. However, where VAT is charged by an assessment, interest does not run from more than three years before the date of the assessment. Where the VAT was paid before an assessment was raised, interest does not run for more than three years before the date of payment.

In practice, interest is only charged when there would otherwise be a loss to the Exchequer. It is not, for example, charged when a company failed to charge VAT but if it had done so another company would have been able to recover the VAT.

10.4 Reasonable excuse

A penalty may not be due if the trader can show that there is reasonable excuse for the failure, or the penalty may be mitigated by HMRC or by the Tribunal. There is no definition of 'reasonable excuse'. However the legislation states that the following are not reasonable excuses:

- An insufficiency of funds to pay any VAT due
- Reliance upon a third party (such as an accountant) to perform the task in question

Many cases have considered **what constitutes a reasonable excuse** but decisions often conflict with one another. Each case depends on its own facts. Here are some examples:

(a) Whilst **'ignorance of basic VAT law'** is not an excuse, ignorance of more complex matters can constitute a reasonable excuse.

(b) There have been a number of cases where it has been accepted that **misunderstandings as to the facts** give rise to a reasonable excuse.

(c) Although the law expressly excludes an insufficiency of funds from providing a reasonable excuse, the Tribunal will, in exceptional circumstances, look behind the shortage of funds itself and examine the case of it – this is generally restricted to cases where an unexpected event (eg bank error) has led to the shortage of funds.

Exam focus point

You are not required to know any of the other VAT penalties for your exam.

11 Imports, exports, acquisitions and dispatches

11.1 Introduction

The terms **import and export** refer to purchases and sales of goods with countries **outside the EU.**

The terms **acquisition and dispatch** refer to purchases and sales of goods with countries **in the EU**.

The EU comprises of: Austria, Belgium, Bulgaria, Croatia, Republic of Cyprus, Czech Republic, Denmark, Estonia, Finland, France, Germany, Greece, Hungary, Ireland, Italy, Latvia, Lithuania, Luxembourg, Malta, Netherlands, Poland, Portugal, Romania, Slovakia, Slovenia, Spain, Sweden and the UK.

Exam focus point

> There are different rules for transactions between EU member states and for transactions with non-EU countries.

The long term implications of the **process which has started for the UK to leave the European Union** are not fully known, in particular whether there will be a transitional period. However, until the UK has gone through the process of ceasing its membership, **European Union rules will continue to apply to the UK**.

11.2 Place of supply

The place of supply of goods and services is important because it determines how the supply is treated for VAT. For example, if a supply is made in the UK, it is subject to the rules and rates of UK VAT.

If the supply is a **supply of goods**, it will be treated as **made in the UK if the goods are in the UK at the time they are supplied**. Similarly, a supply of goods which are not in the UK when they are supplied will not be treated as made in the UK and so will not be subject to UK output tax.

If the supply is a **supply of services**, the basic rule for services made to a **business** (B2B supplies) is that the **supply is made where the customer has established their business**.

The basic rule for **supplies of services to other consumers** (B2C supplies) **is that the supply is made where the supplier has established their business**. There are some exceptions to this rule. For example, certain services relating to land are treated as made where the land is located.

11.3 Trade in goods outside the European Union

11.3.1 Imports

6/18

An importer of goods from outside the EU:

(a)   Must usually account for the output VAT at the point of entry into the UK; and

(b)   Can claim the input VAT payable on their next VAT return.

There are **special rules** about the accounting for output VAT on imports in the following circumstances:

(a)   **The trader is approved under the Duty Deferment Scheme**: deferred charges are calculated for imports for each calendar month and must be paid in one sum by direct debit on the 15th of the month following the month of importation. Thus this scheme gives deferral of payment for between two and six weeks and simplifies administration for both the trader and HMRC.

(b)   **Goods are held in an HMRC warehouse**: the import of the goods into the warehouse is disregarded, but output VAT is accounted for either when the goods are removed from the warehouse or under the Duty Deferment Scheme if the trader is approved.

11.3.2 Exports

The export of goods outside the EU is zero rated.

The trader must provide evidence of the export such as copy invoices and consignment notes.

11.4 Trade in goods within the European Union

11.4.1 Purchases (acquisitions)

Goods acquired by a VAT registered person in the UK from another EU member state are liable to VAT in this country. Consequently, output tax has to be accounted for on the relevant VAT return.

The 'tax point' for such acquisitions is the earlier of:

- **The fifteenth day of the month following the month of acquisition, and**
- **The date of issue of an invoice.**

The transaction is entered on the relevant VAT return as an output **and** an input so, subject to the partial exemption provisions, the effect is neutral. Thus the trader is in the same position as they would have been if they had acquired the goods from a UK supplier.

If the goods acquired are zero-rated or exempt under UK VAT legislation there is no requirement to account for VAT at the standard rate.

11.4.2 Sales (dispatches) 6/18

Where goods are sold to a customer in another EU member state, the supply is zero-rated if the following conditions are satisfied:

- **The supply is made to a registered trader**
- **The supplier quotes their customer's VAT number on the invoice**
- **The supplier holds evidence that the goods were delivered to another member state**

If these conditions are not satisfied, the trader will usually account for VAT in the same way as for a supply to a customer within the same member state as the trader. This is called 'distance selling'.

If the trader exceeds the distance selling threshold for the customer's member state, the trader is required to register for VAT in the customer's member state. The trader then accounts for VAT in the customer's member state instead of the trader's member state.

11.5 International services 12/17

International services between VAT-registered businesses require the customer to account for both output and input tax under the reverse charge rules. Output tax on other international services is usually accounted for by the supplier in the usual way.

As we have seen, B2B services are treated as supplied in the place where the customer has established their business. Where the supply is treated as made in the UK under these rules, the UK business customer must apply the 'reverse charge'. This means that the UK business charges itself output tax which it recovers as input tax in the normal way. This means that the foreign supplier has no obligation to register for VAT in the UK or to charge UK VAT on such supplies. Instead, the customer is required to account for VAT.

If the customer is not registered for VAT, the purchase of the services counts as a deemed supply in measuring the registerable turnover for the customer. This might lead to the customer becoming liable to register for VAT.

If the business customer only makes taxable supplies, the overall effect of the reverse charge will normally be tax-neutral as the output tax and input tax will cancel each other out. However, if the business customer is partially exempt, not all of the input tax may be recoverable and so the reverse charge will lead to a net payment of output tax.

The tax point for a single supply to which the reverse charge applies is the earlier of:

- **The time the service is completed**
- **The time the service is paid for.**

If the supply is continuous, the tax point will be the end of each billing or payment period, Where the service is not subject to billing or payment periods, the tax point will be 31 December each year unless a payment has already been made, in which case the tax point will be the date of the payment.

For B2C services, the supply will be made by the supplier where they have established their business and the supplier will charge output tax in the normal way. No input tax is recoverable on B2C supplies since, by definition, the consumer is not a VAT-registered business.

Exam focus point

> The special place of supply rules for B2C supplies of telecommunications, broadcasting and e-services are **excluded** from the Advanced Taxation (ATX – UK) syllabus.

12 Special schemes

FAST FORWARD

> Special schemes include the cash accounting scheme, the annual accounting scheme and the flat rate scheme. These schemes make VAT accounting easier for certain types of trader usually with relatively low turnover.

> One of the competencies you require to fulfil Performance Objective 17 Tax planning and advice of the PER is to review the situation of an individual or entity advising on any potential tax risks and/or additional tax minimisation measures. You can apply the knowledge you obtain from this section of the text to help to demonstrate this competence.

12.1 The cash accounting scheme

The cash accounting scheme enables businesses to account for VAT on the basis of cash paid and received. The date of payment or receipt determines the return in which the transaction is dealt with. This means that the cash accounting scheme gives automatic impairment loss relief (bad debt relief) because VAT is not due on a supply until payment has been received.

The scheme can only be used by a trader whose annual taxable turnover (exclusive of VAT) is not expected to exceed £1,350,000 over the following 12 months and whose returns and VAT payments are up to date. A VAT group can use the cash accounting scheme if the expected annual taxable turnover of the whole group satisfies this condition.

If the value of taxable supplies exceeds £1,600,000 in the 12 months to the end of a VAT period a trader must leave the cash accounting scheme immediately.

Advantages of the scheme are:

- Automatic relief for impairment losses
- Cash flow

12.2 The annual accounting scheme   12/13

The annual accounting scheme is only available to traders who regularly pay VAT to HMRC, not to traders who normally receive repayments. It is available for traders **whose VAT exclusive taxable turnover is not expected to exceed £1,350,000 over the following 12 months.**

Traders file annual VAT returns and must make nine monthly payments on account equal to 90% of their previous year's VAT liability, with the first payment due at the end of the fourth month of the year. An annual VAT return must be submitted to HMRC along with any balancing payment due within two months of the end of the year. There is an option to pay three larger interim instalments. Late payment of instalments is not a default for the purposes of the surcharge liability notice system.

To use the scheme all payments must have been made up to date. Annual accounting is not available where VAT registration is in the name of a VAT group.

If the expected value of a trader's taxable supplies exceeds £1,600,000 notice must be given to HMRC within 30 days and they may then be required to leave the scheme. If the £1,600,000 limit is actually exceeded, the trader must leave the scheme.

Advantages of annual accounting:

- Only one VAT return each year so fewer occasions to trigger a default surcharge
- Ability to manage cash flow more accurately
- Avoids need for quarterly calculations for partial exemption purposes and input tax recovery

Disadvantages of annual accounting:

- Need to monitor future taxable supplies to ensure turnover limit not exceeded
- Timing of payments have less correlation to turnover (and hence cash received) by business
- Payments based on previous year's turnover may not reflect current year turnover which may be a problem if the scale of activities has reduced

12.3 Flat rate scheme   6/14

The flat rate scheme enables businesses to calculate VAT due to HMRC by simply applying a flat rate percentage to their VAT inclusive turnover, including all zero-rated and exempt income. The percentage depends upon the trade sector into which a business falls. The percentage usually depends upon the trade sector into which a business falls. It ranges from 4% for retailing food, confectionery or newspapers) to 14.5% for accountancy and book-keeping. A 1% reduction off the flat rate % can be made by businesses in their first year of VAT registration.

Businesses using the scheme must issue VAT invoices to their VAT registered customers but they do not have to record all the details of the invoices issued or purchase invoices received to calculate the VAT due. Invoices issued will show VAT at the normal rate rather than the flat rate.

To join the flat rate scheme businesses must have a tax exclusive annual taxable turnover of up to £150,000. A business must leave the flat rate scheme if the total value of its tax inclusive supplies in the year (excluding sales of capital assets) is more than £230,000.

The **main advantage of the flat rate scheme** is the **reduction in VAT administration**, rather than a substantial saving of VAT itself.

There is a special flat rate of 16.5% which applies if the trader either does not purchase any goods or purchases only a limited amount of goods.

If the **16.5% rate is applicable**, it will **usually not be advantageous** for a trader to use the flat rate scheme unless the amount of input VAT is very low.

12.4 Example: flat rate scheme

Kevin is a VAT-registered trader who makes supplies to individuals who are not VAT-registered and to other VAT-registered traders. In a VAT year, the supplies to VAT-registered traders amount to £25,000 and Kevin will issue VAT invoices totalling £30,000 (£25,000 plus VAT at 20%). Turnover from supplies to individuals totals £60,000, including VAT. Total gross sales are therefore £90,000. The flat rate percentage for Kevin's business is 10.5%. The special 16.5% rate does not apply.

VAT due to HMRC will be 10.5% × £90,000 = £9,450. Under the normal VAT rules the output tax due would be:

	£
£25,000 × 20%	5,000
£60,000 × 1/6	10,000
	15,000

Whether Kevin is better off under the flat rate scheme depends on the amount of input tax incurred as this would be offset, under normal rules, from output tax due. The reduced VAT administration should also be taken into account.

Chapter roundup

- VAT is charged on turnover at each stage in a production process, but in such a way that the burden is borne by the final consumer.

- VAT is charged on taxable supplies of goods and services made by a taxable person in their business.

- Some supplies are taxable (either standard-rated, reduced-rated or zero-rated). Others are exempt.

- A trader becomes liable to register for VAT if the value of taxable supplies in any period up to 12 months exceeds £85,000 or if there are reasonable grounds for believing that the value of the taxable supplies will exceed £85,000 in the next 30 days. A trader may also register voluntarily.

- VAT incurred on goods and services before registration can be treated as input tax and recovered from HMRC subject to certain conditions.

- Not all input VAT is deductible, eg VAT on most motor cars.

- If fuel is supplied for private purposes all input VAT incurred on the fuel is allowed and the business will normally account for output VAT using a set of scale charges.

- Relief for VAT on impairment losses (bad debts) is available if the VAT has been accounted for, the debt is over six months old (measured from when the payment is due) and has been written off in the trader's accounts.

- The transfer of a business as a going concern is outside the scope of VAT provided certain conditions are satisfied.

- VAT is accounted for on regular returns which are usually filed online within one month plus seven days of the end of the VAT period. Extensive records must be kept.

- VAT is charged on the VAT-exclusive price. Where a discount is offered for prompt payment, VAT is chargeable on actual amount received for the supply.

- VAT is administered by HMRC and the Tax Tribunal hears appeals.

- A default occurs when a trader either submits their VAT return late, or submits the return on time but pays the VAT late. A default surcharge is applied if there is a default involving late payment during a default surcharge period.

- There is a common penalty regime for errors in tax returns, including VAT. Errors in a VAT return up to certain amounts may be corrected in the next return.

- Default interest is charged on unpaid VAT if HMRC raise an assessment of VAT or the trader makes a voluntary payment before the assessment is raised. It runs from the date the VAT should have been paid to the actual date of payment but cannot run for more than three years before the assessment or voluntary payment.

- Imports from outside the EU are subject to VAT and exports to outside the EU are zero-rated. Taxable acquisitions from other EU states are also subject to VAT and sales to registered traders in other EU states are zero-rated.

- International services between VAT-registered businesses require the customer to account for both output and input tax under the reverse charge rules. Output tax on other international services is usually accounted for by the supplier in the usual way.

- Special schemes include the cash accounting scheme, the annual accounting scheme and the flat rate scheme. These schemes make VAT accounting easier for certain types of trader usually with relatively low turnover.

1   On what transactions will VAT be charged?

2   What is a taxable person?

3   When may a taxable person be exempt from registration?

4   How are transfers between group companies treated under a VAT registration?

5   When may a person choose to be deregistered?

6   What is the time limit in respect of claiming pre-registration input tax on goods?

7   What input tax is never deductible?

8   What relief is available for bad debts?

9   What is a default?

10   What are the turnover limits for the annual accounting scheme?

11   What is the optional flat rate scheme?

1   VAT is charged on taxable supplies of goods and services made in the UK by a taxable person in the course or furtherance of any business carried on by them.

2   Any 'person' whose taxable turnover exceeds the registration limit, or a person with no UK establishment, making taxable supplies in the UK. The term 'person' includes individuals, partnerships, companies, clubs, associations and charities.

3   If a taxable person makes only zero-rated supplies they may request exemption from registration.

4   Any supplies between VAT group members are ignored for VAT purposes.

5   A person is eligible for voluntary deregistration if HMRC are satisfied that the value of their taxable supplies in the following year will not exceed £83,000.

6   VAT on:

   •   Motor cars (where there is an element of private use)
   •   Business entertaining (UK customers)
   •   Expenses incurred on domestic accommodation for directors
   •   Non-business items passed through the accounts

7   Where a supplier has accounted for VAT on a supply and the customer fails to pay, then the supplier may, after 6 months, write it off in the accounts and claim a refund of the VAT.

8   The VAT must have been incurred in the four years prior to the effective date of registration.

9   A default occurs when a trader either submits their VAT return late or submits the return on time but pays the VAT late.

10 Turnover not exceeding £1,350,000 to join the scheme. Once turnover exceeds £1,600,000 must leave the scheme.

11 The optional flat rate scheme enables businesses to calculate VAT simply by applying a percentage to their tax-inclusive turnover ie the total turnover generated, including all zero-rated and exempt income. The percentage usually depends upon the trade sector into which a business falls or may be 16.5% if the trader makes no, or limited, purchases of goods.

Now try the questions below from the Practice Question Bank

Number	Level	Marks	Time
Q31	Introductory	10	20 mins

Value added tax 2

Topic list	Syllabus reference
1 Land and buildings	A6(a)(i)
2 Partial exemption	A6(a)(ii)
3 Capital goods scheme	A6(a)(iii)

Introduction

In this chapter, we continue our VAT studies by looking at aspects which are new in Advanced Taxation (ATX – UK).

First we consider the rules about land and buildings. It is possible to opt to tax certain supplies as taxable instead of being exempt.

Next we deal with the restriction on recovery of input tax under partial exemption.

Finally, we look at the capital goods scheme which ensures that the recovery of VAT on certain capital expenditure reflects its taxable use over a longer period of time than the usual VAT period in which the expenditure is incurred.

In the next chapter, we will draw together all of our Advanced Taxation (ATX – UK) studies by looking at the impact of taxes and tax planning.

Study guide

6	Value added tax, tax administration and the UK tax system	Intellectual level
(a)	The contents of the Taxation - United Kingdom (TX – UK) study guide for value added tax (VAT) under heading:	2
•	F2 The computation of VAT liabilities	
	The following additional material is also examinable:	
(i)	Advise on the VAT implications of the supply of land and buildings in the UK	3
(ii)	Advise on the VAT implications of partial exemption	3
(iii)	Advise on the application of the capital goods scheme	3

Exam guide

In the exam, you may be required to advise on almost any aspect of VAT. A question may require you to consider the effect of following a particular course of action, for example commencing to make exempt supplies may lead to a greater than expected VAT cost as the partial exemption rules result in the disallowance of a proportion of input tax.

Knowledge brought forward from earlier studies

Land and buildings, partial exemption and the capital goods scheme are all new topics in Advanced Taxation (ATX – UK).

1 Land and buildings   12/15, 3/16, 6/17

FAST FORWARD

Transactions in land may be zero rated, standard rated or exempt.

1.1 Transactions in land

Transactions in land may be zero rated, standard rated or exempt.

(a) **The construction of new dwellings or buildings to be used for residential or charitable purposes is zero-rated.**

(b) **The sale of the freehold of a 'new' commercial building is standard-rated. The definition of 'new' is less than three years old.** The construction of commercial buildings is also standard-rated.

(c) Other sales and most leases of land and buildings are exempt.

1.2 Option to tax

Owners may elect to treat sales and leases of land and *commercial* buildings as taxable instead of exempt. This is known as 'waiving the exemption' or the option to tax.

The owner must become registered for VAT (if they are not already so registered) in order to make the election. The election replaces an exempt supply with a standard rated one, usually to enable the recovery of input VAT.

A taxpayer may make a 'real estate election' (REE) instead of making separate elections for each property they own. **If a taxpayer makes a REE, they will be treated as having made the election for each property they acquire after making the REE**, although they may revoke the option on a particular property under the 'cooling-off' provisions described below.

The election may be revoked:

(a) **During the 'cooling off' period**: within six months of the election taking effect, provided that no use (including own use) has been made of the land, no tax has been charged on a supply of the land as a result of the option, no TOGC has occurred and HMRC has been notified of the revocation on the appropriate form

(b) **Where no interest has been held in the property for over six years**

(c) **Where more than 20 years have elapsed since the election first had effect**, provided certain conditions are met or with the prior consent of HMRC

2 Partial exemption $\qquad$ 12/13, 6/15, 12/15, 6/18

FAST FORWARD A trader making both taxable and exempt supplies may be unable to recover all of their input tax.

2.1 Introduction

A trader may only recover the VAT on supplies made to them if it is attributable to their taxable supplies. **Where a person makes a mixture of taxable and exempt supplies, they are partially exempt. In this case, not all their input tax may be recoverable because some of it is attributable to their exempt supplies.**

2.2 The standard method of attributing input tax

For a trader who is partially exempt, input tax must be apportioned between that relating to **taxable supplies** (and recoverable) **and** that relating to **exempt supplies** (exempt input tax). The standard method of attributing input tax is to:

Step 1 **Calculate how much of the input tax relates to making taxable supplies**: this input tax is deductible in full.

Step 2 **Calculate how much of the input tax relates to making exempt supplies**: this is exempt input tax.

Step 3 **Calculate how much of any residual (ie remaining) input tax is deductible using the percentage:**

Formula to learn

$$\frac{\text{Taxable turnover excluding VAT}}{\text{Total turnover excluding VAT}} \times 100\%, \text{ rounded up}$$

Where the residual input tax does not exceed £400,000, the figure is rounded up to the nearest whole percentage. Otherwise, the figure is rounded to two decimal places.

For each VAT return period, the trader usually works out the amount of input tax they can recover (subject to the *de minimis* tests – see further below). The trader can either use the previous year's recovery percentage or the percentage for the return period. However, the trader must use only one of these methods in a year ie either the previous year's recovery percentage for all return periods in the year or the actual percentages for each return period. Note that the same amount of input VAT will be recoverable for the year overall because the difference between the percentages used will be adjusted at the end of the year (see further below).

In the three-month VAT period to 30 June 2018, Arun makes £105,000 of exempt supplies and £300,000 of taxable supplies. Most of the goods purchased are used for both types of supply which means that much of the input tax cannot be directly attributed to either type of supply. After directly attributing as much input tax as possible the following position arises.

	£
Attributed to taxable supplies	1,200
Attributed to exempt supplies	600
Unattributed VAT	8,200
	10,000

How much input tax can Arun recover, assuming that Arun uses the percentage for the return period?

Answer

The amount of unattributed VAT which is apportioned to the making of taxable supplies is

$$\frac{300,000}{405,000} = 74.07\% \text{ rounded up to } 75\% \times £8,200 = £6,150$$

Note. The percentage is rounded up since residual (unattributed) input tax does not exceed £400,000 per month.

Arun can therefore recover £1,200 + £6,150 = £7,350 of his input tax.

The balance of input tax of £2,650 (£600 + £(8,200 − 6,150)) is exempt input tax.

An alternative method of attributing input tax ('special' method) may be agreed in writing with HMRC.

2.3 *De minimis* tests

All the input VAT is recoverable if one the amount of input VAT relating to exempt supplies is small (*de minimis*) under one of the following tests:

Test 1

The **total input VAT incurred is no more than £625 per month on average** and the **value of exempt supplies is no more than 50% of all supplies.**

Test 2

The **total input VAT incurred less input VAT directly attributed to taxable supplies is no more than £625 per month on average** and the **value of exempt supplies is no more than 50% of the value of all supplies.**

Test 3

The **input VAT wholly attributable to exempt supplies plus the residual VAT attributed to exempt supplies (ie the total of exempt input tax) is no more than £625 per month on average** and **no more than 50% of its input tax.**

2.4 Annual test

The annual test gives a trader the option of applying the *de minimis* test once a year instead of every VAT return period.

To use the annual test, **the trader must satisfy the following conditions:**

(a) Have been *de minimis* in the previous partial exemption year;

(b) **Consistently apply the annual test throughout any given partial exemption year** (ie does not switch between the quarterly tests and the annual test in the year);

(c) Have reasonable grounds for **not expecting to incur more than £1 million input tax in its current partial exemption year**.

If these conditions are satisfied, the trader can opt to treat himself as *de minimis* in the current partial exemption year. The trader can therefore recover input tax in full in each VAT return period without needing to see if one of the *de minimis* tests is satisfied for each VAT return period. This means that there is provisional recovery of all input tax in the year which will give a cash flow benefit and an administrative time saving.

At the end of the year, the trader must review their *de minimis* status using the *de minimis* tests applied to the year as a whole. If **one of the tests is failed**, the trader must carry out an **annual adjustment** as described below and which will result in a repayment of part of the input VAT previously recovered in full.

Exam focus point

> The annual test for partial exemption was tested in June 2015 Question 3(c)(ii) Nocturne Ltd. The examining team commented that this part of the question was 'not done well. The problem here was that the majority of candidates addressed the annual accounting scheme rather than the subject of the question. This was unfortunate and meant that very few candidates did well on this part of the question.'

2.5 Test for each return period

If the trader does not use the annual test, they must apply the *de minimis* tests for every VAT return period.

Tests 1 and 2 are simple to apply because they do not require the trader to make a calculation of residual VAT.

Test 3 is more complicated as it requires the calculation of residual VAT, usually using the standard method explained in Section 4.2.

Question

De minimis tests

Sue makes the following supplies in the quarter ended 31 October 2018.

	£
Taxable supplies (excl. VAT)	28,000
Exempt supplies	6,000
	34,000

Sue analyses her input tax for the period as follows.

		£
Wholly attributable to:	taxable supplies	1,500
	exempt supplies	900
Non-attributable (overheads)		1,200
		3,600

How much input tax is available for credit on Sue's VAT return assuming that she uses the percentage for the return period, where relevant?

Test 1

Total input VAT is $\frac{3,600}{3}$ = £1,200 per calendar month, more than £625 per calendar month.

Proportion of exempt supplies $\frac{6,000}{34,000}$ = 17.6%

Test 1 failed as only one part of test satisfied.

Test 2

	£
Total input VAT for period	3,600
Less wholly attributable to taxable supplies	(1,500)
	2,100

Monthly average $\frac{2,100}{3}$ = £700 per calendar month, more than £625 per calendar month.

Proportion of exempt supplies $\frac{6,000}{34,000}$ = 17.6%

Test 2 failed as only one part of test satisfied.

Test 3

	£
Wholly attributable to taxable supplies	1,500
Partly attributable to taxable supplies	
$\frac{28,000}{28,000 + 6,000}$	
ie 82.35% rounded up to 83% × £1,200	996
	2,496

£(900 + (1,200 − 996)) = 1,104

	£
Exempt input tax is *de minimis* (W)	1,104
Input tax recoverable	3,600

ie all input tax is recoverable

Working

Monthly average $\frac{1,104}{3}$ = £368 ie not more than £625

Proportion of total $\frac{1,104}{3,600}$ = 30.7% ie not more than 50%.

Both parts of Test 3 satisfied so Test 3 passed.

2.6 Annual adjustment

6/15

An annual adjustment is made with the *de minimis* tests applied to the year as a whole.

If **Tests 1 or 2 passed** for the year, **the trader can recover all of their input tax for the year and does not need to carry out a partial exemption calculation.**

If Tests 1 or 2 are failed, the trader will need to carry out a **full partial exemption calculation for the year to determine whether Test 3 is passed.** If it is, **the trader can recover all of their input tax for the year.**

The result for the year is compared with the total of results for the individual VAT periods and any difference is added to or deducted from the input tax either on the return for the last period in the year or on the return for the first period after the end of the year, at the option of the trader.

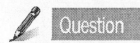
Following on from the example in Section 2.2 Arun has the following results in the remaining VAT quarters of his VAT year ended 31 March 2019.

| | | Input tax attributed to | |
Quarter to	Taxable supplies £	Exempt supplies £	Unattributed £
30.9.18	1,500	1,000	5,000
31.12.18	2,000	500	1,800
31.3.19	1,900	850	7,000
	5,400	2,350	13,800

| | Turnover | |
Quarter to	Taxable £	Exempt £
30.9.18	400,000	100,000
31.12.18	500,000	150,000
31.3.19	450,000	120,000
	1,350,000	370,000

It has already been ascertained that neither Test 1 nor Test 2 is satisfied for any of the four quarters nor for the year as a whole.

Calculate the annual adjustment required assuming that Arun uses the percentage for the return period in each of the quarters and state the latest return it will be made on.

Answer

First we calculate the recoverable input tax in each VAT return.

	£	Recovered £
Return to 30.6.18		
See above Taxable	7,350	7,350
Exempt (more than £625 per month)	2,650	
	10,000	
Return to 30.9.18		
$\frac{400,000}{500,000}$ = 80% × £5,000 = Non-attributable	4,000	
Wholly taxable	1,500	
Taxable total	5,500	5,500
Exempt £(1,000 + 1,000) (more than £625 per month)	2,000	
	7,500	
		12,850
Return to 31.12.18		
$\frac{500,000}{650,000}$ = 76.92% rounded up to 77% × £1,800	1,386	
Non-attributable		
Wholly taxable	2,000	
Taxable total	3,386	
Exempt £(500 + 414)	914	
	4,300	4,300

The exempt input tax at £914 is less than £1,875 (£625 × 3 months) and 50% of total input tax (50% × £4,300 = £2,150) so is *de minimis* and recoverable under Test 3.

Return to 31.3.19

$\dfrac{450,000}{570,000}$ = 78.94% rounded up to 79% × £7,000

		5,530

Non-attributable

Wholly taxable	1,900	
Taxable total	7,430	7,430
Exempt £(850 + 1,470) (more than £625 per month)	2,320	
	9,750	
Recovered over the VAT year		24,580

Now we do the same calculation again but using the results for the whole VAT year to 31.3.19.

Annual adjustment

$\dfrac{1,350,000 + 300,000}{1,720,000 + 405,000}$ = 77.64% rounded up to 78% × £(13,800 + 8,200) (note)

	17,160	
Wholly taxable £(5,400 + 1,200)	6,600	
Taxable total	23,760	(23,760)
Exempt £(31,550 − 23,760) (more than £625 per month)	7,790	
	31,550	

VAT to repay to HMRC on VAT return (latest)
to 30 June 2019 as annual adjustment

820

Note. We must include the quarter to June 2018's results.

3 Capital goods scheme

12/14

FAST FORWARD

> The capital goods scheme (CGS) allows HMRC to ensure the VAT claimed on the purchase of certain capital items accurately reflects the taxable use to which they are put over a period of time.

The scheme mainly affects partially exempt businesses and enables the amount of VAT recovered to be adjusted for each year's use.

The CGS applies to:

(a) Computers, boats and aircraft costing £50,000 or more, which are dealt with over five VAT years, and

(b) Land and buildings costing £250,000 or more, which are dealt with over ten VAT years.

In the VAT year the asset is acquired the input recovery is initially based on use for the quarter of purchase, and is then subject to the annual adjustment as described below.

For each subsequent VAT year over the recovery period of five or ten years an adjustment is made to the VAT recovery.

Formula to learn

> The adjustment is equal to the difference in percentage use between the first VAT year and the VAT year under review × 1/5 (for computers, boats and aircraft) or 1/10 (for land and buildings) × the original input tax on them

The adjustment is made in the second VAT return following the end of the VAT year.

If the asset is sold before the end of the recovery period, two adjustments are needed:

(a) The normal adjustment for the VAT year of sale as if the proportion of use for the period from the start of the year until the date of sale had applied for the whole VAT year

(b) An additional adjustment for each remaining VAT year of recovery calculated assuming 100% use for taxable supplies.

Question

Zoran Ltd purchased a computer for £100,000 + 20% VAT on 1 July 2018. It used it 58% for taxable use in the quarter of purchase and 60% for taxable purposes in the year to 31 December 2018.

The taxable use in the year to 31 December 2019 was 50%. The computer was sold on 10 May 2020. The taxable use in the period 1 January 2020 to 10 May 2020 was 50%.

Calculate the initial input recovery and adjustments required for all other years. Assume that the standard rate of VAT is 20% throughout.

Answer

For the first VAT year to 31 December 2018 the recovery (after the annual partial exemption adjustment) is £100,000 × 20% = £20,000 × 60% = £12,000.

For the second VAT year to 31 December 2019 the adjustment is £20,000 × 10% (ie 60% − 50%) × 1/5 = £400, payable to HMRC.

For the third VAT year to 31 December 2020 there are two adjustments:

(a)   £20,000 × 10% × 1/5 = £400, payable to HMRC

(b)   £20,000 × 40% (ie 100% − 60%) × 2/5 = £3,200

The net adjustment for the third VAT year to 31 December 2020 is £400 − £3,200 = £2,800 recoverable from HMRC.

Exam focus point

The capital goods scheme was tested in June 2012 Question 2 Janus plc group. The examining team commented that: 'Part (b)(ii) was done well by those candidates who both knew what to do and had practised applying the rules prior to the exam. Weaker candidates had a vague, confused knowledge of the rules or simply tried to describe them as opposed to apply them to the specific circumstances of the question. Very few candidates knew how to handle the adjustment following the sale of the building.'

Chapter roundup

- Transactions in land may be zero rated, standard rated or exempt.

- A trader making both taxable and exempt supplies may be unable to recover all of their input tax.

- The capital goods scheme (CGS) allows HMRC to ensure the VAT claimed on the purchase of certain capital items accurately reflects the taxable use to which they are put over a period of time.

Quick quiz

1   What is partial exemption?

2   Are goods exported from the EU standard-rated or zero-rated?

3   Higgins is registered for VAT in the UK. He only makes taxable supplies. Higgins is supplied with services by a French business. The value of the supply is £50,000. What are the VAT consequences of the supply?

4   What types of goods are included in the capital goods scheme?

5   What is the adjustment to VAT recovery required under the capital goods scheme?

Answers to quick quiz

1   Where a 'person' makes a mixture of taxable and exempt supplies they are partially exempt and cannot recover input tax incurred by the business in full.

2   In general, exports from the EU are zero-rated.

3   Higgins will have to account for output tax of £50,000 × 20% = £10,000 on the supply and also £10,000 of input tax. The reverse charge is therefore tax neutral for him.

4   Computers, boats and aircraft costing £50,000 or more, land and buildings costing £250,000 or more.

5   The adjustment is equal to the difference in percentage use between the first VAT year and the VAT year under review × 1/5 (for computers, boats and aircraft) or 1/10 (for land and buildings) × the original input tax on them.

Now try the question below from the Practice Question Bank

Number	Level	Marks	Time
Q32	Introductory	10	20 mins

Impact of taxes and tax planning

Impact of taxes and tax planning

Topic list	Syllabus reference
1 Impact of taxes	B1, B2(a), B4, B5, D1-5
2 Personal finance	B3(a)
3 Business finance	B3(b),(c),(d)
4 Tax planning	C1-4, C6
5 Ethics	B5, C5
6 Tax avoidance schemes	B6

Introduction

You have now completed your studies of the individual taxes covered in the syllabus so we will turn our attention to how to use your knowledge. First we consider how to answer questions about the impact of taxes on a given scenario.

Next, we look at the tax treatment of sources of finance and investment products for individuals. We also compare the tax implications of businesses raising equity and loan finance, and leasing an asset rather than buying it.

We then turn to tax planning, which is an integral part of any tax advice you give. We have dealt with various tax planning aspects as they have arisen earlier in this text. In this chapter, we bring together topics by considering ten specific scenarios in personal and business tax.

We next consider the ethical rules which should be applied to every situation that you are required to consider. Up to five marks on every exam will be given for your comments on ethical matters. It is therefore important that you identify ethical issues and comment as appropriate.

Finally, we look at HMRC's powers in relation to tax avoidance schemes which is a current issue in taxation.

Study guide

		Intellectual level
B	**THE IMPACT OF RELEVANT TAXES ON VARIOUS SITUATIONS AND COURSES OF ACTION, INCLUDING THE INTERACTION OF TAXES**	
1	Identify and advise on the taxes applicable to a given course of action and their impact.	3
2	Identify and understand that the alternative ways of achieving personal or business outcomes may lead to different tax consequences.	3
(a)	Calculate the receipts from a transaction, net of tax and compare the results of alternative scenarios and advise on the most tax efficient course of action.	3
3	**Advise how taxation can affect the financial decisions made by businesses (corporate and unincorporated) and by individuals.**	
(a)	Understand and compare and contrast the tax treatment of the sources of finance and investment products available to individuals.	3
(b)	Understand and explain the tax implications of the effect of the raising of equity and loan finance	3
(c)	Explain the tax differences between decisions to lease, use hire purchase or purchase outright.	3
(d)	Understand and explain the impact of taxation on the cash flows of a business.	3
4	**Assess the tax advantages and disadvantages of alternative courses of action.**	3
5	**Understand the statutory obligations imposed in a given situation, including any time limits for action and advise on the implications of non-compliance.**	3
C	**MINIMISE AND/OR DEFER TAX LIABILITIES BY THE USE OF STANDARD TAX PLANNING MEASURES**	
1	Identify and advise on the types of investment and other expenditure that will result in a reduction in tax liabilities for an individual and/or a business.	3
2	Advise on legitimate tax planning measures, by which the tax liabilities arising from a particular situation or course of action can be mitigated.	3
3	Advise on the appropriateness of such investment, expenditure or measures given a particular taxpayer's circumstances or stated objectives.	3
4	Advise on the mitigation of tax in the manner recommended by reference to numerical analysis and/or reasoned argument.	3
5	Be aware of the ethical and professional issues arising from the giving of tax planning advice.	3
6	Be aware of and give advice on current issues in taxation.	3

		Intellectual level
D	**COMMUNICATE WITH CLIENTS, HM REVENUE AND CUSTOMS AND OTHER PROFESSIONALS IN AN APPROPRIATE MANNER**	
1	**Communicate advice, recommendations and information in the required format:**	3
	For example the use of Reports, Letters, Memoranda and Meeting notes	
2	**Present written information, in language appropriate to the purpose of the communication and the intended recipient.**	3
3	**Communicate conclusions reached, together, where necessary with relevant supporting computations.**	3
4	**State and explain assumptions made or limitations in the analysis provided; together with any inadequacies in the information available and/or additional Information required to provide a fuller analysis.**	3
5	**Identify and explain other, non-tax, factors that should be considered.**	3

Exam guide

A significant number of marks in the exam will be available for evaluation and advice. Before you start to write your answer, assess what is required. You may simply be asked to advise on the tax consequences of one course of action, or you may have to compare the tax consequences of two or more options. The options may be specified in the question, or you may be required to identify possible options. You may have to cover all taxes, or to restrict your answer to a single tax. Present your answer in the required format; if you are asked for notes do not write an essay and if you are asked to write a letter, do so.

There will be five marks awarded for your comments on ethical matters in Section A. You need to know the fundamental principles of the ACCA's code of conduct, and when presented with a scenario you should quickly review these to make sure that they are not compromised. If there is a threat then consider how serious it is and how you should respond.

One of the competencies you require to fulfil Performance Objective 17 Tax planning and advice of the PER is to review the situation of an individual or entity advising on any potential tax risks and/or additional tax minimisation measures. You can apply the knowledge you obtain from this chapter of the text to help to demonstrate this competence.

1 Impact of taxes

FAST FORWARD

Questions on impact of taxes require you to use your technical knowledge of taxation in relation to particular scenarios. Avoid writing about technical areas in general terms as opposed to in relation to the question's requirements.

1.1 Answering questions involving impact of taxes

In the Advanced Taxation (ATX – UK) examination, most of the questions will require you to identify and advise on the taxes applicable to a given course of action and their impact. Here are some tips which will help you prepare for answering such exam questions.

1.1.1 Practise questions from past exams

Practise questions from past exams with the aim of adopting the style of the model answers. Questions 38 and 39 in the Questions Bank are examples of past exam questions which you should attempt when you have finished studying this chapter. **BPP's Practice and Revision Kit contains over 50 such questions** and should be the core of your revision.

Avoid looking at the model answers whilst attempting questions – the biggest problem most students face is knowing how to approach answering questions. You do not want to be attempting this for the first time in the exam! Remember that you are not required to make all the points shown in the model answer, so don't be discouraged if there are some that you miss when attempting a question. However, there will be a core of marks in each question which you should be aiming to obtain.

1.1.2 Address the requirement

Make sure you understand what you are required to do. In Section B questions, this means reading the requirement of the question. In Section A questions, you will usually need to look also at the more detailed instructions in one of the documents you are given (for example, an email or notes of a meeting) to find out exactly what is required. Look for key phrases in the question such as 'I need the following ....' or 'Please prepare the following for me...'.

Apply your knowledge to the facts by reference to the requirement. Marks are awarded for satisfying the requirements and not for other information even if it is technically correct. Avoid writing about technical areas in general terms as opposed to in relation to the requirements of the question.

The requirements of each question are carefully worded in order to provide you with guidance as regards the style and content of your answers. You should note the command words (calculate, explain etc), any matters which are **not** to be covered, and the precise issues you have been asked to address.

You should also note **any guidance given in the question or in any notes following the requirement** regarding the approach you should take when answering the question. For example, you may be asked to provide explanations 'briefly' or, on the other hand, 'in detail'. A brief explanation requires a succinct statement of the main points, a detailed explanation requires a wider consideration of the issues.

Pay attention to the number of marks available – this provides you with a clear indication of the amount of time you should spend on each question part. There is no point writing a page of explanation for a part which is allocated two or three marks.

Only provide explanations when you are asked to. For example, if you are asked to calculate, there is no need to explain what you are going to do before you do it; just get on with it.

1.1.3 Think before you start

Before you start writing, think about the issues and identify all of the points you intend to address and/or any strategy you intend to adopt to solve the problem set.

You should be methodical in your approach. Unless you are asked to consider only one or more specific taxes, you should get into the habit of **running through all the taxes,** even if to eliminate them from consideration. For Advanced Taxation (ATX – UK), the taxes in the syllabus are:

(a) Income tax
(b) Capital gains tax
(c) Inheritance tax
(d) National insurance contributions
(e) Stamp taxes
(f) Corporation tax
(g) Value added tax

If you are asked to compare the tax consequences of two or more options, you must consider the impact of **each** tax on **each** option in order to produce a complete picture.

1.1.4 Consider future consequences

Make sure that you consider the future consequences of your proposals, not just the immediate tax impact. In particular, remember that deferred gains crystallise on certain events; it may not be a good idea to claim gift relief if the donee will not be entitled to entrepreneurs' relief to reduce the tax on a subsequent sale, and paying tax now at a lower rate is usually better than delaying paying tax at a higher rate. Sometimes it is better to make a gift of a business asset as part of a will where a CGT uplift will be given – BPR may extinguish any IHT charge.

1.1.5 Present your answer appropriately

One of the competencies you require to fulfil Performance Objective 16 Tax compliance and verification of the PER is to correspond appropriately and in a professional manner with the relevant parties in relation to both routine and specific matters/enquiries. You can apply the knowledge you obtain from this chapter of the text to help to demonstrate this competence.

Read the question carefully to ascertain the type of answer that may be required. You may have to prepare a formal report, letter or memorandum, or you may have to write notes for a colleague. In other cases you may just be required to prepare explanations or calculations.

Where the answer is formal, **marks will be specifically awarded for the presentation of the material and the effectiveness with which the information is presented**. There will be four such professional marks available in question one of the exam. You should get used to setting out the points in your answer in a logical order, giving full explanations and yet still being concise. You may find using headings will help you organise your answer. It is often better to present any calculations as an appendix, unless they are extremely short. Look back to the question; if you are asked to draw conclusions or make recommendations have you done so?

It is important to know who the report, letter etc is being prepared for. If you are writing to a client they are unlikely to understand technical terms, and certainly will not know, for example, what 'early trade losses relief' is. If, on the other hand, you are writing a memorandum to a partner you can assume a certain degree of familiarity with the underlying concepts.

1.1.6 Consider non-tax factors

Sometimes **the information not given in the question is just as important as the information which is. You may have to make assumptions** about what the taxpayer has done, or intends to do, or about their personal circumstances. If so, state them in your answer, so that if your assumptions are wrong the reader's attention will be drawn to them. Otherwise the course of action that you are recommending may be totally unsuitable. You may be able to give some indication of how your answer would differ, but do not go wildly off on a tangent.

Remember also that **tax should never be the only factor** in a decision. For example, if you are advising someone to invest under the enterprise investment scheme to obtain a tax reducer and also to defer a gain, stop and think about the nature of the investment. Small unquoted companies often fail, and your client may prefer to pay the tax rather than lose their investment. There may be hints and clues in the question; a 74-year old is not likely to want to invest in a personal pension.

1.2 Alternative ways of achieving outcomes and different tax consequences

In the exam, you will often be asked to compare alternative ways of achieving personal or business outcomes and advise on the most tax efficient course of action.

For example, an individual may which to raise funds, to buy a house. Conversely, they may have funds which they can invest to generate an income or for capital growth. The tax treatment of the different sources of finance or investment products available (as detailed in this chapter), may affect the individual's decision regarding which source or product to use.

2 Personal finance

2.1 Sources of finance for individuals

FAST FORWARD

There are many sources of finance available for individuals, long or short term, secured or unsecured.

2.1.1 Introduction

Investments can only be made if funds are available. The private investor will generally have their own funds to invest, accumulated from salary or from business profits, but they may even decide to borrow money in order to make an investment which is expected to be particularly profitable. And of course, many private individuals borrow money to invest in land and buildings, buying their homes with mortgage loans.

2.1.2 Sources of finance for private purposes

The following **sources of finance** are available to individuals for private purposes:

- Bank overdrafts
- Unsecured bank and building society loans
- Mortgage loans from banks and building societies, secured on the borrower's home
- Credit cards
- Hire purchase facilities
- Credit facilities provided by retailers

If the individual wishes to **buy or improve a house**, a **mortgage loan** is likely to be the most suitable source of finance. The fact that it is secured reduces the risk to the lender, and therefore the interest charged. For other large purchases, hire purchase facilities or the credit facilities provided by retailers may be the most suitable: the cost may be reduced as an incentive to make the purchase concerned, and using a specific facility avoids tying up a large proportion of a more general facility such as an overdraft or a credit card. An alternative to such specific facilities is an unsecured bank or building society loan, which must be repaid by agreed instalments over a fixed period.

Small and varied purchases may be made using a credit card, although if credit is taken the interest rate is very high, to reflect the risk of non-payment accepted by the credit card company. A bank overdraft facility can be useful to allow the individual to cope with times when expenditure temporarily exceeds income, perhaps because of fluctuating business profits or because of occasional worthwhile new investment opportunities such as new share issues.

2.1.3 Mortgage products

FAST FORWARD

> A mortgage may be a repayment or interest only mortgage. Pensions or ISAs may be used to accumulate the capital required to repay an interest only mortgage.

Most people who buy a house need to **borrow** to finance the purchase. Mortgage loans are normally repayable not later than the end of a fixed term agreed at the start of the loan.

Key term

> A **mortgage** is a loan given on the **security** of a property. The purchaser pays a proportion of the purchase price of a property – a **mortgage deposit** – and the balance is lent by the mortgage lender.

The borrower gives the lender **legal rights over the property** for the duration of the loan. While the loan is outstanding the property is the lender's security that the loan will be repaid. If the borrower does not keep up repayments on the loan – defaults – **the lender has the right to take possession of the property**, sell it, recover the amount of the loan (assuming the sale price is higher than the loan) and pay the balance to the borrower. If the loan is repaid according to the terms of the mortgage, the legal rights of the lender over the property cease **at the end of the term**.

During the term of the mortgage the borrower must pay **interest**. The **interest rate** charged by a lender may be variable (**variable rate mortgage**). Some variable rates of interest are limited to a specified maximum but may rise or fall subject to that maximum. These are **'capped' mortgages**. **Fixed rate mortgages** are available at a rate of interest which is fixed for a specific period of time.

There are two methods of **repaying the capital**: during the term or at the end of it. It is possible to **combine the two types of mortgage**. For example, a borrower might borrow £70,000 on a repayment basis and £30,000 on an interest only basis.

With a **repayment mortgage** each time interest is paid to a lender, part of the capital is repaid at the same time. Payments are often of a fixed regular amount. However, flexible mortgages may allow underpayments (ie less than the regular monthly amount), overpayments or payment holidays. There may also be additional borrowing facilities.

With an interest only mortgage **the entire capital sum is repaid on the last day of the mortgage**. Most lenders will want the borrower to take some action over the term of the mortgage to accumulate sufficient money to repay the loan, for example by investing in a pension or individual savings account.

2.1.4 Tax treatment of borrowings

Tax relief is only available for interest paid in limited circumstances.

Apart from business borrowings or in connection with a property letting business, where the interest paid is a deduction from profits, interest relief is only available if the interest is charged on a qualifying **loan** such as for loans to invest in close companies or partnerships. This precludes relief for interest on overdrafts or credit card borrowings. There is also a restriction for individuals on the deduction of finance costs on a property letting business.

Note that **interest relief is not available** on a loan to buy shares in a close company **if EIS relief is claimed** for the investment.

Unless tax relief is available for interest, it may be advisable to repay loans if surplus funds are available. In evaluating the situation, however, as well as comparing the interest charge on the borrowing with the income generated by the surplus funds you need to take into account any capital return which may be generated if the surplus funds are invested.

2.2 Investment products for individuals

2.2.1 Introduction

There is a **very wide range of investment products available to individuals**, ranging from an almost risk free bank deposit to a high risk investment in shares in a small unquoted trading company under the seed enterprise investment scheme.

It may be preferable to **invest for capital growth**, rather than income, since capital gains are taxed at 20% for most assets for an individual who is a higher or additional rate taxpayer compared with the higher and additional rates of income tax of 40% and 45% (or 32.5% and 38.1% for dividends).

2.2.2 Deposit based investments

Most deposit based investments are fairly low risk investments in which an investor receives a low rate of interest in return for depositing their capital with the institution.

Some of the products available and their tax treatment are:

Provider	Type of account	Tax treatment
Banks and building societies	Instant access accounts, notice accounts, fixed term deposits, money market accounts	Interest taxable as savings income. No tax provided within savings income nil rate band.
Banks and building societies, National Savings and Investments (NS&I)	Cash ISAs	Tax free
National Savings and Investments (NS&I)	Direct Saver accounts, Investment accounts	Interest taxable as savings income. No tax provided within savings income nil rate band.
National Savings and Investments (NS&I)	Savings certificate, fixed interest or index linked	Tax free

2.2.3 Fixed interest securities

> A fixed interest security pays a fixed rate of interest and has a known maturity value so long as it is held until its redemption date.

Key term

> A **fixed interest security** is a loan to a government, a local authority, a company, or a building society. **The security pays a fixed rate of interest and has a known maturity value so long as the stock is held until its redemption date**.

Government securities and corporate bonds are negotiable and can therefore be traded in the market.

The securities available and their tax treatment are:

Investment	Income tax	Capital gains tax
Government securities, Local authority bonds	Interest is taxed as savings income. Paid gross.	Exempt gains, losses not allowable
Company loan stock which is qualifying corporate bond	Interest is taxed as savings income. Paid net of 20% tax unless loan stock is listed on a recognised stock exchange, when paid gross.	Exempt gains, losses not allowable
Company loan stock which is not a qualifying corporate bond	Interest is taxed as savings income. Paid net of 20% tax unless loan stock is listed on a recognised stock exchange, when paid gross.	Taxable gains, losses allowable

2.2.4 Individual savings accounts (ISAs)

> Individual savings accounts (ISAs) provide a tax-free wrapper for investments in cash, and stocks and shares.

Investments within ISAs are exempt from both income tax and capital gains tax. The introduction of the savings income nil rate band and the dividend nil rate band means that ISAs are not as advantageous as they were previously. However, **additional rate taxpayers and individuals who have already used their savings income nil band will still benefit from using a cash ISA**. The **main benefit of using a stocks and shares ISA** is the **capital gains tax exemption** where an individual already uses the annual exempt amount.

2.2.5 Equities

> Equities are high risk investments as neither the income nor the capital is secure.

When an investor buys a share in Marks and Spencer plc that is exactly what they have done; they have bought a share in the ownership of the company.

Dividends are subject to income tax as described earlier in this text.

A capital gain arising on shares, calculated using the matching rules, is subject to CGT. Losses are allowable losses.

Equities are **high risk investments** as neither the income nor the capital is secure. Equities in companies listed on a recognised stock exchange are generally less risky than those in unlisted companies.

2.2.6 The enterprise investment scheme (EIS)

> The enterprise investment scheme (EIS) is a scheme designed to promote enterprise and investment by helping high-risk, unlisted trading companies raise finance by the issue of ordinary shares to individual investors who are unconnected with that company.

Individuals who subscribe for EIS shares are entitled to income tax relief. This has already been discussed earlier in this text, but as a summary the rules are that individuals can claim a **tax reducer of the lower of 30% of the amount subscribed for qualifying investments** (maximum qualifying investment is £1,000,000 and the individual's tax liability for the year after deducting VCT relief).

The investor may claim to have all or part of the shares treated as issued in the previous tax year. This is subject to the total actual and deemed investment not exceeding the limit for the previous year.

The relief may be withdrawn if certain events, such as the sale of the shares, occur within three years.

Where EIS income tax relief is available there are also **capital gains tax reliefs**:

(a)   Where EIS shares are **disposed of after the three year period** any gain is **exempt** from CGT. If the shares are disposed of within three years any gain is computed in the normal way.

(b)   If EIS shares are **disposed of at a loss at any time**, the loss is **allowable** but the acquisition cost of the shares is reduced by the amount of EIS relief attributable to the shares. The loss is eligible for share loss relief against general income (see earlier in this text).

EIS deferral relief may be available to defer chargeable gains if an individual invests in EIS shares in the period commencing one year before and ending three years after the disposal of the asset (see earlier in this text). Note that this relief is not conditional on income tax relief being available.

2.2.7 Seed enterprise investment scheme (SEIS)

FAST FORWARD

The seed enterprise investment scheme (SEIS) is similar to the EIS scheme but rewards investment in small, start up unquoted trading companies with a greater tax reducer.

Individuals can also invest in SEIS shares and obtain income tax relief and capital gains tax reliefs as detailed earlier in this text.

The **qualifying companies are smaller, start up companies** and the **greater tax reducer of 50%** (available on up to £100,000 of investment) reflects the **greater risk of investing in these companies**. In the exam, you may advise investing in an EIS or SEIS company: remember to **point out the risks as well as the tax reliefs**.

SEIS reinvestment relief can exempt 50% of a gain matched with an investment under SEIS made in the same tax year.

2.2.8 Venture capital trusts (VCTs)

FAST FORWARD

Venture capital trusts (VCTs) are listed companies which invest in unquoted trading companies, so enabling investors to spread their risk over a number of higher-risk, unquoted companies whilst obtaining income tax and capital gains tax reliefs.

Venture capital trusts (VCTs) are listed companies which invest in unquoted trading companies and meet certain conditions. **The VCT scheme differs from EIS in that the individual investor may spread their risk over a number of higher-risk, unquoted companies.**

An individual investing in a VCT obtains the following tax benefits on a maximum qualifying investment of £200,000:

•   A tax reduction of 30% of the amount invested. There is a withdrawal of relief if the shares are disposed of within five years or if the VCT ceases to qualify.

•   Dividends received are tax-free income.

•   Capital gains on the sale of shares in the VCT are exempt from CGT (and losses are not allowable).

In addition, capital gains which the VCT itself makes on its investments are not chargeable gains, and so are not subject to corporation tax.

Note that there is no minimum holding period requirement for the benefits of tax-free dividends and CGT exemption.

3 Business finance

3.1 Sources of finance for business

Businesses may require short or long term finance to start up, carry on or expand.

Businesses need funds in order to start up and expand, and their requirements are often far beyond the means of the entrepreneurs concerned. Outside capital may be sought from banks, from other lenders or from new shareholders or partners.

The following sources of finance are available for businesses.

- The entrepreneur's own capital
- Bank overdrafts
- Bank loans (which may be short term, medium term or long term)
- Loans secured by mortgages of land
- Leasing and hire purchase arrangements
- Sale and leaseback arrangements
- Loans from private individuals
- Capital invested by partners
- Share issues (for incorporated businesses)
- Loan stock issues (for incorporated businesses)
- Venture capital institutions

The tax treatments of equity and loan finance differ, as do the tax implications of leasing equipment compared with buying it outright.

3.2 The tax implications of equity finance and of loan finance

A business may obtain finance through loans and obtain tax relief for interest paid. A company can raise finance by issuing shares to shareholders.

3.2.1 Loan finance

You saw earlier in this text that if a company is a party to a loan relationship for the purposes of its trade, any debits are deductible in computing its trading profits. If, however a loan relationship is not one for the purposes of a trade any debits or credits are pooled. A net credit on the pool is chargeable as interest income. A net deficit may be relieved in the various ways described earlier in this text.

It is not only the interest costs of borrowing that are allowable or taxable. The **capital costs are treated similarly**. Thus if a company issues a loan at a discount and repays it eventually at par, the capital cost is allowed.

A sole trader or partnership will not obtain a deduction in respect of capital repayments of loan finance. A trading deduction will only be available in respect of interest incurred wholly and exclusively for trade purposes.

3.2.2 Equity finance

Companies can raise finance by issuing shares to shareholders. Capital can be raised in this way for trading and non-trading purposes. Companies can distribute profits to shareholders in a variety of ways, of which the payment of dividends is the most common. **The cost of making distributions to shareholders is not allowable in computing taxable profits.**

The **main types of share** are:

Type of share	Features
Ordinary shares	The shareholder is entitled: (a) To a share of profit distributed as a dividend (b) To the right to vote on matters affecting the company (c) In the event of a winding up, to a share of assets, but note that shareholders do not take precedence over the creditors
Preference shares	(a) These shareholders are placed ahead of the ordinary shareholders for dividend payments and in the event of a liquidation (b) The dividend is usually a guaranteed amount but if the distribution to the ordinary shareholders is higher, the preference shareholders do not receive the increase
Convertible preference shares	The dividend paid on these is usually less than the non-convertible preference share but there is the option to convert to ordinary shares in the future at pre-set dates and at pre-set prices

3.2.3 Legal and professional expenses

Legal and professional expenses relating to capital or non-trading items are disallowable. This includes fees incurred, for example, in issuing share capital. However, a deduction is allowed to companies under the loan relationship rules for the incidental costs of obtaining medium or long term business loans and for issuing loan stock.

3.2.4 Investors

Interest income received from a company on loan stock etc is taxable income for the recipient (and will have suffered 20% tax at source if paid on unlisted loan stock which can be repaid).

Dividend income received from a shareholding in a company is taxable on an individual investor only to the extent it exceeds the dividend nil rate band.

UK dividend income is not taxable in the hands of a company shareholder, for the purposes of the Advanced Taxation (ATX – UK) examination.

No gain or loss can arise to the original creditor when they dispose of their debt. A purchaser of a debt may have a chargeable gain and (unless they are connected with the original creditor) **an allowable loss.**

A debt on a security can give rise to a gain or loss to the original creditor.

3.3 The lease or buy decision

FAST FORWARD

A business may lease or buy assets. Short term leasing costs may be deductible expenses. Longer term costs may attract capital allowances in a similar way to buying an asset outright.

If assets are leased and the term of the lease is less than five years, then the lease payments are in general deductible in computing taxable profits. If they are bought on hire purchase or leased under a long term lease, then the cash price of the assets may qualify for capital allowances and the finance charges are deductible in computing taxable profits, making the tax effects very similar to those of taking out a loan and then buying the asset.

If assets are bought outright then capital allowances may be available on the purchase cost. These will be given on a reducing balance basis each year. The ultimate lease or buy decision is likely to depend on the availability of funds and whether leasing the asset allows the company to keep funds free to finance other activities.

4 Tax planning

4.1 Introduction

It would be impossible to write a definitive section on tax planning and mitigation, as no two scenarios are ever the same. This section covers nine scenarios, highlighting the points which need to be considered, both tax and non-tax. You may well think of other situations where taxpayers may seek advice.

4.2 Employment and self-employment

As a general rule, self-employment leads to lower overall tax and NIC burdens than employment.

A taxpayer who has a choice between being employed and being self-employed, on similar gross incomes, should consider the following points.

(a) An employee must pay **income tax and NICs as salary is received, under the PAYE system** and on a current year basis. A self-employed person pays **income tax and NICs which are at least partly payable after all of the profits concerned have been earned**. There is thus a cash flow advantage in self-employment.

(b) **An employee is likely to suffer significantly higher NICs in total than a self employed person**, although the employee's entitlement to state benefits will also be higher.

(c) An **employee may receive benefits as well as salary**. Taxable values of benefits may be less than their actual value to the employee and benefits do not attract employee NICs. Most benefits attract employer's Class 1A NIC.

(d) The **rules on the deductibility of expenses are much stricter for employees** (incurred wholly, exclusively and necessarily in the performance of duties) than for the self-employed (normally incurred wholly and exclusively for the purposes of the trade).

4.3 Remuneration packages

If someone is to be an employee, the tax effects of the remuneration package should be taken into account.

4.3.1 Income tax planning for employment situations

An employee will usually be rewarded largely by salary, but several other elements can be included in a remuneration package. Some of them bring tax benefits to the employee only, and some will also benefit the employer.

Bonuses are treated like salary, except that if a bonus is accrued in the employer's accounts but is paid more than nine months after the end of the period of account, its deductibility for tax purposes will be delayed.

The general position for **benefits** is that they are subject to **income tax and employer Class 1A NICs**. The cost of providing benefits is generally deductible in computing trading profit for the employer (but if a car with carbon dioxide emissions over 110g/km is provided, the employer's capital allowances (or deductions for lease payments) are reduced). However, there are a large number of **tax and NI free benefits** and there is a great deal of planning that can be done to ensure a tax and NIC efficient benefits package for directors and employees. The optimum is to ensure that the company receives a tax deduction for the expenditure while creating tax and NI free remuneration for employees.

Amy is employed by Wright Ltd and Bernard is employed by Turn plc.

Amy receives a salary of £33,850.

Bernard receives a salary of £28,700, the use of a new digital camera which cost £800 on 6 April 2018 and the use of a car purchased by Turn plc on 6 April 2018 which has a list price of £15,000 and has CO_2 emissions of 90g/km, so the taxable percentage is 19%. No fuel is supplied.

Bernard is also in an occupational pension scheme to which he contributes 5% of his gross salary (excluding benefits) and his employer company contributes 10% of his gross salary (excluding benefits).

Show the tax and the NIC effects of the two remuneration packages on both Amy and Bernard and Wright Ltd and Turn Ltd. Use 2018/19 tax rates and allowances and assume that both companies prepare accounts to 31 March each year and that the companies will only claim writing down allowances for capital allowance purposes. Amy and Bernard both have no other income. Ignore the Employment Allowance for employer's NICs.

Answer

Amy's income tax and NIC computations are as follows.

	£
Earnings	33,850
Less personal allowance	(11,850)
Taxable income	22,000

Income tax

£22,000 × 20%	£4,400

NICs

£(33,850 − 8,424) × 12%	£3,051

Wright Ltd must pay NICs of (£33,850 − £8,424) × 13.8% = £3,509, and can deduct £(33,850 + 3,509) = £37,359 in computing trading profits.

Bernard's income tax and NIC computations are as follows.

	£
Salary	28,700
Use of digital camera £800 × 20%	160
Car £15,000 × 19%	2,850
	31,710
Less pension contribution £28,700 × 5%	(1,435)
Earnings	30,275
Less personal allowance	(11,850)
Taxable income	18,425

Income tax

£18,425 × 20%	£3,685

NICs

£(28,700 − 8,424) × 12%	£2,433

Turn plc must pay NICs as follows:

	£
Class 1 NICs	
£(28,700 − 8,424) × 13.8%	2,798
Class 1A NICs	
£(2,850 + 160) × 13.8%	415
	3,213

Turn plc will have the following deductions in computing profits.

	£	£
Salary		28,700
Pension contribution £28,700 × 10%		2,870
NICs		3,213
Capital allowances		
Car £15,000 × 18%	2,700	
Digital camera £800 × 18%	144	
		2,844
		37,627

4.3.2 NIC planning for employment situations

NIC is payable on 'earnings' which is defined as 'any remuneration or profit derived from employment'. Remuneration packages structured to include the following items which are not 'earnings' would reduce the NIC burden.

(a) **Dividends** – director/shareholders could take remuneration in the form of dividends. Dividend waivers and adjustments to bonuses would probably be required. There are CT implications as salary and NIC costs are allowable business expenses whereas dividends are not.

Dividends are an efficient way of avoiding NIC. However dividend income is not earnings for pension purposes. There is also a cash flow impact since PAYE does not apply to dividends.

(b) **Rents** – a director owning a property used by a company could be paid rent instead of remuneration. However, this will impact entrepreneurs' relief for associated disposals (if available) on the subsequent sale of the property. The rental expense is a deductible business expense for the company but the income is not earnings for pension contribution purposes for the individual.

4.4 The choice of a business medium

FAST FORWARD

An individual can choose between trading as a sole trader or trading through a company. That choice, and if a company is chosen, the choice between dividends and remuneration, can significantly affect the overall tax and NIC burden. Cash flow is also an important consideration.

4.4.1 General considerations

When starting in business the first decision must be whether to trade as a company (with the individual as a director taxable on earnings) or as an unincorporated business, either as a sole trader or a partnership. Certain professions may not be practised through a limited company (although unlimited companies and limited liability partnerships may be allowed).

The attraction of incorporation lies in the fact that a sole trader or a partner is liable for business debts to the full extent of their personal assets. A limited company's shareholder's liability is limited to the amount, if any, unpaid on their shares. However, limited liability is often reduced by the demands of bankers or landlords for personal guarantees from company directors. In addition, compliance with the statutory obligations (eg annual returns, audits etc) that apply to a company can be costly.

A company often finds raising finance easier than an unincorporated business. This is partly because of the misguided view that a company has greater reliability and permanence. A company can obtain equity finance through venture capital institutions and can borrow by giving a floating charge over its assets as security whereas a sole trader or partnership cannot do this.

A business may be seen as **more reputable or creditworthy if conducted through the medium of a company.** Companies, however, have to comply with disclosure requirements and this may be unattractive to proprietors who wish to keep information from employees, potential competitors etc. This could be avoided by using an unlimited company but in that case any advantage of limited status is lost. The disclosure requirements could be reduced by filing abbreviated accounts.

4.4.2 The effect of marginal tax rates and national insurance

A trader's profits whether retained or withdrawn are taxed at a marginal rate of 40% on taxable income between £34,500 and £100,000, at a marginal rate of 60% between £100,000 and £123,700 (due to the withdrawal of the personal allowance), **at a marginal rate of 40% between £123,700 and £150,000 and at a marginal rate of 45% on taxable income above £150,000.** In addition **Class 2 and Class 4 National Insurance contributions are payable.**

A controlling director/shareholder can decide whether profits are to be paid out as remuneration or dividends, or retained in the company. The Employment Allowance of up to £3,000 per tax year reduces the employer's Class 1 NICs payable by the company but is not available if there is a sole employee who is also a director. The national insurance cost of extracting profits by way of remuneration will often be a significant factor.

If profits are retained, the consequent growth in asset values will increase the potential capital gain when shares are sold. Where remuneration is paid the total national insurance liability is greater than for the proprietor of an unincorporated business.

Where a spouse is employed their salary must be justifiable as, 'wholly and exclusively for the purposes of the trade'. HMRC may seek to disallow excessive salary cost. On the other hand, a spouse as active partner can take any share in profits, provided that they are personally active in the business and there is evidence of a bona fide partnership. Thus the spouse's personal allowance, basic rate and higher rate bands can be used.

In choosing a business medium, we should also remember that a sole trader will be denied the enhanced state benefits that are available to an employee who pays Class 1 national insurance contributions.

Question — Net income from a business

Alan is starting a new business and expects to make annual profits of £39,000 before tax and national insurance.

Consider the tax effects of his choosing to trade as a sole trader or, alternatively, through a company, paying him a salary of £13,500 and then the largest possible dividend not giving rise to a loss of capital. Assume that accounting profits equal taxable trade profits and that Alan will be the sole employee and a director of the company. Use 2018/19 tax rates.

Answer

As a sole trader

	£
Profits	39,000
Less personal allowance	(11,850)
Taxable income	27,150
Tax thereon at 20%	5,430
National Insurance Classes 2 (52 × £2.95) and 4 (£(39,000 − 8,424) × 9%)	2,905
	8,335
Net income £(39,000 − 8,335)	30,665

Through a company

	£
Profits	39,000
Less: salary	(13,500)
employer's NI (13,500 − 8,424) × 13.8%	(700)
Taxable profits	24,800
Less corporation tax 19% × £24,800	(4,712)
Net profits	20,088

A dividend of £20,088 can be paid without loss of capital.

	Non-savings income	Dividend income	Total
	£	£	£
Earnings	13,500		
Dividend		20,088	
Net income	13,500	20,088	33,588
Less personal allowance	(11,850)		
Taxable income	1,650	20,088	21,738
Non-savings income			
£1,650 × 20%			330
Dividend income			
£2,000 × 0%			0
£18,088 (20,088 − 2,000) × 7.5%			1,357
Income tax payable			1,687

Net income		£
Salary		13,500
Dividend		20,088
	£	33,588
Less: income tax	1,687	
employee's NIC £(13,500 − 8,424) × 12%	609	
		(2,296)
		31,292

Trading through a company would give annual net income of £(31,292 − 30,665) = £627 more than trading as a sole trader.

Question · Small business as sole trader versus company

Let's say we have a business earning profits of £18,000.

Compare the retained profit for the business owner if they operate the business as a sole trader with a year ended 31 March 2019 to that of a company with the same year end but paying out £8,400 as a salary (no Class 1 NIC but preserving the business owner's state benefits) and the remaining post-tax profits as dividend.

Answer

Sole Trader

Trading profits of £18,000 in 2018/19

Year ended 31 March 2019

	£
Income tax	
£(18,000 − 11,850) = £6,150	
£6,150 × 20%	1,230
National Insurance	
Class 2	153
Class 4	
£(18,000 − 8,424) × 9%	862
Total Income Tax and NIC	2,245
Net income	
£(18,000 − 2,245)	£15,755

Company   £

Year ended 31 March 2019
Taxable total profits = £(18,000 – 8,400)   9,600
Corporation tax
£9,600 × 19% before distribution   (1,824)
Maximum distribution is   7,776

Income tax
Salary covered by PA
Dividend income = £7,776, of which £(11,850 – 8,400) = £3,450 covered by PA and
£2,000 covered by the dividend nil rate band
Remaining £(7,776 – 3,450 – 2,000) = £2,326 × 7.5%   £174

Net income £(8,400 + 7,776 – 174)   £16,002

As a sole-tradership the business would typically pay £2,245 in the 2018/19 tax year as income tax and National Insurance contributions. The same business operating as a limited company for the same year would have a tax bill of £(1,824 + 174) = £1,998.

4.4.3 Benefits and expenses

The restrictions on deducting expenses against earnings may make self-employment rather more attractive than employment as a company director. Although the same expense deduction rules apply to a company and a sole trader, the company's deductible business expenses may give rise to taxable benefits as earnings for directors.

On the other hand, the provision of fringe benefits can be an advantage of incorporation. Tax exempt benefits can be used to maximise directors' net spendable income, although care is required because not all benefits are tax-efficient.

4.4.4 Opening years

Companies have no equivalent of the opening year rules that apply for income tax purposes. For a sole trader or partnership, profits earned when basis periods overlap are taxed twice. Relief is available for such overlap profits but that may not take place for many years, by which time inflation may have reduced the value of the relief for overlap profits.

If a partnership is envisaged it may be worthwhile to commence trading with the prospective partner as a salaried employee for a year or so, thereby obtaining tax relief twice on their salary during the overlap period.

4.4.5 Losses

Losses in the first four years of an unincorporated business can be used to obtain tax repayments (using early trade losses relief). In these and later years a loss relief claim against general income permits **relief for trading losses against other income** (and capital gains) of either or both of two tax years. However, **trading losses carried forward can only be set against the future profits of the same trade.**

With **corporation tax**, there is **considerable flexibility for use of losses by the company itself,** including the ability to **carry forward trading losses against total income.** However, **a company's losses are not available to reduce shareholders' taxable income** and there is **no equivalent to an early trade loss relief claim.**

4.4.6 Capital gains tax

One difference between companies and individuals is that **companies do not benefit from an exempt amount of the first £11,700 of total gains** (for 2018/19).

Chargeable gains of an individual are usually charged to capital gains tax at 10% or 20%. In contrast, companies' gains are always charged at 19% and are calculated with an indexation allowance so the amount of the chargeable gain may be lower as well.

The principal disadvantage of incorporation is the double charge to tax which arises when a company sells a chargeable asset. Firstly, the company may pay corporation tax on the chargeable gain. Secondly, the shareholders may be taxed when they attempt to realise those proceeds, either in the form of dividends or, when the shares are sold, incurring a further charge on capital gains.

If there are no tax advantages in the company owning an asset, the asset should be held outside the company, perhaps being leased to the company. The lessor may receive rent without restricting IHT business property relief. However, rent received will restrict entrepreneurs' relief for CGT.

4.4.7 Tax cash flows

A sole trader/partner is assessable to income tax and NICs on a current year basis but will use a prior year basis to calculate two payments on account due on 31 January in and 31 July directly following the tax year. The balance of tax is due on 31 January following the tax year. Thus tax on profits earned in the year to 30 April 2018 (assessable 2018/19) will not be payable in full until 31 January 2020 and will be used to calculate payments on account due 31 January 2020 and 31 July 2020. **Where profits are rising this lag gives a considerable benefit**. A sole trader's/partner's drawings do not of themselves attract or accelerate a tax charge.

A company usually pays corporation tax nine months after the end of its accounts period. Large companies are required to make **quarterly payments on account** based on the current year's estimated liability. As an employer it will have to account for **PAYE and NICs 14 days after the end of each tax month** in which the pay date falls.

Generally therefore a business held by a company will pay tax earlier than a business held by a sole trader or partnership.

4.4.8 What if things go wrong?

Sound tax planning should always take account of possible changes in circumstances. A successful business may fail or a struggling concern may eventually become profitable.

Running down an unincorporated business does not normally give rise to serious problems. The proprietor may be able to cover any balancing charges with loss relief.

Taking a business out of a company (disincorporation), or winding up a corporate trade altogether is more complex and involves both tax and legal issues. Consider the following:

- No subsequent relief is available for a company's unused losses once the trade ceases

- Liquidation costs may be considerable

- A double charge on capital gains may arise

4.4.9 Personal service companies (PSCs)

The 'IR 35 provisions' (see earlier in this text) are anti-avoidance rules which attack the provision of personal services by personal service companies (PSCs). If an individual would have been an employee if they had been working directly for a client, they will generally be subject to tax and NIC on income from the PSC as if they were in fact an employee of the client.

4.5 The incorporation of a business

FAST FORWARD

The incorporation of a business should be carefully planned, taking account of consequent tax liabilities. There are both advantages and disadvantages to incorporating a business. A disposal of shares can also have several tax consequences.

4.5.1 Advantages of incorporating a business

(a) Retained profits subject only to corporation tax not income tax or NIC.

(b) More flexible trading loss relief within the company for carried forward losses.

(c) Easier to dispose of shares in a company than interest in a business – thus advantage for raising equity and selling to outside investors.

(d) Pension provision can be made by employer (the company) for employees (eg directors) with no national insurance liability.

(e) Benefits for employees can be more tax efficient.

(f) Loan finance easier to arrange as lender can take out charge on company assets.

(g) Limited liability for shareholders if the company is a limited company.

(h) A company arguably has a more respectable image than a sole trader or partnership.

(i) Incorporation is a means of converting the value of a business into shares which could eventually become listed on a recognised stock exchange. This provides for succession of ownership and can make the original proprietors very wealthy.

4.5.2 Disadvantages of incorporating a business

(a) Potential double capital gains charge on assets (see above).

(b) Trading losses restricted to set-off against corporate profits.

(c) No carry back of trading losses in opening years (ie no early trade losses relief equivalent).

(d) Partner's share of profit not openly challenged by HMRC provided the recipient is a genuine partner. Conversely excessive remuneration to employee/director can be challenged.

(e) NIC for employer company and employee will generally exceed the contributions required of a self-employed person.

(f) Tax payment dates for tax for a company and shareholder/employees (CT, PAYE and NIC) are generally well in advance of those for self-employed.

(g) Assets used in a business but held outside the business entity can qualify for 50% BPR for IHT. In the case of a partnership the owner merely has to be a partner but in the case of a company using an asset the owner must be a controlling shareholder.

(h) There may be statutory requirements of audit, keeping books, filing accounts etc.

(i) Disclosure requirements of published accounts may give information to employees/ competitors that business owners would not have willingly disclosed.

4.5.3 Income tax

When an unincorporated trade is transferred to a company the **trade is treated as discontinued for tax purposes and the cessation rules apply.** Careful consideration of the level of profit, available overlap profits and date of transfer is required **to avoid large taxable profits in one year and to utilise the personal allowance and basic rate tax band as effectively as possible.**

For example, if a trader with a 31 December year end incorporates their business on 31 March 2019, the year of cessation will be 2018/19. If the individual makes profits of £3,000 per month, they will be taxed on profits in 2018/19 between 1 January 2018 to 31 March 2019 (15 months) which will be £45,000 (less any overlap relief). If, however, the individual delayed incorporation until 30 April 2019, the year of cessation will be 2019/20. They will be taxed on profits of £12,000 in 2019/20 (again less any overlap relief) and on 12 months of profit in 2018/19 (£36,000). This may be more advantageous if they do not have other income to use up their personal allowance and/or their basic rate band in 2019/20.

On the transfer of a trade to a company **a balancing charge will usually arise as plant and machinery are treated as being sold at market value.** However, where the company is controlled by the transferor, **the two are connected and an election may be made** so as not to treat the transfer as a permanent discontinuance for capital allowances purposes. **Plant is then transferred at its tax written down value.**

Unrelieved trading losses cannot be carried forward to a company as such, but **may be set against any income derived from the company** by way of dividends, remuneration and so on, provided the business is exchanged for shares and those shares are still held at the time the loss is set off. Terminal loss relief may also be available for the loss of the last twelve months of trading.

4.5.4 Capital gains tax

When the transfer takes place the **chargeable assets are deemed to be disposed of to the company at their open market values.** Capital gains tax liabilities are likely to arise, particularly on land and buildings and on goodwill.

If the whole business (or the whole business other than cash) **is transferred to the company as a going concern in exchange for shares in the company, any chargeable gains are automatically rolled over through incorporation relief,** reducing the base cost of the shares on a subsequent disposal. If the shares are held until death the tax liability may never arise as no capital gains tax arises on death.

Individuals who incorporate a business can elect that incorporation relief should not apply. This election must usually be made within two years of 31 January following the end of the tax year in which the business was incorporated. Making the election could be advantageous if the gains are quite small and entrepreneurs' relief would apply. However, entrepreneurs' relief will not apply on the disposal of goodwill to a close company of which the individual(s) are participators.

It may not be desirable for all the assets comprised in the business to be transferred to the company. **As an alternative**, an individual can **use gift relief** to transfer chargeable business assets to a company and **defer any gains by deducting them from the base costs of the assets** for the company.

4.5.5 Value added tax

The transfer of assets will not be treated as a supply for VAT purposes if it is a transfer of a going concern (TOGC).

An application may be made for the company to take over the existing VAT registration number. In this case the company will take over all the debts and liabilities of the business but it will be able to claim VAT impairment loss relief in respect of supplies made before the transfer.

If the conditions for a TOGC cannot be satisfied, VAT will be charged on the transfer, but this will only represent a cash flow problem in most cases.

HMRC should be notified of the incorporation within 30 days.

4.5.6 Stamp duty land tax

The transfer of land will be subject to Stamp Duty Land Tax as a transfer at market value. The use of the gift relief route should be considered so that land can be retained outside the company.

4.6 Tax efficient profit extraction   6/16, 6/17, 12/17

FAST FORWARD 〉〉

There are several methods by which profit can be extracted from a company.

4.6.1 Methods of extracting profits

When trading activities are carried on through a limited company, careful thought needs to be given to the level and method of extraction of the profits generated. This decision should take into account both the needs of the individual shareholders and directors as well as the needs of the company itself. For instance, the company may need to retain a certain level of profit in order to reduce its bank overdraft or fund an expansion project.

The table below compares the various methods of extracting profits in outline. They are looked at in more detail below:

Method of extraction	Company	Individual
Remuneration Salary Benefits Tax free benefits	Deductible/Class 1 NICs Deductible/Class 1A NICs Deductible/No NICs	Taxable/Class 1 NICs Taxable/NI free Tax free/NI free
Dividends	Not deductible	Dividend nil rate band, then 7.5% within basic rate band Higher rate tax at 32.5% or additional rate at 38.1% No NICs
Loan interest	Deductible on accruals basis as interest on a loan relationship	Taxable as savings income
Rental income	Deductible	Taxable non-savings income
Pension contributions to registered pension schemes	Deductible on paid basis	Tax free

4.6.2 Dividends or remuneration

Director/shareholders may wish to consider either extracting profits as dividend or remuneration. Payments of dividends or remuneration will reduce a company's retained profits which means a reduction in net asset value and hence the value of the shares, ultimately reducing any chargeable gain on the disposal of those shares. However, the immediate tax cost of paying dividends or remuneration must be weighed against this advantage.

Remuneration and the cost of benefits will be allowed as deductions in computing the company's total profits. However, **the national insurance cost must also be borne in mind**. A combination of dividends and remuneration may give the best result.

Question

Dividends and remuneration

Air Ltd is wholly owned by Alex who is also the sole director. There are no other employees. Air Ltd makes a profit before remuneration of £40,000 in the year to 31 March 2019.

Consider Alex's disposable income available by paying out the profit entirely as salary (of £36,171, allowing for employer's national insurance contributions of £3,829 since there is no Employment Allowance) or by paying it out as a mixture of salary (of £8,424, so that no national insurance contributions are payable but preserving Alex's entitlement to state benefits) and the remaining profits as a dividend.

Answer

		Salary only £	Salary and dividend £
(a)	**The company's tax position**		
	Profits	40,000	40,000
	Less: salary	(36,171)	(8,424)
	employer's national insurance	(3,829)	
	Taxable profits	0	31,576
	Corporation tax at 19%	£0	£5,999
	Dividend £(31,576 – 5,999)		£25,577

(b)   **The director's tax position**

	Non-savings income £	Dividend Income £	Total £
Salary only			
Earnings	36,171		
Less personal allowance	(11,850)		
Taxable income	24,321		24,321
Salary and dividends			
Earnings	8,424		
Dividends		25,577	
Less personal allowance	(8,424)	(3,426)	
Taxable income	–	22,151	22,151

	Salary only £	Salary and dividend £
Non-savings income		
£24,321 × 20%	4,864	–
Dividend income		
£2,000 × 0%		0
£20,151 (22,151 – 2,000) × 7.5%		1,511
Tax payable	4,864	1,511
Disposable income		
Salary	36,171	8,424
Less employee's national insurance		
£(36,171 – 8,424) × 12%	(3,330)	
Dividend		25,577
Less tax payable	(4,864)	(1,511)
	27,977	32,490

The overall saving through paying a dividend is £(32,490 – 27,977) = £4,513.

4.6.3 Dividend payments

If dividends are paid, timing can be important. The tax year in which a dividend is paid affects the due date for any additional tax, and if a shareholder's other income fluctuates it may determine whether or not there is any additional tax to pay.

There is a dividend nil rate band of £2,000. Basic rate taxpayers must pay tax at 7.5% on any other dividends within the basic rate band. Higher rate taxpayers must pay tax at 32.5% on dividend income and additional rate taxpayers tax at 38.1%.

The payment of dividends does allow flexibility, ie family members need not work for a company in order to receive a dividend. However, this must be weighed against the fact that the company must generate sufficient profit to pay a dividend. Furthermore, HMRC may seek to invoke anti-avoidance legislation if dividends are paid to non-working family members if those who do work for the company do not draw a commercial salary. Most lenders will recognise regular dividends from an owner managed company as income for mortgage or other loan purposes. This takes away a potential drawback of extraction of funds in the form of investment income.

Dividends are not subject to NICs. They do not give rise to an entitlement to pay pension contributions whereas remuneration and benefits do. They are not an allowable trading expense for the company.

4.6.4 Liquidation

An alternative to both dividends and remuneration is to retain profits in a company and then liquidate it. The company itself may have capital gains on the sale of its assets, and the shareholders will have

capital gains on the liquidation, which will be treated as a disposal of their shares for the amounts paid to them. The CGT charges on the shareholders may be mitigated by spreading the capital distributions over two tax years, so as to use both years' annual exempt amounts. Entrepreneurs' relief may be available, in which case the rate of CGT will be 10%.

This route may be worth considering when a company is set up to undertake a single project which will be completed within a few years.

4.6.5 Loans

A director/shareholder may choose to lend money to the company and extract profits as interest income in return.

Interest income is taxed on the director/shareholder as savings income but it is not subject to NIC. It does not count as relevant earnings for pension purposes.

From the company's point of view, tax relief for the interest will be available under the loan relationship rules (ie either as a trading expense or as a deficit on a non-trading loan relationship).

4.6.6 Loans by close companies

Although loans by close companies to participators are not treated as distributions, on making such a loan the company suffers a tax charge: a payment equal to the amount of the loan × 32.5% is made to HMRC. This tax charge cannot be recovered until the loan is repaid or written off.

4.6.7 Rental income

On incorporation the owner(s) may decide to retain business premises outside the company and charge rent for its use. **The advantages of this method of profit extraction are that the company will obtain a trading income deduction for rent charged up to a commercial rate. Also, no NIC is payable.**

The disadvantage is that income from a property business does not qualify as relevant income for pension purposes. The payment of rental income will also restrict entrepreneurs' relief on a subsequent disposal of the premises.

For many small companies, the directors' own homes are often used for company business. It is possible to claim a deduction in the company for reasonable rent paid by the company. Care should be taken so as not to deny principal private residence relief on a proportion of the home. To do this, it must be shown that the room(s) are not used exclusively for company business, ie the occasional guest stays in the 'study'.

4.6.8 Pension provision

It is becoming increasingly important to save for one's own retirement. Fortunately, it is also something the government recognises as important and, as a result, pension provision has become the most efficient way of extracting funds from a family company.

Employers are required to make pension contributions for their employees under automatic enrolment and may set up an **occupational pension plan** for their employees. Employees may contribute to the occupational pension plan and all individuals may contribute to a **personal pension plan**. Employers may also contribute to an employee's personal pension plan.

The tax breaks for registered pension schemes are listed below:

(a)   No taxable benefit for employer contributions
(b)   No NIC is due on employer contributions
(c)   The individual receives tax relief on their contributions
(d)   The employer obtains tax relief for normal contributions actually paid during its accounting period.
(e)   Pension fund grows tax free
(f)   Tax free lump sum available up to 25% of the fund

4.7 Tax efficient exit routes

FAST FORWARD

Capital gains and inheritance tax planning are important when disposing of a family business.

4.7.1 Introduction

Advice on tax efficient exit routes is probably the biggest area that a professional adviser is asked to deal with in tax planning for an owner managed business. This section will explore the key tax implications of passing on and selling the family business or company and suggest useful planning tips to help structure the business in the most efficient manner from the outset.

4.7.2 Capital gains tax planning

Regardless as to whether the business or company is to be sold or passed down to the next generation, a capital gain is likely to arise. It is therefore **essential to maximise the reliefs available**. Entrepreneurs' relief may be particularly valuable especially since the lifetime limit for gains is £10 million.

4.7.3 Inheritance tax planning

IHT is only a consideration where the family business or company is to be passed on to the next generation. An outright sale of the business to a third party does not constitute a transfer of value for IHT.

When a taxpayer wants to pass on his family business a major question exists as to whether to gift the assets now or wait until death.

If the assets are given during lifetime there may never be an IHT liability, either because the PET does not become chargeable or because the gift is covered by BPR provided the transferee still owns it (or has replaced it with other relevant business property) at the time of the transferor's death.

A lifetime gift will be subject to CGT at some point, either on transfer or on sale of the assets by the transferee assuming a gift relief claim is made.

However, a **transfer of assets on death receives a free uplift in the CGT base cost to current market value and any business property is passed on with the benefit of 100% BPR.**

There are strong arguments in favour of the approach to hold business property until death but other points are worthy of serious consideration:

(a)   If a business is hit by recession the gain itself may be fairly low in any case.

(b)   The gain may be deferred through EIS reinvestment relief.

(c)   BPR at 100% may not be around forever.

(d)   Free CGT uplift on business assets may be abolished in the future on the basis that such assets should either be taxed under capital gains tax or under inheritance tax.

Some other tax pitfalls exist which can be avoided provided they are identified and acted upon. The main areas as to consider include:

(a)   Holding assets, such as business premises, outside the company or partnership restricts BPR to a rate of only 50%. This reduces to nil if the shares or partnership interest are disposed of before the business premises.

(b)   Where a lifetime gift is made it is important that the property remains 'business property' for the next seven years and that the transferee retains ownership of it (or owns alternative business property) to prevent a charge to IHT on a sudden death.

(c)   Beware of buy and sell arrangements included in the Articles of Association or partnership or shareholder agreements as BPR may be denied.

(d)   It will be important to ensure that a gift does not fall foul of the 'reservation of benefit' rules.

4.7.4 Repurchases of own shares

It may be advantageous for individuals to sell shares back to the issuing company as a repurchase of own shares (see earlier in this text). This will be treated as a capital gain (if the conditions are satisfied) or, if not, as a distribution. If distribution treatment is preferable it may be necessary to alter the proposal to ensure the conditions are **not** satisfied.

4.8 Planning for corporate growth

FAST FORWARD

At each stage of a 'company's life' from its beginning, through growth and future expansion overseas, tax planning strategies should be adopted.

Exam focus point

This section looks at a company as it begins trading, acquires additional business, and eventually expands abroad. It looks at the commercial decisions taken by the company and its shareholders at the different stages in the company's development, and summarises the tax implications of those decisions. It focuses, in particular, on those elements of corporation tax that are likely to be examined.

4.8.1 New company

Companies often start small. **One or two individuals will set up a company using their own funds (or borrowed funds) to do so.** Some shareholders may be active in running the company on a daily basis whilst others will be passive investors looking for a return on their investment.

Points to consider:

- **Is the company a close company?**
  If so, are any benefits provided to participators (treated as dividends) or loans made to participators (trigger a charge at 32.5% on the company)?

- **Can the shareholders receive tax relief for their investment?**
  If the company is a close company interest paid on a loan to invest in the company is deductible from total income.

  EIS income tax relief may be available to small investors.

- **Level of tax paid on company profits**
  Salaries paid to employees reduce total profits, dividends paid to shareholders do not.

- **Losses** made can be relieved by carry back up to 12 months (if there are any profits to carry back against) or carry forward and claim to offset against future total profits.

- Don't forget to consider registration for VAT.

4.8.2 Expansion in UK

A company can grow bigger by increasing its own activities or purchasing the activities of another business and either assuming those activities within itself or setting up a subsidiary company.

Points to consider:

(a) Single company (no related 51% group companies) or group of companies. Number of related 51% group companies affects CT payment dates (see (c) below)

(b) If a group is formed: group relief for losses; asset transfers and tax planning regarding asset groups in respect of capital gains and losses; VAT group registration

(c) As taxable total profits grow, may need to consider payment of CT and VAT in instalments (large company)

(d) When a company acquires the trade of another company, capital losses remain within the vendor company. Trading losses will also remain with the vendor company unless the two companies are under common ownership.

4.8.3 Expansion overseas

As a company grows it may consider expanding overseas.

The tax implications of the overseas business depend on the legal structure used. From a tax point of view, there are two distinct ways of establishing the business:

1   **It could be owned by the UK company**. Under this option, it would be an overseas PE of a UK resident company

2   The UK company could **incorporate a new subsidiary in the overseas country** to acquire the business. Under this option, it would be an overseas subsidiary of a UK resident company.

Points to consider:

(a)   **Overseas permanent establishment (PE)**

A PE is not a separate legal entity but is an extension of the company that owns it. **The profits or losses of the PE belong directly to the company.**

Provided the PE is controlled from the UK, **any trading loss made could be offset by the UK company (or group) against its income and gains of that year**, reducing the company's UK corporation tax liability. Once the PE is profitable, the company owning the PE will be subject to overseas corporation tax on the PE profits, because it is trading within the boundaries of the overseas country from a PE.

The profits will also be subject to UK corporation tax because a UK resident company is subject to tax on its worldwide income and gains. However the **UK corporation tax liability, in respect of the PE profits, will be relieved by double tax relief.**

A UK company may make an election to exempt the profits and losses of all its overseas PEs from UK corporation tax. The election means that the profits of a PE are only taxed overseas, but the election will disallow loss relief or overseas PEs against UK profits. Once made, the election must apply to all of the UK company's PEs and is irrevocable, so it is important to consider whether PEs in the future are likely to make a loss.

Double tax relief should also be taken into account when deciding whether to make the election. If the operation of DTR means that there is little or no UK corporation tax payable on overseas profits, it may be better not to make the election, and keep loss relief available in future accounting periods.

(b)   **Overseas subsidiary**

A subsidiary is a separate legal entity. **A company incorporated in an overseas country will be resident in that country for tax purposes**, provided it is not managed and controlled from the UK. Its profits or losses will then be subject to the tax regime of the overseas country.

Any trading loss of the year would usually be carried forward and deducted from the company's future trading profits arising out of the same trade.

Once the company is profitable, it will be subject to tax in the overseas country. Any dividends paid to the UK parent company will normally be exempt from corporation tax.

(c)   It is usually suggested that a **PE should be used where an overseas enterprise is expected to make initial losses**. This strategy enables the losses to be offset against any other profits of the company (as long as the exemption election is not made). The PE can be incorporated once it is profitable. However, the particular facts of the situation must be considered carefully.

4.9 Group tax minimisation strategies

FAST FORWARD

There are several tax planning opportunities available to groups of companies.

4.9.1 Tax planning for groups

There are many **tax planning opportunities for groups of companies**. The following points should be considered, in addition to the points made earlier in this text.

(a) **Minority interests should be restricted so as to ensure that the holding company has a 75% effective interest in every company. This will enable losses to be group relieved** to whichever company can make the best use of them.

(b) **The group can be regarded as one unit for the purposes of rollover relief** on the replacement of business assets.

(c) **VAT will arise on intra-group trading unless a VAT group is formed. It may be best to concentrate all exempt supplies in one or two companies which can be left outside the VAT group, and zero rated supplies in one or two other companies which can also be left outside the VAT group (or can form their own separate VAT group) and can make monthly repayment claims.**

(d) **Capital losses cannot be group relieved. However, an election can be made to transfer gains and losses between group members.** There are restrictions on the use of pre-entry losses.

4.10 Divisionalised v group company structure

FAST FORWARD

Careful consideration needs to be given as to whether a group structure or a divisionalised company would be better.

4.10.1 General principles

In certain circumstances a business can be operated through a group company structure or through a single divisionalised company.

The setting up of a **trading group has a number of implications**, namely:

(a) It is **easier to give status to a key employee** by appointing them as a director of a subsidiary company.
(b) **Group relief of losses** is available.
(c) **Assets may be transferred between the group without giving rise to a charge to tax.**
(d) **Group wide rollover relief** may be claimed.

There are a number of disadvantages to a group structure that must be considered, particularly where the parent company or subsidiaries are to be sold.

Where the parent company is sold then the group would either:

(a) **Sell the group and then buy back the required subsidiaries**
(b) **Reconstruct the group which would need tax clearances and cause delays**, or
(c) **Sell assets**

Where a subsidiary is sold this could give rise to a capital gain although the relief for substantial shareholdings may be available.

The advantages of divisionalised company structure are:

(a) **Automatic set-off losses** in respect of the various divisions
(b) **Automatic set-off of capital gains and losses**
(c) **Administration is simplified**

On the other hand, the disadvantages include:

(a) **Lack of incentive for divisional directors**
(b) **Difficulty in giving equity interest in a venture** (but may consider profit-related bonuses)
(c) It may be **difficult to find a prospective purchaser for the whole company**

5 Ethics

5.1 Introduction

In common with most professional organisations, the ACCA require members and students to observe the highest professional standards in all aspects of their work. This section discusses how these standards can be maintained, with particular reference to giving tax planning advice. The requirements apply equally to members and students, and in this section the term 'members' should be taken to include students.

In addition to the ACCA's own requirements, there are many instances where **members are required to comply with statutory and regulatory requirements**. If a member is in doubt as to the course of action they should take, they should approach the ACCA for guidance. **Failure to observe the ACCA's standards may result in disciplinary action**.

The ACCA publish a **Code of Ethics and Conduct** covering the standards and ethical requirements which they expect. It details the **fundamental principles and sets out a framework for applying those principles**. Members must apply this framework to particular situations to identify instances where compliance with the ethical standards may be compromised so that safeguards may be put in place to avoid threats, or to reduce them to below the minimum level that can be regarded as acceptable. The ACCA, jointly with certain other professional bodies, also publishes more specific guidance for members working in tax called **Professional Conduct in Relation to Taxation**.

Normally a member's responsibility will be to a client, or to an employer, but there may be instances where a member may need to act in the public interest.

5.2 The fundamental principles 9/15

> **FAST FORWARD**
>
> The fundamental principles of ethics should underlie all of a member's professional behaviour.

The fundamental principles are:

(a) **Integrity**: Requires all members to be straightforward and honest in professional and business relationships.

A member should not be associated with information if they believe that the information contains a materially false or misleading statement, statements or information furnished recklessly, or omits or obscures information required to be included where such omission or obscurity would be misleading.

(b) **Objectivity**: Imposes an obligation on members not to compromise their professional or business judgement because of bias, conflict of interest or the undue influence of others.

Relationships that bias or unduly influence the professional judgement of the member should be avoided.

(c) **Professional competence and due care**: Requires members to:

(i) Maintain professional knowledge and skill at the level required to ensure that clients or employers receive competent professional service based on current developments in practice, legislation and techniques; and

(ii) Act diligently in accordance with applicable technical and professional standards when providing professional services.

Any limitations relating to the service being provided must be made clear to clients and other users to ensure that misinterpretation of facts or opinions does not take place.

(d) **Confidentiality**: Imposes an obligation on members to refrain from:

(i) Disclosing outside the firm confidential information acquired as a result of professional and business relationships without proper and specific authority or unless there is a legal or professional right or duty to disclose; and

(ii) Using confidential information acquired as a result of professional and business relationships to their personal advantage or the advantage of third parties

A member should consider the need to maintain confidentiality of information within the firm. A member should also maintain confidentiality of information disclosed by a prospective client or employer.

The need to maintain confidentiality continues even after the end of relationships between a member and a client or employer. When a member changes employment or acquires a new client, the member is entitled to use prior experience, but not confidential information obtained from the previous relationship.

(e) **Professional behaviour**. Imposes an obligation on a member to comply with relevant laws and regulations and avoid any action that may bring discredit to the profession.

This includes actions which a reasonable and informed third party, having knowledge of all relevant information, would conclude negatively affects the good reputation of the profession.

Members should be honest and truthful and should not:

(i) Make exaggerated claims for the services they are able to offer, the qualifications they possess, or experience they have gained

(ii) Make disparaging references or unsubstantiated comparisons to the work of others

5.3 The conceptual framework

5.3.1 Introduction

A member may find himself in a situation where there is a **specific threat to compliance with the fundamental principles**. There are many possible scenarios, and rather than trying to specify how each situation should be dealt with, the ACCA provide a conceptual framework that requires members to identify, evaluate and address such threats. Unless an identified threat is clearly insignificant, members should apply safeguards to eliminate the threat or reduce it to an acceptable level so that compliance with the fundamental principles is not compromised.

5.3.2 Threats

The member is obliged to evaluate any threat as soon as they know, or should be expected to know, of its existence. Both qualitative and quantitative factors should be taken into account.

Most threats to compliance with the fundamental principles fall into the following categories:

(a) **Self-interest threat**, which may occur as a result of the financial or other interests of a member or of an immediate or close family member

(b) **Self-review threat**, which may occur when a previous judgment needs to be re-evaluated by the member responsible for that judgement

(c) **Advocacy threat**, which may occur when a member promotes a position or opinion to the point that subsequent objectivity may be compromised

(d) **Familiarity threats**, which may occur when, because of a close relationship, a member becomes too sympathetic to the interests of others

(e) **Intimidation threats**, which may occur when a member may be deterred from acting objectively by threats, actual or perceived

5.3.3 Safeguards to offset the threats

If a member cannot implement appropriate safeguards, they should decline or discontinue the specific professional service involved, or where necessary resign from acting for the client.

Safeguards that may eliminate or reduce threats to an acceptable level fall into two broad categories:

(1) **Safeguards created by the profession, legislation or regulation**, such as education and training, continuing professional development, professional or regulatory monitoring and disciplinary procedures

(2) **Safeguards in the work environment**, such as effective, well publicised complaints systems operated by the employing organisation

The nature of the safeguards to be applied will vary depending on the circumstances. In exercising professional judgement, a member should consider what a reasonable and informed third party, having knowledge of all relevant information, including the significance of the threat and the safeguards applied, would conclude to be unacceptable.

5.4 Ethical conflict resolution

There may be instances where a particular situation leads to a **conflict in the application of the fundamental principles**.

When initiating either a formal or informal conflict resolution process, a member should consider five factors:

1   **Relevant facts**
2   **Ethical issues**
3   **Fundamental principles related to the matter**
4   **Established internal procedures**
5   **Alternative courses of action**

Having considered these issues, the appropriate course of action can be determined which resolves the conflict with all or some of the five fundamental principles. If the matter remains unresolved, the member should consult with other appropriate persons within the firm for help in obtaining resolution.

Where a matter involves a conflict with, or within, an organisation, a member should also consider consulting with those charged with governance of the organisation.

It is advisable for the member to **document the issue and details of any discussions held or decisions taken, concerning that issue**.

If a significant conflict cannot be resolved, a member may wish to obtain **professional advice from the ACCA or legal advisors**, to obtain guidance on ethical and legal issues without breaching confidentiality.

If, after exhausting all relevant possibilities, **the ethical conflict remains unresolved, a member should, where possible, refuse to remain associated with the matter creating the conflict**.

The member may determine that, in the circumstances, it is appropriate to withdraw from the engagement team or specific assignment, or to resign altogether from the engagement or the firm.

5.5 Disclosure of information   6/16, 6/17

5.5.1 When to disclose

A member may disclose confidential information if:

(a)   Disclosure is permitted by law and is authorised by the client or the employer

(b)   Disclosure is required by law, such as under anti-money laundering legislation

(c)   There is a professional duty or right to disclose, when not prohibited by law, such as under a quality review

5.5.2 Factors to consider regarding disclosure

In deciding whether to disclose confidential information, members should consider:

(a) Whether the interests of all parties, including third parties, could be harmed if the client or employer consents to the disclosure of information

(b) Whether all the relevant information is known and substantiated, to the extent it is practicable to do so. When the situation involves unsubstantiated facts, incomplete information or unsubstantiated conclusions, professional judgement should be used in determining the type of disclosure to be made, if any

(c) The type of communication that is expected and to whom it is addressed; in particular, members should be satisfied that the parties to whom the communication is addressed are appropriate recipients

5.6 Conflicts of interest   6/13

FAST FORWARD

A conflict of interest is a commonly met threat to compliance with the fundamental principles.

5.6.1 The threat of a conflict of interest

A member should take reasonable steps to identify circumstances that could pose a conflict of interest. These may give rise to threats to compliance with the fundamental principles.

A conflict may arise between the firm and the client or between two conflicting clients being managed by the same firm. For example, where a firm acts for both a husband and wife in a divorce settlement or acts for a company and for its directors in their personal capacity.

Evaluation of threats includes consideration as to whether the member has any business interests or relationships with the client or a third party that could give rise to threats. Safeguards should be considered and applied as necessary.

5.6.2 Safeguards

Depending upon the circumstances giving rise to the conflict, safeguards should ordinarily include the member in public practice:

(a) **Notifying the client** of the firm's business interest or activities that may represent a conflict of interest

(b) **Notifying all known relevant parties** that the member is acting for two or more parties in respect of a matter where their respective interests are in conflict

(c) **Notifying the client that the member does not act exclusively for any one client** in the provision of proposed services (for example, in a particular market sector or with respect to a specific service)

In each case the member should obtain the consent of the relevant parties to act.

Where a member has requested consent from a client to act for another party (which may or may not be an existing client) and that consent has been refused, then they must not continue to act for one of the parties in the matter giving rise to the conflict of interest.

The following additional safeguards should also be considered:

(a) The use of separate engagement teams

(b) Procedures to prevent access to information (eg strict physical separation of such teams, confidential and secure data filing)

(c) Clear guidelines for members of the engagement team on issues of security and confidentiality

(d) The use of confidentiality agreements signed by employees and partners of the firm

(e) Regular review of the application of safeguards by a senior individual not involved with relevant client engagements

Where a conflict of interest poses a threat to one or more of the fundamental principles that cannot be eliminated or reduced to an acceptable level through the application of safeguards, the member should conclude that it is not appropriate to accept a specific engagement or that resignation from one or more conflicting engagements is required.

5.6.3 Example

You have acted for Robenick Ltd for several years, and also for the three director shareholders, Rob, Ben and Nick. During 2018 Rob has a disagreement with Ben and Nick over the direction of the company. What should you do?

When you commenced acting for both the company and Rob, Ben and Nick you should have advised each that you were acting for the others, and asked their permission to act. Providing there were no areas where the interests of the clients conflicted, there is no reason why you should not have acted for all the clients, although it may be advisable to have ensured that, for example, a different tax manager was responsible for each client.

However, now that there has been a disagreement between Rob and the other clients the situation has changed and there is a conflict of interest. It is most likely that it would be inappropriate to continue to act for all the clients, and you will need to cease to act, either for Rob, or for Ben, Nick and the company.

5.7 Prospective clients   6/13, 12/13, 6/15, 12/17, 6/18

Members invited to act as tax advisers by clients must **contact the existing tax advisers** to ascertain if there are any matters they should be aware of when deciding whether to accept the appointment.

5.7.1 Acceptance

Before accepting a new client, members should consider whether acceptance of the client or the particular engagement would create any threats to compliance with the fundamental principles.

Potential threats to integrity or professional behaviour may be created from, for example, questionable issues associated with the client, or a threat to professional competence and due care may be created if the engagement team does not possess the necessary skills to carry out the engagement. Where it is not possible to implement safeguards to reduce the threats to an acceptable level, members should decline to enter into the relationship.

Exam focus point

> Ethical issues in relation to acting for a new client were tested in Sample Questions September/December 2017 Question 2 Florina, Kanzi and Winston in relation to Winston who wanted to carry out some sophisticated tax-planning in order to reduce the inheritance tax payable in respect of his death estate and wished to appoint your firm to replace his existing tax advisers. The examining team commented that: 'a reference to 'sophisticated tax planning' required by the client (to elicit discussion of whether the firm had the necessary expertise), appeared to be regarded by a good number of candidates as alluding to possible tax evasion, and this was followed by a discussion of evasion, money laundering etc, a topic which the candidates had no doubt revised, but candidates should generally take the information provided in a question at face value, unless there is a clear indication that for some reason it is not to be relied upon.'

There are also client identification procedures to be followed (see later in this chapter).

5.7.2 Changes in professional appointment

Members who are asked to replace another accountant should ascertain whether there are any professional or other reasons for not accepting the engagement. This may require direct communication with the existing accountant to establish the facts and circumstances behind the proposed change so that members can decide whether it is appropriate to accept the engagement.

Communication with the existing accountant is not just a matter of professional courtesy. Its main purpose is to enable members to ensure that there has been no action by the client which would on ethical grounds, preclude members from accepting the appointment and that, after considering all the facts, the client is someone for whom members would wish to act. Thus, members must always communicate with the existing accountant on being asked to accept appointment for any recurring work.

The existing accountant is bound by confidentiality. This means the extent to which a client's affairs may be discussed with a prospective accountant will depend on the nature of the engagement and on whether the client's permission has been obtained. **If the client refuses permission, the existing accountant should inform the prospective accountant, who should then inform the client that they are unable to accept the appointment**.

If the existing accountant fails to communicate with the prospective accountant despite the client's permission, the prospective accountant will need to make other enquiries to ensure there are no reasons not to accept the appointment. This could be through communications with third parties, such as banks.

Where the member is the existing accountant then, subject to obtaining the client's permission, they should disclose all information requested without delay.

5.7.3 Example

You have acted for Alexander but have discovered a serious tax irregularity which Alexander has refused to correct and you have advised Alexander that you can no longer act for him. You receive a letter from another ACCA member advising you that they have been asked to act for Alexander. Alexander has forbidden you to divulge any information about him. What should you do?

You should advise the new accountant that Alexander has not given you permission to divulge any information. The new accountant should then refuse to act for Alexander.

5.7.4 Acting as agent or principal

Where you are performing tax compliance work eg preparing and submitting tax returns, you will be acting as agent to the client. This means that the client remains responsible for all of the information provided in the return.

When you are **providing tax planning advice, however, you will be acting as 'principal'** which means that you are fully responsible for the advice you give.

5.7.5 Tax planning concerns

One of the competencies you require to fulfil Performance Objective 17 Tax planning and advice of the PER is to advise clients responsibly about the differences between tax planning, tax avoidance and tax evasion. You can apply the knowledge you obtain from this chapter of the text to help to demonstrate this competence.

At the very least, **anything you recommend must be legal**. You should understand the basic distinction between tax avoidance (tax mitigation through legal means) and tax evasion (illegal, such as fraud). Apart from the specific rules regarding disclosure of avoidance schemes (see below), you must understand that the taxpayer has the responsibility of preparing a tax return that is complete and correct (see above), and this will include an accurate disclosure of the facts.

That is not to say that you may not suggest a course of action where HMRC might disagree with your conclusion as to the tax consequences. You need to explain to the client that full details must be given to enable HMRC to consider the matter, and you should warn them that any negotiations with HMRC will take time and incur expense.

Make sure that you **know the time limits for any claims** that need to be made. If you miss the limit, the relief will be denied. Late returns incur penalties, and late payment of tax leads to an interest charge.

5.8 Tax irregularities

6/14, 12/14, 3/16, 9/16

If a member discovers that a client has misled them in order to obtain a tax advantage, the member has to consider their position in relation to both the client and the tax authorities.

5.8.1 Discovery of errors

A member may discover that a client has committed a taxation offence. Tax legislation prescribes monetary penalties for a number of offences. There is also the possibility of criminal proceedings being brought against the client.

The evasion or attempted evasion of tax may be the subject of criminal charges under both tax law and money laundering legislation. This applies not only to direct taxes such as income tax or corporation tax, but also to indirect taxes such as VAT.

The member has the following responsibilities:

(a) If the information obtained concerns computations or returns that the member is currently preparing, the member must ensure that the information is accurately reflected therein. **If the client fails to provide any information requested by the member, or objects to way in which the member has presented the information, the member needs to consider whether they can continue to act for that client.**

(b) If the information obtained concerns computations or returns that the member has already prepared and submitted to HMRC, the member cannot allow HMRC to continue to rely on them. **They should advise their client to make full disclosure to HMRC, or to authorise them to do so, without delay. If the client refuses, then the member can no longer act for the client.** The client should be advised of this, and also that the member must inform HMRC that they have ceased to act for the client. If the documents submitted to HMRC contain any accountant's report, the member must also advise HMRC that the report should no longer be relied on. The member should not, however, advise HMRC in what way the accounts are defective unless the client has consented to such disclosure.

(c) If the information relates to a new client and concerns computations or returns that have been prepared by the client or a third party and submitted to HMRC, the member should advise the client to make full and prompt disclosure. If the error affects the current computations or returns then the member must inform the client that an appropriate adjustment must be made in the current accounts, and **if the client refuses the member should consider whether they should act for that client.** Indeed, even if the error does not affect current returns and computations the member should consider whether they should act for the client if the client refuses to disclose the error to HMRC.

Whether or not the member feels able to act for a client, they are still under a **professional duty to ensure that the client understands the seriousness of offences against HMRC.** They should also warn the client that notification that they are no longer acting for a client may alert HMRC, and urge the desirability of making a full disclosure, subject to any legal advice obtained. Any accounts, returns, computations or reports submitted on behalf of taxpayers are deemed to be submitted by the taxpayer and/or with their consent unless they prove otherwise.

This emphasises the need for members to ensure that clients have approved computations and returns, and signified their approval by signing them. There should always be a letter of engagement in place setting out the precise responsibilities of both the member and the client.

5.8.2 Example

You are preparing the tax return for Sonia and amongst her papers you find a bank statement for a new account which was opened with the transfer of a significant amount from her own account. Sonia says that this new account belongs to her young son, and that the interest should not be put on her tax return. What should you do?

572 **30: Impact of taxes and tax planning** | Part H Impact of taxes and tax planning

BPP
LEARNING MEDIA

First, you should explain that income from funds provided by a parent are taxed as the parent's income, unless the income is less that £100, so that the interest must be shown. If Sonia still refuses to enter the interest on her return you should advise her that you can no longer act for her, and you must also advise HMRC that you no longer act. You are not obliged to disclose the reason to HMRC.

At this stage you have a suspicion that a tax offence may be committed, and you should discuss this with your firm's money laundering officer.

5.8.3 HMRC powers

HMRC have certain statutory powers to compel disclosure in particular instances. Where information is sought under such powers, members must check that the statutory power being invoked actually covers the information sought and, if in any doubt, should take legal advice.

In some cases HMRC will ask for information to be provided voluntarily, rather than resorting to the use of their statutory powers. In this case the member must consider carefully whether it is in the client's interest to make voluntary disclosure, rather than await a statutory demand, and again may wish to take legal advice.

5.8.4 Errors by HMRC in the taxpayers' favour

Problems may arise if HMRC erroneously makes an excessive repayment of tax to taxpayers, even though they have received full disclosure of the facts.

If the repayment is made directly to the client, the member should urge them to refund the excess sum to HMRC as soon as possible. Failure to correct the error may be a civil and/or criminal offence by the client. **If the client refuses the member must consider whether they should continue to act for the client.** If they cease to act, they must notify HMRC that they no longer act for the client, but are under no duty to give HMRC any further details, although it may be necessary to consider whether a report should be made under the money laundering rules.

If the repayment is made to the member on the client's behalf, the member must notify the tax authorities. Failure to do so could involve both the member and client in a civil and/or criminal offence.

It should be noted that if HMRC make the repayment because they have adopted a different treatment of a transaction to that taken by the member and client, this is not an excessive repayment, it merely arises from a different interpretation of the legislation. This is subject to the proviso that full details of the transaction has been returned, so that HMRC have reached their decision on an informed basis.

<table>
<tr><td>Exam focus
point</td><td>Tax evasion may include keeping a repayment of tax to which the client is not entitled. This point was tested in December 2012 Question 1 Flame plc group in relation to a group member, Bon Ltd. The examining team commented that: 'Most candidates recognised this situation and were able to list the actions that the firm needed to take and the matters that needed to be drawn to the attention of Bon Ltd.'</td></tr>
</table>

5.9 Money laundering

Money laundering is the process by which criminals attempt to conceal the true origin and ownership of the proceeds of their criminal activity, often with the unwitting assistance of professionals such as accountants and lawyers.

Members are bound by legislation to implement preventative measures and to report suspicions to the appropriate authority. Failure to follow these legislative requirements will often be a criminal offence, leading to a fine and/or imprisonment. The legal position and its application to any given set of facts may not be straightforward and members are advised to take legal advice whenever they are uncertain as to their conduct.

Members should have appropriate procedures to ensure that client identification procedures are carried out correctly and that knowledge and suspicions of money laundering are reported to the firm's money laundering officer.

5.9.1 Client identification procedures

Where a new client is taken on a member should verify their identity by reliable and independent means. This could comprise the following:

(a) Where the client is an individual: by obtaining independent evidence, such as a passport, driving licence, HMRC document such as a notice of coding, and proof of address

(b) Where the client is a company: by obtaining proof of incorporation; by establishing the primary business address; by identifying the members and directors of the company; and by establishing the identities of those persons instructing the member on behalf of the company and verifying that those persons are authorised to do so.

If satisfactory evidence cannot be obtained, no work should be undertaken.

Members should **retain all client identification records for at least five years after the end of the client relationship**, together with records of all work carried out for the client.

5.9.2 Suspicions of money laundering

During the course of the engagement, members should regularly review the client's actions to satisfy themselves that they are consistent with the client's usual activities. Anything which appears to be out of the ordinary should be closely examined and a written record made of the member's conclusions. **If members' suspicions are aroused, a money laundering report should be made**.

Suspicion is more than mere speculation, but which falls short of proof based on firm evidence. What is suspicious in relation to one client may not be suspicious in relation to another client. Therefore, the key to recognising a suspicious transaction or situation is for members to have a full understanding of the client and their activities.

Transactions which appear to have no apparent economic or visible lawful purpose should be looked at carefully to establish their purpose and any findings recorded in writing. If no purpose for the transaction can be established, this may be a ground for suspicion.

Where members know or suspect that funds are directly or indirectly the proceeds of crime, they should report their suspicions promptly to the National Crime Agency. Where tax evasion is involved members will also need to examine their responsibilities to the tax authorities.

Where the work done by members for their clients is covered by legal professional privilege, members are not required to report their suspicions. Whether or not legal professional privilege applies to members and in what circumstances will depend on local law and members are strongly advised to seek legal advice as and when the issue arises.

5.9.3 Tipping off

Members should not 'tip off' a client that a report has been made. This may cause a member difficulties if a client refuses to disclose tax irregularities to HMRC as ceasing to act for the client might tip off the client that a report has been made. Any attempts to persuade a client not to proceed with an intended crime will not constitute tipping off.

Members faced with money laundering issues may call upon the Advisory Services Section of the ACCA for confidential advice.

6 Tax avoidance schemes

6.1 Disclosure of tax avoidance schemes

FAST FORWARD

> There are disclosure requirements for promoters of direct tax avoidance schemes. Businesses may be required to disclose use of VAT avoidance schemes.

6.1.1 Direct tax avoidance schemes

Promoters of tax avoidance schemes have disclosure obligations. There is also an obligation on taxpayers to disclose details of schemes in certain cases.

Notification is required from a promoter of arrangements or proposed arrangements, the main benefit of which is to enable any person to obtain an advantage in relation to tax. A 'promoter' is defined as a person who, in the course of a trade, profession or business involving the provision of tax services to other persons, is to any extent responsible for the design of the arrangements, or who makes a proposal available for implementation by other persons.

The information to be given by a promoter must be provided within a prescribed period of five days after being made available. The information to be provided and the manner in which it is to be provided is set out in the regulations.

A taxpayer is required to provide details of arrangements where the arrangements have been purchased from an offshore promoter, and that promoter has made no disclosure. Disclosure must also be made by large businesses which have **entered into arrangements not involving a promoter.**

HMRC may allocate a reference number to arrangements notified under the disclosure rules. Promoters are required to notify clients of that reference number so that they can enter that number on their tax return.

Any person that fails to comply with any of the disclosure provisions is liable to a penalty not exceeding £5,000. If the failure continues after that penalty has been imposed, that person is liable to a further penalty or penalties not exceeding £600 for each day on which the failure continues.

A tax advantage is defined as relief or increased relief from tax, repayment or increased repayment of tax, avoidance or reduction of a charge to a tax. It also includes the deferral of any payment of tax or advancement of any repayment of tax or the avoidance of any obligation to deduct or account for tax. Hallmarks are laid down by regulations specifying types of notifiable schemes.

The taxes covered by these provisions are IT, NIC, CGT, CT, IHT, and stamp taxes.

6.1.2 VAT avoidance schemes

Businesses using VAT avoidance schemes must disclose their use. Certain VAT avoidance schemes ('notifiable' schemes) are put on a statutory register.

Businesses with an annual turnover of £600,000 or more that use designated schemes must inform HMRC. A designated scheme is one which has been designated by the Treasury.

Businesses with an annual turnover of £10 million or more must also inform HMRC if they use notifiable schemes, that are not designated schemes, for the purpose of securing a tax advantage.

Detailed regulations deal with the notification procedure to be used.

The **penalty for failure to notify HMRC of the use of a designated scheme is 15% of the VAT saving** as a result of the use of the scheme. The **penalty for using other arrangements is £5,000.**

Exam focus point

> Various changes were made in Finance (No.2) Act 2017 in order to strengthen the regime designed to prevent aggressive tax avoidance schemes and to reduce tax evasion. You should be aware of this general tightening of the rules but the details of the changes are **beyond the scope** of the Advanced Taxation (ATX – UK) syllabus.

6.2 Serial tax avoidance

Taxpayers who use **more than one tax avoidance scheme which has been defeated on or after 6 April 2017 may be classed as serial tax avoiders by HMRC.**

A **defeated scheme** is one which either one whether the taxpayer:

(a) Has **reached an agreement with HMRC** so the **tax advantage** that would have been expected under the scheme is **not available**; or

(b) **HMRC has obtained a favourable court or tribunal ruling about its assessment of the scheme.**

Such taxpayers will be issued with a **serial tax avoidance warning notice** which has effect for **five years** that requires them to **submit additional information to HMRC about their tax affairs annually,** for example their use of tax avoidance schemes.

Sanctions against serial tax offenders include:

(a) **Penalties** if **further tax avoidance schemes are entered into** during the notice period **increasing with the number of such schemes entered into.**

(b) Being **publicly named** as a serial tax avoider.

(c) **Restrictions on direct tax reliefs** for up to three years.

6.3 General anti-abuse rule (GAAR)

6.3.1 Introduction

The GAAR provides **additional means for HMRC to 'counteract' tax advantages arising from abusive 'tax arrangements'.**

6.3.2 Tax arrangements

Tax arrangements are arrangements with a main purpose of obtaining a tax advantage.

Arrangements are **abusive** if they **cannot be regarded as a reasonable course of action**, for example, where they **lead to unintended results involving one or more contrived or abnormal steps and exploit any shortcomings in the tax provisions.**

Examples of **abusive arrangements** include those that result in:

(a) Significantly less income, profits or gains

(b) Significantly greater deductions or losses; or

(c) A claim for the repayment or crediting of tax (including foreign tax) that has not been, and is unlikely to be paid.

A **'tax advantage'** includes:

(a) Relief or increased relief from tax
(b) Repayment or increased repayment of tax
(c) Avoidance or reduction of a charge to tax
(d) Avoidance of a possible assessment to tax
(e) Deferral of a payment of tax or advancement of a repayment of tax
(f) Avoidance of an obligation to deduct or account for tax

6.3.3 Counteracting tax advantages

HMRC may counteract tax advantages arising by, for example, increasing the taxpayer's tax liability. HMRC must follow certain procedural requirements and, if it makes any adjustments, these must be on a 'just and reasonable' basis.

A **penalty** will also be imposed if a taxpayer enters into arrangements which are countered by the GAAR. The penalty is **60% of the tax advantage** counteracted by the GAAR.

Chapter roundup

- Questions on impact of taxes require you to use your technical knowledge of taxation in relation to particular scenarios. Avoid writing about technical areas in general terms as opposed to in relation to the question's requirements.

- There are many sources of finance available for individuals, long or short term, secured or unsecured.

- A mortgage may be a repayment or interest only mortgage. Pensions or ISAs may be used to accumulate the capital required to repay an interest only mortgage.

- Most deposit based investments are fairly low risk investments in which an investor receives a low rate of interest in return for depositing their capital with the institution.

- A fixed interest security pays a fixed rate of interest and has a known maturity value so long as it is held until its redemption date.

- Individual savings accounts (ISAs) provide a tax-free wrapper for investments in cash, and stocks and shares.

- Equities are high risk investments as neither the income nor the capital is secure.

- The enterprise investment scheme (EIS) is a scheme designed to promote enterprise and investment by helping high-risk, unlisted trading companies raise finance by the issue of ordinary shares to individual investors who are unconnected with that company.

- The seed enterprise investment scheme (SEIS) is similar to the EIS scheme but rewards investment in small, start up unquoted trading companies, with a greater tax reducer.

- Venture capital trusts (VCTs) are listed companies which invest in unquoted trading companies, so enabling investors to spread their risk over a number of higher-risk, unquoted companies whilst obtaining income tax and capital gains tax reliefs.

- Businesses may require short or long term finance to start up, carry on or expand.

- A business may obtain finance through loans and may be able to obtain tax relief for interest paid. A company can raise finance by issuing shares to shareholders.

- A business may lease or buy assets. Short term leasing costs may be deductible expenses. Longer term costs may attract capital allowances in a similar way to buying an asset outright.

- As a general rule, self-employment leads to lower overall tax and NIC burdens than employment.

- If someone is to be an employee, the tax effects of the remuneration package should be taken into account.

- An individual can choose between trading as a sole trader or trading through a company. That choice, and if a company is chosen, the choice between dividends and remuneration, can significantly affect the overall tax and NIC burden. Cash flow is also an important consideration.

- The incorporation of a business should be carefully planned, taking account of consequent tax liabilities. There are both advantages and disadvantages to incorporating a business. A disposal of shares can also have several tax consequences.

- There are several methods by which profit can be extracted from a company.

- Capital gains and inheritance tax planning are important when disposing of a family business.

- At each stage of a 'company's life' from its beginning, through growth and future expansion overseas, tax planning strategies should be adopted.

- There are several tax planning opportunities available to groups of companies.

- Careful consideration needs to be given as to whether a group structure or a divisionalised company would be better.

- The fundamental principles of ethics should underlie all of a member's professional behaviour.

- A conflict of interest is a commonly met threat to compliance with the fundamental principles.

- If a member discovers that a client has misled them in order to obtain a tax advantage, the member has to consider their position in relation to both the client and the tax authorities.

- There are disclosure requirements for promoters of direct tax avoidance schemes. Businesses may be required to disclose use of VAT avoidance schemes.

- Serial tax avoiders may have to provide additional information to HMRC for five years. Sanctions against serial tax avoiders include penalties, public naming and restrictions on direct tax reliefs.

- There is a general anti-abuse rule to enable HMRC to counteract tax advantages gained from abusive tax arrangements.

Quick quiz

1 What are the main sources of finance for private purposes?

2 What are the two main methods of repaying the capital of a mortgage?

3 How are the returns on NS&I savings certificates taxed?

4 What are the features of a preference share?

5 What are the main NIC differences between the tax positions of employees and the self employed?

6 What is a major attraction of incorporation?

7 Why might a newly commencing trader employ a prospective partner at first, before forming a partnership?

8 What is the major disadvantage for an individual shareholder of an incorporated business where losses are anticipated?

9 List the methods by which profit may be extracted from a company.

10 What are the advantages of a divisionalised company structure?

11 Can an ACCA member act for both parties in a marriage/civil partnership?

12 What should you do if you suspect that a client may have taken a bribe from a customer?

13 What is the maximum initial penalty for failure to notify a tax avoidance scheme relating to income tax?

14 What sanctions may HMRC use against serial tax avoiders?

15 When may HMRC use the general anti-abuse rule?

30: Impact of taxes and tax planning | Part H Impact of taxes and tax planning

Practice question and answer bank

1 Eric and Melanie

39 mins

Eric is a partner in a firm of architects. His taxable trade profits for 2018/19 are £102,900. In 2017, he took out a loan to buy some plant and machinery used in the partnership business. The amount of loan interest in 2018/19 was £1,000.

Eric has a bank account with the Halifax Bank. His account was credited with interest of £2,000 on 31 March 2019. In October 2018 Eric invested £11,000 in a venture capital trust.

Eric is married to Melanie and they live in England. Melanie is employed as an educational consultant. In 2018/19 she had earnings of £155,415. PAYE of £53,000 was deducted from these earnings.

Melanie received dividends of £2,000 during 2018/19. She also cashed in National Savings & Investments Certificates and received £250 interest in addition to the repayment of the capital invested.

Eric and Melanie are considering buying a cottage together on 6 April 2019 and renting it out. The cottage will cost £120,000. The net rental income will be about £12,000 per year. There will be no finance costs incurred. Eric and Melanie have not decided exactly in what proportions they will contribute to the cost of buying the cottage.

Assume Eric and Melanie have the same other income and expenditure in future years as in 2018/19 and that the rates of tax and allowances also remain the same in future years.

Required

(a)   Compute the income tax payable by Eric and Melanie for 2018/19.   **(10 marks)**

(b)   Explain how the rental income from the cottage will be taxed on Eric and Melanie. What advice would you give them to reduce their total tax liability?   **(5 marks)**

(c)   A friend of Melanie has offered her the opportunity to subscribe £12,000 for shares in an EIS company. If Melanie does so she will borrow the money from the bank at an interest rate of 8%. Melanie's friend assures her that the company will start to pay dividends in five years' time. Alternatively Melanie could invest £12,000 to buy a 10% stake in a company currently owned by another friend, and in this case dividends are likely to be paid at the rate of £1,200 each year. Melanie would like to know how much her cash outlay will be over five years for each investment.

(5 marks)

(Total = 20 marks)

2 Lee and Harry

35 mins

(a)   You have received the following e-mail from a client, Lee:

'I am just about to start a new job and thought that I ought to start making some pension provision now that I am in my mid-30s. My initial salary is £30,000 a year, but I am hoping that, with bonuses, it may increase in the next few years. I've been told that it could be as much as £250,000. I don't have any other sources of income. I live in England.

My new employer operates a workplace pension scheme and I have been given a booklet about it which says that I will be automatically enrolled into the scheme but that I can opt out of the scheme. The booklet says that the scheme is a 'money purchase' scheme and that my employer will make contributions to the scheme in addition to the amount that I pay into it.

Could you answer the following questions:

(1)   Should I opt out of my employer's workplace pension scheme and make other pension arrangements? What is a 'money purchase' scheme?

(2)   If I stay in my employer's pension scheme, how much can I contribute to the scheme and how much can my employer contribute? The booklet refers to an annual limit and a lifetime limit. How do these work?

(3)   I have heard that there is tax relief on my contributions to a pension scheme. How does that work if I am in my employer's pension scheme?

Required

Draft an email in response.   **(13 marks)**

(b)   It is March 2019. Another of your clients, Harry will have employment income of £123,700 for 2018/19. Harry has no other income in 2018/19.

Required

(i)   Compute Harry's tax liability for 2018/19 based on this information.

(ii)   Advise Harry how he can make a personal pension contribution which would be most tax efficient.   **(5 marks)**

(Total = 18 marks)

3 Hamburg   29 mins

(a)   Hamburg retired in January 2018 and used income from his investments to live on. He lives in England.

On 31 December 2018, he received interest of £1,260 from an investment account with his bank.

Hamburg received an income payment of £17,333 on 1 February 2019 from a discretionary trust set up by his aunt. The whole of the trust fund was invested in quoted shares.

Hamburg also received dividends of £18,250 during 2018/19 from his own investments.

Hamburg bought a house on 1 July 2018. He financed this purchase with a mortgage secured on the house and he paid an arrangement fee of £500 on 1 July 2018 and interest of £3,550 from 1 July 2018 to 5 April 2019. Hamburg let the house from 6 August 2018 for £2,400 a month payable on the 6th of each month. Hamburg paid a buildings insurance premium of £440 for the period from 1 July 2018 to 30 June 2019.

During 2018/19 Hamburg also rented out one furnished room of his main residence. He received rent of £7,850 and incurred allowable expenses of £875.

Required

Compute Hamburg's income tax repayable for 2018/19.   **(9 marks)**

(b)   Hamburg is thinking about investing in two holiday cottages in Cornwall.

Required

Outline the requirements for the cottages to be furnished holiday lettings and the income tax treatment of such lettings.   **(6 marks)**

(Total = 15 marks)

4 Taker   25 mins

(a)   Taker is employed by Ruby plc at an annual salary of £50,000. He is not in a pension scheme, but receives the following benefits in 2018/19.

(i)   He has the use of a motor car provided by Ruby plc with a petrol engine, which cost £20,000. Its CO_2 emissions are 107g/km. Fuel is provided for both business and private motoring, and Taker contributes £500 a year (half the cost of fuel for private motoring) for fuel.

(ii)   He makes occasional private calls on a mobile phone provided by Ruby plc.

(iii)   He has private use of Ruby plc's digital camera (which cost £600).

(iv)   He has an interest free loan of £7,000 from Ruby plc.

(v)   His 2-year old son attends Ruby plc's workplace nursery for 48 weeks at a cost of £80 per week.

(vi)   He was bought a cake by Ruby plc to celebrate his birthday at a cost of £40.

In 2018/19, Taker pays expenses out of his earnings as follows:

(i)   He pays subscriptions to professional bodies (relevant to his employment) of £225.

(ii)   He pays a golf club subscription of £150. He does not play golf at all, but goes to the club to discuss business with potential clients. These discussions frequently lead to valuable contracts.

Required

Compute Taker's taxable earnings for 2018/19.   **(6 marks)**

(b)   Taker is considering changing his employment and has received two offers, both in England. One is from a nearby company which is offering a salary of £50,000 a year and a choice of the provision of a company car with a taxable benefit of £3,250 (no private use fuel would be provided) or an increase in salary of £3,000 and a mileage allowance of 40p per business mile. If he does not accept the company car Taker would need to buy a new car costing £15,000 with annual running expenses of £2,200, including private use fuel of £500. Taker would sell the car after 3 years for £5,000, and estimates that extra interest charges over the period would amount to £1,800. Taker would drive 6,000 business miles a year.

The other offer is from a company 100 miles away, and it offers a salary of £55,000. Taker would be required to relocate, and the company would pay allowable relocation expenses of £12,000. Taker does not wish to sell his old house and would let it out unfurnished for £6,000 a year renting a property at the new location for £4,000 a year. Alternatively the company would pay only £6,000 of relocation expenses but would provide Taker with a company flat which cost the company £120,000 four years ago and which has an annual value of £2,500. Taker could obtain an additional £1,000 rent for letting out his old house furnished. Taker estimates that he would spend three years in this job before moving back to his old house. He thinks his actual relocation costs will be £2,000 lower if he chooses the company flat.

Required

For each offer, compute the effect on Taker's net income of the available options. (You should ignore NICs.)   **(7 marks)**

(Total = 13 marks)

5 Poster plc   20 mins

(a)   Albert works for Poster plc. He receives a salary of £53,500. He is entitled to a company car (benefit £4,500). No private fuel is provided. Albert is also provided with private medical insurance at a cost to the company of £750.

Required

Show all NICs payable for 2018/19 in respect of Albert, before any deduction is made for the employment allowance.   **(3 marks)**

(b)   Poster plc has had a good year and wants to reward its employees. Instead of paying bonuses it has decided that the employees should all have an additional holiday and it is offering the following options:

(i)   A week on a health farm. The place will be booked by Poster plc, and will cost £2,000.

(ii)   A week's sailing on a yacht chartered directly by the employees. The charter costs £5,000 per week, and a professional skipper a further £1,000 per week. Three members of staff must charter together, and each will take a partner.

(iii)   A voucher which may be exchanged for a holiday at a high street travel agent. The face value (the amount for which the voucher can be exchanged) is £2,200, but the voucher cost the company £2,000.

(iv)   For employees with commitments that mean they cannot leave home, a payment of £1,500 cash.

Required

Explain the NICs payable under each of these options.   **(7 marks)**

(Total = 10 marks)

6 Envirotech plc   **39 mins**

You have received the following letter from Colin, who is managing director of Envirotech plc, a trading company.

1 April 2019

Dear Brian,

I wonder if you could help me with three issues relating to employment taxation. All our employees live in England.

Bonus schemes

For the last 10 years we have been paying relatively modest cash bonuses to our workforce. It has been suggested that if we pay the bonuses in the form of shares, our employees would be committed to our company, and could see their hard work reflected in the value of their shares. We don't envisage that the employees would be required to give up any of their employment rights in exchange for shares. Is there a tax advantaged way of dealing with this?

Share options

You will be aware that Derek (assistant Chief Executive on a salary of £200,000 a year) is due to retire on 30 June 2019 after 20 years with the company.

In 2015 Envirotech plc granted him the right to buy 100,000 shares for £1.50 each. These options are not tax advantaged options. Derek could exercise at any time until 2021 but actually did so last week as he is keen to get the shares before he leaves the company. The share price is currently up around £3.60. Derek wants to know what the position is for income tax and CGT.

Retirement bonus

We are considering awarding Derek a 'thank you' bonus of £30,000 in cash as a retirement gift. Derek doesn't know yet. The company has no obligation to do this, but Derek who was born in 1961 and has been with us since the beginning. He has been talking about retiring to the Algarve to play a bit of golf and the rest of the Board thought that this would be a nice gesture.

Yours sincerely,

Colin

You are required to write a letter to Colin dealing with his queries.   **(20 marks)**

7 Helen and Gemma   **39 mins**

(a)   Helen started trading on 1 July 2013. Her accounts were initially prepared to 30 June each year but in 2016 she changed her accounting date to 30 September by preparing accounts for the 15 months to 30 September 2016. She ceased trading on 31 December 2018 and accounts were prepared for the three months to 31 December 2018.

Helen's trade profits were as follows.

	£
Year to 30 June 2014	36,000
Year to 30 June 2015	48,000
Fifteen months to 30 September 2016	60,000
Year to 30 September 2017	30,000
Year to 30 September 2018	24,000
Three months to 31 December 2018	10,000

Required

Show the taxable trade profits for each tax year. Show clearly when overlap profits arise and how these are relieved. **(10 marks)**

(b) Gemma, who lives in Wales, has traded for some years preparing accounts to 30 April each year. Her business has been making profits at the rate of £2,300 per month for the last three years. She has decided to sell her business and is unsure whether to sell on 31 March 2019 or 30 April 2019. Gemma has no other income in 2018/19 and expects to have property business income of £27,850 in 2019/20 onwards (no finance costs). She had overlap profits on commencement of £1,100.

Required

For each of the proposed sale dates, compute Gemma's combined income for 2018/19 and 2019/20 after tax and Class 4 national insurance contributions and so advise her whether she should sell the business on 31 March 2019 or 30 April 2019 to maximise her income after tax and Class 4 national insurance contributions. **(10 marks)**

(Total = 20 marks)

8 Sheila   20 mins

Sheila began trading as a dress designer on 1 January 2019, prepared her first accounts to 31 March 2019 and thereafter prepared accounts to 31 March each year.

Sheila incurred the following expenditure on plant and machinery.

Date	Item	£
4.1.19	General plant	10,000
1.3.19	Integral feature in building (air conditioning system)	51,100
25.9.19	Delivery van	11,800
15.10.19	General plant	191,000
15.11.19	Car for Sheila CO_2 emissions 120 g/km	18,600
30.11.20	General plant	10,000
30.3.21	Car for salesperson CO_2 emissions 90 g/km	9,000

The private use of Sheila's car is 35%.

Required

Calculate the maximum capital allowances for all periods of account. Assume that the rates and rules applying to capital allowances in 2018/19 apply in later years. **(10 marks)**

9 Arrol and Louisa   49 mins

Arrol, a dentist, has been employed for several years as a representative by Bean Ltd, dental equipment manufacturers. His salary was £27,000 in the year ended 5 April 2018 and £30,000 in the year ended 5 April 2019. His employer provides him with a motor car which has a petrol engine (list price £19,370) and has CO_2 emissions of 167g/km. All petrol is purchased on Bean Ltd's account at a garage. Arrol makes a nominal £25 a month reimbursement to Bean Ltd for part of the petrol used by him in private usage of the motor car.

On 1 May 2018 Arrol and his wife Louisa received substantial gifts in cash from a relative. On that day Arrol exchanged contracts and completed purchase of a private dental practice. Since then he has continued his employment and has worked part time in his practice. The result of the practice for the first year of trading to 30 April 2019 as adjusted for income tax but before capital allowances was a loss of £30,834. Indications are that the practice will have profits of about £70,000 in the year ending 30 April 2020.

Dental furniture (chairs, lamps etc) was purchased with the practice for £12,800. Additions to this equipment in the year ended 30 April 2019 cost £11,960 on 26 January 2019. Arrol wishes to claim the maximum capital allowances as soon as possible.

In 2018/19 Arrol and Louisa had other income as follows.

	Arrol £	Louisa £
Bank interest received	300	
Building society interest received	308	6,735
Interest on National Savings & Investments investment account		2,832
Salary as part-time receptionist in Arrol's practice		8,985

Both Arrol and Louisa live in England.

Required

(a) Calculate Arrol's income tax liability in 2018/19 on the assumption that he claims to have the loss incurred in 2018/19 set against his general income of that year.

(b) Calculate Louisa's income tax liability in 2018/19.

(c) Calculate the loss of 2018/19 remaining unrelieved after the loss relief given in part (a), state the alternative ways in which this loss may be relieved and give Arrol any advice you consider beneficial to maximise the tax relief.

(25 marks)

10 ABC Partnership and Ernie   49 mins

(a) Adam, Bert and Charlie started trading as the ABC partnership on 6 April 2015, sharing profits in the ratio 2:2:1, after charging annual salaries of £15,000, £12,000 and £10,000 respectively.

On 5 July 2016 Adam retired and Bert and Charlie continued to trade in partnership, taking the same salaries as before, but dividing the balance of the profits in the ratio 3:2.

On 6 May 2018 Donald was admitted as a partner on the terms that he received a salary of £18,000 a year, that the salaries of Bert and Charlie should be increased to £18,000 a year each and that of the balance of the profits, Donald should take one tenth, Bert six tenths and Charlie three tenths.

The trade profits of the partnership as adjusted for tax purposes are as follows:

Year ending 5 April	Profits £
2016	102,000
2017	208,000
2018	126,000
2019	180,000

Required

Show the taxable trade profits for each partner for 2015/16 to 2018/19 inclusive.   **(15 marks)**

(b) Ernie has been running a hardware store for several years. His shop assistant is retiring. Ernie has no other employees. Ernie would like to take his wife Freda into the business. He is unsure whether to take her on as a part time salaried assistant, or to take her into partnership sharing profits 2:1. Ernie's profits are £76,950 a year before deducting his assistant's wages. If Ernie took on a new assistant, on the same terms as he would employ Freda, he would expect to pay wages of £25,650 a year. Freda has no other income.

Required

Advise Ernie of the advantages or disadvantages of employing Freda as an employee or of taking her into partnership with him:

(i)   assuming Freda would receive £25,650 of gross income in both scenarios.

(ii)   assuming a profit share for Freda that would maximise the couple's tax saving. **(10 marks)**

(Total = 25 marks)

11 Maria, Felix and Susan   39 mins

(a)   Maria was born in Brazil and had lived there all her life until she married Henry, a UK resident, in June 2018. Maria owns a house in Brazil. She does not work.

Maria and Henry bought a flat in London in July 2018. Maria spent 150 days in the UK during the tax year 2018/19 living in the flat. She spent the remaining 215 days living in her house in Brazil.

Required

Explain, giving reasons, whether Maria is UK resident in the tax year 2018/19.   **(5 marks)**

(b)   Felix was born in Denmark and is domiciled there under general law. He is resident in the UK in the tax year 2018/19 and lives in England. In that tax year Felix has UK trading income amounting to £15,000 and overseas property business income amounting to £135,000 of which he remits £18,000 during the tax year. Felix will claim the remittance basis if possible.

Required

(i)   Explain Felix's UK income tax status for the tax year 2018/19 if he has been resident in the UK for 18 tax years immediately preceding that tax year and compute his income tax liability for the tax year 2018/19.   **(5 marks)**

(ii)   Explain Felix's UK income tax status for the tax year 2018/19 if he has been resident in the UK for 8 tax years immediately preceding that tax year and compute his income tax liability for the tax year 2018/19.   **(5 marks)**

(c)   Susan is UK resident and domiciled, lives in England, and received the following income in 2018/19.

	£
UK employment income	33,000
Overseas property business income (before deduction of tax)	14,705

Overseas tax of £4,705 was deducted before the overseas property business income was paid to Susan.

Required

Calculate the UK income tax payable by Susan if she has suffered £4,200 of tax under PAYE for the year.   **(5 marks)**

(Total = 20 marks)

12 Sophie

37 mins

Sophie made the following disposals in 2018/19:

(a) A painting for proceeds of £50,000 at auction on 12 October 2018. The auctioneer's costs of sale were 1% of the gross proceeds. Sophie had bought the painting for £2,500.

(b) A holiday cottage on 1 February 2019 for £85,000. The cottage was acquired by Sophie's husband Terry for £40,000. He had transferred the cottage to Sophie in 2008 when it was worth £60,000. The cottage has never been the main residence of either Sophie or Terry.

(c) Two acres of land on 10 July 2018 for £18,000. This was part of a 10 acre plot of land acquired by Sophie for £11,000. Immediately before the sale, the 10 acre plot as a whole was valued at £92,000. At the date of the sale, the remaining eight acres was valued at £70,000. The land has always been used for agricultural purposes.

(d) 4,000 shares in JKL plc to her son Jason for £20,000 (their market value) on 23 December 2018. Sophie bought the shares on 1 February 2007 for £51,000. Jason sold the shares in January 2019 for £18,000.

Sophie has taxable income of £50,000 in 2018/19.

Terry has made no capital disposals during the year. He has taxable income of £31,000 in 2018/19.

Jason is a student with no capital assets and no taxable income in 2018/19.

Required

(a) Calculate the capital gains tax liability for Sophie for 2018/19, giving details of your treatment of the disposals.

(b) Advise Sophie of any steps that could have been taken to reduce the capital gains tax liability for 2018/19.

(19 marks)

13 John and Matilda

29 mins

John acquired 20,000 shares in Miller plc on 1 May 2008 for £40,000. On 10 July 2018, Miller plc was taken over by Wall plc. Clearance was obtained from HMRC that this was a bona fide commercial arrangement. John received 1 ordinary share (worth £4.90) in Wall plc and cash of £1.60 for each Miller plc share.

John's wife, Matilda, made the following purchases of ordinary shares in Read plc, a quoted company.

Date	Number	Cost
		£
15 May 2008	1,800	1,900
1 October 2018	2,000	25,750

On 12 July 2018, there was a 1 for 1 bonus issue.

On 30 September 2018 Matilda sold 3,200 of the shares for £42,000.

Entrepreneurs' relief does not apply to any of the disposals. John and Matilda each have taxable income of £20,000 in 2018/19. John had £16,160 of allowable losses brought forward at 6 April 2018.

Required

(a) Compute the chargeable gain on the takeover of Miller plc for John. Show the base cost of his shares in Wall plc. **(4 marks)**

(b) Explain whether there would have been any advantages for John if instead of receiving cash on the take over of Wall plc shares he had received loan stock. **(4 marks)**

(c) Compute the chargeable gain or allowable loss on the sale of Matilda's shares. **(4 marks)**

(d) State how much capital gains tax John and Matilda will have to pay for 2018/19 if they have no other chargeable gains or allowable losses in that tax year. Show any amounts carried forward.

(3 marks)

(Total = 15 marks)

14 Hazel   23 mins

Hazel has been running a retail business as a sole trader for the past three years. She wishes to incorporate the business and will hold 100% of the shares issued. She also wishes to receive some of the consideration for incorporation other than in shares provided that this does not trigger a tax charge.

Hazel estimates that her business is worth £155,000, comprising the following assets which would result in the following gains on disposal:

Asset	Market value	Gain
	£	£
Cash	25,000	n/a
Goodwill	30,000	30,000
Freehold shop	90,000	50,600
Inventory	20,000	n/a
Creditors	(10,000)	n/a

Hazel has no other chargeable assets.

Required

Prepare a report for Hazel addressing the following issues set out below, and where appropriate, include supporting calculations.

(a) State the conditions that must be satisfied If Hazel's business is to be sold to a company without incurring an immediate CGT charge. **(2 marks)**

(b) Assuming the relief **is** available, advise Hazel on the maximum amount of non-share consideration she could receive on incorporation without triggering a CGT liability. **(5 marks)**

(c) State any disadvantages in using the relief that Hazel should be aware of. **(3 marks)**

(d) Identify and describe another relief that Hazel might use without incurring an immediate CGT charge. **(2 marks)**

You may assume that the rates and allowances for the tax year 2018/19 continue to apply for the foreseeable future.

(Total = 12 marks)

15 Wendy, Henry and Robert   41 mins

(a) On 30 June 2018 Wendy assigned the lease of a building originally acquired as an investment for £30,750; the lease expires on 30 June 2034. She had acquired the lease for £8,000 on 1 January 2010 and the building had never been her principal private residence.

You may assume that the relevant percentages from the lease percentage table are as follows:

16 years   64.116
24 years   79.622
25 years   81.100

Required

Calculate Wendy's gain or loss on the assignment. **(5 marks)**

(b) Henry is a sole trader. He bought a factory for use in his trade on 10 July 2017 for £150,000.

On 9 November 2018, the factory was damaged in a flood. Henry received compensation from the water company of £20,000 on 1 September 2019. He had incurred costs of £15,000 in July 2019 on renovations. The value of the factory after the renovations is £250,000.

On 1 December 2020, Henry sold the factory for £260,000.

Required

Show the chargeable gains (if any) for Henry for 2018/19, 2019/20 and 2020/21 assuming that any claims to defer gains are made. Henry made no other disposals except to utilise his annual exempt amount each year. **(8 marks)**

(c) Robert is a non-UK resident who requires advice about two residential properties situated in the UK. Robert was UK resident until 5 April 2015. He was not UK resident in 2015/16, 2016/17 or 2017/18 and will not be UK resident in 2018/19 nor any future year.

Robert owns two residential properties in the UK, a house (Redacre) and a holiday cottage (Bluesky). He used Redacre as his main residence from its purchase on 6 April 2006 for £150,000.

Robert had Redacre valued on 5 April 2015 at £325,000. He stays in Redacre during his visits to the UK which do not exceed 30 days in a tax year. He will sell Redacre on 5 October 2019 for net proceeds of £450,000.

Robert has always rented out Bluesky as a furnished holiday letting. He is considering gifting Bluesky to his daughter Emily who is also non-UK resident.

Required

(i) Advise Robert, with supporting calculations, of the taxable gain that will arise on the sale of Redacre, assuming any relevant elections are made and that this is the only disposal that Robert will make in the tax year 2019/20. **(6 marks)**

(ii) Advise Robert whether or not he can claim gift (holdover) relief on the proposed gift of Bluesky to Emily. **(2 marks)**

(Total = 21 marks)

16 Mark and Sarah
33 mins

Mark and Sarah are a married couple who have asked your advice about some tax administration issues.

Mark's income tax liability for 2017/18 was £16,000. He had suffered tax under PAYE of £4,000 and paid two payments on account of £6,000 each on the due dates.

He submitted his 2017/18 return on 31 January 2019 and made a claim to reduce his payments on account for 2018/19 on the basis that his total liability for 2018/19 would be £14,000 with PAYE of £5,000.

He made the payments on account of £4,500 on 28 February and 31 August 2019.

Finally, on 31 March 2020 he submitted his return for 2018/19 which showed total tax due of £17,000 and PAYE of £4,000. He therefore paid a further £4,000 on the same date.

Sarah's tax return for 2018/19 included a transaction which it was commonly understood gave rise to a tax liability of £10,000. The return was filed in December 2019. In February 2020 another taxpayer who had undertaken a similar transaction challenged HMRC's interpretation of the legislation, succeeding before the Tax Tribunal and the case is expected to proceed to the Court of Appeal during early 2021. If the alternative interpretation was correct it would have saved Sarah tax of £8,000.

Required

(a) Outline the time limits for submission of returns and payments of tax under self assessment for 2018/19 and detail the provisions for failure to comply. **(9 marks)**

(b) Calculate the interest on overdue tax chargeable in respect of Mark's tax payments for 2018/19. **(3 marks)**

(c)   Advise Sarah of any action she should take to enable her to take advantage of the alternative interpretation should the other taxpayer be successful before the Courts.   **(5 marks)**

(Total = 17 marks)

17 Rodin   31 mins

Rodin died unexpectedly on 20 December 2018. His record of gifts is as follows:

Date	£	Recipient
25.12.06	60,000	Son
21.1.09	321,000	Discretionary trust (Rodin paid the IHT)
20.8.12	31,000	Daughter
19.2.14	91,000	Discretionary trust (Trustees paid the IHT)
1.8.15	73,000	Cousin, Canova
1.9.15	400,000	Wife, Bertha

Both Rodin and Bertha have always been UK domiciled.

Required

(a)   Compute all amounts of inheritance tax due on these gifts.   **(10 marks)**

(b)   Comment on whether your answer would have been the same had Bertha not been domiciled, nor deemed domiciled, in the UK at the time of the transfer to her. Assume that no election has been made in respect of her domicile.   **(2 marks)**

(c)   Canova wishes to give £50,000 to each of his son and daughter and to transfer £350,000 to a discretionary trust for his grandchildren. His daughter is widowed, and he thinks it likely that in the next few months she will remarry. Canova has not made any gifts recently. What advice would you give Canova?   **(4 marks)**

(Total = 16 marks)

18 Hubert   49 mins

Hubert, for whom you act as tax adviser, had over the years acquired 3,000 £1 ordinary shares in Bod Ltd, an unquoted trading company with an issued share capital of 5,000 ordinary shares. None of the shares were acquired under the Enterprise Management Incentive scheme. All the assets of Bod Ltd are in use for the purpose of its trade. Hubert has been a director of the company since 1992. His wife, Rose, also owns 1,000 ordinary shares in the company.

Hubert had acquired his shares as follows:

	Shares	Cost
		£
1.11.95	2,200	3,300
15.6.05	200	1,366
18.8.11	600	3,000

The current market values attributable to various percentage shareholdings in Bod Ltd are estimated as follows:

% Shareholding	Value of £1 ordinary share
100	40.50
80	36.67
60	25.00
40 or below	18.00

On 1 April 2019 Hubert sold 2,000 of his shares in Bod Ltd for £10,000 to his daughter Maxine, who sold them to an unconnected buyer ten days later. Hubert has taxable income of £100,000 in 2018/19.

He has made no previous transfer of assets other than a gift of £349,000 cash to a discretionary trust (which did not include Hubert as a beneficiary) on 1 May 2018. Hubert had agreed to bear any costs or taxes in respect of the gift. Apart from his shares in Bod Ltd, Hubert currently has no other assets apart from cash of £40,000. He has left everything in his will to his son Roger. You should assume that today's date is 14 April 2019.

Required

(a) Advise Hubert of his potential inheritance tax and capital gains tax liabilities.

(b) Advise Hubert on the inheritance tax implications which would arise if he were to die on 20 April 2019. (Assume that any CGT on lifetime gifts is unpaid at the date of death but that any IHT has been paid.)

(c) Roger has suggested to Hubert that he should gift his shares in Bod Ltd now rather than retaining them until his death. Prepare brief notes of matters which will have a bearing on a decision in preparation for a meeting with Hubert.

Assume that the IHT nil rate band is £325,000, the CGT annual exempt amount is £11,700 throughout and that the rules and rates of CGT and IHT are the same in 2019/20 as in 2018/19.

(25 marks)

19 Rhys
21 mins

On 17 July 2011 Rhys settled his portfolio of quoted shares on the RJ discretionary trust. Rhys died on 3 September 2018.

Under his will Rhys left his estate on discretionary will trusts for his sister Blodwen and her children, with the trust to be wound up and the capital to be distributed to Blodwen's children on her death.

Blodwen died on 28 February 2023.

Half of the assets of the RJ discretionary trust were distributed to beneficiaries on 5 March 2020 and the remainder was finally distributed on 18 April 2024.

Rhys made no other gifts other than to use his annual exemptions each year.

Required

(a) Explain the occasions of charge to IHT in respect of the above transactions. Calculations are not required. **(9 marks)**

(b) Comment on how your answer would have been affected had Rhys died on 3 July 2018. **(2 marks)**

(Total = 11 marks)

20 Dan
6 mins

Dan was involved in the following transactions during 2018/19.

(a) Purchased a freehold warehouse in England for £520,000.

(b) Purchased 1,000 ordinary shares in Ursale Ltd (an unquoted company) for £15,000.

(d) Purchased, through the CREST system, 5,000 ordinary shares in HSBC plc (a company listed on the London Stock Exchange) for £30,000.

(e) Received a non-residential freehold plot of land in England worth £80,000 as part of a divorce settlement.

Required

State the stamp taxes consequences of these transactions. **(3 marks)**

21 Fraser Ltd

Fraser Ltd is a trading company. It prepares accounts to 31 March in each year.

The statement of profit or loss for the year ended 31 March 2019 showed a profit before taxation of £413,278.

The following items were included in the accounts.

Income	£
Dividend from an unconnected UK company	1,655
Interest on bank deposits	6,834
Interest from gilts (gross)	2,208
Surplus on the disposal of an office building and a lease	61,806

Expenditure	
Directors' remuneration	62,075
Miscellaneous	3,837
Depreciation	13,876

The company's bank deposits and gilts are held for non-trading purposes.

The company sold an office building for £116,683 on 15 August 2018. It had cost the company £79,000 in May 2008. The relevant indexation factor is 0.293.

A lease of one of the company's retail outlets was sold on 30 April 2018 for £39,213. The term of the lease was 30 years from 1 November 2005 and the company acquired it on 1 November 2010 at a cost of £17,500. The lease percentage for 17 years is 66.470, for 18 years is 68.697 and for 25 years is 81.100. The relevant indexation factor is 0.226.

Miscellaneous expenses comprise the following.

	£
Hire purchase interest on two new fork lift trucks	783
Christmas gifts to customers: 40 executive desk diaries bearing the company's name	2,085
Entertaining customers	969
	3,837

The main pool value of plant at 1 April 2018 was £nil. With the exception of the acquisition of the two new fork lift trucks under the hire purchase agreements at a cash price of £9,800 each on 1 December 2018 there were no purchases or sales of plant in the year ended 31 March 2019.

Fraser Ltd has build up a cash surplus and is considering several schemes.

Fraser Ltd is considering acquiring a new office building. There are two possible options.

(i) Office building A could be acquired at a cost of £150,000.

(ii) Office building B could be acquired at a cost of £400,000. Fraser Ltd would need to raise additional finance of £250,000, partly through a bank loan and partly through the issue of loan stock. Initially the office building would be too large, and Fraser Ltd would let out approximately half of the building to another company.

Alternatively, Fraser Ltd would purchase all of the issued share capital of Simmonds Ltd. The cost of the investment would be £250,000, and Fraser Ltd would need to raise £100,000 through bank loans.

To do well in the new area in which Simmonds Ltd operates, Fraser Ltd is likely to have to buy patents which it expects would cost £50,000. These will be written off over their useful lives in the accounts.

Instead of raising loan finance, Fraser Ltd is contemplating issuing new shares.

Required

(a) Compute Fraser Ltd's corporation tax liability for the year ended 31 March 2019. **(10 marks)**

(b) Advise Fraser Ltd of the corporation tax consequences of its proposals. **(5 marks)**

(Total = 15 marks)

22 Melson Ltd

20 mins

Melson Ltd, a UK resident trading company, made the following disposals in the year ended 31 December 2018.

(a) On 31 May 2018 it sold a warehouse for £125,000. The company had bought the warehouse for £65,000 on 1 July 2005. It has always been rented out to another company. Melson Ltd had invested £100,000 in another warehouse for use in its own trade on 1 May 2018.

(b) On 18 June 2018 Melson Ltd sold a retail shop for £77,000. It had bought it for £20,000 on 1 April 2000, had spent £4,000 extending the shop in July 2002 and a further £2,000 establishing its title to the shop in May 2018. The shop has always been rented out to another company.

(c) On 25 July 2018 Melson Ltd sold an office building for £180,000. It had bought the office building for £65,000 on 16 October 2000 and it has always been rented out to another company.

(d) On 30 July 2018 Melson Ltd sold 4,000 ordinary shares in Leigh Ltd, a trading company, for £180,000. This was a 4% holding. Melson Ltd had acquired a 12% holding in Leigh Ltd in July 2002 for £12,000 and had sold 8,000 of the shares in August 2014.

Required

Compute Melson Ltd's chargeable gains for the year ended 31 December 2018.

Indexation factors

July 2005–December 2017 = 0.447	July 2002–June 2018 = 0.597
July 2005–May 2018 = 0.458	May 2018–June 2018 = 0.002
April 2000–December 2017 = 0.635	October 2000–December 2017 = 0.621
April 2000–June 2018 = 0.651	October 2000–July 2018 = 0.640
July 2002–December 2017 = 0.581	July 2002–July 2018 = 0.600

(10 marks)

23 Hogg Ltd

12 mins

(a) Hogg Ltd prepares accounts for the year to 31 March 2019. In September 2018 it estimates that its corporation tax liability for the year will be £500,000. In April 2019 it revises its estimate to £520,000. In January 2020 it submits its corporation tax return, showing a total liability of £525,000. The company has always been a large company.

Required

State the amounts that would have been paid and due dates for the payment of corporation tax by Hogg Ltd in respect of the year to 31 March 2019. **(3 marks)**

(b) Explain the maximum late-filing penalty that would arise if Hogg Ltd did not submit its corporation tax return for the year to 31 March 2019 in January 2020 but instead submits the return on 10 October 2020. **(3 marks)**

(Total = 6 marks)

24 Norma

20 mins

Norma is intending to start a new business on 1 April 2019, and anticipates a profit of £60,000 in the first year of trading. She is undecided whether to:

(a) Operate as a sole trader,

(b) Operate as a limited company and draw out all the profits as a dividend, or

(c) Operate as a limited company, draw a salary of £15,000 a year and draw out all the remaining profits as a dividend. Norma will be the sole employee and director.

Required

Compare the tax and national insurance resulting from each alternative. You should assume that the tax rates and allowances for the tax year 2018/19 and for the financial year to 31 March 2019 will continue to apply for the foreseeable future.
(10 marks)

25 Clarke Ltd
20 mins

Alex, one of the directors of Clarke Ltd, has had a serious disagreement with the other directors over the direction in which the business should be moving, and as a consequence wishes to resign as a director and dispose of his shares. It has been agreed that Clarke Ltd will repurchase Alex's shares for £5 per share, either in March 2019 or in June 2019.

In January 2001, Alex subscribed for 5,000 shares at par. In May 2014 he purchased a further 2,000 from another director, Benny, at a cost of £3 per share. Benny had also subscribed for these share at par in January 2001. Clarke Ltd is an unquoted trading company and has 150,000 ordinary shares in issue. Alex has utilised his capital gains tax annual exempt amount on the disposal of other assets in both 2018/19 and 2019/20. He has taxable income of £160,000 in 2018/19 and 2019/20, including more than £2,000 of dividend income.

Required

Explain how the repurchase will be dealt with for tax purposes for Alex and indicate whether it would be preferable for the repurchase to take place in March or June 2019, assume the tax rules and rates in 2018/19 continue to apply.
(10 marks)

26 Major Ltd
31 mins

Major Ltd is a trading company resident in the United Kingdom. It has one wholly owned subsidiary, which it acquired several years ago. Until 2018 Major Ltd prepared accounts each year to 31 July, but decided to change its accounting date to 31 March. The information below relates to the eight month period to 31 March 2019:

	£
Income	
Adjusted trading profit	425,000
Rents received less expenses	30,000
Loan interest received – (see Note 1)	24,000
Capital gains	40,000
Dividends (received from unconnected company September 2018)	20,000
Payments	
Qualifying charitable donation (paid September 2018)	3,000
Loan interest paid (see Note 2)	30,000

Notes

1 The loan interest was received in respect of a loan of £100,000 made by the company to Zero Ltd, a main supplier of materials to Major Ltd. The directors of Major Ltd are concerned about the financial position of Zero Ltd, but have decided to take no action at present.

2 The loan interest paid was to a UK bank in respect of funds raised to acquire the subsidiary company.

Major Ltd is considering investing in another supplier and has identified two possibilities. 20% of the shares of Shape Ltd are being offered for sale by one of the retiring directors at a cost of £40,000. Alternatively Major Ltd could subscribe for new shares in Tower Ltd, taking an 8% holding at a cost of £15,000. Whichever acquisition is made Major Ltd would hope to sell the shareholding after a few years at twice its original cost, although it is possible that either of the two target companies could collapse. Major Ltd would have to borrow to fund the purchase.

Required

(a) Compute the corporation tax payable by Major Ltd in respect of the above accounting period, assuming any relevant claims are made, and advise how it should be paid.

(b) Advise the directors of Major Ltd in a brief memorandum of the taxation implications of the loan to Zero Ltd proving irrecoverable.

(c) Advise Major Ltd of the tax consequences of its alternative share acquisitions.

(16 marks)

27 Daley plc   31 mins

Assume that it is December 2022.

Daley plc has recently become a client, having previously prepared its own accounts and corporation tax computations on the basis that reliefs should always be claimed as soon as possible. The return for the year to 30 June 2022 has been prepared but not yet filed. A new managing director, Cameron, has recently been appointed and he wishes to understand how the company's losses have been relieved and whether there is an alternative method of using the loss arising in the year ended 30 June 2022 which may result in a greater tax saving.

The company has had the following results since it started to trade.

	Year ended 31.12.18	Year ended 31.12.19	Year ended 31.12.20	Six months ended 30.6.21	Year ended 30.6.22
	£	£	£	£	£
Trading profit/ (loss)	(29,000)	3,000	110,000	85,000	(202,000)
Interest income	10,000	2,200	10,000	12,000	14,000
Chargeable gains/(losses)	18,000	0	(5,000)	2,000	(1,000)
Qualifying charitable donation	Nil	5,000	2,000	3,000	1,000

It is expected that Daley plc's total profits in the year to 30 June 2023 will be in the region of £150,000, and that this level will be maintained in the future. It will not make any qualifying charitable donations for the foreseeable future.

Required

(a) Compute the corporation tax liability for all five periods on the basis that relief is claimed on the stated basis, and show all amounts to be carried forward at 30 June 2022.

(b) Write a letter to the managing director of Daley plc. You should cover the following issues.

  (i) An outline of how capital loss relief operates.

  (ii) An explanation of how Daley plc's capital losses have been relieved.

  (iii) An outline of how current period, carry back and carry forward trading loss reliefs operate, including the effect of accounting periods of less than 12-months.

  (iv) An explanation of how Daley plc's trading loss for the year ended 31 December 2018 was relieved.

  (v) An explanation of how Daley plc's trading loss for the year ended 30 June 2022 will be relieved if claims are made for current period relief, carry back relief and carry forward relief and the tax saving arising.

  (vi) An explanation of alternative claims for using Daley plc's trading loss for the year ended 30 June 2022 which will result in a greater tax saving and any disadvantage of these alternative claims.

Assume that tax rates and allowances for FY 2018 apply to all years.   **(16 marks)**

28 Huis Ltd
29 mins

(a) Huis Ltd is a close company which is not required to pay corporation tax by instalments. On 31 May 2018, six months before the company's year end, it lent £45,000 to Sartre, a shareholder. Sartre is not an employee of the company. The loan carried a market rate of interest.

The company advised Sartre on 31 March 2020 that he would not be required to repay the loan. It has also agreed to include Sartre in its medical insurance scheme at an annual cost of £1,000, and to allow him to use the company yacht (annual value £24,000) for a month each summer.

Required

Set out the tax consequences of the transactions with Sartre, giving the dates on which any amounts are payable to HMRC.

(b) Beauvoir Ltd is an investment company. It has had the following results for the last two years.

	Year ended 31.3.18 £	Year ended 31.3.19 £
Property income	14,000	25,000
Interest income	20,000	100,000
Management expenses	36,000	45,000

Required

Compute the company's corporation tax liability for both years assuming that any beneficial claim is made. **(15 marks)**

29 Hawthorn Ltd, Linden Ltd and Maple Ltd
39 mins

Hawthorn Ltd has owned 60% of the issued ordinary share capital of Linden Ltd since its incorporation, the remaining 40% being held by individuals. Both UK companies have always prepared accounts to 30 June, their most recent accounts showing the following.

	Hawthorn Ltd		Linden Ltd	
	Year ended 30.6.18 £	Year ended 30.6.19 £	Year ended 30.6.18 £	Year ended 30.6.19 £
Adjusted trading profit	2,000		30,000	100,000
Adjusted trading loss		(48,000)		
Qualifying charitable donation paid			12,000	12,000

On 1 January 2018, Hawthorn Ltd acquired 100% of the issued ordinary share capital of Maple Ltd, a company which had always previously prepared accounts to 31 December.

Maple Ltd's accounts for the period of 1 January 2018 to 30 June 2019 show the following.

	£
Adjusted trading profit, before capital allowances	65,250
Investment interest, amount accrued over six months to 30 June 2019	20,000

Maple Ltd had capital allowances of £4,250 in the year to 31 December 2018 and £17,569 in the 6 months to 30 June 2019.

The group is planning several property transactions for 1 January 2020:

(i) Maple Ltd will sell a factory for £200,000 realising a loss of £13,333. Maple Ltd also has an unused capital loss of £26,667 which arose on a disposal of a warehouse in November 2017.

(ii) Hawthorn Ltd will sell an office block for £250,000 realising a chargeable gain of £80,000.

(iii) Linden Ltd will sell a warehouse for £300,000 realising a gain of £70,000.

(iv) Linden Ltd will acquire a new warehouse at a cost of £290,000.

In the year to 30 June 2020, Hawthorn Ltd will make a trading loss of £80,000 and Linden Ltd and Maple Ltd will make trading profits of £5,000 and £7,000 respectively. In the year to 30 June 2021, Linden Ltd and Maple Ltd are likely to make trading profits of £40,000 and £90,000 respectively, and Hawthorn Ltd is likely to make a trading profit of £3,000. All of the companies will have interest income of £500 in the year ended 30 June 2021 but no other income or gains nor any qualifying charitable donations in these years.

Required

(a)   Compute the corporation tax payable by Hawthorn Ltd, Linden Ltd and Maple Ltd for the accounting periods ending 30 June 2018 and 30 June 2019 assuming all available claims and surrenders are made to minimise the corporation tax payable by the group. Assume the rates for FY18 apply throughout.

(b)   Draft a memorandum to the directors of Hawthorn Ltd suggesting the extent to which Hawthorn Ltd, Linden Ltd and Maple Ltd can minimise the corporation tax on chargeable gains for the year to 30 June 2020. For this part you should ignore any claims that could be made for current period or carry forward loss relief against total profits.

(c)   Explain the amount of trading losses that Hawthorn Ltd has unrelieved at 1 July 2020, assuming that all possible current period and carry forward reliefs are claimed in the accounting period ending 30 June 2020, and how those unrelieved losses could be relieved in the year ended 30 June 2021.

(20 marks)

30 Exotica Inc and Willow Ltd   29 mins

(a)   Exotica Inc (for which you act as United Kingdom tax adviser) is a company resident and incorporated in Ruritania, a country which is outside the European Union and does not have a double tax agreement with the UK. The company manufactures items of advanced industrial equipment and now wishes to increase its sales within the UK.

It intends to acquire an office in London and to staff it with full-time salesmen assigned from its head office in Ruritania. Exotica Inc is still considering whether the salesmen will be given the authority to conclude contracts with UK customers or whether such authority will be reserved for the head office only. It is also considering whether customers' orders should be met from stocks held in Ruritania or whether stocks should be maintained in the UK. While tax considerations will be taken into account, other commercial factors are likely to influence these decisions strongly.

Required

Advise Exotica Inc on the corporation tax implications of the various alternative courses of action still under consideration.

(b)   The directors of Willow Ltd have decided to set up an operation in a country where the rate of corporation tax is 18%.

They are considering two alternative approaches:

(i)   to run the overseas operation as a permanent establishment of the UK company; or
(ii)   to run it as a foreign-registered subsidiary of the UK company.

Required

Draft a report to the board on the taxation implications of each of the alternative proposals.

(15 marks)

31 VAT groups

20 mins

It is February 2019. Barry, the Finance Director of Banner plc, has written to you, asking for your advice on certain VAT matters. Banner plc has two wholly owned subsidiaries, Flag Ltd and Ensign Ltd. All three companies are fully taxable and are included in a group registration for VAT. Two months ago, in December 2018, Banner plc acquired 75% of the ordinary share capital of Union Ltd, a partly exempt company. Union Ltd generally recovers around 60% of its input tax. To date, no action has been taken to include Union Ltd in the group registration.

As Union Ltd is not wholly owned, other group companies will be required to pay for any losses surrendered to them as group relief.

Barry has specifically asked whether Union Ltd should be included in the group registration and, if so, what action he should take in this regard.

All four companies are UK resident with an established place of business in the UK.

Required

Write a letter in reply to Barry.

(10 marks)

32 Stewart Ltd

20 mins

Stewart Ltd, a partially exempt trader, has the following information for the year ended 31 March 2019:

Supplies

Quarter ended	Taxable (excl VAT) £	Exempt £	Total (excl VAT) £
30.6.18	403,920	52,072	455,992
30.9.18	*384,177	23,194	*407,371
31.12.18	467,159	18,791	485,950
31.3.19	520,321	37,439	557,760
	*1,775,577	131,496	*1,907,073

* This includes £25,000 in respect of a computer used in the business and subsequently sold. The computer was originally purchased for £45,000 in 2016.

Input tax

Quarter ended	Re taxable supplies £	Re exempt supplies £	Non-attributable £	Total £
30.6.18	44,404	3,120	14,719	62,243
30.9.18	39,098	2,775	12,613	54,486
31.12.18	24,926	1,374	10,412	36,712
31.3.19	36,020	1,876	11,919	49,815
	144,448	9,145	49,663	203,256

Stewart Ltd has decided to use the actual recovery rate percentage to account for VAT in each quarter in the year ended 31 March 2019 rather than the recovery rate for the year ended 31 March 2018. You may assume that neither of the *de minimis* Tests 1 nor 2 apply and the conditions for the annual test are not satisfied.

Required

Calculate the amount of recoverable input tax for each quarter and the annual adjustment, if any.

(10 marks)

33 Tax planning

49 mins

You are a partner in a firm of certified accountants with particular responsibility for tax planning.

Required

Draft an answer to each of the following queries which have been passed on to you by your fellow partners. You should assume that today's date is 1 April 2018.

(a) Client A is about to commence business as a management consultant on 1 May 2018. She was previously employed as a school headteacher for several years at a salary in excess of £55,000 a year. The business involves virtually no expenditure on capital assets. She expects to make operating losses in her first two years of trading, after which she expects the business slowly to become profitable. She will have no other taxable sources of income. For reasons of prestige she is proposing to trade through a specially formed company, A Ltd. However, she could delay forming the company for a short while and she asks what the best course of action would be from a tax viewpoint.

(b) Client B currently manufactures fitted bedroom furniture for the general public from a small workshop. The market is highly competitive. He has a turnover of £60,000 a year which yields a current gross profit percentage of 40% and he incurs minimal overheads. He has been offered a contract to manufacture bookcases for a VAT registered trader at a price of £30,000 a year from 1 March 2019 (exclusive of any VAT). B estimates that this project would involve a similar cost structure to his existing operations. B is concerned that, since he will become liable to register for VAT if he takes on the new contract, it may not be worthwhile to accept it.

He has asked for calculations showing the net annual gain to him from taking on the contract. (**Note.** You are required to consider VAT issues **only**.)

(c) Client C is about to acquire shares in a publicly quoted company for £350,000 out of his own funds. The shares currently yield a dividend of £28,000 a year paid in September and March each year. The prospects for significant capital appreciation in the future are excellent. At the end of ten years C may decide to sell some or all of the shares. It has been suggested to C by a friend, D, that instead of buying the shares himself he should form a new investment company, C Ltd. C would subscribe for 350,000 £1 shares in C Ltd, which would then use the cash to buy the shares. D has told C that he could draw out director's remuneration of up to £11,850 a year and that C Ltd could deduct this against the dividend income and that the balance of £16,150 would only be liable to corporation tax of 19%. D has also said that C could obtain tax relief by paying premiums into a personal pension scheme. C has asked whether the advice which he has received from D is correct.

(d) Client D is setting up in business as an aromatherapist. She is considering structuring her business either as a sole trader or through a limited company. If she operates as a sole trader she will be starting in business on 6 April 2018, making up her first accounts to 5 April 2019 with an expected trading profit of £30,000. If she uses a limited company, it will start in business on 1 April 2018, make up accounts to 31 March 2019, with expected taxable trading profits of £30,000. Client D would extract all available profits by way of dividends on 31 March 2019.

Client D has property business income which exactly covers her personal allowance for 2018/19. Client D wants to know how much net spendable income she would have from the business in each of these cases. She lives in England. **(25 marks)**

34 Hulse Finds Ltd

35 mins

Paul and his friend Nick set up the company Hulse Finds Ltd on 1 April 2017 with Paul and Nick holding 40% of the shares each. The remaining 20% of the company is held by five of their friends. Hulse Finds Ltd runs a shop in Didsbury selling unusual objects which are sourced from around the world. Paul and Nick work full time in the management of the company but their five friends are passive investors in the business.

Paul took out a bank loan of £150,000 secured on his apartment in central Manchester to purchase his shares whereas Nick used his redundancy payout from his old employer (a large bank).

Hulse Finds Ltd incurred significant start-up costs in its first 18 months of trade. Taxable total profits were £60,000 and £160,000 in the years to 31 March 2018 and 2019 respectively.

During June in the second year the company made a loan to Chris (one of the investor friends) of £10,000.

Nick has identified a company Sweet Nothings Ltd (SNL) as a possible acquisition. The company sells furniture and fixtures which it imports into the UK. After negotiations with the board of directors of SNL it has been agreed that Hulse Finds Ltd can purchase the trade and assets of SNL on 1 April 2020.

SNL has trading losses which are being carried forward of £50,000 and capital losses being carried forward of £25,000. Hulse Finds Ltd will set up a wholly owned subsidiary SN2 Ltd to acquire the trade and assets of SNL.

Predicted taxable total profits for the two companies for year ended 31 March 2021 are:

Hulse Finds Ltd		£250,000
SN2 Ltd	Trading profits	40,000
	Capital gains	10,000

By 2022 Paul and Nick expect the existing business to have grown considerably and they expect to have taxable profits of £1 million in the year ended 31 March 2022. SN2 Ltd is expected to have taxable profits of £100,000 in the same period.

Paul and Nick have been looking to expand overseas in order to take advantage of new emerging markets. They intend to start a new business in Newland on 1 April 2021.

It is anticipated that the overseas business will make a trading loss of £60,000 in the year ended 31 March 2022, a profit of £80,000 in the year ended 31 March 2023 and a profit of £100,000 per year in future years.

The system of corporation tax in Newland is broadly the same as that in the UK, although loss relief is only available to companies resident in Newland. In addition, the rate of corporation tax is 25% and there is no withholding tax when dividends are paid to overseas shareholders. There is no double tax treaty between the UK and Newland.

You are meeting with Paul and Chris next week. Assume that the rates of corporation tax in FY18 also apply in later years.

Required

Make brief notes on the following for discussion at that meeting:

(a) Any relief for Paul's investment in the company? **(2 marks)**

(b) What is the impact to the company, if any, of the loan to Chris and would this be different if Chris was an employee of the company? **(4 marks)**

(c) What are the tax implications of the acquisition of SNL? **(5 marks)**

(d) Discuss the tax implications of the proposed expansion overseas. **(7 marks)**

(Total = 18 marks)

35 Financial planning

29 mins

The directors of Moor Ltd, a medium-sized unquoted company engaged in manufacturing, have decided to embark on a major expansion of the business.

The company has a significant amount of unissued share capital and, to finance the expansion, the directors have been considering issuing further shares. They have also considered raising loan capital, using as security identified pieces of valuable property owned by the company.

Required

Draft a report to the board, dated 19 May 2018, setting out the taxation implications for the company under each of the alternative methods of raising finance.

Your report should also identify any taxation implications for the providers of this finance. **(15 marks)**

36 Daniel

49 mins

An extract from an email from your manager is set out below.

> I had a telephone conversation with Daniel, the managing director of Saturn Ltd, first thing this morning. We discussed the anticipated results of the Saturn Ltd group of companies and the proposed acquisition of a majority holding in Tethys Ltd. All the relevant details are included in the attached memorandum.
>
> I need the following:
>
> (i)   A memorandum that I can use to prepare for my telephone call to Daniel. I realise that he did not give me all of the information we need so please identify any additional information that you think could have an effect on our advice.
>
> (ii)   A summary of the information we need and any action we should take before agreeing to become tax advisers to the Saturn Ltd group.
>
> Tax manager

The memorandum attached to the email is set out below.

> **To**:   Internal filing
> **From**:   Tax manager
> **Date**:   2 June 2019
> **Subject**: Saturn Ltd group of companies
>
> This memorandum sets out the matters discussed with Daniel, the managing director of Saturn Ltd, earlier today.
>
> **Group structure**
>
> Saturn Ltd has three wholly-owned subsidiaries: Dione Ltd, Rhea Ltd and Titan Inc. Titan Inc trades in and is resident in the country of Galactica. The other three group companies are resident in the UK. Saturn Ltd has owned all three subsidiary companies for many years.
>
> **Budgeted results for the year ending 30 June 2019**
>
> It is estimated that Dione Ltd will make a tax adjusted trading loss of £187,000 in the year ending 30 June 2019; it will have no other income or capital gains in the period. The budgeted taxable total profits of the other companies in the group are set out below.
>
> | | £ |
> |---|---|
> | Saturn Ltd | 385,000 |
> | Rhea Ltd | 90,000 |
> | Titan Inc | 265,000 |
>
> Rhea Ltd is expected to make a trading loss of £(200,000) in the year ending 30 June 2020 and will have no other income or gains, Dione Ltd is expected to make minimal profits in that year.
>
> **Proposed acquisition of 65% of Tethys Ltd**
>
> On 1 August 2019, Saturn Ltd will purchase 65% of the ordinary share capital of Tethys Ltd for £235,000 from the personal representatives of George Jetson. The whole of the balance of the company's share capital is owned either by Edith Clanger or by her family company, Clangers Ltd; Daniel cannot remember which.

It is anticipated that Tethys Ltd will make a tax adjusted trading loss of approximately £80,000 in the year ending 31 December 2019.

In early 2020, Tethys Ltd will sell its manufacturing premises for £240,000 and move to a rented factory. The premises were acquired new for £112,000 in January 2011 and immediately brought into trade use. The indexation factor from the date of acquisition to December 2017 is 0.214, and to the date of disposal is 0.302.

Information requested by Daniel

(i)   The best use of the loss of Dione Ltd, and the amount of tax that can be saved.

(ii)   The amount of the trading loss of Tethys Ltd for the year ending 31 December 2019 that can be used by Saturn Ltd and the ability of Tethys Ltd to use this loss in the future.

(iii)   In respect of the sale of the manufacturing premises:

–   Whether or not Tethys Ltd should charge value added tax (VAT) on the sale of the property

–   The taxable profit arising in respect of the sale

–   The amount of the gain that could be rolled over if Tethys Ltd or any of the other Saturn Ltd group companies acquired assets costing £200,000, the types of asset that would have to be purchased and the period during which the assets would need to be acquired

(iv)   Any stamp taxes payable by the Saturn Ltd group in respect of the proposed transactions.

Tax manager

Required

(a)   Prepare the memorandum requested by your manager. The memorandum should include explanations together with supporting calculations and should identify any further information that you think is required. The following marks are available for the four components of the memorandum:

(i)   The best use of the loss of Dione Ltd; **(3 marks)**
(ii)   The use of the trading loss of Tethys Ltd for the year ending 31 December 2019; **(6 marks)**
(iii)   Advice in connection with the sale of the manufacturing premises by Tethys Ltd; **(7 marks)**
(iv)   The stamp taxes payable by the Saturn Ltd group. **(2 marks)**

Additional marks will be awarded for the appropriateness of the format and presentation of the memorandum and the effectiveness with which the information is communicated. **(2 marks)**

(b)   Prepare a summary of the information needed to satisfy our obligations under the money laundering legislation and any action that should be taken before agreeing to become tax advisers to the Saturn Ltd group. **(5 marks)**

(Total = 25 marks)

37 Stuart and Rebecca

51 mins

Your manager has had a meeting with Stuart and Rebecca, who are a married couple, and has sent you a copy of the following memorandum.

To: The files
From: Tax manager
Date: 1 December 2019
Subject: Stuart and Rebecca – Estate planning

Stuart has recently been diagnosed with a serious illness. He is expected to live for another two or three years only. He is concerned about the possible inheritance tax that will arise on his death. Rebecca is in good health.

In November 2019 Stuart sold a house in Plymouth for £422,100. Stuart had inherited the house on the death of his mother on 1 May 2007 when it had a probate value of £185,000. The subsequent pattern of occupation was as follows:

1 May 2007 to 31 August 2009	Occupied by Stuart and Rebecca as main residence
1 September 2009 to 30 June 2013	Unoccupied
1 July 2013 to 30 September 2015	Let out
1 October 2015 to 31 May 2016	Occupied by Stuart and Rebecca as main residence
1 June 2016 to 30 November 2019	Used occasionally as second home

Both Stuart and Rebecca had lived in rented accommodation in London from 1 September 2009 to 30 September 2015. On 1 June 2016 Stuart and Rebecca bought a house in London in their joint names which was then occupied as their main residence. No other capital disposals were made by Stuart in the tax year 2019/20. He has £28,550 of capital losses brought forward from previous years.

Stuart intends to invest the gross sale proceeds from the sale of the Plymouth house, and is considering two investment options, both of which he believes will provide equal risk and returns. These are as follows:

(1) Acquiring shares in Omikron plc, a listed UK trading company, with 50,250,000 shares in issue. Its shares currently trade at 42p per share, or

(2) Acquiring further shares in Omega plc. The issued share capital of Omega plc is currently 10,000,000 shares. The share price is quoted at 208p – 216p with marked bargains at 207p, 211p, and 215p

Stuart and Rebecca's assets (following the sale of the Plymouth house but before any investment of the proceeds) are as follows:

Assets	Stuart £	Rebecca £
Family house in London	450,000	450,000
Cash from property sale	422,100	–
Cash deposits	165,000	165,000
Portfolio of quoted investments	–	250,000
Shares in Omega plc	see files	see files
Life insurance policy	note	note

Note. The life insurance policy will pay out a sum of £200,000 on the death of the first spouse to die.

Tax manager

An extract from an email from your manager is set out below.

Please prepare a letter from me to Stuart incorporating the following:

1 State the taxable capital gain on the sale of the Plymouth house in November 2019, setting out the amounts of any reliefs claimed.

2 Given his recent diagnosis, advice for Stuart on which of the two proposed investments (Omikron plc/Omega plc) would be the more tax efficient alternative.

Give reasons for your choice.

3 Assuming that Stuart:

(i) uses proceeds from the house sale to purchase 201,000 shares in Omega plc on 3 December 2019; and

(ii) dies on 20 December 2021,

calculations of the potential IHT liability which would arise if Rebecca were to die on 1 March 2022, and no further tax planning measures were taken.

Assume that all asset values remain unchanged.

4 Advice on any lifetime IHT planning that could be undertaken to help reduce the potential liability calculated above.

Tax manager

You have extracted the following further information from client files.

• Stuart is a self-employed business consultant.

• Stuart and Rebecca have one adult child, Sam, who is single.

• Both Stuart and Rebecca have wills whose terms transfer all assets to the surviving spouse, with the surviving spouse transferring all assets to Sam.

• On 1 June 2016 Stuart and Rebecca elected for their London house to be their principal private residence with effect from that date, up until that point the Plymouth property had been their principal private residence.

• Omega plc was formerly Omega Ltd and Stuart and Rebecca helped start up the company. The company was formed on 1 June 1998, when they each bought 24,000 shares for £1 per share. The company became listed on 1 May 2007. On this date their holding was subdivided, with each of them receiving 100 shares in Omega plc for each share held in Omega Ltd.

• Neither Stuart nor Rebecca has made any previous chargeable lifetime transfers for IHT purposes.

Required

Prepare the letter requested by your manager. Marks are available for the four components of the letter as follows:

1 Relevant calculations of the taxable capital gain on the sale of the Plymouth house in November 2019. **(8 marks)**

2 Advice on which of the two proposed investments would be more tax efficient alternative. **(3 marks)**

3 Calculations of the potential IHT liability which would arise if no further tax planning measures are taken and Rebecca dies in March 2022. **(6 marks)**

4 Advice on any lifetime IHT planning that could be undertaken for both Stuart and Rebecca to help reduce their potential IHT liability (in three above). **(7 marks)**

Appropriateness of the format and presentation of the report and the effectiveness with which its advice is communicated. **(2 marks)**

You may assume that the rates and allowances for the tax year 2018/19 continue to apply for the foreseeable future.

(Total = 26 marks)

38 Landscape Ltd

Landscape Ltd is an unquoted trading company that operates a nationwide chain of retail shops.

(a)   Landscape Ltd employed Peter as a computer programmer until 31 December 2018. On that date he resigned from the company, and set up as a self-employed computer programmer. Peter has continued to work for Landscape Ltd, and during the period 1 January to 5 April 2019 has invoiced them for work done based on an hourly rate of pay. Peter works five days each week at the offices of Landscape Ltd, uses their computer equipment, and does not have any other clients. The computer function is an integral part of Landscape Ltd's business operations. Peter considers himself to be self-employed but Landscape Ltd's accountant is not sure if this is correct.

(b)   On 15 March 2019 Landscape Ltd dismissed Simon, the manager of their shop in Manchester, and gave him a lump sum redundancy payment of £55,000. This amount include statutory redundancy pay of £2,400, payment in lieu of notice of £1,500, and £5,000 for agreeing not to work for a rival company. The balance of the payment was compensation for loss of office, and £10,000 of this was not paid until 31 May 2019.

(c)   Trevor is one of the Landscape Ltd's shareholders, and is not a director or employee of the company. On 6 April 2018 Landscape Ltd provided Trevor with a new motor car that had a CO_2 emissions figure of 170g/km and that had an original list price of £14,000. No private petrol was provided. On 1 July 2018 Landscape Ltd made an interest free loan of £40,000 to Trevor. He repaid £25,000 of the loan on 31 August 2018, and the balance of the loan was written off on 31 March 2019.

(d)   On 1 October 2018 Landscape Ltd opened a new shop in Cambridge, and assigned three employees from the London shop to work there on a temporary basis.

   (1)   Ursula is to work in Cambridge for a period of 18 months. Her ordinary commuting is a daily total of 90 miles, and her daily total from home to Cambridge to home again is 40 miles. She uses her private motor car for business mileage.

   (2)   Violet was initially due to work in Cambridge for a period of 30 months, but this was reduced to a period of 20 months on 1 January 2019. Violet walks to work whereas the cost of her train fare from home to Cambridge is £30 per day. This is paid by Landscape Ltd.

   (3)   Wilma is to work in Cambridge for a period of six months. Her ordinary commuting is a daily total of 30 miles, and her daily total from home to Cambridge is 150 miles. Wilma passes the London shop on her daily journey to Cambridge. She uses her private motor car for business mileage.

   All three employees worked at Cambridge for 120 days during 2018/19. Landscape Ltd pays a mileage allowance of 41p per mile for business use.

(e)   Landscape Ltd is considering setting up a share incentive plan to reward its key employees. The company would like to know how many tax and NIC free shares it can give to each employee and how long the employees concerned must hold the shares for in order to obtain this advantage.

Required

Explain the income tax implications arising from the payments and benefits that have been made or provided by Landscape Ltd to Peter, Simon, Trevor, Ursula, Violet and Wilma. Your answer should be confined to the implications for 2018/19 and should assume that Landscape Ltd meets the definition of a close company.   **(25 marks)**

Marks for this question will be allocated on the basis of:

6 marks to (a)
4 marks to (b)
4 marks to (c)
7 marks to (d)
4 marks to (e)

Approaching the answer

You should read through the requirement before working through and annotating the question as we have done so that you are aware of what things you are looking for.

Landscape Ltd is an unquoted trading company that operates a nationwide chain of retail shops.

Employment v self employment

(a) Landscape Ltd employed Peter as a computer programmer until 31 December 2018. On that date he resigned from the company, and set up as a **self-employed** computer programmer. Peter has

Suggest self-employed

continued to work for Landscape Ltd, and during the period 1 January to 5 April 2019 has

Suggest employee

invoiced them for work done based on an **hourly rate of pay**. Peter works **five days each week at the offices of Landscape Ltd**, **uses their computer equipment**, and **does not have any other clients**.

Suggest employee

Suggest employee

The computer function is **an integral part** of Landscape Ltd's business operations. Peter now

Suggest employee

considers himself to be self-employed but Landscape Ltd's accountant is not sure if this is the correct interpretation.

(b) On 15 March 2019 Landscape Ltd dismissed Simon, the manager of their shop in Manchester, and gave him a **lump sum redundancy payment of £55,000**. This amount includes

£30,000 exempt if _ex gratia_

statutory redundancy pay of £2,400, **payment in lieu of notice** of £1,500, and

£30k exempt

£5,000 for **agreeing not to work for a rival company**. The balance of the payment

Taxable

Taxable

was compensation for loss of office, and £10,000 of this was not paid until

31 May 2019. **Taxed 19/20**

(c) Trevor is one of the Landscape Ltd's shareholders, and is not **a director or an employee** of the

Calculate benefit

company. On 6 April 2018 Landscape Ltd provided Trevor with

Participator taxed on distribution

a **new motor car** that had a CO_2 emissions figure of 170g/km and that had an original list price of

Calculate benefit

£14,000. No private petrol was provided. On 1 July 2018 Landscape Ltd made an **interest free loan** of £40,000 to Trevor. He repaid £25,000 of the loan on 31 August 2018, and the balance of the loan

was **written off** on 31 March 2019.

Taxable

(d) On 1 October 2018 Landscape Ltd opened a new shop in Cambridge, and assigned three

Travel deductible

employees from the London shop to work there on a **temporary basis**.

(1) Ursula is to work in Cambridge for a period of **18 months**. Her ordinary commuting is a

Temporary

daily total of 90 miles, and her daily total from home to Cambridge to home again is 40

miles. She uses her **private motor car for business mileage**.

Approved mileage rates

(2) Violet was initially due to work in Cambridge for a period of 30 months, [Not temporary] but this was reduced to a period of 20 months on 1 January 2019. Violet walks to work whereas the cost of her train fare from home to Cambridge is £30 per day. This is paid by Landscape Ltd.

[Temporary] (pointing to "30 months")

[Not temporary] (pointing to "30 months")

(3) Wilma is to work in Cambridge for a period of six months. **[Temporary]** Her ordinary commuting is a daily total of 30 miles, and her daily total from home to Cambridge is 150 miles. Wilma passes the London shop on her daily journey to Cambridge. She uses her private motor car for business mileage. **[Approved mileage rates]**

All three employees worked at Cambridge for 120 days using 2018/19. Landscape Ltd pays a mileage allowance of 41 pence per mile for business use.

['Free' shares plus matching and partnership]

(e) Landscape Ltd is considering setting up a share incentive plan in order to reward its key employees. The company would like to know how many tax and NIC free shares it can give to each employee and how long the employees concerned must hold the shares for in order to obtain this advantage.

Required

Explain the income tax implications arising from the payments and benefits that have been made or provided by Landscape Ltd to Peter, Richard, Simon, Trevor, Ursula, Violet and Wilma. Your answer should be confined to the implications for 2018/19 and should assume that Landscape Ltd meets the definition of a close company.

Marks for this question will be allocated on the basis of:

6 marks to (a)
4 marks to (b)
4 marks to (c)
7 marks to (d)
4 marks to (e)

39 Marilyn

Marilyn was widowed on 20 May 2017. Under the terms of the will of her late husband Max she inherited his main residence which became her main residence. In addition Marilyn inherited bank balances and a portfolio of quoted investments, all of which had previously been owned by Max personally. Under Max's will the chattels passed to his brother Mark. Max, who had died suddenly, had made no lifetime gifts. The base cost, probate value and current market value of the items contained in Max's estate are as follows:

	Base cost	Probate value May 2017	Market value February 2019
	£	£	£
Main residence	323,000	430,000	470,000
Quoted investments			
Spiro plc 10,000 ordinary shares	50,000		
quoted at		685-677	635-647
with bargains marked at		690, 670, 675	630, 642, 641
Unit trusts	50,000	60,300	81,000
Unit trusts contained in ISAs	40,000	48,800	67,600
Bank deposits contained in ISAs	9,000	11,000	11,300
Bank deposit account	20,000	20,000	20,000
Chattels			
Chirico painting – Creation	4,000	5,000	7,000
Rene writing desk	8,000	7,000	4,000
Beckman's Diary – first edition	3,500	3,000	4,500

Marilyn also has £33,400 on deposit at Berkley's Bank, unit trust units invested in stocks and shares ISAs valued at £145,000 and a cash ISA of £10,600.

Marilyn's will leaves her estate equally to her twin sons, Douglas and Archie, aged 24, absolutely. She is concerned about the exposure to inheritance tax in the event of her death.

Required

(a) Calculate the inheritance tax liability that arose on Max's estate as a result of his death on 20 May 2017 and that which would arise on Marilyn's estate if she were to die in February 2019. Assume that no claims are made which might reduce the inheritance tax liability on either estate.

(8 marks)

(b) Advise Marilyn about any beneficial claims that may be made to reduce the inheritance tax liability on her death. **(9 marks)**

(c) State how Marilyn can retain the tax benefits on the ISA investments owned by Max at his death.

(1 mark)

(Total = 18 marks)

Approaching the answer

You should read through the requirement before working through and annotating the question as we have done so that you are aware of what things you are looking for.

Spouse exemption

Marilyn was widowed on 20 May 2017. Under the terms of the will of her late husband Max she inherited his main residence which became her main residence. In addition Marilyn inherited bank balances and a portfolio of quoted investments, all of which had previously been owned by Max personally. Under Max's will,

Taxable?

the chattels passed to his brother Mark. Max, who had died suddenly, had made no lifetime gifts. The base cost, probate value and current market value of the items contained in Max's estate are as follows:

	Base cost £	Probate value May 2017 £	Market value February 2019 £
Main residence	323,000	430,000	470,000
Quoted investments			
Spiro plc 10,000 ordinary shares	50,000		
quoted at		685-677	635-647
with bargains marked at		690, 670, 675	630, 642, 641
Unit trusts	50,000	60,300	81,000
Unit trusts contained in ISAs	40,000	48,800	67,600
Bank deposits contained in ISAs	9,000	11,000	11,300
Bank deposit account	20,000	20,000	20,000
Chattels			
Chirico painting – Creation	4,000	5,000	7,000
Rene writing desk	8,000	7,000	4,000
Beckman's Diary – first edition	3,500	3,000	4,500

Lowest of
(i) ¼ up
(ii) Average highest and lowest marked bargain

Marilyn also has £33,400 on deposit at Berkley's Bank, unit trust with units invested in stocks and shares ISAs valued at £145,000 and a cash ISA of £10,600.

All subject to IHT

Marilyn's will leaves her estate equally to her twin sons, Douglas and Archie, aged 24, absolutely. She is concerned about her exposure to inheritance tax in the event of her death.

Required

(a) Calculate the inheritance tax liability that arose on Max's estate as a result of his death on 20 May 2017 and that which would arise on Marilyn's estate if she were to die February 2019. Assume that no claims are made which might reduce the inheritance tax liability on either estate.

Transfer of unused nil rate bands

(8 marks)

(b) Advise Marilyn about any beneficial claims that may be made to reduce the inheritance tax liability on her death. **(9 marks)**

(c) State how Marilyn can retain the tax benefits on the ISA investments owned by Max at his death. **(1 mark)**

(Total = 18 marks)

1 Eric and Melanie

> **Tutorial note.** By this stage you should be proficient at setting up an income tax computation in three columns. Watch out for the savings income and dividend nil rate bands. This question also tests a new area in Advanced Taxation (ATX – UK) – tax reducers for investments – and introduces an element of tax planning which will usually be found in questions in Advanced Taxation (ATX – UK).

(a) (i) *Eric*

	Non-savings income £	Savings income £	Total £
Taxable trade profits	102,900		
Bank interest		2,000	
Total income	102,900	2,000	104,900
Less qualifying interest	(1,000)		
Net income	101,900	2,000	103,900
Less personal allowance (W1)	(9,900)		
Taxable income	92,000	2,000	94,000

Tax

	£
Non-savings income	
£34,500 × 20%	6,900
£57,500 (92,000 – 34,500) × 40%	23,000
Savings income	
£500 × 0% (higher rate taxpayer)	0
£1,500 (2,000 – 500) × 40%	600
	30,500
Less: tax reducer	
VCT £11,000 × 30%	(3,300)
Tax liability/tax payable	27,200

(ii) *Melanie*

	Non-savings income £	Dividend Income £	Total £
Earnings	155,415		
Dividends		2,000	
Taxable income	155,415	2,000	157,415

No personal allowance is available as net income exceeds £123,700.

Tax

	£
Non-savings income	
£34,500 × 20%	6,900
£115,500 (150,000 – 34,500) × 40%	46,200
£5,415 (155,415 – 150,000) × 45%	2,437
Dividend Income	
£2,000 × 0%	0
Tax liability	55,537
Less PAYE	(53,000)
Tax payable	2,537

Note. Interest on the National Savings & Investments Certificates is exempt from income tax.

(b) The total income will be split 50:50 between Eric and Melanie if no declaration of underlying interests is made.

The tax liability would be:

	£
Eric £6,000 × 40%	2,400
Add tax on reduction in personal allowance (W2)	1,200
Melanie £6,000 × 45%	2,700
Total extra tax	6,300

It would be better for the cottage to be bought by Melanie as despite the additional income being taxed at 45%, this is lower than Eric's effective rate of 60%. If Eric wished to have some interest in the cottage he could be given a notional 5% (say) as this would only have a marginal extra tax cost. A declaration for this treatment, to tax income in terms of their actual interests, would need to be made. If Eric's other income increases in future, such that the personal allowance is fully abated before taking account of the extra income, then it may be better for Eric to own the cottage if his income does not reach the higher rate limit.

Workings

1   Personal allowance

	£
Net income as above	103,900
Reduction £(103,900 – 100,000) × 1/2	1,950
Personal allowance £(11,850 – 1,950)	9,900

2

	£
Net income including rent	109,900
Reduction £(109,900 – 100,000) × 1/2	4,950
Personal allowance £(11,850 – 4,950)	6,900

So there is a tax increase resulting from the further loss of personal allowance of £9,900 – £6,900 = £3,000 × 40% = £1,200.

(c)   *EIS investment*

Assuming the shares are subscribed for the initial investment will qualify for EIS relief at the rate of 30%. In this case the interest paid on the bank loan will not qualify for tax relief. Her outlay over five years will be:

	£
Subscription for shares	12,000
Interest on bank loan £12,000 × 8% × 5	4,800
Less tax reducer on EIS shares £12,000 × 30% tax reducer	(3,600)
Net outlay	13,200

Purchase of 10% stake

In this case the bank interest paid will be allowed as qualifying interest, but the dividends received will be liable to additional rate tax since her existing dividends use her dividend nil rate band. Her outlay over five years will be as follows:

	£	£
Subscription for shares		12,000
Interest on bank loan £12,000 × 8% × 5		4,800
Less: dividends received £1,200 × 5	6,000	
additional rate tax £6,000 × 38.1%	(2,286)	
		(3,714)
Less tax relief on qualifying interest £4,800 × 45%		(2,160)
Net outlay		10,926

2 Lee and Harry

> **Note.** Although you are asked to reply by email, you must remember that you are writing to a client and present a structured reply.

(a) **To:**   Lee@red.co.uk
From: An Advisor@taxadvice.co.uk
Date: [   ]
Re: Pension advice

Thank you for your email about pension advice. My answers to your questions are as follows:

(1)   If you opt out of your new employer's workplace pension scheme, you could start a pension with a financial institution such as a bank or insurance company. However, your employer would probably not contribute to private pension arrangements so you need to bear this in mind when considering whether or not to opt out of your employer's scheme.

A money purchase scheme is one where the value of your pension benefits depends on the value of the investments in the pension scheme at the date that you start to receive pension benefits. This is distinct from a defined benefits scheme where the pension benefits are defined from the outset. If you decide to use private pension arrangements, these are also likely to be money purchase arrangements.

(2)   You can contribute an amount up to your earnings into the pension scheme and obtain tax-relief on those contributions (although the annual allowance which I explain below, effectively limits relief). You can also make any amount of further contributions, for example out of capital, but these will not obtain initial tax relief. However, since there is no income tax or capital gains tax payable by a pension fund, it may still be beneficial for such extra contributions to be made into this tax-exempt fund.

In addition, your employer can make any amount of contributions provided these are at least the minimum prescribed by law and provided that the tax authorities are happy that such contributions are wholly and exclusively for the purposes of the employer's trade.

The annual allowance limits the inputs that can be put into the pension fund and still receive tax relief. For 2018/19, this limit is £40,000. However, the annual allowance is reduced if you have adjusted income (basically your employment income without any deductions for pension savings) in excess of £150,000. The reduction is £1 for every £2 by which your adjusted income exceeds £150,000. There is a minimum allowance of £10,000 which will apply if your adjusted income is £210,000 or more.

If you are a member of a pension scheme but do not use your full allowance for a tax year, you can carry forward the excess amount to be used against pension contributions for up to three tax years. The amounts that you contribute and obtain tax relief on, plus any contributions made by your employer, will count towards the annual allowance. If those contributions exceed the annual allowance, there will be a tax charge on the excess which is payable by you. This might be relevant in later years when your earnings may be above the annual allowance limit.

The lifetime allowance limit is the maximum value of the pension fund that you are allowed to build up to provide pension benefits without incurring adverse tax consequences. The lifetime allowance is £1,030,000 in 2018/19. This limit is tested against the value of your pension fund when you receive pension benefits. If your fund exceeds the lifetime allowance at that time, there will be a tax charge of 55% on funds used to provide a lump sum and 25% on funds used to provide a pension income. Although there are no adverse tax consequences if your pension fund exceeds the lifetime allowance other than at the time that pension benefits are received, it would be wise to keep an eye on how your fund is growing so that you can adjust your contributions accordingly so as to keep within the lifetime allowance.

(3)   Your employer will deduct your pension contributions gross from your pay before applying PAYE. This means that tax relief is given automatically at your highest rate of tax and no adjustment is needed in your tax return. As an example, if you contribute £1,000 to your pension and that amount of income would have been taxed at 40%, your pay will be reduced by £1,000 but the amount of tax that would be deducted from your pay would be reduced by £400, so that the net amount of the contribution payable by you would be £600.

The above is only an outline of the basics of pension provision as this is very complex area, so I suggest that we meet once you have decided how you wish to proceed.

AN Advisor

(b)   (i)   *Harry Tax liability 2018/19*

	Non-savings income £
Employment income/Net income/Taxable income (no PA available)	123,700

Tax

	£
£34,500 × 20%	6,900
£(123,700 – 34,500) =89,200 × 40%	35,680
Tax liability	42,580

(ii) *Pension contribution*

If Harry made a gross pension contribution of £23,700 in 2018/19, his adjusted net income would be reduced by this amount which would bring it down to £100,000. This would mean that there is no excess over the income limit and his personal allowance would be available in full.

Harry's tax liability would then be:

	Non-savings income £
Employment income/Net income	123,700
Less personal allowance	(11,850)
Taxable income	111,850

Tax

	£
£34,500 × 20%	6,900
£23,700 × 20% (increased limit)	4,740
£(111,850 – 34,500 – 23,700) = 53,650 × 40%	21,460
Tax liability	33,100

This is a tax saving of (£42,580 – 33,100) = £9,480.

3 Hamburg

(a)

	Non-Savings Income £	Savings income £	Dividend income £	Total £
Income from UK property business (W)	17,085			
Trust income £17,333 × 100/55	31,515			
Interest bank a/c		1,260		
Dividends			18,250	
Net income	48,600	1,260	18,250	68,110
Less personal allowance	(11,850)			
Taxable income	36,750	1,260	18,250	56,260

Tax

	£
Non-savings income	
£34,500 × 20%	6,900
£2,250 (36,750 − 34,500) × 40%	900
Savings income	
£500 × 0% (higher rate taxpayer)	0
£760 (1,260 − 500) × 40%	304
Dividend income	
£2,000 × 0%	0
£16,250 (18,250 − 2,000) × 32.5%	5,281
	13,385
Less property income finance costs tax reducer £(500 + 3,550) × 50% × 20%	(405)
Tax liability	12,980
Less tax deducted on trust income £31,515 × 45%	(14,182)
Tax repayable	(1,202)

Working

	£	£
Rent received		
£2,400 × 8		19,200
Expenses paid		
Finance costs £(500 + 3,550) × 50%	2,025	
Buildings insurance	440	
		(2,465)
Net income		16,735

Hamburg should claim rent a room relief in respect of the letting of the furnished room in his main residence, since this is more beneficial than the normal basis of assessment (£7,850 − £875 = £6,975). This means that Hamburg will be taxed on additional income of £350 (£7,850 − £7,500) from the UK property business.

Total property income £(16,735 + 350)	£17,085

(b) If the cottages are to be treated as furnished holiday lettings, the first condition is that the lettings must be made on a commercial basis with a view to the realisation of profit.

Each property must be available for letting to the public for not less than 210 days in a tax year. Between them, the properties must be let for at least 105 days each in the 210 day period. For example, if the first cottage is let for 135 days in the year, the second cottage must be let for at least 75 days in the year to give an average of 105 days. If one of the cottages satisfies the 105 day test but the aggregation of the other cottage would pull the average down to below 105 days, the landlord can choose to treat the cottage which satisfies the 105 days test as furnished holiday accommodation.

In addition, each property must not normally be in longer term occupation (ie for more than 31 days) for more than 155 days in the year.

If the cottages satisfies these conditions, the income from the lettings is taxed as income from a UK property business but as if the landlord was carrying on a trade (except for the basis period rules). This means that there is no restriction on finance costs, expense relief is available on furniture (cash basis) or capital allowances (accruals basis) (instead of replacement domestic items relief) and the income qualifies as relevant earnings for pension contribution purposes. However, loss relief is restricted to carry forward loss relief against future income from this accommodation.

4 Taker

> **Tutorial note.** The CO_2 emissions of the car are rounded down to 105g/km. The baseline figure for CO_2 emissions given in the Tax Rates and Allowances is 95g/km at which the % is 20%. The % increases by 1% for each 5g/km that this figure is exceeded, ie here to 22%.
>
> Part (b) requires you to compare the after tax effects of different options based on your knowledge of the benefits rules.

(a)

	£	£
Salary		50,000
Car £20,000 × 22%		4,400
Fuel £23,400 × 22% (partial contribution gives no reduction)		5,148
Mobile telephone – exempt		0
Use of digital camera £600 × 20%		120
Loan – exempt (does not exceed £10,000)		0
Workplace nursery – exempt		0
Cake for birthday – exempt (trivial benefit)		0
		59,668
Less: professional subscriptions	225	
golf club: fails wholly, exclusively, and necessarily test	0	
		(225)
Earnings		59,443

(b) *Company car*

If Taker chooses the company car he will be charged 40% income tax on a car benefit of £3,250, ie a cost of £1,300 per tax year.

If Taker accepts the higher salary the position will be:

	£
Extra salary	3,000
Less tax @ 40%	(1,200)
	1,800
Add mileage allowance 6,000 × 40p	2,400
Add tax relief on expenses claim 6,000 × (45p – 40p) × 40%	120

Net additional income from company	4,320
Less running costs (excluding private use fuel) (2,200 – 500)	(1,700)
Less depreciation (15,000 – 5,000) × 1/3	(3,333)
Less extra interest paid £1,800 × 1/3	(600)
Net cost per tax year	(1,313)

Taking the additional salary would only cost Taker an extra £13, so the decision should be made on non-cash flow grounds.

Note. The cost of private use fuel is excluded from running costs as it would also be a cost of accepting the company car.

Company flat

If Taker moves to rented accommodation for three years the position is as follows:

	£
Relocation cost paid	12,000
Less tax on excess (12,000 – 8,000) @ 40%	(1,600)
	10,400
Net rent on old house £6,000 × 3 × (100 – 40)%	10,800
Less rent paid £4,000 × 3	(12,000)
Net inflow (before actual relocation costs)	9,200

If Taker moves to the company flat for three years the position is as follows:

	£
Relocation cost paid (not taxable)	6,000
Less tax on benefit of company flat £(2,500 + (120,000 – 75,000) × 2.5%) × 3 × 40%	(4,350)
	1,650
Net rent on old house £(6,000 + 1,000) × 3 × (100 – 40)%	12,600
Net inflow (before actual relocation costs)	14,250

If Taker chooses to rent accommodation he will be £(14,250 – 9,200) = £5,050 worse off over three years and will also have to pay an extra £2,000 in relocation costs. The relative merits of the different accommodation must also be taken into account.

5 Poster plc

> **Tutorial note.** Part (a) is revision of the basic rules of NICs for an employee which should be familiar from your Taxation (TX – UK) studies.
>
> Part (b) illustrates how different payments and benefits can have different NIC implications.

(a) *Albert*

	£
Employee's contributions	
Total earnings exceed UEL	
£(46,350 – 8,424) = £37,926 × 12% (main)	4,551
£(53,500 – 46,350) = £7,150 × 2% (additional)	143
Total employee's contributions	4,694
Employer's contributions	
£(53,500 – 8,424) = £45,076 × 13.8%	6,220
Class 1A contributions	
£(4,500 + 750) = £5,250 × 13.8%	724

(b) (i) A week on a health farm. This is a payment in kind and Poster plc will be liable to Class 1A NICs on each place, at a cost of £2,000 × 13.8% = £276. There will be no NICs for the employee.

(ii) A week's sailing on a yacht chartered by the employee. This is the payment of the employee's personal liability and so is liable to Class 1 NICs. Each employee's share of the bill is £(5,000 + 1,000)/3 = £2,000 and Class 1 NICs for each employee will be £2,000 ×

12% = £240, or £2,000 × 2% = £40 if the upper earnings limit is exceeded. Poster plc will be liable to employer's Class 1 NICs, at a cost of £2,000 × 13.8% = £276 per employee.

(iii)   A voucher which may be exchanged for a holiday at a high street travel agent. Vouchers are liable to Class 1 NICs even if they cannot be exchanged for cash. The cost to the employee will be £2,000 × 12% = £240, or £2,000 × 2% = £40 if the upper earnings limit is exceeded. Poster plc will be liable to employer's Class 1 NICs, at a cost of £2,000 × 13.8% = £276 per employee.

(iv)   Payment of £1,500 cash. This is liable to employee's Class 1 NICs of £1,500 × 12% = £180 per employee, or £1,500 × 2% = £30 if the upper earnings limit is exceeded. Poster plc will be liable to employer's Class 1 NICs, at a cost of £1,500 × 13.8% = £207 per employee.

6 Envirotech plc

Tutorial note. You need to identify which type of share scheme is appropriate for the particular needs of the employer. In this case, the Share Incentive Plan would best fit the requirements of the employer.

Our address

Your address

Date

Dear Colin,

Thank you for your letter, I shall reply to your queries in turn.

Bonus scheme

There is indeed a tax advantaged scheme, the Share Incentive Plan (SIP) which can be used to reward employees with shares. I set out the main features of the scheme below.

The company establishes a UK trust which acquires shares and appropriates them to employees in accordance with the plan. These shares are free of charge ('free shares'). The value of these free shares cannot exceed £3,600 to any employee in any tax year (although the award can be less). These free shares must stay in the trust for a period of five years if the award is to be completely free of income tax in the hands of the employee. If the employee removes the shares between three and five years after appropriation, there is an income tax charge on the value of the shares at award (or at withdrawal if lower). If the employee removes the shares from the trust before three years have elapsed, there will be an income tax charge on the value of the shares at the date of withdrawal.

The 'free shares' could replace your existing cash bonus scheme. The SIP provisions provide further incentives to your employees to invest in the company as outlined below.

'Partnership shares'

Employees who are awarded free shares can purchase up to £1,800 worth of 'partnership shares' from their pre-tax salary. Thus, for example, an employee can authorise Envirotech plc to deduct up to £150 per month from gross salary. This money is passed to the trustees who then acquire shares on behalf of the employee.

The income tax rules on the withdrawal of partnership shares from the trust are the same as the rules for the free shares.

'Matching shares'

Where an employee buys partnership shares, the company can award free 'matching shares'. The ratio of matching shares to partnership shares must be specified and cannot exceed 1:2 (ie the maximum value of 'matching shares' award to an employee in any tax year will not exceed £3,600).

The income tax rules on withdrawal of these shares from the trust are the same as for free and partnership shares.

'Dividend shares'

Employees can opt to reinvest the dividends on their SIP shares to acquire further shares. Any such dividends reinvested are not treated as taxable income for the participant.

The company may specify what percentage of dividends can be used to acquire dividend shares.

General Conditions

All employees (full or part-time) must be invited to participate in the scheme. Employees with less than 18 months service can be excluded.

The shares must be ordinary shares of a class listed or a recognised stock exchange, fully paid up and not redeemable.

An employee can only participate in one SIP in any given tax year.

Share options

As the options granted to Derek were not tax-advantaged, Derek will have an income tax charge at the date he exercised his options. You will see from the Appendix attached that his income tax liability will be £94,500 since Derek is a 45% taxpayer.

Assuming Derek sells his shares in the very near future, he will have no CGT to pay as his allowable cost is effectively equal to the market value of the shares at the date of exercise. If he retains the shares, any growth will be subject to CGT.

Retirement bonus

It is likely that the £30,000 'thank you' bonus will be taxable in full and will not be eligible for the usual exemption given to ex-gratia payments.

HMRC may argue that the payment is made in return for services thereby making the bonus taxable under normal principles. It is therefore important that any documentation stresses that the payment is ex-gratia and not part of Derek's contractual entitlement.

However, failing this, HMRC could contend that as a payment is made to an employee 'at or near the age of retirement' the payment should be taxable in full in the same way as a benefit under a non-registered pension scheme.

I hope this deals with your queries but do please let me know if I can be of further help.

Yours sincerely

Brian

Appendix

Derek

	£
Tax on exercise of share options	
100,000 × £(3.60 − 1.50)	210,000
Income tax @ 45%	94,500

7 Helen and Gemma

> **Tutorial note.** Part (a) of this question tests both the basis of assessment rules which should be familiar from Taxation (TX – UK) and the change of accounting date procedure which is a new topic in Advanced Taxation (ATX – UK). Part (b) is an example of how the rules on cessation of a sole trade can be used in a tax-efficient manner.

(a)

	£
2013/14 (1.7.13 to 5.4.14)	
9/12 × £36,000	27,000
2014/15 (1.7.13 to 30.6.14)	36,000
2015/16 (1.7.14 to 30.6.15)	48,000

Overlap profits of £27,000 arise as a result of the trade profits accruing in the 9 months to 5.4.14 being taxed in both 2013/14 and in 2014/15.

There is a change of accounting date which results in one long period of account ending during 2016/17. As a result the basis period is the 15 months to 30 September 2016 and 3 months' worth of the overlap profits can be relieved:

2016/17	£
Basis period (1.7.15–30.9.16)	60,000
Less overlap profits £27,000 × 3/9	(9,000)
	51,000

2017/18 (year to 30.9.17)	£30,000

2018/19 (1.10.17 to 31.12.18)	£
Year to 30.9.18	24,000
Three months to 31.12.18	10,000
Less overlap profits £(27,000 – 9,000)	(18,000)
	16,000

The trade ceases during 2018/19 so the basis period for this year runs from the end of the last basis period to the date of cessation. Overlap profits which were not relieved on the change of accounting date are relieved against this final year's taxable profits.

(b) **Sale on 31 March 2019**

Taxable trading profits

Y/e 30.4.18

	£
Profits 12 × £2,300	27,600

P/e 31.3.19

	£
Profits 11 × £2,300	25,300
Less overlap profits	(1,100)
Taxable trading profit	24,200

Income tax 2018/19

Final year of trading: basis period 1 May 2017 to 31 March 2019.

	£
Trading income £(27,600 + 24,200)/Net income	51,800
Less personal allowance	(11,850)
Taxable income	39,950

(a) Income tax computation for Arrol

	Non-savings income £	Savings income £	Total £
Earnings: salary	30,000		
car benefit £19,370 × 34% (W1)	6,586		
fuel benefit £23,400 × 34%	7,956		
Bank interest		300	
Building society interest		308	
Total income	44,542	608	45,150
Less loss relief against general income (W2)	(44,542)	(608)	(45,150)
Net income	0	0	0
Income tax liability: nil			

Workings

1 Car and fuel benefit

167 g/km is rounded down to 165 g/km. Excess over base figure 165 – 95 = 70 g/km.

70/5 = 14. Taxable % = 20 + 14 = 34%.

Partial contributions towards the cost of petrol do not reduce the fuel benefit.

2 The loss available for relief

	£
Loss in y/e 30.4.19	30,834
Capital allowances: AIA £(12,800 + 11,960)	24,760
	55,594
Loss in 2018/19: £55,594 × 11/12 (1.5.18–5.4.19)	£50,961

(b) Income tax computation for Louisa

	Non-savings income £	Savings income £	Total £
Earnings	8,985		
Building society interest		6,735	
NS&I interest		2,832	
Net income	8,985	9,567	18,552
Less personal allowance	(8,985)	(2,865)	(11,850)
Taxable income	0	6,702	6,702

Income tax		£	£
Savings starting rate band	5,000 × 0%		0
Savings income nil rate band	1,000 × 0%		0
Basic rate band: savings income	702 × 20%		140
	6,702		140

(c) The loss of 2018/19 remaining unrelieved

	£
2018/19 loss available for relief	50,961
Less used in 2018/19 (part (a))	(45,150)
Unrelieved balance	5,811

Relief for the remaining loss may be obtained:

(i) In 2017/18 against Arrol's general income

(ii) Under early trade losses relief against Arrol's general income for 2015/16, 2016/17 and 2017/18 in that order, or

(iii) By carry forward loss relief against future profits of the practice.

Income tax:		
£34,500 @ 20%		6,900
£5,450 @ 40%		2,180
Income tax liability		9,080

Class 4 national insurance contributions 2018/19

	£
Trading income	51,800
Class 4 NICs:	
£(46,350 – 8,424) = 37,926 @ 9%	3,413
£(51,800 – 46,350) = 5,450 @ 2%	109
Class 4 NICs	3,522

Income tax 2019/20

	£
Property business income/Net income	27,850
Less personal allowance	(11,850)
Taxable income	16,000
Income tax:	
£16,000 @ 20%	3,200

Class 4 national insurance contributions 2019/20

Nil as Gemma does not trade in this year.

Sale on 30 April 2019

Taxable trading profits

	£
Y/e 30.4.18	27,600
Profits 12 × £2,300	

	£
Y/e 30.4.19	27,600
Profits 12 × £2,300	(1,100)
Less overlap profits	26,500
Taxable trading profit	

Income tax 2018/19

Current year basis: basis period 1 May 2017 to 30 April 2018.

	£
Trading income/Net income	27,600
Less personal allowance	(11,850)
Taxable income	15,750

	£
Income tax:	
£15,750 @ 20%	3,150

Class 4 national insurance contributions 2018/19

	£
Trading income	27,600
Class 4 NIC:	
£(27,600 – 8,424) = 19,176 @ 9%	1,726

Income tax 2019/20

	£
Trading income	26,500
Property business income	27,850
Net income	54,350
Less personal allowance	(11,850)
Taxable income	42,500
Income tax:	
£34,500 @ 20%	6,900
£8,000 @ 40%	3,200
Income tax liability	10,100

Class 4 national insurance contributions 2019/20

	£
Trading income	26,500
Class 4 NIC:	
£(26,500 – 8,424) = 18,076 @ 9%	1,627

Summary

	Sale on 31.3.19 £	Sale on 30.4.19 £
Trading income (before overlap relief)	52,900	55,200
Property business income	27,850	27,850
Less: income tax 2018/19	(9,080)	(3,150)
income tax 2019/20	(3,200)	(10,100)
Class 4 NIC 2018/19	(3,522)	(1,726)
Class 4 NIC 2019/20	(0)	(1,627)
Income after tax and Class 4 NIC	64,948	66,447

Gemma should therefore sell her business on 30 April 2019 to maximise her income after income tax and class 4 NIC.

Tutorial note

Class 2 NIC contributions would also be a factor in making this decision since four weeks of extra contributions (£12) would be payable if the business continued until 30 April 2019.

8 Sheila

> **Tutorial note.** Watch out for special rate pool assets such as integral features. Use the annual investment allowance first against special rate pool assets for maximum tax efficiency.

	AIA £	Main pool £	Special rate pool £	Private use car £	Allowances £
p/e 31 March 2019					
Additions qualifying for AIA					
1.3.19 Integral feature	51,100				
AIA 3/12 × £200,000	(50,000)				50,000
Transfer balance to special rate pool	1,100		1,100		

	AIA £	Main pool £	Special rate pool £	Private use car £	Allowances £
Additions not given AIA		10,000			
4.1.19 Plant					
WDA @ 18% × 3/12		(450)			
WDA @ 8% × 3/12			(22)		
TWDV c/f		9,550	1,078		50,4...
Allowances					
y/e 31 March 2020					
Additions qualifying for AIA					
25.9.19 Van	11,800				
15.10.19 Plant	191,000				
	202,800				200,000
	(200,000)				
AIA	2,800	2,800			
Transfer balance to main pool		12,350			
Additions not qualifying for AIA				18,600	
15.11.19 Car		(2,223)			2,223
WDA @ 18%			(86)		86
WDA @ 8%				(1,488) × 65%	967
WDA @ 8%		10,127	992	17,112	
TWDV c/f					203,276
Allowances					
y/e 31 March 2021		10,127	992	17,112	
TWDV b/f					
Additions qualifying for AIA	10,000				10,000
30.11.20 Plant	(10,000)				
AIA					
Addition not qualifying for AIA		9,000			
30.3.21 Car		19,127			3,443
		(3,443)			992
WDA @ 18%			(992)		890
WDA small pool				(1,369) × 65%	
WDA @ 8%		15,684	0	15,743	15,325
TWDV c/f					
Allowances					

9 Arrol and Louisa

> **Tutorial note.** The disadvantage of a loss relief claim against general income can be that it wastes the personal allowance, demonstrated here in the current year. Note how restricting the capital allowances claimed can avoid the wastage of personal allowances.

A claim against general income for 2017/18 or early years trade losses relief will obtain tax relief at the basic rate (as Arrol would have been a basic rate taxpayer given the probable level of investment income, and the reduced salary, in earlier years).

Carry forward loss relief will obtain tax relief in 2020/21 against the trading profits of the year to 30 April 2020 at the higher rate as Arrol's income will exceed the basic rate band.

£24,760 of the loss derives from Arrol making the maximum claim to capital allowances. A proportion of this loss is wasted by being set against income covered by the personal allowance and the savings income nil rate band in the current year. Arrol should consider restricting his claim for capital allowances to avoid this wastage. Capital allowances not claimed are effectively carried forward in the pool of expenditure, and although they can then only be relieved on a reducing balance basis, relief will be obtained at a higher rate.

10 ABC Partnership and Ernie

> **Tutorial note.** Always divide the profits of a period of account between the partners before you begin allocating them to tax years. In part (b) do not forget to consider national insurance as well as tax, and also non-tax advantages/disadvantages.

(a)

	Total £	A £	B £	C £	D £
Year ending 5 April 2016					
Salaries	37,000	15,000	12,000	10,000	
PSR (balance) (2:2:1)	65,000	26,000	26,000	13,000	
Total	102,000	41,000	38,000	23,000	
Year ending 5 April 2017					
6 April to 5 July					
Salaries	9,250	3,750	3,000	2,500	
PSR (balance) (2:2:1)	42,750	17,100	17,100	8,550	
Total	52,000	20,850	20,100	11,050	
6 July to 5 April					
Salaries	16,500		9,000	7,500	
PSR (balance) (3:2)	139,500		83,700	55,800	
Total	156,000		92,700	63,300	
Totals for the year	208,000	20,850	112,800	74,350	
Year ending 5 April 2018					
Salaries	22,000		12,000	10,000	
PSR (balance) (3:2)	104,000		62,400	41,600	
Total	126,000		74,400	51,600	
Year ending 5 April 2019					
6 April to 5 May					
Salaries	1,833		1,000	833	
Balance (3:2)	13,167		7,900	5,267	
Total	15,000		8,900	6,100	
6 May to 5 April					
Salaries	49,500		16,500	16,500	16,500
Balance (6:3:1)	115,500		69,300	34,650	11,550
Total	165,000		85,800	51,150	28,050
Totals for the year	180,000		94,700	57,250	28,050

Taxable trade profits are as follows.

	A £	B £	C £	D £
Year				
2015/16	41,000	38,000	23,000	
2016/17	20,850	112,800	74,350	
2017/18		74,400	51,600	
2018/19		94,700	57,250	28,050

(b) (i) If Freda is employed on a salary of £25,650 a year the tax and NI costs and savings will be:

	£
Employer's NI £(25,650 – 8,424) × 13.8%	2,377
Less employment allowance	(3,000)
	0
Employee's NI £(25,650 – 8,424) × 12%	2,067
Income tax payable by Freda £(25,650 – 11,850) = £13,800 × 20%	2,760
Income tax saved by Eric £25,650 × 40%	(10,260)
Class 4 NI saved by Eric £25,650 × 2%	(513)
Total saving	(5,946)

If Freda is taken on as a partner with a one-third profit share, ie £25,650, the tax and NI costs and savings will be:

	£
Class 4 NI payable by Freda £(25,650 – 8,424) = £17,226 × 9%	1,550
Class 2 NI payable by Freda £2.95 × 52	153
Income tax payable by Freda £(25,650 – 11,850) = £13,800 × 20%	2,760
Income tax saved by Eric £25,650 × 40%	(10,260)
Class 4 NI saved by Eric £25,650 × 2%	(513)
Total saving	(6,310)

In this case the savings are £364 (£6,310 – £5,946) greater because the reduction in NI contributions due, even after deducting the employment allowance.

(ii) If Ernie increased Freda's share of partnership profits so that Ernie did not pay higher rate tax, the savings would be maximised. Freda's share of profits would be £(76,950 – 34,500 – 11,850) = £30,600. The savings would be:

	£
Class 4 NI payable by Freda £(30,600 – 8,424) = £22,176 × 9%	1,996
Class 2 NI payable by Freda £2.95 × 52	153
Income tax payable by Freda £(30,600 – 11,850) = £18,750 × 20%	3,750
Income tax saved by Eric £30,600 × 40%	(12,240)
Class 4 NI saved by Eric £30,600 × 2%	(612)
Total saving	(6,953)

Note that as Ernie's share of profits is not reduced below £46,350 there is no Class 4 NI advantage in increasing Freda's share of profits because she would pay Class 4 NI at 9% whilst Ernie would only save Class 4 NI at 2%.

In addition to the tax and NI advantages/disadvantages of taking Freda into partnership as opposed to employing her there are other considerations. These include the unlimited liability of partners, employment law, PAYE obligations and an employee's entitlement to contributory benefits (such as Jobseeker's Allowance).

BPP
LEARNING MEDIA

11 Maria, Felix and Susan

> **Tutorial note**. Remember that the tax tables contain useful information to help you determine whether an individual is UK resident or not in a tax year. The new rules on deemed domicile are highly examinable. You need to be able to determine the taxpayer's tax status and then compute income tax as a result of that status.

(a) Maria is arriving in the UK. She is not automatically non-UK resident during 2018/19 as she is in the UK for 46 days or more. She also does not work full time overseas.

Maria is not automatically UK resident during 2018/19 as she is not in the UK for 183 days or more, she has a home outside the UK in which she is present for at least 30 days, and she does not work in the UK.

Maria's residence status will therefore be determined by 'sufficient ties'. Since she is in the UK for between 121 and 182 days, she will be UK resident if she has 2 UK ties. She does have 2 UK ties since she has close family (her spouse) in the UK and accommodation in the UK which is available to her for at least 91 days in the tax year in which she spends at least one night.

Maria is therefore UK resident in the tax year 2018/19.

(b) (i) In the tax year 2018/19, Felix is UK resident, not UK domiciled but UK deemed domiciled since he has been resident in the UK for at least 15 of the 20 tax years immediately preceding this tax year. He is therefore liable to UK income tax on his worldwide income on an arising basis.

His income tax liability for the tax year 2018/19 is computed as follows.

	Non-savings income £
UK trading income	15,000
Overseas property business income	135,000
Net income	150,000

No personal allowance available as adjusted net income at least £123,700.

	£
Income tax on non-savings income:	
£34,500 × 20%	6,900
£115,500 (150,000 − 34,500) × 40%	46,200
	53,100

(ii) In the tax year 2018/19, Felix is UK resident, not UK domiciled and not UK deemed domiciled since he was not born in the UK and has not been resident in the UK for at least 15 of the 20 tax years immediately preceding this tax year. He is therefore liable to UK income tax on his UK income on an arising basis and will make a claim for the remittance basis for his overseas income (as this results in a lower total income tax liability). He is liable to the Remittance Basis Charge of £30,000 because he has been resident for 7 of the 9 tax years immediately preceding this tax year (but not yet 12 of the last 14 tax years).

His income tax liability for the tax year 2018/19 is computed as follows.

	Non-savings income
	£
UK trading income	15,000
Overseas property business income remitted	18,000
Net income	33,000

No personal allowance available as Felix claims the remittance basis.

	£
Income tax on non-savings income:	
£33,000 × 20%	6,600
Remittance basis charge	30,000
	36,600

(c) **Susan – Income tax computation 2018/19**

	Non-savings income
	£
UK employment income	33,000
Overseas property business income	14,705
Net income	47,705
Less personal allowance	(11,850)
Taxable income	35,855

	£
Income tax on non-savings income:	
£34,500 × 20%	6,900
£1,355 (35,855 − 34,500) × 40%	542
	7,442
Less DTR (W)	(3,212)
	4,230
Less PAYE	(4,200)
Tax payable	30

Working

UK tax on overseas income:	Non-savings income
	£
Taxable income	35,855
Less overseas property business income	(14,705)
	21,150

Income tax	£
Income tax on non-savings income:	
£21,150 × 20%/Tax on UK taxable income	4,230
Tax on taxable income (above)	(7,442)
UK tax on overseas income	3,212

DTR is lower of:

(1) UK tax on overseas income £3,212
(2) Overseas tax £4,705

12 Sophie

Tutorial note. This question covers the basics of CGT with which you must be completely familiar by the time you sit Advanced Taxation (ATX – UK). You are also required to consider how the CGT liability could have been reduced; there are several basic strategies.

(a)   *Summary*

	Other gains £	Residential property gains £
Painting	47,000	
Holiday cottage		45,000
Two acres of land	15,750	
Less annual exempt amount (best use)		(11,700)
Taxable gains	62,750	33,300
CGT @ 20% on £62,750		12,550
CGT @ 28% on £33,300		9,324
Total CGT		21,874

Workings

1   *Painting*

The costs of sale (auctioneer's costs) can be deducted from the sale proceeds.

	£
Proceeds	50,000
Less costs of sale	(500)
Net proceeds of sale	49,500
Less cost	(2,500)
Gain	47,000

2   *Holiday cottage*

The transfer of the holiday cottage between the spouses is on a no gain/no loss basis. The base cost for Sophie is therefore £40,000. The value of holiday cottage at the transfer is not relevant.

The gain is:

	£
Proceeds	85,000
Less cost	(40,000)
Gain	45,000

3   *Two acres of land*

This is a part disposal of the land. The fraction of cost used is:

$$\frac{\text{Proceeds of sale}}{\text{Proceeds of sale} + \text{value of part remaining}} \times \text{cost}$$

that is: $\dfrac{18,000}{18,000 + 70,000} \times £11,000 = £2,250$

The gain is:

	£
Proceeds	18,000
Less cost	(2,250)
Gain	15,750

4   *JKL plc shares*

	£
Proceeds	20,000
Less cost	(51,000)
Loss	(31,000)

This is a loss on a disposal to a connected person. The loss is only allowable against a gain on a disposal to the same connected person.

(b)   There are several ways in which Sophie's CGT liability could have been reduced.

(i)   Sophie should have sold the JKL plc shares and gifted the proceeds to her son. She would then have generated an allowable loss of £51,000 – £18,000 = £33,000 (assuming she had achieved the same proceeds as did Jason), instead of realising a restricted loss of £31,000 and Jason generating the loss of £2,000 which can only be used if Jason makes capital gains, which is likely to be some time in the future. Sophie would save CGT of £33,000 × 28% (set against residential property gain for best use) = £9,240.

(ii)   Terry has made no capital gains in 2018/19 so his annual exempt amount of £11,700 is unused and not all of his basic rate band is utilised. Sophie could have transferred the holiday cottage back to Terry so that the gain was realised by him thereby saving CGT of £11,700 × 28% = £3,276 plus £(34,500 – 31,000) = £3,500 × (28 – 18)% = £350. However, Sophie would only have saved tax at 20% on her annual exemption instead of 28%, a difference of £11,700 × (28 – 20)% = £936. The overall saving is therefore £(3,276 + 350 – 936) = £2,690.

(iii)   Sophie has made a part disposal of two acres of land. This does not qualify for the small part disposal relief in Sophie's hands as the proceeds of this disposal plus the proceeds of the disposal of the holiday cottage exceed £20,000.

It might, however, have been possible to have transferred the land to Terry so that he could make a disposal which would fall within the limits (provided the holiday cottage is not transferred as recommended in part (ii)). Sophie would transfer the land to Terry (at nil gain nil loss). The disposal by Terry would then fall within the small part disposal rules because the proceeds are less than £20,000 and do not exceed 20% of the market value of the entire holding of land prior to the part disposal. Terry may then deduct the proceeds of the land sold from the base cost of the land retained. Sophie would therefore save CGT of £15,750 × 20% = £3,150.

13 John and Matilda

> **Tutorial note.** The key to a question in parts like this is to ensure that you make an attempt at each individual requirement.

(a)   *Total value due to John on takeover*

	£
Shares 20,000 × £4.90	98,000
Cash 20,000 × £1.60	32,000
	130,000

Cash element exceeds both £3,000 and 5% of £130,000, so there is a part disposal

	£
Disposal proceeds (cash)	32,000
Less cost $\dfrac{32,000}{32,000 + 98,000} \times £40,000$	(9,846)
Gain	22,154
Base cost of Wall plc shares	
£(40,000 – 9,846)	£30,154

(b) If John had received loan stock instead of cash there would not be an immediately chargeable gain. If the corporate bonds were qualifying corporate bonds the gain of £22,154 would be deferred until the QCBs were sold. This would enable John to sell the QCBs in tranches realising sufficient gains to utilise the annual exempt amount over a couple of years, and preserve brought forward losses.

If the bonds are not QCBs the base cost of the original shares would simply be apportioned between the new shares and bonds, and no gain would arise until the bonds were disposed of. Again, this allows for phased disposals.

(c) *Match acquisitions in next 30 days first*

1 October 2018

	£
Disposal proceeds (£42,000 × $\frac{2,000}{3,200}$)	26,250
Less cost	(25,750)
Gain	500

Then match with share pool

15 May 2008

Shares held after bonus issue 1,800 + 1,800 = 3,600

No change to base cost

	£
Disposal proceeds (£42,000 × $\frac{1,200}{3,200}$)	15,750
Less cost (£1,900 × $\frac{1,200}{3,600}$)	(633)
Gain	15,117

The total chargeable gain on the sale of Matilda's shares in Read plc is £15,617 (£500 + £15,117).

(d) *Summary: John*

	£
Gain	22,154
Less loss brought forward	(10,454)
	11,700
Less annual exempt amount	(11,700)
Taxable gains	0
CGT payable	£nil

The losses brought forward are only set against gains to bring the gains down to the annual exempt amount.

Loss carried forward £(16,160 – 10,454)	£5,706

Summary: Matilda

	£
Gain	15,617
Less annual exempt amount	(11,700)
Taxable gains	3,917
CGT payable	
£3,917 × 10% (within unused basic rate band of £34,500 – £20,000 = £14,500)	£392

14 Hazel

> **Tutorial note.** This question requires you to write a report so it is important that you did so. Marks may be specifically allocated for report writing or letter writing skills.

Report

To: Hazel
From: An Advisor
Date: [date]
Subject: Incorporation of your business

(a)   If you sell your business to a company you will make a disposal of all the business's assets. You can avoid an immediate charge to capital gains tax through incorporation relief.

This relief applies automatically where:

- There is a transfer of a going concern
- All assets (or all the assets except cash) are transferred
- The consideration is wholly or partly for shares

An election can be made to disapply the relief, for example if you wished to use another relief (see further below).

(b)   The gains on disposal are wholly deferred against the cost of shares received on incorporation where all of the consideration is received as shares.

If any of the consideration is received in cash (or loan notes or left on a loan account) a proportion of the gain will remain chargeable.

The maximum amount of cash that you could receive without triggering a charge to capital gains tax is £22,500 (see Appendix).

(c)   The disadvantages to incorporation relief are as follows:

- The cost of the shares that you will be able to use when you eventually dispose of the shares will be reduced by the relief given to £63,600 (£132,500 – £68,900).

- You have to transfer all the assets (with the exception of cash) even if you wanted to retain, for example, the freehold shop outside the company

- The transfer of assets (such as the shop) may lead to a double tax charge in the future as corporation tax would be due from the company on the disposal of the asset and then when the proceeds are paid out to you as the shareholder there may be a further tax charge (either income tax or capital gains tax depending on how the proceeds are extracted from the company).

(d)   As an alternative, you could consider gift relief. In this case you would need to gift the business's assets to the company. You would therefore be able to choose which assets to transfer and which to retain, eg the shop.

Gift relief defers your gain by reducing the base cost of the asset for company. The company then has a lower cost when it comes to sell the assets and therefore a higher gain.

Appendix – Maximum non-share consideration to take on incorporation

	£
Total consideration	155,000
Less share consideration (W1)	(132,500)
Cash consideration	22,500

Workings

1 Share consideration

	£
We want relief of (W2):	68,900
Gain before reliefs is:	80,600
Total consideration is:	155,000

Therefore share consideration must be:

$$\frac{68,900}{80,600} \times £155,000$$

£132,500

2 Relief to bring gain to nil

	£
Total gain:	
Goodwill	30,000
Property	50,600
	80,600
Less incorporation relief (balance)	(68,900)
Gain	11,700
Less annual exempt amount	(11,700)
Taxable gain	Nil

15 Wendy, Henry and Robert

> **Tutorial note.** Note the different methods of calculating the post 5 April 2015 gain in part (c)(i).

(a) **Wendy**

The lease

	£
Proceeds	30,750
Less $\dfrac{64.116\,(16\text{ years})}{80.361\,(24\frac{1}{2}\text{ years})} \times £8,000$	(6,383)
Gain	24,367

The percentage for 24½ years is $79.622 + (81.100 - 79.622) \times 6/12 = 80.361$.

(b) **Henry**

2018/19

No CGT event on the damage to the factory.

2019/20

Receipt of compensation is treated as part disposal. The amount not used in restoration is not 'small'. The restoration must also be taken into account.

	£
Amount not used in restoration £(20,000 – 15,000)	5,000
Less cost plus restoration	
$\dfrac{5,000}{5,000 + 250,000} \times £(150,000 + 15,000)$	(3,235)
Gain	1,765

2020/21

Sale of factory

	£
Sale proceeds	260,000
Less cost £(150,000 + 15,000 – 3,235 – 15,000)	(146,765)
Gain	113,235

(c) **Robert**

    (i) *Redacre*

Non-UK resident individuals are subject to capital gains tax on the disposal of interests in UK situated residential property. However, only the gain accruing since 6 April 2015 is chargeable. The default method of computing the gain on 5 October 2019 is as follows:

	£
Proceeds	450,000
Less market value at 5 April 2015	(325,000)
Gain	125,000

However, Robert can elect to use an alternative straight line time apportionment of the gain calculated under normal CGT rules over the whole period of ownership with the part accruing after 5 April 2015 being chargeable. This would result in the following gain:

	£
Proceeds	450,000
Less cost	(150,000)
Gain	300,000

Robert owned the house from 6 April 2006 to 5 October 2019 (13 and a half years). The period from 6 April 2015 to 5 October 2019 is 4 and a half years.

Post 5 April 2015 gain 4.5/13.5 × £300,000	100,000

Robert should therefore make an election to use the straight line time apportionment method.

Robert is also entitled to principal private residence (PPR) relief on Redacre since it had been his main residence. Only the period of ownership after 5 April 2015 has to be considered. However, as Robert is non-UK resident and does not stay overnight at the property for at least 90 days in any tax year, there is no actual occupation taken into account for any of the tax years after 5 April 2015. Nonetheless, Robert is entitled to treat the last 18 months of ownership as if it were a period of occupation. He is also entitled to the annual exempt amount.

Robert's taxable gain will therefore be:

	£
Gain before PPR relief	100,000
Less PPR relief 1.5/4.5	(33,333)
Gain after PPR relief	66,667
Less annual exempt amount	(11,700)
Taxable gain	54,967

    (ii) *Bluesky*

This is a furnished holiday letting and so is a business asset for the purposes of gift relief.

Gift relief is available on a gift to Emily who is a non-UK resident person because the residential property remains within the charge to CGT.

16 Mark and Sarah

Tutorial note. Administration should be a very familiar topic from your previous Taxation (TX – UK) studies. It is also frequently examined in Advanced Taxation (ATX – UK) so you should ensure that you have a thorough knowledge of it.

(a)   *Returns*

For the tax year 2018/19, a tax return must usually be submitted by 31 January 2020 (electronically) or 31 October 2019 (paper).

However, if the notice to file the tax return is issued by HMRC to the taxpayer after 31 July 2019 but on or before 31 October 2019, the latest filing date is the end of three months following the notice if a paper return filed. The latest date for filing electronically remains 31 January 2020. If the notice to file the tax return is issued by HMRC after 31 October 2019, the latest filing date is the end of three months following the notice. This applies whether the return is filed electronically or on paper.

An individual is liable to a penalty where a tax return is filed after the due filing date. The penalty date is the date on which the return will be overdue (ie the date after the due filing date). The initial penalty for late filing of the return is £100.

If the failure continues after the end of the period of three months starting with the penalty date, HMRC may give the individual notice specifying that a daily penalty of £10 is payable for a maximum of 90 days.

If the failure continues after the end of the period of six months starting with the penalty date, a further penalty is payable. This penalty is the greater of 5% of the tax liability which would have been shown in the return and £300.

If the failure continues after the end of the period of 12 months starting with the penalty date, a further penalty is payable. This penalty is determined in accordance with the taxpayer's conduct in withholding information which would enable or assist HMRC in assessing the taxpayer's liability to tax. The penalty is between 5% and 100% of the tax liability which would have been shown on the return depends on the taxpayer's conduct in withholding information which would enable or assist HMRC in assessing the taxpayer's liability to tax. The penalty is computed as follows:

Type of conduct	Penalty
Deliberate and concealed	Greater of: • 100% of tax liability which would have been shown on return; and • £300
Deliberate not concealed	Greater of: • 70% of tax liability which would have been shown on return; and • £300
Any other case (eg careless)	Greater of: • 5% of tax liability which would have been shown on return; and • £300

Self assessment of tax

If the taxpayer files their return electronically, the calculation of the tax liability is made automatically when the return is made online.

If the taxpayer files their return non-electronically on or before 31 October 2019 (or within two months of the notice if the notice is issued after 31 August 2019), the taxpayer may ask HMRC to make the tax calculation. Otherwise, the taxpayer must make the calculation.

Payments of tax

An individual may be required to make payments on account of their income tax and Class 4 NICs liability for 2018/19 on 31 January 2019 and 31 July 2019. A balancing payment of income tax and Class 4 NICs, and the whole of the individual's capital gains tax liability, is due on 31 January 2020. Class 2 NICs will also be due on 31 January 2020.

Payments on account for 2018/19 are required where the individual's income tax and Class 4 NICs due in 2017/18 exceed the amount deducted at source: the excess is called the 'relevant amount'. The payments on account are 50% of the relevant amount for 2017/18. Payments on account are not required if the relevant amount is less than £1,000 nor if the tax deducted at source in 2017/18 was 80% or more of the total tax liability of that year.

The taxpayer may make a claim to reduce their payments on account if they expect their 2018/19 tax liability to be lower than their 2017/18 liability. The payments may be reduced to a stated amount or to nil. The claim must state why the taxpayer believes their liability will be lower. If the eventual liability is more than estimated, interest will be charged on the over-reduction. If the claim was made fraudulently or negligently, a penalty up to the amount of the over-reduction may be imposed.

Interest on overdue tax is charged on all unpaid tax from the due date. Where the balance of the tax due on 31 January 2020 is not paid within 30 days (the penalty date), a penalty for later payment is charged. Where payment is made within five months of the penalty date, the penalty will be 5% of the unpaid tax, rising to 10% where the payment is made more than five months but less than 11 months after the penalty date and 15% thereafter.

(b)   *Mark*

Due dates of tax – 2018/19

Payments made	Paid	No claim to reduce payments on account	Due date
£		£	
4,500	28 February 2019	6,000	31 January 2019
4,500	31 August 2019	6,000	31 July 2019
4,000	31 March 2020	1,000	31 January 2020
13,000		13,000	

Interest due

Payments on account:

	£
£4,500 × 1/12 × 3.00%	11
£4,500 × 1/12 × 3.00%	11
£1,500 × 14/12 × 3.00%	52
£1,500 × 8/12 × 3.00%	30
Final payment:	
£1,000 × 2/12 × 3.00%	5
	109

(c)   Sarah's tax return was prepared in accordance with the practice prevailing at that time. She will therefore be precluded from making a claim for the revised treatment if the court case should go in the taxpayer's favour.

Sarah is, however, able to amend her tax return at any time up until 31 January 2021. She should therefore file an amendment to her return, using the more favourable treatment.

It is likely that HMRC will open a compliance check enquiry into her tax return, thereby enabling them to amend the return should the taxpayer fail in the Courts. Even at that stage Sarah could appeal against any amendment HMRC made on closing a compliance check enquiry if it was likely that the matter would progress to higher courts.

17 Rodin

> **Tutorial note.** This answer follows the 'steps' set out within the text but in a streamlined format which is equally acceptable in the exam.

(a) **IHT paid during Rodin's lifetime was as follows.**

25.12.06

		£
Gift		60,000
Less: A/E (2006/07)		(3,000)
A/E (2005/06) b/f		(3,000)
PET		54,000

This gift was a PET so no lifetime tax was due.

21.1.09

No gross chargeable transfers were made in the seven years prior to 21.1.09 so all of the nil band remained available for use.

This means the IHT paid by Rodin was:

		£
Gift		321,000
Less: A/E (2008/09)		(3,000)
A/E (2007/08) b/f		(3,000)
		315,000

		£
IHT	£312,000 × 0% =	0
	£3,000 × 20/80 =	750
	£315,000	750

The gross chargeable transfer was: £315,000 + £750 = £315,750.

Check: tax £(315,750 − 312,000) = £3,750 × 20% = £750.

20.8.12

		£
Gift		31,000
Less: A/E (2012/13)		(3,000)
A/E (2011/12) b/f		(3,000)
PET		25,000

This was a PET so no lifetime tax was due.

19.2.14

Gross chargeable transfers of £315,750 had been made in the seven years prior to 19.2.14 so £(325,000 − 315,750) = £9,250 of the nil band remains and the lifetime IHT due was:

		£
Gift		91,000
Less: A/E (2013/14)		(3,000)
A/E (2012/13) b/f		(3,000)
		85,000

		£
IHT	£9,250 × 0% =	0
	£75,750 × 20% =	15,150
	£85,000	15,150

1.8.15

	£
Gift	73,000
Less: A/E (2015/16)	(3,000)
A/E (2014/15) b/f	(3,000)
PET	67,000

This was a PET so no lifetime tax was due.

1.9.15

This was an exempt transfer to Rodin's UK domiciled spouse so no lifetime tax was due.

IHT due as a result of death.

As a result of death, IHT will be due on transfers made in the seven years before the death.

Lifetime transfers

25.12.06

This PET was made more than seven years before death, so no IHT arises as a result of death.

21.1.09

Gross transfer	£315,750

This CLT was made more than seven years before death, so no additional IHT arises as a result of death.

20.8.12

Gross chargeable transfers of £315,750 had been made in the seven years prior to 20.8.12 so £(325,000 – 315,750) = £9,250 of the nil band remains and the death IHT due is

	£
PET	25,000

			£
IHT	£9,250	× 0% =	0
	£15,750	× 40% =	6,300
	£25,000		6,300
Less taper relief @ 80% (6-7 years)			(5,040)
IHT payable by daughter (20%)			1,260

19.2.14

All of the nil band has been used in calculating death tax on the gifts made in the seven years prior to 19.2.14, so the death tax due on this gift is:

Gross chargeable transfer	£85,000

	£
£85,000 × 40% =	34,000
Less taper relief @ 40% (4-5 years)	(13,600)
	20,400
Less lifetime tax	(15,150)
IHT payable by trustees	5,250

1.8.15

No nil band remains so IHT due on this now chargeable PET is:

PET (valued at 1.8.15)	£67,000

	£
£67,000 × 40%=	26,800
Less taper relief @ 20% (3-4 years)	(5,360)
IHT payable by cousin (80%)	21,440

1.9.15

No IHT arises on an exempt transfer to a spouse.

(b) If Bertha had not been domiciled, nor deemed domiciled, in the UK at the time of the transfer to her, only the first £325,000 of the transfer would have been exempt. The balance of the transfer would still be a PET, so there would be no IHT to pay unless Rodin died within seven years. The IHT that would be due following Rodin's death would be £(400,000 – 325,000) × 40% = £30,000.

(c) The gift by Canova into the discretionary trust is a CLT which is in excess of the nil rate threshold of £325,000. He should therefore make this gift first to ensure that the annual exemption for the current year and the previous year are set against this transfer, so reducing the amount of lifetime IHT payable. If Canova pays the tax the gift would need to be grossed up, so the immediate IHT saving would be £3,000 × 2 × 20/80 = £1,500, whereas if the trustees paid the tax the saving would be £3,000 × 2 × 20% = £1,200.

The gifts to the two children are PETs and no tax will be payable unless Canova dies within seven years of the gifts.

Canova could delay his gift to his daughter until her marriage so that he can utilise the marriage exemption. For a parent the exemption is £5,000. Should Canova die within three years of the gift this will save IHT of £5,000 × 40% = £2,000, with reduced savings (because of taper relief) if death is between three and seven years from the gift. There is a small element of risk should Canova die more than seven years after the gift to the son, but within seven years of the gift to the daughter.

18 Hubert

> **Tutorial note**. Note the different valuation rules for CGT and IHT. The shares are valued at market value for CGT purposes. For IHT purposes the diminution in value principle is used to value the shares.

(a) *Capital gains tax liability*

	£
Gain on shares (W)	30,889
Less annual exempt amount	(11,700)
Taxable gain	19,189

The CGT is £19,189 × 10% – £1,919.

Inheritance tax liability

The gift to the discretionary trust is a chargeable lifetime transfer. As he pays the tax, grossing up is necessary. Two annual exemptions of £3,000 each (for 2018/19 and 2017/18) are available to reduce the net transfer.

	£
Transfer	349,000
Less: A/E (2018/19)	(3,000)
A/E (2017/18) b/f	(3,000)
Net transfer	343,000

There have been no previous transfers so all of the nil band remains available for use in calculating the IHT on this transfer.

		£
£325,000	× 0%	0
£18,000	× 20/80	4,500
£343,000		4,500

Gross transfer is thus £347,500 (£343,000 + 4,500). The IHT payable by Hubert is £4,500.

Check: tax £(347,500 – 325,000) = £22,500 × 20% = £4,500.

The gift to Maxine on 1 April 2019 is a potentially exempt transfer so no tax is due during Hubert's lifetime.

Working

Share Pool

	No. of shares	Cost
		£
1.11.95 Acquisition	2,200	3,300
15.6.05 Acquisition	200	1,366
18.8.11 Acquisition	600	3,000
	3,000	7,666
1.4.19 Disposal	(2,000)	(5,111)
c/f	1,000	2,555

	£
Disposal proceeds (2,000 × £18) (market value)	36,000
Less cost	(5,111)
Gain qualifying for entrepreneurs' relief	30,889

Entrepreneurs' relief applies because

- there is a disposal of shares in a company which is the individual's personal company (owns at least 5% of ordinary share capital); and

- the individual is an officer of the company; and

- these conditions were met throughout the period of one year ending with the date of disposal.

(b) If Hubert was to die on 20 April 2019, the potentially exempt transfer to Maxine on 1 April 2019 would become chargeable. The amount of this transfer, applying both the diminution in value principle and the related property rules (since Rose owns 1,000 shares) is as follows.

	£
Before the transfer, Hubert had 3,000 shares	
in a holding of 3,000 + 1,000 = 4,000 shares (80%), worth £36.67 a share	110,010
After the transfer, Hubert had 1,000 shares	
in a holding of 1,000 + 1,000 = 2,000 shares (40%), worth £18 a share	(18,000)
	92,010
Less actual proceeds	(10,000)
	82,010
Less business property relief: unavailable because shares sold by date of Hubert's death	(0)
Transfer of value (no annual exemptions available)	82,010

On Hubert's death, his remaining shares would also be valued using the related property rules, as follows.

	£
1,000 shares in a holding of 2,000 shares, worth £18 a share	18,000
Less business property relief at 100% (unquoted shares)	(18,000)
	0

The inheritance tax liabilities which would arise on Hubert's death on 20 April 2019 are as follows.

1 May 2018 transfer

Gross transfer (valued on 1 May 2018)	£347,500

IHT at death (no taper relief – death within 3 years)

		£
£325,000	× 0%	0
£ 22,500	× 40%	9,000
£347,500		9,000
Less lifetime tax paid		(4,500)
Tax payable at death		4,500

1 April 2019 transfer

	£
Transfer of value 2019	82,010
Less: A/E (2018/19 – already used)	0
A/E (2017/18 – already used)	0
	82,010

All nil band used in previous seven years so IHT due on death is:

£82,010 × 40% = £32,804

Death estate

	£
Shares	Nil
Cash	40,000
Less CGT liability	(1,919)
	38,081

IHT at 40% = £15,232

The trustees of the settlement must pay IHT of £4,500.

Maxine must pay IHT of £32,804.

Hubert's personal representatives must pay IHT of £15,232.

(c) Notes for meeting

Immediate gift of shares in Bod Ltd:

(i) PET for IHT purposes, only chargeable if Hubert dies within seven years.

(ii) BPR only available on Hubert's death within seven years if Roger retains the shares and they are still eligible for BPR.

(iii) Disposal for CGT purposes. Entrepreneurs' relief will reduce tax rate. Gift relief will also be available.

(iv) Loss of influence over running of Bod Ltd; Rose has a 20% holding

Retention of shares in Bod Ltd until death:

(i) BPR likely to be available on Hubert's death, so no IHT.

(ii) Tax free uplift to market value at date of death for CGT purposes.

(iii) Retention of influence over running of Bod Ltd; Hubert and Rose each have a 20% holding.

(iv) If Roger is involved in the business he may be unhappy not to have received shares whilst his sister purchased shares at an undervalue.

19 Rhys

> **Tutorial note.** Work through the transactions methodically to identify when an IHT charge will arise.

(a) Death 3 September 2018

RJ discretionary trust

The occasions of charge are:

17 July 2011: CLT by Rhys. If Rhys pays the tax this will be grossed up. The full nil rate band at 17 July 2011 is available. There is no additional tax the death of Rhys as he survived 7 years from the gift.

5 March 2020: exit charge on the assets distributed. This is calculated using 30% of an assumed rate of tax scaled down by 34/40 to reflect the number of complete quarters that have elapsed since the settlement was created. The assumed rate is calculated using a transfer equal to the initial value of the settlement with prior transfers equal to the chargeable transfers made by Rhys in the seven years prior to the settlement (£nil).

17 July 2021: principal charge calculated using 30% of an assumed rate. The assumed rate is calculated using a transfer equal to the value of the settlement at the date of the anniversary with prior transfers equal to the chargeable transfers made by Rhys in the seven years prior to the settlement (£nil) plus the transfers made on 5 March 2020.

18 April 2024: exit charge on the assets distributed. This is calculated using 30% of the assumed rate of tax calculated at the last principal charge scaled down by 11/40 to reflect the number of complete quarters that have elapsed since the anniversary.

Rhys discretionary will trust

3 September 2018: charge on death estate. The full nil rate band is available as the RJ discretionary trust was set up more than seven years earlier.

28 February 2023: exit charge on death of Blodwen causing capital to pass to her children (the actual date of distribution is not relevant). This is calculated using 30% of an assumed rate of tax scaled down by 17/40 to reflect the number of complete quarters that have elapsed since Rhys' death. The assumed rate is calculated using a transfer equal to the initial value of the settlement with prior transfers equal to the chargeable transfers made by Rhys in the seven years prior to the death (£nil).

(b)   Death 3 July 2018

RJ discretionary trust

If Rhys dies on 3 July 2018 this will be within seven years of the settlement and there may be additional IHT to pay by the trustees. Taper relief will be available to reduce the death tax and any lifetime tax paid will be deducted.

Rhys discretionary will trust

As death occurred within seven years of the transfer to the RJ discretionary trust, the available nil rate band at death will be reduced by the transfer of value and this will increase the IHT due on the death estate.

When computing the exit charge due on death of Blodwen on 28 February 2023 the chargeable lifetime transfer by Rhys to the RJ discretionary trust will be an assumed prior transfer, so increasing the rate of IHT payable on the exit charge.

20 Dan

> **Tutorial note**. Stamp taxes are a small part of the Advanced Taxation (ATX – UK) syllabus but can yield valuable marks. There is useful information in the rates and allowances table available in the exam.

(a)   Stamp duty land tax is payable on non-residential property as follows.

	£
£150,000 × 0%	0
£100,000 (£250,000 – 150,000) × 2%	2,000
£270,000 (£520,000 – 250,000) × 5%	13,500
£520,000	15,500

(b)   Stamp duty payable is £15,000 × 0.5% = £75.

(c)   Stamp duty reserve tax is £30,000 × 0.5% = £150.

(d)   No charge to stamp duty land tax on transfer on divorce.

21 Fraser Ltd

> **Tutorial note.** The first part of this question is revision of material that you should know well from your Taxation (TX – UK) studies. The second part requires you to apply your knowledge to several different proposals.

(a) **Corporation tax liability for year ended 31 March 2019**

	£
Trading income (W1)	338,105
Interest income £(6,834 + 2,208)	9,042
Chargeable gains (W3)	35,870
Taxable total profits	383,017
Corporation tax liability £383,017 × 19%	72,773

Workings

1   *Adjusted profit computation*

	£	£
Profit before taxation		413,278
Add: depreciation	13,876	
gifts (over £50 each)	2,085	
entertaining	969	
		16,930
		430,208
Less: dividend	1,655	
bank interest	6,834	
interest from gilts	2,208	
surplus on disposal of office building and lease	61,806	
capital allowances (W2)	19,600	
		(92,103)
Taxable trading profit		338,105

2   *Capital allowances*

	£
AIA £9,800 × 2	£19,600

3   *Chargeable gains*

(a)   *The lease*

	£
Proceeds	39,213
Less cost	
$£17,500 \times \dfrac{66.470 + \frac{1}{2}(68.697 - 66.470)}{81.100} = \dfrac{17.5 \text{ years}}{25 \text{ years}}$	(14,583)
Unindexed gain	24,630
Less indexation allowance	
0.226 × £14,583	(3,296)
Chargeable gain	21,334

(b)   *The office building*

	£
Proceeds	116,683
Less cost	(79,000)
Unindexed gain	37,683
Less indexation allowance	
0.293 × £79,000	(23,147)
Indexed gain	14,536

Total gains are £(21,334 + 14,536) = £35,870.

(b) *Purchase of office building A*

The building will cost £150,000. The two disposals by Fraser Ltd during the year to 31 March 2019 realised proceeds of £155,896, so Fraser Ltd can make a claim to roll over all but £5,896 of the gains realised in the year ended 31 March 2019.

Purchase of office building B

If Fraser Ltd is to use half of the office building itself, the cost of that half will be £200,000, so that full rollover relief will be available. Rollover relief is not available against let property.

Rent received, less property expenses, will be taxed as property income.

Any interest paid on bank borrowings or loan stock would be allowable, either as a trading deduction or as a deduction from interest income, but not as a deduction from property income. It would be necessary to identify how the borrowings had been applied, and to apportion the interest payable between trading and non-trading.

Purchase of subsidiary

If a subsidiary is purchased Fraser Ltd will not be able to roll over any of the gains from the disposals in the year ended 31 March 2019 as shares are not qualifying assets.

No tax relief will be available for the cost of the shares until Fraser Ltd disposes of them, and the disposal may then be exempt as the disposal of a substantial shareholding.

Any interest paid on borrowings for the share purchase will be allowed as a deduction from non-trading interest.

Purchase of patents

The tax treatment of patents follows the accounting treatment. Fraser Ltd will therefore obtain a deduction for the cost of these intangible fixed assets over their useful lives. As the patents are to be used in the trade the costs will be trading expenses; if Fraser Ltd acquires the subsidiary the patents should therefore also be acquired by the subsidiary.

Equity capital

If Fraser Ltd realises funds through the issue of shares rather than by raising loans, then there will be no interest payments to deduct in the accounts. Investors may require the payment of dividends; these are not tax deductible.

22 Melson Ltd

> **Tutorial note.** Rollover relief is not available to defer the gain arising on the sale of the warehouse or the other properties because they were not used in the trade of Melson Ltd. Watch out for substantial shareholding exemption on a sale of trading company shares.

Chargeable gains computation

	£
Warehouse (W1)	30,945
Shop (W2)	35,976
Office building (W3)	74,635
Shares (W4)	0
Chargeable gains	141,556

Workings

1   *Warehouse*

		£
Proceeds		125,000
Less cost		(65,000)
		60,000
Less indexation allowance 0.447 × £65,000		(29,055)
		30,945

Rollover relief is not available as the old asset was not used by Melson Ltd in its trade.

2   *Shop*

		£
Proceeds		77,000
Less: cost		(20,000)
extension		(4,000)
establishing title		(2,000)
		51,000
Less indexation allowance		
0.635 × £20,000		(12,700)
0.581 × £4,000		(2,324)
		35,976

There is no indexation allowance on the expenditure on establishing title to the shop as this was incurred after December 2017.

3   *Office building*

		£
Proceeds		180,000
Less cost		(65,000)
		115,000
Less indexation allowance 0.621 × £65,000		(40,365)
		74,635

4   *Shares*

The gain on the disposal of the shares in Leigh Ltd is exempt under the substantial shareholding exemption because:

- Leigh Ltd is a trading company

- Melson Ltd held 10% of the ordinary share capital of Leigh Ltd for a continuous period of at least twelve months in the six years preceding the disposal

23 Hogg Ltd

Tutorial note. The information required in this question should be very familiar knowledge to you from your Taxation (TX – UK) studies.

(a)   The due dates for the payment of corporation tax by Hogg Ltd in respect of the year to 31.3.19 are:

	£	£
14 October 2018 (1/4 × £500,000)		125,000
14 January 2019 (1/4 × £500,000)		125,000
14 April 2019 (1/4 × £520,000)	130,000	
plus underpaid 2 × £(130,000 − 125,000)	10,000	
		140,000
14 July 2019 (1/4 × £520,000)		130,000
1 January 2020 100% × £525,000		
− £125,000 − £125,000 − £140,000 − £130,000		5,000
Total		525,000

(b) Hogg Ltd's corporation tax return for the year to 31 March 2019 was due by 31 March 2020, and so the return is more than six months late. Therefore a fixed penalty of £200 is due (or £1,000 if Hog Ltd's return was late (or never submitted) for each of the preceding two accounting periods).

If Hogg Ltd waited until the submission date of 10 October 2020 to finalise its tax liability and pay any outstanding tax, then £5,000 was unpaid six months after the return was due (30 September 2020), and so a tax geared penalty of 10% (£500) would also arise.

24 Norma

> **Tutorial note**. This question takes a situation of an individual commencing a new trade and contrasts the tax treatment of trading as a company or as an unincorporated business. It is simply a question of applying your knowledge of the tax rules to the given scenario.

	(a) Sole trader £	(b) Dividend £	(c) Dividend + salary £
Company			
Profits	N/A	60,000	60,000
Less: salary			(15,000)
employers' NI (15,000 – 8,424) × 13.8%			(907)
(No employment allowance as sole employee and a director)			
			44,093
Less corporation tax @ 19%		(11,400)	(8,378)
Profits available for dividend		48,600	35,715
Individual			
Profits/salary	60,000		15,000
Dividend		48,600	35,715
Less PA	(11,850)	(11,850)	(11,850)
Taxable income	48,150	36,750	38,865
Income tax payable			
34,500/nil/3,150 @ 20%	6,900		630
Nil/2,000/2,000 @ 0% (dividend nil rate band)		0	0
Nil/32,500/29,350 @ 7.5%		2,437	2,201
13,650/nil/nil @ 40%	5,460		
Nil/2,250/4,365 @ 32.5%		731	1,419
	12,360	3,168	4,250
National insurance			
Class 2 52 × £2.95	153		
Class 4 (60,000 – 46,350) × 2% + (46,350 – 8,424) × 9%	3,686		
	3,839		
Class 1 employees (15,000 – 8,424) × 12%			789
Net cash received			
Profit/Salary	60,000		15,000
Dividend		48,600	35,715
Less: income tax	(12,360)	(3,168)	(4,250)
national insurance	(3,839)		(789)
	43,801	45,432	45,676

From this it can be seen that Norma's net receipt is greatest if she operates as a company and draws a £15,000 salary and the balance as dividend. The net inflow is only marginally lower if she draws all the profits as a dividend. Drawing a salary also ensures that her national insurance record is up to date and would enable her to pay pension contributions in excess of the £3,600 limit available to all individuals.

It should also be noted that corporation tax is payable 9 months and one day after the year end, PAYE and class 1 NI are payable monthly during the tax year, and any income tax not collected through PAYE and Class 4 NI is payable by instalments on 31 January in and 31 July following the tax year, and any balance on the following 31 January, along with the Class 2 NI liability.

25 Clarke Ltd

> **Tutorial note**. This question concerns the purchase of a company's own shares. The choice of dates should have alerted you to the likelihood of the conditions not being satisfied on one of the disposals.

Since Clarke Ltd is an unquoted trading company the capital treatment will automatically apply if the conditions are satisfied. Alex is selling all of his shares, so the reduction to 75% or less of his interest is clearly satisfied. The buying out of a dissident shareholder/director is generally accepted by HMRC as being for the benefit of the company's trade. The shares subscribed for in 2001 have been held for more than the requisite five years, whereas the shares purchased in May 2014 will only qualify if the repurchase is delayed until June 2019. Entrepreneurs' relief does not apply because Alex holds less than 5% of the ordinary shares in the company.

Disposal March 2019

May 2014 acquisition – distribution treatment.

	£
Distribution – excess of proceeds over subscription $2,000 \times £(5-1)$	8,000
Additional rate tax £8,000 × 38.1% (dividend nil rate band already used)	3,048
Capital gain	
Proceeds not treated as distribution 2,000 × £1	2,000
Less cost 2,000 × £3	(6,000)
Capital loss	(4,000)

January 2001 acquisition – capital treatment.

	£
Capital gain	
Proceeds 5,000 × £5	25,000
Less cost 5,000 × £1	(5,000)
	20,000
Less capital loss on May 2014 shares (above)	(4,000)
Gain	16,000
CGT payable @ 20%	3,200

Total tax liability £3,048 + £3,200 = £6,248.

Disposal June 2019

May 2014 acquisition – capital treatment.

	£
Capital gain	
Proceeds 2,000 × £5	10,000
Less cost 2,000 × £3	(6,000)
Gain	4,000

January 2001 acquisition – capital treatment.

	£
Capital gain	
Proceeds 5,000 × £5	25,000
Less cost 5,000 × £1	(5,000)
Gain	20,000

Total gains £(4,000 + 20,000) = £24,000.

CGT liability £24,000 × 20% = £4,800.

Delaying the disposal until June 2019 enables the capital treatment to apply to the total shareholding and saves tax of £6,248 – £4,800 = £1,448. It also delays the due date for payment of the tax by one year.

26 Major Ltd

> **Tutorial note.** It is important to distinguish between trading and non-trading loan relationships. Interest on the former is dealt with as trading income whilst interest on the latter is dealt with as interest income.

(a)   Corporation tax

	£
Taxable trading income	425,000
Property income	30,000
Capital gains	40,000
Total profits	495,000
Less non-trade deficit (£24,000 – £30,000) claim in full	(6,000)
Less qualifying charitable donation	(3,000)
Taxable total profits	486,000

Corporation tax

	£
£486,000 × 19%	92,340

Payment of tax

	£
Taxable total profits	486,000
Add dividends	20,000
Profits	506,000
Profit threshold £1,500,000 × 8/12 × ½	500,000

If Major Ltd was a large company in the previous accounting period, it must pay its corporation tax for the period ending 31 March 2019 in instalments. The amount of the first two instalments is 3 × £92,340/8 = £34,628 and the balancing instalment is £23,084. The instalments are due on 14 February 2019, 14 May 2019 and 14 July 2019.

If Major Ltd was not a large company in the previous accounting period it does not have to pay its corporation tax in instalments. Instead the due date for payment of the whole liability is 1 January 2020.

(b)   To: The Directors of Major Ltd
        From: Certified Accountant
        Date: 31 March 2019
        Re: Tax implications of the loan to Zero Ltd becoming irrecoverable

It will not be possible for any amount of the loan written off to be deducted in computing Major Ltd's trading profits. This means that if the loan is written off in the company's statement of profit or loss, the amount written off must be added back to compute trading profits. Instead any amount written off will be treated as a debit on a non-trading loan relationship. This means that it will initially be deducted from income arising on non-trading loan relationships in the same accounting period (if any, given Zero Ltd may also be unable to pay interest on the loan). Any overall net deficit can be:

(i)   Set against the company's total profits in the same accounting period, or

(ii)   Set against income from non-trading loan relationships arising in the previous 12 months, or

(iii)   Set off against total profits in the following period(s), or

(iv)   Surrendered as group relief in the same accounting period or the following period(s).

Any of these reliefs may be claimed in whole or in part.

Signed: Certified Accountant

(c) *General considerations*

Any dividends received on the shares acquired are not subject to corporation tax, but will be taken into account when determining when corporation tax payments are due. Any interest paid on borrowings to fund the purchase would be allowed as a deduction from non-trading interest, and if there is a deficit it can be relieved as described above.

Purchase of 20% holding from a retiring director

If Major Ltd purchases a 20% holding from a retiring director no tax relief will be obtained for the cost of the shares until they are sold. Provided the shares are held for at least twelve months and the target company is a trading company, the conditions for the substantial shareholding exemption to apply are likely to be satisfied so that any gain on disposal would be exempt. Conversely, if the target company collapses the loss would not be allowable. If it appears that the target company is declining it may be worthwhile attempting to sell the shares within twelve months of acquisition to ensure the loss is allowable.

Subscription for 8% holding

As the shareholding will be less than 10%, it will not qualify for the substantial shareholding exemption. If a gain is made on the disposal it will be fully taxable. If there is a loss it will be allowable.

27 Daley plc

Tutorial note. Your discussion of loss relief is required to take the form of a letter to the managing director, and you should ensure that you give a full and clear explanation.

(a) *Taxable total profits*

	Year ended 31.12.18 £	Year ended 31.12.19	Year ended 31.12.20 £	6 months ended 30.6.21 £	Year ended 30.6.22 £
Trading profits	–	3,000	110,000	85,000	–
Interest income	10,000	2,200	10,000	12,000	14,000
Chargeable gains	18,000	–	–	–	–
Total profits	28,000	5,200	120,000	97,000	14,000
Less current period loss relief	(28,000)		–	–	(14,000)
Less carry back loss relief	–		(60,000)	(97,000)	–
Less carry forward loss relief	–	(200)	(800)	–	–
Less qualifying charitable donation	–	(5,000)	(2,000)	–	–
Taxable total profits	–	–	57,200	–	–
CT @ 19%	–	–	10,868	–	–
Unrelieved qualifying charitable donation	–		–	3,000	1,000

Loss memorandum – trading loss y/e 31.12.18	£
Loss	29,000
Less current period loss relief y/e 31.12.18	(28,000)
Less carry forward relief y/e 31.12.19 (claim in part)	(200)
Less carry forward relief y/e 31.12.20 (claim in full)	(800)
Loss unrelieved	0

Loss memorandum – trading loss y/e 30.6.22

	£
Loss	202,000
Less current period loss relief y/e 30.6.22	(14,000)
Less carry back loss relief (6 months) p/e 30.6.21	(97,000)
Less carry back loss relief y/e 31.12.20	
6/12 × £120,000 (restricted)	(60,000)
Loss carried forward at 30.6.22	31,000

Loss memorandum – capital losses

	£
Loss y/e 31.12.20	5,000
Less used in p/e 30.6.21	(2,000)
	3,000
Loss y/e 30.6.22	1,000
Loss carried forward at 30.6.22	4,000

(b)

My address

Managing Director of Daley plc

His address

Date

Dear Cameron

Relief for losses

I am writing to set out for you how Daley plc has obtained relief for losses that it has incurred during its first few years of trading and to advise on an alternative method of using the loss arising in the year ended 30 June 2022.

Capital losses

(i)   Capital losses incurred must first be set against any capital gains made in the same accounting period. Any capital losses which cannot be so offset are carried forward and set against capital gains in future accounting periods, as soon as they arise. The offset is automatic, and cannot be disapplied. Capital losses cannot be carried back.

(ii)   Daley plc incurred a net capital loss of £5,000 in the year ended 31 December 2020. This cannot be carried back against the chargeable gains of £18,000 arising in the year to 31 December 2018 but is carried forward. £2,000 must be offset against the chargeable gains arising in the 6 months to 30 June 2021, leaving £3,000 of unrelieved capital losses to carry forward. Further capital losses of £1,000 arose in the year to 30 June 2021, and these are added to the £3,000 brought forward, so that capital losses of £4,000 are carried forward at 30 June 2022.

Trading losses

(iii)   A claim can be made for trading losses to be relieved by set off against other profits of the same accounting period. Other profits includes interest income, property business income, and chargeable gains. The trading loss is, however, set off against total profits which is calculated before qualifying charitable donations are deducted, so that if the trading loss exceeds the other income, the qualifying charitable donation is unrelieved. If the claim is made, the amount of trading loss that is set off is the lower of the company's other income or the trading loss. It is not possible to restrict the claim, for example to prevent qualifying charitable donations from being unrelieved.

If a claim has been made for current period relief but not all of the trading loss has been relieved, then a claim may be made for the unrelieved amount to be carried back against the company's other income of the previous twelve months. Other income is as above, before the deduction of qualifying charitable donations. Again, the amount of trading loss that is set off is the lower of the company's other income or the trading loss, and the claim cannot be restricted.

As Daley plc's previous accounting periods are not all 12 months long, the loss will be carried back against the other profits of the previous accounting period, then against the relevant proportion of the other income of the accounting period before that. Thus because there is an accounting period which is six months long immediately before the loss making period, any loss carried back is set against the profits of the six month accounting period, then against 6/12ths of the profits of the twelve month accounting period before that. When apportioning the profits it is acceptable to apportion the profits before deducting qualifying charitable donations and then to deduct the qualifying charitable donations from the profits which fall outside the twelve month carry back period.

Any trading loss, which has not been relieved by current period and carry back claims, is carried forward and a claim can usually be made to set it off, in whole or in part, against the company's total profits. This means that relief for qualifying charitable donations may be retained by keeping sufficient profits in charge to cover the donations.

Loss of year ended 31 December 2018

(iv)   A claim was made for this loss to be set against other income of the same accounting period. This meant that £28,000 was relieved in the year ended 31 December 2018 at the rate of 19%.

The remainder of the loss of £1,000 was carried forward to the next accounting period. A claim should have been made to set £200 of the loss against total profits, thus preserving relief for the qualifying charitable donation. The unrelieved loss of £800 would then have been carried forward to the next accounting period and a claim should have been made to set it off in full against total profits of that period.

Loss of the year to 30 June 2022

(v)   It is proposed that a claim should be made for the loss of the year to 30 June 2022 to be relieved against current and prior period profits as far as possible and then the unrelieved loss carried forward and set against total profits in the following accounting period. This will result in relief of £38,380 being obtained as follows:

Y/e 30.6.22	£14,000 × 19% = £2,660, and qualifying charitable donation of £1,000 is wasted
6m/e 30.6.21	£97,000 × 19% = £18,430, and qualifying charitable donation of £3,000 is wasted
y/e 31.12.20	£60,000 × 19% = £11,400
y/e 30.6.23	£31,000 × 19% = £5,890

(vi)   Alternatively, if the whole loss of £202,000 is carried forward and a claim made to set it against total profits in the two following accounting periods, the relief initially obtained will also be £38,380:

y/e 30.6.22	£150,000 × 19% = £28,500
y/e 30.6.23	£52,000 × 19% = £9,880

But, in addition, relief will be obtained for qualifying charitable donations of £4,000 that would otherwise have been wasted, ie a further £760 (£4,000 @ 19%), giving total relief of £39,140.

However, the disadvantage of these claims is that the relief will be delayed compared to current period, carry back and carry forward claims.

If I can provide any further information please do not hesitate to contact me.

Yours sincerely

Certified Accountant

28 Huis Ltd

> **Tutorial note**. The tax consequences of close company status are designed to ensure that people do not use this type of company as a means of avoiding tax.

(a) The loan to Sartre will lead to Huis Ltd being required to make a payment of £45,000 × 32.5% = £14,625 to HMRC. This amount is payable at the same time as the corporation tax for the accounting period, so it is payable by 1 September 2019. (Note that if Huis Ltd were a 'large' company the tax on the loan would be subject to the quarterly instalment regime.)

When the loan is written off on 31 March 2020 the company will be entitled to a refund of 32.5% of the amount waived (ie £45,000 × 32.5% = £14,625 refund). This refund will be due nine months and one day after the end of the accounting period of the write off, ie it will be due on 1 September 2021.

Sartre will be deemed to receive dividend income of £45,000 in the year in which the loan is written off, 2019/20. There will be no further tax liability to the extent that this is covered by the dividend nil rate band of £2,000 and then basic rate tax will be payable at 7.5%. For the income falling above the basic rate limit or the higher rate limit, tax at 32.5% or 38.1% will be payable. The tax will be due by 31 January 2021. That is, Sartre will be taxed just as if he had received a dividend of £45,000.

The provision of private medical cover and the use of the yacht are provisions of benefits to a shareholder who is not an employee. Each year they will be treated as distributions of £(1,000 + 24,000 × 1/12) = £3,000. Sartre will not be a basic rate tax payer in 2019/20 due to the loan write off. If Sartre is a higher rate taxpayer in 2019/20 he will have a higher rate tax liability of £3,000 × 32.5% = £975 and if he is an additional rate taxpayer an additional rate tax liability of £3,000 × 38.1% = £1,143, payable by 31 January following the end of the tax year through self-assessment.

Huis Ltd will not be able to deduct the medical insurance premium nor the running costs of the yacht for that month in its corporation tax computation.

(b) Beauvoir Ltd – corporation tax liabilities

	Year ended 31.3.18 £	Year ended 31.3.19 £
Property income	14,000	25,000
Interest income	20,000	100,000
	34,000	125,000
Less management expenses – current	(34,000)	(45,000)
– brought forward (note)		(2,000)
Taxable total profits	–	78,000

Note. Claim can be made to treat excess management expenses of £2,000 carried forward from y/e 31.3.18 as expenses of y/e 31.3.19.

Corporation tax at 19%	£14,820

29 Hawthorn Ltd, Linden Ltd and Maple Ltd

> **Tutorial note.** Current period group relief is only available for corresponding accounting periods.

(a)   *Hawthorn Ltd: corporation tax computations for the accounting periods of 12 months to*

	30.6.18	30.6.19
	£	£
Trading profit	2,000	–
Less loss carried back	(2,000)	–
Taxable trading profits	–	–
Corporation tax payable	£–	£–

Linden Ltd: corporation tax computations for the accounting periods of 12 months to

	30.6.18	30.6.19
	£	£
Trading profits	30,000	100,000
Less qualifying charitable donations	(12,000)	(12,000)
Taxable total profits	18,000	88,000
Corporation tax		
£18,000 × 19%	3,420	
£88,000 × 19%		16,720
Corporation tax payable	3,420	16,720

Maple Ltd: corporation tax computations for the accounting periods of 12 months and 6 months to

	31.12.18	30.6.19
	£	£
Adjusted profit split 12.6	43,500	21,750
Less capital allowances	(4,250)	(17,569)
Trading profits	39,250	4,181
Interest income	–	20,000
Total profits	39,250	24,181
Less group relief surrendered by Hawthorn Ltd (W1)	(19,625)	(24,000)
Taxable total profits	19,625	181

Corporation tax		
	£	£
£19,625 × 19%	3,729	
£181 × 19%		34

Working

Group relief / loss relief

	£
Loss of Hawthorn Ltd y/e 30.6.19 available for current period group relief	48,000
Surrendered to Maple Ltd	
6 months to 31.12.18 lower of ($^6/_{12}$ × £48,000) or ($^6/_{12}$ × £39,250)	(19,625)
6 months to 30.6.19 lower of ($^6/_{12}$ × £48,000) or £24,181	(24,000)
	4,375
Loss of Hawthorn Ltd carried back	(2,000)
Loss of Hawthorn Ltd carried forward	2,375

Group relief is not available for Linden Ltd because it is only a 60% subsidiary.

(b) To: The Directors of Hawthorn Ltd
    From: Certified Accountant
    Date: 31 December 2019
    Re: Minimisation of corporation tax on property transactions

Hawthorn Ltd and Maple Ltd are in a chargeable gains group because Hawthorn Ltd holds 100% of the shares in Maple Ltd. Linden Ltd is not part of a group with Hawthorn Ltd because Hawthorn Ltd only has a 60% shareholding (75% required for a chargeable gains group)

There are several factors which will affect the corporation tax liability on the proposed disposals.

(i)   The loss of £26,667 made by Maple Ltd in November 2017 is a pre-entry loss and so cannot be offset against gains on the disposals by Hawthorn Ltd.

(ii)   Rollover relief is available against the purchase of the new warehouse. As the cost is only £290,000, only £60,000 of the gain on the old warehouse can be rolled over into the purchase of the new warehouse acquired by Linden Ltd. The balance of £10,000 cannot be rolled over, as there are surplus proceeds of £10,000 and Linden Ltd is not in a group with Hawthorn Ltd and Maple Ltd so cannot benefit from group rollover relief.

(iii)   The gain of Hawthorn Ltd of £80,000 and the post-entry loss of Maple Ltd of £13,333 should be matched by electing that Maple Ltd transfer the loss to Hawthorn Ltd.

The net position for Hawthorn Ltd is then:

	£
Sale of factory	(13,333)
Sale of office block	80,000
Total gains	66,667
Corporation tax £66,667 × 19%	12,667

Linden Ltd will have a gain of £10,000 taxed at 19%, giving corporation tax of £1,900 (plus the corporation tax on its trading profits of £5,000).

Maple Ltd will have a pre-entry loss of £26,667 carried forward.

Signed: Certified Accountant

(c)   Hawthorn Ltd has an unrelieved trading loss of £2,375 brought forward from the year ended 30 June 2019. It will also have a trading loss of £80,000 for the year ended 30 June 2020. Both of these amounts could be claimed to be offset against the £66,667 of total profits (ie the chargeable gains arising in the period). In addition, £7,000 of the £80,000 loss should be surrendered to Maple Ltd under current period group relief to cover that company's total profits for the year ended 30 June 2020. This will have left Hawthorn Ltd with unrelieved losses of £(2,375 + 80,000 − 66,667 − 7,000) = £8,708 at 1 July 2020.

Hawthorn Ltd's unrelieved trading losses will be carried forward to the year ended 30 June 2021 and a claim should be made to set £(3,000 + 500) = £3,500 of the losses against its total profits for that year. This is required before Hawthorn Ltd can surrender the remainder of its trading loss of £(8,708 − 3,500) = £5,208 under carry forward group relief to Maple Ltd to be set against that company's total profits of £(90,000 + 500) = £90,500.

30 Exotica Inc and Willow Ltd

> **Tutorial note.** In part (b) you were asked to produce a report so it is important that you did so. Marks may be specifically allocated for report writing or letter writing skills.

(a)   If the salesmen have authority to conclude contracts, there will almost certainly be a permanent establishment in the United Kingdom, and its profits would therefore be liable to UK corporation tax. The holding of stocks would not, however, by itself show that there was a permanent establishment.

Taxable profits would be determined as if the permanent establishment had an arm's length relationship with the company, so that tax liabilities could not be manipulated by transfer pricing.

(b) **REPORT**

To: The Board of Directors
From: Certified Accountant   Date: 1 November 2018
Subject: Taxation implications of the overseas operation

(i) UK taxation arises on the profits of an overseas permanent establishment (PE), and any losses of such a PE will, provided that the PE is controlled in the UK, be aggregated with the profits or losses of the UK division. It is possible to make an election so that the profits of the overseas PE are exempt from UK corporation tax. However, this means that no relief would be available if the PE were to make a loss. The election is irrevocable and applies to all permanent establishments, so may not be appropriate if you anticipate that you may set up further PEs in the future that may initially be loss-making.

There will normally be no UK taxation on dividends paid by an overseas subsidiary to a UK company. Losses of an overseas subsidiary cannot usually be relieved against the UK company's profits.

(ii) Foreign tax will arise on the profits of both PEs and subsidiaries. To the extent that the profits of the PE suffer both foreign and UK taxation, double taxation relief will be available, either under a treaty or under the UK's unilateral relief provisions. The usual effect is that the overall tax rate is the higher of the UK rate and the foreign rate. Since any dividends paid by a subsidiary will not normally be subject to UK tax, double taxation relief will not be relevant.

(iii) Assets cannot be transferred outside the scope of UK taxation to a foreign subsidiary on a no gain/no loss basis, so capital gains may arise. However, any such gains may be deferred until shares in the subsidiary are sold. If assets are transferred to a PE, there is no change of ownership so CGT is not triggered.

(iv) A subsidiary will only be treated as not UK resident if it is not incorporated in the UK and its central management and control are abroad.

Signed: Certified Accountant

31 VAT groups

> **Tutorial note**. Marks may be specifically allocated for letter writing skills. Would you have gained them here?

Our address

Your address

Date

Dear Barry

Group registration

I am writing in reply to your recent enquiry regarding Union Ltd, specifically the question of whether that company should be included in the group VAT registration and the procedure for so doing.

First, I confirm that group registration is possible, since all the companies are either established or have a fixed establishment in the UK and they are all under common control.

It would be advisable for Union Ltd to be included in the group registration, for two reasons:

(1)   To avoid the need to account for VAT on intra group transactions and hence minimise the risk of VAT being underdeclared in error. For example, the group relief payments to which you refer in your letter would not normally constitute consideration for taxable supplies and so would not give rise to the need to account for VAT, even between companies which are not in a group registration. However, in certain circumstances HMRC might argue that the 'group relief payments' in fact amount to consideration for a taxable supply, giving rise to an output tax liability; for example, if the payments were linked to services provided by Union Ltd to other group companies.

By including Union Ltd in the group registration, such potential problems are avoided.

(2)   As Union Ltd is partly exempt, around 40% of any input tax it incurs is irrecoverable. If Union Ltd is not included in the group registration, any standard-rated supplies which it receives from other group companies would generate additional irrecoverable VAT.

It is also necessary to consider, however, the effect of including a partly exempt company in the group registration. This will depend in part on the partial exemption method used by Union Ltd at present and the method to be used by the group if Union Ltd is included. Under the standard method, more of Union Ltd's overhead input tax would become recoverable but some of the group's would be lost.

It should however be borne in mind that the partial exemption *de minimis* limit will apply to the group as a whole and is not multiplied by the number of companies in the group registration.

So far as the procedure is concerned, an application needs to be made to HMRC for Union Ltd to be added to the group registration. All applications to join an existing VAT group will automatically be approved by HMRC and will take effect from the date they are received by HMRC (or such earlier or later time as HMRC may allow). HMRC will not normally permit retrospective grouping, so Union Ltd will have to be accounted for separately until you make the application.

HMRC do have the power to refuse an application within 90 days of its receipt if the application does not meet all of the eligibility criteria (which should not be a problem in your case) or presents a risk to the revenue. It is not thought that a slight improvement in the partial exemption position would be sufficient to warrant a refusal on the grounds of risk to the revenue; the improvement would have to go beyond the simple effects of grouping, so something 'artificial' would have to be involved.

Please do not hesitate to contact me if I can be of further assistance.

Yours sincerely

Certified Accountant

32 Stewart Ltd

(a) Residual input tax

	6/18 £	9/18 £	12/18 £	3/19 £	Total £
'T' (note 1)	403,920	359,177	467,159	520,321	1,750,577
'T + E'	455,992	382,371	485,950	557,760	1,882,073
T/T + E (note 2)	89%	94%	97%	94%	94%
Residual tax	14,719	12,613	10,412	11,919	49,663

Notes

Excludes sale of capital asset used in the business.
Rounded up to nearest whole percentage point.

(b) Exempt input tax

	6/18 £	9/18 £	12/18 £	3/19 £	Total £
Direct	3,120	2,775	1,374	1,876	9,145
Share of residual	1,619	757	312	715	2,980
	4,739	3,532	1,686	2,591	12,125
De minimis test 3? (note)	N	N	Y	N	N

Note. Less than £625 pm and less than 50% of the total

(c) Recoverable input tax

	6/18 £	9/18 £	12/18 £	3/19 £	Total £
Direct	44,404	39,098	24,926	36,020	144,448
Exempt de min.			1,686		
Share of residual	13,100	11,856	10,100	11,204	46,683
	57,504	50,954	36,712	47,224	191,131

Total recovered in the four quarterly returns: 192,394
Annual adjustment – due to HMRC (1,263)

The annual adjustment will be made by reducing the input tax for the return period to June 2019.

33 Tax planning

(a) Incorporation should take place when the business starts to make profits, on 1 May 2020.

Advantage can then be taken of early trade loss relief, which is only available to unincorporated businesses. This relief is against income of the three tax years preceding the year of loss, taking earlier years first. Relief will be obtained against the salary of the last few years before Client A became self-employed, leading to repayments of tax.

(b) B's current annual profit is £60,000 × 40% = £24,000.

With the contract, B's turnover will be over the registration limit so he will have to register for VAT. He will be able to charge VAT on top of the contract price, as the customer is registered and will be able to reclaim the VAT. However, as the business is highly competitive he will have to absorb the VAT which he will have to charge to other customers, and not increase his prices. This will be offset to some extent by the fact that he will be able to reclaim VAT suffered on his purchases.

Thus his overall profit margin on normal sales will be reduced to 40% × 100/120. The new annual profit will be as follows.

	£	£
Normal sales		60,000
Less VAT on normal sales × $^1/_6$		(10,000)
		50,000
Less normal purchases £60,000 × 60%	36,000	
VAT on normal purchases × $^1/_6$	(6,000)	
		(30,000)
Profit on normal sales		20,000
Contract sales	25,000	
Less cost of contract sales £25,000 × 60%	(15,000)	
		10,000
Revised annual profit		30,000

Therefore annual profit will only increase by £6,000, despite the new contract having a value of £25,000.

(c) It is in general bad planning to hold an asset likely to rise in value in a company. When the asset is sold, the company will have to pay corporation tax at 19% on the gain. If the proceeds are paid out as a dividend, further tax will be suffered on amounts above the dividend nil rate band. If they are paid out in the course of winding up the company, the shareholders will have chargeable gains on their shares.

The scheme has several other flaws. Dividend income is not taxable in the hands of a UK company so there is no question of a deduction for the director's fees from the company's taxable income, as it will not have any taxable income. Also, the payment of the fees will have adverse consequences as employee's and employer's Class 1 NICs will arise. The employment allowance would not be available to offset against the Class 1 employer's NIC assuming C is the sole employee of the company. Finally, tax relief is only available on pension premiums up to the level of his earnings, not on any dividends he draws out from the company.

(d) *Sole trader*

	£
Profits	30,000
IT £30,000 × 20%	(6,000)
NIC: Class 2 £2.95 × 52	(153)
Class 4 £(30,000 – 8,424) × 9%	(1,942)
Net spendable income	21,905

Company

	£
CT £30,000 × 19%	5,700
Net profits (£30,000 – £5,700) paid as dividend	24,300
IT: £2,000 @ 0% (dividend nil rate band)	(0)
£22,300 (24,300 – 2,000) @ 7.5%	(1,672)
Net spendable income	22,628

34 Hulse Finds Ltd

> **Tutorial note**. Although the question may appear long on first reading note how it breaks down into a series of points.

(a)   The interest paid by Paul on the loan to acquire the shares in the company is qualifying annual interest. This is because Hulse Finds Ltd is a close company (it is controlled by Paul and Nick) and Paul works full-time for the company. Qualifying annual interest is a deductible payment that is deducted from Paul's total income, and consequently reduces his net income.

(b)   Hulse Finds Ltd is a close company and has made a loan to a participator, Chris. Accordingly, the company should have paid HM Revenue & Customs (HMRC) £3,250 (32.5% of the loan) by 1 January 2020 (ie nine months and one day after the end of the accounting period). HMRC will repay the £3,250 when the loan is repaid by Chris or waived by Hulse Finds Ltd. The company would not have had to make any payment if Chris had worked full-time for the company, as the loan is for less than £15,000 and Chris does not own more than 5% of Hulse Finds Ltd.

(c)   The tax implications arising out of the acquisition are:

   (i)   The capital losses of SNL will remain with SNL. SNL will sell its trade and assets to SN2 Ltd and capital losses remain with a company when it sells its trade. SNL can use its capital losses to relieve any gains arising on the assets sold to SN2 Ltd.

   (ii)   The trading losses of SNL will also remain with SNL and will not be transferred with the trade. Where a company sells its trade to an unconnected company, any trading losses remain with the vendor company. SNL may be able to offset the losses against any capital allowance balancing charges arising on the sale.

   It is possible for trading losses to be transferred to the purchaser when a company sells its trade to another company, but only when certain conditions are satisfied. Broadly, the same persons must beneficially own at least 75% of the business both before and after the sale. These conditions would have been satisfied if SNL had formed a subsidiary, Newco, sold its trade to Newco, and then sold Newco to SN2 Ltd.

   SNL is the legal and beneficial owner of its trade prior to the sale. If the trade had been sold to Newco, SNL would no longer be the legal owner of the trade but would still be the beneficial owner as it owns Newco.

   In such circumstances, Newco could have used the trading losses against future total profits, provided there was no major change in the nature or conduct of its trade within a period of five years starting no earlier than three years before and no later than the purchase by Hulse Finds Ltd.

(d)   The tax implications of the Newland business depend on the legal structure used. From a tax point of view, there are two distinct ways of establishing the business:

   (i)   It could be owned directly by Hulse Finds Ltd (or SN2 Ltd). Under this option, it would be an overseas permanent establishment of a UK resident company.

   (ii)   Hulse Finds Ltd (or SN2 Ltd) could incorporate a new subsidiary in Newland to acquire the business. Under this option, it would be an overseas subsidiary of a UK resident company.

Overseas permanent establishment

A permanent establishment is not a separate legal entity but is an extension of the company that owns it. The profits or losses of the permanent establishment belong directly to the company.

Provided the permanent establishment is controlled from the UK, the trading loss made in the year ended 31 March 2022 could be offset by Hulse Finds Ltd (or SN2 Ltd) against its income and gains of that year, reducing the company's UK corporation tax liability. Once the permanent establishment is profitable, the company owning the permanent establishment will be subject to 25% Newland corporation tax on the permanent establishment profits, because it is trading within the boundaries of Newland from permanent establishment.

The profits will also be subject to UK corporation tax because a UK resident company is subject to tax on its worldwide income and gains. However, the UK corporation tax liability, in respect of the permanent establishment profits, will be fully relieved by double tax relief as the rate of corporation tax in Newland is higher than that in the UK. Accordingly, there will be no UK corporation tax to pay on the permanent establishment's profits.

It is possible to make an election to exempt the profits and losses of an overseas permanent establishment from UK corporation tax. However, this election would not be appropriate here. The losses in the first year would not be available for relief against Hulse Finds Ltd's (or SN2 Ltd's) profits as described above, and it is not necessary to exempt the profits in future years, because, as explained above, double tax relief means there will be no UK corporation tax on these profits anyway.

Overseas subsidiary

A subsidiary is a separate legal entity. A company incorporated in Newland will be resident in Newland for tax purposes, provided it is not managed and controlled from the UK. Its profits or losses will then be subject to the tax regime of Newland.

The trading loss of the year ended 31 March 2022 would be carried forward and deducted from the company's future total profits (assuming that the loss relief regime in Newland is similar to that in the UK).

Once the company is profitable, it will be subject to tax in Newland at the rate of 25%. No UK tax will be due on the overseas dividends.

Choice of business medium

It is usually suggested that a permanent establishment should be used where an overseas enterprise is expected to make initial losses. This strategy enables the losses to be offset against any other profits of the company. However, the particular facts of the situation must be considered carefully.

The use of a permanent establishment in Newland will enable Hulse Finds Ltd (or SN2 Ltd) to offset the losses against its profits for the year ended 31 March 2022. This will save UK corporation tax at a rate of 19%.

The use of a subsidiary would mean that the losses could not be offset in the year ended 31 March 2022, as the subsidiary will not have any other income. However, in the following year the losses will reduce that year's profits and save tax in Newland at 25%.

Accordingly, provided the group is willing to wait for a year (from a cash flow point of view) a greater tax saving can be achieved by using a subsidiary in Newland rather than a permanent establishment. This assumes, of course, that the anticipated profits materialise in the year ended 31 March 2023.

35 Financial planning

Tutorial note. The choice between equity and debt finance is a very important consideration when raising additional funds. The implications you discuss must be relevant to the situation outlined. For example, an individual subscribing for shares in a seed enterprise investment company (SEIS) can receive 50% income tax relief on investment up to £100,000 in 2018/19, but Moor Ltd is unlikely to be a qualifying company, as it is not a small start up.

Report

To: The Board of Moor Ltd

From: Certified Accountant

Date: 19 May 2018

Re: Taxation consequences of alternative methods of raising finance

The choice of raising additional funds to finance a major expansion of the business can be summarised as being between loan capital or equity. A major distinction between the two forms of financing is that interest payable on borrowings is deductible for corporation tax purposes whereas dividends payable to shareholders are not.

Loan capital

Interest is tax deductible on an accruals basis under either from trading profit (if put to a trading use) or from interest income.

If the loan interest being paid represents an annual payment other than to a UK bank or a UK resident company, income tax should be deducted at source and accounted for to HMRC.

Costs of obtaining loan finance will be treated as tax-deductible in the same manner as interest payable on the loan. In contrast, costs in respect of issuing share capital are not deductible for CT purposes.

Interest income received by the providers of loan finance is taxable. It will be interest income of a company and subject to tax at the normal corporation tax rate of 19%. Individuals in receipt of interest income will be subject to tax on the gross amount at 0%, 20%, 40% or 45%.

Equity finance

Dividends represent appropriations of profit after tax. They are not tax deductible and any costs associated with the raising of share capital are not tax deductible.

With regard to providers of equity finance, there are tax benefits available to investors who invest in Enterprise Investment Scheme (EIS) shares:

(1)   An individual subscribing for new ordinary shares in an unquoted trading company can claim income tax relief at 30% for an investment of up to £1,000,000 in a tax year. The individual can also make a claim to carry back an investment to the previous tax year, subject to the maximum for that year. For example, if an individual has not previously made any EIS investment, he can invest £2,000,000 in EIS shares in 2018/19 and treat £1,000,000 as invested in 2017/18 and £1,000,000 in 2018/19.

        If the EIS shares are held for three years, there is exemption from capital gains tax on a disposal of the shares. A capital loss may arise on a disposal before or after expiry of the three year period but it is restricted by reducing the issue price by the amount of relief obtained.

(2)   Chargeable gains realised by individuals may be deferred provided that those gains are reinvested in the ordinary shares of a qualifying EIS unquoted trading company. The reinvestment of gains must be made in the period twelve months before to three years after the relevant disposal. The gain is deferred and does not therefore crystallise before a subsequent disposal of the new EIS shares.

If you wish to discuss further any of the above points do not hesitate to contact me.

Signed: Certified Accountant

36 Daniel

> **Tutorial note.** There are only a very few calculations needed here. You need to write a memo and include the figures at the relevant points. Take care to plan your answer well ensuring you know what headings are needed so you cover all the points.

MEMORANDUM

To: Tax manager
From: Tax assistant
Date: 2 June 2019
Subject: Saturn Ltd group of companies

This memorandum considers a number of issues raised by Daniel, the managing director of Saturn Ltd.

(a)   (i)   **Dione Ltd – Use and value of tax loss**

                Any amount of the loss can be surrendered to the UK resident members of the 75% loss group, ie Saturn Ltd and Rhea Ltd.

The best use of the loss will be achieved by surrendering it to Saturn Ltd. Rhea Ltd will make a loss in the year to 30 June 2020 and will be able to set this against its total profits for the year to 30 June 2019.

Surrender to Saturn Ltd is also better than carrying the loss forward as this could take several years for the loss to be relieved, given Dione Ltd is expected to make minimal profits in the year ended 30 June 2020.

The surrender of the loss to Saturn Ltd will save corporation tax at the rate of 19% ie £187,000 × 19% = £35,530.

Further information required

Income and gains of Dione Ltd for the year ended 30 June 2018.

The loss could be carried back for offset against the total profits of Dione Ltd for the year ended 30 June 2018 which would be a cashflow benefit.

(ii) **Tethys Ltd – Use of trading loss**

The two companies will not be in a group relief group as Saturn Ltd will not own 75% of Tethys Ltd.

For a consortium to exist, 75% of the ordinary share capital of Tethys Ltd must be held by companies which each hold at least 5%. Accordingly, Tethys Ltd will be a consortium company if the balance of its share capital is owned by Clangers Ltd but not if it is owned by Edith Clanger.

If Tethys Ltd qualifies as a consortium company: 65% of its trading losses in the period from 1 August 2019 to 31 December 2019 can be surrendered to Saturn Ltd, ie £21,667 (£80,000 × 5/12 × 65%). Saturn Ltd must have taxable profits in excess of this in the period 1 August 2019 to 31 December 2019.

If Tethys Ltd does not qualify as a consortium company, none of its loss can be surrendered to Saturn Ltd.

The acquisition of 65% of Tethys Ltd is a change in ownership of the company. If there is a major change in the nature or conduct of the trade of Tethys Ltd within a period five years starting no earlier than 1 August 2016 and no later than 1 August 2019, the loss arising prior to 1 August 2019 cannot be carried forward for relief in the future.

Further information required

Ownership of the balance of the share capital of Tethys Ltd.
Estimate of taxable profits of Saturn Ltd for the year ended 30 June 2020.

(iii) **Tethys Ltd – Sale of the manufacturing premises**

Value added tax (VAT)

The building is not a new building (ie it is more than three years old). Accordingly, the sale of the building is an exempt supply and VAT should not be charged unless Tethys Ltd has opted to tax the building in the past.

Taxable profits on sale

The capital gain arising on the sale of the building will be £104,032 (£240,000 − (£112,000 × 1.214)).

Rollover relief

Tethys Ltd is not in a capital gains group with Saturn Ltd. Accordingly, rollover relief will only be available if Tethys Ltd, rather than any of the other Saturn Ltd group companies, acquires sufficient qualifying business assets.

The amount of sales proceeds not spent in the qualifying period is chargeable, ie £40,000 (£240,000 – £200,000). The balance of the gain, £64,032 (£104,032 – £40,000), can be rolled over.

Qualifying business assets include land and buildings and fixed plant and machinery. The assets must be brought into immediate use in the company's trade.

The assets must be acquired in the four-year period beginning one year prior to the sale of the manufacturing premises.

Further information required

Whether or not Tethys Ltd has opted to tax the building in the past for the purposes of VAT.

(iv) **Stamp duty and stamp duty land tax**

The purchase of Tethys Ltd will give rise to a liability to stamp duty of £1,175 (£235,000 × 0.5%). It is not an allowable revenue expense for the purposes of corporation tax.

There are no stamp duty land tax implications for the Saturn Ltd group, unless Tethys Ltd acquires land and buildings (see part (iii)).

(b) **Before agreeing to become tax advisers to the Saturn Ltd group**

Information needed

Proof of incorporation and primary business address and registered office.

The structure, directors and shareholders of the company.

The identities of those persons instructing the firm on behalf of the company and those persons that are authorised to do so.

Action to take

Consider whether becoming tax advisers to the Saturn Ltd group would create any threats to compliance with the fundamental principles of professional ethics, for example integrity and professional competence. Where such threats exist, we should not accept the appointment unless the threats can be reduced to an acceptable level via the implementation of safeguards

Contact the existing tax adviser in order to ensure that there has been no action by the Saturn Ltd group that would, on ethical grounds, preclude us from accepting appointment.

37 Stuart and Rebecca

> **Tutorial note.** Read the question requirements carefully. Part 2, for example, asks you to consider two alternatives. There are no marks available for doing anything else.

PRIVATE AND CONFIDENTIAL

[Our address]

[Your address]

[Date]

Dear Stuart

TAX POSITION AND ESTATE PLANNING

This letter deals with the capital gains implications of your recent property sale and your current and potential inheritance tax liabilities.

1 **Capital gains on property disposal 2019/20**

The capital gain arising on the disposal of the Plymouth house is £15,532.

This is after taking account of principal private residence relief of £141,318, based on an exempt period of 90 months out of a total ownership period of 151 months, and letting relief of £40,000.

The calculation of the above figures can be found in Appendix 1.

2 **Proposed investment**

As you are considering making an investment in a quoted company you will only be able to obtain business property relief for inheritance tax purposes if you, together with Rebecca, control the company, ie over 50% of the shares.

You could buy approximately 1 million shares in Omikron plc. This would be in the region of a 2% holding, so no business property relief would be available.

Alternatively you could buy approximately 195,000 shares in Omega plc with the proceeds, at a cost of 216p. Currently you and Rebecca jointly hold 4.8 million shares. Provided you achieve a slightly lower price or invest slightly more so that you purchase 201,000 shares as intended, you and Rebecca will have a controlling holding. Provided you then survive for at least two years you will achieve 50% business property relief on your Omega plc shares. Therefore, it would be preferable to invest in future Omega plc shares.

3 **Inheritance tax on Rebecca's estate 1 March 2022**

Upon your death, the transfer of your assets to Rebecca would be exempt from IHT. If, following your death, Rebecca were to die on 1 March 2022, and no IHT planning is implemented, the IHT liability would be £2,512,420 (Appendix 2).

As your will leaves all of your estate to Rebecca you have not taken advantage of your nil rate band. However on Rebecca's death her nil rate band will be increased by the proportion of nil rate band unused at your death. She will therefore have an additional 100% of your nil rate band available on her death. This will be based on the value of the nil rate band at that time. Neither you nor Rebecca will be entitled to the residence nil rate band because each of your net estates is £2,250,000 or more.

4 **Lifetime IHT planning**

The Omega plc shares should be left to Rebecca so that the 50% BPR would be available on her death or earlier gift of the whole shareholding.

Rebecca should consider making lifetime gifts, perhaps to Sam, in the hope that she will survive for seven years, so that they become completely exempt. If she survived more than three but less than seven years, and IHT was payable on the lifetime gifts, then the IHT payable would be tapered.

Both of you should make lifetime gifts utilising your annual exemptions. Each of you would have a current year and a prior year annual exemption available, as you have made no earlier gifts. You may also be able to establish a regular pattern of giving to use the exemption for normal expenditure out of income. Your wealth would appear to be such that it would be simple to demonstrate that capital was not being eroded by this strategy, and that you can maintain your usual standard of living.

It could be possible to give away the life policy before death at a lower value than the death benefit. It would then be excluded from the death estate and escape any IHT liability.

If you wish to discuss further any of the above points do not hesitate to contact me.

Yours sincerely

Certified Accountant

Appendix 1 – disposal of Plymouth property

	£
Sale proceeds	422,100
Less cost May 2007	(185,000)
	237,100
Less PPR exemption $\dfrac{90}{90+61} \times £237,100$ (W)	(141,318)
	95,782

Less letting exemption, lowest of:

(a) PPR relief given: £141,318

(b) Gain in let period: $\dfrac{27}{90+61} \times £237,100 = £42,395$

(c) Maximum: £40,000

	£
	(40,000)
Gain	55,782
Less capital losses brought forward	(28,550)
	27,232
Less annual exempt amount	(11,700)
Taxable gain	15,532

Working

Periods of occupation		Exempt Months	Non-exempt Months
1 May 2007–31 Aug 2009	Occupied	28	
1 Sept 2009–30 June 2013	Unoccupied – absence for any reason	36	
	Unoccupied		10
1 July 2013–30 Sept 2015	Let		27
1 Oct 2015–31 May 2016	Occupied	8	
1 June 2016–31 May 2018	Unoccupied		24
1 June 2018–30 Nov 2019	Last 18 months	18	
		90	61

Appendix 2 – Rebecca's IHT liability with no IHT planning

	£	£
London property		900,000
Cash deposits (including £200,000 from life policy)		530,000
Quoted investments		250,000
Shares in Omega plc 5,001,000 × 210p (1/4 up is lower)	10,502,100	
Less BPR @ 50%	(5,251,050)	
		5,251,050
		6,931,050
Less nil rate band (£325,000 + 100% × £325,000)		(650,000)
Taxable at 40%		6,281,050
IHT liability		2,512,420

38 Landscape Ltd

> **Tutorial note.** Make sure you make an attempt at each part of the question and do not spend too long on any one part.

(a) *Peter*

The distinction between employment and self employment is a fine one. Employment involves a contract of service, whereas self employment involves a contract for services. Taxpayers tend to prefer self employment because the rules for the deductibility of expenses are more generous but the following factors suggest that HMRC will regard Peter as an employee rather than self employed:

(i)   Peter works five days each week: If Peter cannot work when he chooses it suggests the company has control over him and he is an employee

(ii)   Peter uses the company's equipment

(iii)   Peter does not have any other clients

(iv)   The computer function (and hence Peter) is an integral part of the company's business.

Other factors HMRC may consider are:

- whether Peter must accept further work
- whether the company must provide further work
- whether Peter hires his own helpers
- what degree of financial risk Peter takes
- what degree of responsibility for investment and management Peter has
- whether Peter can profit from sound management
- the wording used in any agreement between Peter and the company.

(b)   *Simon*

Both the payment in lieu of notice (PILON) of £1,500 and the £5,000 in respect of the agreement not to work for a rival company are taxable in 2018/19.

The statutory redundancy pay of £2,400 and the balance of the lump sum redundancy payment of £46,100 (£55,000 – £2,400 – £1,500 – £5,000) are taxable as specific employment income. However, if the lump sum payment is a genuine *ex gratia* redundancy payment it, together with the statutory redundancy payment, is exempt up to £30,000 so that only £((46,100 + 2,400) – 30,000 –10,000) = £8,500 is taxable in 2018/19. The balance of £10,000 is taxable when received in 2019/20.

(c)   *Trevor*

Landscape Ltd is a close company and Trevor is a participator. This means that Trevor will be treated as though he has received dividends equal to the earnings that would have arisen in 2018/19 if he had been a director or an employee of Landscape Ltd.

	£
Car (£14,000 × 35%) (W)	4,900
Loan (£40,000 × 2/12 × 2.5%) + (£15,000 × 7/12 × 2.5%)	385
Loan written off	15,000
Taxable benefits = dividend	20,285

Working

CO_2 emissions = 170 g/km
Above baseline figure 170 – 95 = 75g/km
Divide by 5 = 15
% = 20 + 15 = 35%

(d)   *Ursula, Violet and Wilma*

Ursula, Violet and Wilma are all working in Cambridge in the performance of their duties. Tax relief is available for the cost of travel between home and Cambridge, if Cambridge is a 'temporary' place of work. A place of work is classed as a temporary workplace if the employee does not work there continuously for a period which lasts (or is expected to last) more than 24 months.

Therefore, the cost of all of Ursula's travel to Cambridge qualifies for tax relief. The mileage allowance that Ursula receives from the company falls within the approved mileage rates and so is tax free and she can make an expense claim as follows:

	£
Approved mileage rates	
(120 × 40) = 4,800 × 45p	2,160
Less mileage allowance received (4,800 × 41p)	(1,968)
Expense claim	192

As Violet was initially expected to work in Cambridge for more than 24 months the train fare initially paid by Landscape Ltd is a taxable benefit. However, from 1 January 2019 no taxable benefit arises in respect of the train fare because Violet's period of secondment to Cambridge is no longer expected to exceed 24 months.

Wilma should be entitled to full tax relief for the cost of her journeys to Cambridge. Wilma will be assessed on a benefit as follows:

	£
Mileage allowance received (120 × 150) = 18,000 × 41p	7,380
Less approved mileage rates 10,000 × 45p	(4,500)
8,000 × 25p	(2,000)
Taxable benefit	880

(e) Landscape Ltd can give an employee up to £3,600 worth of 'free' shares a year. Employees can buy 'partnership' shares with their pre-tax salary up to a maximum of 10% of gross earnings, subject to an upper limit of £1,800 per year.

In addition, employers can give employees up to two free matching shares for each partnership share purchased. Provided the shares are held for five years before disposal, employees will not be subject to income tax or NIC on them. If the shares are held for more than three years but less than five years, tax and NIC is due on the lower of the market value of the shares on the date they were given to the employee and the market value at the date of withdrawal.

39 Marilyn

> **Tutorial note.** In part (a) it was essential to recognise that the spouse exemption applied to the bulk of Max's estate. Part (b) concerned the rules on transfer of unused nil bands between spouses on the death of the survivor. Make sure you learn this topic, especially the rules on the residence nil rate band which applies from 6 April 2017.

(a) *Inheritance tax liability on the death of Max 20 May 2017*

All of Max's estate (except the chattels) passes to Marilyn for IHT purposes. Therefore the **spouse exemption** applies to these assets.

The chattels passing to Max's brother total £15,000 (£5,000 + £7,000 + £3,000) and are covered by the nil rate band.

Therefore, there is no IHT payable on the death of Max.

Inheritance tax liability on death of Marilyn February 2019

	£
Berkley's Bank a/c	33,400
Unit trust units in ISAs	145,000
Cash ISA	10,600
Ex-cash ISA from Max	11,300
Bank deposit a/c from Max	20,000
Spiro plc (W)	63,600
Unit trusts	81,000
Unit trusts – ISAs	67,600
Main residence	470,000
Gross estate	902,500

Tax is:	£
£125,000 × 0% (residence nil rate band)	0
£325,000 × 0% (nil rate band)	0
£452,500 × 40%	181,000
£902,500	181,000

Working

Valuation of Spiro plc shares at February 2019 is lower of:

¼ up

$$\frac{(647-635)}{4}+635=638$$

Mid-bargain

$$\frac{642+630}{2}=636$$

ie 636 × 10,000 = £63,600

(b) Claims can be made to transfer Max's unused nil rate bands to increase the maximum nil rate bands available on the death of Marilyn. The claims will usually be made by the personal representatives of Marilyn's estate within two years following the end of the month of Marilyn's death (ie by 28 February 2021).

Max's residence nil rate band is £125,000 and it is all available for transfer to Marilyn since he left his main residence to her so the spouse exemption applied. The maximum residence nil rate band for Marilyn is therefore £(125,000 + 125,000) = £250,000. The available residence nil rate band is the lower of £250,000 and the value of the main residence of £470,000, which is £250,000.

Max's unused nil rate band is £(325,000 – 15,000) = £310,000. Since the nil rate bands are the same in 2017/18 and 2018/19, this is also the amount available to transfer to Marilyn. Therefore the maximum nil rate band for Marilyn is £(325,000 + 310,000) = £635,000 and this is also the available nil rate band since Marilyn did not make any lifetime transfers.

The IHT on Marilyn's estate is therefore:

	£
£250,000 × 0% (residence nil rate band)	0
£635,000 × 0% (nil rate band)	0
£17,500 × 40%	7,000
£902,500	7,000
The inheritance tax saving is £(181,000 – 7,000) (which is 40% of £435,000)	174,000

(c) Since Max owned ISA investments at his death, Marilyn, as his spouse, is entitled to an additional ISA allowance equal to the value of the ISA investments held by Max at his death (ie £59,800).

Tax tables

SUPPLEMENTARY INSTRUCTIONS

1   You should assume that the tax rates and allowances for the tax year 2018/19 and for the financial year to 31 March 2019 will continue to apply for the foreseeable future unless you are instructed otherwise.

2   Calculations and workings need only be made to the nearest £.

3   All apportionments should be made to the nearest month.

4   All workings should be shown.

TAX RATES AND ALLOWANCES

The following tax rates and allowances are to be used in answering the questions.

Income tax

		Normal rates	Dividend rates
Basic rate	£1 – £34,500	20%	7.5%
Higher rate	£34,501 – £150,000	40%	32.5%
Additional rate	£150,001 and over	45%	38.1%

Savings income nil rate band – Basic rate taxpayers		£1,000
– Higher rate taxpayers		£500
Dividend nil rate band		£2,000

A starting rate of 0% applies to savings income where it falls within the first £5,000 of taxable income.

Personal allowance

	£
Personal allowance	11,850
Transferable amount	1,190
Income limit	100,000

Where adjusted net income is £123,700 or more, the personal allowance is reduced to zero.

Residence status

Days in UK	Previously resident	Not previously resident
Less than 16	Automatically not resident	Automatically not resident
16 to 45	Resident if 4 UK ties (or more)	Automatically not resident
46 to 90	Resident if 3 UK ties (or more)	Resident if 4 UK ties
91 to 120	Resident if 2 UK ties (or more)	Resident if 3 UK ties (or more)
121 to 182	Resident if 1 UK tie (or more)	Resident if 2 UK ties (or more)
183 or more	Automatically resident	Automatically resident

Remittance basis charge

UK resident for:	Charge
7 out of the last 9 years	£30,000
12 out of the last 14 years	£60,000

Car benefit percentage

The base level of CO_2 emissions is 95 grams per kilometre.

The percentage rates applying to petrol cars with CO_2 emissions up to this level are:

50 grams or less per kilometre	13%
51 grams to 75 grams per kilometre	16%
76 grams to 94 grams per kilometre	19%
95 grams per kilometre	20%

Car fuel benefit

The base figure for calculating the car fuel benefit is £23,400.

Individual savings accounts (ISAs)

The overall investment limit is £20,000.

Property income

Basic rate restriction applies to 50% of finance costs relating to residential properties.

Pension scheme limits

Annual allowance	£40,000
Minimum allowance	£10,000
Threshold income limit	£110,000
Income limit	£150,000
Lifetime allowance	£1,030,000

The maximum contribution that can qualify for tax relief without any earnings is £3,600

Approved mileage allowances: cars

Up to 10,000 miles	45p
Over 10,000 miles	25p

Capital allowances: rates of allowance

Plant and machinery

Main pool	18%
Special rate pool	8%

Motor cars

New cars with CO_2 emissions up to 50 grams per kilometre	100%
CO_2 emissions between 51 and 110 grams per kilometre	18%
CO_2 emissions over 110 grams per kilometre	8%

Annual investment allowance

Rate of allowance	100%
Expenditure limit	£200,000

Cash basis accounting

Revenue limit	£150,000

Cap on income tax reliefs

Unless otherwise restricted, reliefs are capped at the higher of £50,000 or 25% of income.

Corporation tax

Rate of tax: Financial year 2018	19%
Financial year 2017	19%
Financial year 2016	20%
Profit threshold	£1,500,000

Value Added Tax (VAT)

Standard rate	20%
Registration limit	£85,000
Deregistration limit	£83,000

Inheritance tax: nil rate bands and tax rates

	£
Nil rate band	
6 April 2018 to 5 April 2019	325,000
6 April 2017 to 5 April 2018	325,000
6 April 2016 to 5 April 2017	325,000
6 April 2015 to 5 April 2016	325,000
6 April 2014 to 5 April 2015	325,000
6 April 2013 to 5 April 2014	325,000
6 April 2012 to 5 April 2013	325,000
6 April 2011 to 5 April 2012	325,000
6 April 2010 to 5 April 2011	325,000
6 April 2009 to 5 April 2010	325,000
6 April 2008 to 5 April 2009	312,000
6 April 2007 to 5 April 2008	300,000
6 April 2006 to 5 April 2007	285,000
6 April 2005 to 5 April 2006	275,000
6 April 2004 to 5 April 2005	263,000
Residence nil rate band	125,000
Rate of tax on excess over nil rate band: Lifetime rate	20%
Death rate	40%

Inheritance tax: taper relief

Years before death	Percentage reduction
Over 3 but less than 4 years	20%
Over 4 but less than 5 years	40%
Over 5 but less than 6 years	60%
Over 6 but less than 7 years	80%

Capital gains tax

	Normal rates	Residential property
Rates of tax: lower rate	10%	18%
higher rate	20%	28%
Annual exempt amount		£11,700
Entrepreneurs' relief: Lifetime limit		£10,000,000
Rate of tax		10%

National insurance contributions

Class 1 Employee	£1 – £8,424 per year	Nil
	£8,425 – £46,350 per year	12%
	£46,351 and above per year	2%
Class 1 Employer	£1 – £8,424 per year	Nil
	£8,425 and above per year	13.8%
	Employment allowance	£3,000
Class 1A		13.8%
Class 2	£2.95 per week	
	Small profits threshold	£6,205
Class 4	£1 – £8,424 per year	Nil
	£8,425 – £46,350 per year	9%
	£46,351 and above per year	2%

Rates of Interest (assumed)

Official rate of interest	2.50%
Rate of interest on underpaid tax	3.00%
Rate of interest on overpaid tax	0.50%

Standard penalties for errors

Taxpayer behaviour	Maximum penalty	Minimum penalty – unprompted disclosure	Minimum penalty – prompted disclosure
Deliberate and concealed	100%	30%	50%
Deliberate but not concealed	70%	20%	35%
Careless	30%	0%	15%

Stamp duty land tax

Non-residential properties

£150,000 or less	0%
£150,001 – £250,000	2%
£250,001 and above	5%

Stamp duty

Shares	0.5%

Case bibliography

Bamford v ATA Advertising Ltd 1972 .... [1972] 48 TC 359
Benson v Yard Arm Club 1979 .... [1979] 53 TC 67
Blackwell v Mills 1945 .... [1945] 2 All ER 655
Bradley v London Electricity plc 1996 .... [1996] STC 1054
Brown v Bullock 1961 .... [1961] 3 All ER 129
Brown v Burnley Football and Athletic Co Ltd 1980 .... [1980] 53 TC 357

Caillebotte v Quinn 1975 .... [1975] 50 TC 22
Cape Brandy Syndicate v CIR 1921 .... [1921] 1 KB 64
Carmichael and Anor v National Power plc 1999 .... [1999] UKHL 47
CIR v Barclay Curle & Co 1969 .... [1969] 45 TC 221
CIR v Fraser 1942 .... [1942] 24 TC498
CIR v Scottish and Newcastle Breweries Ltd 1982 .... [1982] 55 TC 252
Cole Brothers Ltd v Phillips 1982 .... [1982] 55 TC 188
Cooke v Beach Station Caravans Ltd 1974 .... [1974] 49 TC 514
Croydon Hotel & Leisure Co v Bowen 1996 .... [1996] STC (SDC) 466

Donald Fisher (Ealing) Ltd v Spencer 1989 .... [1989] STC 256

Edwards v Clinch 1981 .... [1981] STC 617
Elwood v Utitz 1965 .... [1965] 42 TC 482

Fitzpatrick v IRC 1994 .... [1994] STC 237

Gordon & Blair Ltd v CIR 1962 .... [1962] 40 TC 358

Hampton v Fortes Autogrill Ltd 1979 .... [1979] 53 TC 691
Hall v Lorimer 1994 .... [1994] IRLR 171
Harvey v Caulcott 1952 .... [1952] 33 TC 159

Jarrold v John Good and Sons Ltd 1963 .... [1963] 40 TC 681

Law Shipping v. CIR 1923 .... [1923] 12 TC 621
Lawson v Johnson Matthey plc 1992 .... [1992] STC 466
Leeds Permanent Building Society v Proctor 1982 .... [1982] 56 TC 293
Lucas v Cattell 1972 .... [1972] 48 TC 353
Lupton v Potts 1969 .... [1969] 45 TC 643

Mallalieu v Drummond 1983 .... [1983] 57 TC 330
McKnight (HMIT) v Sheppard (1999) .... [1999] STC 669
McLaren v Mumford 1996 .... [1996] 69 TC 173
Munby v Furlong 1977 .... [1977] 50 TC 491

Odeon Associated Theatres Ltd v Jones 1971 .... [1971] 48 TC 257

Pickford v Quirke 1927 .... [1927] 13 TC 251

Samuel Jones & Co (Devondale) Ltd v CIR 1951 .... [1951] 32 TC 513
Sanderson v Durbridge 1955 .... [1955] 36 TC 239
Smith v Abbott 1994 .... [1994] STC 237
Strong & Co of Romsey Ltd v Woodifield 1906 .... [1906] AC 448

Vodafone Cellular Ltd and others v Shaw 1995 .... [1995] 69 TC 376

Wimpy International Ltd v Warland 1988 .... [1988] 61 TC 51
Wisdom v Chamberlain 1969 .... [1969] 45 TC 92

Yarmouth v France 1887 .... [1887] 19 QB D

Index

Review Form – Advanced Taxation (ATX – UK) Finance Act 2018 (10/18)

Please help us to ensure that the ACCA learning materials we produce remain as accurate and user-friendly as possible. We cannot promise to answer every submission we receive, but we do promise that it will be read and taken into account when we update this Study Text.

Name: _____   Address: _____

_____

_____

How have you used this Study Text?
(Tick one box only)

☐ On its own (book only)

☐ On a BPP in-centre course _____

☐ On a BPP online course

☐ On a course with another college

☐ Other _____

Why did you decide to purchase this Study Text? *(Tick one box only)*

☐ Have used BPP Study Texts in the past

☐ Recommendation by friend/colleague

☐ Recommendation by a lecturer at college

☐ Saw information on BPP website

☐ Saw advertising

☐ Other _____

During the past six months do you recall seeing/receiving any of the following?
(Tick as many boxes as are relevant)

☐ Our advertisement in *ACCA Student Accountant*

☐ Our advertisement in *Pass*

☐ Our advertisement in *PQ*

☐ Our brochure with a letter through the post

☐ Our website www.bpp.com

Which (if any) aspects of our advertising do you find useful?
(Tick as many boxes as are relevant)

☐ Prices and publication dates of new editions

☐ Information on Study Text content

☐ Facility to order books off-the-page

☐ None of the above

Which BPP products have you used?

| *Study Text* | ☑ | *Passcards* | ☐ | *Other* | ☐ |
| *Kit* | ☐ | | | | |

Your ratings, comments and suggestions would be appreciated on the following areas.

	Very useful	Useful	Not useful
Introductory section	☐	☐	☐
Chapter introductions	☐	☐	☐
Key terms	☐	☐	☐
Quality of explanations	☐	☐	☐
Case studies and other examples	☐	☐	☐
Exam focus points	☐	☐	☐
Questions and answers in each chapter	☐	☐	☐
Fast forwards and chapter roundups	☐	☐	☐
Quick quizzes	☐	☐	☐
Question Bank	☐	☐	☐
Answer Bank	☐	☐	☐
Index	☐	☐	☐

| *Overall opinion of this Study Text* | Excellent ☐ | Good ☐ | Adeqate ☐ | Poor ☐ |

Do you intend to continue using BPP products?   Yes ☐   No ☐

On the reverse of this page is space for you to write your comments about our Study Text. We welcome your feedback.

The author of this edition can be emailed at: learningmedia@bpp.com

TELL US WHAT YOU THINK

Please note any further comments and suggestions/errors below. For example, was the text accurate, readable, concise, user-friendly and comprehensive?